COMMERCIAL MORTGAGE-BACKED SECURITISATION

DEVELOPMENTS IN THE EUROPEAN CMBS MARKET

AUSTRALIA
Law Book Co
Sydney

CANADA AND USA
Carswell
Toronto

HONG KONG
Sweet & Maxwell Asia

NEW ZEALAND
Brookers
Wellington

SINGAPORE AND MALAYSIA
Sweet & Maxwell Asia
Singapore and Kuala Lumpur

COMMERCIAL MORTGAGE-BACKED SECURITISATION

DEVELOPMENTS IN THE EUROPEAN CMBS MARKET

ANDREW V. PETERSEN

With a foreword by

RONAN FOX
Chair, CMSA Europe

First edition 2006

Published in 2006 by
Sweet & Maxwell Limited
110 Avenue Road
London NW3 3PF
http://www.sweetandmaxwell.co.uk

Typeset by YHT Ltd, London
Printed and bound in Great Britain by MPG Books Ltd, Bodmin, Cornwall

No natural forests were destroyed to make this product, only farmed timber
was used and re-planted.

ISBN–10 0421 960 906
ISBN–13 978 0421 960 909

A CIP catalogue record for this book is available from the British Library

The commentary and precedents contained in this publication are not
tailored to any particular factual situation. They may be used as a guide for
the drafting of legal documents *but not otherwise reproduced*. The publishers
and the author cannot accept any responsibility for loss occasioned to any
person acting or refraining from action as a result of the material in this
publication.

FOREWORD

The development of the CMBS product over the past 10 years in Europe has been remarkable. Freed from the restrictions of REMIC rules, the product has been able to address both needs of borrowers, loan originators and investors in a way few would have thought possible 10 years ago.

In the early days, securitisation was a seen by some in Europe as an unnecessarily complex real estate financing tool. For that constituency, the hope of "here today, gone tomorrow" did not materialise and CMBS issuance in Europe has continued on its growth trajectory. Issuance volume in 2006 is likely to exceed €50bn. This publication is a timely review of many facets of the European CMBS industry and the extent to which European solutions to European problems have emerged.

For those with a global focus, some topics will engender feelings of déjà vu. These include regulatory issues, the challenges of subordinated debt to CMBS structures and impact of "car crash" intercreditor agreements where just about the only certainty is litigation between the creditors at some future point in time.

Although many remark on the size of the European market, either in terms of population or GDP, few comment on the number of jurisdictional challenges that transactions in Europe pose. Consequently, a number of the chapters specialise on jurisdictions such as France and Italy that are less creditor-friendly than say the United Kingdom or the Netherlands. The widespread change in ownership in the German multi-family sector has given rise to several large scale CMBS financings and this too is covered.

Synthetic transactions, where effectively a portfolio lender buys protection against losses, have long been a feature of European CMBS. The main purpose of these transactions is usually capital relief or risk management. Newer pay-as-you-go swap transactions are also considered in the chapter on synthetic CMBS.

Structured Finance transactions have also included a number of Islamic finance techniques in *Sukuks* and *Ijara* lease structures. The application of securitisation to *shari'ah* complaint finances is also reviewed.

For CMSA Europe, its unique role as a trade body representing the wide number of parties in a typical CMBS transaction remains key. With a single focus on real estate debt capital markets, the membership harnesses the input of borrowers, loan originators, arrangers, issuers, investors, servicers, trustees, lawyers and accountants; all the hallmarks of a "CMBS village".

The CMBS industry remains inventive in developing solutions that meet the needs of real estate borrowers, originators and investors. The first European Collateralised Debt Obligation of Commercial Real Estate Debt are slated for 2006, hopefully melding some of the best of traditional European CMBS transactions with the structural protections of a CDO in terms of interest cover and over-collateralisation tests.

I would like to thank Andrew Petersen at Dechert for his drive in conceiving and executing this project. A special thanks to the expert contributors who put aside their time in a frenetic years to set out their insights with such lucidity.

Enjoy the read!

Ronan Fox
Chair, CMSA Europe
Managing Director, Structured Finance, Standard & Poor's London

PREFACE

In 2004, I temporarily left the UK to immerse myself in the seasoned US CMBS market. It was an unforgettable experience and it allowed me to experience a world where every week there were issuances a plenty. I was not to know, that when I returned to the UK at the end of 2005, I would arrive to an explosion of issuance, as the CMBS market in Europe reached €46 billion (more than double the total for 2004). With commercial mortgage-backed securities representing the largest growing asset class within European asset backed securities and 2006 annual issuance expected to grow by 50–60 per cent, it is hoped that this work is timely in giving the complete insider's view of current practice and legal issues in this highly topical and rapidly expanding area of financial law.

The journey of CMBS is a fascinating one, and Rick Jones, a past president of CMSA, tracks the story of the birth and growth of the CMBS market, by highlighting a story of innovation, a central theme to the book. Whilst the book then moves on to provide excellent detailed coverage of the "nuts and bolts" of the CMBS process, four chapters that particularly demonstrate the inventiveness of CMBS and the new innovations entering the market are the chapter by Dick Frase on synthetics and swaps, the chapter by Dave Hall and Mark Battistoni on the growth of property derivatives (a subject I am sure we will hear and see a lot more of), the chapter by John Timperio, Todd Stillerman (experts on the US CRE CDO process) and John Gordon and James Spencer (awaiting the first European CRE CDO, coming in 2006), and the chapter on Islamic Financing by Abradat Kamalpour and Mike McMillen (Islamic law experts with real experience of this versatile and exciting emerging area of law). The book can also be commended for its excellent industry knowledge on investors' perspectives presented by Hans Vrensen and its coverage of an issue that has taxed the industry since its emergence in July 2005: how to address and comply with the market abuse rules on disclosure and post-issuance reporting. Finally, no book on European CMBS should be considered complete, as pointed out by Ronan Fox in the foreword, without an examination of Continental European CMBS markets. This book includes coverage of numerous markets in depth.

When conceiving this book at the end of the first CMSA European conference in Brussels in 2005, my desire was to produce a book that included a vital mix of business chapters alongside legal chapters. A new generation of legal textbook spanning the sometimes achingly visible gap between business people and their professional advisors. I approached Sweet & Maxwell, not knowing if such a book was possible. The publication of this book is testament to the fact that such books are and I hope I succeeded in my vision.

On a customary note, I would like to thank our publishers, Sweet & Maxwell, for their efforts in ensuring this book was published efficiently and promptly and in particular, our Publishing Editor, Jasmin Naim, first for making all of this possible with her foresight to commission the book, and secondly for her encouragement and support in completing it.

In addition, I would especially like to thank the book's Technical Editor, Fiona Mullen, for her editing skills and her vigorous pursuit of contributor's chapters. This book owes a great deal to her. Then there are the authors, to all of whom I am very grateful. Without their selfless undertakings, this book would have not reached publication.

Finally, on a personal note, I want to thank my wife, Sarah, and daughters, Livia and Isobel, for their understanding of the time I spent on this book at the absence of time spent with them.

Needless to say any errors contained herein remain those of the authors.

Andrew V. Petersen
November, 2006

ACKNOWLEDGMENT

Many people have been involved in bringing this work to fruition. It is hoped that the mentioning of the names below will go some way to thanking those listed for all the time and effort they spent contributing to the book and helping, in different ways, to achieve this publication.

First and foremost the team of authors receive their just recognition at the beginning of their chapter(s). In addition this book would not have been possible without the following persons from Dechert: Gary Walker, Patrick Gloyens, Michael Beanland, and Puzant Merdinian for diligent reviews of various chapters; Peter Crockford, for his help on the legal contracts; Heather Taylor, Lindsey La Roche, Adele Davis and Tara Hall for their invaluable administrative assistance to the project; Paul McAleer for his contribution to Chapter 1; Nadine Young, Jaqueline Breen and Justin Nuttall for their contribution to Chapter 9; Ral Turbeville and Katie Burton for their contribution to Chapter 11 and Matt Ginsberg for producing the US form Intercreditor agreement.

A special mention must also go to Duncan Batty of Dechert, who single handedly faced the mammoth task of producing the glossary of terms.

We would like to thank Dottie Cunningham and the Commercial Mortgage Securities Association, Inc. for permission to reproduce their "CMSA European Investor Reporting Package" (E-IRP) in Appendix 3.

Finally, mention should also be made of the enthusiasm for the project from within Dechert, especially from the finance and real estate executive committee (Ciaran Carvalho, Jack Gillies, Rick Jones, Mac Dorris and Steven Fogel) for being supportive and permitting the Dechert contributors the time to undertake this work.

TABLE OF CONTENTS

CHAPTER 1
THE EMERGENCE OF CMBS
Richard D. Jones

CHAPTER 2
THE BUSINESS ECONOMICS OF CMBS
Caroline Philips

CHAPTER 3
THE EUROPEAN CMBS MARKET
Nassar Hussain

CHAPTER 4
STANDARD & POOR'S RATING OF EUROPEAN CMBS: LEGAL AND STRUCTURAL CONSIDERATIONS
Judith O'Driscoll

CHAPTER 5
THE CMBS LOAN ORIGINATION PROCESS
Jonathan Braidley

CHAPTER 6
DERIVATIVES AND CMBS BORROWERS: HOW DERIVATIVES AFFECT FINANCING STRATEGY
Mark Battistoni and David R. Hall

CHAPTER 7
SYNTHETIC CMBS AND THE USE OF SWAPS AND DERIVATIVES
Dick Frase

CHAPTER 8
THE EMERGENCE OF SUBORDINATED DEBT STRUCTURES IN EUROPEAN CMBS
Andrew V. Petersen

CHAPTER 9
INTERCREDITOR AGREEMENTS
Melissa Hamilton

CHAPTER 10
SERVICING CMBS
Kathleen Mylod and Katherine Burroughs

CHAPTER 11
COMMERCIAL REAL ESTATE CDOs: THE US AND EUROPEAN MARKETS
John Gordon, John Timperio, Todd Stillerman, James A. Spencer

CHAPTER 12
CMBS: A EUROPEAN INVESTOR'S PERSPECTIVE
Hans J. Vrensen

CHAPTER 13
THE MARKET ABUSE RULES AND THEIR LEGAL IMPACT ON THE EUROPEAN CMBS MARKETS
James A. Spencer and Andrew V. Petersen

CHAPTER 14
INVESTOR REPORTING
Jaymon Jones

CHAPTER 15
THE SECONDARY MARKET IN EUROPEAN CMBS
Rob Ford and Hans J. Vrensen

INTRODUCTION TO CONTINENTAL EUROPEAN CMBS MARKETS

CHAPTER 16
AN INSIGHT INTO GERMAN MULTI-FAMILY
Dr Olaf Fasshauer, Andrew Currie, Gioia Dominedo,
Grif Winkler and Stefan Baatz

CHAPTER 17
THE CMBS MARKET IN FRANCE
Joseph Smallhoover

CHAPTER 18
THE CMBS MARKET IN SPAIN
Javier Ybañez, Gonzalo Garcia-Fuertes and Eduardo Barrachina

CHAPTER 19
THE CMBS MARKET IN ITALY
Alberto Giampieri and Andrea Giannelli

CHAPTER 20
THE PORTUGUESE CMBS MARKET
MORTGAGE-COVERED BONDS: A BRAVE NEW TOOL
Pedro Cassiano Santos and Hugo Moredo Santos

CHAPTER 21
AN INNOVATION IN FINANCING—ISLAMIC CMBS
Michael J. T. McMillen and Abradat Kamalpour

CHAPTER 22
RISK ASSESSMENT GROWS UP
US-STYLE TITLE INSURANCE IN THE EUROPEAN
SECURITISATION MARKET
Jean-Bernard Wurm

CHAPTER 23
WHAT NEXT FOR EUROPEAN CMBS?
Jack Toliver

APPENDICES

ABBREVIATIONS

[A full glossary is provided at Appendix 5]

AAOIFI	Accounting and Auditing Organisation for Islamic Financial Institutions
ABS	Asset Backed Securities
AFC	Available Funds Cap
ALTA	American Land Title Association
AMF	*Autorité des Marchés Financiers* (France)
ARM	Adjustable Rate Mortgage
BIS	Bank for International Settlements
bppa	Basis Points Per Annum
CAGR	Compound Annual Growth Rate
CBO	Collateralised Bond Obligation
CCA	Cash Collateral Account
CDC	*Caisse des Dépôts et Consignations* (France)
CDO	Collateralised Debt Obligation
CDS	Credit Default Swaps
CEE	Central and Eastern Europe
CESR	Committee of European Securities Regulators
CIS	Collective Investment Scheme
CLO	Collateralised Loan Obligations
CMBS	Commercial Mortgage Backed Securitisation
CMO	Collateralised Mortgage Obligation
CMSA	Commercial Mortgage Securities Association
CMVM	Portuguese Securities Commission
CNMV	National Securities Market Commission (Spain)
COMI	Centre of Main Interest
CP	Commercial Paper
CPR	Constant Prepayment Rates
CRE	Commercial Real Estate
CRE CDO	Commercial Real Estate Collateralised Debt Obligation
CSA	Credit Support Annex
CSWA	Capital Structure Weighted Average
CTH	*Certificados de Transmission De Hipoteca* (Spain)

DOL	Department of Labor (US)
DSCR	Debt Service Coverage Ratio
EAD	Exposure At Default
E-IRP	European Investor Reporting Package
EL	Expected Loss
ERISA	Employee Retirement Income Security Act 1974 (US)
ESF	European Securitisation Forum
EUIR	European Union Insolvency Regulation
EURIBOR	Euro Inter-Bank Offered Rate
FCC	*Fonds Commun de Créances* (France)
FHCMC	Federal Home Loan Mortgage Corporation (Freddie Mac)
FIRREA	Financial Institutions Reform, Recovery and Enforcement Act 1989 (US)
FNMA	Federal National Mortgage Association (Fannie Mae)
FSA	Financial Services Authority
FSMA	Financial Services and Markets Act 2000 (UK)
FTA	*Fondos de Titulización Activos* (Spain)
FTC	*Fundos de Titularização De Créditos* (Portugal)
FTH	*Fondos de Titulización Hipotecaria* (Spain)
GAAP	Generally Accepted Accounting Principals
GIC	Guaranteed Investment Contract
GNMA	Government National Mortgage Association (Ginnie Mae)
GSE	Government Sponsored Entities (US)
HEL	Home Equity Loans
HVRE	High Volatile Real Estate
ICR	Issuer Credit Rating
ICR	Interest Cover Ratio
IDB	Islamic Development Bank
IFSB	Islamic Financial Services Board
IO	Interest-Only
IPD	Interest Payment Date
IPRE	Income Producing Real Estate
IRAP	Italian Regional Tax On Productive Activities
IRB	Internal Ratings-Based
IRES	Italian Corporate Income Tax
IRP	Investor Reporting Package
IRR	Internal Rate of Return
ISDA	International Swap Dealers Association
ISE	Irish Stock Exchange
LGD	Loss Given Default
LIBOR	London Inter-Bank Offered Rate
LMA	Loan Market Association
LOC	Letter of Credit
LSE	Luxembourg Stock Exchange

LTV	Loan-To-Value
M	Effective Maturity
MAD	Market Abuse Directive
MBMP	Multi-Borrower Multi-Property
MBS	Mortgage Backed Securities
MFC	French Monetary and Financial Code
MFH	Multi-Family Housing
MGS	Malaysian Global Sukuk Inc.
MiFID	Markets in Financial Instruments Directive
MTN	Medium-Term Note
NIM	Net Interest Margin
NOCF	Net Operating Cash Flow
NRSRO	National Recognised Statistical Rating Organisations
NSMIA	National Securities Markets Improvement Act 1996 (US)
OIC	Organisation of the Islamic Conference
OTC	Over-The-Counter
PD	Default Probability
PH	*Participaciones Hipotecarias* (Spain)
PMA	Property Market Analysis
PMP	Professional Market Parties
PSA	Pooling and Servicing Agreement
RBA	Ratings Based Approach
RBC	Risk Based Capital
REIT	Real Estate Investment Trusts
REMIC	Real Estate Mortgage Investment Conduit
REO	Real Estate Owned Through Enforcement Action
RIS	Regulatory Information Services
RMBS	Residential Mortgage Backed Securities
RTC	Resolution Trust Corporation
RW	Risk Weight
S&L	Savings & Loan
SEC	Securities and Exchange Commission
SF	Supervisory Formula
SGR	*Società di Gestione del Risparmio* (Italy)
SIV	Structured Investment Vehicle
SME	Small And Medium Enterprises
SMMEA	Secondary Mortgage Market Enhancement Act 1984 (US)
SPE	Special Purpose Entity
SPV	Special Purpose Vehicle
STC	*Sociedades de Titularização de Créditos* (Portugal)
UL	Unexpected Loss
UNCITRAL	United Nations Commission on International Trade Law
WAC	Weighted-Average Coupon
WAFF	Weighted-Average Foreclosure Frequency
WALS	Weighted-Average Loss Severity

| WAM | Weighted-Average Maturity |
| WBS | Whole Business Securitisation |

CHAPTER ONE

COMMERCIAL MORTGAGE BACKED SECURITIES—THE EMERGENCE OF CMBS

Richard D. Jones, Partner,
Dechert LLP

INTRODUCTION

The short but compelling story of the birth and growth of the CMBS market is the story of innovation. Conceived of necessity, birthed by technology, and nurtured by the ever growing appetite of the fixed income investor marketplace, it is a story of transformational innovation. Today's $700 billion US CMBS marketplace was inconceivable from the perspective of 1985, just as the commercial real estate market devoid of CMBS is almost inconceivable today.

The explosion of issuance in the CMBS markets of Europe underway today culminated in total European CMBS issuance for 2005 of around €46 billion (in 63 transactions), up from around €14 billion in 2004 (33 transactions). While perhaps modest compared with 2005, total US CMBS issuance of $169.2 billion (€140 billion) in 99 transactions, strong demand, increasing standardisation, and the launch of new bank conduit programs indicate broad expectations of continued growth from European CMBS's present 11 per cent share of total European mortgage financings toward the US's 40 per cent share.

All this makes CMBS critically important to Europe. In an EU market place which exceeds the population of the US, and where CMBS issuance is expected to grow by 50 to 60 per cent in 2006, there is good and timely reasons for this book and investor attention to this growing CMBS market. This chapter will examine the growth of CMBS as a product, before Chs 2 and 3 deal in detail with the economics driving CMBS and the growth of the CMBS European market place.

1

INNOVATION

Securitisation has transformed the commercial real estate market. What was an isolated, self-contained business funded by domestic (and often geographically local) banks and insurance companies which invested a fixed "real estate" allocation of capital into the commercial real estate markets for portfolio purposes and held those mortgage loans on their balance sheets to maturity, is now a business funded by the broad, global capital markets.

Fixed income investors now buy and trade rated bonds up and down the risk curve from AAA to BBB- while a small universe of boutique, high-yield real estate players buy the below investment grade segment of the risk curve. These investors, broadly speaking, see bonds backed by commercial mortgage debt, not as an isolated "alternative investment" but simply as one among many core investment opportunities which are pursued with more or less vigour depending upon perceptions of relative value.

In 1985, the question of how much your mortgage loan was worth would have only confused. A loan was good if the lender had a good "gross spread" and bad if it didn't. Today, a loan is a tradeable asset and not knowing its worth in the marketplace is unthinkable. While loans may certainly be held to maturity on balance sheets as a portfolio asset, the most useful way to analyse the commercial mortgage loan business today is as a manufacturing activity, with the loan as a product to be produced, priced and ready for sale.

SECURITISATION DEFINED

Securitisation, broadly speaking, is a methodology for financing commercial real estate by selling tradeable debt instruments ("certificates" or "bonds") to the fixed income investor marketplace which are backed or secured by a pool of commercial mortgage loans. The transforming insight of the structure is that the cash flows from the whole loans can be stripped and decoupled from the individual whole loans and reassembled in myriad ways to pay principal and interest on debt instruments, stratified by interest rate, risk and duration. These debt instruments or certificates can be designed to meet investor appetites such that the value of the sum of the certificates is equal or greater to the par amount of the loans backing these certificates.

Transforming granular and illiquid whole loans into tradeable securities desired by a wide range of fixed income investors has, over the years, been a fairly lucrative business for bankers. In the process, a deep and less expensive source of capital is tapped for the commercial real estate industry.

To illustrate, if an 80 per cent loan-to-value (LTV) whole commercial loan with a debt service coverage ratio (DSCR) of 1.20 secured by a generic commercial property is generally considered to be roughly a BB+ credit, there are relatively few investors who have an appetite for that paper as a whole loan. This results in a thin investor pool rendering the market vulnerable to disruptions affecting that relatively small and homogenous investor pool. When credit crunch conditions occur, spreads will widen dramatically and the commercial real estate market will be starved for leverage if something causes those lenders to limit lending. If, however, mortgage loans can be pooled with many other similar loans and tranched into tradeable certificates with credit quality ranging from AAA down to unrated,[1] many investors and not just traditional mortgage lenders will be attracted to invest in a deep market for those securities. Deep markets are less sensitive to negative events, affecting just one segment of the economy (commercial banks and life companies) and tend to self-repair following negative events more rapidly.

How the transformation is engineered is the story of innovation, which is the centrepiece of this book. What follows in this chapter is a historical review of the development of CMBS and a brief primer on the structure and dynamics of the modern market.

THE EARLY DAYS

While to many, CMBS may appear to have exploded onto the stage in the early 1990s, full-blown and without any obvious antecedents, that was, in fact, not the case. The headwaters of CMBS can be found in the housing market of the 1970s when the Government National Mortgage Association ("Ginnie Mae"), one of the three government sponsored entities (GSE) dominating the residential mortgage finance business, first guaranteed a pool of mortgage loans. Its sister organisation, the Federal Home Loan Mortgage Corporation ("Freddie Mac") issued its first mortgage-backed participation certificates in 1971 and private label mortgage backed securities (MBS) began in the late 1970s. These early efforts at directly tapping the capital markets to finance real estate (albeit residential real estate) were far removed in structure, scale and design from the broad, robust real estate capital markets of the first decade of the twenty-first century. Highly rated securities only were issued and credit support was predominantly in the form of the GSE's guarantee, which was (and still is) viewed as nearly equivalent to the full faith and credit of the United States government. Nevertheless, it was a beginning and reflected the transforming insight that

---

[1] The ratings process within Standard & Poor's is more fully explored in Ch. 4.

cash flows could be severed from the whole loans from which they arose and used to pay interest and principal on bonds backed by those underlying loans.

It was during the 1980s that many of the legal structural foundations of the modern US securitisation market were put into place. Many forward thinking people and institutions foresaw the possibility of a securitisation market and worked hard during these years to eliminate the legal and regulatory impediments to the market's development. In 1984, numerous regulatory constraints affecting securitisation were eliminated by the passage of the Secondary Mortgage Market Enhancement Act 1984 ("SMMEA"),[2] which eliminated many overlapping blue sky and federal securities regulations and facilitated broader ownership of CMBS. In 1986, the Real Estate Mortgage Investment Conduit ("REMIC") was added to the law as part of the Tax Reform Act 1986.

Prior to 1986, the only available issuance structure for mortgage-backed securities was the grantor trust. Limitations in the structure of this vehicle, such as the need to avoid double taxation of the interest income of the commercial loans pooled for purposes of issuing securities, made multi-class securitisation structures, one of the hallmarks of modern securitisation, almost unworkable. The REMIC statutory scheme eliminated the problem of potential double taxation (the taxable mortgage pool problem) and permitted the creation of multiple classes of certificates differentiated by duration and yield without the concern of a separate level of taxation at the trust or pool level. At the time, however, the United States Congress was concerned that the elimination of taxation at the vehicle level would have a negative impact on governmental tax revenues and consequently imposed various limitations and structural requirements on the vehicles to achieve tax neutrality. The result was an elaborate series of complex rules regarding the structure, nature, composition and performance of these pools and attendant inefficiencies, which the industry continues to work with today.

The 1980s witnessed legal and regulatory constraints being lifted, paving the way for the growth of a real securitisation industry. Following this, the major rating agencies (enterprises which are given special status to provide credit ratings of securities by the United States Securities and Exchange Commission as "Nationally Recognised Statistical Rating Organisations" or "NRSROs") began to develop models for the rating of certificates or securities backed by pools of mortgage loans. In 1987, Standard & Poor's issued the first set of guidelines and the other agencies soon followed.

---

[2] SMMEA was followed 12 years later by the National Securities Markets Improvement Act 1996 ("NSMIA").

Although many of the predicates for modern securitisation were in place by the mid-1980s, and the investor marketplace was developing some appetite for MBS through the slowly growing residential securitisation market place, CMBS was still not a factor in the market place. The commercial real estate finance market was awash in capital provided by traditional mortgage portfolio lenders, in hindsight busily mispricing risk and ignoring the signs of an impending real estate crash. In 1985 and 1986, a small number of highly visible unique securitisations occurred. The most well-known was in connection with the 1985 sale of Rockefeller Centre. In each of these cases, the assets financed were not mainstream assets and, after 1986, there was little further material activity in the CMBS arena. CMBS remained a curiosity.

All this changed with the savings and loan crisis which began in 1988 and deepened into a crisis affecting all commercial mortgage lenders in the early 1990s. Economists view a depression as an economic event involving more than a 30 per cent deflation of prices of goods. The US commercial real estate industry in the late 80s and early 90s experienced what was, indeed, a depression. Real estate value decreased between 30 per cent and 40 per cent all over the country. Traditional sources of capital evaporated, and hundreds, if not thousands, of financial institutions failed.

The crisis led to a seminal event in the development of the modern CMBS industry with the passage of the Financial Institutions Reform, Recovery and Enforcement Act ("FIRREA") in August, 1989. Among other things, it imposed stricter capital standards on regulated commercial lenders and created the Resolution Trust Corporation ("RTC"). The Resolution Trust Corporation was charged with resolving failed thrift institutions and disposing of the assets of these failed institutions.

In the early 1990s, the RTC was confronted with a mounting wave of failed institutions with tens of thousands of whole commercial mortgage loans still on the books of these institutions. The RTC realised that selling those loans one by one was neither efficient, nor, in the final analysis, even achievable. Searching for a solution, the RTC turned to the then novel concept of securitisation as a way to dispose of this overhang of now publicly owned private debt.

In those early days, the RTC was highly price insensitive. Whatever it took to move the loans would be done. Investors were wary as the loans were a mixed bag of under and often non-performing loans and the securitisation structure was novel. These investors were incented to buy largely through the combination of governmental guarantees and vast amounts of cash as additional security for the bonds. In the early 1990s, no investors specialised in securities backed by commercial real estate and, in short, it

5

took a very good deal to attract fixed income investors into the segment. The RTC offered that very good deal. By the time the RTC wound up its affairs in 1995 it had resolved 747 thrifts and liquidated assets in excess of $450 billion, and a robust and growing appetite for bonds backed by commercial real estate had been created. Through this process the RTC jump-started demand for CMBS.

Moreover, while the RTC was pioneering the CMBS business and building an investor base, the traditional mortgage portfolio lending community was not lending much money. Between new and more onerous capital standards and with too much real estate debt already on their books, they were cautious. In the same way it's said that generals always fight the last war, banking management had developed a powerful allergy to commercial real estate that lasted many years. This created credit crunch conditions and offered the entrepreneurial investment bankers enormously rich spreads to fill the gap left by traditional lenders making commercial mortgage loans to be financed through the CMBS market. A number of US investment banks, having been exposed to the new technology as underwriters for the RTC, began to pursue the private CMBS market segment with real vigour. In 1992, with the assistance of the Mortgage Bankers Association America, the National Association of Realtors and the National Realty Committee, a far-sighted group of industry leaders, organised the Capital Consortium to facilitate the growth of the still infantile CMBS industry. Ultimately, the Capital Consortium involved a wide range of market participants including investment banks, specialty finance companies, traditional lenders, RTC servicers, rating agencies, accountants and lawyers who worked diligently throughout the early 1990s to facilitate the development of an effective commercial real estate capital market. The group focused on the development of standardised documents, uniform and comprehensive investor information standards, ratings models, and the elimination of numerous perceived tax and legal and regulatory impediments to the growth of the capital markets.

RETURN TO GROWTH

With the RTC having led the way and a dearth of credit alternatives, when the commercial real estate market began to recover after 1992, CMBS began to play an increasingly important role in financing that growth. Figure 1, below, shows the growth of CMBS from 1990 through to 1998.

In the years following 1992, several of the impediments to the growth of the CMBS market were, in fact, eliminated. In 1994, REMIC was given more clarity with additional regulatory guidelines which, among other things, provided (for the first time) for defeasance which played a large role

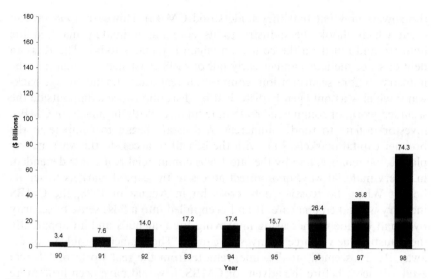

Figure 1: US CMBS issuance

Source: Commercial Mortgage Alert. US only, non-agency, non-CDO.

in the successful growth of the industry in later years. In 1997, the Department of Labor ("DOL") began issuing Underwriter Exemptions which permitted ERISA[3] plans to invest in CMBS bonds without risk of violating the prohibited transactions rules. In November 2000, DOL expanded the underwriting exemptions to permit such plans to invest in subordinate bonds. In 1996, NSMIA was passed, further facilitating the distribution of bonds by the elimination of many conflicting blue sky regulatory schemes.

In 1994, the main initiatives of the Capital Consortium were adopted by a new trade organisation, the Commercial Mortgage Securitisation Association (CMSA), whose charter and mission is to facilitate the growth and success of the CMBS market. The CMSA which recently saw its tenth anniversary, has been an incredibly successful steward of the industry and has played a very material role in the growth of the CMBS industry from its infancy in the early 1990s.

As can be seen from Figure 1, above, the CMBS industry grew from a curiosity to a major source of capital through the mid-1990s. By 1997, CMBS was a $100 billion business and its enthusiastic participants felt the sky was the limit. The underlying commercial real estate markets were strong and borrower appetite for CMBS sourced loans was insatiable

---

[3] Employee Retirement Income Security Act 1974 (US).

(borrowers now felt that they understood CMBS). However, 1998 saw an event which shook the industry to its core but ultimately matured the industry and put it on the course on which it remains today. The Russian debt crisis of the late summer-early fall of 1998 chastened and matured the industry. Before securitisation, commercial real estate finance was a backwater which was only gently disturbed by disruptions occurring outside the secluded world of commercial real estate finance. With the advent of CMBS, investor dollars to fund commercial real estate began to compete in the broader capital markets. But, with the benefit of access to this vast market place came reliance, and by the late 1990s commercial real estate depended, in a very material way, upon direct access to the capital markets to sell its bonds. When the Russian debt crisis hit in August of 1998, the CMBS industry was taken unaware. It had been lulled into a false sense of security by a half decade of increasing improving fundamentals and an apparently inexhaustible new source of investor capital. The financial problems of far away Russia seemed, at the time, remote from the real world of US real estate. Indeed, before the advent of CMBS, it would have been little more than a news item on the evening news for people in the commercial real estate business. But not in this late summer of 1998 when, in brief, the Russian debt crisis caused a flight to quality which drained capital from more arcane investment products, such as CMBS, into Treasuries. This pushed down the yield on Treasuries while virtually eliminating a bid for CMBS, creating an enormous and rapidly widening spread between CMBS and corresponding Treasuries. Immediately after the crisis, swap spreads widened almost 40 basis points in less than 36 hours. Commercial mortgage loan originators were caught with fixed income assets on the books that were mispriced (in not a good way) to the market for the resulting bonds. Many major commercial mortgage loan originators carried their portfolio of loans unhedged and had enjoyed for many years the "free profit" of the continued appreciation of the value of the loans warehoused for securitisation while fixed income interest rates gently declined. When spreads exploded out, portfolios were worth consistently less than par. Moreover, the consequences of the Russian debt crisis were exacerbated because not only were originators saddled with commercial mortgage loans that could not be sold at market clearing prices, but many bond buyers were similarly impaired as the value of their portfolios decreased precipitously. As both originators and many bond buyers used vast amounts of leverage to run their businesses, defaults cascaded throughout the sector. The consequence was that many major participants in the CMBS industry failed during the latter half of 1998. For example, the number of CMBS loan originators fell from 75 in 1998 to less than half, 37 in 2000.

The CMBS industry bounced back rapidly in 1999, validating what many had said about the self-correcting and risk mitigating characteristics of CMBS when compared to traditional, highly granular mortgage portfolio

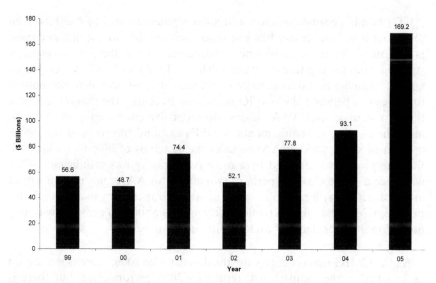

Figure 2: US CMBS issuance

Source: Commercial Mortgage Alert. US only, non-agency, non-CDO.

lending. It also came back with a new commitment to "hygiene." The accumulation of loans was now hedged.[4] The period of accumulation was shortened and this began an era of partnering amongst major CMBS players to ensure they accessed the market regularly and reasonably quickly. For a time (an issue now subject to quite a lot of debate) underwriting standards tightened and the quality of CMBS loans improved.

Since 1999, the US CMBS market has been on a tear. Figure 2, above, reflects the growth of CMBS through to 2005, a record-setting year.

Ongoing creativity and innovation continued to make the CMBS sector dynamic and productive. In the early years of the new century, a high-yield market for the subordinate tranches of mortgage loans (AB Structures[5]) and for mezzanine loans developed which, partnered with the CMBS execution, met borrower demand for proceeds. This has led to the creation of a brilliantly nuanced but complicated structure involving "in the pool" and "out of the pool" tranches of debt which has continued to enhance the competitiveness of CMBS both in the US and throughout Europe.

As investor bond demand increased and broadened, the market responded by creating new securities to meet unmet investor demand. Interest-only

---

[4] See Chs 6 and 7.
[5] See Ch. 8 for detailed discussion.

("IO") bonds became common and soon segmented into "PAC IOs" and "Support IOs", the former being stripped only off the most secure and most prepayment protected long-timed certificates, while the latter generally stripped from the top to the bottom of the credit stack. The PAC IO created a more valuable and durationally stable security and provided alternatives for investors between the two IO securities. Recently, the market has seen the advent of special AAA classes supported by multi-family property to meet the regulatory requirements of GSEs as bond buyers, and the development of super-senior AAAs to meet the demands of investors which felt that the protection afforded by a mere AAA rating was insufficient. What was once a single class, or perhaps two classes of AAAs has now morphed into a structure with multiple classes of AAAs tranched by maturity. In this process, CMBS has shown its flexibility and its ability to grow by carefully nurturing investor demand and meeting investor needs.

As the CMBS market enters the third quarter of 2006, there is a question as to whether the industry will repeat its 2005 performance, but there is every indication it will do so. Whatever it ends up doing, there is no doubt that CMBS, some 15 years after its birth in the 1990s is here to stay as perhaps the most important funding source for commercial real estate in the years to come.

But what is this transformational "technology" for the funding of commercial real estate that makes it work so well?

RATINGS, TRANCHING, THE B PIECE BUYERS, ADVANCING, LEGAL ISOLATION AND PROFESSIONAL SERVICING

Ratings

Ratings models were developed for the CMBS industry in the late 1980s. Figure 3, below, shows the ratings levels of the three major NRSROs. Ratings levels are based on an analysis of the likelihood of default of each of the underlying loans and an estimate of the severity of the losses resulting from such a default. An AAA rating for a bond indicates a credit quality meaning the certificates are extraordinarily unlikely to suffer losses, whereas a B or a lower rated bond indicate a class that is very likely to suffer losses. In most CMBS transactions, the rating reflects the likelihood of the timely receipt of interest and the ultimate receipt of principal. Rating takes into account the underwriting characteristics of each loan in the pool, analysing underwritten (and stressed) loan-to-value and debt service coverage of each loan, asset type, the rent stream, locational and market issues, property

Standard & Poor's	Moody's	Fitch
AAA	Aaa	AAA
AA+	Aa1	AA+
AA	Aa2	AA
AA-	Aa3	AA-
A+	A1	A+
A	A2	A
A-	A3	A-
BBB+	Baa1	BBB+
BBB	Baa2	BBB
BBB-	Baa3	BBB-
BB+	Ba1	BB+
BB	Ba2	BB
BB-	Ba3	BB-
B+	B1	B+
B	B2	B
B-	B3	B-
NR	NR	NR

☐ Investment grade

▨ Non-investment grade

Figure 3: Overview of tranching and subordination levels: ratings.

condition, the geographic diversity of the pool and other factors. Ratings are dependent upon a particular securitisation structure including subordination of lower rated bonds to higher rated, professional servicing, legal isolation, and advancing. Each are discussed in more detail below.

Subordination

Subordination is the heart of modern CMBS. In early RTC transactions, cash collateral was used as the primary credit enhancement to spin BB-credits (or less) into investment grade gold. In the years following the RTC, private label securitisations turned to subordination and sequential pay structures to achieve the same end. AAA rated certificates are entitled to the first payment available for the payment of interest and principal. Each lower rated bond (typically with a higher alphabetic designation) is subordinate to the AAA and superior in rights to all the certificates with a later alphabetic designation. Similarly, when losses accrue due to defaults on the underlying loans, the lowest rated classes are the first to absorb losses with losses penetrating up the capital stack from the lowest rated (and typically highest alphabetically designated class) to the highest AAA class. Figure 4, below, graphically depicts this structural feature of securitisation.

11

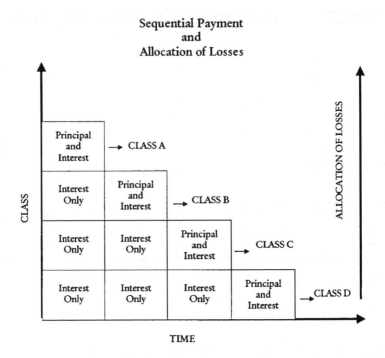

Figure 4: Overview of tranching and subordination levels. Tranching and subordination explained.

Legal isolation

Fundamental to the model that rating agencies and investors use to analyse pools of loans and to make the decision to purchase certificates, is the notion that they only need to analyse the performance of the underlying mortgage properties in isolation from any other business enterprise. Legal isolation of a mortgage property from any other business interests or liabilities of the party controlling the mortgaged property is, hence, a hallmark of the securitisation structure. This has led to set of rules which encourages, and for larger loans, requires, the underlying borrowers to be structured as SPVs which have no material assets other than the real estate and no material liabilities other than the secured mortgage loan. A complexity of rules and practices has grown up around such provisions and SPE (or "LPE" throughout Europe) compliant structures are rewarded in terms of valuation in the rating models and by investors.

In the US, in order to meet the so-called "SPE criteria", the organisational documents of the borrower must contain covenants to create legal isolation and include independent directors (on its or board of managers or board of directors) whose vote will be required for bankruptcy filings or

certain other matters and the delivery of the legal non-consolidation opinion, supporting a legal conclusion that the underlying mortgage borrower
is unlikely to be drawn in to and consolidated into the bankruptcy of any
other legal entity. (Many of these features are designed specifically to deal
with United States bankruptcy law which provides for the possibility of a
bankruptcy court to ignore the juridical separateness of a borrower entity
and consolidate that entity into the bankruptcy of an affiliate).

Similarly, legal isolation occurs at the pool level when a separate and
distinct trust is created to hold all the loans and to issue the rated
certificates.

The B Piece buyer

During the early years of securitisation, investor appetite for mortgage
backed securities was first developed. Over the years since then, appetite has
become robust. Bonds are designed (in terms of rating, fixed or floating,
based interest calculation, yield protection, amortisation, duration and
principal window) to meet investor desires. The investment grade market
has always been sufficiently wide and deep since investors discovered
CMBS. However, the CMBS model is entirely dependent upon some
investors buying the lowest rated (and unrated) certificates. These investors,
generically referred to as the "B Piece Buyers", or B Buyers, buy the BB, B
and unrated certificates. While these certificates represent typically less than
6 per cent to 7 per cent of the capital stack, finding a buyer for these bonds is
an absolute predicate for the success of this market place.

In addition to very wide spreads (which produces marvellous profits if not
overwhelmed by losses resulting from too many defaulting loans) to attract
the B buyer, the market has developed several structural features that have
now become standard. The B buyer is given substantial control on how the
underlying loans are serviced. As these buyers are the first to absorb losses,
this is thought to strongly align the interests of the party in control of
servicing with the interest in all of the other certificate holders. The holders
of the lowest rated bonds are designated the "controlling class" and must be
consulted by the pool servicer on many issues and have material veto rights
over critical decisions about enforcing loan documents and foreclosing on
underlying loans.

As the industry has matured, these B buyers have gone from a handful to
over a dozen institutions who believe that they understand real estate fundamentals and are equipped to deal with the consequences of credit problems and defaults. As the model has developed, the B buyers have often
also acted as special servicer (see section on servicers, below). The combination of the rights held as a controlling class together with the rights of the

special servicer gives the B buyers substantial control over how the pool is managed and serviced. The investment grade buyers take substantial comfort from knowing that the party servicing the loans are also to have "skin in the game" as the holder of the first loss bonds.

Professional servicing and advancing

A securitisation transaction can be thought of in some sense as the deconstruction of old fashioned portfolio lending. Prior to securitisation, a single institution originated a loan, owned the loan, reaped the rewards of good spread income and suffered losses when the underlying property deteriorated, and serviced the loan. In a securitisation structure, many of those functions, organic to portfolio lending are now provided by multiple specialised investors and service providers. A wide range of investors with appetites from AAA to unrated fund the loan. Specialised enterprises service them. The loans are held legally by institutional trustees, documents are managed by specialised custodians and advancing is the responsibility of others. From the early days of the RTC, entire industries have grown up to provide the professional services required of a securitised loan.

In the first instance, the loans are held by a trustee. Driven by the need to isolate the cash flows and manage payments to bond holders in a securitisation structure, trustees must be and are highly rated institutions which have adequate credit quality and legal structures to ensure isolation and processes and systems to act for the bond holders. The trustee's purpose is to act as the owner of the loans for the benefit of the certificate holders and distribute information provided by the servicers to the certificate holders. The trustee may act as custodian and physically hold loan files, or the structure may include a separate custodian whose job is to manage loan files. This is a distinct function from the party providing trustee services.

Mortgage loans are highly dynamic assets with substantial duration and must be serviced and managed. Servicing includes the day-to-day transmittal of information from borrowers to certificate holders, the posting of mortgage payments, dealing with borrowers on a day-to-day basis, dealing with borrower requests about the mortgaged property or the terms of the loans, funding or withdrawing funds from reserves, approving leases, budgets and the like. Servicing also includes dealing with the borrower when the loan defaults. This may involve realising on the loan through foreclosure and managing and ultimately selling real estate owned property.

Through the RTC days, a pattern developed in the industry of dividing this universe of servicing functions into three separate service packages often provided by different institutions: master servicing, special servicing and primary servicing.

14

The master servicer mainly deals with day-to-day servicing issues and manages the cash flow of the underlying borrowers to the trustee for distribution to the certificate holders, and is also responsible for the advancing function discussed below. The primary servicing is usually an institution more closely connected to the loan originator and often within geographic proximity to the mortgaged property to which the master servicer can delegate certain servicing functions such as annual appraisals and site visits. The special servicer deals with the borrower when default occurs or default is imminent. The special servicer is the place where genuine real estate expertise resides and the special servicer has a professional staff which is particularly trained in dealing with problem of non-performing credits.

The master servicing has, in addition to its servicing function, an advancing function. Advancing is one of the hallmark characteristics of US securitisation. As described above, CMBS ratings are not only of the ultimate recovery of principal but the "timely" receipt of interest.

Delays in the payment of interest or principal by a mortgage borrower, even those not in severe stress, are not uncommon (e.g. when there is a mismatch between the date the underlying borrower makes payment on its loan and the dates bondholders must by paid). Moreover, when loans default, the underlying borrower may simply cease making payments of interest and principal. In order for the ratings model to work and to meet the expectations of investors, payments of interest to certificate holders must not be interrupted except in the final exigency of the actual losses by the securitisation trust. To achieve that, the industry has developed the notion of advancing. The master servicer is obligated to advance for property protection purposes or to make principal and interest payments not timely made by the related borrowers so long as the servicer can determine, in its professional judgment, it will be able to recover the amount of that advance from the underlying collateral. A servicer which makes an advance is entitled to reimbursement of that advance from payments by the related borrower obligor unless and until the servicer determines that the payment is not recoverable, in which case it's entitled to repayment from any money available in the trust. This structure assures that the higher rated bonds receive full payment as long as the fundamental economics are there to pay these bond holders and, of course, the lower rated bonds absorb the losses and costs associated with the structure.

Because the ratings model and investor expectations require that the party providing advances be rated no less than one ratings level below the highest rated bonds in the pool (typically AA ratings), there are only a handful of master servicers.

Figure 5, below, depicts the structure of a typical US securitisation.

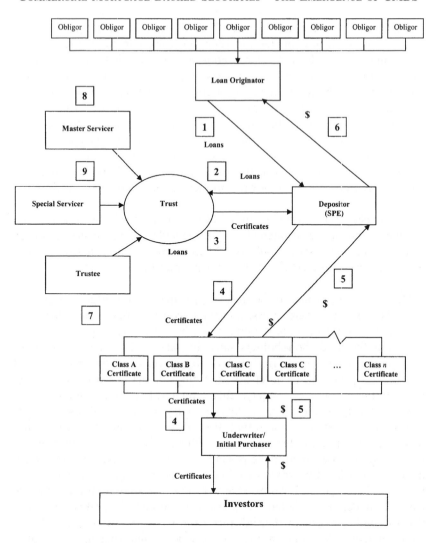

Figure 5: US Securitisation schematic.

This shows each of the parties to a traditional securitisation described above and the bilateral relationships among the various participants.

The structure is described and created by the legal document at the core of a securitisation transaction, generally known as a pooling and servicing agreement ("PSA"). The depositor which contributed loans to the pool, the master and special servicer, the trustee or custodian, sometimes a fiscal agent and several others are all parties. This lengthy and complex document attempts to govern all aspects of the transaction. The PSA imposes the trust upon the pool assets, creates and describes each of the certificates representing an interest in the trust, contains the cash waterfall which allocates the cash flow from the mortgage loans in the pool sequentially to the certificate holders, establishes and articulates the duties of the trustee, master servicer and special servicer, and many other technical provisions including those assuring the appropriate tax treatment of the vehicle.

CONCLUSION

CMBS in the United States has been a huge success. In its infancy barely 15 years ago, it has transformed in a permanent way the commercial mortgage finance landscape. A complex and curious novelty in the early 1990s has matured into a large, robust and structurally stable, albeit still complex, replacement and supplement to the traditional portfolio lending model. Whole new industries have grown to fill the need to manage this enterprise. A lender to originate, an array of professional servicers to service, the whole world of investors up and down the risk curve to buy the bond that was once a single portfolio lender's domain. The model has expanded the availability of credit to the commercial mortgage market place in what fundamentally is a more stable and sustainable format, and has led to more accurate pricing of credit to real estate markets.

This transformational experience in the United States is now spreading to other markets around the world and will continue to do so until it ultimately is the dominant form of credit formation for sophisticated real estate markets worldwide. It is simply the better way to provide credit to real estate markets and it is here to stay.

CHAPTER TWO

THE BUSINESS ECONOMICS OF CMBS

Caroline Philips, Managing Director, Head of Securitisation
Eurohypo AG

PRICING AND UNDERWRITING STANDARDS

Spreads

The business economics of CMBS in the European markets changed fundamentally during the first half of 2004, when spreads tightened dramatically. This structural shift in pricing has been followed by a period of unprecedented pricing stability. Other than a blip at the end of last year arising from a surge in supply, spreads have been broadly constant for a year; as shown in the graph below:

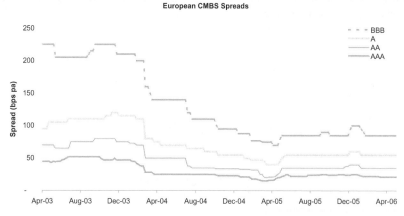

Figure 1: European CMBS spreads.

Source: Eurohypo.

   This new pricing environment lead to a surge in European CMBS issuance volumes in 2005, and which the market expects will continue in 2006 and beyond. The drivers behind this volume growth are broadly two-fold:

(1) Investment banks seeking to maximise profit from their CMBS conduit programmes.

(2) Real Estate borrowers seeking competitively priced financing.

Conduit programmes

The rise of the CMBS conduit programme has been dramatic. For some years Morgan Stanley's ELoC programme was the only active conduit in the market, but, at the time of writing, there are 21 conduits which have issued CMBS and three more have announced that they intend to issue securities later in 2006.

	Conduit Name	2005 Euro Issuance
1	Opera Finance (Eurohypo)	4.7 bn
2	DECO (Deutsche Bank)	2.5 bn
3	ECLIPSE (Barclays Capital)	2.3 bn
4	Titan (Cornerstone) (CSFB/GMAC)	1.8 bn
5	Windermere (Lehman Brothers)	1.7 bn
6	Real Estate Capital (Rothschild)	1.7 bn
7	Talisman (ABN Amro)	1.3 bn
8	EPIC (Royal Bank of Scotland)	1.2 bn
9	ELoC (Morgan Stanley)	1.1 bn
10	Taurus (Merrill Lynch)	0.9 bn
	Seven others	4.9 bn
	Total	**23.8 bn**

Figure 2: Top 10 European CMBS Conduit programmes.

Source: Barclays Capital (y/e 2005).

The proliferation in European CMBS conduit issuance is being driven by a desire to increase profits. For many years US investment banks have been seeking to emulate the successes of their US CMBS businesses in Europe, but until recently the fundamentals did not make much sense. However, the fall in European CMBS spreads during 2004 has changed all that; the business economics underlying CMBS conduits are now clearly positive, and in 2005 conduit issuance leapt to over €23bn, up from €8.6bn in 2004. At the time of writing total issuance is approaching €11bn, and given the traditional surge in activity during the last quarter, 2006 is expected to be another record year for European CMBS conduit issuance.

Pricing

The basic business premise driving CMBS is that a commercial mortgage loan margin is greater than the cost of fully securitising that commercial mortgage loan. This is especially so when such loans are packaged together to improve risk diversity. So, for example, let us take a hypothetical portfolio of commercial mortgage loans:

Number of loans:	10
Total loan amount outstanding:	Euro 1 billion
Weighted average margin:	85bppa
Weighted average loan maturity:	Seven years
Weighted average up front fee received:	35bps
Weighted average loan to value ratio ("LTV"):	75 per cent

This hypothetical portfolio could be securitised in full with a credit structure something like the following:

	Amount	% total	LTV	Spread (bppa)
AAA Notes	720	72.0%	54%	20
AA Notes	100	10.0%	62%	35
A Notes	80	8.0%	68%	55
BBB Notes	80	8.0%	74%	85
BB Notes	20	2.0%	75%	250
	1,000	100.0%	75%	**34**
Issuer costs				7
Amortisation of Up Front Costs				7
Total CMBS costs				**48**
Excess spread				**37**

So on this hypothetical portfolio, the return post securitisation is 37bppa, with no on-going risk exposure to the loan originator: an infinite return on equity. In addition, many issues are now structured to monetise some or all of this excess spread up front, typically via Class X Notes or Net Interest Margin (NIM) certificates.

The pricing of loans destined for conduit issuance would normally be expected to be driven by the overall lending market, and in particular the traditional commercial mortgage portfolio lending banks who are the historic drivers of the markets. However, with so many CMBS conduits looking to originate loan products, there has been a steep increase in competition, and a natural consequence of this increased competition is that pricing falls. Where a loan is suitable for securitisation, the conduit lenders will drive the pricing down to whatever level can still (just about) make a decent return via securitisation. Views on what a decent return is differ from bank to bank, but will often be less in a start up situation. With so many new conduits vying for the same business, loan pricing in some markets has fallen dramatically.

This has lead the conduits to look further afield for their loan product, both on a geographic and sector basis. Germany is now vying with the UK as the biggest source of loan collateral for conduit issuance, and there are an increasing number of asset types being funded alongside each other.

Underwriting standards can come under pressure within such a competitive environment, but unlike the traditional commercial mortgage portfolio lending market, where each bank makes up it own mind about what risk it is prepared to take, the CMBS market has the consistency afforded by the rating agencies. The rating agencies' universal and standardised approach to credit analysis across all CMBS transactions is a great strength of the market, and should give investors significant comfort at a time when there remain significant differences between all the various types of CMBS issuance.

GROWTH IN FLEXIBILITY

Property companies, particularly those based in the UK, have historically used securitisation as a means to raise large amounts of long-term finance, and this remains the case today. However, increasingly, in addition to this, property companies are now looking to the capital markets for shorter maturity finance—traditionally provided by the syndicated loan markets—and in 2005 there was a significant amount of refinancing as companies sought to benefit from the attractive pricing available in the capital markets.

One consequence of this use of securitisation by property companies has been the increased amount of flexibility being built into transactions.

Prepayment flexibility

In the early days of the market, securitisation was often criticised by European real estate borrowers for being inflexible compared to normal secured bank lending. This criticism was based primarily on prepayment inflexibility; even for shorter dated finance, securitised loans typically had severe early repayment penalties that involved a full margin make-whole. This was ideal for loan originators and investors, as it allowed excess spread to be sold up front, and it created greater certainty of average life. However, borrowers disliked it, and in response to pressure from these borrowers, prepayment fees in securitised real estate loans are now pretty much in line with that seen in the commercial lending markets.

Prepayment remains a hot topic of debate in the industry as recent prepayment rates across all European CMBS issues have been high, as indeed they have across the whole of the European commercial mortgage market.

Loans prepayments are driven by borrower activity:

- refinancing at cheaper levels—both loan spread and underlying interest rates,

- increasing leverage off the back of increasing values,

- restructuring of repayment terms, and

- disposing of assets.

All of these activities occur more in an environment of increasing values and falling spreads.

Traditionally loan prepayment penalties paid by the borrower to the lender should partially compensate for loss of margin, and fully compensate for administrative costs and any loss that may arise due to underlying interest rate changes. Currently, with strong competition between lenders, most borrowers do not need to accept prepayment penalties which fully compensate the lender.

Prepayment is unattractive for noteholders, even though most European conduit CMBS transactions are floating-rate, as it exposes buy-and-hold investors to reinvestment risk if spreads have tightened since issue, and similarly it exposes secondary investors who have bought at a premium if the notes are redeemed at par. In addition there is the cost and inconvenience of sourcing new assets and re-matching portfolio maturity against liabilities. In particular, investors complain about the costs in terms of wasted effort analysing a deal and its underlying assets when early prepayment occurs.

Note that in a spread tightening environment, loan prepayments will increase as borrowers have more refinancing options; likewise as spreads widen, prepayments should fall, as borrowers have less incentive to refinance.

Asset management flexibility

Another topic close to a borrower's heart is asset management flexibility. The area of debate broadly splits into two:

(1) restrictions relating to the secured properties; and

(2) substitution of secured properties.

Restrictions relating to the secured properties are typically the same in both the traditional commercial mortgage portfolio banking and the capital

22

markets, and are driven more by the expertise of the borrower or property manager and the nature of the underlying secured properties. Indeed, in certain cases, the flexibility offered in the capital markets can be greater than that generally available in the traditional commercial mortgage portfolio bank market.

The ability to substitute properties is more challenging. Historically investors have been wary of funding portfolios that can change over time through the substitution of assets. Hours of time have been spent negotiating tortuous clauses in loan agreements and offering circulars that endeavour to set conditions on asset substitution—conditions that are often difficult to apply in practice, and yet still do not give investors the clarity that they desire. The benchmark is typically that a maximum of around 30 per cent of the secured properties can be substituted over the life of the transaction subject to certain other criteria (typically relating to valuation, income and geographic diversity, amongst others) being met.

However, in more recent CMBS transactions, the boundaries have been pushed to new levels of substitution flexibility. Perhaps the most extreme example of this is Land Securities' "corporate" securitisation launched in late 2004. Here securitisation replaced corporate bonds as the core funding source, and at lower leverage levels, the structure permitted unlimited disposal and acquisition of assets of all types. The financing was governed by a tiered covenant regime which increases in flexibility provided LTV and interest coverage ratios are kept at healthy levels. If coverage levels reduce, more and tighter covenants are imposed which slowly reduce flexibility and impose a covenant regime more similar to other CMBS transactions. The Land Securities transaction did not target AAA ratings, preferring the greater degree of flexibility afforded by a AA rating. However, even at the AA level, the flexibility was unprecedented for a European CMBS transaction.

What is clear, as we have see in Ch. 1, and will be examined in detail in the central theme to this book, is that the European CMBS market is seeing increasing levels of innovation and structural complexity in single-loan CMBS issues, as arrangers seek to tailor transactions to the underlying borrowers.

VOLUME OUTLOOK

Figure 3, below, shows European CMBS issuance levels over the last few years:

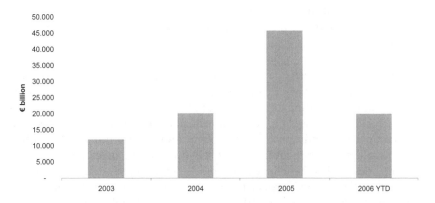

Figure 3: European CMBS issuance 2003–2006 YTD.

Source: Eurohypo.

At the beginning of 2006, market forecasters were predicting 2006 European CMBS issuance of around €60m, a growth rate of around 30 per cent compared to 2005. Announced issuance at the time of writing was €19bn, almost the same as during the same period in 2005. Notwithstanding this, the continued positive business economics for real estate securitisation are likely to lead to a continuation in the growth of issuance. The pipeline looks healthy for the rest of 2006, and in particular a large number of German multi-family issues are expected to fuel growth.[1] Most market forecasters have left their forecasts intact.

CONCLUSION

To underline the growth potential of CMBS in Europe, it is worth remembering that CMBS accounts for only 11 per cent of the overall commercial mortgage lending market, although the figure is slightly higher in the UK at 25 per cent.[2] Both figures are well below the US average which is estimated at between 35 and 40 per cent.

To achieve a 40 per cent share of the total commercial lending market, European CMBS still has a way to go, but most market commentators reckon it is well on its way.

---

[1] The popularity of German assets, such as multifamily shows no inclination of decreasing as may be seen in Ch. 16.
[2] Source: Barclays Capital/DTZ.

CHAPTER THREE

THE EUROPEAN CMBS MARKET

**Nassar Hussain, Managing Director of Debt Markets,
Head of Real Estate Trading, CMBS and Distribution (EMEA)
Merrill Lynch International**[1]

INTRODUCTION

The European CMBS market has experienced impressive growth in recent
years and has matured into a diverse and robust arena for innovative and
sophisticated financing of real estate assets and receivables. It is one of the
most dynamic and fastest growing sectors in the capital markets. European
CMBS issuance levels reached €46bn in 2005, compared with only €14bn
in 2004, and are forecast to reach €55bn+ in 2006. It has become both
an integral part of the European commercial real estate debt market
(directly influencing lending terms across Europe) and the European structured finance market (accounting for 14 per cent of the total funded
structured finance market in 2005).

The issuers in the market are diverse and varied and include sovereigns,
private and public property companies, corporate owner occupiers (such as
retailers and telecom companies) and investment and commercial banks.
The reasons for utilising CMBS are equally diverse and include regulatory
capital arbitrage, risk exposure management, cost-efficient financing, conduit funding arbitrage, off-balance sheet financing and diversifying an
investor base. In addition, funding structures reflect the innovation and
diversity of players, with term bond funding up to 35 years (particularly in
the UK), revolving commercial paper funding; part-bond, part-commercial
paper structures; synthetic structures; part-cash, part-synthetic; and with the
huge growth of the B note market we are now seeing an abundance of part-

---

[1] The views and opinions contained in this article are those of the author and do not reflect in
any way the views of Merrill Lynch.

bond and part-bank/fund driven lending. In recent times, issuance has been dominated by conduit programmes established by investment banks and other multi-borrower transactions, single borrower issuances by large property companies and sovereign transactions relating to government disposal of real estate (in particular Italy).

This chapter will begin with a brief history of the emergence of CMBS in Europe and will then look at various aspects of European CMBS including, key participants, why CMBS is used, CMBS spreads, CMBS issuance, ratings transition, transaction types, transaction motivation, property types and valuations, legal issues peculiar to the European market and the impact of Basel II.[2]

ORIGINS AND EARLY DEVELOPMENT OF THE EUROPEAN CMBS MARKET

The European CMBS market developed for very different reasons to the US CMBS market, where it developed and grew as a result of distress in the commercial real estate market, financial regulatory changes and retrenchment of traditional lenders, as a result of which, borrowers and financial institutions turned to the capital markets to raise funds by issuing CMBS. Whilst the initial impetus for CMBS transactions in the US came from the Resolution Trust Corporation ("RTC")[3] (the federal agency responsible for clearing up the savings and loans (thrift) institutions), this was complemented very quickly by private sector issuance especially as the commercial real estate market improved.

Whilst the very first real estate capital market transactions in Europe were developed at a time of distress in the UK market, such as the £150m Kings Cross House PLC (1989), the number of transactions were very limited and short-lived as the immense liquidity and relationship-based lending practices, which epitomise the real estate lending arena in Europe, came back to the forefront. Consequently, many of the deals that followed tended to be opportunistic and, with the development of all new markets, were focused on the easier jurisdictions and collateral types and typically with only one rating agency involved. In the early 1990s, a number of agented single-borrower deals, secured against Central London offices, and credit tenant leases were completed, including the £120m 135 Bishopsgate Funding (1991) and the £42.3m Grays Inn Road transaction (1992). This pattern was fol-

---

[2] Basel Committee on Banking Supervision: *International Convergence of Capital Measurement and Capital Standards: A Revised Framework*. June 2004, available at http://www.bis.org/publ/bcbs107.htm.
[3] See Ch.1.

lowed by subsequent deals such as the £40m Solar transaction (1995) secured against a Central London office building let to the UK Government.

The initial multi-borrower deals were driven by balance sheet/capital management, risk transfer and funding requirements. The very first multi-borrower CMBS was completed in the UK in 1993 by UCBH, in a securitisation of a nursing home loan portfolio in the £183m Hog 1 transaction (1993), and similar deals were completed by Citibank under the Sonar programme in 1994 and 1995. Bristol & West Building Society completed the £145.5m UK CLIPS CMBS in 1994 and the United Bank of Kuwait commenced the popular Acres programme in 1995, completing three multi-borrower CMBS deals including a separate sell-down of the pooled residuals (£109m Acres 1 (1995), £121.3m Acres 2 (1996), and £118m Acres 3 (1997)).

The late 1990s saw a number of landmark deals which were to shape the European CMBS market for many years to come with innovative structuring and increased deal sizes. These included the £555m Canary Wharf Finance securitisation in 1997, the largest transaction to have been completed to date, which tapped into both the floating rate market and a unique feature of the UK market, the long dated fixed rate sterling bond market. The £343.2m CIT transaction in 1997, also secured on offices with credit tenants, was the first single-borrower deal to have exposure to refinancing risk as well as being funded partly in the commercial paper market (senior tranches), with the junior tranches being structured for placement in the banking market (not dissimilar to the AB structures very common today). In 1996 and 1997, the first non-UK CMBS transactions were completed, with several transactions being completed in France including the Ffr1.5bn Belenus for UIC-Sofal and the Ffr2bn La Defense transaction, which secured office buildings in Paris. The first European conduit programme was established by Morgan Stanley in 1998, with the pioneering £168.9m ELOC 1 transaction. Anglo Irish Bank Corporation, shortly thereafter, completed the first deal in its Monument CMBS programme of highly granular commercial mortgages in the UK, which was driven by capital management requirements. 1999 witnessed the first jumbo CMBS transaction in the form of the £1.5bn Broadgate securitisation, a trophy asset securitisation with a highly innovative security structure driven by compliance with restrictions in the borrower's existing corporate bonds/debentures. In 1999 one of the first synthetic CMBS transactions was completed by Deutsche Hypothekenbank in relation a pool of second lien commercial rate mortgages (€267m Deutsche Hypothekenbank, Hannover).

Examples of some key European CMBS transactions since 2000 include the following:

- Europa 1 (2000)—one of the first multi-jurisdictional synthetic CMBS in Europe.

- Global Hotel 1 (2001)—first synthetic CMBS secured on global hotel portfolio.

- Pan European Industrial Properties 1 (2001)—one of the first multi-jurisdictional cash CMBS in Europe (UK, Holland and France).

- SCIP Series—€2.3bn SCIP 1 (2001) sovereign securitisation by Italian Treasury backed by commercial and residential property followed by €6.6bn SCIP 2 (2002) (refinanced April 05) being one of the largest CMBS transactions to date.

- Imser Securitisation S.r.l. (2002)—first performing Italian CMBS.

- Eiger Trust (2003)—first Swiss CMBS.

- ELOC 17 (2003)—first multi-jurisdictional conduit CMBS.

- Business Mortgage Finance 1 (2004)—first non-conforming small commercial loan CMBS in Europe.

- Self Storage Securitisation B.V. (2004)—first self storage CMBS in Europe.

- Land Securities (2005)—quasi corporate/CMBS flexible financing structure.

- Taurus 1 CMBS (2005)—first co-pooled conduit CMBS in Europe.

- Fleet Street Finance 1 (2005)—first securitisation of predominantly operating real estate assets to apply CMBS analysis in order to achieve superior rating levels.

- Taurus 2 CMBS (2005)—first multi-borrower conduit CMBS in Italy.

- Real Estate Capital 3 (Foundation) (2005)—one of the most flexible CMBS transactions to date including securitisation of blind pool of assets.

- Forest Finance (2005)—first CMBS in Austria.

- Opera Finance (CMH) (2006)—first CMBS in Ireland.

KEY PARTICIPANTS IN EUROPEAN CMBS

Issuers

The issuers are varied and encompass most entities that own real estate assets or some form of direct or indirect real estate risk including corporates (publicly listed and private real estate companies, publicly listed and private

28

companies that own real estate (such as retailers and telecom companies), investment banks, commercial banks, mortgage banks, sovereigns, funds and individuals.

Motives

- All: cost efficient financing, diversification of funding sources, access to a deep investor base, capacity for much larger deal sizes, enhanced market profile, innovative and flexible structuring techniques, strategic funding tool.

- Financial institutions: also includes regulatory arbitrage, off balance sheet financing, risk exposure management, improving return on equity, conduit funding arbitrage.

- Sovereigns: also includes improving sovereign balance sheets and fiscal credibility.

- Corporates/Funds: also includes access to longer funding maturities (particularly in the UK), maintain existing banking relationships through B notes.

Rating agencies[4]

The dominant three rating agencies in Europe, Fitch Ratings (acquired Duff & Phelps in 2000), Moody's Investor Service ("Moody's") and Standard & Poor's, are all active in rating CMBS transactions in Europe. The analytical approach followed by these agencies is varied in relation to modelling methodology, qualitative analysis and legal and structural analysis and it is not unusual to see split ratings or certain parts of the capital structure where not all rating agencies on a deal participate. In the early years of the CMBS market, it was not uncommon for rating analysts to focus on a number of asset classes, however, with the huge growth of the structured finance market and the increased specialisation and sophistication of the market, each have product teams that specialise in CMBS and, in some cases, country teams (rather than London based) that specialise in CMBS only in their respective jurisdiction. Moody's and Standard & Poor's globally have the largest market share in the structured finance market and benefit from many investors such as CP conduits, SIVs and CDOs requiring both a Moody's and Standard & Poor's rating. The notching requirements, in many cases, make its difficult for such investors to invest in bonds without a Moody's and Standard & Poor's rating. Fitch Ratings has sought to differentiate itself through increased focus on customer service and investor education. The estimated market share by volume of these three agencies on European CMBS in recent years has been:

---

[4] For details of the ratings process within Standard & Poor's, see Ch. 4.

- Fitch Ratings: 80–90 per cent.

- Moody's: 70–90 per cent.

- Standard & Poor's: 85–90 per cent.

In recent months, the Canadian-based Dominion Bond Rating Service has announced plans to enter the European CMBS market and is in the process of establishing a team in Europe.

Investors

The CMBS investor base is diverse and comprises numerous types of financial institutions including banks, building societies and fund managers, CP Conduits, SIVs, CDOs, insurance companies, pension funds, opportunistic/hedge funds, corporates and in the case of sub-investment grade debt even high net worth individuals.

The arguments for CMBS investment relative to other asset classes include:

- yield pick compared to consumer finance asset classes;

- the capital structure of deals is conservative—credit enhancement for AAA in the region of 25 to 30 per cent on many deals;

- many deals have exposure to investment grade tenants—which are a superior credit to B leverage loan CLOs; and

- portfolio granularity can be found in some deals—for example large shopping centres with a wide range of tenants, business finance deals with a large number of SME-like borrowers, and even portfolio office deals with a range of properties, tenants and re-letting options.

Many deals are pricing around the recently established benchmark levels because of:

- novelty—the first deals from a certain country or property sector;

- supply levels; and

- analytical complexity for investors to get comfortable with deals.

Servicers[5]

The servicer administers the loan or loans secured on the underlying real estate. The administration of the underlying real estate is typically undertaken by managing agents on behalf of the underlying borrower. This administration includes payment collections, maintaining systems and undertaking data management, maintaining a dialogue with borrowers and dealing with their day-to-day administration requirements (including col-

---

[5] For details of servicing CMBS, see Ch. 10.

lateral changes), checking covenant compliance, insurance renewals, providing payment instructions to the paying agent and other parties to the securitisation and investor reporting and, in some instances, cash management duties on the securitisation. The servicers duties also include controlling the workout of defaulted loans, although in recent years more structured servicing practices have been adopted in Europe which follow the more mature US market in the form of primary servicing and special servicing. The primary servicer performs the general servicing duties, however, on a loan default or a pre-defined trigger breach, a special servicer takes over negotiations with the borrower to remedy the breach or liquidate the assets. A key point of debate in the European market is the level and ranking of special servicing fees, which are considered high compared to European standards, although these are mainly designed to encourage the maximisation of recoveries and are indirectly borne by the most junior debt holder in the securitisation structure, who also, in many cases, has the ability to change the appointment of the special servicer.

Many issuers in the CMBS market, which are financial institutions, will undertake their own servicing and special servicing. The key third party primary servicers in the market are Capmark Services Ireland, Hatfield Philips International and Crown Mortgages Management. Recently the in-house servicing teams of certain banks, such as Morgan Stanley (Morgan Stanley Mortgage Servicing), have started to offer their services to third parties. The key third party special servicers are Capmark Services UK and Hatfield Philips International/LNR Partners.

CMBS SPREADS

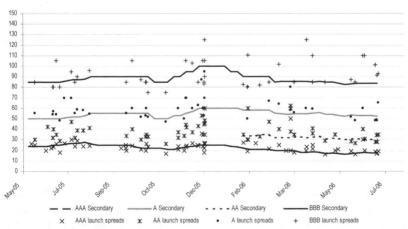

Figure 1: CMBS Spreads 2005–06.

Source: Merrill Lynch; Primary spreads reflect weighted-average where more than one similar-rated tranches from a transaction.

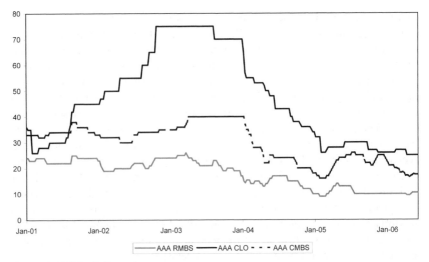

Figure 2: Triple-A Spreads.

Source: Merrill Lynch.

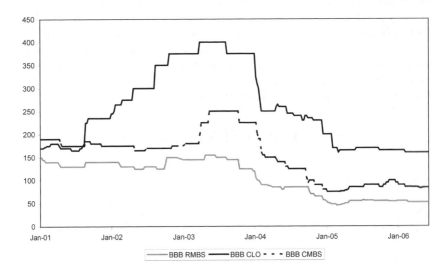

Figure 3: Triple-B Spreads.

Source: Merrill Lynch.

One of the key factors for the rapid growth in the European CMBS market in recent years has been the spread tightening, as shown in Figures 1, 2 and 3, above, witnessed across the whole structured finance market as a result of general trends in the credit market but also increased appetite from structured finance investors. Although the recent spread tightening began in late 2003/early 2004, due to the lead time that CMBS transactions take the surge in volume of issuance came through in 2005. Notwithstanding this significant reduction in funding costs through CMBS, the benchmark pricing levels we are now witnessing are not dissimilar to the pricing levels pre-1998 although supply and the sophistication of the market in those years was more limited.

CMBS ISSUANCE

Securitisation techniques are often used to package disparate exposures together, allowing for diversification. However, the range of commercial real estate securitisations available is even wider than for traditional MBS or ABS: from single-loan or single-borrower transactions to multiple-loan portfolio transactions. Such transaction diversity requires different analytical approaches and investor considerations. Nevertheless, one can always begin with an assessment of debt-service coverage, tenant quality, lease types, and property valuation.

Unlike other types of securitised collateral, European CMBS are not homogeneous asset pools that are automatically suited to statistical analysis. In fact, CMBS transactions in Europe come in a variety of shapes and sizes, and often different property types and geographic locales are packaged together to enhance diversification benefits for investors.

Issuance by issuer type

Figure 4, below, shows issuance by issuer type with the two largest components being single borrower issuances and conduit and multi-borrower

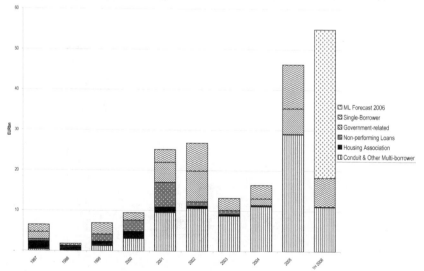

Figure 4: CMBS issuance by issuer type (EURbn).

Source: Merrill Lynch.

issuance. The largest component of the market has tended to be the single borrower deals, although in recent years we have seen a significant increase from conduit issuers and sovereigns such as the State of Italy. In Europe, however, conduit terminology has not always followed the principal and multi-borrower nature of the conduit market in the US and many issuers such as Eurohypo, RBS and NM Rothschild have branded single borrower agented deals under their respective conduit branding. These agented "conduit" transactions have tended generally to be less profitable than more traditional "principal" conduit transactions. If one takes into account this branding approach then single borrower deals continue to form the largest component of the CMBS market in Europe.

Issuance by country

As Figure 5, below, shows the source of collateral for CMBS transactions has traditionally been dominated by the UK, which has the most developed CRE investment market, a very creditor friendly legal regime, and is where structuring techniques were adopted early on as the securitisation markets developed. In 2005, partly due to the expansion of conduit lending outside the UK and the lack of activity of domestic German real estate lenders, Germany has emerged as a major source of loans for conduit lenders whose traditional international customer base have been aggressively acquiring assets in Germany. In addition, Italy has also produced some purely private sector CMBS transactions, sovereign deals and more recently conduit deals. CMBS transactions have recently been completed in Austria and Ireland and the growth of and demand for multi-jurisdictional transactions will

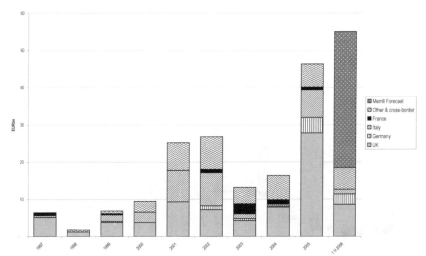

Figure 5: CMBS issuance by country (EURbn).

Source: Merrill Lynch.

ensure that issuance increasingly is derived from a broad range of European jurisdictions. Central and Eastern Europe remain difficult jurisdictions as sources of collateral for CMBS mainly due to legal impediments.

Issuance by property type

Offices have been the most popular source of asset class for CMBS deals which is not surprising bearing in mind its dominance of the commercial real estate asset base. There have been a significant numbers of deals monetising retail assets in all its forms from large regional shopping centres and secondary shopping centres to high street retail and retail warehouse parks. As can be seen in Figure 6, below, the market has witnessed a significant growth in non-traditional real estate asset classes such as hotels, hospitals, public houses, self-storage and nursing homes. Multi-family especially now out of Germany (traditionally from Sweden and France) has become a major source of collateral for CMBS deals in the last 18 months.

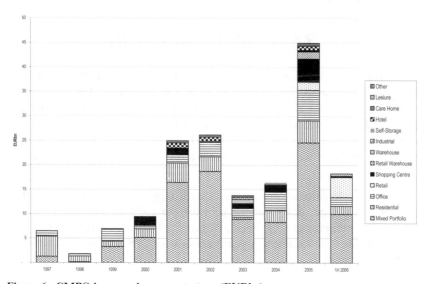

Figure 6: CMBS issuance by property type (EURbn).

Source: Merrill Lynch.

Issuance by currency

Figure 7, below, demonstrates that Sterling has dominated the European CMBS market reflecting the dominance of the UK as the source of collateral for most CMBS deals. However, with increased issuance from continental Europe and the depth and importance of the € investor base its dominance is expected to decline in coming years.

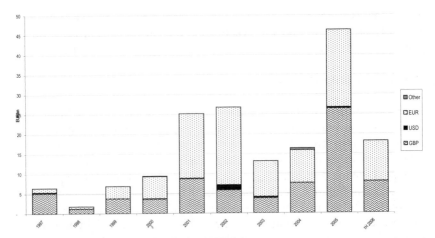

Figure 7: CMBS issuance by currency (EURbn).

Source: Merrill Lynch.

RATINGS TRANSITION

As European CMBS issuance has grown, the asset class can be looked at independently from other structured finance asset clauses. The case for the stability of the asset class is set out in recent rating agency transition data. Perhaps European CMBS is considered a more volatile asset class, more exposed to single-tenant or event risk. However, ratings transition studies place CMBS quite well relative to other structured finance asset classes.

Moody's calculated a downgrade rate for CMBS of 2.9 per cent in 2005, and average 3.6 per cent over the period from 1998 to 2005, see Figure 8, below. This compares to a 4.7 per cent rate for European Structured finance as a whole over the same seven-year period, with CDOs at 11.4 per cent and ABS at 1.6 per cent.

Looking at upgrades, CMBS averaged 4.9 per cent rate compared to 3.7 per cent for all structured finance. The upgrade rate in 2005 was 12.2 per cent—largely driven by high prepayment. Calculating a downgrade to upgrade ratio, CMBS come out at 0.73 per cent, similar to the 0.64 per cent for ABS, but well below the 2.71 per cent for CDOs. Compared with US CMBS, European CMBS also comes out well. Weighting ratings changed by notches, Moody's calculated rating volatility for European CMBS at 11.8 per cent, but 28.4 per cent for US CMBS. To put that in context European RMBS had a rating volatility of 9.1 per cent and European CDOs of 39.7 per cent.

	Downgrade Rate				Upgrade Rate			
	2005	2004	1998–05	1998–05 (US)	2005	2004	1998–05	1998–05 (US)
Overall SF	2.0%	4.0%	4.7%	4.4%	7.3%	1.8%	3.7%	3.8%
ABS	0.7%	1.8%	1.6%	5.4%	2.9%	2.4%	2.5%	1.9%
CDOs	3.8%	7.5%	11.4%	9.9%	8.1%	1.9%	4.2%	0.8%
CMBS	**2.9%**	**4.6%**	**3.6%**	**3.6%**	**12.2%**	**3.6%**	**4.9%**	**8.8%**
RMBS	0.3%	0.7%	0.4%	1.0%	8.0%	0.8%	3.9%	5.2%
Global SF	1.9%	5.0%	4.3%	n/a	6.2%	4.4%	3.9%	n/a
Global Corporate	8.3%	8.1%	14.3%	n/a	13.8%	13.3%	9.5%	n/a

* common to Europe/US.

Figure 8: Moody's European structured finance rating transitions, 1988–2005.

Source: Moody's.

Standard & Poor's ratings show a similar picture. Of 430 CMBS ratings, in 2005 the downgrade transition rate was 2.3 per cent compared to 0.3 per cent for RMBS and 3.9 per cent for CDOs. The upgrade rate was 6.5 per cent compared to 6.3 per cent for RMBS and 3.4 per cent for CDOs. The downgrade to upgrade ratio is again low for CMBS, given upgrades balance out the downgrades.

A further source of comfort for CMBS investors can be had from Fitch Ratings reporting that of the CMBS transactions rated by Fitch Ratings, 100 per cent of all investment grade tranches in 2005 maintained their rating or moved to a higher category with just one downgrade of a tranche at speculative level.

Perhaps relative to RMBS, CMBS is more volatile and does not always benefit so much from the structural de-levering seen in RMBS. However, this is against very benign economic circumstances for the consumer and high residential mortgage refinancing and prepayment, which may not always be the case. A selection of ratings change in 2006 can be seen in Figure 9, below.

Relative to CDOs, the same level of downgrade activity is not seen. CDOs seem to suffer from credit events with major names, which then affect a wide number of deals. CMBS have little of this cross-deal exposure and, in that way, offer a diversification opportunity. One point to note is that Standard & Poor's recognised that only one downgrade in 2005 was related to a problem with a corporate tenant—perhaps indicating that concern over tenant risk is exaggerated.

High loan prepayment rates in the CRE market translate to high pre-payment activity in CMBS bonds. Over the period from 2004 to 2005, this

Deal	Issue Date	Agency	Class	New Rating	Previous Rating	Portfolio Repaid
Coronis (ELoC No. 8)	Nov 01	Standard & Poor's	D	AAA	A+	75%
		Fitch Ratings	C	AAA	A	
			D	AA−	A−	
			F	CCC+	B	
Nereus (ELoC No.20)	Aug 04	Moody's	D	A1	Baa1	53%
Whiter Tower 2004–1	Mar 04	Standard & Poor's	C	AA	A+	50%
Real Estate Capital No.2	May 04	Standard & Poor's	B	AAA	AA	71%
			C	AAA	A	
Victoria Funding	Oct 05	Standard & Poor's	B	AAA	AA	61%
			C	AAA	A	

Source: Rating Agencies.

Figure 9: Selected CMBS ratings changes January–February 2006.

has had a beneficial effect on ratings transition, as many transactions have been upgraded as sequential structures de-lever on receipt of prepayment principal. This strongly positive effect may recede, either as prepayment activity slows as more recent deals have been originated at tight loan margins, and as some recent deals have been structured with less conservative modified pro-rata payment structures. As a result, future ratings transition tables may reveal lower upgrade rates, although downgrade performance should not be significantly affected.

The vast majority of upgrades have been due to prepayments in sequential pay structures and by improved ratings of corporates in credit-linked deals. Downgrades have predominantly been due to declines in ratings of corporates in credit linked deals or ratings assigned to supporting financial institution debt collateral on partly funded synthetic structures. Whilst there have been some notable downgrades for other reasons in the European CMBS market, such as the HOTELOC PLC transaction (loan default) and on the Coronis (ELoC No.8) PLC (loan default) transaction, to-date no investors in European CMBS have suffered a loss due to credit reasons although interest may not have always been met on the most junior bonds predominantly due to available fund cap type issues (e.g. Heritage (Mortgage Securities PLC)). Based on recent Standard & Poor's reports, however, it appears that a loss is increasingly likely on the Coronis (ELoC No.8) transaction.

MAJOR TRANSACTION TYPES

In creating European property securitisations, there are three major types of transactions employed, each of which require a somewhat different analysis:

- portfolio transactions;
- property transactions; and
- single-property transactions.

With each type of transaction, a different risk is contemplated, and each transaction type may include one or more property types.

Portfolio transactions

Whilst it is difficult to clearly categorise, portfolio transactions generally refer to multi-borrower, multi-property diversified loan pools with 30+ loans. Multi-borrower diversified loan portfolios (UK balance sheet, German and Italian transactions to-date) best employ a similar analysis to that of US conduit transactions—primarily an actuarial analysis.

Property transactions

Property transactions generally refer to multi-borrower loan pools with less than 15–20 loans (in many cases less than 10) with a potentially wide or narrow range of properties. These transactions are often classified as "conduit" transactions. Although as mentioned above many European conduit transactions are not principal transactions but are agented transactions branded as conduits where the underlying borrower gets the direct benefit of the bond margins.

European conduits, despite their moniker, in many ways, do not resemble the US-style CMBS conduits, which are more akin to the portfolio-type transactions, above. European conduits warrant instead a large-loan, or fundamental, analysis. These large-loan transactions may be further broken down into two sub-groups, based upon whom the cash flows of the loan and, hence, the notes rely:

- those containing properties with a diversified tenant base; and
- those with a few tenants.

The former group requires predominately a property analysis, whereas the latter requires both a property and a tenant analysis.

Multi-borrower pools with between 20 and 50 loans require a hybrid approach, both an examination of the large and/or riskier loans, as well as scenario analysis to determine portfolio impact of loan delinquencies and defaults. Tenant transactions generally refer to sale-leaseback, single-borrower single-property loans and single-borrower multi-property loans with long tenancies.

Single-property transactions

Single-property transactions resemble traditional securitisations even less, and are really more of an investment in a particular property, particular tenant or group of tenants and precise property market (or business district). Although risk is tranched, the normal benefits of property diversification seen in most securitisations are not present. These transactions do, however, vary considerably if the property in question is an office building, retail establishment, industrial warehouse or hotel property, each of which has a different cycle, expenses and tenant mix.

Finally, due to an emergent trend of European corporations and governments (particularly on the Continent) shifting from owner-occupants to tenants, sale-leaseback CMBS have become increasingly common. Sale-leasebacks are effectively secured bonds of the property tenant—again, very different from other CMBS transactions.

TRANSACTION MOTIVATION

Not only do the risk profiles differ among the three exposure types, but the motivation behind the transactions and often the ongoing servicer commitment also vary. Transaction motivation is differentiated, by originator, among:

- Conduits—these are programmes operated by investment banks and more recently commercial banks, which originate loans to investors or companies holding commercial real estate. Loans are structured for securitisation, but may vary widely in terms of structure and underlying collateral. Loans may also be acquired from, or originated in partnership with other lenders. In many cases the loan is bifurcated and only the senior tranche is securitised with the junior tranche (typically known as the B Note) being sold into the banking or specialist fund investor market.[6]

- Commercial Banks (balance sheet lenders)—diversified multi-borrower portfolios generally represent part of the commercial property book of a financial institution seeking to transfer risk from its balance sheet to the capital markets.

- Developers/property companies—these often employ large-loan "property exposure" CMBS in order to achieve lower financing costs than in the traditional bank lending market.

---

[6] See Ch.8 for more detail.

- Corporates and Governments—these often become the sole and long-term tenants of properties within a "tenant-type" CMBS transaction. In these cases, such institutions have sought to divest of non-core assets, restructure the balance sheet, or have desired a source of long-term financing.

Conduits

In Europe the term conduit is loosely applied to a variety of "brand name" transactions and originators. Compared with programmes in the US, European conduits vary widely in terms of transaction scale and standardisation. Prior to 2003, most conduit issuance came from Morgan Stanley's ELoC programme. In 2004, nine names were counted in the market. Over the 18 months to June 2006, 49 transactions were counted (from conduit programmes or branded issuers) with a total value of €30bn. Only 10 programmes have issued more than twice (see Figure 10, below), and 18 transactions have come from the leading four.

Arranger	Programme	# Deals
Eurohypo	Opera	7
CSFB	Titan	6
Deutsche Bank	DECO	6
Barclays Capital	Eclipse	5
ABN Amro	Talisman	3
Lehman Brothers	Windermere	3
Merrill Lynch	Taurus	3
Morgan Stanley	ELoC	3
Royal Bank of Scotland	Epic	3
Societe Generale	White Tower	3

Figure 10: Conduit programmes issuing more than twice.

Profitability amongst conduit programmes vary based on different priorities which as well as revenue generation include profile and league table status and defensive positioning to retain clients.

One of the benefits of the expansion of conduits should be better ability to price risk in CMBS transactions. To achieve this, transactions should offer a more homogenous exposure to property markets and to mitigate risks appropriately—something which has not always been available in Europe to date. With the development of the European conduit market, there is expected to be improvement and innovation in these areas.

Currently, European CMBS conduits do not consistently offer the same level of diversification and standardisation as US structures. Starting with size, average US conduit deal size in 2005 was around $1.8bn; in Europe average deal size is lower although rising, €668m in 2005 compared with €467m in 2004. Granularity is also often a problem: while US investors commonly seek uniform loan size of around €50 to 100m, many European deals may contain one or two very large loans or be backed by a single borrower. Diversification may also be limited in European transactions to one country, property type or industry. On a positive note, some transactions have offered exposure to several countries, and loans backed by multiple tenants do increase diversification.

Turning to transaction structure, conduits should offer a variety of means to eliminate unwanted risks and create a more standardised product for the investor. Critical issues are payment priority between tranches (particularly for prepayments), interest rate hedging,[7] liquidity support and limiting interest payment to available funds. Again European transactions have varied widely in their approach to these risks.

CORE PROPERTY TYPES

Commercial property is generally divided into four major types: office, retail, industrial and hotel. Although tenant quality, property management and location impact all sectors, each property type is also influenced by a range of distinctly different factors that necessitate a more nuanced analysis and differentiation among the property types and the bonds they support through securitisation.

CMBS transactions are backed by one or more properties, representing one or more types of commercial property. The market broadly characterises these property types into the same four types listed above (and multi-family, in Germany and the US). Although, overall, issues such as economic factors, location/accessibility and supply and demand affect all types of properties and their performance as an investment, a number of issues are property-type specific.

Office

Office properties are generally located in a central business district of a medium or large city, or in suburban areas. The looser the planning regime and the more dependent an area is upon service industries, the more cyclical the market is likely to be. Office properties are susceptible to planning regime restrictions, in part due to lengthy construction periods. Each major

---

[7] For further details, see Ch. 7.

European property market has very different office supply and demand dynamics.

Office properties require significant capital expenditure and improvements to avoid obsolescence when attempting to re-lease. Depending on the state of obsolescence, or lack thereof, office properties are generally classified as Class A, Class B or Class C:

- Class A properties are generally less than 15-years-old, have up-to-date amenities, more than 10,000 square meters of leaseable area, and are located in a prime area.

- Class B properties are older, well-constructed and managed, but have not been renovated recently.

- Class C properties are generally smaller, and often functionally obsolescent.

The average property in a diverse multi-property "portfolio" CMBS transaction is Class B or C, whereas the average property in a large-loan or single-property CMBS transaction is Class A or B.

The key considerations when investing in an office property include:

- proximity to service industry businesses;
- employment trends in the service sector (such as financial and insurance);
- competing properties or business districts;
- structure and flexibility of design;
- tenant quality and leases, and
- management and servicer track record.

Retail

Retail properties include regional malls, strip centres and free-standing stores. Outside of major cities, retail properties rely on automobile traffic to allow customers access to the property. Hence, proximity to one or more major thoroughfares is among the primary credit concerns of an investor. For large shopping malls, a good location may also be determined based upon the size and quality of the residential base surrounding the property, or "catchment". Quality is typically assessed based upon household income levels and property values of the catchment.

43

In a transaction backed by a single-property retail loan, the property must dominate its location, and opportunities for new competition should be mitigated by planning restrictions and/or a limited amount of nearby developable land. In retail properties, turnover, occupancy costs per square meter and "zone A" rents (rents in the prime trading space of a store) are the chief indicators of a property's performance relative to its peers.

Management also plays an important role. While in the UK and Germany, retail shopping centres are owned and managed by a single entity, other jurisdictions may have more than one owning entity. In France, it has been common to engage multiple parties to develop a large retail shopping centre. This kind of arrangement, although suitable for capital raising, can result in a weakened management structure as consensus must be obtained for any refit expenses. In France, a few centres are overdue for refurbishment, as a result of the inability of the multiple owners to agree.

The key considerations when investing in a retail property include:

- accessibility and proximity to residential developments and major roads;
- outlook for retail sales growth;
- planning restrictions and ownership structure;
- area population growth, density and disposable income;
- tenant mix, including presence and quality of anchor tenants;
- parking availability; and
- management and servicer track record.

Industrial

Industrial properties are generally single-story buildings located in either a city warehouse district or suburban area. Industrial properties include storage and distribution warehouses, R&D facilities, light manufacturing (or "light industrial"), and "flex space"—buildings that tend to be smaller than warehouses, with lower ceilings, optional loading docks and more attractive facades making them flexible for use as a warehouse, office, or even a retail centre. Flex space properties can exhibit characteristics resembling office properties, and likewise, the associated risks.

Due to the less rigorous design requirements and larger potential range of desirable land on which to build, industrial properties demonstrate the shortest construction times of the major property types. Due to this, industrial properties are generally built into a market for which demand doesn't differ significantly from that under which it was originally envisaged.

Industrial buildings are generally built to specification for one to five tenants. This has the impact of minimising speculative development, but also limits the alternative use potential for a given property. Light industrial properties are, however, less customised and have the advantage of appealing to a broad tenant mix. Nevertheless, the credit quality of light industrial tenants is generally weaker than that of a warehouse property, and hence, more susceptible to a downturn in the area economy.

Key considerations when investing in an industrial property include:

- access to transport (rail, road and air);
- tenant quality and lease term;
- proximity to labour sources;
- column spacing, floor thickness, ceiling heights, and general flexibility (or lack thereof, e.g. custom fit);
- area employers, proximity to suppliers; and
- employment trends in the manufacturing sector.

Hotel

Hotel properties differ significantly from other commercial property types as they are subject to a high degree of operating leverage, or fixed costs. In addition, a large portion of hotel occupants change every day, making hotel occupancy heavily dependent on tourist and business travel, and the ability of the management to react quickly to seasonal and cyclical volatility. Hotels are, hence, far more susceptible to the ups and downs of the regional, national and, in large cities, international consumer and business cycles. That said, regional hotel cycles are often more muted than their city counterparts. As hotel properties must "re-lease" nightly, they are strongly correlated to tourism and the business economy.

Key considerations when investing in a hotel property include:

- franchise strength, market penetration;
- economic growth;
- seasonality;
- source of demand; and
- of crucial importance, management.

Operating costs

On the most basic level, the costs to operate and maintain each type of property differ, see Figure 11, below. Hotel properties, for example, exhibit the highest "operating leverage" or expense-to-income ratios, and hence, are the most volatile type of property investment. Not only do hotel properties have high fixed costs, but also hotel management must effectively re-lease the property on a daily basis.

Property Type	Range
Office	40–55%
Retail	20–40%
Industrial	20–35%
Hotel	65–80%

Figure 11: Operating expense ratios for European commercial property.[1]

[1] Operating Expenses ÷ (Gross Income—Vacancy and Collection Allowances).

Source: Moody's Investor Service, Merill Lynch.

Industrial properties have the lowest expense ratios, but may require greater management for secondary properties, for which lease terms are often shorter in term, requiring more frequent re-leasing. The low expense ratios of industrial properties are a result of tenant improvements that are often only necessary on a much smaller proportion of the leaseable area than that which a modern office building requires. As a result of the relative expense bases as well as the nature of planning and property development, industrial and retail properties exhibit less performance volatility than the other two major property types.

PROPERTY VALUATION

The key factor to determining the quality of valuation is market liquidity. Liquidity is imperative when determining comparison values and appropriate capitalisation rates for properties similar to those within a selected portfolio. Liquidity may be assessed by the frequency of commercial properties changing hands within a given jurisdiction. This ranges broadly across Europe, from London and Paris, with the most liquid commercial property markets, to Italy and Scandinavia, with the least liquid markets. Although less liquid than Paris and London, the key German markets, including Berlin and Frankfurt, exhibit a fair degree of transaction evidence, as does Amsterdam and, increasingly, Spain. Professional organisations provide for consistent valuation methodology in the UK, Ireland, the Netherlands and Germany.

Some European countries offer greater impartiality (and frequency) in the appraisal process than others, see Figure 12, below. Most Continental appraisers use initial yields and recent prices of similar properties to value a property. The UK, Ireland, the Netherlands, and Germany have national professional organisations of which a valuer must be a member. On the other end of the spectrum lies Italy, where the appraisal process is far more subjective and national guidelines are not present. Spain and France fall somewhere in the middle.

In Spain, although valuation companies are independent, they lack a professional association to ensure uniform practices. In the absence of a professional association, valuers may market themselves based upon relatively aggressive valuations.

Country	Responsibility for Appraisal
UK	Valued by surveyors who are members of the Royal Institute of Chartered Surveyors
Ireland	Independent valuers from Irish Association of Valuers
Germany	Federal Office for Supervision of Credit Sector verifies appraiser's expertise
France	Appraisal non-standard, varies by region
Italy	Surveyors may be in-house, pre-selected, or selected by borrower
Netherlands	Dutch Association of Estate Agents (NVM) and lenders determine foreclosure value
Spain	Several large independent valuation companies
Sweden	Independent valuation companies, discounted cash flow driven

Figure 12: Appraisal varies by country.

Source: Merrill Lynch.

These discrepancies in valuation methodologies are of particular import when analysing Continental bank portfolio transactions, often containing loans from more than one European locale. For continental transactions where the originator of the commercial loan is a developer or a conduit, internationally recognised agents and their approved appraisers are used almost exclusively. These property appraisers typically use valuation techniques established by the UK Royal Institute of Chartered Surveyors, without regard for the location of the property.

SECONDARY TRADING

The vast majority of European CMBS investors tend to be "buy and hold" investors, although they typically all require the ability to trade CMBS positions should the need ever arise. Hence the liquidity of a transaction is a very important feature to many investors and is influenced by deal size, tranche sizes, number of rating agencies, actual ratings of tranches, underlying collateral and transaction structure, programme branding and, more importantly in recent years, the quality and availability of investor reporting and ongoing cashflows.

The vast majority of secondary trading is in AAA rated bonds, as these tend to be easier to analyse and with most mezzanine and junior investors being spread hungry or placing their investments into funds, SIVs or CDOs, they tend to be less likely to trade such positions. It is estimated that approximately €40m of European AAA CMBS trades on a weekly basis. CMBS tends to trade less than more generic asset classes, such as RMBS, as deal sizes tend to be smaller and there is a smaller investor base.

The secondary market is driven by four principal ABS brokers, as well as approximately 15 secondary ABS trading teams within the investment and commercial banks which most actively issue structured finance products. The latter are generally required to make a market in bonds they lead manage as well as trading products on their own account.

The ability to trade on the secondary market has improved significantly over recent years. Increasing pressure has been applied by investors on issuers for information flow as supply levels have increased dramatically and there has been a shift in bargaining power to the investor base. Other important developments have included the issuance of CMSA reporting standards, software programmes by the likes of Trepp and Bloomberg, providing the ability to model cashflows on an ongoing basis, increased sophistication of the investor base, use of third party servicers with enhanced systems capabilities (such as Capmark and Hatfield Philips), increase in investor reporting websites (such as CTSLink) and investor reporting grading by Fitch Ratings.

LEGAL ISSUES PECULIAR TO THE EUROPEAN MARKET

Understanding of the legal framework of one European commercial property market does not transfer directly to that of another, except perhaps in terms of the questions that an investor must ask. The answers will differ according to the structural differences in lease terms, tenant rights, planning regulations, valuation methodologies, and asset security and enforcement procedures. These also influence the timing and nature of commercial property cycles between countries and cities and consequently impact the appropriate timing of investments. Understanding these features allows

48

investors to properly compare the plethora of European CMBS transactions, their underlying properties and to make adequate investment decisions.

In analysing CMBS, experience in one European country's property market does not transfer directly to that of another. The most fundamental tenet, that of fully understanding location desirability and competition, remains applicable regardless of the country in which a property resides. However, the next few major concerns of a credit investor may be influenced by the statutory environment in which the property resides, including:

- security of the rental stream;

- projected growth of rental flows (DSCR); and

- maintenance or improvement of property value (LTV).

Commercial implications of different legal systems must therefore be borne in mind in order to ensure that rental income flows, loan security and the structural protections of similar CMBS investments in different jurisdictions are comparable.

Lease terms vary

Lease terms range from landlord-friendly in the UK and Ireland to tenant-focused in the southern European countries. Commercial leases across Europe vary as to the balance of property rights and costs allocated between the tenant and landlord. Lease terms and tenant rights also vary between office or industrial tenants, and retail tenants, the latter of which may have greater rights in some jurisdictions. All leases other than UK and Irish leases are generally indexed to inflation, in the form of a proportion of the cost of living index in the respective country. In any case, the basic factors determining the strength of a lease include:

- term;

- rental rate;

- rent review;

- landlord obligations and tenant rights; and

- tenant quality.

Lease terms range from considerably landlord-friendly in the UK and Ireland, to more tenant-focused as one moves south across the Continent.

Customary and statutory recovery procedures vary

Unlike the US, there are very few non-performing commercial property specialists in Europe. Those that do exist usually have an element of US ownership or management. As such, commercial mortgage originators, as in the residential market, are vertically integrated, managing all aspects of the property loans. As most bank originators felt the pain of the last commercial property recession, many are now well equipped to handle (or avoid) problem loans. In fact, as vacancies trend upwards in a number of jurisdictions, LTVs on new financings have declined, as lenders required additional equity in the properties. Originating lenders typically service both performing and non-performing loans.

Regardless, in most CMBS transactions, it is crucial that an investor understands the likely recovery value of the property upon loan default. Three key elements determine this value:

- procedure to obtain the property;

- time from property possession until sale; and

- costs associated with the property sale.

The right to obtain the property lies in the insolvency framework of the relevant jurisdiction. The extent and duration of the possession process

Country	Foreclosure Process
UK	Legal repossession process commences, with court order required, and lasts 12 months, on average. Eviction and sale in open market. No government mandated auction system.
Ireland	Period of beginning of arrears status to forced sale no longer than 18 months. Presentation of civil bill, notice of trial/court hearing, order for repossession, execution order, repossession by county sheriff.
Germany	one to two-year recovery period.
France	Foreclosure, 50 percent more than one year, 33 per cent more than two years. Creditor must have court decision to seize property.
Italy	Lengthy court process with a period of as long as eight years from time of default to recovery.
Netherlands	Foreclosure process usually within three months.
Spain	Regulated, new law reduces number of required auctions from three to one to speed up process. However, foreclosure or auction is rare, normal course of action renegotiation of rate or term of debt. Typically three years to foreclose.

Figure 13: Foreclosure periods vary by country.

Source: Merrill Lynch.

varies by legal jurisdiction, ranging from a lengthy court-driven process in Italy (as much as several years in length), to creditor friendly foreclosure environments in the UK and the Netherlands, see Figure 13, above. Depending on the length of the foreclosure process, potential losses relating to accrued interest could be substantial. In jurisdictions where long foreclosure and recovery periods are possible, the maturity date on underlying loans should be several years earlier than those on the issued securities.

The costs of selling the possessed property depend on loan size and cost of carry, as well as legal fees, commissions, improvement expenses, and management fees. As an example, stamp tax payable upon property transfer in the event of a possession, differs by jurisdiction and ranges from 3 per cent of the property value in Sweden to 10 per cent in Italy.

THE IMPACT OF BASEL II

The main focus of this section is to:

- consider the relative change in capital required against assets pre- and post-BIS2 implementation for both originators and investors involved with commercial mortgage-backed securitisation; and

- consider the relative difference in capital required under BIS2 to hold commercial real estate (CRE) assets either on balance sheet or in a securitisation structure.

There are some issues not covered by this section, as there are more than a few grey areas concerning the implementation and interpretation of the new rules. This section does not address liquidity facilities, but focuses on the capital requirements for assets. On top of that, the new rules give rise to a range of possibilities as to how assets are held, and what capital will be required against them—at this stage only a suggestion as to some of the potential trends can be offered.

- Under BIS2, banks which use the internal ratings-based (IRB) approach and are able to perform portfolio analysis may hold significantly less capital compared to most CRE exposures, but particularly low-risk ones, than under BIS1 or under the BIS2 standardised approach. This may encourage IRB banks to increase lower-risk CRE lending and off-load higher-risk real estate assets.

- Under BIS2, under both IRB and standardised approaches, like-for-like, less capital may be required for the full CMBS capital structure than for holding the whole portfolio on balance sheet. This may incentivise banks with identical CRE loan portfolios to securitise the loans into a CMBS and trade all tranches to each other.

- For both IRB and standardised banks considering originating a CMBS transaction, the capital charge for retaining the first-loss piece may be significantly lower than the charge for retaining the whole CRE loan portfolio on balance sheet—particularly if the tranche can be rated BB or higher. This may further stimulate securitisation of CRE loans.

- The sharp "cliff" in capital charge between BBB and BB+ may encourage all banks to sell-off non-investment grade tranches to non-bank investors. Despite this, standardised banks have an advantage relative to IRB banks in holding BB/BB- tranches. Under the standardised approach itself, investor banks have an advantage relative to originator banks in holding BB tranches.

- Separate mezzanine or B note lending may attract lower capital requirements than BB-rated CMBS tranches. As a result CRE loan origination may change to facilitate full CMBS funding without any equity or tranche rated below BBB.

Capital requirements for originators and investors

BIS capital requirements apply to most banks worldwide and are implemented by national banking supervisory authorities. It is estimated that about 60 per cent of all structured finance issuance is held by bank investors, hence the importance of the BIS2 new regulatory capital guidelines for the securitisation market. The proportion of CMBS investors formed by banks may be similar, although this is difficult to estimate; with the rise of CDOs buying CMBS alongside institutional investors, the proportion may decline. On the origination side, bank lending remains a prime source of CRE finance and securitisation origination, and it is very likely to continue to do so. In the UK alone, bank CRE lending has risen to £130bn. Therefore, on both sides of the origination/investor equation BIS requirements have a large impact.

The capital a bank is required to hold against a particular loan is usually expressed as percentage risk weight (RW) of a fixed percentage (usually at 8 per cent, but it can be greater at the supervisory authority's discretion) of the loan amount. Currently, under BIS1, commercial property loans attract a RW of 100 per cent in most countries—that means that for every $100 of loan, 100 per cent × 8 per cent × $100 = $8 must be funded by capital. Germany is a notable exception which generally applies a 50 per cent RW, i.e. 50 per cent × 8 per cent × $100 = $4 of capital is required for $100 of loan; the UK usually requires the full 100 per cent. Holding CMBS rated notes also attracts a 100 per cent RW; although holding non-investment grade junior tranche from a transaction, or a first-loss reserve, would require a dollar-for-dollar deduction from capital.

BIS2 rules will completely overhaul this simple regime, with the aim of setting a more credit-focussed system. In general, BIS2 will be implemented by banks in most European countries. However implementation in the US is limited, although it is expected that similar rules will be adopted for securitisation exposures. The US is planning to implement BIS2 rules to the top international UK banks, starting the transition period one year after the rest of the world, that is, as of January 1, 2008. This gives rise to the so-called "gap year", during which non-US banks will be using BIS2 and the major international US banks will not. The implementation schedule started in January 2006, with banks performing parallel BIS1 and BIS2 calculations for their capital base. From 2007, depending on the type of BIS2 rules adopted, banks can benefit from a reduction in capital under BIS2, subject, broadly-speaking, to a floor set as a ratio of the BIS1 requirement, see Figure 14, below.

	From year-end 2005	From year-end 2006	From year-end 2007	From year-end 2008
Foundation IRB Approach	Parallel Calculation	95%	90%	80%
Advanced Approaches for credit and/ or operational risk	Parallel calculation or impact studies	Parallel calculation	90%	80%

Figure 14: Transition to BIS2.

Source: BIS.

Under BIS2, RWs for CRE loans and CMBS bonds will be calculated on a more graduated basis depending on the perceived credit risk of the asset. Credit risk is determined by referring to the rating agency credit ratings for the asset, a bank's own calculation based on its historical portfolio performance, or, if neither of the former is possible, a blanket assumption for the asset class. The treatment for securitisation bonds is only applied where the securitisation achieves "significant risk transfer", which is difficult to define. If an originating bank retains a securitisation structure on the balance sheet it cannot benefit from the regulatory capital relief.

Banks have the option of two different methodologies for doing this depending on their level of sophistication, known as standardised and the

IRB approaches. Banks must select which one to use and apply it to all assets of a certain sector, for example, CRE. The IRB methodology is then split into two options, foundation and advanced, which differ in the degree to which a bank is allowed to use its own data to determine the inputs in the regulatory capital calculation. Surveys carried out by the market suggest 80 per cent of European banks may become IRB banks. There is little clear information, but it is believed a similar proportion of those banks involved with CRE and CMBS may implement IRB.

The standardised approach use a fixed RW of 100 per cent for CRE lending, and for investing in a securitisation structure sets a RW depending on the rating of the tranche. For holding securitisation tranches, a distinction is made between a bank as an originator of a transaction and as a third party investor in a transaction. The IRB approach for CRE lending requires a statistical analysis of the loan portfolio to form estimates for default probability (PD), loss given default (LGD), exposure at default (EAD), and effective maturity (M). These are then used as the basis of a calculation of the expected loss (EL), and unexpected loss (UL), of the portfolio. Capital is required to cover UL and is comparable to the capital determined by the RW $\times$ 8 per cent, as under BIS1 or the BIS2 standardised approach. Foundation IRB banks are only expected to assess PD, their national supervisor will supply standard LGD and other factors. Advanced IRB banks will be able to estimate all the factors. Depending on the risk profile of the portfolio, capital required can vary widely—in Figure 15, below, column 7 sets out are some estimates Fitch Ratings recently published based on historical performance data for portfolios backing CMBS. There is a further exception. Where an IRB bank is unable to produce the PD and other estimates for a loan, then, as a fall-back option, RWs for "specialised lending", are used, see Figure 15, columns 3–5. Since many CRE portfolios may have limited performance history, for example, where banks move into new areas of property finance, the use of specialised lending RWs may be quite commonplace.

RWs depend on an assessment of the risk level of the loan, and whether the CRE is fairly standard, leased, income-producing real estate (IPRE); or high volatile real estate (HVRE) which includes more specialised lending, such as development or infrastructure, which may exhibit highly volatile losses. RWs for loans deemed strong or good range between 70 to 120 per cent; those for satisfactory and weak loans between 115 to 250 per cent. BIS 2 proposes a specific set of criteria to differentiate between IPRE and HVRE. Under this approach, IRB may require more capital under BIS2 for higher-risk CRE loans than under BIS1. This may encourage banks to either sell-off these loans, or securitise them depending on the size and rating of the junior/equity tranches retained.

As indicated above, there are specific guidelines regarding the regulatory capital treatment of specialised lending and regarding securitisation under BIS2. For most real estate exposures, the distinction between specialised lending and securitisation is fairly straightforward. In some cases, however, that distinction is, at best, unclear. Typical examples include: securitisations of a single real estate exposure or senior/subordinated (AB) commercial real estate loans. Regulatory clarification is needed regarding the capital treatment in such situations and that may be left to national discretion, suggesting subjective decisions and potential divergence in treatment among national regulators. The IRB approach for investing in a securitisation structure, or for an originator retaining some tranches of a CMBS, sets RWs by referring to the bonds' external credit ratings. Unlike the standardised approach, the RBA does not distinguish between originator and investor banks, but does have a much more graduated set of RWs referring to ratings' notches, see Figure 15, columns 13–16. The RBA system also has a separate, lower set of RWs for the senior-most tranche in a transaction, see Figure 15, column 14. For transactions backed by a concentrated portfolio, where the "effective number of loans" (based on a specific calculation) is less than six, there is a more punitive set of RWs, see Figure 15, column 15. There is a definition for the effective number of loans in a portfolio, which is meant to address portfolios with a mix of granular and concentrated exposure. The resulting capital under the product of the RBA approach cannot be greater than the requirement for the same portfolio of loans under the IRB approach. In other words, a securitising bank cannot hold more capital after securitisation than before securitisation, although the capital held in the banking system as a whole may be more after securitisation.

This leaves the issue of how unrated securitised tranches would be treated. For these, under IRB, a supervisory formula (SF) may be used which calculates the capital requirement based on the IRB factors and tranche specifics, such as thickness, size, enhancement level and pool diversity. Figure 15, below, sets out the current BIS1 and future BIS2 capital requirements for holding unsecuritised CRE assets on balance sheet, and for holding securitisation tranches, either as an investor or originator. The table can be used to compare the RWs on-balance sheet portfolios and rated CMBS bonds attract. For comparison purposes, the Fitch Ratings estimates of capital required for UL for low-, medium- and high-risk CRE portfolios are also shown. These ratios are the first examples of what capital levels on-balance sheet CRE portfolios might be expected to attract. These have been used for the basis of the conclusions as to the relative impact of BIS2 on banks' decisions whether or not to securitise loans. With regard to RWs, the table sets out the RW required for: the whole loan on-balance sheet (BIS1 and BIS2 Standardised); the whole loan by portfolio risk level (IRB "specialised lending"); or by rating of a securitised tranche (Standardised and IRB RBA). The RW would then be multiplied by the standard 8 eight per

On-Balance Sheet Commercial Mortgage Loans | Securitisation Tranches

Column	1	2	3	4	5	6	7	8	9	11	12	13	14	15	16	17
	BIS 1	BIS 2 Standardised	BIS 2 RW IRB Specialised Lending			IRB Unexpected Loss Estimate		BIS1	BIS 2 Standardised Approach			BIS2 IRB RBA Approach for rated Securitised Tranches				BIS2 IRB Approach for Unrated Securitised Tranches
	RW Applied to all commercial mortgages	RW Applied to all commercial mortgages	Risk Category	RW for IPRE	RW for HVRE	Portfolio Risk Level	*Capital Level Required	Applied to all investment grade CMBS tranches	Rating of CMBS bond	RW for Originator Bank	RW for Investor Bank	Rating of CMBS Bond	RW for Senior Tranche	Base RW for CMBS Tranches	RW for Non-Granular CMBS	**Supervisory Formula by Portfolio Risk Level
	100%	100% for all CRE loans, or 50% if loan LTV is <50% (or 60% of mortgage value), and losses less than 0.3% pa, and 0.5% for whole CRE pool	Strong BBB- or better	70%	95%	Low	4.57%	100%	AAA to AA-	20%	20%	AAA	7%	12%	20%	Low: 6.41%
												AA	8%	15%	25%	
									A+ to A-	50%	50%	A+	10%	18%	35%	
						Medium	6.45%					A	12%	20%	35%	Medium: 8.70%
			Good BB+/BB	90%	120%							A-	20%	35%	35%	
									BBB+ to BBB-	100%	100%	BBB+	35%	50%	50%	
			Satisfactory BB- or B+	115%	140%	High	7.17%					BBB	60%	75%	75%	High: 7.57%
												BBB-	100%	100%	100%	
									BB+ to BB-	Deduction	350%	BB+	250%	250%	250%	
			Weak B to C	250%	250%							BB	425%	425%	425%	
												BB-	650%	650%	650%	
			Default	0%	0%				B+ and below	Deduction	Deduction	Below BB-	Deduction	Deduction	Deduction	
									Not rated	Deduction	Deduction	Not rated	Deduction	Deduction	Deduction	

* Capital Level Required under IRB Unexpected Loss Estimate is an example level calculated by Fitch Ratings for various CMBS portfolios in its report ''Basel II: Bottom-Line Impact on Securitisation''.
** Capital Level Required under Supervisory Formula is an example level calculated by Fitch Ratings, for the same portfolio as for the above, Unexpected Loss Estimate.
Deduction from capital results in a dollar-for-dollar reduction of the bank's capital.

Figure 15: Comparative table for treatment of on-balance sheet CRE lending and securitisation tranches.

Source: BIS, Fitch Ratings, Merrill Lynch.

cent capital ratio to determine per cent capital required against the exposure amount.

Conclusions as to the relative impact of BIS2 on originators and investors

Using this table, some assessments have been made of where treatment varies either pre- and post-BIS2, between on-balance sheet lending and securitisation, or where treatment varies between standardised and IRB banks post-BIS2.

- Under BIS2, compared with BIS1, both standardised and IRB banks gain a large reduction in capital in holding securitisation tranches rated A- and above. IRB banks also gain on tranches rated BBB and above. The effect of this may be for spreads on these tranches to tighten.

- Under BIS2, both approaches may require less capital for holding securitised tranches vs. holding CRE loans on balance sheet (less so for CRE loans below 50 per cent LTV). Although for IRB banks, the capital requirement for CRE loans on-balance sheet is dependent on the IRB calculation (unlike the 100 per cent RW required for standardised banks) it appears that this calculation is more conservative than the RBA approach for securitised tranches. The effect appears to be greatest for low-risk loans. Since an originator cannot retain the full capital structure of a CMBS and hold less capital than that for the portfolio on balance sheet, banks with similar portfolios may be incentivised to securitise and trade CMBS transactions.

- IRB banks have an advantage over standardised banks in holding all tranches rated BB+ and above, see Figure 15, columns 9–16.

- Similarly standardised banks have an advantage over IRB banks in holding BB and BB- tranches. This may have the effect of encouraging IRB banks to sell junior-most tranches in CMBS structures to standardised banks.

- Under the standardised approach, investor banks have an advantage over originator banks in holding BB-rated tranches, see Figure 15, columns 11–12. This may encourage standardised originating banks to sell/transfer the most junior-rated part of a CMBS capital structure to other standardised banks.

- Under the IRB approach, RBA also seems to require less capital against a securitisation structure, than the supervisory formula (SF) method for an unrated securitisation structure. Fitch Ratings' analysis, referred to above, shows SF is much more punitive than RBA for tranches which would be rated BBB and below, although less is required by SF at the A rating level. Overall, RBA and SF appear aligned for senior and junior tranches but vary widely for middle tranches.

Assessing the capital requirement across a CMBS capital structure

Figure 16, below, sets out the capital calculations for the full capital structure of a recently issued CMBS transaction, Cornerstone Titan 2005–1. The capital requirement is calculated based on the assumptions that the capital charge is 8 per cent multiplied by the RW for the tranche. The total capital required for the whole structure is expressed as a ratio of the total note value, based on the given proportion for the note tranches. This shows that the total capital required in the banking system for holding all of this rated structure would be 2.88 per cent under the IRB approach and 3.57 per cent or 5.95 per cent under the standardised approach depending on whether the originator holds the most junior tranche, which is quite a wide variation.

	Ratings-Based Approach		Standardised Originator		Standardised Investor		
Note Class	%of Total Amount	Rating	Risk Weight	Capital Required	Risk Weight	Capital Required	Risk Weight	Capital Required
A1	54.0%	AAA	7%	0.30%	20%	0.86%	20%	0.86%
A2	14.0%	AAA	12%	0.13%	20%	0.22%	20%	0.22%
B	6.5%	AA	15%	0.08%	20%	0.10%	20%	0.10%
C	8.0%	A	20%	0.13%	50%	0.32%	50%	0.32%
D	13.0%	*BBB–	100%	1.04%	100%	1.04%	100%	1.04%
E	1.2%	BBB	75%	0.07%	100%	0.10%	100%	0.10%
F	3.3%	BB	425%	1.12%	**1250%	3.30%	350%	0.92%
Total	100.00%			2.88%		5.95%		3.57%

* Assumed ratings meet BIS2 criteria, in this example use of different agencies has produced a lower rating on Class D than the more junior Class E. Use of the same rating agency for the whole capital structure would be required under BIS2.
** Equivalent to the actual capital deduction which would occur.

Figure 16: Example of capital calculation for a CMBS transaction (Cornerstone Titan 2005–1).

Source: Merrill Lynch.

More interestingly, this example also shows the capital charge an originating bank would attract if it securitised a portfolio and retained just the most junior, or equity, piece–rated BB here. For an IRB bank using RBA, the capital charge would be 1.12 per cent and for a standardised bank, 3.30 per cent. Even with additional charges for any reserves of liquidity facilities provided to the transaction, this looks attractive against an estimated capital charge for holding the entire portfolio on balance sheet of around 4 per cent under IRB, or 8 per cent under standardised. On this basis, it would appear that banks wishing to use capital efficiently will be encouraged to securitise portfolios of CRE loans. In all cases, it can be seen that the junior BB-rated tranche is relative to its size the biggest contributor to the capital requirement. This may encourage banks originating CMBS, particularly standardised banks, to minimise the size of the first loss piece retained, and to sell-off a senior-ranking double-B rated tranche.

One issue arises concerning the treatment of CMBS junior tranches, which frequently have available funds cap (AFC) features. AFC restricts payment of interest under certain portfolio events. BIS2 generally requires that ratings used for RWs must not be principal-only ratings and must address timely payment of interest. If junior CMBS tranches cannot meet BIS2 rating requirements, then these exposures may attract a full deduction from capital. This may encourage banks to sell such tranches to non-banks, however pricing for such tranches may be more costly. Overall the impact of this treatment of AFC will marginally reduce the capital saving under securitisation as outlined above.

The "Cliff" in capital requirements between BBB and BB-rated bonds will impact the CRE mezzanine lending and B note market. As noted above, it is relatively costly for banks to hold tranches rated BBB and below. Therefore, it may be likely that banks will start to originate loans for CMBS that are of sufficient credit quality (that is, low enough LTV) to fully fund a CMBS structure without any BB-rated or non-rated junior/equity tranche. This may increase the volume of separate mezzanine lending or B note lending which occupies the band in property lending between 70 to 85 per cent LTV. What is not entirely clear is what the RW or IRB capital charge would be for this type of lending. Without sufficient portfolio history it will be difficult to perform either the foundation or advanced IRB calculation. In which case IRB lenders could benefit by attracting 90 to 250 per cent under "specialised lending" rules. Standardised banks might just get a 100 per cent RW.

Either way there may be an advantage in separating the mezzanine area of CRE lending from conventional bank lending suitable for CMBS. This could further tighten spreads for non-rated B notes lending relative to BB-rated CMBS tranches.

The author would like to thank members of Merrill Lynch's International Structured Product Research Group's contribution to this chapter.

CHAPTER FOUR

STANDARD & POOR'S RATING OF EUROPEAN CMBS: LEGAL AND STRUCTURAL CONSIDERATIONS

Judith O'Driscoll, Assistant General Counsel
Standard & Poor's

INTRODUCTION[1]

The securitisation of commercial mortgage loans in Europe has grown significantly over the past five years and the general expectation is that this trend will continue as more institutional lenders use securitisation to manage their balance-sheet exposure to commercial mortgage loans and to access the capital markets for funding.

This growth has brought CMBS beyond the familiar shores of the UK into Europe where it has seen healthy activity in countries such as France, Germany and Italy (countries which will be dealt with in detail in Chs 16, 17 and 19). More recently new countries have appeared on the European CMBS map: Austria and Ireland, to name a few. These real estate markets with their disparate legal and tax frameworks present exciting challenges for originators seeking to securitise their loans in Europe.

Summary

A Standard & Poor's issue credit rating is a current opinion of the creditworthiness of an obligor with respect to a specific financial obligation.

---

[1] A more detailed discussion of the issues addressed in this chapter can be found in our criteria articles titled "European CMBS Loan Level Guidelines" published in September 2004 and "European Legal Criteria for Structured Finance Transactions" published in March 2005. Both articles are available on RatingsDirect, the real-time Web-based source for Standard & Poor's credit ratings, research, and risk analysis, at www.ratingsdirect.com. The criteria can also be found on Standard & Poor's Web site at www.standardandpoors.com.

In the case of a rating of CMBS notes, a Standard & Poor's rating addresses the issuer's ability to pay interest and principal in accordance with the terms of the notes. This involves an analysis of associated credit, structural and legal risks and the protections against those risks in order to assess the likelihood that an issuer will meet all of its promised payment obligations.

In standard CMBS transactions, credit risk is pinned almost entirely on the underlying real estate and the sustainable revenues it can generate. Consequently, the property's ability to sustain its value and to produce cash-flow throughout the transaction term lies at the heart of Standard & Poor's rating analysis. The extent to which the CMBS structure provides for protection of property value and cash-flow, and the ability of issuers to access the property and cash-flow in a default scenario by enforcement of the security, are also relevant. These are typical "loan level" concerns and will range from consideration of such questions as:

- Could tenancy rights hamper a re-letting of the property or its sale?

- Could insolvency trigger a freeze on enforcement?

- Will there be any burdensome taxes on a sale of the property that will reduce funds available to the issuer?

At issuer level in a CMBS, as with any securitisation, Standard & Poor's concerns are well known: it considers whether assets are isolated from (de-linked from) originator risk, whether a safe harbour has been created for the assets through an insolvency remote SPE, whether taxes can reduce funds available to issuer, and whether adequate liquidity is available to fund timing delays.

What follows is a discussion of some of the key elements in the analysis that can affect the rating outcome.

THE ASSETS: PROPERTY AND CASH-FLOW

The property

As mentioned above, Standard & Poor's credit analysis begins with the assessment of the property and its ability to produce income and sustain value for the life of the rated notes. The ability of the issuer to meet its payment obligations will depend on the borrower's ability to make ongoing debt service payments which in turn depends on the underlying cashflow from the property. In addition, on the maturity date of the rated notes the underlying property must have an inherent value sufficient either to allow a refinancing by another lender, or a sale to a third party for a sum equal to or in excess of the remaining outstanding principal balance of the notes. With this in mind, property issues that Standard & Poor's generally considers will include the following:

Condition of the property

Day 1 Condition: Standard & Poor's expects originators, acting as prudent commercial mortgage lenders, to have undertaken their own due diligence on the property. Originators' representations in the loan sale documents will usually reflect the results of that due diligence. Standard & Poor's expects these representations to confirm that the property is not damaged in any way that would adversely affect the use or value of the property. Property valuations provide additional key information about the property, as do environmental and other reports.

Maintenance: Borrower obligations to maintain and keep the property in good repair over the term of the rated transaction are also key to the maintenance of property value and it is expected that borrowers will covenant, amongst other things, to maintain, or procure the maintenance of, the property in good and tenantable repair and condition throughout the term of the rated obligations.

Management: Given the importance of competent management to the sustainability of cashflows, property management is expected to be competent and reliable. Standard & Poor's often therefore considers whether the property manager has the appropriate experience in the management of similar property portfolios. Depending on the circumstances, it would expect that trustee (or the servicer on its behalf) will be able to require the borrower to replace the property manager following a loan default. It is also common for the loan holder to be able to require a replacement of the property manager following events that indicate a deterioration in the value of the mortgaged property.

Insurance: Standard & Poor's expects that the borrowers will maintain property insurance from appropriately rated insurers and in amounts sufficient to protect against losses and disruptions in the cash flows, and to preserve the lender's asset security. Insurance coverage typically includes, at a minimum, fire and casualty (including coverage for acts of terrorism), general liability, and rental interruption insurance. Flood, windstorm, and earthquake coverage may also be required, depending on the location of the property. Insurance coverage should be for the life of the loan and all insurance policies are expected to have a clause in favour of the originator, stating that there can be no changes, including modifications, amendments, or cancellations, to the policy without 30 days' written notice to the lender.

Where permitted by applicable laws and insurance policies, insurance proceeds should be paid directly to the lender.

Permitted development and alterations: Alterations to or developments of the property are usually prohibited. Occasionally, however, some development or alterations may be appropriate. In some instances, Standard & Poor's has accepted loan provisions that permit limited alterations where the loan documents contain specific provisions that ensure that alterations do not adversely affect:

- the borrower's financial condition;
- the value of the property; or
- the borrower's ability to make scheduled debt service payments.

Substitution of property: Substitutions of properties in the pool generally require various approvals before the substitution is made and the applicable mortgages released. In limited circumstances, Standard & Poor's has seen provisions that allow substitution without approval. However, in these cases, substitution is limited to a relatively small portion of the collateral pool and subject to tests designed to ensure, for instance, that the substitute property is equal in quality and value to the released property and pool diversity is maintained (based on, for example, geography, property type and tenant concentrations). Where substitution is permitted without approval, Standard & Poor's would generally consider the effect of substitutions on the collateral. This potential impact would then be reflected in the credit analysis.

The leases: As a general rule, Standard & Poor's assessment of the ability of the property to produce a sustainable income does place a great deal of emphasis on the leases in place at the time of the closing of the transaction. However, in transactions that rely significantly on in-place occupational leases or which have significant income concentration, the current lease terms may become more relevant to the rating assessment. In these cases, issues such as lease term and break options, rent reviews, the ability of the tenant to assign or terminate the lease, and landlord and tenant remedies are relevant.

After the rating is assigned: surveillance and reports

After Standard & Poor's has assigned the rating, it will undertake surveillance of the CMBS transaction. This generally involves scrutiny of the issuer level matters (such as cash flows, swap payments and amortisation) but it also looks to the loan level and property level so as to track the underlying risk profile of the transaction. As a result, Standard & Poor's expects to receive reports from the servicer and/or cash manager on an ongoing basis on issues that could impact the issuer's ability to meet its obligations on a timely basis—loan arrears, breaches of financial covenants and material changes affecting property value or income (including amendments to tenancy schedules, changes in net operating income emanating from the property, substitutions and vacancy rates) are the kinds of issues that would be relevant.

The cash flows

In a CMBS transaction, the cash generally flows from the tenants to the borrower(s), to the issuer and finally to the note holders, with diversions along the way to originator accounts, property managers, and other third-party servicers. In almost all cases, the manner of collection and the legal and structural protections of the cash from risks (insolvency, set-off, commingling to name a few) are relevant to the rating analysis at Standard & Poor's.

The optimum collection arrangement would generally involve the immediate payment or transfer of rental income by the tenants by way of an irrevocable direction from the borrower into an account held with a suitably rated account provider in the issuer's name, and over which the issuer has full security and control. In practice, arrangements are generally weaker and the rating analysis is likely to reflect potential losses to the cash flows or delays in collection after consideration of the following matters.

Commingling issues

Commingling issues at all levels (borrower, property or asset manager, originator and issuer) are generally considered when evaluating risk to cash flows. Commingling occurs whenever cash belonging to a debtor is mixed with general cash or with cash belonging to another entity, or where cash goes into an account in the name of another entity in such a way that, in the insolvency of the debtor or the other entity, the cash is "lost" or "frozen".

The cash would become "lost" if, following a debtor's insolvency, the creditor's claim to the money were treated at law as an unsecured debt of the insolvent entity. Under Standard & Poor's criteria, an unsecured debt claim would be treated as a total credit loss for the issuer. On the other hand, cash may merely be "frozen" where the issuer has a recognisable and valid claim over the funds, for example because an account is subject to a valid security interest in its favour.

Insolvency of borrower, property or asset manager, or other account holding entity: The most common type of commingling seen in CMBS transactions arises where underlying tenants make payments to accounts in the name of the borrower or a property or an asset manager. Rental payments are often paid directly into a segregated account (over which security is granted or a trust is declared) so as to protect the cash against the insolvency of these account holders. The success of these types of arrangements can vary significantly across different European jurisdictions. In some jurisdictions, for example, pledges on running accounts are quite difficult to create as they may need to be "refreshed" every time new sums are credited to the account.

Standard & Poor's expects confirmation of the validity and effectiveness of the trust or other security arrangement before credit is given in the rating analysis. Information should also be provided about the likely delays in enforcing that security, taking into account any potential bankruptcy stays. If these delays could result in the issuer not being able to meet its obligations under the rated notes in a timely fashion, then the rating is likely to be adversely affected unless arrangements (such as liquidity) are in place to meet payment obligations due on the notes during those delays.

Account bank risk: Consistent with Standard & Poor's approach to unsecured debt of an insolvent company, all cash held with a bank that does not meet Standard & Poor's rating requirements is treated as lost or unavailable to the issuer. This is the case even where valid security has been granted over the accounts because that security provides protection against the account holder's insolvency but not the account bank's insolvency. As a mitigant to the risk of an account bank insolvency, loans are structured so that:

- account providers at the loan level are suitably rated; and

- in the event of a downgrade of the account provider, the account is transferred to a suitably rated account or cash is invested in suitably rated eligible investments, which, in turn, should be chosen to ensure that proper security may be given over them, thereby protecting the issuer's interests in the event of insolvency of the bank holding the investments.

Account bank set-off

Commingled cash may also be lost in the insolvency of the account holder where the account bank is allowed to assert a right of set-off. In other words, it may be lost where the bank is allowed under the account terms or by law to set off the amounts owed to it by the borrower pursuant to dealings outside the CMBS transaction against funds standing to the credit of the account. This could affect the funds ultimately available to the issuer.

Ideally, the account bank should not have any right of set-off in relation to the funds held in the applicable account. However, most bank account standard terms explicitly allow the account bank to set off obligations of the account holder against amounts standing to the credit of the bank account.

If Standard & Poor's is to give credit to cash collections standing in a borrower account, it will expect set-off to be waived.

ASSESSING ACCESSIBILITY OF THE ASSETS POST-DEFAULT: THE SECURITY, ENFORCEMENT, AND THE EFFECT OF INSOLVENCY ON CASH FLOWS

The security

Given that the credit risk is pinned almost entirely on the underlying property and the sustainable revenues it can generate, it is of paramount importance that the cash flows from the property and the rights to the property itself are protected for the benefit of the note holders.

Therefore, the structural and legal analysis considers the ability of creditors to access the assets in a default scenario. Consequently, the nature of the security package and the procedures available in each jurisdiction for enforcing that security are core elements of the Standard & Poor's rating analysis.

The basic security package granted by the borrowers at the loan level usually includes:

- first-ranking security over the property;

- assignment of the rental income and insurance;

- first-ranking security over all agreements relating to the ownership and management of the property;

- first-ranking security over rental accounts and any other accounts (such as reserve accounts);

- first-ranking security over all relevant shares, goodwill, and uncalled capital;

- first-ranking security over the benefit of any guarantees and sub-ordination agreements that the borrowers may have;

- equivalent security over any other assets of the borrowers; and

- additional third-party security in the form of guarantees is sometimes provided to support the borrowers' obligations.

At issuer level, the issuer will generally grant security to a security trustee over all of its assets (accounts; contractual rights; security package received from loan level entities). When assessing the efficacy of the security package at loan level, Standard & Poor's will generally consider if, in a default situation:

- the security can be enforced effectively and without undue delay;
- enforcement could result in additional costs to the transaction, loss to the transaction, or loss of value in respect of the secured assets;
- enforcement would require further formalities to be met; and
- insolvency proceedings could materially affect the enforcement process.

Insolvency regimes

How long it is likely to take to enforce a loan and supporting security is of key importance in assessing the issuer's ability to pay in full and on time, as is the extent to which the issuer has control of, or real influence over, the enforcement process. This is because delay in enforcement could lead to a reduction in value of the collateral property and an increase in third-party costs, such as legal fees or property expenses. Of course, enforcement, control, delay, cost and similar issues vary from jurisdiction to jurisdiction in Europe—this invariably means that there is no uniform answer.

The property-owning borrower

Underlying loans made to property owning borrowers are the actual assets that support the notes and it is at this level that borrowers could default and in some cases become insolvent. It is fundamental to make this distinction because these underlying borrowers are rarely, if ever, bankruptcy-remote borrowers in the sense understood by structured finance professionals. This is so even if the borrower is a special purpose vehicle because ownership of property involves a degree of insolvency risk that cannot be fully eliminated. (For example, a borrower who owns property would be exposed to environmental law risks and third-party liability risks.) For these reasons, Standard & Poor's seeks to understand how the insolvency of the borrower would affect the enforcement of the security package, and the degree to which the risks posed by an insolvency have been mitigated.

Assessing how insolvency affects the enforcement process

To understand the effect of a borrower insolvency in any CMBS transaction, Standard & Poor's expects to receive from the transaction's legal experts a detailed analysis of the effects of applicable insolvency proceedings on enforcement and recovery expectations to enable it to make appropriate assumptions as to the outcome of enforcement in an insolvency scenario. The reason is that insolvency proceedings of the borrower are likely to:

- lead to an event of default under the loan, resulting in an acceleration and enforcement of security;

- in some jurisdictions, trigger a freeze on proceedings against the borrower, resulting in delays in enforcement of security and delays in receipt of cash, leading in turn to delays in payment due under the rated notes; and

- result in a "haircut" or reduction in the amount of cash available to repay the notes because of the costs and expenses of insolvency.

If a borrower has offices, assets or business activities in more than one EU jurisdiction, Standard & Poor's also expects the legal analysis to indicate which laws would apply to the insolvency proceedings and to confirm that the courts in the other relevant jurisdictions will recognize and give effect to the insolvency court's determinations.

An additional consideration in the enforcement analysis and one which brings a further level of complexity to investors in European CMBS is the lack of uniformity in insolvency rules across Europe. When creditors assess how long it will take to recover the properties and other assets in a European context in an insolvency scenario, the quick answer is that the outcome varies from jurisdiction to jurisdiction. In France, social policies favouring rehabilitation of failing businesses tend to delay recoveries. In Germany, the Netherlands and the UK the process is generally quicker (assuming, of course, no creditor compromise and sufficient liquidation value of the collateral security). In most jurisdictions, administration proceedings impose a stay or moratorium on enforcement and the length of stay varies widely across jurisdictions. In all jurisdictions the size and complexity of financial arrangements are a complicating factor.

Timing to liquidation; moratorium on enforcement

Where local laws impose a freeze on enforcement in an insolvency, Standard & Poor's would expect liquidity coverage to be provided for the duration of the assumed moratorium and thereafter until completion of liquidation and realisation of the security—a period that can be lengthy in some jurisdictions. In the absence of liquidity coverage, the credit analysis is likely to be affected.

Costs of enforcement

Where the borrower's assets and commercial relationships are more complex, it may take longer for an insolvency officer to realise the assets and/or determine claims. In such a case, it is likely that its costs would be increased and an allowance may need to be made for this in rating levels. Similar allowances would be made where local law regimes (such as the insolvency regime in Germany) provide for haircuts on enforcement proceeds.

Set-off

Set-off risks where relevant (whether this involves set-off by underlying tenants or account banks) may also require rating assumptions.

Other issues that may affect the security

The validity and/or enforceability of security interests may be adversely affected by legal principles of general application, such as preference rules, over-collateralisation, financial assistance, capital maintenance and related rules, as well as corporate laws on the subordination of claims and related security. Standard & Poor's expects all these issues to be reviewed by the originator (and, where relevant, covered by legal opinions).

OTHER CONSIDERATIONS

The issuer, borrowers and property owners

The issuer

Standard & Poor's methodology of forecasting a default and potential insolvency of the underlying borrower(s) within a CMBS transaction and assessing managed recoveries from this process must not be confused with a default of the CMBS issuer or issuing vehicle.

Structured finance is predicated on ensuring the solvency of the issuer, and all securitisation transactions generally focus on how assets can be isolated so that a bankruptcy of the underlying obligors does not adversely affect the payment of principal and interest on the rated notes. Generally to achieve this goal the assets (in CMBS, the CMBS loans and security) are transferred to an "insolvency remote" special purpose entity; that is, an entity unlikely to be subject to voluntary or involuntary insolvency proceedings. An entity that satisfies Standard & Poor's "SPE Criteria" is generally regarded by Standard & Poor's as being sufficiently protected against voluntary and involuntary insolvency risks. (These criteria include restrictions on objects and powers, debt limitations, independent direct separateness covenants and security interests over assets.) In this regard the CMBS asset class is no different from other asset classes.

The form of the borrower

As indicated earlier, property owner/borrowers in CMBS transactions are not considered by Standard & Poor's to be insolvency remote. Therefore, CMBS ratings are intended to survive the enforcement of underlying loan security and account for the potential effect of an insolvent borrower. Rating an underlying borrower through enforcement of security and using the proceeds, together with liquidity during that period, enables Standard & Poor's to assume that the solvent issuer is able to maintain payments to note holders. Nonetheless, the structure of the borrower is relevant in the overall analysis of enforcement, particularly in an insolvency scenario. Where the actual borrowers limit their ownership to the assets backing the loans, own no assets other than the mortgaged property, have no employees, have no liabilities other than the mortgage or related debt, and restrict their activities to the owning and managing of the mortgaged property, the timing of enforcement is likely to be more favourable.

Ownership structure/control of borrower

If the borrower is part of a group of companies (which is often the case in CMBS transactions), detailed information about the borrower's shareholders and ultimate parent company should be provided. In addition, an assessment needs to be made as to whether the parent and/or ultimate holding company could interfere in the smooth running of the loan transaction. Standard & Poor's expects these risks to be mitigated. In jurisdictions where the issue of substantive consolidation arises or cannot be completely excluded, appropriate legal opinions are required to confirm that this is not applicable to the transaction being considered. Absent these opinions, and Standard & Poor's would need to assume that the consolidation risk would materialise and they would need to understand the consequence of that event for the transaction.

Similar principles apply to the assessment of risks related to non-corporate entities—such as limited partnerships, individuals, or charities.

Tax issues

Understanding the tax implications in a CMBS transaction is also an important part of the rating process. Failure by the transaction parties to correctly assess the tax liabilities, which can be substantial, could result in an under-estimation of borrower cash flows, and even in some cases increase the likelihood of borrower default.

In CMBS transactions, at the note and loan levels, Standard & Poor's needs to be satisfied that, with the potential exception of withholding taxes from payments on the rated notes, there are no taxes payable by the issuer or the borrower that could unexpectedly dilute the cash flow, including recovery proceeds. If taxes are payable, then the originator is expected to demonstrate that there is sufficient cash flow to meet the tax liabilities as well as principal and interest on the rated debt.

Therefore, information regarding the tax analysis (generally in the form of **4–031** tax opinions) is expected to consider all tax issues that the structure raises along with confirmation that:

- the issuer and borrower are not liable for corporate tax (or, if so liable, that the tax position is either neutral or quantified and factored into the cash flows);

- VAT is not applicable to cash flows owed to or by the issuer in the transaction (or, if so applicable, that the amount of any irrecoverable VAT has been quantified);

- withholding taxes are not applicable to cash flows owed to the issuer (or, if so applicable, that the amount of potential withholding tax liability is quantified);

- withholding taxes are not applicable to payments by the issuer under swaps and other derivative instruments (or, if so applicable, that the amount of potential withholding is quantified);

- stamp duties are not payable in respect of the documents and stamp duty land tax is not payable in respect of any property transfers (or if so payable, the amount has been quantified); and

- either there are no other taxes applicable, or that these taxes have been identified, quantified and funded.

SOME FINAL NOTES

Finally, for reasons of space, this chapter has not attempted to address all the legal and structural issues that are considered by Standard & Poor's when assigning a rating to CMBS notes. So, asset isolation issues (true sale and secured loan equivalence) have not been discussed here; nor have AB Structures[2] and the challenges they pose. Jurisdiction specific issues concerning security can bring another level of complexity to the analysis—springing mortgages, for example. Increasingly, CMBS transactions are structured so as to incorporate properties across a number of European jurisdictions. These pan–European securitisations (given the variety of legal, tax, land law, tenant and other issues that are dealt with differently from one jurisdiction to the next in Europe) add additional layers of complexity to the analysis. When considering these issues, Standard & Poor's common concern will be to understand how the applicable risks, should they materialise, impact the ability of the issuer to meet its payment obligations in accordance with the terms of the rated notes.

---

[2] For further details, see Ch. 8.

CHAPTER FIVE

THE CMBS LOAN ORIGINATION PROCESS

Jonathan Braidley, Director
Hypo Real Estate Bank International

INTRODUCTION

So far this book has covered the CMBS product and the CMBS market. However, without the raw material—commercial mortgage loans—neither would exist. This chapter is therefore concerned with the origination of commercial mortgage loans for incorporation into a CMBS transaction. It is intended to explore some of the issues that mark the difference between a loan originated for retention on a traditional commercial mortgage portfolio lender's balance sheet and one intended for a securitisation. Does the origination process differ between the two, or is it solely the structure and documentation that separates a balance sheet loan from a securitisation loan?

As outlined in Ch. 4, the structure of a loan can affect its credit analysis by the rating agencies and thus the rated loan proceeds at each rating category. To achieve the best possible capital structure for a CMBS transaction (that is, to maximise proceeds at AAA and minimise proceeds at BBB or below), any loan that is intended to form part of a CMBS transaction must be structured and documented carefully to ensure that the integrity of the loan cashflows are preserved as robustly as possible in a variety of scenarios. This chapter will also look at some of the typical structural features and covenants found in loans intended for securitisation and contrast these with those intended to remain on balance sheet.

SOURCING THE DEAL

For the established lenders in the property finance market with established origination teams, personal contacts are a significant source of new business opportunities. In addition, the refinance of existing loans often presents a steady stream of funding opportunities. Refinancing by property investors seeking to minimise their interest burden or consolidate their borrowings has been a significant driver behind the recent growth in European CMBS issuance. Referrals from other parts of a lender's business are also a good source of new lending opportunities.

With new CMBS conduits, commercial banks and property investors arriving into the property markets all the time, competition for funding opportunities and investment properties is fierce. Faced with myriad different lenders, many investors use the services of a finance brokers to source the most competitive funding terms. Thus, for many lenders, whether sourcing loans for a CMBS programme, or to hold on balance sheet, a combination of direct client relationships and broker introductions will provide the majority of funding opportunities.

LOAN TYPES

CMBS transactions are dependant on the cashflows from a loan or loans (depending on the transaction) to ensure that the payment obligations under the issued notes are met in full and on time. This will have a bearing on the type of loans that are originated with a view to their incorporation in a CMBS transaction. Typically, only loans that are secured on income-producing properties are suitable for securitisation. Thus development projects, or loans secured on properties requiring extensive refurbishment and repositioning will not usually lend themselves to a CMBS exit. Balance sheet lenders on the other hand may have the ability to capitalise interest, the appetite for the increased risks and rewards associated with development funding and the expertise to properly monitor such development projects.

With increased competition for loan opportunities, those lenders with CMBS programmes have increasingly found themselves having to be creative when looking at new lending opportunities. This means for example, that they will consider advancing loans incorporating capital expenditure facilities to fund property upgrades. Prior to drawing any money to fund capital expenditure however, the borrower must satisfy certain criteria, for example confirmation that asset value will not be reduced by the proposed development, maintenance of cashflow at a specified level for the duration of the works, confirmation of funding for the works and a restriction on the size of the development works. In contrast, a balance sheet loan may have fewer restrictions, for example, no requirement for confirmation of funding for the works, or less stringent cashflow tests.

A further consideration, when originating loans for CMBS, is their size. This will be determined in part by the nature of the market at the time, but also on the lender's CMBS programme. Do they want to securitise large pools of smaller loans and achieve a degree of granularity (for example, the Dolerite transactions or the Sandwell transactions), or do they want to focus on larger loans and issue large loan or single loan CMBS—the approach adopted by most of the European CMBS programme lenders to date. Typically, most multi-borrower European CMBS transactions comprise between five and 10 loans of between €5 million and €30 million each.

Origination of smaller loans is seen by many CMBS houses as commercially unattractive, requiring significant investment in staff and IT infrastructure to enable the origination of a sufficient volume of loans on a regular basis to maintain a regular CMBS issuance. Traditional portfolio balance sheet lenders, in particular the retail banks, do not have the same constraints with a significant origination capacity through their branch networks and, as a result, tend to dominate the market for small loans secured on commercial property.

PROPERTY TYPE

One of the key ingredients for achieving an optimal CMBS execution is a sound, predictable and unbroken income stream arising from the loan pool. Aside from structuring considerations (see, below), this will largely be determined by the nature of the underlying properties and the occupational leases. When considering a lending opportunity, originators should bear in mind the on-going income generating capabilities of the underlying secured property or properties. That is to say, they should consider the re-letting prospects of the property should it become vacant—how long would it take to re-let the space and will all of the space ultimately be occupied, or will there be a permanent void at the property? If so, what level of void is likely having regard to the quality of the property and its location?

The answers to these questions are generally more predictable for the more conventional property types than for a hotel or petrol filling station for example. As a consequence, the vast majority of loans originated for a CMBS exit have been secured by properties in the office, retail and industrial/distribution warehouse sectors. These property sectors are considered to offer the greatest continuity and security of rental income and are most likely to be occupied by investment grade tenants. They are also readily understood by CMBS investors and the rating agencies.

However, increased competition has lead some CMBS lenders to fund assets in other property sectors, including leisure, hotels, residential, student accommodation, nursing homes, self storage and petrol filling stations.

These sectors have traditionally been funded by portfolio balance sheet lenders as operating businesses.

The move into these more unconventional asset classes has also been facilitated in part by the emergence of OpCo-PropCo[1] structures in these business sectors. Originators reliant on a CMBS exit who are considering lending on assets in any of these sectors, will need to look carefully at the operating business itself to satisfy themselves that the contracted rent is sustainable in a range of operating environments.

The quality of the secured property or properties is also important. This may be assessed both in terms of a building's specification and its condition. Specification does inevitably vary from property sector to property sector and what is regarded as good for the office component of a distribution warehouse will not generally be regarded as good for a city centre office block. Similarly, what is regarded as a good specification for a retail warehouse property would not be regarded as a good specification for a retail unit or a shopping centre.

Specification extends beyond the quality of fixtures, fittings and fit-out to include "softer" issues, such as car parking provision, landscaping, age, building flexibility and staff facilities. Clearly, all other things being equal, a higher specification building would be more attractive to a larger range of tenants than a poorer specification building. Whilst lenders originating loans for retention on their balance sheet do generally have a preference for a well specified building over a poorly specified one, the likely continuity of rental income from a good quality property should give CMBS lenders in particular, added comfort when advancing a loan.

A further consideration for the collateral property in those jurisdictions where leasehold tenure is common, in the UK and Germany (*Erbbaurecht*) for example, is the unexpired term of the leasehold at loan maturity. Typically, a CMBS lender would look for an unexpired lease term of more than 50 years on final maturity of the loan, including any extension options. In addition, the leasehold interest should not be subject to forfeiture on borrower insolvency. It is also important that if required, the consent of the lessor to the leasehold interest being taken as loan security is or has been

---

[1] OpCo-PropCo structures arise where an operating business with significant property assets—for example hotels, pubs and care homes—is acquired and restructured into two separate companies. One company "OpCo" is the operating company, which operates the business. The other company is "PropCo" which holds all the property assets and the majority, if not all, or the debt. OpCo then takes a lease from PropCo on all of the operating properties. Rents paid under the leases provide the income to meet the debt service payments due under the PropCo loan.

obtained. This latter point is a matter of prudent lending practice and would not be restricted to those lenders contemplating a CMBS exit.

For any secured property, registration of title in the name of the Borrower must be completed as soon as practical following purchase, where the loan is funding the purchase of a property or properties. For loans refinancing existing indebtedness, title should be registered in the name of the Borrower. If this has not yet occurred, then generally the loan funds would be held in a reserve, to be disbursed only on registration of title.

In England and Wales, there are a significant number of properties where the title has been divided between the legal interest and the beneficial interest. In these cases, it is important for a CMBS lender to establish the ownership of the legal title. To maximise the loan proceeds rated to investment grade by the rating agencies, the legal title should be held jointly by two trustees, with the beneficial interest held by the borrower. Any departure from this structure whilst not affecting the ability to securitise the loan will affect the investment grade proceeds of that loan. Lenders advancing loans for retention on balance sheet are more flexible on this point however.

GEOGRAPHIC LOCATION

On a macro-level, increased competition and aggressive expansion plans have led lenders to seek funding opportunities away from the UK, in continental Europe. Europe provides a range of independent jurisdictions, each with its own legal framework and property market. The challenges these pose to lenders intending to securitise their loans have been significant, however, most hurdles have now been overcome and CMBS are issued in respect of loans in all the major European jurisdictions.[2]

To date, with one exception, loans secured on property located in the EU's new Member States and EU accession countries[3] have not featured in any CMBS issue. This is for a number of reasons, including the sovereign rating of these jurisdictions and uncertainty surrounding the legal processes and timing of loan security enforcement. These uncertainties give rise to questions over the economics of CMBS backed by loans in these countries and has so far lead to those lenders with a CMBS exit staying away from these markets. In contrast, balance sheet lenders, particularly those with a pan-European presence, are active in a number of these countries.

---

[2] See Ch. 3 for further details.
[3] For example, Poland, Czech Republic, Hungary and Turkey.

Whether originating loans for CMBS or for retention on the balance sheet, the micro-location of the collateral property or properties will be important. Proximity and access to transport infrastructure, access to a large catchment population (particularly important for retail properties), location within an established commercial area and proximity to complimentary and/or competing properties are all important considerations.

TENANT COVENANT

The credit analysis undertaken by the rating agencies as a part of a CMBS transaction is not solely restricted to a Monte Carlo simulation of rents. However, all other things being equal, high tenant quality will have a beneficial effect on the amount of loan proceeds rated to investment grade. Thus, those loans secured by properties with a high proportion of investment grade tenants on long unexpired lease terms would generally achieve a more advantageous capital structure within a CMBS transaction compared to loans without such leases and tenants. This type of loan has, therefore, been keenly sought after by those institutions with a CMBS programme. However, there is a relative scarcity of properties with this type of tenant and lease profile, which also appeal to a range of purchasers not reliant on debt finance.

An alternative to a single or small number of highly-rated tenants would be to finance properties let to a large number of smaller tenants. This diversity of income will generally provide a relatively stable rental cashflow over time with which to make debt service payments under the loan. Income diversity is often demonstrated in shopping centres, which have been collateral for a significant number of loans appearing in European CMBS transactions to date. Similarly, multi-let offices and industrial estates provide a diversity of income which should provide a stable income stream over time.

It should be borne in mind that irrespective of the quality of the occupational tenant or tenants, asset quality (see "Property Type", above) remains an important consideration in the origination process.

LOAN UNDERWRITING

Loan underwriting is a topic in itself and, given the focus of this chapter, it will not be considered here in any detail. However, no discussion on loan origination would be complete without some reference to loan underwriting and the issues considered. Clearly underwriting procedures will vary from organisation to organisation, but the standards applied should be consistent with those of a prudent lender of money secured on commercial property.

These standards should not vary, whether the loan is destined for a CMBS issue, or to be retained on the balance sheet.

Typically, for each secured property, consideration would be given to the number of tenants and their covenant strength, the length of the occupational leases, the rental income, the market rent payable under the leases and lease rollover. In particular, the rental income and lease length at loan maturity would be analysed in detail. At the loan level, the loan-to-value (LTV) ratio and cover ratios (interest cover (ICR) and debt service cover (DSCR)) will be examined throughout the term of the loan and, in particular, at loan maturity. The requirement for, and amount of, amortisation will also be examined.

Typical assumptions made when assessing the loan cashflows during the underwriting process would include:

- no rental growth;
- tenants vacating their premises at the earlier of lease break date or lease expiry;
- premises re-letting at current rents after a suitable void period (in multi-let properties);
- space currently vacant not re-letting (in multi-let properties);
- deduction of void costs; and
- nominal interest rate stress a little above the current LIBOR/EURIBOR rates.

Underwriting a single asset or a single tenant loan is generally more involved, with a greater focus on tenant credit quality and property quality and location.

LOAN STRUCTURE

The structure of a loan is the principal area of difference between a loan destined for a CMBS exit and one to be retained on a traditional portfolio lender's balance sheet. Particular areas of divergence would include term, hedging, bank accounts, substitutions, prepayments, additional drawings and insurance. However, as CMBS structures have become more accommodating, and traditional balance sheet lenders generally have become a little more rigid in their requirements, partly in response to offering lower pricing, the structural differences between a balance sheet loan and a CMBS loan are not as great as they once were. Readers should also refer to Ch. 4

dealing with the rating process within Standard & Poor's for greater detail on specific issues that need to be addressed in the documentation for a loan intended for a CMBS exit.

Loan term

The majority of CMBS programme loans are medium term, five to seven year facilities. This profile fits with the note maturity profile most CMBS investors now expect. Loans with longer maturities or extension options can be securitised, although investor appetite for longer dated bonds may be more muted, which will adversely affect the economics of the CMBS issue. There are however a number of current floating rate CMBS transactions which had final maturities 10 or 12 years after their closing date. Longer-term CMBS issues (20 to 25 years) tend to be of fixed rate notes and the loan or loans securing the issue would be expected to amortise down to a nominal sum by maturity of the CMBS transaction. This permits noteholders significant certainty that they would be repaid their principal at or by maturity of the rated CMBS transaction.

Balance sheet lenders have greater flexibility in the term of the loans offered and the amount of debt outstanding at maturity. For example, a good quality asset let to a strong investment grade tenant on a 25-year lease could be funded for a term equal to the unexpired lease term. With limited amortisation, at loan maturity, the debt outstanding may be significant when expressed as a percentage of day one value, but should be covered by the property's then vacant possession value. It is unlikely that such a loan would work well within a CMBS transaction because of the exit loan balance in 25 years time. As outlined above, noteholders require certainty of repayment of principal and in this case, given the limited amortisation, the only way to achieve a nominal exit loan balance in 25 years would be to limit the day one loan amount appropriately.

Hedging

As a general rule, a loan intended for a CMBS exit should be fully hedged against interest rate movements. The majority of CMBS lenders achieve this by advancing funds to the borrower at a fixed rate. This removes a significant element of uncertainty from the loan cashflows and should help maximise loan proceeds rated to investment grade. Many traditional portfolio balance sheet lenders also require full interest rate hedging. However, this is often achieved by the borrower entering into an interest rate swap directly with a counterparty (a "Borrower swap"). The swap counterparty in these arrangements is often the originating the bank. In addition, the traditional portfolio balance sheet lenders may be more flexible with their hedging requirements at lower levels of loan-to-value, perhaps only requiring, for example, 75 per cent of the principal balance to be hedged at any one time.

Borrower level swaps can be, and are, used in loans destined for a CMBS, but it is imperative that the swap documentation contains provisions that ensure it complies with rating agency swap criteria. Copies of the relevant swap criteria are available from the individual rating agencies directly. Rating agency swap criteria covers a range of issues, including that the swap counterparty has a minimum rating. For example, Standard & Poor's require that the hedging counterparty should have a minimum short-term rating of A–1 (for interest rate and basis rate hedging) and A–1+ (for currency hedging). Should a counterparty not have these ratings, or be downgraded during the loan term, then it must take one of a number of alternative courses of action, so called downgrade language. Typically these would include lodging collateral (in accordance with a Credit Support Annex (CSA), see below), providing a guarantee by an entity with the minimum rating (as outlined, above) or transferring the swap to an entity with the minimum rating (as above).

Additional issues which need to be covered within the hedging documentation and dealt with in a way that complies with the requirements of the rating agency criteria include: the disapplication of certain events of default and termination events in respect of the borrower; early termination provisions; and transfer provisions relating to the counterparty.

Should the loan be advanced at a fixed rate to the borrower, the swap involved at the originator level is generally novated to the CMBS issuing vehicle. As a consequence, the swap documentation should also comply with the rating agency swap criteria, outlined above. In addition, there are a couple of points that need to be considered, including for example, withholding tax.

Originators should also be aware of rating agency criteria in respect of CSA. These documents govern the nature, type and amount of collateral required to support the payment obligations of a swap counterparty no longer having the requisite minimum ratings.

It should also be borne in mind that, in the event of a borrower default, in most cases the swap agreement would terminate and swap break costs will be incurred, which will be paid out of enforcement proceeds senior to the rated noteholders. Using a fixed rate loan would allow swap break costs to be deferred or even avoided in the event of borrower insolvency. This is achieved by the securitisation trustee (or the servicer on his behalf), using a liquidity facility at the CMBS issuing vehicle level to keep making swap payments whilst the loan is rehabilitated. Thus to date, fixed rate loans have seen a greater portion of their proceeds rated to investment grade relative to floating rate loans hedged at the borrower level[4].

Bank accounts

Bank account arrangements in loans intended for CMBS transactions tend to be more complex than those used by traditional portfolio balance sheet lenders. As the loan cashflows are the only source of income for a CMBS issuer required to make regular payments on time and in full to the CMBS note holders, they need to be protected from the potential insolvency of the borrower, the managing agent (if applicable) and the account bank.

To protect the cashflows from potential borrower insolvency, arrangements should be put in place to ensure that the borrower has no control over the bank account into which rental income from the secured properties is paid. However, assuming no default under the loan, after debt service payments have been met and any expenses paid to third parties (for example head rents, insurance premiums) any excess may flow back to the borrower. This is achieved via a priority of payments, or waterfall. These arrangements are very similar to those now used by the majority of balance sheet lenders. In the event that a borrower is permitted to dispose of properties, then disposal proceeds should also be paid into an account over which the borrower has no control. Similarly for the proceeds from any insurance claim and compulsory purchase proceeds.

To protect funds from the potential insolvency of the account bank, the bank should carry a minimum rating consistent with rating agency criteria. For example, should the account bank be downgraded below a Standard & Poor's rating of A−1+, then all funds must be transferred to a new account bank having the appropriate (i.e. A−1+) rating within a specified time frame, usually 30 days. Such downgrade provisions have traditionally been absent from balance sheet loans.

Substitutions

For most borrowers with a loan or loans secured on a portfolio of commercial properties, the flexibility to substitute one property into the security pool whilst removing another is a priority. This flexibility gives them the ability to actively manage their portfolios, for example selling those assets they consider have limited future potential and replacing them with assets having better relative prospects. Traditionally, this requirement for flex-

---

[4] For further information on the use of Derivatives in CMBS transactions, see Ch. 6.

ibility has been better accommodated by the portfolio balance sheet lending institutions.

CMBS noteholders are understandably wary of any changes to the collateral securing the loans underpinning the CMBS issue and in particular at any perceived reduction in the quality of that collateral. However, in response to increased pressure from both borrowers and the competition, substitution flexibility is now regularly included in loans originated for a CMBS exit, although this flexibility is not limitless. In order to address CMBS noteholder concerns, loans originated for a CMBS exit have restrictions on substitutions. Typically, these may include:

- a limit on the total amount of property that can be substituted, expressed as either a number of properties, or a percentage of the portfolio by value;

- limits on the type of property that may be substituted;

- a time limit on any substitutions, that is, a date after which substitutions are not permitted;

- comparative tests on the substitute and substituted property in terms of value, lease profile, location; and

- portfolio tests, post substitution.

Generally, these restrictions are referred to as substitution criteria, or substitution tests and their intention is to ensure that the overall quality of the loan collateral does not decline over time following numerous substitutions.

A further substitution test that may be incorporated is one of rating agency consent, whereby prior to any proposed substitution, the rating agencies rating the CMBS issue confirm that the existing ratings on the notes will not be adversely affected by the proposed substitution. However, such a test may add delays and uncertainty to any substitution. As a consequence, the substitution restrictions are often drafted in such a way that, should the proposed substitution meet all of the criteria/tests, rating agency consent is not required. Substitution criteria should therefore be the focus of early attention to ensure they are comprehensive and relevant. Clearly, tests will have to be tailored for the specific loan and property collateral, but the incorporation of substitution mechanics into loans intended for a CMBS exit is a good example of the increased flexibility of CMBS.

Prepayments

Rather like substitutions, the ability to prepay the loan in full or in part, for example following the sale of a collateral asset, is a flexibility most borrowers feel they require. Originally, prepayments in loans originated for a CMBS exit were not permitted. However, as with substitutions, increased competition between lenders and pressure from borrowers means that loans within CMBS transactions now permit prepayments. In order to achieve this however, a number of issues at the CMBS transaction level have to be addressed. These issues are outlined briefly below, although their solutions are beyond the scope of this chapter.

For an originator contemplating a CMBS exit, there are three principal issues related to prepayment which need to be addressed:

- loss of excess margin income to the originator and its effect on the economics of the CMBS transaction,
- the effect of prepayments on the CMBS transaction itself, and
- the timing of the prepayment.

As regards the first issue, an originator will levy prepayment fees on a borrower who repays all or part of their debt prior to its maturity date. These prepayment fees are designed to compensate the lender for the loss of excess of margin over the life of the loan plus any outstanding costs of the securitisation that have not been amortised. It is likely therefore that the prepayment fees will be substantial in the early years of the loan and all other things being equal, greater than those levied by a balance sheet lender.

The effect of prepayments on the CMBS transaction itself arises as a consequence of adverse selection if the better quality loans prepay, leaving a pool of potentially lower credit quality loans. This can be and often is addressed within the structure of the CMBS transaction itself. An added complication arises however, in that whilst avoiding the adverse selection risks, a situation may arise where following loan prepayments a mismatch arises between the loan margins received by the CMBS issuer and the margin that is due to the CMBS noteholders. Again, there are now structural features incorporated into CMBS transactions which deal with this mismatch should it arise.

The timing of a prepayment of all or part of a loan destined for a CMBS exit is important in order to avoid the situation where the CMBS issuer has funds sat on deposit yielding less than the coupon required to be paid on the CMBS notes. As the loan cashflows are the only source of income a CMBS issuer has in order to make the payments due to noteholders, any reduction in these cashflows following a loan prepayment, without a commensurate reduction in the amount of CMBS notes outstanding, will potentially leave the issuer short of funds to pay its obligations. As a consequence, for those loans originated for a CMBS exit, there should be a restriction preventing loan prepayments on anything other than a loan payment date. Assuming that the loan payment date and the CMBS note payment date are the same, this would enable the prepayment of the loan and notes to happen simultaneously. In contrast, a loan arranged for retention on a balance sheet does not have to fit within a broader transaction framework, and so would generally have greater flexibility to accommodate the timing of loan prepayments.

Additional drawings

A traditional balance sheet lender will generally have the ability to make additional advances to a borrower, if required and permitted under the loan documentation. However, one of the key shortcomings of a loan intended for a CMBS exit is its relative inflexibility to accommodate additional debt at a future date. This arises because the CMBS issuer, post the securitisation, has limited assets, comprising solely the loans in the CMBS transaction. It does not therefore have the resources to enable it to make additional term advances to a borrower. As a consequence, a loan intended for a CMBS exit will generally preclude additional advances.

For larger loans, it is possible to accommodate a borrower's desire for additional funding at a future date by the introduction of provisions into the CMBS transaction which would facilitate the advance of additional debt by the CMBS issuer to a borrower. However, such provisions tend to be restricted to single borrower (i.e. single loan) CMBS transactions. Thus if a large loan is being originated with a view to it being the only loan in a CMBS transaction, it should be possible, if required by the borrower, to include provisions for additional debt.

Loan covenant package

Competition between lenders and pressure from borrowers has lead to a convergence of loan covenants between those found in loans intended for a CMBS exit and those found in loans intended for retention on balance sheet. As a consequence, the majority of loan covenants are common to both loan types. Some of the principal differences in loan structure between a CMBS and a balance sheet loan have been dealt with above. These differences are given effect by the loan covenants governing those issues. Some additional covenants that should be incorporated in to a loan intended for a CMBS exit are outlined below. In addition, readers should refer to Ch. 4 which outlines a number of the areas where a loan agreement needs to address specific issues in order to maximise rated loan proceeds.

In a CMBS transaction, the CMBS noteholders will require quarterly investment reports containing information at both the loan and property level. Examples of such information would include amortisation and interest payments received under the loan, rent reviews settled and at what level of rent, new leases agreed and the associated terms and any lease expiries that have happened or are due to happen in the next quarter. In order to provide this level of detail to investors, the loan agreement must contain covenants to ensure the borrower provides comprehensive information on the property collateral on a quarterly basis. Clearly the level of detail will vary from loan to loan and property to property, but should be in line with the CMSA reporting requirements. In any event, the amount of information required from the borrower will generally be greater than that required by a balance sheet lender, who does not have the same investor reporting requirements.

The structure of the borrower and its activities are an important consideration when making a loan which will end up in a CMBS transaction. Borrower structure and an explanation as to why it is important is covered below. However, the loan agreement should contain covenants controlling and restricting the activities of the borrower. For example, the borrower should, in so far as is possible, be restricted to the ownership and management of the collateral properties only. Other restrictions would include the borrower having no employees, debt limitations and limits on the borrower's ability to reorganise, merge or change its ownership. In addition, the borrower should provide a negative pledge and non-petition covenants within the loan agreement. In contrast, loans advanced for retention on balance sheets tend not to have such stringent requirements, although as a matter of good practice, many of the restrictions outlined here would be incorporated into the loan.

Insurance arrangements are often different between CMBS and balance sheet loans. The items of cover tend to be the same (terrorism is an absolute requirement in those jurisdictions where it is available) and the provisions for payment of insurance proceeds are also often the same. However, for those loans where a CMBS exit is anticipated, the credit rating of the insurance provider is important and needs to be incorporated into the loan agreement. The minimum credit rating for an insurance provider is, for example, A by Standard & Poor's. The rating agencies criteria on insurance in CMBS transactions are available from the rating agencies directly.

Financial covenants in loans, principally cover ratios and the loan-to-value ratio, have been disappearing in the face of increased lending competition. Although they have not disappeared completely, very often the only financial covenant is an interest cover ratio. For a loan advanced with a view to a CMBS exit, it is advantageous to have both a loan-to-value ratio and coverage ratios incorporated into the covenant package. The rating agencies view these as beneficial, giving the securitisation trustee (or the servicer on his behalf) a greater ability to take control of the loan should it be underperforming, thus reducing the probability and/or severity of loss on the loan. However, the absence of a comprehensive financial covenant package in itself would not preclude a successful CMBS exit for the loan.

The ability to negotiate and agree new leases, surrenders, rent reviews and changes to lease terms is important to any borrower. The loan covenants governing these activities will need to be tailored to the individual loan and property but need to balance the borrower's requirement for flexibility, with a CMBS noteholder's desire to ensure that the quality and value of the collateral property and its cashflow are not adversely affected by the borrower's actions.

As discussed in "Loan Types", above, some loan facilities may incorporate the flexibility for a borrower to make physical alterations to the secured property/properties. This flexibility can be incorporated into a loan destined for a CMBS exit, subject to certain controls. Typical controls would include:

- a restriction on the total value of the works undertaken at any one time;

- compliance with the loan financial covenants before, during and after the proposed works;

- appointment of a professional team, including a project monitor and a reputable contractor to complete the works; and

- demonstrated ability to fund the works—in certain cases this may include the requirement to place 110 per cent (or more) of the contract sum on deposit.

As loan cashflow is critical in a CMBS transaction to ensure noteholders receive their interest payments on time and in full, the collection of rents and property management is important. Loan covenants in a loan originated with a CMBS exit in mind should require that a suitable managing agent has been appointed and that it has entered into a duty of care agreement with the borrower and the loan security trustee. Generally, a managing agent should be regulated by the Royal Institution of Chartered Surveyors, or an equivalent body if the property is located in continental Europe. The property management agreement should specify that all rents collected in respect of the secured property or properties will be held separately from all other rental income collected by the managing agent. Replacement of the property manager should be restricted to specific circumstances and any replacement must be acceptable to the loan security trustee.

Finally, central to any CMBS transaction is the transfer of the loan or loans to the CMBS issuing vehicle. As a consequence, it is essential that any loan intended for a CMBS exit contains language that permits the assignment and transfer of that loan and its associated security to a third party.

BORROWER STRUCTURE

The vast majority of commercial mortgage lending is made on a non-recourse basis, with funds advanced to a borrower which is a special purpose vehicle. Where a loan is advanced in anticipation of a CMBS exit however, borrower structure and domicile assume a greater importance when structuring the loan. This importance arises from the desire of a CMBS lender to maximise rated loan proceeds to investment grade. As a property owning company will always be subject to some insolvency risk that is unrelated to the credit quality of its assets, for example a third party claim or environmental liabilities, this insolvency risk should be minimised. Loan covenants (some of which are outlined above) restricting the powers and activities of the borrower should help to minimise the insolvency risk.

However, assuming that the borrower becomes insolvent, it is likely this will lead to an event of default under the terms of the loan, which will result in acceleration and enforcement of security. The longer and more complex the enforcement process, the lower the enforcement proceeds are likely to be, and thus the greater the loss on the loan. An insolvent borrower may add additional complexity and delay to enforcement proceedings and as a consequence, it is important that the borrower is structured to be as clean and simple as possible. This should help minimise the time it would take to enforce security and thus maximise recoveries on the loan.

In addition to the structure of the borrower, its domicile is also important as this too may have a bearing on enforcement timing. For example, the insolvency of a borrower may give rise to a moratorium on enforcement of security for a specific period. In France, for example, this may be between three and 20 months. However, most single purpose borrowers are incorporated off-shore, in locations such as the Channel Islands, Gibraltar, or the British Virgin Islands where moratoria may not be applicable depending on the circumstances. It is important that a loan originator contemplating a CMBS exit understands the effect of borrower insolvency on its ability to enforce the loan security and avoids, in so far a possible, borrowers domiciled in borrower friendly, or little known jurisdictions.

LOAN SECURITY

The basic security package normally granted by a borrower would include:

- first ranking security over the property;

- assignment of the rental income from the property;

- first ranking security over all agreements relating to the ownership and management of the property, including insurance where possible;

- first ranking security over all bank accounts;

- first ranking security over any relevant shares in the borrower and/ or property owning entity; and

- first ranking security over the benefit of any guarantees or other agreements the borrower may have.

The basic security package would not generally differ between a loan originated for a CMBS exit and one originated to remain on the balance sheet. However, balance sheet lenders have greater flexibility to accommodate variations to the above, in particular, no mortgage loans, where a loan is secured by a share pledge over the property owning company, or low mortgage loans, where a nominal mortgage is registered against the property. Both of these structures are designed to save the borrower money in circumstances where mortgage registration duties are significant.

The absence of a mortgage will present an originator with a CMBS exit significant challenges. However, to date there have been a very few CMBS transactions in Europe involving loans without mortgage security.

CONCLUSIONS

The process of originating loans for incorporation into a CMBS transaction is not significantly different to that required for loans to be retained on balance sheet. Where differences arise, it is as a result of the structural differences between the two types of loan. However, competition within the property finance market has intensified over recent years and as a consequence loan pricing has fallen. In order to price loans as competitively as possible, all lenders are looking carefully at the risk profile of any proposed loan and are seeking to build protections into the loan structure to reduce their risk to a level commensurate with the pricing offered. As a consequence, the differences between loans originated for a CMBS exit and loans originated for retention on balance sheet are currently limited. The principal differences primarily come about because of the involvement of the rating agencies and their criteria requirements, particularly in relation to hedging and bank accounts. However, many of these requirements do help to provide a more robust loan structure, and so are often incorporated into loans intended for retention on balance sheet.

Traditionally, balance sheet lenders have been better able to fund development projects, provide longer loan terms and be more flexible regarding loan covenants generally. However, as this chapter has outlined, loans intended for a CMBS exit can incorporate significant flexibility, for example in relation to property substitutions, prepayments and development works which allow the borrower to actively manage their portfolio or portfolios. The type and geographic location of the secured property or properties has also seen significant diversification over recent years. Given the speed with which the CMBS market and the loans underlying it have evolved over recent years, continuing innovation in loan structures is a given, particularly in the face of continued competition. The requirement to provide comprehensive information on a quarterly basis on those loans and secured properties underpinning CMBS transactions should also help to further develop liquidity in both the property and the property finance markets by improving information quality and flow within the property market.

CHAPTER SIX

DERIVATIVES AND CMBS BORROWERS: HOW DERIVATIVES AFFECT FINANCING STRATEGY

Mark Battistoni and David R. Hall
Chatham Financial

INTRODUCTION

It is well known that derivatives perform important interest rate and currency risk management functions for borrowers and lenders alike in most modern financings. However, the extent to which derivatives can shape costs over the life of a CMBS financing is not always fully appreciated. The decision to choose a CMBS financing in Europe begins similarly to the decision on any loan. Among other variables, the decision involves finding an appropriate balance of the following:

- *initial equity outlay*: securing the desired loan proceeds relative to purchase price, net of any entry costs, such as those associated with hedging;

- *ongoing interest expense*: managing projected cash flows to service the debt and satisfy all ongoing financial covenants over time; and

- *exit costs*: retaining flexibility to prepay or refinance the debt as efficiently as possible, when appropriate.

The impact of derivatives on each of these three sets of costs can be significant; indeed, a financing strategy is incomplete without at least a basic understanding of its associated derivatives. It could be argued that this understanding should be robust and as quantitative as reasonably possible, following analysis of each of the above areas' contribution to the bottom line. This is especially relevant for European CMBS transactions because borrowers are confronted with packages that are ultra-efficient in many respects, but the derivatives explicitly or implicitly accompanying the package may affect their all-in financing costs in less than obvious ways.

To be clear from the start, the purpose of this chapter is not to imply that CMBS financings are better or worse than any other funding source for property investors in Europe. Rather, it is to show the importance of considering the derivatives involved in an asset financing. European CMBS transactions are typically structured in ways that are more derivatives-intensive for borrowers than other funding sources, such as traditional commercial mortgage syndicated bank lending or even CMBS in the United States or Japan. Understanding basic derivative instruments, hedging strategies and their role in shaping costs is therefore critical for European CMBS borrowers.

This focus of this chapter is purposefully narrow: how derivatives typically employed in European CMBS affect the three main cost areas driving financing strategy decisions. It is worth noting that a comprehensive analysis of the plethora of derivative structures in all European CMBS could fill many books. The same would apply to a proper comparison of typical European versus typical US or Japanese CMBS structures from a derivatives perspective. For brevity and (we hope) clarity, this chapter uses a single representative transaction to illustrate the connection between interest rate derivatives and financing strategy. The hypothetical transaction is a portfolio in a single currency (in this example, euros: EUR or €);[1] it is important to note that financing strategies are similarly affected by currency hedging environments within multi-currency portfolio transactions. Therefore, the main emphasis is on the three cost areas outlined above, and the case study is introduced near the beginning. It serves as a good platform for discussion on these costs and a few other related peculiarities of derivatives and European CMBS transactions. But first, this chapter takes a broader and historic view of derivatives to set the stage properly.

BACKGROUND ON INTEREST RATE DERIVATIVES

Quite simply, derivatives are instruments whose value is somehow linked to the value of something else. To use an engineering reference, (when used in hedging) they act as the counter-weights of the financial world by moving in synch with, but opposite to, other objects. Owing to misuse that has led to (or at least contributed to) financial calamities every so often since their proliferation in the 1980s, financial derivatives have been regarded with almost universal suspicion and they have not yet shaken the reputation for mind-numbing complexity. This belies the fact that these financial instru-

---

[1] It is beyond the scope of this chapter to discuss how currency derivatives are employed on multi-currency portfolios.

ments can be fairly simple and commodity-like when "vanilla" and backed up by liquid markets (i.e. when they conform to certain standard conventions, remain unbundled from other derivatives, and are heavily traded on and off exchanges globally). Owing to the increasing depth and efficiency of global capital markets over the past 20-plus years, some derivatives have proliferated to such an extent that vanilla products are approaching commodity status in some markets.

The "something else" referred to above is usually an index or market rate that is widely published or easily verifiable, such as LIBOR[2] in the case of variable interest rates, or a traded rate that can be negotiated on a live basis in the case of currencies or commodities, e.g. the "spot" market. Interest rate derivatives provide a very efficient and effective means of managing tailored interest payment characteristics over a defined period of time. Their over-the-counter and exchange-traded markets are some of the deepest in the world, and transactions are greatly facilitated by internationally standardised documentation. For leveraged property transactions with essentially fixed cash flows (underlying rental income) but variable interest rates,[3] interest rate derivatives can insulate a borrower's interest costs from encroaching on (or exceeding!) their rental income over a certain designated term. The extent of insulation is defined by the type of derivative instrument chosen, and also its term.

A derivative instrument can therefore act as a hedge against rising variable interest rates if its value rises and falls in step with the level of variable interest rates. The hedge is the "good news" offsetting the "bad news" in the case of rising rates, and vice versa in the case of falling variable interest rates. For a hedge to be truly effective from a technical standpoint, its critical terms must exactly match those of the underlying exposure, which sits uneasily (from a contractual perspective) with the loan market's perception of swap documentation as standard (as opposed to standardised). Since the documentation of over-the-counter derivatives is so flexible, this is not problematic. Prior to a transaction, one has almost complete freedom to select the proper interest calculation periods, floating rate index reference rates and dates, maturity date and any other terms to match that of the underlying loan. It is therefore reasonable to expect that that a loan will require hedging terms exactly matching those of the loan.[4] This equivalency may appear as either implicit (bank-level or internal) hedges underlying a

---

[2] London Inter-Bank Offered Rate, published daily by the British Bankers' Association.
[3] This reflects market practice whereby even a fixed-rate lender finances itself with variable-rate debt, then uses derivatives to provide the fixed rate, as alluded to later in this section and elsewhere in the chapter.
[4] Certain borrowers may opt to enter into hedges that do not match their loan for a variety of reasons. Some entities, however, may have restrictions related to entering derivative contracts and may not legally be able to adjust the hedge in certain ways.

fixed-rate financing or explicit (borrower-level or external) hedges required by variable-rate financings.

A typical interest rate derivative is an obligation to pay a fixed interest rate to a party, in exchange for receiving a variable rate. The value of this series of payments will therefore rise and fall with variable interest rate levels over time, offsetting the fixed-rate party's exposure to variable interest rates. The following diagram shows cash flows of a typical interest rate derivative enabling the borrower to synthetically fix a variable-rate financing (see top two rows). The direction of each arrow indicates the direction of each cash flow.

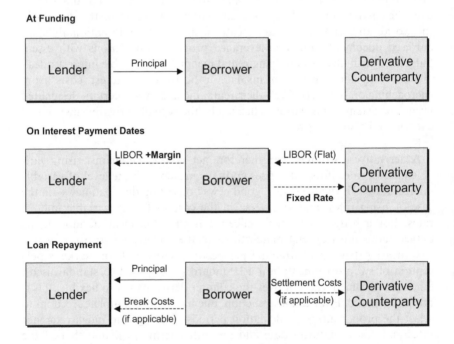

Figure 1: A typical borrower's derivative usage.

For this example hedge to match the loan, each cash flow on the derivative would apply to the same amount and calculation basis as the loan, and they would occur on the same frequency and payment dates as well, including the scheduled repayment date. On interest payment dates, the variable index (LIBOR/EURIBOR) payment from the Derivatives Counterparty to the

Borrower equals the index payment from the Borrower to the Lender, exclusive of the Margin. On a net basis, the Borrower is left paying the Fixed Rate plus the Margin. This continues until the maturity date of the loan, which is normally the final interest payment date; or, in the event of an early loan repayment, this could be the early termination date leading to the settlement of the derivative contract. The bottom row shows that early repayment might lead to Break Costs on the loan and Settlement Costs on the derivative contract. These are not to be confused; to be clear, these costs would not be equivalent or otherwise offsetting in any way unless by a remarkable coincidence. These settlement costs are introduced in this section but covered in more detail later in this chapter.

Derivatives are extremely efficient, useful, and predictable when employed properly, but they are certainly not magical. As the later sections will highlight in detail, interest rate derivatives generally cover a defined time period; that is, they do not generally disappear conveniently when a borrower might no longer require their services. In general, one can elect to terminate a derivative instrument prior to its maturity date, but the cost or benefit of this early termination depends on prevailing market conditions and the settlement characteristics of the hedge product, as specified in the underlying contract. Since accurately predicting these market conditions is impossible, the settlement cost or benefit of early termination is indeterminable; however, it should not be ignored. In some structures the possibility of these costs cannot be ignored to the extent that they relate to certain financial covenants, ratios and security cover. Normally referred to as hedge breakage risk, it can be limited, banded or at least quantified given certain assumptions as part of a financing strategy analysis. Of the three cost areas explored in this chapter, breakage risk most directly relates to exit costs, but it also indirectly affects the others.

DERIVATIVES CASE STUDY: PORTFOLIO FINANCING

A hypothetical investment taking place a few years ago can illustrate the impact of derivatives on a financing decision using actual historical interest rate movements. The time was January 2002. A property investor (ABC Property Ltd., or "ABC") with an internal rate of return ("IRR") target of 13–15 per cent was to purchase a portfolio of ten equal-value office properties for €125 million and finance it with €100 million of debt, or 80 per cent loan-to-value. The business plan was to sell the portfolio for €150 million after seven years, but ABC believed they would probably face compelling offers on four of the assets sometime in the first few years. ABC found that the most attractive margin could be achieved via a CMBS structure that was effectively marketed as a fixed-rate loan. This was priced at a margin 100 basis points over the prevailing EURIBOR-based swap rate, a full 25 basis points less than the most competitive variable-rate loan for identical proceeds on similar terms (fees, prepayment characteristics, reserves, financial covenants and all other details are assumed to be comparable). Similar, that is, but for hedging requirements.

The fixed-rate loan, as the name implies, required the borrower to fix the rate on the entire notional for the entire term.[5] ABC correctly understood this to be that the arranging bank would engage in an internal interest rate swap on its own variable-rate funding and "pass" the fixed rate along to the borrowing vehicle as part of the securitisation. This would result in a fixed rate of 4.70 per cent plus margin.

The floating-rate loan was 25 basis points more expensive in margin, and it also required the borrower to hedge the full initial balance at the prevailing swap rate. However, it left room for floating on a portion of the debt for the final three years of the seven-year term. The borrower could hedge any debt earmarked for early repayment with a purchased interest rate cap as long as the cap strike rate was low (very close to the prevailing swap rate) and the cap covered a prudent term of not less than four years, regardless of projected disposal timing. If ABC elected to partially hedge with a cap, the cash for the cap premium (€600,000) would have to come out of equity, which was clearly a negative.

Below is a summary of the major decision points with a graphic of the hedging profile plotting the hedge type and amount over each year of the financing.

Which loan?

The main cost difference between the two loans begs the question, "To what extent does the margin really matter, compared to hedge breakage risk that could be avoided by the loan's hedge closely following the likely business plan?" Qualitatively, the 25 basis point margin savings is a high-visibility, clear and tangible benefit, whereas the risk of hedge breakage costs is nebulous conceptually and probably difficult to quantify.

To quantify the possible benefit of the flexibility afforded by the variable-rate loan from an IRR perspective, ABC would need to weigh the likelihood and timing of dispositions with the likelihood of unfavourable interest rate

---

[5] This example is not meant to imply that CMBS financings are without choice; certain flexibility for prepayment can be part of otherwise fixed-rate structures.

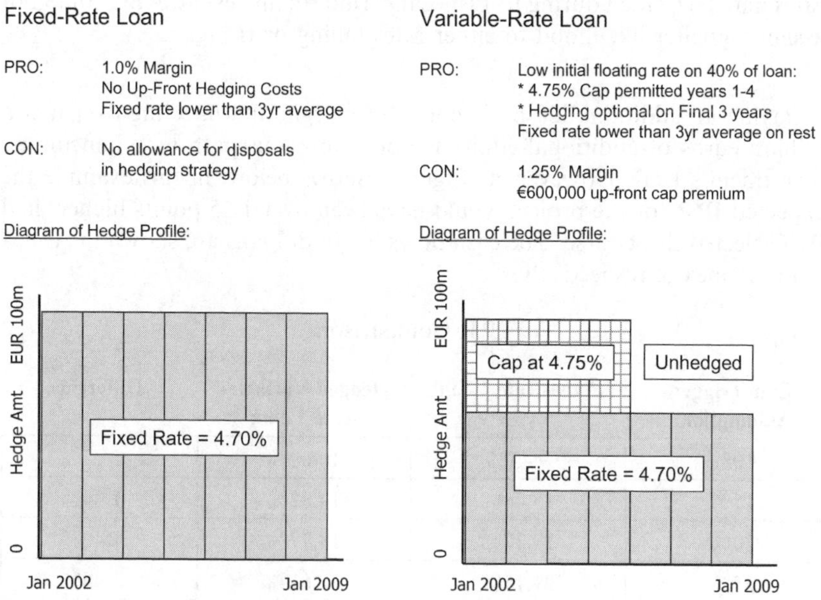

Fixed-Rate Loan

PRO: 1.0% Margin
    No Up-Front Hedging Costs
    Fixed rate lower than 3yr average

CON: No allowance for disposals
    in hedging strategy

Diagram of Hedge Profile:

Variable-Rate Loan

PRO: Low initial floating rate on 40% of loan:
    * 4.75% Cap permitted years 1-4
    * Hedging optional on Final 3 years
    Fixed rate lower than 3yr average on rest

CON: 1.25% Margin
    €600,000 up-front cap premium

Diagram of Hedge Profile:

Figure 2: Comparing ABC's loan offers.

movements (in the micro sense for this loan, the likelihood of rates falling). If confident that the sales would take place, ABC could easily discount the risk of not hedging past four years on the variable-rate financing. If asset sales then failed to materialise, the obligation to hedge up to €40 million for the final three years would be irksome but probably not disastrous. After all, rates could be lower and hedging costs could therefore be minimal. Or, if rates were higher, then it would only be a three-year hedge, which was less than half the overall loan term. But in the fixed-rate loan, ABC had no allowance for disposals in the loan profile and would therefore be liable to settle the costs of the bank's internal swap breakage on any partial pre-payment. This would hurt their IRR if the interest rate environment was generally lower at prepayment than at funding, but the breakage could be a gain, and therefore IRR accretive, if rates were higher at the time of sales.

The extent of this IRR impact was unclear, though, without knowing where interest rates would travel. ABC was not interested in speculating on interest rate movements, but they were clearly exposed to falling rates if they sold the assets under the fixed-rate loan. Were there any clues in the market? Not from their perspective; although the swap rate at the time was below the average seven-year swap rate since the inception of the Euro, it was not decidedly lower (see Annex 1). Further, the paucity of historical data on the new currency was not helpful in giving ABC a cyclical hint of where interest rates may be headed during its disposal period. In any event, ABC could not assign a greater likelihood to either rates falling or rising.

Paying an additional 25 basis points of margin and injecting over half a million euros of additional equity is not an obvious path to enhancing an investment's IRR. However, as Figure 3 shows below, in this example the expected IRR for the project would have been over 1.25 points higher[6] had ABC elected this course. The cash flows for both loans are shown in Annex 2 and Annex 3, respectively.

IRR Comparison

Exit Trigger Assumption:	Fixed-Rate Loan:	Hedged Variable-Rate Loan:	Difference:
10%	9.43%	10.69%	1.27%
15%	13.48%	14.82%	1.34%
20%	17.37%	18.77%	1.40%
25%	21.15%	22.61%	1.46%

Figure 3: IRR comparison of loans at various exit triggers for four of 10 assets.

In hindsight, Eurozone interest rates were mostly lower during the period in which ABC made its disposals, after having initially spiked in early 2002. This resulted in hedge breakage payments under the fixed-rate financing but not under the variable-rate loan. Additional to breakage, the variable interest rates on the capped debt for the 40 per cent of debt held prior to disposition were lower than the fixed rate. By comparison, the margin on the fixed-rate loan would have needed to be 0.64 per cent in order for the two loans to have been IRR-neutral in this example.

Does this imply that the loan margin is insignificant? Not at all; in leveraged finance, as was seen in Ch. 2, the margin is an important cost and a factor driving levels of CMBS origination that cannot be ignored. The lesson for ABC is that a superior loan margin will not necessarily compensate for a mismatch between the loan profile and the business plan. As some readers may have already noted, there are steps ABC could have taken to address this mismatch whilst still enjoying the efficiency of the CMBS package—even with a fixed-rate loan as "cut and dry" as in the example. This chapter unfolds several possible solutions for ABC in the main sections of the chapter that follow. To ensure that their courses of action are clear,

---

[6] The impact depends on the gross profit trigger assumed for all hypothetical asset sales. Additionally, had the variable-rate loan also had a 100bp margin, the IRR benefit would have been roughly a further 1 per cent.

however, this chapter will first review the basic interest rate derivative products.

STEP-BY-STEP INTEREST RATE DERIVATIVES DESCRIPTIONS

Interest rate swaption

Most people correctly guess that a swaption is an option on an interest rate swap. By definition, swaptions are over-the-counter ("OTC") purchased contracts giving the buyer the right, but not the obligation, to pay (or receive) a fixed rate of interest and to receive (or pay) a floating rate of interest over a defined term. This term can contain many periods in which future payments are exchanged, or it can be a single period. A "pay-fixed" swaption protects its purchaser from interest rates rising above a chosen rate, the "strike rate." Likewise, a "receive-fixed" swaption protects its purchaser from falling interest rates. The cost ("premium") of the swaption depends on several factors; but for otherwise equivalent pay-fixed swaptions the lower the fixed rate, the higher the swaption premium.

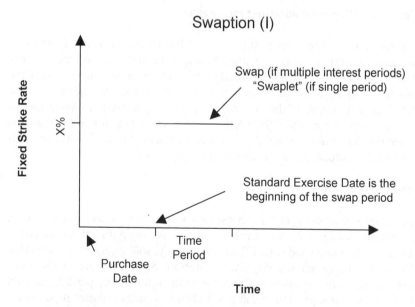

Figure 4(a): Diagram of an interest rate swaption.

The opposite dynamic holds for receive-fixed swaptions. The interest rate at which the cost of a pay-fixed swaption equals the cost of an otherwise equivalent receive-fixed swaption is referred to as the "at the money" swap rate for that period.

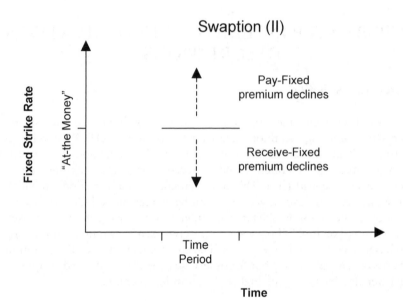

Figure 4(b): Diagram of an interest rate swaption.

Importantly, at any given time for a defined future period of time in a particular currency, there is a unique swap rate that is at the money. The strike rate for a swaption is normally referred to as a certain distance from this rate. For example, 25 basis points "out of the money" means 0.25 per cent higher than an "at the money" swap rate for a pay-fixed swaption, or 0.25 per cent lower than the at the money swap rate for a receive-fixed swaption. Although it is possible to purchase "in the money" swaptions, it is not usually rational to do so due to their high cost.

Interest rate swap

An interest rate swap can be constructed as merely a combination of a purchased swaption of one variety with a sold swaption of the opposite variety at the same fixed rate. Effectively, it is the sold receiver swaption that "finances" the purchased pay-fixed swaption. Since they are at the same rate, one party or the other will exercise its swaption in any period, except if the variable rate equals the fixed rate (when it wouldn't matter if payments are made, as they would net to zero). The result is that at for each swap period (which can be many), there will be a two-way payment obligation in which one counterparty always pays the fixed rate and the other always pays the variable rate. This two-way obligation means that, depending on where

100

variable rates are expected to be, the value of each obligation will not be zero; the swap will either be an asset or a liability (its mark-to-market valuation will fluctuate with interest rate movements).

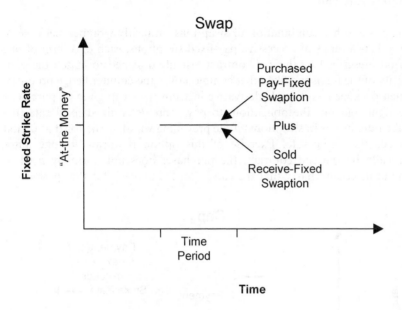

Figure 5: Diagram of an interest rate swap.

Each swap has a fixed-rate payer and a floating-rate payer, and swaps are described as being entered into, not purchased. Thus a borrower will normally enter into a pay-fixed swap with a lender or other bank counterparty, in which it has purchased a pay-fixed swaption and sold an equal and opposite receive-fixed swaption. From the bank's perspective, it has entered into a receive-fixed swap with the borrower.

Sometimes this is also referred to as a "reverse swap" but again, it is a matter of perspective. A swap can have a term of a single interest period, or dozens or even hundreds strung together. For a five-year swap hedging a loan with quarterly interest payment dates, there will be 20 periods to which the exchange of a fixed rate for a variable rate applies on a standard, or "vanilla", interest rate swap.

Note that a swap is delineated by its effective date—which can be well into the future—and its maturity date. Swaps with an effective date contemporaneous to their trade date are referred to as "spot starting", whereas those with a delay prior to becoming effective are referred to as "forward starting" swaps. Importantly, since the price for each (building block) pay-fixed and receive-fixed swaption will be different based on time to expiration, "at the money" rates for forward starting swaps are likely to be quite different than spot starting swaps.

Interest rate cap

A cap is another combination of swaptions—a neatly wrapped package of sorts. It is a series of successive pay-fixed swaptions, each of a term of one period prescribed by the cap contract, usually designed to match the periodicity of the financing like other common over-the-counter hedge products. When packaged as a single derivative instrument, a cap gives its purchaser the right, but not the obligation, to pay a pre-determined fixed rate (the strike rate, just as in swaptions) if the prevailing variable rate for that period exceeds the strike rate. Exercise of this option is normally done automatically by the cap contract; the purchaser does not normally need to remind its counterparty that the cap is "in the money" for that period.

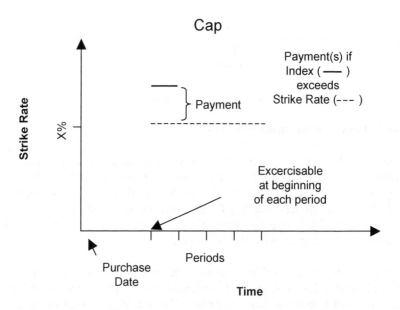

Figure 6: Diagram of an interest rate cap.

Notably, a cap does not prejudice the purchaser's ability to benefit from lower variable rates in later periods if rates fall. The cap therefore provides ongoing, predictable and flexible protection throughout its term. It cannot become a liability to the purchaser, as it only contains one-way obligations after the premium has been paid. Thus, hedge breakage on a cap can only mean that the purchaser receives a payment on early termination, although sometimes this payment can be negligible or zero (if variable interest rates are well below its strike rate). But the payment of this residual value can be substantial if the opposite is true, especially if plenty of time remains until the cap matures.

For all its advantages, the most negative feature of a cap is its cost; a cap requires an up-front payment for the value of the expected payout given the interest rate environment. Although alternate arrangements can be negotiated to work around the standard up-front nature of the premium (e.g. deferral of the premium until a specified event or future date), the premium itself can sometimes be prohibitively expensive for a borrower. A cap with a strike rate close to the market swap rate over the period of its protection can be quite costly. "Out of the money" caps are those with strike rates well above the market expectations; in exchange for a lower premium, they provide commensurately less protection against rising variable interest rates.

Interest rate floor

The inverse of a cap, a floor, is also a purchased series of swaptions. A floor therefore insulates its purchaser from the effects of variable interest rates falling below the prescribed strike rate over the term of the floor contract.

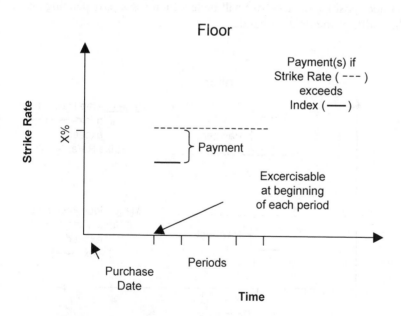

Figure 7: Diagram of an interest rate floor.

103

Interest rate collar

A collar is a combination of a cap and a floor. If paying a cap premium is either not palatable or not possible, a borrower can partially or fully offset the premium by selling a floor to the provider of the cap. The resulting package provides protection against variable interest rates above the cap's strike rate whilst forsaking the benefit of interest rates falling below the floor's strike rate.

By entering into a collar, as with a swap, a borrower is entering into a two-way obligation throughout the term of the instrument, since it would need to make a payment in the event that variable interest rates fell below the floor strike rate. Effectively, the only difference between an interest rate collar and an interest rate swap is the fact that the cap strike rate and the floor strike rate are different. A collar with equal cap and floor rates, technically, would be a swap. For this reason, a collar is a very similar hedging instrument to a swap; depending on the width of the "floating band" delineating the variable rates in which no payment is made by either counterparty, these two derivative instruments possess very similar characteristics. Most noteworthy, terminating a collar early can create hedge breakage very similar to that of a swap—although in every instance the magnitude (positive or negative) will be less than a swap, depending again on the width of the floating band.

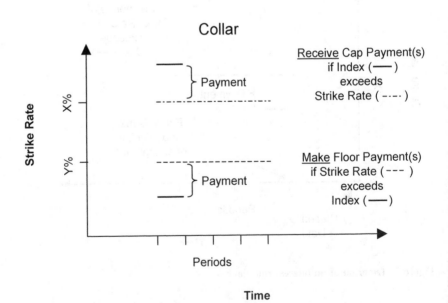

Figure 8: Diagram of an interest rate collar.

Other combinations

Given the combinations already present in the above descriptions of the most basic interest rate derivatives, one should not be surprised that further combinations are possible. To create the desired blend of protection and flexibility, the basic hedge products can be segmented and/or layered on top of each other. For example, a swap strategy may be appropriate for the first half of a financing, but a cap may be better for the back end. A cap can be purchased so that its effective date is timed to match the chosen termination date of a swap on the front end of a financing. Or, a swap strategy may be well suited for a certain percentage of the debt for its full term; the remaining amount hedged could be "topped up" by a collar, for example.

One combination often favoured by ratings agencies (and by extension, CMBS arrangers) when there may be uncertain prepayment characteristics on a certain portion of the loan is a flexi-swap. This is a combination of at least three derivatives. The first and largest is a standard interest rate swap on a defined portion of the debt for the full term. This is not surprisingly the "swap" part of its namesake. The "flexi" part is derived from a two-part instrument layered onto the swap to provide interest rate protection on the difference between the swap amount and the total hedge amount. Comprised of a standard pay-fixed swap with a purchased series of receive-fixed swaptions (a floor or a version of a floor) at the same strike rate as the swap, this layered portion—and this portion only—is effectively a cancellable swap.

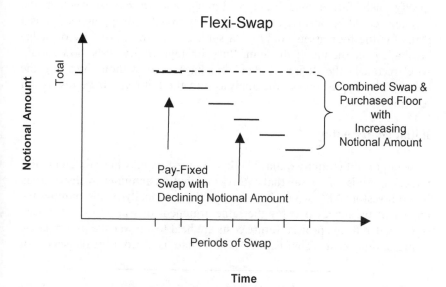

Figure 9: Diagram of an interest rate flexi-swap.

A flexi-swap protects the full amount of the loan balance up to the total hedge amount at a known fixed rate. But if the loan balance is lower than the total hedge amount but above the amount hedged by the standard swap, then the borrower is not subject to hedge breakage on the difference. This difference is shown in the diagram as the area between the total amount (dotted line) and the declining swap amount (solid line stepping down over time). To the extent that the loan balance is less than the amount hedged by the standard swap, the borrower is subject to hedge breakage, however.

STRATEGY DISCUSSION

In the case study, ABC Property was faced with a financing decision perhaps familiar to property investors. Locking into a fixed rate was the "cost-free" and relatively efficient and straightforward choice, whereas structuring a hedge with a bit more flexibility required an extra 2.4 per cent equity contribution,[7] plus higher ongoing interest costs. It turned out for ABC that the bad news of hedge breakage accompanying the fixed-rate loan throughout a partial disposal period was worse than the higher margin and additional equity contribution required by the alternative loan. The term "cost-free" appears above in inverted commas because ABC could not, at the time, quantify the future value of hedge breakage costs on the fixed-rate loan for a present value comparison to other costs. This is not the same as denying there is a cost, however. Hedge breakage costs befuddle many property investors (financing through CMBS or not) because of the inability to specify their future magnitude or timing, and of course whether the breakage could be positive or negative. Only by ABC dropping its disposal plans for the four assets could it "assume away" the possibility of hedge breakage over the life of the loan. But with high equity costs, how should ABC reconcile the desire to avoid breakage costs without breaking the bank? This chapter breaks the analysis into the following three discussion sections.

Initial equity outlay

How important is equity outlay? Different investors may have different IRR targets, but it is safe to say that equity contribution amounts are disregarded by no investor. ABC would have been acting rationally by discounting the impact of breakage costs for the same argument driving most other decisions related to the project: future costs are held to a lower standard relative to present-day costs. That is, even if ABC had assumed a breakage cost of

---

[7] Calculation refers to the €600,000 additional to the €25 million equity accompanying ABC's €100 million financing.

say, X, in the future, the comparison would have to account for its relatively high cost of equity capital by discounting X at its IRR target. From the reverse perspective, any expense at the inception of an investment which effectively comes out of equity should be held to a relatively high standard relative to future costs. This section focuses on this higher standard for the equity part of the equation by exploring what CMBS borrowers should consider as they evaluate, through three lenses, the effects of up-front costs associated with hedging instruments.

The first lens is creating certainty of one's maximum downside risk. The principal benefit of any derivative instrument funded by up-front cash is that the investor's worst-case interest costs, hedging costs, and hedge breakage costs are clearly defined no matter what the future holds. The most prominent of these costs—the most painful in the decision-maker's mind—is the equity required to fund this strategy versus others without the need to inject costly equity. Since hedge breakage costs are avoided when paying cash up-front, these can be ignored. The other main part of the worst-case cost calculation depends on the strike rate chosen for the instrument. This was described briefly in the previous section by reference to setting the strike rate out of the money relative to the market rate for that period and/or periods. Choosing a high (far from the money) strike rate will result in higher interest costs if variable rates rise up to, or indeed beyond,[8] the strike rate. In the case study, ABC's variable-rate financing required a cap very near to the money. Again in hindsight, had ABC been able to elect a cap with a higher strike rate and it followed its disposal plan, its IRR would have been enhanced further (but it would have accepted increased risk of marginally higher interest costs if rates had risen, in turn).

This introduces the second lens: directing the certainty of downside risk to only the necessary portion of the debt to limit expense. From a borrower's perspective, the interest rate derivatives with known downside risks are purchased products such as caps or pay-fixed swaptions. For the moment this section will consider only the cap, as this will typically be the most cost-intensive choice for a hedge; why one might elect a swaption over a cap will be covered later in this section. If a borrower needs to keep interest costs quite low, the strike rate on a cap will likely be relatively low/close to the money. Especially if the loan-to-value level is high, this is usually the case, but at other times it may not be so punitive. For CMBS borrowers, it is likely that a pure cap strategy would lead to quite an expensive cap premium. Is it worth the cost? From a market standpoint, it must be mentioned

---

[8] Since it is often counterintuitive, readers are reminded that exercising an option is worst-case result for the purchaser of an option. This is because the index has risen up to the protection level, increasing costs the entire way. Especially when taking into account the initial premium paid, a different hedge would have been a less costly decision!

that it is never worth over-paying for a cap, even caps for securitisations.[9] It is therefore strongly recommended that, if an investor is paying cash for a cap, it verifies the cap premium with an independent source prior to purchase. From any other perspective, the answer will depend on an analysis of a borrower's wants versus its needs.

In the case study, ABC had the right to fix interest costs (via an interest rate swap) on the entirety of the variable-rate loan had it wanted to do so. It must be assumed that ABC was not very interested in paying cash out of equity for a cap. But in the scenario, due to the possible disposition of four of the 10 assets, ABC had a competing interest—avoiding possible swap breakage payments on partial loan prepayment. As ABC did not need to purchase a cap on the debt for the six assets it intended to hold to term, a hedge strategy of a partial swap and a partial cap against the fully-fixed securitised fixed-rate loan was pitted. This strategy illustrates a proper analysis of wants versus needs: if the flexibility of a cap is not necessary for a certain portion of the debt, then one should not apply the cap to the full loan amount. A pure cap strategy would have added over 5 per cent to the equity amount required to fund the project. A 60 per cent swap plus 40 per cent cap strategy addressed the appropriate balance dictated by the business plan owing to the anticipated disposition strategy.

The third lens is applying this same analysis over time, as well. Recall that ABC was able to negotiate with the variable-rate lender an exception to the 100 per cent hedge requirement; it could remain unhedged for the final three years on the 40 per cent of the debt it planned to repay prior to the end of year four. The case summary did not dwell on the implication of this concession from the lender's perspective, although the duration of a hedge time horizon should be addressed in any thorough analysis. Had ABC not been confident that the four disposals would occur, it would have been prudent to explore (and limit, in practice) exactly what could be the potential hedging costs for the final three years. With only mild confidence of disposals, leaving the final three years without interest rate protection would hardly have been prudent. However, this is a commercial decision best made by those in a position to know about future asset disposals. To be sure, conservative lenders generally resist permitting a borrower's hedging strategy to leave a "naked back-end" if they desire. This is also subject to their legal and regulatory permission to do so, which some types of borrowers do not enjoy. Although due to a different sort of prudence than this strategy brings to

---

[9] Caps for securitised financings almost always come with strict requirements driven by ratings agency criteria. These should not affect the premium substantially, however; there are several specialist securitised cap providers with the ability to provide caps for virtually the same rates as "standard" interest rate caps.

mind, we must report that we do not observe such exhibitionism in European CMBS financings.[10]

Protecting the back end with an out of the money instrument would be a good means for ABC to backstop its worst-case interest expense if it had doubts about the asset sales. If it had a niggling doubt and could afford to service the debt with an out of the money rate on the final three years, for example, should ABC continue with the cap strategy? No. Earlier in this section, the pay-fixed swaption as another viable alternative was identified; this is the appropriate situation for this derivative. The main driver would be the cost. A swaption giving ABC the right to fix a three-year rate at the end of year four would have a lower premium than a cap at the same strike rate. This is because the swaption has one decision point or exercise date—the end of year four—whereas the cap has three years' worth of interest periods in which an exercise is possible. The derivatives markets charge extra for this additional "optionality". Depending on the market expectations underlying swap pricing over the term and some technical reasons, the difference between cap and swaption pricing can be substantial. And possessing a swaption does not obligate the borrower to anything; if prevailing rates are below the strike rate at the time, ABC can choose another strategy. Finally, it would be assumed that if ABC's sales failed to occur by the end of year four and rates had risen to the chosen strike rate, there would be bigger problems to contend with than not having the flexibility of a cap for the final three years.

This section has not yet addressed the single most important point related to hedging costs. Why wait until now? The best advice on how to think about hedging costs' role in marrying financing and hedging strategies is to go through the analysis described above; there is no short-cut. The bottom line on funding a hedging strategy, however, is to only outlay additional equity as a last resort. This is not to suggest that only strategies with no up-front premium (such as swaps, collars and flexi-swaps) should be employed; it is that finding an alternate means to pay for a cap or swaption will generally make far more sense when a cap or a swaption is the appropriate hedge. In other words, selecting a "costless" hedge or fixed-rate product in order to avoid the up-front cost of a cap or a swaption could be the wrong choice made for the wrong reasons. By focusing on possible hedging costs through the lenses of capping downside risk and applying flexibility only where needed, proportionally and temporally, an investor should be able to gauge the appropriateness of derivatives that would typically involve

---

[10] With apologies for this (probably failed) attempt at humour, we note that the colourful vernacular of the derivatives realm does warrant exposure to some of its jargon to prepare the reader for later discussions. But seriously, in European CMBS, large unhedged swathes would most likely fail stress tests by ratings agencies.

spending additional equity. But because funding a hedging cost with equity is so costly and there are more IRR-friendly means at a borrower's disposal to achieve the same flexibility, these should be exhausted prior to resorting to increasing one's equity contribution. The next section will highlight a few of these means as part of its discussion of ongoing interest expense.

Ongoing interest costs

How much interest can a borrower afford to pay while still satisfying the financial covenants imposed by the financing? This is a central question for any lending operation, especially rated issuances such as European CMBS transactions. Ideally, access to unlimited income would render the question moot. In reality, though, the answer lies in controlling interest costs in ways that suit both borrower and lender—the essence of hedging. As the previous sections introduced, interest rate derivatives provide various hedging instruments to fix, limit or otherwise manipulate interest costs. Over the life of the loan, these instruments assure the lender/note holder that interest payments can indeed be fully serviced. Exactly how this assurance is gained, however, can vary from deal to deal. Or, this assurance can vary over time within the same deal. This section commences with an introduction of the best-practice methodology of calculating exactly how much interest a borrower can afford to pay given its financial covenants. It continues by describing how this methodology is likely to apply to a European CMBS transaction using an example hedge strategy. It concludes with a few important notes on the structural and security differences between European CMBS transactions and bank lending from the perspective of their effects on ongoing interest costs.

Although interest-cover ratio ("ICR") and debt service cover ratio ("DSCR") tests can have myriad look-back or look-ahead features to complicate the mathematics, their essential components are fairly straightforward. For a given period's net operating income and interest cost assumption, the ICR can be calculated quite easily. Adding any principal repayment to the cost side of the equation will give the DSCR. Strictly speaking, a coverage test failure in a few interest periods (or even a single period) can cause problems for the loan. Since one is unlikely to be able to renegotiate a lease to provide extra cash over certain periods, or to receive an exception for certain interest periods' financial covenants, one is limited to adjusting the interest cost assumption. To be useful, the interest cost assumption needs to reflect the net payments and receipts after hedging and therefore a fairly accurate estimate of the hedged rate would be necessary to determine whether or not the covenants will be satisfied over all the interest periods of the loan.

The obvious way to address a failure of coverage tests is to compel the borrower to achieve a lower interest rate across the board. This is a simple and straightforward solution, but it could be asking a lot of a borrower since there may only be a few periods failing the required covenants. In the extreme, it could directly affect loan proceeds if the required underwriting rate is below the market swap rate; the borrower would in this case need to "buy down" its hedged rate (usually a swap rate), which can be painful. It is probably not surprising that the best way to achieve ICR and DSCR tests is by getting the most out of the derivatives at one's disposal. The best practice methodology is to calculate the required interest rate given the covenants and income assumption on a period-by-period basis. Thus for a seven-year loan with quarterly interest periods, the result could be up to 28 distinct required interest rates. Recall that derivatives can be extremely flexible. For simplicity, our descriptions of the basic hedging instruments have thus far indicated a single strike rate over the term of the hedge. However, it is possible to set 28 or more[11] different rates on a single instrument, if necessary, without sacrificing efficiency. Depending on the instrument, it can be as simple as borrowing from one period to subsidise another.

Step-Up Swap

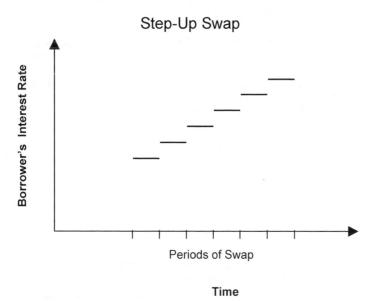

Time

Figure 10: Diagram of a step-up swap.

Critically, though, the process begins with knowing each period's interest rate tolerance. Taking this methodology one step further, the analysis

---

[11] We use 28 to continue with the latest example, which reflects the interest periods for a seven-year loan with four interest periods per year. It is possible, but not advisable, to split the rates within interest periods.

should enable the borrower to exceed the standard for a period's covenant tests, and this should hold true whether the interest costs are managed by a single instrument, or many. The hedging instruments should deliver a "no worse than" interest cost result to the lender on a weighted average basis per period. For example, if it is assumed that the fixed rate for a swap on three quarters of the notional amount for a particular period is 4.0 and the required interest rate is 4.25 per cent for that period, what is the maximum strike rate for the one quarter of the notional amount hedged by the cap? The answer is 5 per cent, and this is important because a 5 per cent cap is likely to be substantially less costly than a 4.25 per cent cap. This example is shown alongside five others in Figure 11 in the penultimate period. In each other period, even if the relevant variable-rate index rises above 8 per cent the borrower will meet the 4.25 per cent weighted average rate.

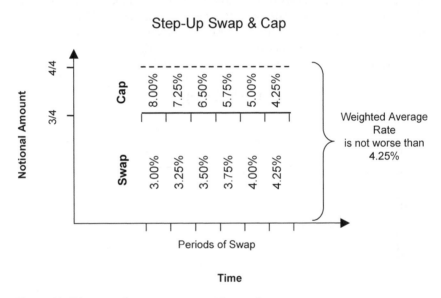

Figure 11: Diagram of a step-up swap with step-down cap.

In a practice, this methodology works exceptionally well. It is not advisable to add complexity where it is not needed, however; there is no real need to blend more than a few instruments given the flexibility the standard derivatives provide. Arriving at a packaged swap and a cap combination with variable rates for each period may seem like a complicated exercise. However, the resulting hedge can be less complicated, more flexible, less costly, and more transparent in pricing than the flexi-swap described at the end of the product description section. One disadvantage, albeit a slight one, is that a cap and swap combination will usually lead to the borrower receiving less of a breakage gain upon partial termination if the hedges are in the money. This is because there can be very rigid procedures for partially terminating the hedge(s) associated with a loan, especially in securitised structures. These will almost always restrict the borrower from partially terminating the swap if its partial termination would result in less favourable financial covenant tests in the future. In contrast, a flexi-swap would result in higher breakage gains if structured such that the borrower can partially terminate future periods, since the cancellable swap portion (which is almost always at the same rate as the rest of the hedge) will contain more value than an out of the money cap.

The preceding section alluded to alternate payment strategies for hedges normally involving up-front premiums. Since this chapter has identified a flexible hedge structure involving a cap layered onto a swap, it should also describe this is best achieved without a cash outlay at the funding date. The ultimate solution from an IRR perspective, which it should be cautioned is not typically possible in European CMBS transactions, is to merely defer the cap premium payment until the loan repayment date. This method is accretive to the property investor's IRR to the extent that their IRR target exceeds the all-in financing rate applied to this deferral. If a derivatives provider was to apply the same margin as the loan to its cost of funding (normally the swap rate to the date of the repayment) then the property investor has effectively increased its loan amount by the cap premium without requiring an additional equity contribution. Reverting to the ABC case, this example cap funding strategy would have increased the IRR by 0.2 per cent versus the conservative assumption of an up-front payment funded by equity.

A slightly less optimal but more commonly applied method is to pay the derivatives counterparty via an increase in the fixed rate on the swap portion. By embedding the cost of the cap into the at-market swap rate, the swap effectively pays down a fixed amount of the premium over time. The implication is higher ongoing costs, but it is assumed those have been calculated properly using the process delineated earlier in this section. The swap portion is also off-market at inception, which can be a negative under some accounting regimes. However, the degree of how much this is "off-market" depends on the proportions of cap and swap, as well as the strike rate of the cap relative to the at the money rate, the main driver of its cost; this degree may not be sufficient to trigger unwelcome accounting treatment.[12] In certain jurisdictions, notably Germany, it is not accepted practice to enter into off-market swaps to blend other costs; in these instances the

---

[12] Hedge accounting treatment under IFRS (IAS 39) is beyond the scope of this chapter. Accommodating shortcut hedge accounting as well as all hedging concerns within an asset financing strategy is complicated but not impossible. For questions related to this area of CMBS, please contact the hedge accounting staff at Chatham Financial or another independent advisor.

same effect can be achieved with a slightly more intensive work-around. The main theme is that it is possible through derivatives to shift hedging costs logically and transparently to periods in which they can be serviced. The process of avoiding up-front costs for otherwise desirable hedging strategies is not overly complicated or risky, but it does take a few extra steps. They are well worth taking.[13]

Exit costs

Repaying a property financing should be a good thing for a property investor. It signals that either a more attractive financing is available to replace the debt, or that an attractive sale has been agreed. Both events would return equity to the investor for more efficient employment elsewhere. Transaction costs lurk, though. Each element of friction encountered along either path will erode the equity returned to the investor, which is a bad thing. This section explains the salient points of hedge breakage costs, a sometimes misunderstood (or forgotten) contributor to this friction. The goal is to conclude the analysis of derivatives' impact on a borrower's overall financing decision by addressing perhaps its most notorious element. Recall from the case study that an interest rate hedge can be terminated early but the cost or benefit associated with this early termination is not predictable at the beginning of a loan. The case highlighted the financial impact of hedge breakage on two otherwise identical property investment projects; the difference of over 1.25 points in the IRR. Whether or not this would classify as a "deal killer" depends on the investor, but certainly hedge breakage can be quite material. What is hedge breakage technically, on what basis was the breakage calculated, and who makes the calculation? What are the best ways to minimise the breakage, if it is unavoidable? What structural factors in European CMBS transactions work in a borrower's favour related to this?

Hedge breakage is actually a misnomer. There are no shards of interest rate swaps laying about the trading floor after a termination transaction, to be sure. A more appropriate term would be "entering into an equal and opposite derivatives transaction at market rates, with any offsetting cash flows discounted at the appropriate market rate to arrive at a single, present value, cash settlement amount." Clearly, the technical description is less catchy. Yet the actions involved in early termination of a derivative instrument can be fairly complex, even though the goal is simply to reduce an ongoing obligation to a single payment. The complexity depends on the original transaction, as an equal and opposite derivative cannot be less

---

[13] It is curious that some lenders or CMBS arrangers might initially discourage the methods described in this section, preferring to offer a flexi-swap even though it is almost always a more complex arrangement with less transparent pricing.

complex than the original. In the product descriptions section, recall that a swap could be a "pay fixed" or a "receive fixed" swap. A cap or swaption could be either purchased or sold. These are the distinctions leading to a termination.

An example termination of a swap may be instructive. A borrower with a variable-rate loan has fixed the loan synthetically with a swap. To terminate this swap it needs to enter into a new receive-fixed swap of the same size, tenor, and with the same payment dates. Execution of this transaction occurs in the same manner, with attention paid to the exact market fixed rate—except the borrower is now on the opposite side of the market (bid side) to when it was entering into the original swap. Assuming the borrower physically enters into this reverse swap, it is now obligated to pay the floating rate and will receive a fixed rate over the appropriate term. With both parties receiving and paying fixed and floating rates on all future payment dates over both transactions, the floating obligations cancel (as they will be the same rate in the future, assuming all the terms match properly). Unless the fixed rates coincidentally happen to match, the difference in fixed payments will result in a fixed cash flow on each future payment date. With the appropriate market discount rate applied to each future cash flow, both parties should be able to agree on the present value of a single payment to offset all future obligations. This is the cash settlement amount which, once paid, means that the documentation of the new transaction would be completely unnecessary. It is therefore market standard to agree on the cash settlement amount, either by going to the market or asking the swap provider to give its best estimate, in lieu of physically transacting the offsetting hedge.[14]

The case study involved swap breakage and cap breakage. The swap was an internal hedge undertaken by the lender, which provided a fixed rate loan by adding the loan margin to its swap rate. In this type of loan, as alluded to earlier in the chapter, the borrower indemnifies the lender for the lender's swap breakage in the event of any repayment of the debt. In European CMBS this structure is quite common. Crucially, almost every loan documented in this manner provides for any gains associated with swap breakage to be for the account of the borrower. A borrower failing to ensure this provision is documented properly would surely regret this oversight if prepaying a loan in a higher interest rate environment, as the breakage gains can in theory be just as large as breakage costs. Caps, on the other hand, have one-way breakage and this can never involve a payment by the borrower that has already paid the cap premium. The process for determining a

---

[14] Further to this market standard, the hedge provider would in most instances be the primary Calculation Agent determining this settlement amount. This does not, however, preclude a competitive process for the early termination of a derivative transaction.

cap's breakage settlement amount is more complicated technically than that of a swap, but the result is the same in that it boils down to a cash amount. The extra step is that additional to the market for interest rates—which will drive swaps as well as cap valuations—there is also a market for a component of the cap's pricing. Depending on whether this component, volatility, is being bought or sold, it will have an offer ("ask") price or bid price, respectively. Again, even with this additional step the cap will never be a liability to the borrower.

There are several important notes for this process. The first primarily involves efficiency but is a good reminder on loan economics. If the fixed rate agreed in the original swap transaction was one basis point higher than it should have been, then the borrower pays an extra basis point of interest until the termination date. But unlike an extra basis point in the loan margin, the borrower must effectively continue paying this extra one basis point until the scheduled term even if the loan is prepaid. The breakage calculation will use the too-high fixed rate in determining the termination settlement amount, thus effectively continuing the borrower's one basis point overpayment until the full term of the hedge. Some readers may be wondering if, given that hedge breakage technically involves a new transaction, that a similar phenomenon must exist for an unnecessarily low fixed rate assumption for the offsetting hedge used in the termination. This is absolutely true. A fixed rate that is too low will also yield a cash settlement amount that is unnecessarily high; the consolation is that the borrower did not overpay on this amount during the term of the loan. A basis point in the interest rate hedging is, mainly for this reason, often much more valuable to the borrower than a basis point in the margin.

Secondly, it is noted that the big-picture task of hedge breakage is to remove the borrower from all future obligations after making or receiving a cash settlement payment. This is normally most practical to execute with the original trading counterparty, but this is not technically necessary. The implication is that it is possible to introduce competition to the hedge breakage process. As mentioned in the previous paragraph, the true cost of an early termination is wholly dependent on the efficiency to which the equal and opposite transaction can be effected. If the fixed rate used to calculate the offsetting trade is, say one basis point too low, the borrower will effectively pay this extra basis point over the remaining term of the hedge. Depending on the notional amount of the hedge and its remaining term, even one basis point can contain a very large value; in Chatham Financial's experience the discrepancy can amount to several basis points in magnitude even on closely-monitored breakage transactions. The value potentially "left on the table" is high. Five-figure amounts are everyday, but six-figure "value per basis point" amounts are not terribly uncommon. If a borrower can find another counterparty willing to transact at a better fixed rate than the original provider on a breakage transaction, involving this third party can be quite worthwhile.

In the event of a discrepancy, the process of arriving at an acceptable solution to all parties can be a dynamic one. From a legal perspective, the process outlined in the standardised derivatives documentation provides a modicum of protection to the borrower. Economically, however, this process could provide only marginal improvement over a very large discrepancy. Knowing that a third-party termination would be the most efficient means to achieve a satisfactory economic result if necessary, the borrower may have provided itself the absolute right to assign its obligations to a third party in the original transaction documents. However, to terminate the hedges from the borrower's perspective, the counterparty (hedge provider) in short needs to document that the borrower is released from the obligations under the hedges. In theory, there is no limit to the paths to this outcome, but the general action would be for the borrower vehicle to be replaced by a financial institution of good standing. The hedge breakage (again, this can be positive or negative) will take place by arrangement between the borrower ("transferor") and the third party ("transferee"). This novation process results in documentation evidencing the borrower's release of future obligations under the original hedge transactions. It should be noted that in European CMBS, just as with a fixed-rate loan structure outside of a CMBS, this assignment process is complicated by the fact that the borrower is not a direct counterparty to a hedging transaction. However, in principle the arranger should co-operate with any process resulting in appropriate, at-market, breakage costs to the issuing vehicle and, ultimately, the property investor financing via the CMBS market.

Thirdly, an important but often invisible component in any hedging transaction is that of credit charges. This applies directly to transactions involving two-way obligations such as swaps and collars, of course, and therefore indirectly applies to termination transactions. The salient point is that hedge breakage involves the removal of a once-existing credit relationship and is therefore a positive credit event from the perspective of the hedge provider. At the termination transaction, it is unfortunately too late for a borrower to retroactively adjust any credit charge levied on the original hedge transaction such as a swap or collar.

Although "credit refunds" for borrowers terminating a hedge early are not yet possible,[15] none of the concepts described in this section should be construed as conveyance that there is a credit component detracting from

---

[15] A small number of large institutions active in the derivatives markets have arranged certain provisions related to this concept, but it is far from mainstream. To be clear, these institutions are not known to be involved in European CMBS transactions.

the hedge breakage cost calculations. Recall that for any derivative transaction with up-front cash settlement, once this cash amount is paid there is no ongoing credit risk. This applies equally to interest rate caps, swaptions, and the termination transactions resulting in a cash settlement as described herein. One could imagine at least one variation of the hedge breakage process that could be exceptional: perhaps it would make sense for a borrower to enter into an offsetting swap transaction to skip the step of discounting the future cash flows to the present. In this case, ongoing payment obligations would remain, but even in this situation the credit exposure is capped and therefore less than what would exist otherwise. Therefore, it would fall under the same credit charges assessed at inception. This perhaps extreme example illustrates a point only; it would not be applicable to a typical property transaction with income apportioned for each amount of debt, however, not least a CMBS transaction with strict rules for borrower/issuer obligations.

European CMBS transactions have other interesting credit characteristics for derivatives worth mentioning. The previous paragraphs show that any reduction in a fixed rate on entry of a hedge carries the indirect effect of reducing the hedge breakage risk. Credit for hedges involving two-way obligations, and for the moment consider a swap, is arguably the largest area of potential savings in the fixed swap rate. The calculation of the appropriate swap credit charge depends on many factors—too many to delve into properly in this chapter. However, the principal driver is the ranking of the hedge provider in the waterfall of payments in the event of an acceleration of the financing. In short, the ranking of hedge providers is very senior in European CMBS transactions, perhaps with a few outliers as exceptions. As a result, compared to borrowing vehicles in typical variable-rate syndicated bank loans, in which the hedge provider will generally rank only *pari passu* to the senior lender(s), the creditworthiness of a borrower as swap counterparty in a European CMBS financing is vastly superior. This is true even when the borrower is not a direct counterparty to the hedge; the internal swap at the arranger level will be indemnified from risk of non-payment in the event of early termination, usually ahead of the highest tranche of the notes. How does this translate into greater efficiency for the CMBS borrower? It is of course dependent to the degree the arrangers are giving proper "credit" to the borrower for this structural benefit. The theoretical savings, which can be appreciable, applies to the entire loan term regardless of prepayment. To reiterate an earlier conclusion, the effect is that a basis point in the hedging spread, notably the swap credit charge, is much more valuable than a basis point in the margin.

A final note on European CMBS hedges and partial terminations deserves mention. The previous strategy discussion section described a hedge strategy that effectively finances a cap or swaption by increasing the fixed rate on an accompanying swap transaction rather than paying cash. This structure contains a swap that could be viewed as an at-market swap plus a stream of fixed payments over the term of the swap. These additional fixed payments effectively finance the cost of the other products "blended" into the overall interest rate hedge structure. Depending on the relative magnitude of the respective hedge components, there may be partial termination scenarios possible in which the amount of "financing payments" remaining outstanding contributes in an unwelcome manner to the debt burden of the borrower(s). Recall that one of the principle advantages of a cap alongside a swap is that in a partial repayment scenario, the termination of the cap would result in lower breakage costs for the borrower, especially if variable interest rates are low relative to the fixed swap rate. Terminating the cap could also result in the return of substantial cash to the borrower, which would often be the case if there was a relatively long term remaining in the partially terminated cap. To the extent that the borrower would only be paying for the cap over the future term of the swap, this dynamic may result in an unfavourable view by ratings agencies. This hedging strategy may still be viable in a CMBS structure, but it would likely result in the insertion of a procedure whereby the cap breakage is not returned in full to the borrower. However, it is important to ensure that the economic value of this cap breakage is captured and beneficial to the borrower. As the cap is financed by a higher fixed rate on the associated swap, the borrower will in one form or another pay for the cap in full over the term of the hedge(s), as this section has described in detail.

CONCLUSION AND INTRODUCTION TO OTHER DERIVATIVES

As mentioned at the onset of this chapter, it would be relatively easy to devote an entire book to the use of derivatives in European CMBS. While this chapter hopefully serves as a primer on the use of interest rate derivatives used by European CMBS borrowers, additional chapters written purely from the borrower perspective could cover other types of derivatives that are increasingly useful in managing unwanted or unnecessary financial risks. There could be chapters written on would be currency derivatives for multi-currency property portfolios in single-currency issuances, inflation derivatives for gaining certainty of CPI-driven rent uplifts, credit derivatives for lease credit enhancement, or even perhaps property derivatives to insulate against particular market devaluations. They could cover related areas of interest rate derivatives—such as documentation terms (under ISDA and trade confirmations, for example), accounting and reporting (under IAS39 or FAS133), derivatives portfolio considerations, negotiation and execution strategies, hedging in anticipation of CMBS financing, or hedging risk of CMBS financings outside of the CMBS framework.

The strategy discussion in this chapter examined the impact of interest rate derivatives on costs at three important stages of the life cycle of a property financing. Despite the differences in loan packages and lender requirements, analysis of the derivatives that will eventually have an impact on the investor's returns is indispensable across property financings. At inception, there is good reason to focus on immediate costs and to defer them in a sensible manner. Although the ideal strategy cannot prevent potential future costs altogether; it should be flexible enough to provide some predictability on breakage costs where appropriate. A portion of the effectiveness and efficiency of a hedging strategy is a function of allocating costless products to debt with low likelihood of prepayment, and/or a high overall penalty to the investor if interest rates were assumed to rise. Creating IRR-friendly means to provide flexibility for other portions of debt is the important as well; the case study highlighted the impact of partial prepayment risks on a hypothetical investor's returns.

The remaining component of efficiency applies more universally to borrowers contemplating prepayment since the value of each basis point on a hedge is larger (and should therefore receive more attention) than that of the loan margin. Whether through partial or full early termination, hedge breakage should not detract from the otherwise good news of loan repayment more than absolutely necessary due to interest rate movements. Also, one should not forget that the good news should not be made "less good" by a borrower failing to receive the full market value of a hedge termination if rates have moved such that the borrower receives a settlement amount. In any financing, but especially those of a fixed-rate variety or of CMBS in Europe, as this chapter has demonstrated, the derivatives involved in the interest rate management need to be carefully considered and implemented.

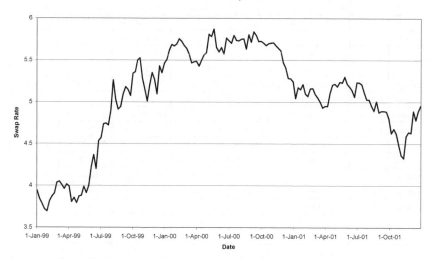

Annex 1: Seven-year EUR swap rate movements 1999–2002.

Source: Bloomberg.

From:	To:	Fixed-Rate Loan Principal Amount:	Interest Costs:	Net Operating Income:	Simple Cash Flow:	Debt Repayment:	Swap Breakage:
1-Jan-02	1-Jan-02	€ 100,000,000			−€ 25,000,000		
1-Jan-02	1-Apr-02	€ 100,000,000	€ 1,405,479	€ 1,570,438	€ 164,959	€ 0	€ 0
1-Apr-02	1-Jul-02	€ 100,000,000	€ 1,421,096	€ 1,570,438	€ 149,342	€ 0	€ 0
1-Jul-02	1-Oct-02	€ 100,000,000	€ 1,436,712	€ 1,570,438	€ 133,726	€ 0	€ 0
1-Oct-02	1-Jan-03	€ 100,000,000	€ 1,436,712	€ 1,570,438	€ 4,135,682	€ 10,000,000	−€ 373,044
1-Jan-03	1-Apr-03	€ 90,000,000	€ 1,264,932	€ 1,413,395	€ 148,463	€ 0	€ 0
1-Apr-03	1-Jul-03	€ 90,000,000	€ 1,278,986	€ 1,413,395	€ 3,884,061	€ 10,000,000	−€ 625,347
1-Jul-03	1-Oct-03	€ 80,000,000	€ 1,149,370	€ 1,256,351	€ 106,981	€ 0	€ 0
1-Oct-03	1-Jan-04	€ 80,000,000	€ 1,149,370	€ 1,256,351	€ 3,829,048	€ 10,000,000	−€ 652,933
1-Jan-04	1-Apr-04	€ 70,000,000	€ 994,767	€ 1,099,307	€ 104,540	€ 0	€ 0
1-Apr-04	1-Jul-04	€ 70,000,000	€ 994,767	€ 1,099,307	€ 3,822,226	€ 10,000,000	−€ 657,313
1-Jul-04	1-Oct-04	€ 60,000,000	€ 862,027	€ 942,263	€ 80,236	€ 0	€ 0
1-Oct-04	1-Jan-05	€ 60,000,000	€ 862,027	€ 942,263	€ 80,236	€ 0	€ 0
1-Jan-05	1-Apr-05	€ 60,000,000	€ 843,288	€ 942,263	€ 98,975	€ 0	€ 0
1-Apr-05	1-Jul-05	€ 60,000,000	€ 852,658	€ 942,263	€ 89,605	€ 0	€ 0
1-Jul-05	1-Oct-05	€ 60,000,000	€ 862,027	€ 942,263	€ 80,236	€ 0	€ 0
1-Oct-05	1-Jan-06	€ 60,000,000	€ 862,027	€ 942,263	€ 80,236	€ 0	€ 0
1-Jan-06	1-Apr-06	€ 60,000,000	€ 843,288	€ 942,263	€ 98,975	€ 0	€ 0
1-Apr-06	1-Jul-06	€ 60,000,000	€ 852,658	€ 942,263	€ 89,605	€ 0	€ 0
1-Jul-06	1-Oct-06	€ 60,000,000	€ 862,027	€ 942,263	€ 80,236	€ 0	€ 0
1-Oct-06	1-Jan-07	€ 60,000,000	€ 862,027	€ 942,263	€ 80,236	€ 0	€ 0
1-Jan-07	1-Apr-07	€ 60,000,000	€ 843,288	€ 942,263	€ 98,975	€ 0	€ 0
1-Apr-07	1-Jul-07	€ 60,000,000	€ 852,658	€ 942,263	€ 89,605	€ 0	€ 0
1-Jul-07	1-Oct-07	€ 60,000,000	€ 862,027	€ 942,263	€ 80,236	€ 0	€ 0
1-Oct-07	1-Jan-08	€ 60,000,000	€ 862,027	€ 942,263	€ 80,236	€ 0	€ 0
1-Jan-08	1-Apr-08	€ 60,000,000	€ 852,658	€ 942,263	€ 89,605	€ 0	€ 0
1-Apr-08	1-Jul-08	€ 60,000,000	€ 852,658	€ 942,263	€ 89,605	€ 0	€ 0
1-Jul-08	1-Oct-08	€ 60,000,000	€ 862,027	€ 942,263	€ 80,236	€ 0	€ 0
1-Oct-08	1-Jan-09	€ 60,000,000	€ 862,027	€ 942,263	€ 26,330,236	€ 60,000,000	€ 0

Annex 2: Cash flows for ABC's fixed-rate loan.

From:	To:	Variable-Rate Loan Principal Amount:	Swap Notional Amount:	Interest Costs on Swapped Portion:	Cap Notional Amount:	Interest Costs on Capped Portion:	Net Operating Income:	Simple Cash Flows:	Debt Repayment:	Hedge Breakage:
1-Jan-02	1-Jan-02	€ 100,000,000						– € 25,600,000		
1-Jan-02	1-Apr-02	€ 100,000,000	€ 60,000,000	€ 892,500	€ 40,000,000	€ 456,900	€ 1,570,438	€ 221,038	€ 0	€ 0
1-Apr-02	1-Jul-02	€ 100,000,000	€ 60,000,000	€ 902,417	€ 40,000,000	€ 475,222	€ 1,570,438	€ 192,799	€ 0	€ 0
1-Jul-02	1-Oct-02	€ 100,000,000	€ 60,000,000	€ 912,333	€ 40,000,000	€ 479,422	€ 1,570,438	€ 178,683	€ 0	€ 0
1-Oct-02	1-Jan-03	€ 100,000,000	€ 60,000,000	€ 912,333	€ 40,000,000	€ 464,804	€ 1,570,438	€ 4,568,301	€ 10,000,000	€ 0
1-Jan-03	1-Apr-03	€ 90,000,000	€ 60,000,000	€ 892,500	€ 30,000,000	€ 308,775	€ 1,413,395	€ 212,120	€ 0	€ 0
1-Apr-03	1-Jul-03	€ 90,000,000	€ 60,000,000	€ 902,417	€ 30,000,000	€ 286,574	€ 1,413,395	€ 4,599,404	€ 10,000,000	€ 0
1-Jul-03	1-Oct-03	€ 80,000,000	€ 60,000,000	€ 912,333	€ 20,000,000	€ 173,676	€ 1,256,351	€ 170,342	€ 0	€ 0
1-Oct-03	1-Jan-04	€ 80,000,000	€ 60,000,000	€ 912,333	€ 20,000,000	€ 172,909	€ 1,256,351	€ 4,546,108	€ 10,000,000	€ 0
1-Jan-04	1-Apr-04	€ 70,000,000	€ 60,000,000	€ 902,417	€ 10,000,000	€ 85,338	€ 1,099,307	€ 111,552	€ 0	€ 0
1-Apr-04	1-Jul-04	€ 70,000,000	€ 60,000,000	€ 902,417	€ 10,000,000	€ 81,091	€ 1,099,307	€ 4,490,799	€ 10,000,000	€ 0
1-Jul-04	1-Oct-04	€ 60,000,000	€ 60,000,000	€ 912,333	€ 0	€ 0	€ 942,263	€ 29,930	€ 0	€ 0
1-Oct-04	1-Jan-05	€ 60,000,000	€ 60,000,000	€ 912,333	€ 0	€ 0	€ 942,263	€ 29,930	€ 0	€ 0
1-Jan-05	1-Apr-05	€ 60,000,000	€ 60,000,000	€ 892,500	€ 0	€ 0	€ 942,263	€ 49,763	€ 0	€ 0
1-Apr-05	1-Jul-05	€ 60,000,000	€ 60,000,000	€ 902,417	€ 0	€ 0	€ 942,263	€ 39,846	€ 0	€ 0
1-Jul-05	1-Oct-05	€ 60,000,000	€ 60,000,000	€ 912,333	€ 0	€ 0	€ 942,263	€ 29,930	€ 0	€ 0
1-Oct-05	1-Jan-06	€ 60,000,000	€ 60,000,000	€ 912,333	€ 0	€ 0	€ 942,263	€ 29,930	€ 0	€ 0
1-Jan-06	1-Apr-06	€ 60,000,000	€ 60,000,000	€ 892,500	€ 0	€ 0	€ 942,263	€ 49,763	€ 0	€ 0
1-Apr-06	1-Jul-06	€ 60,000,000	€ 60,000,000	€ 902,417	€ 0	€ 0	€ 942,263	€ 39,846	€ 0	€ 0
1-Jul-06	1-Oct-06	€ 60,000,000	€ 60,000,000	€ 912,333	€ 0	€ 0	€ 942,263	€ 29,930	€ 0	€ 0
1-Oct-06	1-Jan-07	€ 60,000,000	€ 60,000,000	€ 912,333	€ 0	€ 0	€ 942,263	€ 29,930	€ 0	€ 0
1-Jan-07	1-Apr-07	€ 60,000,000	€ 60,000,000	€ 892,500	€ 0	€ 0	€ 942,263	€ 49,763	€ 0	€ 0
1-Apr-07	1-Jul-07	€ 60,000,000	€ 60,000,000	€ 902,417	€ 0	€ 0	€ 942,263	€ 39,846	€ 0	€ 0
1-Jul-07	1-Oct-07	€ 60,000,000	€ 60,000,000	€ 912,333	€ 0	€ 0	€ 942,263	€ 29,930	€ 0	€ 0
1-Oct-07	1-Jan-08	€ 60,000,000	€ 60,000,000	€ 912,333	€ 0	€ 0	€ 942,263	€ 29,930	€ 0	€ 0
1-Jan-08	1-Apr-08	€ 60,000,000	€ 60,000,000	€ 902,417	€ 0	€ 0	€ 942,263	€ 39,846	€ 0	€ 0
1-Apr-08	1-Jul-08	€ 60,000,000	€ 60,000,000	€ 902,417	€ 0	€ 0	€ 942,263	€ 39,848	€ 0	€ 0
1-Jul-08	1-Oct-08	€ 60,000,000	€ 60,000,000	€ 912,333	€ 0	€ 0	€ 942,263	€ 29,930	€ 0	€ 0
1-Oct-08	1-Jan-09	€ 60,000,000	€ 60,000,000	€ 912,333	€ 0	€ 0	€ 942,263	€ 26,279,930	€ 60,000,000	€ 0

Annex 3: Cash flows for ABC's hedged variable-rate loan.

CHAPTER SEVEN

SYNTHETIC CMBS AND THE USE OF SWAPS AND DERIVATIVES

Dick Frase, Partner
Dechert LLP

INTRODUCTION

This chapter is focused on the use of credit default swaps (CDSs) in relation to two CMBS product areas: the European synthetic CMBS market and the CDOs based on CMBS and similar underlyings. It looks first at the way credit default swaps are used in conventional credit trading. It then discusses how the CDS concept has been used to develop synthetic CMBS and CDO structures, and the characteristic terms of these two types of CDS. Finally, it looks at the use of a repo agreement to manage the collateral arrangements within a synthetic CMBS or CDO.

CREDIT DEFAULT SWAPS

Debt-based derivatives

Debt-based derivatives can be used to facilitate trading, as in the case of a total return swap, designed to replicate (often with some adjustments) the payment flows of an underlying loan. This allows the commercial value of an asset to be moved about without having actually to transfer the underlying physical asset (such as a loan), or extended trading in an asset where underlying physical supply is insufficient to meet market demand. Derivatives are also used to restructure or repackage existing debt to appeal to different types of investor. Restructuring may be used to increase leverage, speculate on or hedge against forward prices, to split out and trade separately different aspects of the underlying instrument or to alter its credit quality.

In the last 10 years, an increasingly important restructuring (and indeed facilitating) product has been the credit default swap, or CDS. CDSs were originally protection-driven, as a way for investment banks to provide accommodation to customers who wanted to hedge their credit exposure to particular companies, investments and counterparties. From the early 2000s, however, they have also come to be used as a form of synthetic investment, with buy-side customers and their managers assuming the investment banker's role of selling protection from credit risk, and the investment bank facilitating this by assuming the more passive, protection-buyer role.

CDSs allow the credit risk of a debt asset to be traded separately from its interest rate risk, with an associated potential for rearranging the risk and return factors associated with the underlying loan. There is relatively little volatility in a conventional debt security compared with an equity, because the capital value is a fixed principal amount, and the investment interest is focused on the interest payments. The only capital-type variation is linked to the creditworthiness of the borrower and the market's assessment of the risk of a default. If this credit risk is separated out and traded separately, it can offer the investor an enhanced risk and return opportunity, comparable to an equity investment, and the hedger an easy way of laying off the credit risk of its debt portfolio. It is this credit default swap structure which can be used as a basis for a synthetic CMBS.

The basic ISDA documentation

A CDS is a particular type of swap which first evolved in the 1990s. Since 1998, it has been standardised in documentation produced by the International Swaps and Derivatives Association (ISDA). The vast majority of OTC ("over-the-counter") derivatives are documented under an ISDA Master Agreement, which lays down a standard set of terms for transactions between the two signing parties (conventionally labelled as Parties A and B, with the sell-side bank usually identified as Party A and its buy-side customer as Party B). It covers the terms on which they will enter into a new transaction, confirmation of the transaction, various representations and warranties as to capacity, tax status and so on, and a series of detailed provisions governing what will happen on a default.

Defaults are divided into two classes:

- events of default proper, such as failure to pay and bankruptcy; and
- termination events, such as illegality or unfavourable tax events, which terminate the transaction on something approximating to a "no fault" basis.

Additional terms, elections and variations are agreed by the parties in a supplementary schedule which, although signed as a separate physical document, legally forms part of the main ISDA Master Agreement. The schedule may also import other standard sets of ISDA terms, such as the standard ISDA definitions, specialist sets of Equity and Commodity Definitions and (most relevant for present purposes) the ISDA Credit Derivative Definitions 2003.

The ISDA material has been developed by and for investment banks and seeks to standardise documentation across a wide range of different products and markets. It also reflects a desire to reduce the points which need to be agreed for an individual trade to an absolute minimum. The use of a menu of standard definitions, designed to operate at different levels of generality, gives the resulting architecture the ability to operate both at the very generalised level of the ISDA Master, and product specific levels (such as equity, commodity and foreign exchange), as well as incorporating transaction and structure-specific provisions at the appropriate level.

For the uninitiated (generally those on the buy-side), this multi-market definition-driven approach, viewed in the context of a single market, often appears (and is) very clumsy compared with what could be drafted up on a bespoke basis for their particular market. In CDSs in particular, ISDA's emphasis on a definitional approach, as distinct from the narrative-based format of a conventional legal agreement, means that the contract does not follow a logical progression, but jumps from concept to concept and from document to document, often without anything which can be identified as an operative clause, requiring the reader endlessly to cross-reference between the different definitions being used.

The confirmation

The Master Agreement (with schedule) for a CDS is not normally materially different from any other ISDA Master. The distinctive CDS provisions are contained in the CDS transaction confirmation, issued under the terms of the Master Agreement. Compared with most types of OTC derivative, a CDS has a particularly large number of individually negotiated and agreed provisions. To address this, the practice has grown up, in the more liquid markets, of agreeing a "master confirmation", which contains a series of standardised elections, reducing the matters which need to be agreed for a specific trade to a few specific points. This presumes that the parties expect to be doing a large number of trades on similar terms and makes the trading process as easy as possible, as well as eliminating basis risk between those trades. However, for more bespoke transactions, the detailed confirmation terms will still need agreeing on a one-off basis.

126

All derivatives may be reduced conceptually to either a future or an option. The basic structure established by the Credit Derivatives Definitions and the individual confirmation is a put option. One party, the option buyer, buys the right (but not the obligation), on the occurrence of a specified credit event, to "put" an agreed quantity of the reference obligation onto the option seller, at an agreed price (the reference price).

The reference obligation is identified as the debt of a particular corporate or public issuer/borrower, known in ISDA-speak as the reference entity, and in market parlance as a "name".

The most commonly used credit events are bankruptcy, failure to pay, and restructuring. These are contained in the Credit Default Definitions, and are similar to the equivalent provisions in the ISDA Master. It is important to keep in mind that they apply, not to a default between the buyer and the seller under the ISDA Master, but a default by the underlying reference entity (borrower) giving rise to an obligation for the protection seller to make a payment to the protection buyer, thereby providing the credit protection for default by the reference entity.

On the occurrence of a credit event, the buyer is entitled to exercise its put option by serving a credit event notice on the seller. The notice must include evidence from public sources that demonstrates the occurrence of the credit event. The seller is then obliged, depending on whether cash or physical settlement was specified in the original confirmation, to cash settle or physically settle the option. Under cash settlement, the seller pays the buyer the difference between the original reference price of the reference obligation and the current market price. Under physical settlement the seller pays the buyer the whole reference price against physical delivery by the buyer of the actual reference obligation (i.e. transfer of the loan).

The price of a reference obligation immediately after a credit event may well be lower than it will be once there has been some sort of workout or recovery, so a seller may ultimately get a better price if it takes physical delivery and holds the reference obligation through this period. On the other hand, for short-term convenience, and for sellers who do not really have the capacity to manage physical holdings, cash settlement is often preferable. Historically, single name CDSs have tended to be physically settled, though with the growth in volume in the credit derivatives market it has been increasingly difficult to find deliverable physical, and there is a move towards universal cash settlement for more actively traded names.

The buyer buys the right to the credit protection provided by the option by paying a premium at periodic intervals during the life of the transaction. In ISDA-terminology the premium is usually known as a fixed rate payment, and the settlement by the seller on the occurrence of a credit event is a floating rate payment. These terms have more to do with the ISDA market's origins in the forex and interest-rate markets than the option-based structure of the CDS transaction.

Portfolio swaps

CDS swaps may also be established as a portfolio of underlying names, as distinct from a single-name swap. This usually means the bank's customer (or its investment manager) identifying a series of names and seeking tenders from counterparties as to what sort of terms they will offer. The best individual trades are then booked to the customer's bank as portfolio swap counterparty. The bank in its turn enters into a matching portfolio swap with the customer.

The portfolio swap counterparty documents the portfolio swap with an ISDA Master and transaction confirmation with its customer. Under the terms of the confirmation the portfolio is given a notional aggregate value and individual names are given weightings, expressed as percentages, within that portfolio. The portfolio swap counterparty deducts a fee for intermediating the trades, but otherwise the fixed payments agreed for each of the portfolio names flow through to the customer.

The portfolio may be static, which means that, once the customer's initial selection is completed the portfolio will never change, apart from minor adjustments as necessary to reflect market events such as mergers and redemptions, or one of the names falling out of the agreed parameters for credit quality. In a managed portfolio, on the other hand, the expectation is that the manager will actively add and remove reference obligations to and from the portfolio with a view to improving the portfolio return.

If the customer is operating the portfolio as an investment, the majority of its trades will be entered into as seller, to obtain the fixed rate payment/ premium on the underlying positions. But it may also trade as buyer from time-to-time to hedge or manage its seller positions, particularly if the portfolio is being actively managed.

If a credit event occurs in respect of a name, the seller makes a floating rate payment (the credit protection payment) according to the name weighting, and the notional amount (on which the fixed payment is calculated) is reduced to reflect the fact that the "option" has been called in respect of the underlying name and that name is no longer part of the portfolio.

Tranching

CDSs can also incorporate tranching, based on the banking idea of different levels of senior, mezzanine and junior indebtedness, with different interest entitlements and different repayment priorities. Under a tranched swap, the seller's fixed payments and settlement liability are structured as if they related, not to the reference obligation at large, but to a notional tranche of credit risk within that reference obligation. This is most relevant for a portfolio swap, where a series of credit events, occurring within the portfolio over a period of time, will generate a gradually rising level of floating rate payments on the part of the seller.

Suppose that the seller is selling credit risk on a notional reference portfolio of £100 million. This would expose it to maximum payments of £100 million. If it does not want this level of exposure it can either write the risk on a smaller portfolio, or write only a percentage of the risk on the portfolio. In the latter case, it might sell £10 million of credit cover in return for a 10 per cent exposure to any credit events in the £100 million portfolio.

Tranching takes this one stage further. The seller can select, not only the percentage of its exposure, but what level it occurs at. So if the seller wants a middle range mezzanine exposure, the CDS confirmation can specify that it has no liability to pay until credit event payments on the portfolio reach, say, £40 million (sometimes called an attachment point) and its liability will cease when payments reach £50 million (the detachment point). The fixed rate payment will be adjusted accordingly, with a lower return payable to the seller the higher and later up the payment ladder it has fixed its liability tranche. As with ordinary portfolio swaps, the notional amount attributable to the tranche will be reduced according to the floating payments made, and once the whole tranche has been used up no further payments will be due.

USE OF CDSs IN A SYNTHETIC CMBS OR CDO

Overview

The use of CDSs in the CMBS market was developed in the CDO market, based on reference obligations which are usually US CMBS. A US CMBS is typically structured as a Real Estate Mortgage Investment Conduits (REMICs). The REMIC is a creation of US tax law and is designed to avoid tax being incurred at the trust level. It comprises a pool of mortgage loans held by a single purpose trustee. The REMIC trustee issues tranches of bonds which pay a return based on, and secured over, an underlying pool of mortgage loans.

The CDO issuer in effect resecuritises these underlying CMBS by issuing its own collateralised debt obligations ("CDOs" or credit-linked notes) to investors and using the proceeds either to buy the underlying CMBS directly (a cash CDO), or to fund a CDS portfolio swap creating synthetic exposure to the underlying CMBS (a synthetic CDO). Although we are concerned in this chapter specifically with CDOs of CMBS, the CDO structure is applied to many other types of investment including RMBS, ABS, REITs, debt securities, whole commercial mortgage loans, mezzanine loans and other CDOs.

In contrast to the above, in the European market, there is no need to use the distinctive tax-driven US structure when setting up a CMBS. Early European synthetic CMBS, principally in the German market, did not use CDSs, and the "synthetic" element often meant no more than that the loans were not sold to the issuer, and that therefore the securities being issued were not secured over the underlying real estate. However, European originators have begun to make use of CDSs, as a CDS makes it easier to produce a CMBS where the underlying loans have not been originated for the CMBS market and do not allow for disclosure of information or transfer to an issuer, or where the originating bank wishes to retain a close banker-customer relationship. The use of the CDS in European synthetic CMBS looks set to increase, as many banks come to terms with the requirements of Basle II and increasingly look to securitise loans which were not originated for the CMBS market.

Figure 2, overleaf, shows a typical synthetic CMBS or CDO transaction using a CDS.

For the benefit of readers with a European CMBS background, in the remainder of this chapter the CDS parties and related terms are generally referred to by their equivalent in a true-sale CMBS transaction. Figure 1, below, sets out the ISDA terminology and the (European) CMBS equivalent.

ISDA term	CMBS term
Party A/Buyer	Originator
Party B/Seller	Issuer
Reference Entity/name	The underlying Borrower or, in the case of a CDO, the underlying CMBS
Reference Obligation	The underlying Loan or, in the case of a CDO, a specified class of securities of the underlying CMBS
Floating Rate Payment	Loss Amount

Figure 1: ISDA terminology and its European CMBS equivalent.

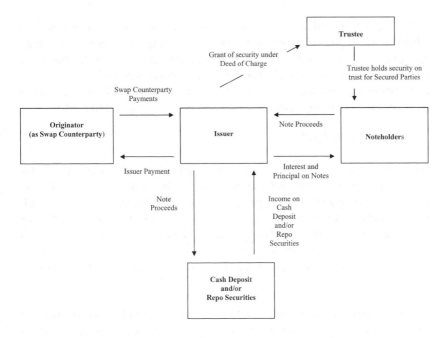

Figure 2: Diagrammatic overview of a synthetic CMBS transaction.

General form of the CDS

The CDS allows the issuer to interface with a swap counterparty (the originator) through a portfolio CDS covering the whole portfolio of underlying reference obligations (such as commercial mortgage backed loans and in the case of CMBS) which the originator wishes to sell and the issuer wishes to buy.

The issuer is the seller under the CDS, selling cover for the credit risk on a notional amount of the reference obligations to the swap counterparty/ buyer. This notional amount may not be 100 per cent of the pool loans, for example, a super senior tranche may be dealt with in a separate CDS outside the CMBS, or if AB loans exist in the portfolio then the notional amount may only relate to the A loan. In return for a fixed rate payment the issuer undertakes to pay any losses attributable to the notional amount of the portfolio.

The portfolio's notional amount is either the full principal balance of the underlying reference obligations on the cut-off date, or sometimes a percentage, usually where the CDS is not intended to cover 100 per cent of the underlying, though a percentage greater than 100 per cent can be attractive to an investor who wants to leverage exposure to reference obligations which are in short supply.

Once the transaction is up and running this notional amount will be adjusted to replicate changes in the underlying reference obligations, including routine events such as principal prepayments, amortisations and repayments, and exceptional events such as writedowns and loss amounts. Principal payments include any scheduled or unscheduled payment of principal on the underlying reference obligations other than capitalised interest.

The issuer's collateral

While the issuer could pay the entire proceeds of its note issue over to the swap counterparty as an up-front payment, in the same way as a cash deal, this would not give it any proprietary right to the underlying assets, while leaving both the issuer and its noteholders exposed to the bank's credit risk for the life of the CDS. Similarly, it would be possible for the issuer simply to sit on the cash and meet any payment obligations as they arise, but this leaves both the originator and the noteholders exposed to the issuer's credit risk.

Accordingly, in a synthetic CDO or CMBS, the standard arrangement is for the note issue proceeds to be held by a note trustee as collateral for payments due under the notes and the CDS. The terms of the various transaction agreements should dove-tail with each other so that the available collateral matches the maximum amounts payable by the issuer under the CDS and the notes. The issuer's note trustee will generally be empowered to invest the proceeds in cash, appropriately rated investments or repo securities (see, below).

The issuer's payment obligations will be secured by a charge over its assets, including the collateral and its rights under the CDS. This security will be held by the note trustee on behalf of all interested parties. If the security were ever enforced, the broad order of payment is: first, the fees of the note trustee and similar expenses, secondly, any amounts due to the swap counterparty, and thirdly, the noteholders in order of seniority. Although there may be variations on this, for instance break costs on cash deposits and fees payable to the swap counterparty which do not form part of the main credit event payments might be negotiated down to a lower place in the waterfall.

A collateralised portfolio swap of the sort just described is sometimes referred to as a "funded" transaction, because the issuer/investor funds its full exposure up-front. Some banks will also enter into a CMBS-based swap with a customer on an unfunded basis, without any related note issue. In practice such an arrangement will only be available to a customer which is itself a bank or other institution with an acceptable credit rating, where there is an established relationship between the parties, and where the unfunded transaction is within the overall credit exposure that the bank is prepared to accept to that customer.

Payments to noteholders

Payments under the notes will be funded from two sources, interest earned on the collateral, and the fixed rate payments made by the originator under the CDS. The collateral is typically designed to produce a LIBOR rate of return—in other words a basic return for the use of money, without any material credit risk element. The price of assuming the credit risk is contained in the fixed rate payment paid by the originator and is known as the credit spread (i.e. the premium over LIBOR).

Payments due under the notes will normally be matched up with the payments due to the issuer under the collateral and the CDS, so that the issuer receives its cash just in time to make the corresponding note payments.

It will also be normal to build certain expenses of the CDO or CMBS into these payments. In a CDO, typically the amount payable on the notes will have been adjusted downwards to allow an element of the CDS fixed rate payments to be used to meet these expenses. In a European CMBS, typically, the fixed rate payments by the originator will be increased to meet any expenses (ordinary or extraordinary) in the CMBS.

Routine payments under the CDS

The standard fixed rate payments from the originator to the issuer have already been mentioned and comprise the credit spread (being the difference between the interest rate payable on the notes, and the interest rate received on the collateral), and an amount in respect of the ordinary and extraordinary expenses of the CMBS/CDO for the relevant payment period.

The fixed rate payments will be adjusted to reflect principal payments and prepayments on underlying loans, which operate to amortise the underlying loans. A proportion of the note trustee's collateral, equivalent to the amortisation amount, will be released at the same time as the amortisation (since the issuer is no longer on risk for a credit event in relation to the repaid amounts). The released collateral will typically be repaid to the noteholders by way of a partial redemption or reduction in value of the notes. However, it will not be released in an actively managed CDO, and in a CMBS structure which allows for substitutions in the portfolio during a specified reinvestment period, it will not be released until the end of such reinvestment period. On such repayment, the notional amount of the CDS will also be reduced by a corresponding amount, giving rise in its turn to a reduction in the fixed rate payments by the originator.

Credit events in the CDS

As with other types of CDS, the most common credit events[1] (in relation to the underlying loans or CMBS) will be:

- failure to pay—any failure to pay a scheduled payment under the loan within an applicable grace period,
- bankruptcy, and
- restructuring—simplistically a reduction in interest rate or principal or a waiver or postponement of principal due on the loan.

A credit event in relation to CMBS assets will initially operate in a similar way to an amortisation. The issuer will pay the floating rate amount in respect of the reference obligation out of the collateral, and the value of the collateral, the notes and the fixed rate payments will all reduce proportionately.

If the floating rate amount is paid immediately, this will be in advance of the mortgage on the underlying real estate being fully enforced. Thereafter, enforcement is likely to result in material recoveries being made on the defaulted loan some time later, and these need to be taken into account in the CDS. There are two possible approaches to this, both of which are based on the loss actually incurred by the originator, in contrast to the standard CDS method of cash settlement using a settlement price based on market quotations.

The actual loss approach

Here (in contrast to normal CDS practice) there is no payment on occurrence of the credit event. In the case of failure to pay and bankruptcy, the servicer proceeds to enforce the loan, and once the servicer determines that full recovery has been made, the calculation of payments is made under the CDS (this could be a number of years, but cannot extend beyond legal final maturity of the notes). In the case of a restructuring (where there is no subsequent failure to pay or bankruptcy) the loan continues to maturity and a calculation of the reduction due to restructuring (generally on a present

---

[1] Note that in the ISDA pay-as-you-go template designed for US CMBS what most people would think of as credit events are classed as floating repayments, and do not follow the ISDA Credit Derivatives Definitions standard process for credit events. See further, below, under "CDOs based on US CMBS".

value or accounting adjustment basis), plus any additional losses on maturity, is made under the CDS.

The issuer then pays this calculated loss amount in respect of the loan out of the collateral, pays the balance (if any) of that reference obligation's notional amount by way of redemption to the noteholders, and the value of the collateral, the notes and the fixed rate payments all reduce proportionately.

The estimated loss approach

Alternatively, the originator may want to receive loss payments earlier than it would in the scenario described above. In that case the CDS will contain a mechanism for estimation and payment of losses before the mortgage on the underlying real estate has been fully enforced. Once full recovery has been made on the mortgage loan an adjustment calculation is performed, and if there was an overpayment of losses by the issuer at the estimation stage, the payment from the originator back to the issuer may need to compensate noteholders for any interest foregone. The estimation process in a European-based CDS will generally be performed by a qualified valuer, with the ability for the trustee to appoint a second valuer if it disputes the estimate of the first valuer. In a CDO structure the valuations are performed at the CMBS level.

CDSs based on US CMBS use the estimated loss approach, also known as "pay-as-you-go", which should be an exact match for the reimbursement payments received from the underlying CMBS. European originators operating at the synthetic CMBS level have tended to use the actual loss approach, which has the advantage of not incurring valuation costs on estimating each loss and having to adjust back (potentially with interest foregone to the noteholders) if there is an overpayment on the initial estimate. The actual loss approach also assists from a ratings perspective, as noteholders are not exposed to the credit risk of the originator in respect of future adjustment payments.

Estimated losses are also used where full recovery has not been made by legal final maturity of the notes. As with a true-sale CMBS, the synthetic European CMBS/CDO will have a scheduled maturity date, which in the European CMBS will be the latest maturity date of the loans in the pool. There will then be a tail period to allow for full recoveries on defaulted loans. If the recovery process has not been completed within a certain period prior to legal final maturity then there will be a mechanism to estimate these losses and allow final payments to be made under the CDS.

Some CMBS originators structure their CDSs so that each loan in the portfolio is given its own "tail period". If the recoveries on that loan have not been fully made within a specified period (for example, 18 or 24 months) then the estimation process is used to close out the swap on that loan, rather than continuing for an extended period until legal final maturity.

Termination of the swap

The CDS will contain the standard ISDA Master termination events as between the issuer and the originator. These will include, for example:

- failure to pay by the issuer or the originator,

- bankruptcy of either party,

- illegality, or

- tax events.

To these may be added additional termination events, such as early redemption of the notes, or an increase in the regulatory capital costs of the CDS to the originator. In these "no fault" situations the normal default provisions of the ISDA Master may be modified to allow for termination on as neutral a basis as possible. Similarly, a termination of, or default under, the CDS, should trigger a compulsory note redemption, and the principal and interest payment terms of the notes will need to be matched to the payment flows and notional value under the CDS and collateral, in exceptional as well as routine situations.

Other features designed to reflect the CMBS/CDO structure include limited recourse and non-petition provisions, making it clear that any swap counterparty claim against the issuer is limited to the amount of collateral and other secured assets available to the note trustee, so that the issuer can never be made insolvent as a result of failure to pay under the CDS.

Downgrade of the swap counterparty (the originator) is generally not a termination event under the CDS where an actual loss approach is used. Since the collateral held by the note trustee already provides full security for the principal amount of the notes, the only risk of counterparty default is on the receipt of the fixed rate credit spread from the originator, and the originator simply needs to provide sufficient protection against non-payment. This can be done by changing the fixed rate payment from a payment in arrear on each note payment date to a payment in advance, often accompanied by an additional payment in escrow. This ensures that the fixed rate payment is already held by the issuer, and not at risk, for a sufficient period to allow for full realisation of the note trustee's collateral (for example, two full interest periods).

Loss amount in the European CMBS

As noted above, the European CMBS swap is usually drafted so as to make one "actual loss" lump sum payment of the aggregate loss on a mortgage loan after full enforcement. Under this approach, the calculation of the loss amount will not occur until the earlier of:

- a final recovery determination being made by the servicer,

- an intervening early termination of the CDS (e.g. for default by the originator or issuer), and

- a period prior to legal final maturity of the notes to allow for full settlement of all payments. This actually results in a more relaxed position as regards tail periods for the notes, because even if recovery is not complete by legal final maturity, a final calculation can be made allowing full payment of all principal amounts to the noteholders by legal final maturity.

The notification of the loss amount must describe in reasonable detail how the loss amount was determined. A verification agent (generally an internationally recognised accounting firm) will then be required to verify certain matters before payment is made. These will often include:

- that the eligibility criteria were met for the relevant loan. This replicates a true-sale deal where, if the originator's representations on sale of the mortgage loans were incorrect, the noteholders would not bear the loss as the loan would be repurchased by the originator. In a synthetic CMBS, if the eligibility criteria (which are broadly in the same form as true-sale originator representations) are not met, no loss is payable by the issuer and the originator bears the loss;

- that the servicing standard was met in relation to the relevant loan; and

- that the calculation of the loss amount is correct.

Once the verification process is complete, the issuer must then pay the loss amount due to the originator on the first fixed rate payer payment date falling after such verification. The loss amount payable by the issuer is based on the actual loss on the underlying loan. This is then multiplied by the relevant percentage, to get the proportion of the loss for which the issuer has accepted liability under the transaction relative to the total loss. Where the loss amount is calculated after full recovery, the issuer, at the same time as paying the loss amount to the originator, will redeem a portion of the notes equal to the balance of the notional amount for that loan less the loss amount.

It is possible in addition to the arrangements described above, for the originator to include a right to settle all or part of the CDS physically following a credit event. This provision has not been used in European CMBS CDSs. There is no need for it under the actual loss approach, and it is in any case inconsistent with the motivation for most European synthetic CMBS—namely the non-transferability of the underlying loans and/or the originator's desire to maintain its relationship with the borrower. For transactions settled on an estimated loss basis, (as is in the case of the pay-as-you-go CDSs described, below), physical settlement has the advantage that the originator can clear the transaction off its books at the time of the initial losses, rather than having to wait and see if there are any recoveries.

CDOs BASED ON US CMBS

Where the reference obligations under a CDS are US CMBS, the swap will need to incorporate a number of distinctive features, making it generally more complicated than its European CMBS CDS equivalent. In particular, US CMBS mortgage pools do not have a conventional maturity date for the repayment of principal, other than a long stop date of 30 years or so, by which time all the underlying mortgage loans are expected to have been either repaid or defaulted and enforced. When an individual mortgagor defaults, the CMBS operator does not call an event of default, it merely estimates the impact of this on the CMBS pool and then writes down the CMBS's value.

As a result of this, the issuer's payment obligations are normally triggered, not by a failure to pay principal, but by a writedown. On the occurrence of a writedown, the issuer is called immediately to pay the originator the amount of the writedown. If later on there is a recovery as a result of the enforcement of the mortgage, the issuer receives a payment in respect of that recovery. Both of these payments are "pay-as-you-go"; that is, a floating rate payment obligation is triggered simply by the occurrence of the specified event. Nor do the parties wait until the actual losses has been quantified; payments are made at the time the writedown or recovery is identified.

The CDS will also include provisions for payment by the seller if interest is not paid on the underlying CMBS. In a European CMBS there is no interest payment of this sort, the assumption being that interest will be received by the CMBS until a default, at which time any interest shortfall will be wrapped in with the actual loss payment.

The following description is based on the ISDA confirmation template:

"Credit Derivative Transaction on Asset-Backed Security with Pay-as-You-Go or Physical Settlement (Dealer Form)".

Notional amount

The notional amount on which the issuer's slice of exposure to the reference obligation is calculated (described in the ISDA template as the reference obligation notional amount) is identified initially as the product of:

(1) the original principal amount. This is the amount of the reference obligation originally issued;

(2) the initial factor. This is a ratio equal to the outstanding principal amount as of the effective date divided by the original principal amount—reflecting any reductions in the principal amount between its original issue and the commencement date of the swap; and

(3) the applicable percentage. This is the percentage of the reference obligation covered by the CDS transaction—which may be greater than 100 per cent. So the applicable percentage for an issuer which wants exposure to $20 million of a $100 million security issue is 20 per cent.

Once the transaction is up and running the notional amount replicates changes in the underlying reference obligation by being:

- reduced by principal payments, any principal shortfall amount, writedowns and partial physical settlement; and

- increased by any writedown reimbursements and other cash payments.

As regards this terminology:

- *"Principal payment"* includes any scheduled or unscheduled payment of principal to the lender of the Reference Obligation other than capitalised interest.

- *"Principal shortfall"* is a failure to pay principal when due.

- *"Writedown"* is a writedown or applied loss, or a forgiveness of principal, resulting in a reduction of the outstanding principal amount, or the attribution of a principal deficiency or realised loss to the reference obligation resulting in a reduction in the current interest payable.

These formulae are designed to adjust the notional amount to reflect any repayments of principal and amortisations, any payment defaults, and any subsequent recoveries. A writedown reflects the fact that one or more

139

mortgagors have defaulted and that the trustee/servicer has concluded that the value of the relevant mortgages should be written down in the CMBS's accounts. Once the security has been enforced and the mortgaged property sold, the proceeds will be applied in or towards satisfaction of the defaulted debt. At this point there may well be a recovery against the original writedown.

First fixed amount (the issuer's premium)

This is the standard ISDA fixed rate payment, payable by the originator to the issuer, also known as the credit spread, and is payable in respect of each fixed rate payer calculation period. This period is as specified in the confirmation. It is usually designed to match underlying pool payment dates, but may be applied across the board as a series of periodic (typically three monthly) payment dates.

The buyer pays this premium at a fixed rate on the outstanding notional amount. The formula for calculating this is the product of:

(1) the fixed rate;

(2) the weighted average of the notional amount as at 5pm in the calculation agent city on each day in the fixed rate payer calculation period; and

(3) the day count fraction (actual number of days in the calculation period divided by 360).

Floating amounts (the originator's protection)

The originator's obligation to pay is triggered on notification by the calculation agent or the originator of a floating amount event, defined as writedown, failure to pay principal or interest shortfall. The notification must describe in reasonable detail how the floating amount was determined. The issuer must pay the floating amount due to the originator on the first fixed rate payer payment date falling at least two business days after such notification.

The floating amount payable by the issuer is based on the actual shortfall or writedown on the underlying reference obligation. This is then multiplied by the applicable percentage, to get the proportion of the shortfall for which the issuer has accepted liability under the transaction relative to the total shortfall.

Note that these floating amount events are usually thought of as credit events, and behave in virtually the same way. However, the documents for

CDO CDSs are drafted in such a manner that only the physical settlement credit events described below technically constitute actual credit events. It is of course open to the parties to redraft the ISDA template so as to eliminate this extra source of confusion.

The amounts payable in respect of an interest shortfall are typically subject to an interest shortfall cap, calculated by reference to the first fixed amount. Under this arrangement the first fixed amount payable to the issuer is reduced by the amount of any outstanding interest shortfall. If the currently payable first fixed amount is not enough to cover this interest shortfall, then the excess is carried over and applied against the next first fixed amount, and so on. The commercial effect is that interest shortfalls are only payable out of the issuer's credit spread, and no further spread will be payable until the whole of the outstanding interest shortfall has been discharged.

Although the floating amount could be treated as due and payable at the date of actual occurrence of the floating amount event, the floating rate payer payment date is conventionally defined as the next fixed rate payer payment date, to reduce operational complexity.

Additional fixed amounts

Additional fixed amounts are payable by the originator to the issuer on the occurrence of additional fixed payment events. These are designed to reflect recoveries in respect of earlier shortfalls which have been paid out by the issuer as floating rate payments. They are defined as:

- *Writedown reimbursement*. This is a payment by or on behalf of the borrower of any amount in respect of the reference obligation in reduction of prior writedowns, or any other decrease in the principal deficiency balance or realised loss.

- *Principal shortfall reimbursement*. This is any payment by or on behalf of the borrower in or towards any deferral or failure to pay principal arising from a prior failure to pay principal.

- *Interest shortfall reimbursement*. This is the payment on any reference obligation payment date of an actual interest amount which is greater than the expected interest amount.

Where there is an interest shortfall cap, and an interest shortfall is still outstanding, the originator will not be required to make an additional fixed payment in respect of an interest shortfall reimbursement until all the interest shortfall amounts in excess of the cap have been reimbursed. An interest shortfall reimbursement does not normally include any provision for payment of lost interest on the recovered interest.

Physical settlement credit events

The ISDA template contemplates that, in addition to the arrangements for floating payments described above, the originator may choose to settle part or all of the CDS physically (partial physical settlement) following a credit event. This provision is an alternative to pay-as-you-go settlement. It is not regularly used, and is probably only of interest to the originator if the originator believes that it might be able to source the underlying asset in the market. The ISDA template suggests the following credit events for triggering physical settlement:

- failure to pay principal,
- writedown,
- distressed ratings downgrade, and
- maturity extension.

On the occurrence of such a credit event, and service of the required credit event notice, the issuer pays the physical settlement amount on delivery of the underlying asset by the originator. The physical settlement amount is equal to par (the outstanding principal balance), except that any writedowns that have occurred but which do not reduce the outstanding principal balance are carved out of the physical settlement amount. The main effect of physical settlement is to reduce the size of the overall CDS transaction, so that the originator is no longer on-risk to pay any subsequent reimbursements/additional fixed amounts. This physical settlement process does not deal with a realised writedown, which must be paid as a floating payment.

Summary

In summary then, there are potentially four different payment obligations under a pay-as-you-go CDS confirmation:

Buyer pays:
- fixed amounts (the swap premium); and
- additional fixed amounts (reimbursement payments).

Seller pays:
- floating amounts (the pay-as-you-go payments, to be distinguished from the single credit event payment which is typical of an ordinary CDS); and

- physical settlement amounts (following physical settlement by the buyer);

as well as the buyer's delivery obligation on physical settlement.

COLLATERALISATION BY USE OF REPOS

Background

The collateral comprising the proceeds of the notes is often simply held as cash in a bank deposit account. The bank makes periodic income payments from the account to the issuer, timed to coincide with the note payment dates, and based on three month LIBOR.

Often the bank which has originated the CMBS or CDO and acts as swap counterparty will also be the account bank which holds the cash collateral. This creates a significant credit risk. If the bank goes into default and is unable to meet its obligations under the collateral arrangements, this is exactly the time when it will also be defaulting under the CDS. If the issuer and the noteholders cannot get their hands on the collateral at this point, the object of taking collateral in the first place is defeated. As with a rated true-sale CMBS, there will be requirements in the documents to change account banks on a downgrade of the account bank below a specified rating level. However, one derivative-based structure used to protect the notes against this credit risk is to hold the collateral under a repo.

A repo is a particular type of sale and repurchase agreement used primarily in the government bond markets. The standard master documentation sponsored by the Bond Market Association[2] is known as the Global Master Repurchase Agreement. Under a repo, the seller enters into a cash or spot sale of securities to the buyer, and a matching forward repurchase contract, under which the seller agrees, at some time in the future, to repurchase equivalent securities from the buyer. The repurchase is at a pre-agreed price which locks in a certain return to the buyer on the original price it paid for the securities. In commercial terms, the seller is borrowing cash from the buyer on the collateral of its securities portfolio.

Establishing the repo arrangement

In the CMBS or CDO context, the mechanism offered by the repo concept is used to convert an unsecured loan by the issuer to the bank (in the form of the original cash deposit) into a fully collateralised loan, documented on a

---

[2] As at July 2006, the Bond Market Association has voted to merge with the Securities Industry Association to form the Securities Industry and Financial Markets Association (SIFMA).

recognised market standard, with valid first ranking security over the repo securities in favour of the noteholders.

The repo may be activated as soon as the notes are subscribed for, it may be delayed until the credit rating of the account bank holding the cash collateral falls below an acceptable level, or there may be a combination of cash and repo from the outset, with the proportions determined by account bank and repo counterparty ratings. Once the repo is activated, the collateral is applied by the issuer (as buyer) to buy securities from the originator (as seller) under the repo agreement.

The securities must meet certain eligibility criteria (including criteria specified by the rating agencies). Typically these would be:

- listed securities issued or guaranteed by an OECD country with a specified rating and certain other attributes,

- commercial paper and treasury bills and short term money market instruments issued or guaranteed by an OECD country with a specified rating and certain other attributes, and

- AAA asset-backed securities subject to a percentage limit on the portion they comprise of the portfolio.

The bank may be required to build an element of over-collateralisation into the securities delivered to the issuer by applying a margin ratio to the price payable by the issuer for the purchase (i.e. the note proceeds are treated as purchasing a greater quantity of securities than would be the case on a straight market price basis). This originates as a rating agency requirement for maintaining the rating of the notes, and might typically be required where the move from cash collateral to repo is triggered by a downgrade in the bank's credit rating.

Operating the repo

Once the repo is in place, the originator holds the cash purchase price and the issuer (to be precise the note trustee) holds the repo securities (which are secured under the issuer security in favour of the secured parties) in a securities account with a third party custodian. Usually, the issuer pays the originator the income it actually receives on the securities, and the originator makes periodic payments corresponding to the LIBOR payments payable on the original collateral. The two payments are normally netted out, so that only the net balance is payable. Other arrangements are possible, and the terms may be such that the originator keeps the interest earned on the cash and issuer keeps the return earned on the repo securities.

If, in between payments, either party has a mark-to-market exposure to the other above a certain level, then there may also be a requirement for it to pay margin cover to the other party equal to that exposure.

The terms of the repo also require the originator to repurchase the securities at a specified repurchase price. This ensures that the issuer is not at risk for any decrease in value of the repo securities. Accordingly, where collateral needs to be liquidated to fund amounts payable by the issuer under the swap or to the noteholders, the bank will buy back the necessary quantity of securities to generate the required cash in the hands of the issuer. The cash is then applied by the note trustee to make those payments, and the principal amount of the notes is written down proportionately. Such repurchases may occur throughout the life of the notes, with the final out-standing balance being repurchased on final redemption of the notes.

The repo includes events of default upon which the date for repurchase of the repo securities will be deemed to occur immediately, the sums payable by each party to the other will be netted, and the net balance paid between the parties. An event of default under the repo should be included as a termination event under the CDS and an early redemption event in the terms of issue of the notes.

The final repo repurchase may also be accelerated (without a default being involved) in other circumstances—notably where payments can no longer be made gross but are required to be made net, to match up with early termination events under the CDS or the notes and on a downgrade of the repo counterparty.

As with the overlying CDS, the procedure on default or early termination of the repo will often be based on the assumption that it is the issuer which will default, rather than the originator. If the originator does default, however, the terms of the repo should allow the note trustee to liquidate the repo securities and apply the proceeds in accordance with the priorities governing the collateral.

OTHER PARTIES IN A SYNTHETIC CMBS

As can be seen above, in addition to the issuer and the originator there are a number of other parties to a synthetic CMBS. These include:

Verification agent: The verification agent will often be an internationally recognised accounting firm. As described above, they will be required to verify certain matters under the CDS before payment of any loss amount is made by the issuer. The verification agent has a distinct role to the valuers appointed in the case of any estimated losses who must be qualified valuers to estimate the extent of potential recoveries on enforcement of the mortgage over the property.

Custodian: The custodian is the party who holds the repo securities. Generally this will need to be a party independent from the originator to ensure that on an originator downgrade the repo securities are not at risk. The custodian is also required to maintain a minimum rating.

Repo counterparty: The repo counterparty at the outset is generally the originator. However the repo counterparty will be required to maintain a certain rating to ensure it can meet its obligations to repurchase the repo securities.

Servicer: Often the originator will retain the role of servicer. The originator as servicer will be required to meet the same servicing standard as would apply in a true-sale CMBS.

Others: As with a true-sale CMBS other parties such as the account bank, the note trustee, the cash manager, the corporate manager of the issuer and various paying agents are usually part of the transaction. Their role will not differ in any material respect between a true-sale and a synthetic CMBS transaction.

CONCLUSION

The nature of the CMBS-based credit default swap owes a good deal to the way it has evolved historically, with the original US-focused product now being adapted for use in European CMBS. The biggest source of synthetic investment still appears to be the US mortgage market, although the entry of European originators into the arena, as an alternative to the true sale CMBS, promises some interesting developments.

CHAPTER EIGHT

THE EMERGENCE OF SUBORDINATED DEBT STRUCTURES IN EUROPEAN CMBS

Andrew V. Petersen, Senior Associate
Dechert LLP

INTRODUCTION TO EUROPEAN SUBORDINATE DEBT STRUCTURES

We saw in Ch. 5, when considering the lifespan and workings of the whole CMBS loan origination process, that a successful CMBS loan should be sufficiently balanced so as to provide a competitive return and sufficient flexibility to the mortgage borrower, whilst providing safety of investment to bond investors. This results in a constant balancing exercise to address differing interests. Furthermore, as we also saw at the beginning of this book, it is the technological innovations which help drive CMBS as a product to address this balancing exercise and to adapt to the market conditions in which CMBS operates. The technological drive and desire to embrace the latest innovations has led to CMBS currently representing the largest growing asset class within European asset backed securities. Within the asset which is CMBS, as a result of an increasingly competitive commercial real estate lending environment and margin compression, European lenders have been forced to be more innovative in structuring CMBS transactions to help achieve the balancing exercise between origination volume and their return on their product, without compromising their securitisation execution, alongside mortgage borrowers' demands for even more flexibility and leverage.

One such method adopted to achieve this balance or alignment of rights is through bifurcating the financing which underlines CMBS transactions. This is nothing new. Commercial mortgage loans with related birfucated subordinate debt have been a long term feature of "traditional" (i.e. non-securitised or non-capital markets) global commercial real estate finance transactions. However, 2003 witnessed one of the first European CMBS transactions to use an AB loan structure, splitting the participation in the underlying loan, with only the senior tranche being securitised. This type of structure is useful in enhancing the securitisable value of a highly leveraged loan and was significant as it was arguably the first to utilise what has become known as the "class-X note" structure. By purchasing the total-return class-X note, the originator is able to efficiently extract the residual profit from the structure as an interest payment to divest itself of its retained profit interest should it so desire. Moreover, in recent years, CMBS has witnessed a proliferation of highly complex subordinate debt structures incorporating a concept of birfurcated or trifurcated real estate loans, comprising of A-1 or A-2, B, C or even D tranches, senior-subordinate tranches and mezzanine or junior debt,[1] and as will be seen, throughout the global CMBS markets, such as the United States and Europe, the practice of introducing subordinate debt into CMBS transactions generates highly flexible structures that allow the subordinate debt to be tailored to comply exactly with the legal and ratings requirements applicable to CMBS. As a result, it has become a rare exception for CMBS transactions not to be structured with some form of multiple separate subordinate debt tranches. Such structures apply to both single and multi-borrower transactions.

In this chapter, the debt underlying such structures will be referred to as "subordinate Debt", whilst the senior-subordinate structures themselves will be referred to as "AB Structures". Equally the phrase "B Lenders" will be used to signify the junior subordinate lenders below the senior A Lenders, and such a phrase can equally apply to the C or even D Lenders (such structures are constantly evolving as the capital structures and investors require further subordination). This chapter will examine:

- the emergence of AB Structures (defined below) and their development within the European CMBS market;

- the reasons behind the introduction of AB Structures;

- the common key features of AB Structures, including the continuing attempts, by those structuring deals, of walking the tightrope of existing tensions between competing rights, based on a senior-subordinate split of economic interests;

- the impact of subordinate debt on the capital structure; and

- the controlling rights when buying into an AB Structure.

---

[1] For an extremely comprehensive article on the US approach to structural issues surrounding subordinate debt structures, see "Slicing and Dicing: A Primer on Selected Legal and Structuring Issues" by David W. Forti, Dechert LLP and William C. Stefko, formerly Dechert LLP in *CMBS World*, Vol. 7, No. 1, Spring 2005, p.17.

AN OVERVIEW OF SENIOR-SUBORDINATE DEBT STRUCTURES

In a senior-subordinate debt structure, the ownership of a single whole mortgage loan, is tranched or split into one or more senior tranches (usually named the "A Loan"), and one or more subordinate tranches (usually named the "B Loan"), essentially in an variation exercise based on a standard participation loan. Each of the A and B Loans is secured by the same mortgage on the property or properties which secure the whole mortgage loan.

As stated, there can also be one or more tranches to both the A Loan and the B Loan: *pari passu* senior, super senior or multiple subordinate tranches can be structured, with each tranche secured by the same security. The senior A Loan with its lower leverage and lower-risk is typically part of the securitisation trust and tranched into rated classes of notes from AAA down to the BBB or BBB- rating level, whilst the subordinate B Loan, higher-leverage, higher-risk, sub investment grade tranche, is generally unrated and may be held outside the securitisation trust by the originator or sold on in an active B Loan market to third party high yield investors outside the securitisation structure, a market that will be examined in greater detail, below. The division of the financing allows a lender to be competitive in terms of loan proceeds without compromising any securitisation it may be planning on execution.

In an AB Structure, the legal relationship between the A and B Lenders is delineated in an intercreditor agreement, which both grants and limits certain important rights (which may have an impact on the A Lenders), to the B Lender. In such structures, the A Loan, being the senior and the B Loan, being the junior, results in the intercreditor agreement setting out in detail the key structural features, as well as specifying how principal and interest from the mortgage loan will be distributed between the A and B Loans before and after a loan event of default. The main distinction between the standard syndicated loan and the AB Structure is in payment priority and loss allocation. Unlike the standard syndicated loan where the payments to the senior-mortgage lender and the syndicatees are *pari passu*, the AB Structure is a classic senior-subordinated structure whereby the B Loan provides credit support for the A Loan. Upon the occurrence of an event of default, all payments are made sequentially, first, to the A Loan holders and, secondly, to the B Loan holders. Furthermore, any losses incurred with respect to the underlying borrower are allocated from the first loss position starting with the B Loan. The intercreditor agreement also defines the rights of the B Lender with on the enforcement and servicing of the loan following a loan event of default. These key structural features will be examined in greater detail, below. A typical simple AB Structure would be as follows in Figure 1, below.

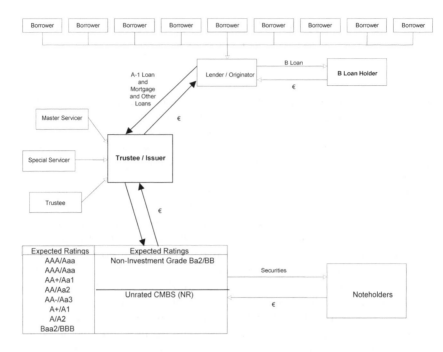

Figure 1: Overview of a securitisation with a B Loan.

As stated, there can be more than two tranches in an AB Structure, including multiple subordinate tranches. A further development in Subordinate Debt structures may be seen in Figure 2, below.

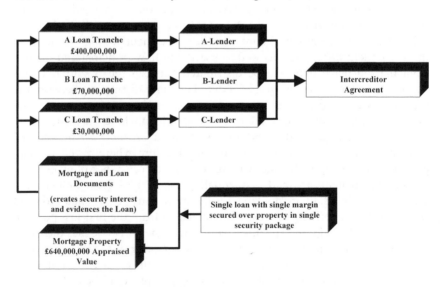

Figure 2: Senior-subordinate (ABC) debt structure.

In the example illustrated in Figure 2, above, a £500 million commercial whole mortgage loan has been originated by a lender under the A Loan (the "A Lender"). The whole loan has then been tranched or trifurcated into: (i) a £400 million A Loan; (ii) a £70 million B Loan, which is subordinate to the A Loan; and (iii) a £30 million C Loan, which is subordinate to both the A Loan and B Loan. The A Lender sells the B Loan and the C Loan to investors, and retains the A Loan for the securitisation. The A Loan, B Loan and C Loan are subject to the terms of an intercreditor agreement between the A Lender, the lender under the B Loan (the "B Lender"), and the lender under the C Loan (the "C Lender"), which regulates the relationship between the originator (and following the transfer of the A Loan into a securitisation, an issuer) and the B and C Lenders. The originator will assign its interest in the intercreditor agreement to an issuer under a loan sale agreement.

Subordinate Debt structures may also consist of senior and mezzanine loans. A mezzanine loan is a separate subordinate loan (behind a first priority mortgage loan), with separate loan agreements, secured by second priority charges on the same security as the senior mortgage loan. This is generally referred to as "mezzanine debt" or "European mezzanine debt".

More recently, European AB Structures have witnessed developments in Subordinate Debt structures, that of the subordinate debt loan and note structure, as may be seen in Figures 3 and 4, below.

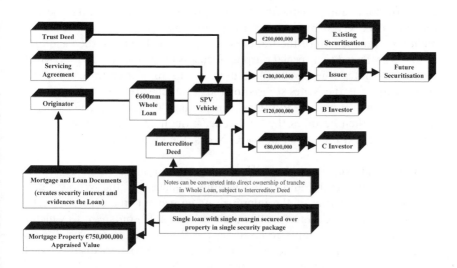

Figure 3: Subordinate debt loan and note structure.

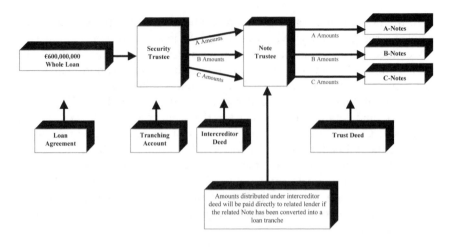

Figure 4: Redistribution of cash flow under subordinate debt loan and note structure.

In Figure 3, above, the €600 million whole commercial mortgage loan (the "Whole Loan") is originated and then trifurcated into three separate tranches. The first tranche, the €400 million A Tranche, is itself sub-divided into two sub-tranches (A-1 and A-2) with rights between the tranche holders related thereto being as agreed between the holders, but subject to the terms of the intercreditor agreement. Payments on those notes are made pro-rata to the A-1 and A-2 note holders. Losses are borne pro rata by the A-1 and A-2 note holders. This structuring allows for further slicing in that, as can be seen from the diagram, the *pari passu* senior tranches can then be sold into and be the subject of differing securitisations, resulting in greater diversification of pools and a reduction of "lumpiness" within pools. The second tranche is the €120 million B tranche and the third tranche is the €80 million C tranche. All of the tranches of the Whole Loan are then acquired by and transferred to a special purpose securitisation vehicle ("SPV"), which then issues notes (the "Notes") secured by the respective tranches of the Whole Loan, i.e. the Notes secured by the A tranche are the "A Notes", the B tranche, the "B Notes" and the C tranche the "C Notes"). The holder of the A Notes then becomes the "A Lender"; the holder of the B Notes, the "B Lender"; and the holder of the C Notes, the "C Lender".

Figure 4, above, shows the SPV entering into an intercreditor agreement to regulate the rights among the various tranches of the Whole Loan. Pursuant to the terms of the intercreditor agreement, the security trustee agrees to open an account (the "Tranching Account") pursuant to which it agrees to hold all amounts received on the Whole Loan, on trust for the holders of the tranches (the A, B and C Lenders) and to disburse such amounts pursuant to the terms of the intercreditor agreement. Pursuant to the terms of the intercreditor agreement, the rights of the B tranche and C tranche shall at all times be subject and subordinate to the rights of the A tranche.

WHY INTRODUCE AB STRUCTURES?

Given the additional complexity caused by the introduction of Subordinate Debt structures, it is appropriate to examine why they are incorporated into CMBS transactions.

Increased leverage?

A factor in introducing Subordinate Debt structures is to accommodate the mortgage borrower's desire to constantly maximise leverage. Traditionally, investors in CMBS are comprised of groups of investors with a range of widely-varying risk tolerances. As such, lenders originating commercial mortgage loans were faced with having to devise a means of packaging the added leverage related to loans destined for CMBS in a way that would appeal to investors across this risk-tolerance spectrum.

In the United States, where Subordinate Debt structures first emerged, originating lenders soon discovered that dividing or splitting a whole loan into multiple tranches enabled them to create a variety of debt instruments which would appeal to a broad array of investors, while meeting the demands of their mortgage borrowers for greater leverage and flexibility. For example, on a highly-leveraged property, the related financing might be structured so as to produce only an investment grade portion of the debt that can be included in a CMBS transaction with the remaining portion of the financing split into one or more subordinated tranches, often tailored to meet the requirements of the anticipated purchaser (for example, a certain investor's risk and return preference might cause such an investor to prefer a slice of the debt that represents 65 to 75 per cent of the overall leverage of the financing; other investors with more aggressive risk and return tolerances may prefer more deeply subordinated, higher risk, higher-yielding tranches of the financing).

Diversification

Even where mortgage borrowers' desire to maximise gearing is not a driving factor, investors' dislike of concentration risk, and the desire for more diversified portfolios of loans to be included in CMBS transactions has led to a decline in the number of stand-alone securitisations. This in turn, has led to more debt being sliced, both horizontally and vertically. One result of this, as we shall see, is that the rights that B Lenders achieve in such structural features have become more contentious as such structures have led to an increased focus on the control/cure rights the junior lender has over the senior lenders prior to a control valuation event (discussed, below) increasing the existing tensions between competing rights, based on a senior-subordinate split of economic interests.

WHAT ARE THE COMMON FEATURES OF AN AB STRUCTURE?

B Lender rights

There are certain common features existing within AB Structures. One such feature of AB Structures versus whole loan standard securitisations is that, although B Lenders lack the right to enforce the mortgage loan security, they do, typically, benefit from certain rights following monetary events of default on mortgage loans, in a recognition that they are in the first loss position. Such rights are not usually available to junior first loss piece holders in standard securitisations, the "B Piece holders". The B Piece holders in a standard securitisation hold the most junior certificate interest in a pool of CMBS loans. They hold the "last pay" "first loss" certificates which do not represent individual loans and have no direct relationship with the mortgage borrower, and are often confused with the B Lenders or B Loan holders.

B Lenders are not obliged to exercise these rights, which vary from deal-to-deal and ultimately depend on the sophistication and the needs of the subordinate investors. B Lenders would generally only do so if expected recoveries from the mortgage loan would thereby be enhanced. The exercise of cure and repurchase rights (which usually include the B Lender's right to purchase the A Loan and to avoid enforcement proceedings by the A Lender following a mortgage loan payment default by making whole a mortgage loan payment) has implications for the A Loan and thereby the rated bonds and in such cases, the structure of the intercreditor agreement and servicing agreements are extremely important to AB Structures. As a result, the following two chapters will examine in greater detail the structural and legal issues surrounding the approach which has developed within Europe in respect of the intercreditor agreement and servicing agreements. However, it is necessary here to consider briefly the origins of such issues, by focusing on the position that B Lenders adopt when purchasing subordinate debt and the positions from where such rights have emerged. These will be examined in more detail below in the section on "Controlling an AB Structure", below.

Getting paid—waterfalls

In a CMBS transaction, an intercreditor agreement, in acknowledging the economic terms of the A and B Loans, sets out the payment priorities (both before and after a loan event of default) of interest and principal payments and the distributions between the lenders. In a standard CMBS structure, principal and interest are repaid on either a sequential or modified pro rata basis, starting with the most senior class of bonds. Losses are allocated initially to the first loss piece (B Pieces) held by the B Piece holders and, once extinguished, in reverse sequential order, starting with the most junior class of rated notes.

Pre-event of default waterfall

The key feature to an AB Structure is the fact that payments to the B Loan holders are junior to payments to the A Loan holders, with the B Loan providing credit support for the A Loan. Reimbursements for additional trust fund expenses are made prior to payments on the A Loan or the B Loan—as a result, shortfalls resulting from such payments affect the B Loan first and the A Loan second. Furthermore, any losses incurred with respect to the mortgage loan must be allocated first to the B Loan up to the outstanding principal balance, and then to the A Loan. As regards repayment of the A and B Loans, as long as no event of default exists with respect to a mortgage loan, payments on such mortgage loan, may be applied pursuant to a waterfall which may be found in the deed of charge created by the issuer as security for payment under the Notes. This usually provides that (following lender expenses such as reimbursements of advances, costs and expenses associated with hedging arrangements and servicing fees) payment is made:

- first, to interest on the A Loan;

- second, to interest on the B Loan;

- third, pro rata to scheduled principal on the A Loan and the B Loan; and

- fourth, to prepayment premiums, late charges, default interest, as negotiated.

Whilst any losses incurred with respect to the mortgage borrower are allocated from the first loss piece starting with the B Loan, this has the result that the interests of both the A and B Lenders are aligned as regards preserving the value of the underlying real estate. However, this creates tensions within the AB Structure. The B Lender has purchased the B Loan for the higher yield (which is higher than the yield on the A Loan in light of the B

Loan's subordination and higher risk), and is ultimately holding the B Loan as a long-term investment. With the B Loan serving as "credit support", the A Lender can rely on the subordination cushion of the B Loan (the B Lender will (as set out below) suffer losses first until wiped out) and may be more willing to take aggressive action against the mortgage borrower, whilst the B Lender, given one of its investment strategies is to hold to maturity, may prefer more conciliatory, restructuring solutions to credit stresses. These are all complex issues which must be addressed in the intercreditor agreement.

Post-event of default waterfall

It is following a material loan event of default, however, that AB Structures and standard CMBS transactions differ in the allocation of principal and interest between the A and B Lenders. Upon the occurrence of a material event of default, all payments shall be applied sequentially (following lender expenses such as reimbursements of advances, costs and expenses associated with hedging arrangements and servicing fees) in the following waterfall:

- first, to interest on the A Loan, and principal on the A Loan until paid in full, including the reimbursement of actual costs;

- second, to interest on the B Loan, and principal on the B Loan until paid in full, including the reimbursement of actual costs; and

- third, prepayment premiums, late charges, default interest, as negotiated.

As can be seen, only after the entire outstanding principal amount of the A Loan has been paid off in full are payments permitted to be applied to the B Loan. This has the effect that all payments of principal and interest to the B Lenders are effectively cut off following a material loan event of default (a "Trigger Event"). The occurrence of a Trigger Event effectively determines when the rights of the B Lender to receive payments of interest and principal become subordinate to the rights of the A Lender, thereby providing for accelerated repayment of the A Lenders, as all such receipts will be (post a material loan event of default) directed to the A Lenders. Having said this, on a negotiated basis, certain deals provide for an escrow account into which cash which is to be used to amortise the A Loan or the element that would have been used to amortise the B Loan is placed. This allows the prospect of cash being released to the B Lenders from escrow if the A Loan is no longer suffering losses.

Trigger event for a loan event of default

What amounts to a Trigger Event will change from deal to deal, but will often include:

(1) a monetary default by the obligor under the loan;

(2) insolvency events relating to any obligor under the loan; and

(3) any default that results in a transfer of the loan to special servicing.

It can also include other events such as a breach of a financial covenant or other material events. Such non-monetary events of default triggers are heavily negotiated between the A and B Lenders. Furthermore, a Trigger Event may be postponed until the subordinate creditor cure periods have expired and will be averted by a cure. This is important as the B Lender avoids being faced with a change to a sequential waterfall when it is trying to cure the underlying mortgage loan event of default. However, if there is some form of restructuring or workout in the event of a default under the whole loan, all payments to the A Lender are made as though no restructuring or workout occurred. If the principal balance, interest rate or scheduled payments on the loan are reduced, or any other material modifications are made to the mortgage loan, the full economic effect of the modifications are borne by the B Lender (up to its then-remaining principal balance). Only after the B Loan has suffered its full loss allocation is the A Loan affected by any restructuring or workout.

Accelerated repayment of the A Lenders is an important factor in AB Structures as it results in the subordination of payments to the B Lender before a shortfall in payments to the A Lender—and therefore to the rated bonds—has occurred. This acts as superior credit support for the rated bonds, as funds are available to the senior classes that would, in a standard CMBS transaction, be allocated to the junior classes. As such, it is important to consider the impact on the capital structure (set out below) following the introduction of Subordinate Debt.

Curing defaults

The B Lender will typically have the right (but not the obligation) to advance the amounts necessary to cure a monetary event of default on the mortgage loan within a defined number of days following the default and to cure certain defaults under the underlying credit agreement.

It should be remembered that the B Lender will want the right to cure the mortgage borrower's defaults so that it continues to receive its payments pursuant to the pre-event of default waterfall and this prevents enforcement and transfer to a special servicer. Furthermore, if the mortgage borrower defaults and the B Lender does not cure the default, the B Lender will not be paid until the A Lender has been paid in full (pursuant to the post-event of default waterfall).

Cure payments may only be reimbursed after all amounts due on the senior debt have been paid. To allow the B Lender time to cure such defaults, the grace period permitted for curing such a default is typically three to five business days after the B Lender has received notice of such default. In relation to a default other than a payment default, the grace period generally mirrors mortgage borrower cure periods of typically 15 to 30 business days after the B Lender receives notice that a default has occurred in connection with the underlying credit agreement (or, if earlier, 10 to 20 business days after the date upon which the B Lender has served a remedy notice on the facility agent in respect of such default). During this period, the issuer and the servicer are prohibited from accelerating the mortgage loan, enforcing any security for the mortgage loan, taking any steps towards placing a mortgage borrower in insolvency proceedings, bringing any legal proceedings, or transferring to a special servicer.

Although it varies from deal-to-deal and will always be the subject of negotiation, the B Lender will usually be permitted to cure two or three consecutive payment defaults or financing covenant defaults in any one 12-month period, and six to eight cures over the life of the mortgage whole loan. This is because the effect of cure rights on the A Loan and, thereby the rated bonds, is to delay proceedings for enforcement or recoveries, which could result in lower overall recoveries on the mortgage loan in an environment where the value of the properties may be declining or deteriorating.

Buying out the senior loan

Following the occurrence of certain mortgage loan events of default,[2] the B Lender may purchase or arrange for a third party to purchase the mortgage loan at par. This typically means (although this is negotiated on a deal-by-deal basis) that a consideration equal to such amount as the special servicer (acting as agent of the facility agent) determines to be outstanding on the mortgage loan in full together with amounts required to compensate the issuer for any breakage or funding costs incurred by it as a result of the transfer (the "Defaulted Mortgage Loan Purchase Price"). If the purchase date specified in the purchase notice is not a due date, this will include the

---

[2] Usually the same mortgage loan defaults that trigger a change in the payment waterfall from the "Pre-Event of Default Waterfall" to the "Post-Event of Default Waterfall," such as any monetary default under the mortgage loan documents together with certain non-monetary events of default (as negotiated between the A Lender and the B Lender).

full amount of the interest that is payable on the immediately succeeding due date (but excluding any fees payable in connection with a prepayment of the mortgage loan or any default interest to the extent that such default interest has not been recovered from the obligors).

Again, the B Lender will want the right to purchase the A Loan, as after the occurrence of a trigger event (discussed, above), the B Lender will not be paid until the A Lender has been paid in full. Moreover, if a "control valuation event" (discussed, below) has also occurred (or may imminently occur), the B Lender may also lose its consent and consultation rights: thereafter, control shifts to the A Lender. In general, the most subordinate tranche holder would be granted priority rights in exercising such a purchase option, and would be required to purchase each tranche which is senior to it at the Defaulted Mortgage Loan Purchase Price.

If the B Lender does not take advantage of this right and buy out the A Lender, then the special servicer must enforce or work out the mortgage loan in the best interests of the whole loan. This provides an incentive to the B Lender to exercise its purchase right and may be viewed as a positive feature of AB Structures, especially in the case of experienced sophisticated B Lenders.

Following an event of default on the mortgage loan that cannot be cured by monetary payments, the rights of the B Loan are subordinated to the rights of the A Loan. One example of this type of loan default would be the mortgage borrower's insolvency.

Choosing the servicer

In an AB Structure, certain rights and conditions in respect of the servicing of the whole loan (the A Loans and the B Loans) are provided for and are incorporated into the servicing agreement. Once sold into the securitisation, the servicing and administration of the whole loan will, in many cases, be performed by the servicers retained by the holder of the senior tranche. The bundle of rights which are important to a lender who wants to control the relationship with the mortgage borrower, usually carried out by the A Lender (or the servicer on behalf of the A Lender and the B Lender) includes (among other things):

- collection of all payments;
- the processing of the mortgage borrower requests under the loan documents;
- modification or waiving provisions of the loan documents;

- calling or waiving of mortgage loan defaults;

- accelerating the mortgage loan;

- taking legal action to enforce the A and B Lenders' interests;

- selling the loan at a discount;

- the day-to-day administration of the whole loan;

- transacting with the mortgage borrower under the whole loan, and

- acting for and on behalf of the A Lenders and the B Lenders in the event of any insolvency proceedings involving the related mortgage borrower, subject, in many cases to the consent and consultation rights granted to the B Lenders.

With the related Subordinate Debt of the whole loan typically not included in the CMBS into which the senior tranche is sold, the subordinate tranches will continue to be held outside of the CMBS trust. Nonetheless, there is a tendency in Europe for servicers (preferably a rated servicer, approved by the rating agencies) to service the whole loan (including the subordinate tranches) for the benefit of the holders of both the A Loan and the B Loan, as a collective whole, acting to maximise proceeds for both and taking into account that the B Loan is subordinate. The servicer is, in accordance with the requirements of the CMBS transaction, governed by the servicing standard. In Europe, the servicing standard at present is a more generally worded standard setting out the concept of the servicer acting as a minimum "as a prudent lender", although there are signs that this is changing to be more in line with the standard laid down in the United States, where the servicing definition is much more detailed. Notwithstanding this difference, the servicing standard is a significant protection that investors, lenders and rating agencies in a CMBS transaction rely upon. This topic will be dealt with in much more detail in Ch. 10.

Counterbalancing the rights of the A Lender to appoint the master servicer for the whole loan, most AB Structures provide that the B Lender will have certain consent and consultation rights over servicing of the whole loan, including appointing or terminating a special servicer. The B Lender may also appoint a new special servicer for the whole loan, who would, subject to the servicing standard and agreed exceptions, be entitled to make all decisions regarding the senior and subordinate debt and direct any enforcement strategy. The rating agencies prefer to see that this right falls away upon a control valuation event (discussed, below). Indeed the point has been made many times that where B Loan holders retain embedded rights as their economic interest erodes, this is probably inappropriate and will result in an adjustment to rated proceeds. It is important to note that the subordinate tranche holder's right to replace the special servicer extends only to the particular whole loan in which it holds a subordinate tranche, and does not permit the subordinate tranche holder to terminate the special servicer for other commercial mortgage loans included in the CMBS transaction containing the senior tranche in the whole loan.

In addition (and while generally the subject of negotiation between the senior tranche holder and the subordinate tranche holder), major servicing decisions and certain other actions proposed to be taken with respect to the whole loan (e.g. changes in the monetary terms of the whole loan, actions to bring the mortgage property in compliance with environmental laws, sales of the whole loan when it is a defaulted mortgage loan, and certain other fundamental items) are generally subject to the consent and/or consultation rights of the holders of the most subordinate tranche. As a check on the ability of the subordinate tranche holders to thwart actions which may benefit the holders of each tranche as a whole (but which might not result in the most favourable outcome for the subordinate tranche holder) the rating agencies prefer that the consent rights of the subordinate holder be over-ridden by the servicer, if the servicer determines that the course of action proposed by the B Loan holders would otherwise violate the servicing standards set forth in the related CMBS servicing agreement. This is the so-called "Servicing Standard Override", so-called as the servicer may always override any proposed course of action.

IMPACT OF SUBORDINATE DEBT ON CAPITAL STRUCTURE

Figure 5, below, illustrates the differences in credit support between a securitisation without a B Loan and one with a B Loan.

In the AB Structure, as can be seen above, the B Loan is an alternative to what would otherwise be the B-piece of a rated transaction if the whole loan were deposited into the securitisation trust. This raises the question of which is more preferable: an AB Structure or a traditional standard securitisation structure.

THE ATTRACTION OF AB STRUCTURES

From the perspective of the most junior investor in the securitisation trust, as payments to the B Loan can be subordinated to the A Loan in an AB Structure, loan level defaults and shortfalls in mortgage loan payments, are preferable to standard securitisations without a B Loan. This is because, depending on the transaction structure, as we have seen above, payments to

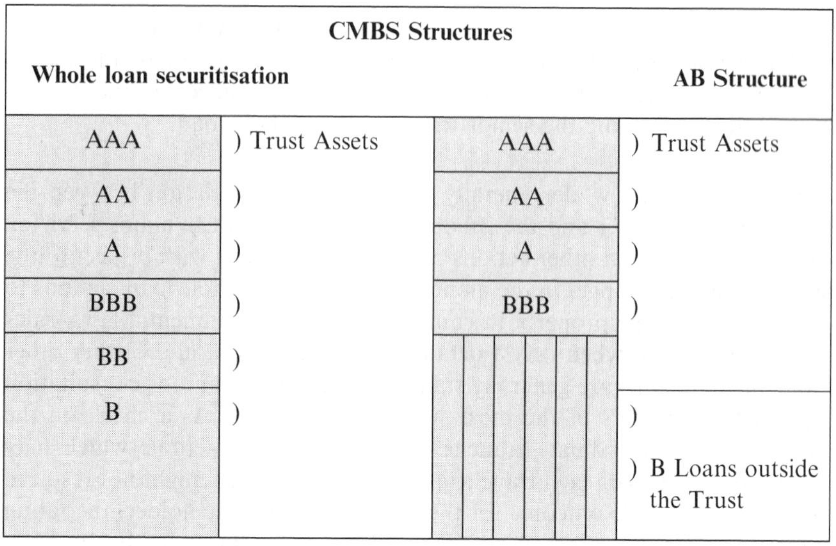

CMBS Structures			
Whole loan securitisation			**AB Structure**
AAA	) Trust Assets	AAA	) Trust Assets
AA	)	AA	)
A	)	A	)
BBB	)	BBB	)
BB	)		
B	)		)
			) B Loans outside the Trust

Figure 5: Differences in credit support.

the B Lender may be cut off entirely following a mortgage loan monetary event of default until the A Loan has been redeemed in full. In a standard securitisation, by contrast, this will not tend to occur until the most senior class has missed a payment.[3] Thus, by creating a B Loan that is held outside the securitisation trust, loss severity can be viewed as having been reduced as, following a loan monetary event of default, the A Lender benefits from the subordination of payments to the B Loan by having the ability to take control over the whole loan and instigate enforcement proceedings before a shortfall has occurred on the A Loan, and therefore the rated bonds. This allocates the risks associated with incorporating the additional debt efficiently throughout the market and is preferable to a standard securitisation, in which senior noteholders gain control only after realised losses have eroded the value of the junior notes. Furthermore, this results in an improvement of the subordination levels of the rated securities versus the subordination levels if the entire loan were included in the trust. Moreover, for multi-borrower transactions, which may pool together various B Loans, the additional credit support provided by the subordinated B Loans is specific to the separate individual mortgage loans and is therefore not provided to the entire transaction, usually resulting in higher credit enhancement being expected for the lowest-rated level of securitised notes. If losses incurred on any one loan exceed the amount of the B Loan, then the

---

[3] See Fitch Ratings Commercial Mortgage/Europe Special Report *"Getting from A to B—An overview of A/B Note Structures"*, June 8, 2004.

excess will be allocated to the lowest-rated class of notes. Where B Loans provide the only credit support to an A Loan in a multi-borrower transaction, there is no pooling benefit for the lowest-rated class of the A Loan.

It is important to note, however, that although a higher percentage of the rated securities are considered investment grade in a pool that is made up of A Loans, the investment-grade debt as a percentage of the first-mortgage debt (the first-mortgage debt equalling the combined total of all A and B Loans) is not higher. In fact, in most cases the investment-grade debt as a percentage of the first-mortgage debt would be lower than if the entire loan were deposited into the securitisation trust. This is due to the weaker form of credit support provided by the B Loans that are not cross-collateralised, compared to subordinate bonds, which are cross-collateralised. For instance, in a pool made up of A Loans, if a loan incurs losses, upon the erosion of the B Loans, losses would continue upward into the rated securities and not to the other B Loans held outside of the securitisation trust.

From a prospective purchaser's perspective there are several benefits to an AB Structure. First, the B Loan is secured by a preferred form of security, a first mortgage. Also, for many of the institutional B Loan purchasers such as insurance companies and banks, risk-based capital reserve requirements are less onerous for B Loans than that of subordinate bonds. Having to reserve less capital against B Loans effectively increases their overall net yield. When contrasted with investing in subordinate bonds, the primary benefit of the B Loan is the ability to isolate risk to one asset. Unlike a subordinate bond where losses can be incurred from any one asset in a pool, the loss potential of a B Loan is limited to the asset(s) serving as security to the B Loan. This makes it easier than in a whole loan securitisation, where the originator, when placing a pooled bottom class of risk, has to try and sell this risk to an investor willing to take the first loss risk on all of the loans in the pool. As a result, risk is effectively dealt with much more discretely and the risk assessment of potential Subordinate Debt investors is also much more efficient since the due diligence process of evaluating one asset (the B Loan) is considerably easier than evaluation of a pool of subordinate bonds. This is especially so in the European market where there is multitude of loans and variety of asset classes within pools. Another benefit, as we have seen above, is the ability to either purchase or cure upon an event of default. While this feature may not always be a viable option, it may be a potential exit strategy.

In AB Structures, liquidity facility advances following a loan event of default are only available to A Loans. This is beneficial to the rated bonds, as repayments of liquidity facility advances rank senior to payments to the notes. In a standard securitisation, by contrast, liquidity advances to the junior classes reduce the funds available to the senior classes of rated bonds.

One disadvantage of the B Loan is its lack of tradability. Currently, as discussed in Ch. 15, there is little or no secondary market in CMBS due to the limited and imperfect nature of investor reporting. Chapters 13 and 14 may have solutions to this problem. However, if the demand for B Loans continues, a broadened market should result in more liquidity for this product.

CONTROLLING AN AB STRUCTURE

It is the more mature US CMBS market where, in recognition of the extremely important function that subordinate debt purchasers undertake, B Lenders have achieved considerable rights. Such rights afford them protection but also afford protection against a tyranny of the minority due to the fact that whatever rights the B Lender has achieved may be eliminated on the occurrence of a "control valuation event". This means that the subordinate lenders may only exercise such consent rights and may only appoint a special servicer over the whole mortgage loan when prior to a control valuation event. AB Structures also generally provide that the servicer is not required to follow the direction of a subordinate creditor with respect to such approval rights if such direction would violate the servicing standard.

A control valuation event occurs when the value of the underlying properties has depreciated to such a level that there is not sufficient value to cover both the senior debt and a specified portion of the subordinate debt. While AB Structures may vary on the formulation of the control valuation event, most provide that a subordinate tranche holder is divested of its consent rights and the ability to appoint a special servicer where the initial principal balance of the most subordinate tranche less any principal payments received on that tranche, any valuation reductions and realised losses allocated to such tranche, is less than a certain percentage (typically, 25 per cent) of the initial principal balance of such tranche less principal payments received on such tranche. On and after the date that the control valuation event would apply to the most subordinate tranche holder, such as the B Lender, the B Lender is no longer considered the controlling class and the rights that are ascribed to the controlling class pass to the next most subordinate tranche holder higher up in the capital structure, which in the case of a securitised A Loan, would likely be the first pooled class.

As a result of the importance of losing the rights to control their destiny, there are several measures of protection that subordinate tranche holders typically attempt to negotiate into an AB Structure which are designed to forestall or mitigate the effects of the control valuation event being triggered. One such measure is the right of the subordinate tranche holder to deliver a "challenging" valuation to the servicer charged with computing the valuation reduction amounts under the CMBS servicing agreement—if the servicer determines in accordance with the servicing standard that the subordinate tranche holder's valuation is a more accurate barometer of mortgaged property value than valuations obtained by the servicer, the valuation reduction amount based on the challenging valuation may be reduced, and consequently, the applicability of the control valuation event averted. When dealing with an ABC structure, the most subordinate lender's valuation will often prevail. Another measure sometimes negotiated by the holders of the tranches in the AB Structure would permit the subordinate tranche holder to post highly-liquid collateral (for example, cash or a letter of credit from highly-rated providers) with the senior tranche holder, that when added to the outstanding principal balance of the subordinate tranche will meet or exceed the thresholds set out in the control valuation event.

In an AB Structure, typically a B Lender will agree that the servicer or the special servicer (in such case as agent for the facility agent and not as agent for the B Lender) may amend, waive a term of, or give consent under the underlying credit agreement or other finance document relevant to the underlying mortgage loan, if the amendment is a procedural, administrative or other change arising in the ordinary course and is not, in the sole opinion of the facility agent, usually acting reasonably, material.

The consent of the B Lender will be required for certain amendments or waivers, typically those that impact on the economic terms of the subordinate creditor's position (e.g. amending the amount or timing of payments by the mortgage borrower) and those that are material to the credit analysis (e.g. provisions dealing with ownership, disposals, additional borrowings, financial covenants) of the underlying credit agreement unless the amendment, waiver or consent is agreed by the originator and the B Lender, and always recognising that provisions enable the senior creditor or the servicer, as applicable, whilst a material default is outstanding, to grant such consents as are necessary for the day to day management of the properties (e.g. the grant or amendment of occupational leases). Examples of amendments or waivers which are material to the credit analysis are:

(1) (a) a change to the currency of any amount payable under the whole loan finance documents;

(b) any change to the basis upon which a payment is calculated in accordance with the original provisions of that whole loan finance document;

(c) a release of any security other than in accordance with the terms of the whole loan finance documents, or a change in such terms;

(d) a change to the clause of the underlying credit agreement that restricts the mortgage borrowers' ability to engage in any busi-

ness other than owning and managing their respective properties; or

(e) an amendment or waiver which relates to:

    (i) the definition of "majority lenders" in the underlying credit agreement;

    (ii) a reduction in the margin or a reduction in the amount of any payment of principal, interest, fee or other amount payable to a lender under the whole loan finance documents;

    (iii) an increase in, or an extension of, a commitment or the total commitments;

    (iv) a release of a mortgage loan obligor;

    (v) other than a release pursuant to the terms of the underlying credit agreement, a release of a security document;

    (vi) a term of a whole loan finance document which expressly requires the consent of each lender;

    (vii) the right of a lender to assign or transfer its rights or obligations under the whole loan finance documents;

    (viii) amending the underlying credit agreement;

    (ix) extending the term of the underlying credit agreement; or

    (x) the regulation of the mortgage borrowers' bank accounts under the underlying credit agreement, unless the amendment, waiver or consent is, in each case, agreed to by all the lenders; or

(2) (a) a change to the clauses of the underlying credit agreement dealing with prepayment, hedging, financial statements, financial covenants, the negative pledge, disposals, financial indebtedness, mergers, acquisitions, arm's-length contractual terms, insurances, environmental matters or events of default;

    (b) a change to the manner or basis on which rental income is collected and applied in accordance with the underlying credit agreement; or

    (c) any change to the right of the mortgage borrowers to assign or transfer their rights under the finance documents.

Standstill periods

In certain deals, the B Lender may also face a restriction on enforcement and not be allowed to call for an enforcement event. During this period, known as a standstill period, if there is a payment default on the B Loan— the B Lender will be restricted from carrying out any enforcement action. Depending on the default, the period usually lasts for anything up to 90 days for payment, 120 days for financial covenants, and 150 days for all other matters. Following the expiry of the standstill period, if there is the likelihood of recovering between 110 per cent and 125 per cent (one rating agency, Standard & Poors, has stated that 120 per cent market value test is typical) of the outstanding principal amount of the A Loan then the B Lender may call for enforcement. Difficulties arise on a jurisdiction by jurisdiction basis as it becomes difficult in certain European jurisdictions to calculate precisely, with any certainty, based on the unpredictability of the enforcement regime, 110 per cent of the outstanding principal amount of the A Loan.

EXITING A SUBORDINATE DEBT STRUCTURE

There is usually some restriction on the transfer of the subordinate debt in the underlying loan documents. The ability of a B Lender to exit a Subordinate Debt structure will typically by regulated by provisions in transactions that restrict the rights of B Lenders to sell their positions according to the financial strength of potential purchasers. All English law loan documents typically have the standard Loan Market Association (LMA) restrictions on transfer, which would limit holders to certain financial institutions, loosely classified as a "qualifying lender". There is also an increase throughout Europe of local jurisdiction transfer restrictions, such as the Dutch "professional market parties" (PMP) exemptions, which provides that the debt may only be transferred to entities which qualify as a PMP. PMPs are defined in the Exemption Regulation[4] and include (amongst others) to the extent relevant:

(1) parties regulated or authorised to operate in the financial markets,

(2) entities that according to their latest (consolidated) annual accounts comply with two of the following three criteria:

    (a) an average number of employees during that year of at least 250,
    (b) a total balance sheet exceeding €43 million, and
    (c) an annual net turnover exceeding €50 million,

(3) entities or persons registered as a professional party,

(4) entities whose sole corporate object is investing in securities, and

(5) entities incorporated solely for the purpose of acquiring assets which serve as security for securities offered or to be offered by them.

---

[4] The Exemption Regulation under the Dutch Act on the Supervision of Credit Institutions 1992 (as amended).

Further, any such transfer restrictions provisions typically provide that while holders of the senior tranche are generally free to transfer all or a portion of their interests in their senior tranche, the holders of a subordinate tranche in the whole loan may not transfer all or more than a certain specified percentage (usually greater than 49 per cent) of their respective interests in such tranche except to—

(1) certain classes of large financial institutions or their closely-held affiliates, known as "Qualified Transferees", on the basis that financially sound B Lenders may be considered advantageous for the rated notes. Examples of Qualified Transferees are:

- banks, insurance companies, pension funds, investment companies, etc. that have total assets in excess of amounts such as €600 million and capital surplus or shareholders' equity of €250 million, and which are regularly engaged in the business of making or owning commercial real estate loans or operating commercial mortgage properties;
- trustees in connection with a securitisation of the B Loan (for example, in CDO or commercial paper conduit transactions); or
- investment funds owned at least 50 per cent by an entity that is otherwise a Qualified Transferee.

It should be noted that this definition is negotiated on a case by case basis; or

(2) if the senior tranche of the whole loan has been included in a CMBS transaction, where the holder of the senior tranche receives written confirmation from each rating agency which rates any securities issued pursuant to the CMBS transaction, that such transfer will not result in the downgrade, qualification or withdrawal of the ratings assigned to such securities.

Tensions increase when the B Loan holder's interests are aligned with those of the mortgage borrower, which would occur when a mortgage borrower-affiliate owns the B Loan. Generally, B Lenders may not transfer all or any part of its interest in the B Loan to the mortgage borrower or its affiliate (although many European deals have not been alive to this), as conflicts may arise from the circular relationship when a mortgage borrower—or its affiliate—effectively acts as its own lender. A mortgage borrower-affiliate owning the B Loan may materially impede the senior lender's rights to recover on its collateral and increase the severity of loss, if the mortgage borrower-affiliate were able to appoint the special servicer and have "consultation rights" or veto rights that delay the inevitable, or be able to repeatedly cure its affiliate's defaults. This has led to a generally accepted position that the rights granted to third-party lenders may not be made available to the mortgage borrower's sponsor through the route of the mortgage borrower-affiliate.

Despite this, however, many AB Structures do provide that the holders of the related subordinate tranches may pledge their interests in the whole loan as collateral (e.g. in connection with a warehouse financing of such interest), provided certain conditions are satisfied.

WHO BUYS SUBORDINATE DEBT?

Subordinate debt structures are also on the increase as a result of the marked increase in the number of players in the real estate capital markets that desire to purchase higher-yielding, subordinate debt. As subordinate debt instruments have become more commonplace, a number of financing and warehousing sources have developed. In Europe many large lenders and CMBS conduit shops operate their own B Loan operations desk, tasked with selling the subordinate tranches of deals they have originated or seeking arrange or purchase subordinate tranches, either from their own deals or other people's deals in the secondary market. Overseas investor numbers are also increasing as can be seen from the data set out in Ch. 12.

Further, we will see in Ch. 11 that a rapidly-evolving financing and exit strategy for the holders of subordinate debt is the collateralised debt obligation ("CDO") market. Generally speaking, a CDO transaction involves an off-shore or domestic special purpose entity issuing notes to investors which are collateralised by certain assets. CDO transactions vary greatly depending on the asset-types to be included into the CDO, the motivation for the CDO transaction (e.g. arbitrage or balance sheet CDOs), and whether the CDO investors are looking through to the market value of the asset (a "market-value" CDO) or the future income stream to be generated by the assets (a "cash-flow" CDO). This topic is dealt with in much more detail in Ch. 11, but in summary, commercial real estate CDOs ("CRE CDOs") typically involve either a static pool of assets (with some period for a "ramp-up" of assets to be included in the CDO vehicle), or, a pool of actively-managed assets (where trading of assets in and out of the pool over all or a portion of the term of the CDO may occur under certain circumstances). At the time of writing, there has not been a CRE CDO carried out in Europe, although the first is predicted by market professionals to be carried out towards the end of 2006. However, assets that have been included in US CRE CDOs include (among other things) CMBS securities, REIT debt securities, other CDO securities and, more recently, whole commercial mortgage loans, B Loans, subordinate participation interests and mezzanine loans. Using CDOs, subordinate debt investors can move their debt instruments off balance sheet, or take arbitrage profit from favourable interest rate movements. Indeed, in the US, in the last few years, the appetite for CDOs which are backed in whole, or in part, by whole commercial mortgage loans, subordinated notes, subordinated participation interests and mezzanine financing has been robust. This growth seems to have, in turn, fuelled the desire for the participants in the subordinated debt markets to acquire appropriate and sufficient collateral for inclusion into these vehicles, which has spurred increased competition for these subordinate debt pieces.

CONCLUSIONS

This chapter has highlighted the purposes, general key features, risks, and benefits provided by typical AB Structures. Many regard the introduction of AB Structures in the European CMBS market as a positive development, since certain features of the structures provide additional benefits that are unavailable to lenders in standard securitisations. However, these benefits may not necessarily translate into improved credit enhancement levels for loans structured as AB Loans. That being said, it is generally recognised that the structural features of an AB Structure ensure that a default of the whole mortgage loan do not necessarily result in a shortfall of funds to, and therefore a default of, the A Loan. In particular, it may be seen that the cure rights of the B Lender, the priority of all payments to the A Loan and the enforcement rights of the A Lender reduce the probability of default of the Whole Loan, leading to the conclusion that AB Structures can provide benefits to rated classes of bonds in single-loan transactions.

In conclusion, it is apparent that whole loan slicing and dicing ultimately creates a variety of interested parties (whose interests are often at odds), having a variety of consent and approval rights over both "routine" mortgage borrower actions such as alterations and lease approvals as well as more complex issues such as material financial modifications. For instance, if a mortgage borrower seeks approval of a material lease at the mortgaged property, it is possible that all of the tranche holders will have some sort of a say. In a whole mortgage loan with multiple *pari passu* senior tranches, subordinate tranches and possibly mezzanine loans, it is easy to see how a once relatively easy process quickly becomes extremely complicated and convoluted, and will likely require more time and effort to process, which inevitably leads to increased costs and possibly delays. While certain deemed consent rights are becoming much more commonplace in an effort to streamline this process, any insolvency proceedings are bound to be infinitely more complex, with the potential for large-scale conflict among the various interest holders. In the end, only time will tell what other impact further slicing and dicing will have on mortgage borrowers, originating lenders, CMBS executions and commercial mortgage loan servicing in general. The European CMBS market seems to have an evolution different to anything that has been seen in the United States. This is what makes it such a dynamic market, and it is clear, that in the interim, the dynamic technological innovations which continue to drive CMBS as a product will, through the increased use throughout the European CMBS markets of more complex Subordinate Debt structures, continue to play an integral and legitimate role in the global liquidity of real estate finance.

CHAPTER NINE

INTERCREDITOR AGREEMENTS

Melissa Hamilton, Associate
Dechert LLP

INTRODUCTION

The aim of this chapter is to explore in greater depth the negotiation and drafting of intercreditor agreements in the context of CMBS transactions. Intercreditor agreements not only govern the relationship between holders of senior and junior loans, but they are also of great interest to rating agencies who rate bonds backed by the senior loans, the investors in those bonds, and the servicer and special servicer of the loans. A properly drafted intercreditor agreement will take into account not only the interests of senior and junior lenders but also the interests of these various non-parties.

As we have seen in Ch. 8, there are several different types of subordinate debt, all of which can generally be covered by an intercreditor agreement. For the purposes of this chapter, the terms "senior loan" and "senior lender" will be used broadly to refer, respectively, to a senior or A loan or tranche and the holder of that loan, including an issuer in a securitisation of the senior loan; "junior loan" and "junior lender" will refer, respectively, to a B or subordinated loan that is either a separate loan (whether originated under a single loan agreement with the senior loan or under separate loan documents) or a subordinated B tranche of a single whole loan, and the holder of such a loan. Generally, the concepts discussed in this chapter would also apply to more subordinate loans or tranches having priority below B loans and the rights of a junior lender can be extended to a C loan holder or a mezzanine loan holder behind a B loan. However it is important to note that the intercreditor agreements described in this chapter are only those between third-party lenders; they do not extend to, nor are they appropriate to cover, subordinate loans held by affiliates of a borrower which, in the context of securitisation, would be expected to be fully subordinated and not afforded control or cure rights or a purchase option.

In structured finance, rating agencies generally look unfavourably upon subordinate debt but a properly structured intercreditor agreement in which a subordinate lender provides credit support to the senior securitised loan or tranche, can enhance the rating agencies' view of the securitised loan.[1] In its most extreme position (for example when a junior lender is an affiliate of a borrower), the senior lender will be looking for full and absolute subordination of payment and rights in security from the junior lender, along with a "standstill" covenant in which the junior lender agrees that it will have no rights to enforce or accelerate its subordinate debt without the consent of the senior lender and a covenant against petitioning the borrower or affiliates into insolvency proceedings. The junior lender in the securitisation-related transactions considered here, while willing to provide subordination, standstill and non-petition covenants, will do so only if it is afforded certain rights to protect its position by way of approval over material decisions, cure rights and a purchase option.

There are generally two junior lender types. The first type are European banks who buy pieces of syndicated loans. They will participate on a subordinated basis under intercreditor agreements that resemble agented syndication agreements, with the agent acting on the instructions of the majority lenders for most decisions and with unanimous approval required for material loan modifications. These lenders may rely more on the judgment of the lead (majority) lender in the day-to-day administration of the loan and in developing a strategy for recovery if the loan defaults. The other type of junior lender will often be a sophisticated real estate investor with in-house expertise in recovery of defaulted loans. This junior lender will often have the inclination and capacity, when necessary to maximise its recoveries, to purchase the senior loan, enforce against security, and take ownership or control of the property. It will expect to have access to all available property data during the loan term, and will monitor the asset performance closely. It will expect to have a voice in material decisions relating to the loan and the security. It will generally favour a workout and restructure over quick enforcement and liquidation of security. The rating agencies generally tolerate significant junior lender rights, within certain limitations. However, the failure to balance the junior lender rights against the concerns of the rating agencies can result in an adverse impact on subordination levels in the securitisation of the senior loan.[2]

---

[1] K.Moretti, G.Gruchet, A.Currie and R.Pelletier, "Getting from A to B—An Overview of A/B Note Structures", *Fitch Ratings*, June 8, 2004, at p.4.
[2] J.Braidley, "A/B Structures Have an Affect on European CMBS Subordination Levels", *Standard & Poor's*, July 14, 2005, at p.1.

For a general discussion of the two principal forms of intercreditor agreements used in Europe which, roughly, correspond to these two junior lender types, see the paper prepared by the AB Task Force of the European Chapter of the Commercial Mortgage Securitisation Association at www.cmbs.org/international/european_chapter_page.htm.

PRINCIPAL BALANCE AND INTEREST RATE ALLOCATIONS

If the senior and junior lenders hold tranches of a single loan, one primary function of the intercreditor agreement, often accomplished in a side letter, is the allocation of the aggregate principal balance of the loan and of the all-in interest rate paid by the borrower between the senior and junior tranches. There are a number of factors senior and junior lenders will consider in this allocation such as rate creep and responsibility for servicing fees (as discussed below, where the junior lender will service the junior loan independently from the securitisation servicing of the senior loan, there may be no discussion of servicing fees in the intercreditor agreement; Fitch[3] and Standard & Poor's[4] have, however, expressed a preference for the joint servicing of multiple tranches of whole loans).

The higher interest rate margin allocated to the junior lender in a tranched loan structure will be subject to the risk of what is termed "rate creep". This arises when principal allocated sequentially (to the senior loan in priority to the junior) causes the weighted average rate on the senior and junior loans as established in the intercreditor agreement to creep above the weighted average whole loan rate that the borrower pays, thereby resulting in an available funds shortfall with an increasing portion of junior loan interest becoming non-recoverable. To overcome this issue the junior lender may seek to ensure that the intercreditor agreement defines the senior loan rate as net of a specified junior rate. If the junior loan is serviced by the securitisation servicer, responsibility for servicing fees (that is, for non-specially serviced loans) may be allocated on something other than a pro rata basis. The following are excerpts from an intercreditor agreement in which the junior lender is assured its margin while the senior lender (through the definition of "senior loan margin") will absorb both the rate creep and the basic servicing fee, including any future increases in that fee. With this definition, the servicing fee will be paid at the top of the waterfall, but the burden of it will fall on the senior lender.

---

[3] *Fitch Ratings*; op.cit. at p.2.
[4] *Standard & Poor's*; op.cit. at p.3.

"Senior Loan Margin" means, on any calculation date, a per annum percentage rate equal to (a) the Senior Interest minus the [annualised servicing fee], divided by (b) the outstanding principal balance of the senior loan, and "Senior Interest" means, on any calculation date, an amount equal to (a) the Whole Loan Margin (as defined in the loan agreement) multiplied by the outstanding principal balance of the whole loan at the calculation date, minus (b) the Junior Loan Margin multiplied by the outstanding principal balance of the junior loan at the calculation date, and "Junior Loan Margin" equals ___ per cent per annum. The Senior Loan Margin will be recalculated from time to time hereafter upon any allocation of principal to the junior and senior loans on other than a pro rata basis, and upon each change in the servicing fee rate.

The more common approach to the servicing fee will be to pay it at the top of the waterfalls as in the examples below, with no allocation between the lenders. Where, instead of one of the approaches described above, the intercreditor agreement provides that the servicing fee strip will be paid only from funds allocated to either the senior loan or the junior loan, the servicer is likely to object on the grounds that, if the portion of the loan that is responsible for the servicing fees is paid off or removed from the securitisation while the other portion of the loan is still serviced, the allocated funds to which the servicer must look for its fee are no longer available and the servicer will be working for no compensation. In fact, as discussed more fully below, the servicer will want to be able to recover its servicing fee relating to the junior loan from the revenues of the securitisation and not just from amounts received on that loan.

PRIORITY OF PAYMENTS AND WATERFALLS

Notwithstanding its agreement to subordinate its tranche of the loan, the junior lender is generally permitted to receive payments of principal and interest in circumstances where the whole loan is performing and the risk of loss is viewed as minimal. An intercreditor agreement will, therefore, include two alternative priority of payment, or "waterfall", provisions, one that applies in a pre-default scenario and the other for post-default. Under the former, both senior and junior loans will receive current interest allocated in accordance with their respective interest rate margins; payment of principal may be allocated in a number of ways including pro rata based on the relative principal balance, stipulated percentages or even first to the junior loan until it has been paid in full. Naturally, the rating agencies will model the senior loan according to the agreed principal allocation and methods of allocation that favour the junior loan will result in less favourable treatment of the senior loan in the securitisation.

The loan agreement may have its own waterfall, which will usually make payments to the facility and security agent and any receiver ahead of principal, interest and other lender payments. Therefore the intercreditor waterfalls may only deal with the payments to the lenders under this loan waterfall, which will usually include interest payments, principal payments, payments under any hedging arrangements and any indemnity/fee/expense payments.

In all cases, the available funds that flow through these waterfalls should include junior lender cure payments, hedge periodic payments and, in the post-default waterfall only, any escrowed amounts allocated to the junior lender after a borrower default and any junior lender cure deposits for purposes of curing financial covenants as discussed below.

The following is an example of a standard pre-default waterfall and shows the various payment priorities. Note that certain expenses are paid at the top of the waterfall.

"At any time that no Material Event of Default is continuing, available funds (including any cure payment made by Junior Lender and any available swap liquidity drawings) shall be distributed as follows:

First, to any payment due under any hedging arrangements entered into with respect to the Whole Loan (including periodic payments and payments as a result of termination, provided that such termination is not due to a default of or termination caused by or resulting from the status of the swap provider);

Second, to payment of all fees, costs and expenses due and payable to the Security Agent and its agents under the Finance Documents, and all fees and expenses of the Servicer and Special Servicer (if appointed) (which fees are payable, for the avoidance of doubt, on the Whole Loan) as agents of the Finance Parties pursuant to the terms of the Servicing Agreement and attributable to the Whole Loan and all amounts expended by the Security Agent or the Senior Lender in connection with the preservation of the rights of the Finance Parties under the Finance Documents, including the preservation of the Property as security for the Whole Loan;

Third, to payment to the Senior Lender: (i) of interest due and payable to the Senior Lender up to the amount necessary to make a complete payment of interest on the Senior Loan at the Senior Loan Rate for the related interest period; and (ii) of the amount due and payable from the Borrower in respect of increased costs of the Senior Lender resulting from a change of law or regulation or otherwise;

Fourth, to payment to the Junior Lender: (i) of interest due and payable to the Junior Lender up to the amount necessary to make a complete payment of interest on the Junior Loan at the Junior Loan Rate for the related interest period; and (ii) of the amount due and payable from the Borrower in respect of increased costs of the Junior Lender resulting from a change of law or regulation or otherwise;

Fifth, as with respect to all principal due and payable (or otherwise received) in respect of the Whole Loan, to payment to the Senior Lender and the Junior Lender, pro rata, according to the principal balances of the Senior Loan and the Junior Loan outstanding;

Sixth, to reimbursement on account of any cure payments made by the Junior Lender;

Seventh, to payment to the Senior Lender and the Junior Lender, pro rata, other than to the extent such amounts are paid above, of all other costs, fees and expenses due and payable under the Finance Documents; and

Eighth, to payment to the swap provider of any subordinated termination payments."

In the post-default waterfall, after expenses paid first in the loan waterfall, payments of interest and principal will be allocated sequentially, that is first to the senior loan until it has been paid in full and then to the junior loan.

"At any time that a Material Event of Default is continuing, available funds (including any cure payments and cure deposits made by the Junior Lender, all escrowed funds of the Junior Lender and any available swap liquidity drawings), shall be distributed as follows:

First, to payment of any amounts due under any hedging arrangements entered into with respect to the Whole Loan (including periodic payments and payments as a result of termination, provided that such termination is not due to a default of or termination caused by or resulting from the status of the swap provider);

Second, to payment of all costs, fees and expenses due and payable to the Security Agent under the Finance Documents, and all fees and expenses of the Servicer and Special Servicer (if appointed) as agents of the Finance Parties pursuant to the terms of the Servicing Agreement and attributable to the Whole Loan) and all amounts expended by the Security Agent or the Senior Lender in connection with the preservation of the rights of the Finance Parties under the Finance Documents, including the preservation of the Property as security for the Whole Loan;

Third, to payment to the Senior Lender: (i) of interest due and payable to the Senior Lender up to the amount necessary to make a complete payment of interest on the Senior Loan at the Senior Loan Rate for the related interest period; and (ii) of the amount due and payable from the Borrower in respect of increased costs of the Senior Lender resulting from a change of law or regulation or otherwise;

Fourth, to repayment of all principal outstanding on the Senior Loan (whether or not such amount is then due);

Fifth, to payment of the Senior Lender's pro rata portion of default interest received on the Whole Loan based on the outstanding principal on the Senior Debt as compared to the Whole Loan as of the beginning of the related interest period;

Sixth, to reimbursement on account of any Cure Payments made by the Junior Lender;

Seventh, to payment to the Junior Lender: (i) of interest due and payable to the Junior Lender up to the amount necessary to make a complete payment of interest on the Junior Loan at the Junior Loan Rate for the related interest period; and (ii) of the amount due and payable from the Borrower in respect of increased costs of the Junior Lender resulting from a change of law or regulation or otherwise;

Eighth, to repayment of all principal outstanding on the Junior Loan (whether or not such amount is then due);

Ninth, to payment of the Junior Lender's pro rata portion of default interest received on the Whole Loan based on the outstanding principal on the Junior Loan as compared to the Whole Loan as of the beginning of the related interest period;

Tenth, to payment to the Senior Lender and the Junior Lender, pro rata, other than to the extent such amounts are paid above, all other costs, fees and expenses due and payable under the Finance Documents; and

Eleventh, in or towards payment to the swap provider of any subordinated termination payments."

Securitisation-related expenses are not always covered by the junior lender's subordination in European CMBS transactions. These may be paid in the intercreditor waterfalls, or paid at the securitisation level (that is, only from the funds allocated to the senior loan). This is negotiated and treated differently in the intercreditor agreements used by the various European arrangers; but it is consistent with the credit-enhancement of the senior loan that, at a minimum, all expenses that can be recovered from the borrower under the senior loan agreement be paid prior to the junior lender under the intercreditor agreement.

The position in the waterfalls of repayment of any junior lender cure payments can vary. Whilst it will always be below the current amounts due to the Senior Lender, if there are multiple Junior Lenders, they may not agree that, if only one of them elects to cure, it will be reimbursed in priority to Junior Loan interest. In addition, certain payments received from the borrower may be allocated within or entirely outside of these waterfalls; prepayment fees, extension fees and default interest are sometimes allocated to one lender or another, or pro rata, without regard to the other payment priorities.

It is common in European intercreditor agreements, particularly when the trigger for the change in waterfalls is enforcement rather than material default, to provide for a so-called "cash trap" of all amounts that would be distributable to a junior lender commencing immediately upon a payment default or borrower insolvency; thus the junior lender's funds would be held in an escrow account pending the senior lender's decision to enforce or the junior lender's decision to cure the borrower default. Typically a junior lender will not agree to the trapping of its funds beyond a limited period of time; if the senior lender has not elected to enforce against the loan security within that time, the funds trapped would be released to the junior lender with interest earned during the trap period. If, on the other hand, the senior lender has enforced, then the junior lender's trapped funds would be distributed in accordance with the post-trigger waterfall.

In the sample pre-trigger waterfall above (under "*Fifth*"), each lender is allocated its pro rata share of any principal payment received on the loan. This is unobjectionable where the borrower is making full principal payments on its loan, but where the intercreditor agreement provides that the pre-trigger waterfall is effective at any time that a default (or other trigger event) "is not continuing" (for example in a post-default restructure where the borrower's principal payment obligations have been reduced), it can have a result inconsistent with the junior loan subordination in that the senior lender receives only a pro rata share of principal collected. One approach for addressing this is to pay first to the senior lender its pro rata share of principal due without regard to any modifications, then to the junior lender its pro rata share. Another approach used in some European intercreditor agreements is to include a so-called "workout override" provision imported from US intercreditor agreements. Under the workout override provision, if the pre-trigger payment priority is reinstated after a workout or restructure of the loan (the loan no longer being in default), any expenses, losses or reductions in borrower payments resulting from the restructure or workout will be borne by the junior lender notwithstanding the agreed pre-trigger payment allocation. An example of a workout override clause is as follows:

179

"Notwithstanding anything to the contrary set forth herein, if the whole loan is modified in connection with a workout of the whole loan (the 'Workout') and such modification: (i) reduces the outstanding principal balance of the whole loan; (ii) reduces the whole loan interest rate or the scheduled amortisation payments under the loan agreement; (iii) waives, reduces or defers any payment of interest or principal under the loan agreement; or (iv) adjusts any other payment term of the whole loan, all payments to the senior lender under this intercreditor agreement whether pursuant to the pre-trigger or post-trigger priority of payments, shall be made to the senior lender as if such Workout had not occurred, and the payment terms of the senior loan shall be deemed to remain unmodified by the Workout, and the junior loan shall bear the full economic effect of all such modifications, waivers, reductions or deferrals attributable to the Workout up to the amount otherwise payable with respect to the junior loan."

PRE-DEFAULT TO POST-DEFAULT TRIGGER

The intercreditor agreement must specify the event(s) or "trigger(s)" that will cause the switch from the pre-default to post-default waterfall; in fact, "default" alone is generally not the trigger. European intercreditor agreements typically define the trigger event as either: (a) enforcement action, or (b) payment default or insolvency of the borrower. The junior lender will, naturally, want the least aggressive trigger event and will therefore negotiate for enforcement being the only trigger event. The senior lender, on the other hand, will not want to be forced to quickly enforce a loan in order to trigger sequential payments where a negotiation with the borrower may provide for better recovery; thus senior lenders will negotiate for payment default or insolvency to be the trigger events. Triggers may also include breach of financial covenants or material non-monetary default. From the perspective of the rating agencies rating the securitisation of the senior loan or the investor in the lowest classes of that securitisation, the logical trigger for the post-default waterfall will be any event that results in a transfer of the senior loan to special servicing. This is because the commencement of special servicing gives rise to increased fees and costs and thus will generally be the point at which losses begin to accrue in the securitisation. The junior lender will negotiate for rights to prevent the switch from pro rata to sequential payments by curing, as discussed below, and will want the pre-trigger waterfall to resume if a loan is no longer in default due to a borrower's cure or a modification or workout.

REIMBURSEMENT OF PROPERTY PROTECTION ADVANCES

The servicer or special servicer of the senior loan will be required, in the securitisation servicing agreement, where necessary and recoverable, to advance funds or draw on a liquidity facility for property protection purposes, such as the cost of an insurance premium or rental payments under any headlease where the borrower has failed to pay these amounts. This will be required whether the senior and junior loans are serviced jointly or separately, and the protective advance will benefit both the senior and junior lenders. The intercreditor agreement should, therefore, include a mechanism for recovery from the junior lender of the property protection advances. This is not difficult where servicing is on a whole-loan basis and all property revenues are collected and administered in the securitisation; the property protection advance will be reimbursed at the top of the waterfall and, if this results in shortfalls, they will be borne at the bottom of the waterfall by the junior lender. However, where the junior lender receives its own debt service payment directly from the borrower or through the facility agent, the intercreditor agreement should include a covenant by the junior lender to reimburse from its collections the protective advance and interest on the advance. The junior lender will want to limit the senior lender's and servicers' recourse for these amounts to the funds received by the junior lender under the loan or intercreditor agreement.

SERVICING

The servicing of loans in CMBS is discussed further in Ch. 10. However in the context of a tranched AB loan certain issues on servicing arise which will be discussed here.

Where the subordinate debt is a separate loan, secured by either second-priority charges on the senior security package or other related security, the senior and junior lenders would each generally service or arrange for servicing of its own loan. In terms of tranched AB-style loans, whilst some European intercreditor agreements provide for the senior and junior loans to be serviced within the senior loan securitisation others provide for servicing of only the senior tranche. In any case, where the subordinate debt is secured by the same security documents, the agreement regarding servicing of the senior and subordinate loans should be specified in the intercreditor agreement. This will give rise to a number of issues, including approval rights over actions of the servicers, the allocation of liability as between the junior and senior lender for the various servicing and special servicing fees, and the point at which the whole loan is transferred to special servicing.

In CMBS transactions it is common for the junior tranche of a whole loan to be sold and the intercreditor agreement signed simultaneously with the securitisation of the senior tranche. Thus rather than setting out the terms of a whole loan servicing arrangement in the intercreditor agreement, the originator may simply require the junior loan purchaser to be a signatory to the securitisation servicing agreement, with its specified servicing standard and fee structure. A concern with this approach is that it does not address how the loan will be serviced if the senior loan is no longer part of the securitisation either because it has been repurchased by the originator due to a breach of representation or has been sold out of the securitisation after a default. In this case it would not be appropriate for the junior loan to continue to be serviced in the securitisation and a junior lender will want the intercreditor agreement to specify how servicing will be conducted when the senior loan is not in the securitisation. This may simply be a covenant that a new servicing agreement will be signed by the junior and senior lenders upon substantially the same terms as the securitisation servicing agreement.

The servicer of the securitisation, whether or not it will be servicing the subordinate debt, will wish to see a clear allocation of responsibility for servicing. If it is servicing both the senior and junior loans, the servicer will have a keen interest in the control rights of the junior lender and the interface with the duties of the servicer. The servicer will also be interested in the allocation of responsibility for its servicing, special servicing, liquidation, and workout fees.

Joint servicing versus separate servicing

In contrast to the US, in Europe there is no consensus that the subordinate loan should be subject to the same servicing arrangements as the senior loan. Whilst some junior lenders prefer the subordinate loan to be serviced by the securitisation servicer, others prefer that it is not (in the latter case with the junior lender either servicing the subordinate loan itself or having its own servicer). There are various reasons for this, including:

- avoiding the servicing expense,

- the junior lender may have originated the whole loan and may have a broader relationship with the borrower, its affiliates and security agent, and

- a junior lender that is building a portfolio (perhaps for a potential CRE CDO) may want the consistency of having all of its subordinate loans serviced by one "junior servicer".

On the other hand, where the senior and junior loans share the same security, a senior lender who has originated the loan and is selling the senior loan into a securitisation may prefer to see a single servicer appointed for the whole loan. This is partly due to the preference of the rating agencies for this approach. The Standard & Poor's view[5] is that separate servicing only works before a loan default (i.e. when the servicing role is essentially the collection of payments, reporting and responding to borrower requests); once there has been a loan default, they consider that there should then only be one special servicer dealing with the security package and the post-default strategy. It may also be preferable from a senior lender perspective, particularly where the senior lender was the originator and wants to assure the borrower it will have a single point of contact on its loan.

Whole loan servicing standard

For loans intended to be serviced on a "whole loan" basis, but with the securitisation servicing not yet in place when the intercreditor agreement is signed, the junior lender will want the key terms relating to servicing of the loan to be set out in the intercreditor agreement. Typically, the securitisation servicing agreement will establish priorities among transaction documents to govern conflicts among them. As the terms of the borrowers' loan cannot be varied without their consent, the loan documents will generally be afforded first priority (after applicable laws), followed by the intercreditor agreement, then the servicing agreement and other securitisation agreements. If, however, the intercreditor agreement does not specify the key servicing terms that affect the junior lender and instead says it will be serviced according to the (to-be-completed) servicing agreement, the servicing agreement will take priority and, if the junior lender is not a signatory to or third party beneficiary of the servicing agreement, it will be at risk of amendments to the servicing agreement without its consent.

Where the senior and junior loans are serviced on a whole loan basis, the intercreditor and servicing agreements should, taken together, include a servicing standard which specifies the required level of skill and care with which the whole loan is to be administered; often this is expressed to be for the loans "as a collective whole", having regard to the subordinated nature of the junior loan. Although this "collective whole" standard may seem vague, special servicers in the US, who have ample experience of applying this standard to defaulted AB loans, think it marks a clear enough path for the servicer between:

- the strategy that will maximise recoveries for both the senior and junior, without taking any substantial risk of making less than full recovery for the senior, and

---

[5] *Standard & Poor's*; op.cit. at p.3.

- the strategy that will assure quick and full recovery to the senior, without any regard for the junior.

Allocation of liability for servicing fees

Where the servicer is only servicing the senior loan, servicing fees will only be payable on the senior loan balance and will be paid from receipts of the senior lender within the securitisation waterfalls. In this case, there may be no mention of servicing fees in the intercreditor agreement. As discussed above, in cases where the servicing fees will be based on the whole loan, the allocation of the servicing fee is often negotiated in the context of the allocation of the interest rate margin. Where both lenders are paying the servicing fee proportionately, the servicer will want to ensure that it is paid at the top of the intercreditor waterfall and not just from funds allocated to each lender, so that if, for example, the payments to the junior lender are insufficient to cover the junior servicing fees, these are payable by the senior, thereby assuring that the servicer receives full payment of its fees. The servicer can be expected to object to any agreement that its fees for servicing the junior loan may only be paid from funds allocated to the junior lender in the intercreditor waterfalls. In a post-trigger sequential waterfall, the junior lender may not have any funds from which the servicer can be paid, but the servicer must continue to act for the whole loan. The following is an example of a protective covenant clause for a pool securitisation servicing agreement which addresses this issue:

> "In respect of any loan that is comprised of a senior loan and a junior loan, if on any interest payment date there are insufficient funds allocated to the junior lender under the payment priorities in the intercreditor agreement to pay all amounts payable by the junior lender to the servicer and special servicer, then the issuer will pay the shortfall to the servicer and special servicer from funds allocated to the issuer as senior lender under the intercreditor agreement or, if such allocated funds are also insufficient, from the issuer's available funds (including the proceeds of any liquidity facility drawing). The issuer will seek reimbursement from the junior lender in respect of any such payment (together with interest at the reimbursement rate or, if applicable, any interest accrued on any relevant liquidity facility drawing at the liquidity facility advance rate) from amounts thereafter allocated to the junior lender under the intercreditor agreement, until the issuer has been fully reimbursed, with such interest."

Limits on liability for liquidation fees

The junior lender will typically request that no liquidation fee be payable to the special servicer where the junior lender exercises its purchase right following a loan default, on the basis that the special servicer has provided no value if the liquidation process has not commenced. Special servicers will often agree to this if the purchase option is exercised within a limited period of time after default. The following is an example of a clause (which should appear in both the servicing and intercreditor agreements) dealing with a junior lender exercising its purchase option without payment of the liquidation fee:

"No liquidation fee will be payable in connection with the exercise by the junior lender of its right to acquire the senior loan pursuant to the terms of the intercreditor agreement if the junior lender gives notice in writing to the special servicer of its intent to purchase the senior loan from the senior lender within 30 days after junior lender's receipt of written notice from the special servicer that the special servicer intends to take action to dispose of the whole loan or to enforce the security granted in relation to the property, and the junior lender completes such purchase of the senior loan within 60 days after the junior lender's notice of intent to purchase the senior loan."

In any event, if and when a liquidation fee is payable to the special servicer for a loan with subordinate debt, it should generally not be borne by the securitisation (except where the junior loan has insufficient recoveries) nor fully waived (thereby eliminating special servicer's incentive to promptly and actively pursue recoveries).

Special servicing transfer events

The servicing provisions contained within the intercreditor agreement would generally specify the trigger for the loan to move from servicing to special servicing; at a minimum it will include payment default and insolvency events. In many cases it will also include other events such as a breach of financial covenant or other material covenant defaults. The junior lender will seek to ensure that the transfer to special servicing does not occur too early or too late; it will not want the transfer to be triggered by immaterial problems, such as a brief payment delinquency since the transfer to special servicing may result in a shift to the post-trigger waterfall. Furthermore, as discussed above, special servicing fees, at a significantly higher rate than servicing fees, will reduce funds that would otherwise be available for the junior lender. However, as it has first-loss exposure, the junior lender will also want to ensure that the move to special servicing occurs early enough to assure prompt action to limit losses on the subordinate loan. In any event, a servicing transfer will generally be postponed until the junior lender cure periods have expired and will be prevented by a cure (see below).

The interface between facility agents and servicers

In a (non-securitised) syndicated facility, a facility agent is appointed to be the interface between the lenders and the borrower and a security agent or trustee holds the lenders' security and enforces upon default. For a securitised loan, the facility agent function is normally delegated or assigned to and assumed by the servicer and special servicer and the same should be the case for a tranched loan serviced on a whole loan basis.

Where the servicing on the loan is for the senior loan only, the facility agent role may remain separate to the servicing role, with the facility agent seeking directions from the lenders, and the servicer providing those directions only for the senior lender while the junior lender acts for itself or through its own servicer. Leaving facility agents in place where there is also a servicer can increase expenses of the transaction and can result in decision-making for a securitised loan being in the hands of a person who is not a recognised CMBS servicer or special servicer and who is not bound by a servicing standard. The intercreditor agreement should be clear about the basis on which decisions are made: generally the senior lender will be the "majority lender" for the purpose of instructing the agent, though subject to the consent/control rights of the junior lender (see below).

CONTROL RIGHTS

As noted above, European style intercreditor agreements, modelled on loan syndication agreements, may give junior lenders rights to approve only material loan modifications. But some buyers of subordinated real estate debt are experienced property investors, with substantial in-house expertise in dealing with defaulted loans. They expect to control the strategy for defaulted loans, enforcement and all pre- and post-default modifications.

It is important that the allocation of approval and consultation rights be clearly set out in the intercreditor agreement. In addition to the senior and junior lenders agreeing this allocation, clarity is important to the servicers and the rating agencies. The servicers need to know when and in what time frames consultation is required. The rating agencies will prefer that in a stress or enforcement situation there is little scope for disputes between lenders which may delay proceedings and increase loss severity.

The scope of junior lender control

Most junior lenders will require, at a minimum, control over all loan modifications affecting payment terms or the loan security. Some junior lenders seek broader control, including all changes in borrowers and property managers, approval of new occupational leases, alterations to the properties and control of enforcement strategy.

The senior lender (who may have an ongoing relationship with the borrower notwithstanding the sale of the loan) and the servicer will be mindful that any delays to the decision-making process will create issues for the borrower, so will prefer to identify in the intercreditor agreement those amendments, waivers and consents which require both the senior and junior lenders' approval with any others being made or given by the servicer. Generally, these identified provisions would be those that impact on the economic terms of the junior lender's position (such as changes to the amount or timing of payments, interest rate, deferrals) and those that are material to the credit analysis (such as disposals, ability to incur debt and financial covenants).

These rights of the junior lender will take the form either of control rights (where consent may be given or refused by the junior lender) or consultation rights (where the servicer is not bound by a consent or refusal of the junior lender but must consult with the junior lender in compliance with a set timetable provided in the intercreditor agreement). Unlike a servicer who must act in the interests of both senior and junior lenders as a collective whole, the junior lender will not owe any duty of care to the senior lender (or securitisation investors) and will act strictly in its own interests.

Where the senior and junior loans are jointly serviced the junior lender will generally also have the right to appoint and replace the special servicer who would, subject to the servicing standard and agreed exceptions, make all decisions regarding the senior and junior debt after a servicing transfer event and direct any enforcement strategy. This is because the junior lender, as the first loss piece, will be the party most interested in ensuring a successful work-out or enforcement of the loan. This is true provided the junior lender retains an economic interest in the loan, hence senior lenders may require that this right revert to the senior lender should the junior lender no longer have a sufficient economic interest. In addition to the senior lender, the rating agencies will also wish to see this right fall away in these circumstances.[6] The mechanism whereby the junior lender's economic interest is determined not to be sufficient is termed a "control valuation event" (see below).

The rating agencies do not require limitations on what matters should be subject to junior lender control; even a loan restructure or discounted payoff can be subject to junior lender approval. However the rating agencies do not

---

[6] *Standard & Poor's*; op.cit. at p.5.

look favourably on the decision-making process of the servicers being unduly encumbered when the senior loan is in default. Standard & Poor's has identified the following key issues which they would expect to be addressed in intercreditor agreements:

(1) the time period within which a consent is to be given or refused, or consultation is to be undertaken, should be clearly specified and be as short as possible;

(2) the rights should be subject to the servicing standard override; and

(3) the rights should fall away after a control valuation event.[7]

If a junior lender retains approval rights and in particular if it can veto the acceptance of a discounted payoff that would fully pay the senior loan in circumstances where the junior lender's economic interest has been substantially eroded, this will be of concern to the rating agencies.

Junior lenders and junior noteholders

The junior lender's consent and control rights are usually much more extensive than those typically granted to the holders of the most subordinate class of notes in a securitisation. However, intercreditor agreements normally provide that the control rights given to the junior lender as the "controlling party" will, upon a control valuation event (discussed below), pass to the senior lender. Where there are multiple layers of subordinate debt, the controlling party will typically be the most junior lender, with control rights moving upward upon control valuation events through the tiers of subordinate debt until they pass to the senior lender. Where the senior loan is to be securitised, the intercreditor and servicing agreements should address the interface of the eventual shift of control rights from junior to senior lender. In the securitisation, these control rights (which will be applicable to the relevant loan only) will vest in the securitisation's controlling class, which is usually defined in a manner similar to the intercreditor agreement: that is, the lowest ranking class that has a principal balance outstanding after adjustment for payments received and losses allocated of at least 25 per cent of its amortised principal balance. The servicing agreement generally refers to a "controlling party" for each securitised loan: loans without junior lender control rights will have as controlling party the controlling class; loans with junior lender control rights will initially have the most junior lender as controlling party, with those rights shifting (if control valuation events occur) upward to the securitisation's controlling class for the senior lender.

---

[7] *Standard & Poor's*; op.cit. at pp.2 and 4.

Operating advisers and controlling class representatives

As with noteholders of the securitisation's controlling class, there will often be more than one holder of a junior loan. Even where there is only one initial buyer, subsequent trades may result in multiple junior lenders in any given tranche. Intercreditor agreements should provide for this eventuality with multiple junior lenders who together hold control rights being able to designate a representative, often called the "operating adviser". The servicer will often request this if junior lenders do not do so; thus the servicer's obligations to consult or seek approval will be limited to a single representative.

Typically the majority junior lender (or junior lenders together representing a specified percentage of all subordinate debt) will have the right to appoint or change the operating adviser. This percentage may change from deal to deal, depending on the requirements of the junior lenders. The servicer will deal only with the operating adviser, who will exercise all of the control rights for all holders of the applicable junior loan.

In securitisation terms the person performing this role for the most subordinate class of noteholders is commonly called the "controlling class representative". Similarly, the majority holders of notes in the controlling class will have the right to appoint or change the controlling class representative; this percentage may change from deal to deal. The servicer will deal only with the controlling class representative, who will exercise all controlling class approval rights and will owe a duty of care only to the holders of that class.

Servicing standard override; immediate action

Standard & Poor's have expressed the view[8] that irrespective of the various consultation or approval rights of controlling parties and whether vested in a junior lender or a controlling class of securitisation noteholders, there should be a "servicing standard override" in the intercreditor and servicing agreements. This will allow the servicer to:

- disregard any exercise of control or approval rights which would cause the servicer to violate the servicing standard, and

- act immediately if delay would violate the servicing standard.

Intercreditor agreements based upon a syndication model are less likely to have this override. An example of such a provision is as follows:

---

[8] *Standard & Poor's*; op.cit. at p.2.

If the Servicer or the Special Servicer determines in accordance with the Servicing Standard that immediate action is necessary to protect the interests of the Senior Lender (or the noteholders) and the Junior Lender (as a collective whole but taking into account the subordination of the Junior Loan), the Servicer or Special Servicer may take any such action without waiting for the Controlling Party's response.

Notwithstanding any right of the Controlling Party to provide any directions to the Servicer or the Special Servicer or to approve or consent to any action of the Servicer or the Special Servicer, the Servicer or the Special Servicer will not be obliged or permitted to take any action or refrain from taking any action that would violate any law of any applicable jurisdiction and/or which would be, in the opinion of the Servicer or the Special Servicer, inconsistent with the Servicing Standard or violate any provisions of the Finance Documents or the Intercreditor Agreement.

Junior lender right to force enforcement

In US-style mezzanine debt, the junior lender holds its own security over separate assets from the senior lender, such as a security over equity in the borrower where that equity is not part of the senior security. In these situations the junior lender will be able to negotiate the right to separately enforce its security to take control of the borrower or real estate-owning company so long as it does not proceed against any part of the senior lender's security.

As noted above, the position in relation to AB structures, or "European" mezzanine debt, is that the security is often shared by both lenders. Thus the junior lender will have an interest in enforcement of the shared security. The junior lender would probably not push for a quick liquidation of security, but would prefer workouts and extensions of time in the hope of greater ultimate recoveries. The junior lender's worst position, however, would be where a loan default has triggered the sequential priority of payments under the intercreditor agreement thus cutting off all payments to the junior lender but the senior lender has delayed commencement of enforcement action which might eventually yield some proceeds to the junior lender after the senior loan has been paid in full. In that case, particularly where the senior and junior loans are not serviced on a whole loan basis or the junior lender does not have the right to replace the special servicer, the junior lender will want the right to accelerate the loan and require the servicer to take enforcement action. Sometimes the senior lender will require a standstill period before the junior lender can require enforcement. In any case, the junior lender's right to require enforcement will generally be subject to a qualification that it may do so only if the expected enforcement proceeds would exceed the senior debt by a particular percentage. The junior lender's position would be that it should not be prevented from taking (or requiring the taking of) enforcement action where it is reasonably clear that the senior lender will be repaid in full.

However, the senior lender on the other hand may suggest that if the junior lender wants to control enforcement, it should use its purchase rights (see below) to acquire the senior debt and then enforce for the whole loan. Whatever position is agreed, the senior lender commonly seeks to direct the enforcement action once triggered, whether by the servicer or the junior lender.

The rating agencies' current position is that any right of the junior lender to force enforcement should only apply if the property value is expected to cover a minimum percentage of the senior loan (Standard & Poor's criteria requires that this percentage be at least 125 per cent[9]) and should be limited by the occurrence of a control valuation event (see below) and the servicing standard override (see above).

TERMINATING CONTROL RIGHTS

Consistent with their first loss position and greater expertise in defaulted loan recoveries, junior lenders negotiate heavily for the control rights discussed above. However, as discussed above, senior lenders and the rating agencies will wish to ensure that a junior lender does not have the ability to delay or restrict enforcement or workout if it has only a minimal interest left in the deal.

Control valuation events

To balance the rights of the senior and junior lenders, it is common in US-style intercreditor agreements to provide for a "control valuation event" upon which all approval and consent rights, the right to appoint a special servicer and the right to require enforcement will move from the junior lender to the senior (or, if there are several tiers of junior lenders, upwards to the next most subordinate lender). A control valuation event occurs when a current valuation of the security property indicates that a diminished property value will not in all likelihood produce recovery by the controlling party of a material portion of its junior debt.

---

[9] *Standard & Poor's*; op.cit. at p.2.

Historically, European intercreditor agreements have given junior lenders enduring rights with no concept of a control valuation event; while the inclusion of a control valuation event is becoming more common in European intercreditor agreements, many do not include it and the junior lender veto over material modifications may continue for the term of the loan.

A junior lender will prefer enduring rights, so that until final recovery it has a say in the management of the enforcement process. Senior lenders will seek to ensure that if a junior lender no longer has an economic interest, and therefore no incentive to devote time and resources to the enforcement process, then they are removed from the decision making process.

Enduring rights are seen as less than optimal because they may preclude an agreed work-out with the borrower. Standard & Poor's has published its view[10] that the recovery period is likely to be extended due to enduring rights of a junior lender, thereby reducing recoveries and they may, as a consequence, adjust the levels on the investment-grade portion of the loan in a securitisation.

Formula for computing value reduction amount

It is common to see a formula set out in the intercreditor agreement in order to determine when the junior lender no longer has sufficient economic interest in the loan.

The "valuation reduction amount" is generally defined as the amount by which combined junior and senior loan balances exceed 90 per cent of property value. An example of such a clause is as follows:

> A "Valuation Reduction Amount" with respect to the whole loan will be an amount equal to (a) the outstanding principal balance of the whole loan minus (b) the amount by which 90 per cent. of the value of the Property (after deduction of the amount of any prior security interest and addition of all reserve balances that may be applied against repayment of the whole loan) exceeds the sum of (i) all unpaid interest on the whole loan that has not been advanced pursuant to a liquidity facility drawing, (ii) all unreimbursed servicer advances or liquidity facility drawings made to pay property related expenses related to the Whole Loan, (iii) interest on all such advances or drawings, (iv) any other unpaid fees, expenses and other amounts of the servicer, special servicer or note trustee that are related to the whole loan and payable in priority to the securitisation notes, and (v) all unpaid ground rents,

---

[10] *Standard & Poor's*; op.cit. at p.6.

insurance premia and all other amounts payable by the borrower and unpaid with respect to the whole loan.

If, after application of the valuation reduction amount to the junior loan, its balance is less than 25 per cent of the amortised junior loan principal balance, a control valuation event will be deemed to have occurred. An example of such is as follows:

> A "Control Valuation Event" will occur with respect to the whole loan for so long as: (a) (1) the then outstanding principal balance of the Junior Loan; minus (2) any Valuation Reduction Amount with respect to the whole loan, plus, without duplication, the amount of all losses realised with respect to any enforcement of security in respect of the property, is less than (b) 25 per cent of the outstanding principal balance of the junior loan after all principal payments received by the junior lender prior to the date of calculation.

Junior lender actions to prevent loss of control

Once the junior lender has negotiated its control rights, it will wish to retain them for as long as possible. In intercreditor agreements with enduring junior lender rights this is not an issue. However on deals with either: (a) control valuation events, or (b) no junior lender involvement after enforcement has been triggered, the junior lender will require options to prevent such a loss of control.

The options available to the junior lenders are:

- *Cure rights*: exercise of a cure right (see below) may defer the servicer's obligation to obtain a new valuation for the purpose of testing whether a control valuation event has occurred.

- *Purchase rights*: exercise of the junior lender's purchase right (see below) will mean that the junior lender owns and therefore controls the whole loan.

These will be discussed in more detail below.

The junior lender may also negotiate for a right to provide its own valuation to challenge the current valuation used by the servicer to assess whether a control valuation event has occurred and for the junior lender's valuation to control if it differs from the servicer's valuation. Its argument is that its valuation should be given preference where there is a risk of the junior lender losing such fundamental rights. Senior lenders may agree to this provided that the valuation is prepared by a qualified valuer, and at the junior lender's sole expense.

CURE RIGHTS

Intercreditor agreements will generally contain a right for the junior lender to temporarily remedy certain borrower defaults, termed a "cure right". Junior lenders will negotiate at the outset of any transaction for these rights given their fundamental importance to the junior lenders' overall investment.

Cure right provisions will provide that the junior lender is given notice of a borrower default and thereafter is allowed a period of time to elect whether to exercise its cure right. Cure periods vary from transaction to transaction but it is not uncommon to see periods of seven days or less. Whilst the junior lender may wish for a longer period of time within which to gather information and investigate the default situation before deciding whether to exercise its cure right, the senior lender, servicers and rating agencies will wish to limit the delay before decisions can be made about how the loan is to be managed, the timing of a transfer to special servicing, and ultimately enforcement.

If the junior lender decides to exercise its cure right then in the case of a borrower payment default the junior lender will pay an amount equal to the particular payment shortfall. In some circumstances the junior lenders will have negotiated a right to make a cash shortfall payment net of any monies due to themselves under the waterfall thus waiving, as between the senior and junior lender only, any monies which would have flowed through the waterfall to pay principal and interest due to the junior lender. Senior lenders will also negotiate for any cash shortfall payment to include additional costs incurred by the senior lender (or the securitisation) as a result of the payment default, such as interest on liquidity facility drawings, special servicing fees and swap break costs. Thus senior lenders will look for a "make whole" payment so that they are put in the position they would have been in had there been no default.

The junior lender may also negotiate for a right to cure breaches of financial covenants (loan to value or debt service cover covenants) by making a cure deposit sufficient to bring the loan to value or debt service cover within the limits prescribed in the loan agreement. As with a payment default, the junior lender will be given notice of such default and an ability to cure within a set period of time. Intercreditor agreements vary in the formula used for calculating the amount of the debt service cover cure deposit. Some require a deposit of a sum sufficient to generate interest earnings on investment to pay the debt service cover shortfall; others require only deposit of the interest shortfall amount. The cure deposit will generally be held in escrow as additional security for the whole loan, and the junior lender will seek the right to direct investment of the cure deposit. Upon a subsequent (uncured) loan default or upon the exhaustion of the junior lender's cure rights, the deposited amount will be treated as a recovery and distributed in the post-trigger waterfall. If, on the other hand, the financial covenant breach is rectified by the borrower, then the junior lender will want the cure deposit to be released to the junior lender, together with all interest earned thereon.

Junior lenders may also negotiate the right to cure other non-monetary defaults, however their ability to cure a default other than by way of payment may be limited where they do not have control over the borrower or its affiliates. For example, a junior lender may be able to cure the failure to maintain insurance by paying the premium but may not be able to cure a breach of a negative covenant or reporting requirements by the borrower.

The effect of the exercise by the junior lender of its cure rights will be to ensure that the waterfall payments remain as they would have done if there had been no borrower default; thus the pre-default waterfall is applied rather than the post-default waterfall, with the consequential pro rata interest and principal payments to the junior lender. Furthermore, whilst these cure rights are being exercised and the particular default is remedied, the underlying loan is not treated as being in default so the cure will prevent the transfer of the loan to special servicing.

RESTRICTIONS APPLIED TO THE EXERCISE OF CURE RIGHTS

Whilst rating agencies have considered cure rights to be a positive aspect of intercreditor agreements, as they provide credit support to the transaction, they have noted that the consequential delays to enforcement could reduce recoveries in a falling real estate market. Therefore rating agencies prefer to see limits on cure rights,[11] principally so that a junior lender's cure rights are subject to limitations as to the number of times during the life of a loan they can be exercised and the time period within which they can be exercised.

Typically the number of times the junior lender may cure loan defaults would be limited to between four and six (depending on the length of the loan term) during the life of a loan and not more than twice in a one-year

---

[11] *Standard & Poor's*; op.cit. at p.4; *Fitch Ratings*; op.cit. at p.3.

period, or on more than two consecutive interest payment dates. Junior lenders may however seek to distinguish cures of the senior loan to those on the junior loan, so that they may cure defaults that relate solely to the junior loan without limitation.

Junior lenders will also generally wish to see a distinction drawn between restrictions on the number and time periods for curing payment defaults and those for breach of financial or non-monetary covenants. Whilst they would generally accept that the former should be limited in number as the junior lender's cure payments are providing artificial support to the transaction, they would argue that a right to cure for breach of financial or non-monetary covenant should not be so limited. Junior lenders might suggest that their cure deposits to remedy borrower breach of financial covenants and the curing of non-monetary covenants actually reduce the transaction risk for the senior lender and as such they should be unlimited.

In any case, where the senior and junior loans are jointly serviced in the securitisation, the special servicer will be able to reduce a junior lender's cure period or act immediately notwithstanding the junior lender's cure rights if a delay would violate the servicing standard (see above).

PURCHASE OPTION

The junior lender's right to purchase the senior loan following the occurrence of specified loan events of default is the junior lender's most significant protection. It becomes the ultimate fallback when the junior lender has exhausted its cure rights or a non-curable loan default triggers a change to sequential payment or when a "control valuation event" will result in the junior lender losing its consent or consultation rights, with a consequent shift of control to the senior lender. Many senior lenders see a purchase option for the junior lender as a positive feature of an intercreditor agreement, and in fact argue strongly for the limitation of cure and consent rights on the basis that if the junior lender wants control it should exercise its purchase option. While rating agencies also have viewed junior lender purchase options as a positive feature of an intercreditor agreement, no explicit credit in the rating process is given as it is, indeed, only an option.[12]

The triggers for the junior lender's option to purchase the senior loan will often be the same as the triggers for change in the payment waterfall from the pre-trigger waterfall to the sequential post-trigger waterfall. From the junior lender's perspective, the minimum trigger should be a change to

---

[12] *Fitch Ratings*; op.cit. at p.3.

sequential payment, but a junior lender may negotiate for the option to also be available when there has been a material non-monetary event of default, a transfer to special servicing or loss of control by the junior lender.

A properly drafted intercreditor agreement will provide a clear formula whereby the consideration payable by the junior lender for the purchase of the senior loan can be calculated. An example of such a formula is set out below:

> "the principal amount outstanding under the senior loan at the date of purchase by the junior lender, plus interest that will accrue up to the next succeeding loan payment date plus all outstanding property protection advances and enforcement costs of the senior lender (and interest on each of them), plus all reasonable out-of-pocket costs and expenses incurred by the senior lender in connection with such purchase, including any swap breakage costs payable by the senior lender, plus any other fees, costs and expenses of any trustee, servicer, special servicer, or any other person in connection with the securitisation of the senior loan arising as a result of such purchase."

The purchase price would typically exclude default interest and any prepayment fees payable under the loan agreement.

The Standard & Poor's position on the purchase option price is that, consistent with the principle of subordination, the purchase price should be sufficient to "make whole" the securitised senior loan, putting the securitisation in the same financial position as if the mortgage loan had not been included in the securitisation.[13] The purchase price would therefore include all of the amounts in the formula above plus interest on liquidity facility drawings and any special servicing fees incurred for the purchased loan. From a senior lender and rating agency perspective the price paid by the junior lender should never be based upon a valuation of the property or matching any offer below par by a third party.

The junior lender may argue that additional costs or fees relating to the securitisation, such as special servicing fees and interest on liquidity drawings, should be included only to the extent that the borrower would be liable to reimburse those items under the loan agreement; thus the option purchase price would only include amounts for which it would be entitled to seek full recovery from the borrower. Borrower indemnities will often not have been drafted broadly enough to cover special servicing fees, liquidity facility costs and other securitisation-related expenses which means these expenses will

---

[13] *Standard & Poor's*; op.cit. at p.3.

cause losses to either the senior loan or the junior loan, depending on the provisions of the intercreditor agreement. As in the sample formula above, a compromise may be to include in the option price all costs and expenses in connection with securitisation of the senior loan to the extent they are directly related to the purchase, but not otherwise; thus, securitisation costs resulting from the default would not be added to the purchase price payable by the junior lender.

If the servicing agreement for the senior loan provides for a liquidation fee to be payable to the special servicer upon a purchase by a junior lender, the senior lender will wish to ensure that the purchase price also includes reimbursement of that fee. The junior lender may seek to limit its obligation for the liquidation fee, but the rating agencies prefer that, if it is payable under the servicing agreement, it should be part of the junior lender purchase price.[14] As discussed above in regard to servicing issues, the junior lender's best approach may be to address this in the servicing agreement by seeking to limit accrual of the liquidation fee to allow a period within which the fee is not payable if the junior lender has given notice of intent to purchase.

The junior lender may also be concerned to have senior loan swap agreements novated to the junior lender on the exercise of the purchase option and the intercreditor agreement may include a covenant by the senior lender to use reasonable endeavours to procure such novation and transfer of the swap agreement if requested. Any such transfer will be subject to the consent of the swap counterparty who may be less willing to have exposure to the credit of the junior lender than the credit of a securitisation issuer.

The junior lender's option to purchase will generally continue until any outstanding event of default has been cured, or enforcement of the loan security has been completed, or the senior loan has been transferred to another party.

CONCLUSION

In contrast to US intercreditor agreements[15] which have become fairly standardised but with significant differences between the rights afforded to B noteholders and those afforded to mezzanine lenders, European intercreditor agreements generally treat all types of subordinate lenders in a similar fashion, but with little standardisation among the forms used by

---

[14] *Standard & Poor's*; op.cit.
[15] For an example of a US Intercreditor Agreement, see Appendix 1.

different originators. There is no discernable trend toward convergence, even on those issues identified by the rating agencies as having a bearing on subordination levels. For that reason, no model intercreditor agreement is offered here; instead the author has identified the issues that might be addressed, with examples of some key clauses. With low default rates on European securitised commercial mortgage loans, European intercreditor agreements have not been tested and it remains to be seen whether they will impact recoveries positively or negatively. No matter which of the approaches are adopted by the senior and junior lenders, to the extent that a well-crafted intercreditor agreement clearly sets out the rights of the senior and junior lenders, thereby avoiding disputes and litigation it will be, in large part, successful.

Chapter Ten

SERVICING CMBS

Kathleen Mylod, Associate
Katherine Burroughs, Partner
Dechert LLP

INTRODUCTION: LOAN SERVICING

CMBS loan servicing is the administration of commercial mortgage loans that have been securitised. One significant difference between portfolio lending and securitisation is the separation of the post-closing loan relationship from the pre-closing loan origination process. Specifically, whereas in portfolio lending the servicing of a loan post-closing is likely to be done (or controlled) by the same institution that originated the loan, in securitisation transactions the loan originator is often not involved in loan servicing and administration. Even if the loan originator (or its affiliate) does continue to have a role in post-securitisation servicing, because of the requirements of the securitisation structure, its discretion will be constrained by a servicing agreement.

APPOINTMENT OF SERVICER AND SPECIAL SERVICER

In CMBS transactions a servicing agreement is entered into at the closing of the transaction, pursuant to which the CMBS issuer, as the new owner of the underlying mortgage loans, and the note trustee as representative of the CMBS noteholders, for which the mortgage loans are collateral security, appoint a "servicer" (sometimes referred to as a "master servicer") to administer the performing loans, and a "special servicer" to administer any loans that become non-performing.

To the extent that a facility agent and/or collateral (or security) trustee have been appointed in conjunction with any of the mortgage loans, those entities may also be parties to the servicing agreement, and will often delegate their respective rights and obligations under the loan documents to the servicer and special servicer. The servicer and special servicer are essentially responsible for exercising all of the rights, obligations and discretions that the holder of the loans possessed prior to their being securitised. In addition, if any of the underlying commercial mortgage loans have been tranched, the servicer and special servicer may also be appointed to exercise the rights and obligations guaranteed under any intercreditor related to the portion of the loan that has not been securitised.

In the event that one or more of the mortgage loans have been tranched, and an interest sold to investors outside of the CMBS transaction, the other investors, as co-owners of the participated loans, may also be parties to the servicing agreement for the purpose of appointing the servicer and special servicer to act on their behalf in administering their loans.

SERVICING STANDARD

In performing their respective functions, the servicer and special servicer agree to do so in accordance with a "servicing standard", which is defined in the servicing agreement. While the exact wording may vary, the servicing standard typically includes the following:

The "Servicing Standard" shall mean diligent service and administration of the mortgage loans pursuant to the servicing agreement in the best interests of and for the benefit of the holders of the CMBS notes (as determined by the servicer or the special servicer, as the case may be, in its good faith and reasonable judgment):

- in accordance with applicable law;
- the terms of the applicable finance documents and applicable intercreditor or participation agreements and the terms of the servicing agreement; and
- to the extent consistent with the foregoing, in accordance with the customary and usual standards of practice of prudent commercial mortgage lenders servicing their own mortgage loans;

with a view to the timely collection of all sums due in respect of the mortgage loans and if a mortgage loan comes into default, the maximisation of timely recovery of principal and interest on a net present value basis of such mortgage loan, as determined by the servicer or the special servicer as the case may be, in its reasonable judgment.

In applying the servicing standard, neither the servicer nor the special servicer shall have regard to:

- any fees or other compensation to which the servicer or special servicer may be entitled;

- any relationship the servicer or the special servicer or any of their respective affiliates may have with any borrower or any affiliate of any borrower or any party to the transactions entered into in connection with the issue of the CMBS notes; and/or

- the ownership of any CMBS note by the servicer or special servicer or any of their respective affiliates.

The importance of the servicing standard is twofold. First, it provides a benchmark for evaluating the servicer's or special servicer's standard of performance with respect to administering the mortgage loans including the exercise of any discretion, for example, in the enforcement of any security. Secondly, it requires the servicer and special servicer to act without regard to any personal interest, the servicer or special servicer (or their respective affiliates) might have, including without limitation other roles that they or their affiliates may have in the transaction.

This latter point is important because it is common for the servicer and special servicer to be affiliated with other parties in the transaction, including the mortgage loan originator/seller, subordinate investors in the mortgage loans, and the holders of the most subordinate classes of the CMBS notes. Accordingly, in order to protect the interests of the holders of the CMBS notes (as a collective whole) it is critically important that the servicer and special servicer agree to act without regard to these potentially conflicting interests.

SERVICER AND SPECIAL SERVICER OBLIGATIONS

After securitisation, the mortgage loan borrowers will generally interact only with the servicer and the special servicer, as applicable, and not with any other parties to the securitisation transaction or with the lenders that originated their mortgage loans and sold them into the securitisation pool. The other parties to the securitisation transaction, such as the CMBS issuer and note trustee, delegate their authority and rights under the securitisation transaction documents to the servicer and special servicer so that they have the full authority to perform their respective servicing functions. Those functions (described in more detail below) include:

(1) monitoring the loan and collecting debt service payments,

(2) collecting data, issuing reports and maintaining loan files,

(3) monitoring payments to certain third parties such as tax authorities and the insurers of the secured properties,

(4) enforcing the loan sale agreement,

(5) initiating property protection advances,

(6) administering loan related swaps, and

(7) consenting to modifications of or waivers and consents under the mortgage loan documents.

These functions are ordinarily the obligations of the servicer; however, if a mortgage loan becomes non-performing, then certain obligations will transfer to the special servicer. The exact circumstances which result in the transfer of the servicing of the mortgage loan to the special servicer comprise what is described as the special servicing transfer event (which is discussed further, below).

Monitoring the loan and collecting debt service payments

A primary obligation of the servicer is to actively monitor the serviced mortgage loans and to calculate, as specified under the applicable facility agreements, the amount of debt service due from the mortgage borrowers. On the applicable loan payment dates, the servicer collects the amounts due from the mortgage borrowers, often by directly withdrawing such amounts from the mortgage borrowers' accounts, to which the servicer may have access in accordance with the provisions of the mortgage loan documents. The servicer deposits the payments from the mortgage borrowers into what is commonly referred to as the "issuer collection account", which is an account opened in the name of the CMBS issuer at the CMBS issuer's cash management bank. For any period that the servicer holds any mortgage borrowers' payments, it does so on trust for the CMBS issuer and the servicer must keep such money separate from all other funds in its possession.

If any mortgage borrower fails to pay such amounts on the due date, then the servicer must provide prompt notice to the CMBS issuer, the cash manager and other relevant securitisation parties so that there is sufficient time for a drawing to be made on the liquidity facility in place for the securitisation, subject to the requirements of that facility, in order to fund any resulting shortfall in interest payments due to CMBS noteholders. Even where a special servicing transfer event has occurred, the servicer generally retains the obligation to calculate and monitor debt service payments.

Collecting data, issuing reports and maintaining loan files

Data and reports

The servicer has three primary responsibilities with regard to the collection of data about the borrowers and the secured properties. First, the servicer must keep records regarding the mortgage borrowers and payments they make for debt service and to other third parties. Secondly, the servicer must periodically collect the financial statements of the mortgage borrowers and analyse them. Thirdly, the servicer uses the data acquired to prepare reports for the securitisation parties, the investors in the securitisation and the rating agencies who monitor the ratings of the CMBS notes.[1]

Periodically, as required under the terms of the servicing agreement, the servicer will prepare and issue various reports. It is not unusual for a servicing agreement to dictate that the servicer use specific forms for the reports, such as those generated by the Commercial Mortgage Securitisation Association, including, but not limited to comparative financial status, loan periodic update, property file, financial file, and delinquent loan status reports.[2]

From the investors' perspective,[3] the servicer's reports are critical—they are periodic snapshots of the stability, or instability, of the securitisation pool. These reports are the primary sources of information about the financial performance of the mortgage borrowers, the status of the loans, and the condition of the secured properties.

Loan files

When a securitisation transaction closes and the obligations of the servicer commence, the servicer receives a file on each of the loans that it will service. This "loan file" provides the servicer with the information that it requires to properly service each of the mortgage loans and includes, among other documents, the mortgage loan agreement and related documents, the loan sale agreement, and other documents relating to the secured properties, such as environmental reports.

As the servicer compiles data about the mortgage borrowers and their loans and generates reports using such data, the servicer adds that information and reports to the appropriate loan files. Throughout the period of

---

[1] See Ch. 4.
[2] These and other forms may be located at the CMSA website: www.cmbs.org. An example of such a report, the E-IRP, is set out in Appendix 3.
[3] As will be seen in Ch. 14.

its appointment, the servicer will add to the loan files records of debt service and third party payments, records of any property protection advances (discussed below), property inspection reports, borrower financial statements, subsequent property level diligence such as further environmental reports, modifications to any of the mortgage loan documents, and records of any special servicing transfer events.

Reporting obligations of the special servicer

The obligations of the special servicer with regard to data collection, issuance of reports and maintenance of the loan files will differ across securitisation transactions. Some servicing agreements may provide that the obligations always remain with the servicer, even when a loan has been transferred to the special servicer. In such servicing agreements, the special servicer will have the obligation to provide information to the servicer about the mortgage loans that it is specially servicing. Other servicing agreements may provide that upon the occurrence of a special servicing transfer event, all data collection, post-issuance reporting and loan file maintenance transfer to the special servicer with respect to the particular mortgage loan in need of special servicing. In such situations, the special servicer is charged with those responsibilities until the mortgage loan is no longer in need of special servicing, at which point the servicer resumes those responsibilities.

Monitoring third party payments

In addition to calculating debt service payments and monitoring timely payment by the mortgage borrowers, the servicer also oversees borrower payments to third parties, such as tax, insurance, property management and headlease payments. Whereas the goal of the servicer in monitoring the debt service payments is to ensure adequate payments to the CMBS issuer so that timely payments may be made to the CMBS noteholders, the goal of the servicer in monitoring third party payments is to ensure the protection of the properties serving as security for the mortgage loans. In the event that a mortgage borrower fails to make a timely third party payment or is in default under any of its third party agreements related to a secured property, the servicer can make or cause a property protection advance to be made in order to preserve the value of the secured property.

Property protection advances

A property protection advance is a mechanism by which the servicer or special servicer, as applicable, can fund amounts necessary for the protection of a property serving as security for the mortgage loans. If the servicer or special servicer becomes aware that a mortgage borrower has failed to make a third party payment, such as insurance premiums or rent due under a headlease, then the servicer or special servicer, as applicable, will first apply funds that are available in that mortgage borrower's accounts, if any, to make that payment. If those funds are insufficient, or, if the servicer or the special servicer does not have the authority to direct those funds, then under certain circumstances, the servicer or special servicer may make a property protection advance.

Prior to making any property protection advance, the servicer or the special servicer, as applicable, must be satisfied that the amount of the payment to fund the shortfall can be recovered from the mortgage borrower and/or secured property, and that making the property protection advance is in accordance with the servicing standard.

Depending on the terms of the servicing agreement, property protection advances can be made in one of two ways. The servicer or the special servicer, as applicable, can cause a drawing to be made under the securitisation transaction liquidity facility agreement. Alternatively, the servicer or special servicer, as applicable, may have the right (but not the obligation) to fund the payment to a third party from its own funds. The servicer or special servicer who advances the funds itself would be reimbursed, with interest, by the CMBS issuer on the next CMBS noteholder payment date. Not all securitisation transactions, however, authorise the servicer or special servicer to make a property protection advance from its own funds.

Enforcing loan sale agreements

When the originating lenders of the mortgage loans transfer those loans into the securitisation pool, they make certain representations and warranties in the respective loan sale agreements with regard to the mortgage loans and their underlying security. In the event that there is a breach of these representations or warranties, the servicer or special servicer is obligated to enforce the rights of the CMBS issuer under the relevant loan sale agreement. Those rights may include compelling the loan originator in question to re-purchase the deficient loan.

Administration of swaps

Most European CMBS issuances are floating rate notes, though many of the underlying loans are at a fixed rate. To address the discrepancy that may arise with respect to the payments due under these different benchmarks, the CMBS issuer will enter into a swap arrangement with a third party swap provider. The servicer is responsible for monitoring the swap relationship and ensuring that the swap will cover any gap between the fixed and the floating interest rates.[4] If the borrower pays a floating rate under their loans, they will usually be obliged to hedge and the servicer may monitor payment and loan level hedges.[5]

A second kind of funding discrepancy may need to be addressed in the securitisation deal if the floating rates that apply to the mortgage loans are calculated off a different benchmark to that of the CMBS notes. For example, all debt service payments on a particular mortgage loan may be calculated off EURIBOR as determined on a certain day each month, but the payments to the CMBS noteholders may be calculated off EURIBOR determined as of a different day. The role of the servicer in this situation is to monitor the swap that is acquired to cover the gap between the two benchmarks.

A third funding discrepancy may arise in pan-European deals where the underlying mortgage loans are denominated in one currency and the payments made by the CMBS issuer to the CMBS noteholders are in a different currency. Where there are numerous currencies, the CMBS issuer must ensure that despite any fluctuation those currencies experience, enough money is being paid to the CMBS issuer so that it may make payments owed to the CMBS noteholders.

Generally, the servicer must also liaise with the swap provider regarding any modification affecting a mortgage loan, such as a change in the loan amount, a restructuring, or an adjustment to an interest rate. To the extent that any such modification would impact any swap arrangement, the servicer must make certain that the swap is appropriately modified. Similarly, in the event that a swap provider or the CMBS issuer terminates a swap agreement during the term of the securitisation, the servicer is obligated to facilitate replacing the swap. Finally, if a borrower prepays a mortgage loan, or a mortgage loan is sold prior to the end of its term, the servicer is responsible for calculating any break costs payable under the relevant facility agreement, often including those break costs due with respect to any subordinated mortgage loans. The servicer will confirm those break costs with the swap provider and incorporate those costs into the redemption statement. Generally the servicer retains the obligations with regard to the swap provider, even when the mortgage loan becomes a specially serviced loan.

---

[4] For more detail on derivatives and the interest rate products available in CMBS deals, see Chs 6 and 7.
[5] See fn.4, above.

Loan redemption

In the event that a mortgage borrower seeks to prepay its mortgage loan, the servicer or special servicer, as applicable, will calculate the loan payoff amount, including any prepayment penalties or break costs due from the borrower, render a redemption statement and facilitate the remittance of those funds. After the mortgage borrower has paid in full all sums and satisfied all obligations under its mortgage loan documents, the servicer or the special servicer will co-ordinate the release of the security for the loan. After updating the loan file accordingly and transferring it to the appropriate recipient party, the obligations of the servicer and special servicer with respect to the redeemed loan cease.

Modifications, waivers and consents

In the event that a mortgage borrower seeks any kind of modification of the mortgage loan documents, a waiver of any obligation under the mortgage loan, or consent for any action for which the mortgage borrower must seek consent under its facility agreement (collectively, the "modifications"), the borrower must make its request to the servicer, or the special servicer if the mortgage loan is a specially serviced loan. As stated, the servicer or special servicer has the authority to effect these modifications because the various transaction parties, who otherwise would have to provide their consents, have delegated that power to the servicer and special servicer.

Modifications of performing mortgage loans

Some typical modifications that a mortgage borrower may request when it is performing under its mortgage loan documents include alteration of a loan covenant, obtaining a release of part of the property serving as security, or approving a restructuring of or sale of the interests in a mortgage borrower. When a mortgage borrower makes a request for any such modification to the servicer, the servicer must first evaluate, in accordance with the servicing standard, the request itself and the impact that it may have on the mortgage loan.

In some deals, the servicing agreement may obligate the servicer to obtain additional consents, such as from the operating advisor (see below), special servicer or a related subordinated lender, before agreeing to a requested modification. With respect to some significant modifications, such as a new borrower assuming an existing loan, the servicer may also be required to obtain rating agency confirmation from the rating agencies that the ratings of the CMBS notes will not be adversely affected by the modification.

Modifications of non-performing mortgage loans

Generally, the servicer will not be involved in modifications to non-performing mortgage loans as, in most cases, a non-performing mortgage loan will have been transferred to the special servicer (see below).

Modifications involving property managers

Under some mortgage loan documents, the mortgage borrower is required to obtain the consent of the lender before it may replace the property manager that it appointed to manage a mortgaged property. The servicer or special servicer, as applicable, may be prevented from giving consent to a change in property manager unless an acceptable replacement property manager has been appointed to take over immediately upon termination of the existing property manager. Where a property manager is the party seeking to terminate its appointment, the servicing agreement may direct the servicer or the special servicer, as applicable, to take reasonable action to prevent the property manager from terminating until an acceptable replacement has been identified and appointed.

Post-modification responsibilities

Following the granting of any modification, waiver or consent, the servicer, or special servicer, as applicable, must notify the CMBS issuer, who will notify the other relevant securitisation parties. This notice will include the details of the modification, its effective date and any costs and expenses to be charged to the mortgage borrower receiving the benefit of the modification. Further, the servicer or special servicer, as applicable, will update the relevant Loan File.

WHEN A LOAN BECOMES A SPECIALLY SERVICED LOAN

Special servicing transfer events

A number of events give rise to a transfer of a mortgage loan from the servicer to the special servicer. In such circumstances, the special servicer takes primary responsibility for servicing the mortgage loan and addressing the situation giving rise the to the special servicing transfer event.

The servicing agreement will expressly define special servicing transfer events. Common special servicing transfer events include:

(1) a payment default on a mortgage loan on its final maturity date where the date was not extended,

(2) a payment due by a mortgage borrower that is more than 30–60 days overdue,

(3) a mortgage borrower becoming the subject of any insolvency proceedings or other insolvency related events,

(4) the servicer, special servicer or security trustee, as the case may be, receiving notice of any enforcement action taken against the mortgaged property,

(5) any other material default by a mortgage borrower that is not cured to the satisfaction of the servicer within the applicable cure period, and

(6) an imminent default, not likely to be cured within 30 days, that, in the opinion of the servicer, would likely have a material adverse effect on the CMBS issuer or any subordinated lender (collectively, the "special servicing transfer events").

Once the servicer has determined that a special servicing transfer event has occurred, the servicer must provide written notice to the special servicer, the CMBS issuer and other relevant securitisation parties, which may include the operating advisor where one has been appointed by the controlling class of CMBS noteholders, as well as any subordinated lenders where the loan has been tranched into an AB Structure.[6]

Even though the obligations of the special servicer commence upon the occurrence of a special servicing transfer event, in many deals the servicer retains certain responsibilities, such as collecting and monitoring debt service and third party payments, administering the swaps and generating reports on behalf of the CMBS issuer.

Property valuation reports

Strategy

When a non-performing mortgage loan is transferred to the special servicer, the special servicer must determine the optimal strategy for maximising the value of the loan, which may include modifying the mortgage loan, accepting a discounted payment of the loan or enforcing the mortgage loan documents. In order to assist in the development of its strategy, the special servicer may obtain an updated valuation of the mortgaged property in

---

[6] See Ch. 8 for more detail.

order to ascertain the value of the distressed mortgage loan. Most servicing agreements oblige the special servicer to request a property valuation report within a certain period of time following a special servicing transfer event and provided that there is no recent valuation report. A recent property valuation report will assist the special servicer in determining what strategy to employ with respect to the mortgage loan. One of the most important responsibilities of the special servicer is to assess when a greater return will be gained on a non-performing loan by liquidating its related security, or restructuring the loan and keeping its related security in place.

Appraisal reduction

A secondary function of the property valuation report is to assist the special servicer in determining whether, as a result of a reduction in the value of property, it is unlikely to recover all monies outstanding on the loan and that there should be a corresponding reduction in the amount available in the liquidity facility to pay any shortfalls of interest to CMBS noteholders. This is referred to as the appraisal reduction and involves the application of a percentage determined by a formula specified in the servicing agreement where, if the outstanding principal and interest and unreimbursed property protection advances on the mortgage loan amount to more than 90 per cent of the latest value of the property, then the value attributed to the mortgage loan is reduced.

Control valuation events

As we saw in Ch. 8, AB Structures and the introduction of subordinated debt into the European CMBS structures has become increasingly popular, and in deals where a subordinate debt structure has been put in place and there is a subordinate interest not held by the CMBS issuer, an appraisal reduction may also be used to determine whether there is a "control valuation event." If the value of the property serving as collateral for the mortgage loan has decreased to such an extent that a subordinated lender is not likely to get a meaningful economic recovery on its investment, then a control valuation event has occurred. A common formula used in securitisation transactions to determine whether a control valuation event has occurred is when the outstanding balance of the subordinated loan minus the applicable value reduction amount is less than 25 per cent of the outstanding principal balance of the subordinated loan. The significance of this event is that after the control valuation event has occurred, a subordinated lender may lose its consent and/or consultation rights with respect to modifications to, or enforcement of, a mortgage loan.

Modifications of non-performing loans

If a mortgage borrower is not performing under its mortgage loan documents, and the special servicer has determined that a loan modification is the best approach to maximising value, then the special servicer may agree to restructure or modify the distressed loan. Typical economic modifications include a reduction in the amount of principal, a reduction in the interest rate, a change in the amortisation schedule, or the capitalisation of unpaid principal and interest. Prior to agreeing to such modifications, the servicing agreement may require the special servicer to consult with and/or obtain the consent of the operating advisor (discussed below), controlling class of CMBS noteholders (discussed below) or related subordinated lender if the mortgage loan has been tranched.

Corrected loans

A mortgage loan that is specially serviced becomes "corrected" when the situation causing it to be non-performing no longer exists. A typical definition of "corrected" in a servicing agreement is when:

(1) the facts giving rise to the initial special servicing transfer event have ceased to exist for a specified period, and

(2) the mortgage loan is not at risk of another special servicing transfer event.

The concept of what constitutes a corrected loan is deal-specific and may vary among securitisation transactions. Once a specially serviced mortgage loan has been corrected, the special servicer will notify the CMBS issuer, the servicer, and various other securitisation parties of the correction and transfer the loan file for that mortgage loan back to the servicer. It is at this point that the special servicer's obligations with respect to that mortgage loan cease, and the full obligations of the servicer resume.

Loan enforcement

Not all specially serviced mortgage loans will be corrected. For such non performing mortgage loans, the special servicer may determine that the optimal maximisation of value is through enforcement. In such circumstance, the CMBS issuer, acting through the special servicer, will commence enforcement proceedings against the mortgaged property, generally requiring the use of outside local counsel to facilitate the process.

Enforcement proceedings vary greatly across European countries as to matters such as timing and to priority payments. In addition, in deciding whether to pursue enforcement, the special servicer must consider the like-lihood of whether the mortgage borrower will initiate insolvency proceed-ings. Insolvency proceedings also vary from country to country and may significantly complicate and lengthen the enforcement process. The expense and length of an enforcement process may have a significant impact on the ultimate recovery of the CMBS noteholders with respect to a mortgage loan.

Mortgagee-in-possession provisions

Some servicing agreements include detailed provisions with regard to the management of mortgaged property after foreclosure or repossession by the mortgagee, whereas others do not address such management at all. For those servicing agreements that do have these provisions, they mostly per-tain to the creation of a special purpose vehicle to take ownership of the property and the requirement that certain environmental evaluations be conducted prior to foreclosure or repossession of the property. These pro-visions are unlikely to be relevant in relation to English property where foreclosure is seldom the best option.

CONTROLLING CLASS AND OPERATING ADVISORS

Many servicing agreements provide that the most subordinate class of CMBS noteholders is the "controlling class" and that it is therefore entitled to appoint an "operating advisor" or "controlling class representative" with whom the servicer and special servicer, as appropriate, is obliged to consult regarding certain decisions to be made with respect to the mortgage loans. Decisions that require consultation often include modifications to key terms of the loan documents, such as interest rate or maturity date; releases of a mortgage borrower from its obligations under the loan documents; approvals of material alterations to or environmental remediation of a mortgaged property; and decisions regarding enforcement of the mortgage loan documents.

When a decision requires consultation with the operating advisor or controlling class representative, the servicing agreement will usually provide for a designated number of days for the operating advisor or controlling class representative to review the facts underlying the decision and to con-sult with the servicer or special servicer. If the operating advisor or con-trolling class representative and servicer or special servicer fail to reach agreement about the decision within a timeframe of usually 30–45 days, or if the servicer or special servicer determines, in its own discretion and in accordance with the servicing standard, that action must be taken immediately. The servicing agreement wholly provides that the servicer or the special servicer may act without the consent of the operating advisor or controlling class representative.

Similarly, the servicing agreement will generally provide for an override, the so called "servicing standard override", if the operating advisor requests that either the servicer or special servicer take action that would violate the servicing standard. This latter situation may arise because the operating advisor is acting in its own best interest and, although in most situations what would be in the best interests of the most subordinate class of CMBS noteholders, would also be in the interests of all CMBS noteholders, some situations may arise where that is not the case. The servicer and the special servicer are obliged to act in the interests of all CMBS noteholders, and this "override" ensures that they may do that.

SERVICING FEES

As a general matter, all fees and reimbursements payable to the servicer and special servicer are incorporated into the distribution scheme of the securitisation transaction and paid in priority to the CMBS noteholders. The fees payable to the servicer, a quantifiable constant, are generally underwritten into the cash flow of the deal. However, variable and unpredictable fees and expenses, such as special servicing fees, reimbursement for expenses and property protection advances, and other charges are likely to diminish the return that the subordinated CMBS noteholders realise.

The servicer is generally entitled to a servicing fee calculated on the initial principal balance of each mortgage loan in the securitisation pool. The fees vary across deals, but are typically 0.05 to 0.10 per cent of the outstanding principal balance of each serviced mortgage loan. The servicer is entitled to its fees throughout the life of the deal, even during the time that a mortgage loan is specially serviced.

The special servicer is entitled to a special servicing fee for each of the mortgage loans that it specially services. The special servicing fee begins accruing the day that a mortgage loan becomes specially serviced and continues until the mortgage loan is deemed corrected. Special servicing fees vary, but a typical fee is 0.25 per cent of the outstanding principal balance of each mortgage loan being specially serviced.

The special servicer may also be entitled to other additional fees. The first is a "liquidation fee" payable to the special servicer from the net proceeds of any sale of a mortgage loan or related mortgaged property. Liquidation fees often are one per cent of the net proceeds from such a sale. The second is a "workout fee" payable to the special servicer for any specially serviced mortgage loan that becomes corrected. Workout fees are generally a percentage of each collection of interest and principal received on a corrected mortgage loan and are payable for so long as the loan continues to perform. The purpose of the fee structure for specially serviced loans is to incentivise the special servicer to seek correction or liquidation of a non-performing mortgage loan as quickly as possible.

PARTICIPATED DEBT AND SUBORDINATE LENDERS

Servicing participated loans

As we saw in Ch. 8, in securitisation transactions it has become increasingly common for loans to be tranched into both senior and junior or subordinate pieces. The junior or subordinate piece is usually held by outside investors and provides credit enhancement for the securitisation. In many senior and subordinated loan structures where the senior portion has been securitised, the servicer and special servicer often service on behalf of all lenders. In other circumstances, such as where the portions of the loans are *pari passu*, the servicer and special servicer may or may not service on behalf of all lenders. In the event that the servicer and special servicer are not servicing on behalf of all lenders, then the rights of the servicer and special servicer to act will be limited to exercising the CMBS issuer's rights, as detailed in the intercreditor agreement.

Pursuant to the terms of the participation arrangements with respect to a mortgage loan, subordinated lenders may be granted the "controlling class" rights with respect to the mortgage loan, which include the right to appoint an operating advisor that possesses rights with respect to the mortgage loan. Generally these rights will be extinguished upon the occurrence of a control valuation event.

Notice and cure rights

Depending on its level of sophistication, a subordinated lender may negotiate for various notice and cure rights in the event that the senior piece of the loan which is securitised becomes non-performing. For example, many servicing agreements provide that when a special servicing transfer event occurs, the servicer will provide notice to a subordinated lender, who will then have the opportunity to cure the default giving rise to the special servicing transfer event within a certain time period. Often that cure will require the payment of borrower debt service, and if the subordinated lender does so, then the loan will not become specially serviced.

Subordinated lender purchase options

In addition to the cure rights discussed above, in many deals, the subordinated lender may be granted an option to purchase the senior portion of the mortgage loan that has gone into default, a "purchase event of default". What constitutes a purchase event of default is specifically negotiated and defined in each securitisation transaction. Common purchase events of default include the same events that give rise to a special servicing transfer event.

Upon a purchase event of default, the servicing agreement obliges the servicer or special servicer to provide notice to the relevant subordinated lender. If the subordinated lender indicates its intent to purchase the senior portion of the mortgage loan, and the applicable intercreditor deed provides that the subordinated lender may do so, then the servicer or special servicer, as applicable, determines the price of the senior portion and the subordinated lender must make that payment on the next loan payment date. As we have seen, the intercreditor agreement will govern whether the subordinated lender has a finite amount of time or a certain number of payment periods within which to complete the purchase.

In conjunction with its purchase of the senior portion of the mortgage loan, the subordinated lender will generally also be responsible for the payment of out-of-pocket costs and expenses incurred by the servicer or special servicer, as applicable, in connection with their co-operation with the subordinated lender's right to purchase and calculation of the purchase price. During the period in which the subordinated lender is exercising its right to purchase the senior portion of the loan, the loan will not be deemed a specially serviced loan.

When a subordinated lender purchases the whole mortgage loan, that mortgage loan is effectively removed from the securitisation pool; the treatment is similar to a mortgage loan that a mortgage borrower is prepaying. The subordinated lender's purchase results in an accelerated paydown of the CMBS notes. One issue that the servicer, or more likely, the special servicer, must address is what it must include in the calculation of the purchase price. The intercreditor agreement may provide that the purchase price is calculated from the outstanding amounts of principal and interest on the mortgage loan for the senior piece only. In such a case, the purchase price, as provided in the intercreditor agreement, may not provide for the payment of securitisation expenses, such as interest on advances under the liquidity facility, and any property protection advances. Additionally, the intercreditor agreement may not provide for the payment of the fees due to the special servicer, such as the liquidation fee. In the event that there are unreimbursed securitisation expenses and special servicer fees, and their payment by the subordinated lender is not contemplated in the intercreditor agreement, there will be a shortfall to the CMBS noteholders, since those payments are remitted to the servicer and special servicer before any distribution is made to the CMBS noteholders.

Payment to the servicer and special servicer when a loan is participated

Where a mortgage loan has been tranched, the senior and junior lenders can, as a business matter, allocate among themselves how the servicer and special servicer are to be paid their fees and reimbursed for their costs and expenses. In most securitisation transactions, the arrangement between the lenders with respect to the servicing payment obligations is found in the intercreditor deed. Various arrangements exist, for example, the senior and junior lenders may make the payments pro rata, or they may all be paid by either the senior or the junior lender.

Clearly the servicer and the special servicer want to ensure that they will be paid regardless of which lender is obliged to pay them. In transactions where the responsibility to pay the servicer or special servicer is allocated to the subordinated lender, whether in whole or in part, the servicer and special servicer will want to ensure that they are not exposed to any risk of non-payment, particularly in circumstances where loan payments to the junior lender have been stopped. For example, if the subordinated lenders only make payment to the servicer and special servicer from their loan payments, then the servicer or special servicer is at risk of the loan payments received by the junior lender being insufficient to pay the fees of the servicer and special servicer. To protect themselves from such a risk, the servicer and special servicer may negotiate for a provision in the servicing agreement that requires the CMBS issuer to pay any such payment shortfall.

SUB-SERVICING

It is not uncommon for servicing agreements to provide that, under certain circumstances and in accordance with the servicing standard, the servicer and the special servicer may sub-contract some or all of their obligations. One fundamental prerequisite is that in no event may any such sub-contract result in a downgrade in the securitisation rating from any rating agency.

If a servicer or special servicer enters into a sub-servicing agreement, the servicer or special servicer, as applicable, will be liable for payment of all fees to the sub-servicer and remains liable under the servicing agreement for the actions (or omissions) of any sub-servicer. In the event that the sub-servicer breaches the performance of any of its obligations and the servicer or special servicer fails to remedy that breach, then that breach shall be attributed to the servicer or special servicer, as applicable, as a breach under the servicing agreement. Servicing agreements often have express restrictions on certain obligations which may not be delegated and some servicing agreements may provide that only the servicer may delegate to sub-servicers, but not the special servicer.

Any restriction on sub-contracting is separate from the ability of the servicer and special servicer to retain third party service providers, such as accountants, solicitors, property valuers, surveyors and environmental consultants. The servicer and special servicer are entitled to reimbursement for any payments made to such third party service providers.

ENFORCEMENT OF THE CMBS NOTES

A default at the deal level, resulting in enforcement of CMBS notes, might arise where a severe downturn has resulted in significant losses across multiple loans in the securitisation pool. In such a circumstance, the note trustee, pursuant to the relevant transaction documents, has the authority to enforce the CMBS noteholders' security interest in the underlying mortgage loans, which may result in the liquidation of those mortgage loans. Some servicing agreements provide that the note trustee must consult with the servicer and special servicer before taking any CMBS note enforcement action. In contrast, some servicing agreements provide that when the CMBS notes are in default, the note trustee may replace the servicer and/or the special servicer, or may provide that upon a CMBS note default, the appointment of the servicer and special servicer is automatically terminated. Thus, there is no clear consensus on the role of the servicer and special servicer in a CMBS note enforcement situation.

TERMINATION OF THE SERVICER AND SPECIAL SERVICER

Termination due to default

The CMBS issuer may terminate the appointment of the servicer or special servicer if any one of a number of default situations arise (each a "servicer event of default"). Common servicer events of default include, but are not limited to:

- failure to procure the transfer of funds into the collection account in the manner proscribed in the servicing agreement;

- breach of any obligation under the servicing agreement or breach of any representation or warranty;

- insolvency of the servicer or special servicer; or

- any rating agency gives notice that the continued appointment of the servicer or special servicer, as applicable, will result in an adverse rating event.

Voluntary termination

The servicer or special servicer, as applicable, may terminate its appointment although it must generally provide significant advance written notice to the CMBS issuer and the other securitisation parties in order to provide sufficient time for a replacement to be identified and retained. It is usual that no termination shall take effect until a successor servicer or special servicer, as the case may be, has been appointed, the rating agencies have confirmed that such appointment will not result in an adverse rating event, and the successor servicer or special servicer, as the case may be, has entered into a servicing agreement on substantially the same terms and conditions as the initial servicing agreement.

Termination by controlling class or by extraordinary resolution

In many deals, the servicing agreement will permit the controlling class to terminate the appointment of a special servicer. In those and other deals, the servicing agreement may provide that all classes of CMBS noteholders must pass an extraordinary resolution by a majority vote in order to effect the termination of the special servicer's appointment. The threshold that must be met for an extraordinary resolution to be passed will be established in the trust deed and will vary from deal-to-deal.

Payment upon termination

The terminated servicer or special servicer is entitled to receive all fees and other monies accrued up to the date of termination, and will not be entitled to any further compensation with respect of the servicing fee or special servicing fee. However, if the terminated special servicer is entitled to a workout fee, such terminated special servicer shall continue to receive the workout fee until the relevant loan again becomes a specially serviced loan, at which point the entitlement of the terminated special servicer shall cease permanently.

219

MISCELLANEOUS

Insurance

The servicer and the special servicer generally must keep in place a policy covering corporate malfeasance. The servicer and special servicer may fulfil this obligation by purchasing insurance policies, either directly or through an affiliate of the servicer or special servicer if the policy extends to the servicer or special servicer. The servicer and special servicer may also self-insure provided they have a satisfactory credit rating, typically meaning that they are rated at least "A" by Standard & Poor's, "A1" by Moody's and "A" by Fitch.[7]

Indemnification of servicer and special servicer

The CMBS issuer and any other transaction parties remain liable for their own actions or inactions, despite the delegation of any authority to the servicer or special servicer. Similarly, the servicer's and special servicer's participation in the servicing agreement does not constitute a guarantee or similar obligation for any other aforementioned parties, including the mortgage borrowers.

The CMBS issuer is solely liable for the failure to make any payment due under the CMBS notes, unless such failure is the direct result of a failure by the servicer or special servicer. The CMBS issuer should indemnify the servicer or the special servicer, as applicable, against any liabilities that the servicer or special servicer may have incurred in connection with the servicing agreement or as a direct result of the performance of their obligations under it. Conversely, the servicer and the special servicer should have the right under the servicing agreement to refrain from taking any action as a result of which they may incur liability unless they are satisfactorily indemnified by the CMBS issuer.

However, where the servicer's or special servicer's negligence, wilful default, dishonesty or fraud causes the CMBS issuer's failure to pay, then the servicer or special servicer, as appropriate, will be liable and must indemnify the CMBS issuer.

---

[7] The role of insurance in CMBS is examined in Ch. 22.

CONCLUSION

Third party servicing is on the rise as the European CMBS market continues to develop. Both the number of servicers and special servicers, as well as the number of jurisdictions involved in CMBS transactions are expected to increase as the market evolves. This dynamic environment requires that servicers and special servicers adjust to constant change. For example, investors are demanding more detailed and sophisticated reporting requirements, which require increased technological infrastructure and additional personnel. Another potential structural change is whether servicers can or should be securitisation level liquidity providers by advancing loan payment shortfalls as well as property protection payments. While current European deals usually have separate liquidity providers, deals in the United States rely upon the servicer to provide this function. At least some European market participants have expressed an interest in introducing this concept in European deals, however, at least one securitisation transaction has utilised an affiliate of the servicer to fund property protection and loan payment shortfall advances.

Additionally, varying legal and regulatory climates across countries require servicers and special servicers to address pan-European differences. Cross-border CMBS transactions require servicers and special servicers to develop strategies to address localised issues, such as local markets, local legal practices, and language and cultural differences.

These demands to adjust to constant change are at odds with increasing price compression. While bidding competitions are driving down servicing fees, the European CMBS market is requiring servicers and special servicers to provide more detail, possess more localised knowledge, and have more expertise. This pressure on fees may result in a move towards standardisation which would be quite challenging given the diversity of the pan-European CMBS market. Unlike in the United States, a standardised platform for servicing does not currently exist.

Servicing in the European CMBS market is far from being settled. Servicers and special services are required to continue to respond to evolving requirements of investors, and to service increasingly sophisticated and diverse transactions.

CHAPTER ELEVEN

COMMERCIAL REAL ESTATE CDOs: THE US AND EUROPEAN MARKETS

John Gordon, Partner
John Timperio, Partner
Todd Stillerman, Partner
James A. Spencer, Associate
Dechert LLP

INTRODUCTION

A collateralised debt obligation ("CDO") is a debt security backed by a portfolio of debt instruments held by the issuer of the CDO ("CDO issuer") and charged to secure the CDO issuer's obligations to holders of the CDO securities ("CDO investors"). CDOs are backed by an expanding variety of underlying debt instruments, including bank loans (in the case of CLOs), bonds (in the case of CBOs), asset backed securities (in the case of CDOs of ABS), credit derivatives (in the case of synthetic CDOs) and other credit assets.

Since 1999, a new form of CDO, where the assets backing the debt issuance derive from the commercial real estate sector, emerged as an alternative source of funding for the US real estate lending market. Such transactions are known as commercial real estate collateralised debt obligations ("CRE CDOs"). The US witnessed a surge in issuance of CRE CDOs during 2005 which has continued during the early part of 2006.[1]

On the back of a burgeoning European CMBS market, interest in the prospects for CRE CDOs in Europe is also on the rise. Yet despite increasing arranger and investor interest and a number of market partici-

---

[1] US CRE CDO issuance increased by 49 per cent in 2005 to $12.4 billion from $6.4 billion in 2004.

pants in various stages of warehousing portfolios with a view to a CDO take-out, and an increasing number of CDOs allowing portfolios containing commercial real estate debt and securities, at the time of writing the European market has yet to see its first pure CRE CDO although deals are beginning to come to the market.

PART 1: THE US MARKET

CRE CDOs permit lenders to access capital with an average cost of funds that is relatively low when compared to traditional warehouse or repurchase financing and without the associated mark-to-market risk. In addition, CRE CDOs have been used to finance collateral types that are not susceptible securitisation-to-securitisation in traditional real estate vehicles, such as mezzanine debt and preferred equity. From the investor's perspective, CRE CDOs have permitted investors who have typically not invested in subordinate real estate debt to access this asset class without the need to develop the sophisticated infrastructure and employing the personnel necessary to directly invest in these assets.

In the late 1990s, the basic CDO technology that had been developed to repackage high-yield bonds and investment grade bank loans was adapted to commercial real estate finance with the offering of the first CRE CDO. These CRE CDOs were generally backed by pools of fixed-rate, real estate related securities. These early static structures permitted limited sales of the underlying collateral only in the event of changes in credit quality, determined by reference to some objective standard and not within the discretion of the collateral manager. Monitoring credit quality and disposing of assets was undertaken by a collateral manager ("collateral manager") with very limited discretion in disposing of assets and no discretion to acquire replacement assets. Disposition proceeds from credit risk assets and returns on principal were generally allocated to pay down the CDO securities. However, since 2004 two fundamental changes have occurred in the US CRE CDO market; an expanding collateral base and changes in style of collateral management.

Expanding collateral base

The nature and variety of the underlying collateral base expanded in response to various factors, including structural constraints on other types of real estate financing and increasing investor and marketplace sophistication. The initial CRE CDOs were generally backed by pools of real estate related securities, primarily commercial mortgage backed securities, REIT debt or some combination of the two. In 2004, the CRE CDO collateral base began to expand to include interests in single mortgage loans in the form of B loans and rake bonds, and the collateral base continues to expand. Although securities continue to form a part of the collateral base for some CRE CDOs, the prevalence of real estate related securities has declined in favour of direct interests in loans, including whole loans, B loans, mezzanine loans, rake bonds, preferred equity interests, and credit tenant leases. In addition, the development of standard-form documentation for credit derivatives based on asset-backed securities and other market developments has resulted in an increasing use of credit derivatives as collateral for CRE CDOs.

Role of manager

The role of the collateral manager in the typical CRE CDO has changed dramatically and continues to evolve in response to the expanding collateral base and other factors. In a "managed CRE CDO", the collateral manager has greater discretion to sell collateral assets for credit-related and other reasons and the ability to reinvest the proceeds from such sales and from principal repayments within relatively flexible parameters. The ability to replace assets that have been sold, have matured or have been prepaid permits the inclusion of assets that are subject to prepayment or that have relatively short remaining terms, because it allows the fixed transaction costs associated with the formation and operation of the CRE CDO to be amortised over a longer period. In this way, the expansion of the permitted collateral types to include whole loans and other direct interests in loans and the increased role of the collateral manager have complemented one another.

These changes in the nature of the collateral and the role of the collateral manager were possible only in conjunction with changes in the CRE CDO investor base. The first, static CRE CDOs were purchased primarily by investors familiar with the static transactions of the CMBS market. The emergence of managed CRE CDOs was accompanied by an influx of investors who had not been traditional CMBS buyers, including some non-real estate CDO and CLO investors. These investors exhibited a greater willingness than traditional CMBS investors to give the collateral manager trading and reinvestment discretion in light of the benefits of being able to access new asset classes.

Structure and operation of managed CRE CDOs

Basic structure

CRE CDOs are similar in structure to those utilised in CMBS transactions and other asset securitisation transactions. A pool of underlying collateral interests (the "collateral interests") are purchased by the CDO issuer from one or more asset sellers ("asset seller"). The CDO issuer funds the purchase through an offering of various classes of stated return notes ("CDO notes") and a class of preferred equity securities or income notes ("CDO equity" and, together with the CDO notes, "CDO securities"). There may be multiple asset sellers to any one CRE CDO, and often an asset seller is a sponsor of the CDO or may be an affiliate of the collateral manager. The collateral interests may be purchased by a warehousing vehicle or depositor (the "depositor") who is typically a newly-formed, special purpose, bankruptcy-remote, US corporation or limited liability company who in turn conveys the collateral interests to the CDO issuer at the closing date of the transaction. Alternatively, the asset seller may sell the collateral interests directly to the CDO issuer. In both cases, the sale of the collateral interests is made in accordance with a purchase agreement which includes the terms of the sale, representations and warranties of the asset seller with respect to itself and the collateral interests and remedies against the asset seller for breach of any of these representations or warranties. These remedies will usually include a repurchase obligation on behalf of the asset seller in the event of a breach that is not susceptible of cure.

The CDO issuer is typically a newly-formed exempted company incorporated with limited liability under the laws of the Cayman Islands. The CDO issuer's constituent documents and the CDO transaction documents will typically impose single purpose covenants on the CDO issuer similar to the constraints imposed on other securitisation vehicles. There may also be a US entity that acts as co-issuer (the "co-issuer") with respect to, and is jointly obligated for the investment-grade classes of CDO notes. The presence of the co-issuer permits certain institutional investors (primarily insurance companies) that are not authorised to purchase foreign bonds to invest in the co-issued CDO notes.

The collateral interests are charged in favour of a trustee ("trustee") for the noteholders and other secured parties to secure the obligations in respect of the CDO notes pursuant to a trust deed. The trust deed and the conditions of the notes scheduled thereto provides for, among other things, the priority of payments and distributions on the CDO securities, the relative rights among the CDO securities, covenants, representations and warranties of the issuer and co-issuer (if any) and the general conditions precedent for issuance of the CDO notes. In addition, the trust deed sets out the duties and liabilities of the trustee, the events of default and the criteria for ramp-up and reinvestment of proceeds and any remedies upon the occurrence of an event of default. The trustee's role is distinct from the role of the collateral manger. The trustee administers the trust performing such functions as making payments and enforcing remedies, while the collateral manager monitors the asset pool and reinvests principal proceeds and disposition proceeds according to stated reinvestment criteria. The collateral manager's rights and obligations are contained in a separate collateral management agreement between the collateral manager, the CDO issuer and the trustee.

In addition to the collateral manager, transactions which include whole loans, mezzanine loans or other assets which are not securities will require the involvement of an experienced loan servicer (the "servicer") to perform servicing functions similar to those required in connection with a traditional commercial mortgage securitisation.

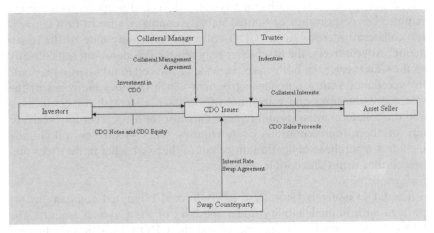

Figure 1: Typical CRE CDO structure.

Capital structure and cash flows

A typical CRE CDO capital structure includes investment-grade CDO notes, sub-investment grade CDO notes and CDO equity. The relative size and subordination levels of each class of CDO notes is determined in consultation with the rating agencies rating the transaction and vary based upon the nature and quality of the collateral interests. Although not required, the CDO equity and/or the lowest-rated CDO notes are typically held in whole or in part by the collateral manager, the sponsor or their affiliates. This provides investors additional assurance that the collateral manager and/or the sponsor have an economic interest in the performance of the deal.

The two or three highest-rated classes of CDO notes typically do not permit deferral of interest payments and will be rated by the rating agencies on the basis of timely payment of interest rather than ultimate payment of interest. Each of the other classes of CDO notes permit the deferral or capitalisation of accrued interest in the event there is insufficient cash flow to pay accrued interest on any payment date. Deferrable interest obligations are sometimes referred to as "payment in kind" or "PIK" instruments. In rating the deferrable interest CDO notes, the rating agencies focus on the likelihood of ultimate payment of interest and repayment of principal.

Most CRE CDO capital structures provide for sequential payment of interest and sequential paydown of principal on a separate basis. Generally, interest proceeds from the collateral interests are used to pay current interest on the CDO notes sequentially to the extent of available interest proceeds. During the reinvestment period (described in more detail below), principal proceeds are generally reinvested in replacement collateral interests and, after the reinvestment period, are generally applied to pay down the principal of the CDO notes on a sequential basis. In addition, CRE CDOs typically include interest coverage and principal value coverage tests which may divert interest proceeds or principal proceeds to the early paydown of principal in the event the cash flows or principal value of the collateral interests deteriorate below specified thresholds.

The interest coverage tests are used to measure, as of a given determination date, whether the aggregate interest collections from the pool of collateral interests equals or exceeds specified interest coverage requirements for specified classes of CDO notes. The principal value coverage tests (usually referred to as over-collateralisation tests) are used to measure as of a given determination date, whether the aggregate principal balance of the pool of collateral interests equals or exceeds specified principal value requirements for specified classes of CDO notes.

Figure 2, below, illustrates a typical CRE CDO capital structure and the cash flows within the deal.

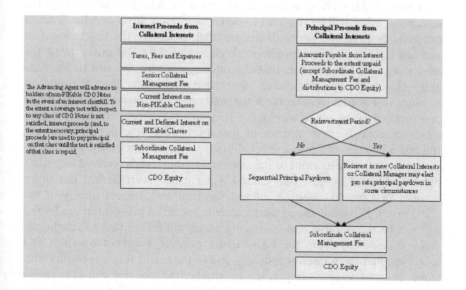

Figure 2: Capital structure and cash flows.

Liquidity advances

For each class of CDO notes that does not permit deferral of interest, an advancing agent (the "advancing agent") will be required to advance scheduled interest payments to the holders of the non-deferrable classes to the extent of any shortfall in the amounts received pursuant to the collateral interests. The advancing agent is typically an affiliate of the sponsor group of the CRE CDO and an affiliate of the collateral manager, asset seller or the holder of the CDO equity. The advancing agent's role is to provide liquidity to the non-deferrable classes and not to provide credit support. The advancing agent is entitled to reimbursement as soon as the applicable shortfall is recovered by the CDO issuer and, if the advancing agent determines that an advance will not be recoverable, the advancing agent is entitled to immediate reimbursement from the CDO issuer. A CRE CDO that includes only CMBS bonds or other assets which already provide for asset-level advancing would not require an advancing agent since under the pooling and servicing agreement the CMBS master servicer would be required to make advances on the loans that underlie the CMBS bonds. As the asset base for CRE CDOs has become more and more diversified and the number of direct interests in loans has increased, the rating agencies have increasingly required advancing agents. Interest advancing is necessary when there are whole loans, mezzanine loans, or similar assets for which an existing servicer or other party is not obligated to make advances.

In most CRE CDOs, as long as no event of default is continuing, the advancing agent will be required to make an interest advance when interest proceeds or principal proceeds are insufficient to pay the full amount of accrued interest on the non-deferrable classes of the CDO notes unless the advancing agent determines that the interest advance will not be recoverable. Generally, the advancing agent may determine that the interest advance will not be recoverable if the amount of the interest advance made or proposed to be made would not be recoverable from subsequent payments or collections in respect of the entire pool of collateral interests. Interest advances generally are reimbursed to the advancing agent together with interest on the amount of the advance from proceeds received in respect of the collateral interest that caused a particular shortfall but not in an amount that would cause an interest shortfall with respect to any of the CDO notes. If the advancing agent determines that a prior interest advance will not be recoverable, the advancing agent will be entitled to reimbursement immediately from the CDO issuer prior to payment on the CDO securities, first from interest proceeds and to the extent they are insufficient, from principal proceeds, regardless of whether the recovery would cause an interest shortfall with respect to any of the CDO notes. The rating agencies impose certain ratings criteria with respect to the advancing agent and typically require a back-up advancing agent. The trustee typically serves as the back-up advancing agent.

Ramp up period

Although some CRE CDOs are fully invested as of their closing date, meaning the pool of collateral interests purchased on the closing date fully invests the proceeds from the offering of the CDO securities, many CRE CDOs are closed prior to a full pool of collateral interests being identified. In these circumstances, the collateral manager is typically required to invest the remaining proceeds of the offering over a period of six to nine months. This period is referred to as the "ramp up period". The ramp up period permits the sponsor to size the CRE CDO efficiently without having to identify a full complement of collateral interests for purchase at closing. CRE CDOs with ramp up periods are typically between 75–80 per cent invested on the closing date of the offering. During the ramp up period, the collateral quality standards described below (such as, geographic concentration) are typically relaxed as long as the pool satisfies the standards by the end of the ramp up period. During the ramp up period, the excess proceeds are deposited into an eligible account at closing and designated specifically for the purchase of additional collateral interests during the ramp up period. Following the ramp up period, the rating agencies will provide confirmation that the target pool size has been met and that the assets comply with the applicable collateral quality standards. If these requirements are not met at the end of the ramp up period, the CDO issuer will de-lever by redeeming bonds on a sequential basis until the rating agencies confirm the required ratings on the CDO notes.

Reinvestment period

The distinctive feature of managed CRE CDOs is the ability of the collateral manager to reinvest principal proceeds from the sale, prepayment or maturity of the collateral interest during a specified period (the "reinvestment period"). The reinvestment Period is typically four to five years. Subject to the interest and principal coverage tests described above, the reinvestment period permits the collateral manager to maintain the size of the transaction (and, therefore, the relative funding cost) for a specified period of time. The ability to reinvest and maintain the size of the transaction for a set period permits the efficient use of the CRE CDO as a funding vehicle for assets which are subject to prepayment or have relatively short remaining terms.

During the reinvestment period, as long as the reinvestment criteria are met and the interest and principal coverage ratios are not such that funds are diverted to pay down principal, the collateral manager may reinvest principal collections from the collateral interests including, scheduled, unscheduled and sale proceeds rather than using such collections for payment on the CDO notes. The conditions that must be satisfied to permit the collateral manager to reinvest principal proceeds include the absence of an event of default and the collateral manager's determination that further reinvestment of principal proceeds would not be impractical or no longer beneficial to the CDO notes. In addition, all eligibility criteria and collateral quality standards must be satisfied in connection with the proposed acquisition. The eligibility criteria and collateral quality standards are typically quite detailed and heavily negotiated with the rating agencies. Figure 3, below, describes a typical set of eligibility requirements and collateral quality standards for a CRE CDO holding a diverse mix of collateral interests.

Once the reinvestment period has expired, typically four to five years from the closing date, the collateral manager's discretion to dispose of assets and the ability to reinvest principal proceeds are typically much more limited than during the reinvestment period. Typically, the collateral manager will not have any discretionary trading authority but may be permitted to sell "credit risk collateral interests" and "defaulted collateral interests" as described, below. The collateral manager typically will not be permitted to reinvest principal proceeds except in very limited circumstances. The reinvestment criteria once again must be satisfied for the collateral manager to make these reinvestments, including satisfaction of the coverage tests and eligibility requirements and collateral quality standards.

Most CRE CDOs permit the collateral manager to sell a "credit risk collateral interest" or a "defaulted collateral interest" and reinvest the proceeds with fewer constraints than those imposed on other reinvestments. A "credit risk collateral interest" is typically defined as any collateral interest which in the collateral manager's reasonable judgment has a significant risk of declining in credit quality or price unrelated to general market conditions prevailing at the time and with the passage of time or is likely to become a defaulted security. This assessment gives the collateral manager substantial discretion to make such a determination. A "defaulted collateral interest" is a collateral interest that has experienced a payment default, a material non-payment default, or in the case of rated collateral, a downgrade of such collateral has occurred. Although the collateral manager is typically permitted to sell a credit risk collateral interest or a defaulted collateral interest at any time (during or after the reinvestment period), the reinvestment of proceeds from these sales will generally be subject to various constraints required by the rating agencies, including requirements as to the rating, term and asset type of the asset in which the proceeds are reinvested.

Collateral requirements:
- Loan, preferred equity interest, security or derivative instrument related to commercial real estate.
- Borrower or issuer organised under US law or other select jurisdictions.
- Instrument must pay periodically and no less than semi-annually.
- Generally, may not require future advances by the holder.
- Maturity dates must generally be prior to maturity of CDO notes though some deals permit a specified percentage of long-dated collateral interests.
- Generally no cross-defaults or cross-collateralisation with loans not include in the pool.
- No "principal only" or "interest only" instruments unless approved by the rating agencies.
- Assets other than securities must generally be subject to CMBS-style servicing regime.

Pool requirements:
- Geographic concentration limitations (e.g. no more than 25 per cent of collateral interests in any single state).
- Borrower and property concentration limitations (e.g. no more than 15 per cent of collateral interests issued by a single obligor or secured by a single property.
- Property type limitations (e.g. no more than 35 per cent of collateral interests secured by retail properties).
- Limitations on interest rate risk (e.g. no more than 5 per cent of unhedged, fixed rate collateral interests).
- Minimum weighted average coupon to ensure sufficient liquidity to cover debt service on CDO notes.
- Maximum weighted average life to ensure sufficient liquidity to repay principal on CDO notes at maturity.
- Required ratings distributions to prevent credit "barbelling".

The requirements and limitations outlined above are meant to be illustrative of the risks typically addressed and are not exhaustive. In addition, each transaction is typically subject to various proprietary tests developed by the rating agencies to facilitate their monitoring of the ratings on the CDO notes.

Figure 3: Typical collateral and pool requirements.

In addition, an increasing number of CRE CDOs today allow for discretionary trading during the reinvestment period up to a specified level (for example, 15 per cent of the aggregate collateral balance in any one year and 25 per cent over the entire reinvestment period), but still limit reinvestment outside of the reinvestment period to collateral interests which are "credit risk collateral interests" or "defaulted collateral interests". Typically, discretionary trades are permitted only if in the collateral manager's judgement, the proceeds from the sale can be reinvested in substitute collateral interests within a certain period of time and the aggregate par amount of the substitute collateral interests will be at least 100 per cent of the par amount of the collateral interest sold. The discretionary trading authority is particularly important in transactions that contain loans secured by transitional or non-stabilised properties, because it permits the collateral manager to manage the CRE CDOs balance sheet in response to changing market conditions prior to any impact on the credit quality of the portfolio. For example, in the event of macroeconomic changes which disproportionately impact a particular real estate sector (such as multifamily or condominium properties), the collateral manager could use the discretionary trading authority to reduce the CRE CDOs exposure to the sector on an accelerated basis even if the particular loans held by the CRE CDO have not experienced any change in credit quality.

Collateral management and asset servicing

The collateral manager monitors and manages the pool of collateral interests securing the CDO notes pursuant to the terms of the trust deed, the collateral management agreement and possibly other transaction documents. The collateral management agreement provides for, among other things, the services to be performed by the collateral manger, the standard of care to be applied with respect to these duties, the representations and warranties of the collateral manager as well as the issuer, the fees to be paid to the collateral manager and the removal and appointment of a successor collateral manager.

In order to align the collateral manager's interests with those of the holders of the CDO notes, the collateral management fee is typically bifurcated into a senior fee and a subordinate fee. The senior fee is payable from the CDO issuer's cash flow prior to payments owing on the CDO notes and the junior fee is payable from the CDO issuer's remaining cash flow after payments owing on the CDO notes. Although collateral management fees vary from deal to deal, a typical range is 10 to 20 basis points on the aggregate collateral balance for the senior fee and 15 to 25 basis points on the aggregate collateral balance for the subordinate fee.

In addition to asset disposition and acquisition, the collateral manager will be involved in loan administration, workouts and resolutions and the management and disposition of real estate owned through enforcement action (REO). These roles will likely overlap with the roles of the servicer and, in transactions with a robust servicing function, much of the day-to-day administration will be delegated to the servicer. Generally among the responsibilities of the servicer, is any day-to-day interaction with the underlying borrowers, the timely collection of monthly payments, handling default situations and making servicing advances. Services preformed by the servicer and any special servicer will vary from one transaction to another depending on the nature of the collateral interests and the role of the collateral manager.

The servicer will be entitled to certain fees, including but not limited to a fixed servicing fee, late fees, defaulted interest, extension fees, prepayment fees and partial release fees. The servicer may also in some instances receive a fee for serviced loans that return to performing status, if the asset remains performing for some set period of time. The servicer may be removed if a rating agency has qualified, downgraded or withdrawn its rating for one or more classes of notes and in so doing, cited servicing concerns as the sole or material factor for the rating action. The servicer may also be subject to termination by the collateral manager.

Amortisation and redemption of CDO notes

If the collateral manager is unable to reinvest principal proceeds due to market conditions or other factors, the unused principal proceeds will be used to redeem a portion of the CDO notes. This is typically referred to as a "special amortisation". If certain rating agency requirements related to interest and principal coverage for the more senior CDO notes are satisfied at the time of the special amortisation, all classes of CDO notes will be redeemed on a pro rata basis. If these requirements are not satisfied (i.e. there is a relatively higher risk that the more senior classes will not ultimately be repaid), then the unused principal proceeds will be used to redeem a portion of the CDO notes on a sequential basis. The ability to redeem the CDO notes on a pro rata basis is important to the efficiency of the deal, because a disproportionate paydown of the most senior notes would cause the weighted average spread to increase making the CRE CDO less attractive as a funding vehicle. A special amortisation is typically the only time that the CDO notes are permitted to be redeemed other than on a sequential basis.

The CDO notes will generally be subject to mandatory redemption

- if any coverage test is not satisfied to the extent necessary for the CRE CDO to be back in compliance with the coverage tests, or
- in whole, upon the occurrence of certain adverse tax events.

In addition, the CDO notes may be subject to redemption at the option of the collateral manager or holder of the CDO equity, in whole but not in part,

- after the expiration of a stated lockout period,
- upon the occurrence of certain adverse accounting events or deter-

minations requiring the consolidation of the CDO issuer with the collateral manager, an asset seller or another third party, and

- in order to effect a "clean-up call", which is typically permitted once the principal balance of the CDO notes has been reduced to 10 per cent of their balance on the closing date of the offering.

The collateral manager is only permitted to effect an optional redemption on a distribution date and only if the sum of the sales proceeds of all the collateral interests and any other amounts available to pay the redemption prices is at least equal to the aggregate redemption price (outstanding principal balance and accrued and unpaid interest) with respect to all outstanding CDO notes.

PART 2: THE EUROPEAN MARKET

Introduction

At this time of writing, there have been no CDOs in the European market consisting solely of commercial real estate assets (whether CMBS, whole loans, or B loans). However, as indicated in the introduction to this chapter, there have been a number of European CDOs with large portfolios of CMBS securities as well as CDOs with small buckets for commercial real estate loans.

As the European CMBS market has taken off since 2004, there has been an increasing amount of interest in replicating the successful development to date of the US CRE CDO market, both in terms of using rated CMBS assets in CDOs and also in terms of using commercial real estate loans and subordinated tranches (B loans) carved out of whole loans, the senior element of which are securitised into CMBS transactions.

At the time of writing, the rating agencies are in discussions with a number of arrangers which are in the process of structuring CRE CDOs in Europe. It is expected that a number of such deals will close by the end of 2006, however it is not anticipated that any deals in the near future will be backed solely by a portfolio of commercial real estate loans (rather than CMBS due to the lack of such assets in the secondary market). No criteria pieces or rating methodologies for European CRE CDOs have yet been finalised but these are in the course of preparation, and are likely to be available by the time this book is published. The development of the European market is anticipated to mirror the rapid development of the CMBS sector in Europe; as more of the commercial real estate sector becomes securitised there will be more assets available to be included in CRE CDOs.

European CDOs—some differences from the US

European CDOs are fundamentally very similar to US CDOs, and the same basic methodologies apply for the analysis of such transactions. However, there are certain parameters and structural elements which frequently differ from the US model.

Issuers

The issuers will be newly formed, special purpose, bankruptcy remote companies incorporated with limited liability, most likely under the laws of Ireland, the Netherlands or Luxembourg. For transactions where some of the senior liabilities are placed into the US market, a co-issuer structure may be used as in US transactions. From a European collateral manager perspective it is important to ensure that the collateral manager acts solely for the issuer and not the US co-issuer to minimise US regulatory issues for the manager.

Split of responsibilities

The split of responsibilities within a transaction tends to differ between European and US CDO transactions. Much of the operational role which is performed by the trustee in US transactions is carried out by a collateral administrator in European transactions, frequently an affiliate of the trustee, whereas the trustee's role is limited to actual operation of the trust and representation of noteholder interests. However, given that the US template has both collateral manager and servicer/special servicer roles, the exact split and responsibilities in European CRE CDOs remains to be seen.

Redemption provisions

Clean-up calls are not that common in European CDOs of ABS, however, subordinated noteholders are frequently given the option to call transactions after the end of a non-call period, provided that the classes of notes ranking senior to the subordinated noteholders can be redeemed in full.

"Equity" format

The most junior class of securities sold will be a subordinated note designed to be paid the residual from the transaction rather than the preferred equity issued in US transactions.

Tax

A number of other structural difference between European and US transactions are driven by the need to comply with divergent tax legislation. These are outside the scope of this chapter.

Collateral: the growth of European CMBS and B loan origination

In Europe, the central problem hindering the development of an active CRE CDO market historically has been the lack of assets (both in terms of volume and diversity) that could realistically form the portfolio of a pure CRE CDO. While the market has seen a number of CDOs allowing significant exposure to CMBS as well as CDOs with small commercial real estate loan buckets, no transaction to date has been completely focused on the real estate sector.

The European CMBS market changed dramatically in 2004 when spreads tightened considerably. As a result there has been a significantly increased interest in the market both from property-rich entities looking to finance their portfolios, and from investment banks looking for product.

Since 2004 there has been a sharp rise in the issuance of CMBS transactions where arrangers have bifurcated whole loans, putting senior pieces or A loans into CMBS transactions in order to get all proceeds at investment grade and minimise subordination levels. The drivers to bifurcate CRE loans are discussed in Ch. 8 but in summary derive from a desire to be able to lend more to underlying borrowers while simultaneously achieving a lower all-in cost of funds on a refinance by way of securitisation.

The increased interest in the European CMBS market from investors at the senior level has been coupled with the development in Europe of a significant knowledgeable investor base at the subordinated level due, at least in part, to the entry into the market of specialist B loan investors, most of whom have affiliates with significant experience buying whole loans or B loans in the US market (where they or affiliates may also act as servicers or special servicers). These investors are developing the necessary skill sets to enable them to underwrite subordinated commercial real estate loans in Europe and so are prepared to buy the increased amount of B loans generated by the market. Such investors are more likely to be comfortable with the credit backing the B loan and prepared to accept the increased risk of holding a subordinated piece of paper for the increased yield it offers. In addition, over the past few years, as interest rates have tightened, a risk premium has been available to investors in this relatively complex asset class which has resulted in increasing investor appetite for B loan paper. One result of this is that ticket sizes have on average remained relatively small and there is substantial competition from specialist investors for allocations in each new transaction.

The attraction of the nascent CRE CDO market for these specialist investors is the ability to refinance their existing holdings of CRE loans on a term basis. The investors would probably always be in the market holding these assets in any event. The CMBS conduit model generates B loans for these investors, the B loans offer a yield pick up which makes them attractive. The CDO market potentially offers a take out once a (relatively) diversified pool of assets has been assembled. The development of the CRE CDO market is potentially restricted by both insufficient volume of assets and insufficiently diverse assets (which prevents the benefits of CDO methodology being fully applicable to transactions).

Management: The importance of manager knowledge

The set of rights which US B loan investors have characteristically acquired includes certain controls over the management of the underlying property and rights as a secured lender under the same mortgage as the A loan lender (likely in practice to be represented by a securitisation servicer). In addition, US B loan lenders have the ability to remedy defaults arising under the A loan ("cure rights") and the ability, in certain circumstance, to buy out the A lender. Although such rights are not universal in the European market, they are frequently seen.

Given the relatively complex nature of the underlying assets of CRE CDOs, such transactions in Europe, as per the US model, are likely to require portfolio managers who have specialist knowledge of the B loan and whole loan markets in order to successfully manage CRE asset portfolios. CDO managers are likely to have to administer mechanisms to allow cash injections to cure defaults in relation to underlying B loan positions. Management of a CRE CDO is perceived as qualitatively different from management of a multi-sector CDO or CDO of ABS, with real estate expertise at a premium. It is expected that the rating agencies will give significantly more weight to the manager's capabilities in their ratings of European CRE CDOs than is the case in the US. CDO managers without extensive real estate experience will need to buy in that expertise either by joint venturing with CMBS servicers or employing appropriately qualified individuals.

This is even more important given that the European CMBS market has been experiencing high levels of prepayment which means that the potential collateral for CRE CDOs is likely to be of relatively short duration, requiring managers to administer relatively rapidly revolving portfolios. Among the risks inherent in this are the potential difficulties of maintaining appropriate asset distribution and diversity, the risk that replacement assets cannot be found, or at least cannot be found at the correct spread, in a tightening market environment.

In addition, managers will most likely be managing assets from multiple real estate markets and potentially from several legal jurisdictions (a factor which does not arise for managers in US deals), requiring an extra dimension of specialist knowledge and raising issues of hedging if there is a change in the geographical distribution of assets in a transaction over time.

In summary, the major requirements placed on managers of CRE CDOs in Europe are likely to include: the ability to source suitable collateral in a cost effective manner; extensive real estate experience; the availability of financial resources to cure defaults; and the ability to service the portfolio day-to-day.

Expected rating approach: The cross over between CMBS and CDO market segments

CRE CDOs are at the intersection of two different rating methodologies. Real estate derived assets have historically been analysed by real estate/CMBS analysts (often with real estate surveyor backgrounds) using a methodology that pays particular attention to the underlying real property asset in terms of looking at LTV ratio, tenant default, etc. The rating approach to CDOs concentrates on interest coverage and over collateralisation ratios, as mentioned earlier in this chapter. The approach which is likely to be adopted by the rating agencies in analysing European CRE CDOs will be a hybrid of the CMBS analysis and CDO analysis. The rating agencies have set up cross-specialism initiatives to produce a combined rating product. Given the complexity of the underlying CRE assets, it is understood that the final methodology to be adopted is likely to borrow more from the CMBS approach in order to better capture variables such as available funds caps and the potential for high prepayments. CDO technology will in all probability be employed in the analysis of diversified asset pools since correlation, default probability and recovery rates become of statistical relevance when analysing larger numbers of assets. For example, in the US, Standard & Poor's has its CMBS group review the collateral, assign recovery rates and consider real estate aspects of the transaction documents, with its CDO group responsible for reviewing the model, the waterfall and the legal documentation from a CDO perspective.

At the time of writing, it is understood that each of the proposed CRE CDO deals in the immediate pipeline propose a transaction comprised of a mix between B loan and CMBS assets. The approach of the rating agencies will probably itself be an amalgam of techniques to analyse these different asset classes. For example, Fitch have in the past indicated that they are likely to use their European CMBS conduit model which covers correlation between different B loan assets to analyse B loan collateral and their VECTOR model to analyse any rated securities in such a transaction. The resulting cash flow model would employ the weighted average default and recovery rates and would then be stressed for foreign exchange movements, interest rate movements and default timings.

The rating agencies are also seeking to prevent arbitrage between different rating methodologies, i.e. a transaction which puts B loans into a CMBS should not produce a markedly different rating outcome than one which puts the same B loans into a CDO.

Risk factors

There are a number of risk factors to be considered in any CRE CDO, some of which are more particular to the European market. Some potentially important ones are briefly discussed, below.

Correlation

In order to be able to apply CDO methodology to CRE assets, there is a need for sufficient diversity between assets in terms of maturity, real estate market sub-sector and country, for example. There is significant correlation between B loans particularly within individual European jurisdictions and this is potentially a major issue for CRE CDOs since the bulk of underlying CRE transactions to date have been in the UK and Germany.

Low recovery rates

Historic low recovery rates attributed by the rating agencies to B loans will tend to result in relatively high credit enhancement levels. It may be possible to use excess spread trapping mechanisms to mitigate potential shortfalls since excess spread is likely to be quite sizeable and of significant value from a rating perspective if it can be trapped ahead of problems and retained in the transaction.

Currency risk

In the US, CRE assets will nearly always be USD-denominated. In Europe, because asset pools are likely to be situated both within and outside the Euro-zone, it is likely that transactions will require currency hedging. It seems probable that perfect currency swaps will not be used leading to the rating analysis needing to deal with the potential costs of over or under hedging.

Prepayment risk

Underlying CMBS A notes have in the recent past been prepaying very rapidly. CRE CDOs comprised of B loan collateral will be exposed to this

239

prepayment risk also, potentially resulting in collateral managers being almost "forced buyers" of replacement collateral as they strive to keep their transactions fully invested. Obviously, the risk here is of a fall off in underwriting standards and increased acquisition costs for replacement collateral, squeezing cashflows in the CDO.

Variability of documentation

Unlike in the US where documentation is well on the way to becoming standardised, the relatively young European CRE market has not yet developed a conformed approach to legal issues in documentation, particularly in matters relating to B loans, for example the intercreditor relationship between A and B lenders (as discussed in more detail in Ch. 9). This variability of rights and obligations necessitates a significant effort to analyse the rights of the parties and therefore the default probability and likely recovery rates of individual B loans.

CONCLUSION

These are interesting times for CMBS and CDO market participants in Europe. A working CRE CDO sector requires sufficient diverse collateral to be available to allow CDO methodology to be applied to the asset class, a cohort of able managers to be developed, and currently favourable pricing in the CMBS sector to continue.

CHAPTER TWELVE

CMBS: A EUROPEAN INVESTOR'S PERSPECTIVE

Hans J. Vrensen, CFA, Drs Econ, MRE,
Director of European ABS Research
Barclays Capital

INTRODUCTION

Throughout Europe, the perspective of investors in CMBS varies widely and depends on the individual investors' background, objectives and restrictions. This chapter will explore all of these areas as well as the due diligence and analyses that are carried out by investors in European CMBS. Finally, it covers investor issues and preferences and spread pricing in the current European CMBS market.

THE EUROPEAN CMBS INVESTOR BASE

There appears to be no dedicated CMBS investor base for European CMBS, which makes the title of this section a bit of a misnomer. This is due, in the most part, to the limited overall issuance in the European CMBS market compared to other bond market segments and a lack of maturity of the sector. As a result, most current investors in European CMBS are investors that consider a wider range of ABS sectors, or even corporate and/or government bonds. However, just because there are no dedicated CMBS investors, does not mean there are not certain things that can be said.

Categorisation of investor base

In November 2005, Barclays Capital Securitisation Research did an investor survey among 50 European ABS investor clients. Barclays Capital believe that the 50 survey respondents were representative of the European ABS investment universe, given their geographic locations (11 different European countries), ABS portfolio size (collectively accounting for 28 per cent of the European ABS universe) and investor types (including banks, funds, structured and other investors). The results of this survey allowed the categorisation of the investor base in a number of different ways.

Investor base by ABS sector

When asked about their global ABS portfolios, the survey respondents total added to over €250bn, of which, approximately 68 per cent or over €170bn was allocated to European ABS. This implied that the survey respondents had 80bn invested in non-ABS assets, confirming that many of them were in fact cross-over investors.

The respondents' global ABS portfolio was allocated to various ABS sub-sectors as shown in Figure 1, below. The survey respondents' allocation broadly matched the European ABS sector breakdown, with some exceptions. Allocation to Consumer ABS and other ABS exceeded the European ABS universe percentages. This was due to allocations to US credit card and US student loans, which are quite popular with European investors. Also, the allocation to whole business securitisation (WBS) was less than half of the universe percentage. This might have been due to an under-representation of fixed rate investors in the survey.

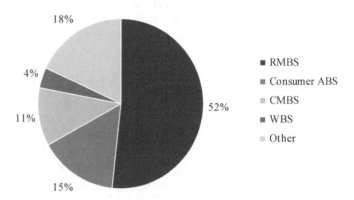

Source: Barclays Capital.

Figure 1: Investor survey respondents' portfolio allocation by sector.

Investor base by investor type

The four main investor types included banks, fund managers, structured vehicles and others (see Figure 2, below). It should be noted that a number of survey respondents had activities in more than one investor category. For example, a bank in addition to its own investments, may have managed an ABCP conduit or a SIV. In general, it was noted that some of the broader categories included a wide range of different investors. For example, the fund manager category included pension funds, hedge funds, insurance company funds, money market funds and general fixed income funds.

Also, despite not having specific figures for previous years, it was apparent that the investor base had broadened significantly compared to only a few years earlier. In particular, it was noted that the banks were no longer the single largest category of investors, despite being a close second.

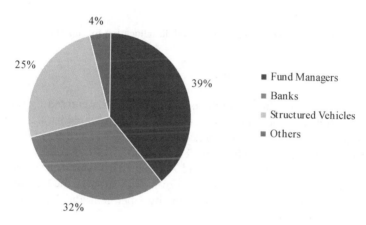

Source: Barclays Capital.

Figure 2: Investor survey respondents by investor type.

Investor base by collateral country

The allocation of survey respondents' European ABS portfolio is presented in Figure 3, below. The dominance of the UK in European ABS was evident in the allocation. However, it should be noted that 23 per cent of the respondents' portfolio was either not specified per country or included multiple jurisdictions. By excluding those non-specific responses from the results, the UK allocation might be overstated. The overall European ABS universe is made up of the UK at 46 per cent of total, Italy at 16 per cent, Spain at 12 per cent and the Netherlands at 9 per cent. It is clear that the survey respondents were over-allocated to the UK and the Netherlands. But the survey respondents were under-allocated to Italy and Spain, which may have been due to the survey respondent sample.

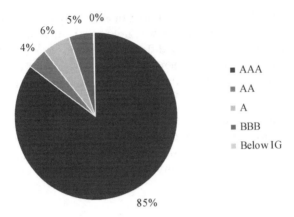

Source: Barclays Capital.

Figure 3: Investor survey respondents' portfolio allocation by country.

Investor base by rating category

The breakdown for the respondents' ABS portfolio, weighted by the size of each respondent's portfolio considering broad rating categories, is presented in Figure 4, below. The large allocation to AAA was representative of the European ABS market, which has 80 per cent AAA issuance to date, followed by 7 per cent each in AA and A-rated. BBB is at 4 per cent for the overall universe, implying a 5 per cent over-allocation of the respondents to AAA, and conversely under-allocations by 3 per cent and 1 per cent in the AA and A-rated categories.

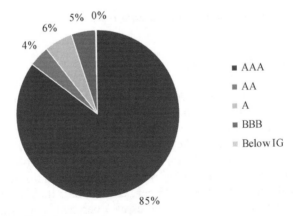

Source: Barclays Capital.

Figure 4: Investor survey respondents' portfolio allocation by rating category.

244

INVESTOR OBJECTIVES AND RESTRICTIONS

Investor's objectives differ, but in general they are focused on achieving the maximum total return at a level of risk acceptable to them. This section of the chapter explores a relative value analysis that Barclays Capital Securitisation Research performed at year-end 2005, which considers both risk and return factors in European ABS. The section goes on to explore additional results from the investor survey which consider investors' growth objectives and re-investment requirements. Finally, the section highlights a number of restrictions that investors impose on themselves in order to manage the overall risk in their portfolios.

Investor objectives

In assessing relative value, one can move from the general to the specific (the deductive or "top-down" approach) or from the specific to the general (the inductive or "bottom-up" approach). The bottom-up approach works best in a relatively homogeneous market, which lends itself to making direct comparisons between different bonds. The wide variation in assets, structures and geographies that make up the global ABS market renders the bottom-up approach cumbersome in this case. The top-down approach, on the other hand, is well suited to comparing different types of bonds at the sector level. Rather than focusing on specific bonds, Barclays Capital's relative value analysis is, for the most part, restricted to comparing different ABS sectors. Within each sector, a bottom-up approach can then be used to identify specific bonds of interest.

Figure 5 provides a schematic representation of an ABS transaction. The major components are the economy, the underlying assets, the structure and the market. The economy forms the backdrop for the performance of assets. It drives what has been identified above as the systemic component of returns. The asset generates the cash flow that ultimately supports the operation of the transaction. The structure allocates this cash flow (principal and interest) to different note holders. Finally, the notes themselves are priced within the context of a wider market. This model is clearly a simplification, but it does allow a complex object to be broken down into simpler pieces, which can then be compared and contrasted across the different ABS sectors.

Using Figure 5, below, the relative value process can be separated into discrete steps:[1]

---

[1] For a full description of the methodology and the results for each of the identified steps, see "Securitisation Relative Value 2006" in Barclays Capital's *Global Securitisation Annual*, January 1, 2006.

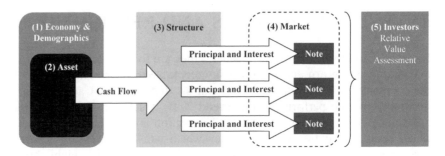

Source: Barclays Capital.

Figure 5: A schematic representation of the components of ABS.

(1) compare the economic and demographic fundamentals of different jurisdictions;

(2) compare the underlying assets;

(3) compare the structures;

(4) take into account market spreads; and

(5) combine risk indicators from Steps 1 to 3 with the market spreads from Step 4 to arrive at a relative value assessment.

This chapter presents only the results of this process, and it should be noted that CSWA means capital structure weighted average, including all investment grade, weighted-average asset classes.

Indicator	US HEL	US Cards	US Autos	Europe Cards	Europe Autos	Europe RMBS	Europe CMBS	Europe Pubs
CSWA Spread	37	6	7	14	11	17	37	46
Structural Protection Index	16	21	21	21	18	22	13	20
CSWA Ratings Implied Three-Year Expected Loss (bp)	3	4	2	4	3	2	5	14
Typical AAA Subordination (%)	18	14	11	12	8	10	30	
Delinquencies (%)	6.55	3.93	0.31	5.05	0.68	0.50	0.36	
Loss rates (%)		5.56	0.48	5.00	1.00	0.00	0.03	
CSWA Downgrade Experience (%)				0.00	0.00	0.16	0.55	0.19
Issuance 2005 ($bn)	500	61	87	14	8	182	45	5

Source: Barclays Capital.

Figure 6: Spreads and summary of risk indicators by sector.

The results are further refined by ranking each indicator for each of the considered ABS sectors and calculating a straight average for the overall risk indicator ranking.

Indicator	US HEL	US Cards	US Autos	Europe Cards	Europe Autos	Europe RMBS	Europe CMBS	Europe Pubs
CSWA Spread	37	6	7	14	11	17	37	46
Structural Protection Index	7	2	2	2	6	1	8	5
CSWA Ratings Implied three-Year Expected Loss (bp)	4	6	2	5	3	1	7	8
Typical AAA Subordination	2	3	5	4	7	6	1	
Delinquencies	7	5	1	6	4	3	2	
Loss rates		6	3	5	4	1	2	
Average risk indicator rank	5.00	4.40	2.60	4.40	4.80	2.40	4.00	6.50
Issuance 2005	1	4	3	6	7	2	5	8
CSWA Downgrade Experience				1	1	3	5	4

Note: Barclays Capital included CSWA downgrade experience and 2005 issuance for information only—it is not included in their average risk indicator rank.

Figure 7: Spreads and summary of ranked risk indicators by sector.
Source: Barclays Capital.

Overall, it was noted that European ABS investors might be coming to similar relative value views even without considering Barclays Capital's relative value framework. Figure 8, below, shows that, according to the ABS investor survey, in a further indication of the popularity of CMBS within Europe CMBS ranked as the favourite ABS sector for 2006.

Finally, the results from the investor survey with regard to what asset types European ABS investors prefer to see increased supply of are presented. The surprise here was that there were many different answers. When the responses were categorised, non specific responses, such as "more BBB" or "more cheaper assets", were excluded. This left 35 responses, some of which included multiple sectors and more specific asset types than others.

Figure 8, below, shows that the survey responses supported further growth in CMBS and RMBS, with 26 per cent and 23 per cent of respondents specifically mentioning these as preferred sectors in which to have an increased supply.

It should be noted however that the financial markets have a tendency to self correct, and attractive value relative to risks is typically not available for

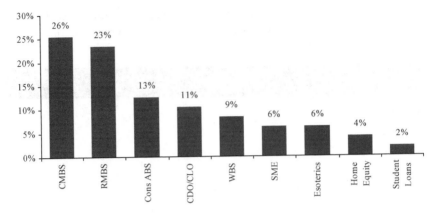

Source: Barclays Capital.

Figure 8: Survey respondents—ABS sector preferences.

very long. As additional investors are attracted to the sector, pricing might tighten to such an extent that it becomes relatively unattractive.

Growth and reinvestment requirements

After several years of strong issuance growth in the European ABS markets, the survey assessed how much more appetite there was with investors, as of year-end 2005, to take on more ABS issuance in the future. The average expectation for growth for the ABS portfolio for 2006, among the 39 survey respondents that answered those questions, was approximately 40 per cent. However, when weighted against the current size of their portfolio, the average expected growth was 21 per cent. The difference between these two

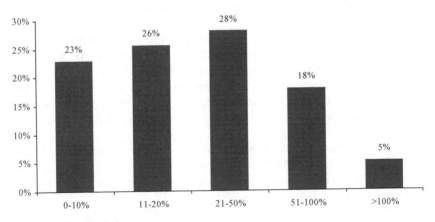

Source: Barclays Capital.

Figure 9: Survey respondents—ABS portfolio growth expectation for 2006.

growth expectations implied that the expected growth rate for smaller investors was much higher compared to investors that already had large allocations to European ABS.

Figure 9, above, shows that a small majority of investors, expected to grow their ABS portfolio by more than 21 per cent. The low growth investors were mostly in the fund manager and bank categories. It should be noted that some additional growth in demand for European ABS assets is expected from investors that are currently not invested in the sector. It is expected that these will include investors from outside the region, including from the US, Australia and Japan.

Due to redemptions and prepayments, investors are required to re-invest principal returned to them from issuers. But exactly how much of this reinvestment are investors required to do? The average re-investment requirement for 2005 among the 30 survey respondents (that answered this question) was approximately 20 per cent, as a percentage of the current portfolio. However, when weighted against the current size of their portfolio, the average requirement was only 9 per cent. The difference between these two growth expectations implies that the requirement for smaller investors is higher then those for large investors. Also, if the 9 per cent was used as a proxy, it could be deduced that the weighted average life of the respondents European ABS portfolio was approximately 11 years. This took into account prepayments, scheduled amortisation and refinancing. The 11 years, upon further reflection, does seem long as, based on Barclays Capital's European ABS database, the average life of European ABS bonds is more like four or five years. Therefore, it is expected that the survey respondents under-estimated the true need for re-investment.

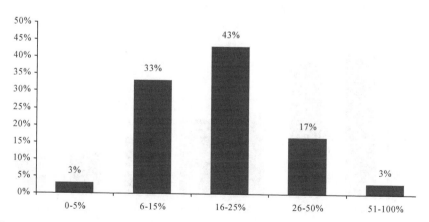

Source: Barclays Capital.

Figure 10: Survey respondents—re-investment requirements.

It is clear from Figure 10 that most investors need to re-invest at least a portion of their current ABS portfolio. The largest category of respondents was in the 16 to 25 per cent category, with 43 per cent of total and the next largest category was in the 6 to 15 per cent category.

The survey noted that, if the weighted average growth expectations of 21 per cent are combined with the 9 per cent re-investment requirement, an estimate could be arrived at, for increase in demand for European ABS, of 30 per cent. If a further 5 to 10 per cent were to be added in from new investors, currently not invested in the sector, the result would be an estimated growth in ABS demand of between 35 and 40 per cent. Finally, another 5 to 10 per cent could be added for CMBS being investors' favourite ABS sector offering the best relative value. This would mean that investor demand for European CMBS in 2006 could be expected to grow by 45 to 50 per cent compared to 2005.

Investor restrictions

In making their investment decisions, many investors are restricted by internal guidelines or client mandates to not invest in certain types of ABS bonds. In identifying these restrictions, it became clear that the restrictions on fixed rate and ratings were most prevalent. Only one third of the survey respondents were able to invest in fixed interest rate ABS, with a further 64 per cent restricted in some way by the credit ratings.

Other restrictions included currency, with 40 per cent of respondents not able to invest in USD, 27 per cent could not buy GBP-denominated ABS bonds and finally 21 per cent were not in a position to allocate to

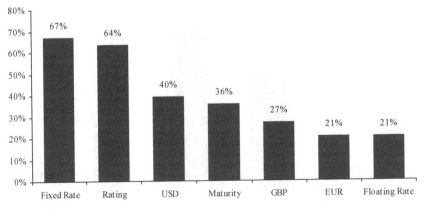

Source: Barclays Capital.

Figure 11: Investor survey respondents – portfolio restrictions.

EUR-denominated ABS. Many USD-restricted investors had separate US-based operations that managed the USD-denominated ABS portfolio. Most EUR-restricted respondents were UK based investors, focused on investing in GBP-denominated ABS (see Figure 11, above).

Furthermore, 36 per cent of respondents were prevented from buying all types of maturities and 21 per cent were not able to buy floating interest rate bonds. Floating rate-restricted ABS investors were typically UK-based fund managers focused solely on GBP-denominated fixed rate ABS.

When taking a closer look at the rating restrictions, it was noted that the two most prevalent rules were AAA only and BBB or better, with 59 per cent and 24 per cent of total respondents, respectively (see Figure 12, below). With the combination of 59 per cent of rating restricted-respondents only able to invest in AAA and 80 per cent of the European ABS universe consisting of AAA-rated bonds, it is not surprising that AAA-rated bonds make up such a large portion of the respondents overall portfolio. Again, 64 per cent of respondents were in some way restricted by the ratings in their investment decisions.

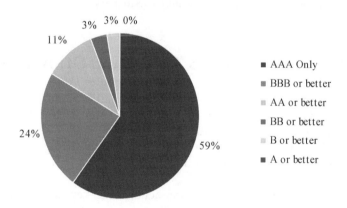

Source: Barclays Capital.

Figure 12: Investor survey respondents—rating restrictions.

Next, the maturity restrictions are considered in a little more detail. These restrictions impact 36 per cent of survey respondents. A wide range of maturity restrictions were reported and it should be noted that some respondents specified that the restriction was on the weighted average life (WAL) and not final maturity. When categorised, it was found that the restrictions of 10 years or less and 15 years or less applied to 39 per cent and 33 per cent, respectively. The balance was made up of 19 per cent of respondents unable to invest beyond a five-year maturity and only 9 per cent restricted from investing beyond 30 years. However, the five-year restriction is expected to be much more limiting than the 30-year limit, as most European ABS bonds have maturities beyond five-years.

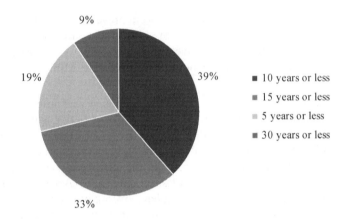

Source: Barclays Capital.

Figure 13: Investor survey respondents—maturity restrictions.

INVESTOR ANALYSES AND DUE DILIGENCE

Since there is no single dominant transaction type in European CMBS, it is difficult to come up with a standard analytical approach for European CMBS investors. However, in order to provide investors with a general framework for analysis of European CMBS transactions, the key criteria for each transaction type is highlighted below (see Figure 14, below).

Starting with credit tenant lease transactions, the key analysis should focus on the quality of the tenant (as reflected in its rating) as well as the underlying lease. Regarding the latter, it is important that the lease agreement is watertight and provides a sufficient term to allow for (full) amortisation of the loan. Other criteria, such as DSCR, LTV, borrower quality and cash flow stability, are of less concern. This does not imply that these criteria can be ignored, but typically, the deals are structured tightly to have a DSCR very close to 1.01x. In some cases, the LTV is above 100 per cent, which is not necessarily problematic as long as the structure allows for full (scheduled) amortisation. Since the borrower is typically a newly-formed SPV, an assessment of its credit quality is not really relevant. The quality of the properties is also immaterial, as long as the lease agreement is watertight, with no breaks and escape clauses.

252

Transaction Type/Key Criteria	Credit Tenant Lease	Single-Borrower Single-Property	Single-Borrower Multi-Property	Multi-Borrower Multi-Property	Synthetic CMBS
Pool Diversity			Depends	Yes	Yes
DSCR		Yes	Yes	Yes	Yes
LTV		Yes	Yes	Yes	Yes
Borrower Quality		Yes	Yes	Depends	
Property Quality		Yes	Yes	Depends	
Tenant Quality	Yes	Yes	Depends		
Lease Quality & Profile	Yes	Yes			

Source: Barclays Capital.

Figure 14: Key analytical criteria in European CMBS transaction types.

At the other end of the spectrum, synthetic CMBS transactions[2] are considered, which typically have a large number of reference loans. Due to this granularity, the quality of any single borrower, property, tenant or lease is not really material to the performance of the loan reference pool. On an overall, weighted average basis, the qualitative borrower, property, tenant and lease criteria are difficult to measure. The rating agencies are likely to "shadow rate" each individual loan in the reference pool based on static (or dynamic) DSCR coverages during the loan term and balloon LTV ratio at refinance. Therefore, it can be seen that DSCR and LTV are the key criteria for investors to focus on for synthetic, as well as multi-borrower multi-property (MBMP) transaction types.

For synthetic CMBS transactions, there is the additional complexity of the public sector German *Pfandbriefe* (and in certain cases, additional cash) collateral. In the case of MBMP transaction types with a limited number of loans, the borrower and property quality can start to matter to a greater extent than in more granular loan pools.

The single borrower deal types require a broad focus on most criteria, except for multi-property transactions with a large number of properties, where detailed tenant and lease analysis provides less added value. The required focus on lower level criteria depends largely on the granularity of the collateral pool. The more properties, the less need to focus on individual leases and tenants.

Based on the above, six different analytical levels in CMBS credit analysis can be identified (see Figure 15, below).

---

[2] See Ch. 11 for further details.

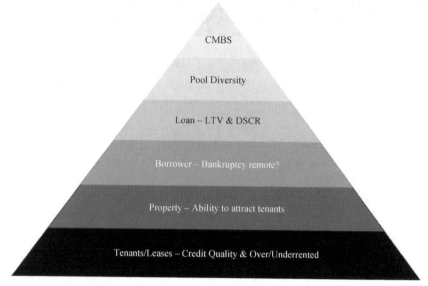

Source: Barclays Capital.

Figure 15: Levels of CMBS analysis.

Need for qualitative analysis

Credit analysis can be thought of, in its most basic format, as an assessment of:

(1) how likely it is that money will be lost. In CMBS, the DSCR can be looked at and it can be assumed that if it is below 1.00, there will be a default because there is insufficient cash flow to cover the debt service. Therefore, DSCR can be used as an indicator for the probability of default; and

(2) how much money is likely to be lost. This can be defined as the severity of the loss. In CMBS, the LTV ratio can be looked at as an indicator for this loss severity. Clearly, the higher the LTV, the higher the likely loss. The final loss will also be affected by the costs involved in enforcing the security, the time delay required to sell the property and any loss in value due to the forced nature of the sale.

By multiplying the probability of default with the loss severity, an expected loss can be identified. Each level of expected loss can be mapped to a rating category, which is discussed in more detail in Ch. 4.

Despite the need to focus on certain criteria, some LTV and DSCR statistics are available which suggest that investors should still consider qualitative factors in their analysis. When considering LTVs at the BBB level, no clear pattern can be discovered for each transaction type. The range of BBB LTV values for MBMP deals is fairly wide. So, despite recommending that investors focus on LTV and DSCR in evaluating these MBMP transactions, it was noted that the LTV is not consistent across deals. This it is most likely due to qualitative factors (such as diversity and quality of the property, tenants, leases and cash flow) that may explain these LTV differences. It is of note that the LTVs for synthetic CMBS have been lower than most other transaction types. However, at this point, much more synthetic CMBS issuance seems unlikely. If DSCRs are considered for the different transaction types, it is again difficult to identify any clear trends or patterns. Data limitations are also unhelpful, but the lack of any clear trends further supports the view that qualitative analysis matters in European CMBS.

Due diligence

Other issues for European CMBS investors to consider include such issues as site visits and property market analyses. An increasing number of more specialised analysts insists on the need for site visits, which many arrangers offer either at issuance or on a periodic basis. In Barclays Capital's view, investors will be well served to understand the underlying security better. Furthermore, clearly investors need to do a detailed legal review of the offering circular and any other transaction documents that are available. Some investors will also use the third party cash flow models that are now available on many conduit transactions.

Ultimately, many AAA investors will also rely on the independent analyses of the rating agencies and the increasing community of CMBS sell-side analysts.

ISSUES AND PREFERENCES IN THE CURRENT MARKET

The following section provides an overview of investor issues and preferences in the current market. The issues include the increased level of prepayments, structural complexity and limitations to secondary market liquidity. Finally, it discusses investor preferences and spreads.

Prepayments

In European CMBS, prepayment rates have varied significantly amongst different transaction types and vintages in terms of profile as well as over time, reflecting the diverse collateral characteristics in terms of granularity in the number of borrowers or the structural features, including pay-down structures. On average, prepayment rates are around 17 per cent of out-standing balances, but have increased significantly in recent years, largely explained by declines in interest rates and increases in the capital values of the underlying properties. Constant prepayment rates ("CPRs") increased in both multi- and single-borrower deal types over most of 2000 to 2005. In addition, multi-borrower ("MB") CMBS transactions showed the most volatility in CPRs during 2000 to 2005 (see Figure 16, below). Given the available data, it is not yet possible to determine on whether this trend or pattern will continue.

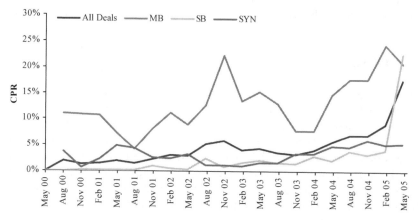

Source: Barclays Capital.

Figure 16: Chronological weighted average CPRs for three CMBS deal types from 2000–2005.

The reasons for investors concern about prepayments are the re-investment risk and the possible impact on the credit quality of the remaining loan pool. The re-investment risk is that investors will be forced to re-invest the redemption of existing high-spread bonds at a lower spread in the current market. This risk will reduce as spreads remain in a broad range over a longer period of time, such as has been the case in the last 12 to 18 months. The impact on the credit quality of the remaining loan pool relates to the possible negative pooling as a result of the better quality loans paying off first leaving the lower quality loans in the remaining collateral pool, but, there is no real evidence of this phenomenon in the European CMBS market at the time of writing.

However, overall CPRs for multi-borrower CMBS for 2006 can be pro-jected using a regression analysis. When considering the European CMBS outlook for CPRs for the following year, the Barclays Capital's economics research team's forecasts for five-year swap rates were taken into account as well as two different forecasts for the IPD capital index. The first forecast of the IPD capital index comes from Property Market Analysis (PMA), which consists of an 8.8 per cent capital growth estimate in 2005 and a 6.6 per cent projection for 2006. Secondly, as an alternative, a scenario of capital value decreases of 5 per cent in the next 12 months, with a further 2 per cent quarterly reduction thereafter were used. This scenario was used as an extreme example to illustrate a reasonable range of CPRs. It is believed these two forecasts represent a realistic range of outcomes for the IPD capital index.

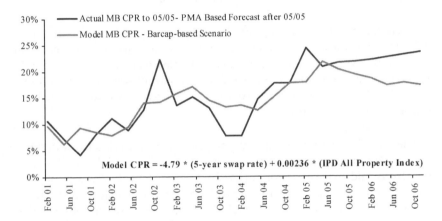

Source: Property Market Analysis, Barclays Capital.

Figure 17: Projected CPR for European multi-borrower CMBS.

The PMA-based forecast results in a moderate increase of CPR to 23.6 per cent in November 2006, just below the February 2005ʹ high for the sector. The alternative scenario results in a 17.3 per cent CPR in the final quarter of 2006. Based on the above, CPRs for European CMBS transactions are expected to remain relatively stable, especially after the large increases of the last few years. For 2006, as interest rates are expected to rise and value increases are expected to be more moderate than the last few years, these factors will provide further support for stable CPRs in European CMBS. This CPR projection is at a sector level only and prepayments on individual deals will invariably differ widely based on the behaviour of individual borrowers in often concentrated loan pools.

Some of the recent industry discussions focus on addressing the increased level of prepayments with lock out periods and prepayment penalties in the loan agreements. However, it is noted that not many European CMBS transactions have loans with these features included, due to the competitive nature of the traditional commercial mortgage portfolio lending market.

Overall, a stabilisation of CPRs in European CMBS is expected, which, in combination with more range bound spreads will result in a reduced investor concern regarding prepayments in the future.

Structural complexities

Another frequently discussed issue in European CMBS is the increased level of structural complexities. This is typically illustrated by more detailed analyses of the pay-down structures, AB Structures,[3] available funds caps and others. In general, Barclays Capital share investors' concerns on these issues, but do note a number of mitigating factors.

Overall, they see a wide range of different pay-down structures, with many different loan bucket structures and pro rata to sequential trigger event definitions. However, some uniformity and consistency in each of the individual conduit programmes can be seen as the start of some standardisation. There has been a general shift from sequential pay down to modified pro rata pay down structures.

The main issues to consider with the priority of payments (or waterfalls) are whether they apply pre- or post-enforcement. The possible variations are numerous and make investor review sometimes difficult. By way of illustration, separate waterfalls for interest first and principal second can be considered, or vice versa. There might be a separate waterfall for deals that have a liquidating portfolio for the allocated loan amount and the release premium payable on sale.

Also, straight sequential or pro-rata pay-down are possible. Modifications of both are also quite common, where perhaps 50 per cent is paid down sequentially and the rest pro rata (or vice versa or a different percentage). There are also CMBS deal structures where each of these pay-downs apply but to a certain subset of loans (i.e. some loans are sequential, others pay down pro rata and the remainder might pay down modified sequential), and there are pay-down structures that switch from pro rata to sequential at different trigger events (and back).

As said before, the variations are numerous, and Barclays Capital do observe a wide range of different pay-down structures in European CMBS. However, some uniformity and consistency in each of the individual conduit programmes can be seen as the start of some standardisation. The exact nature of the pay-down structure has an effect on the credit enhancement and subordination of individual notes classes and should, therefore, be

---

[3] Dealt with in detail in Ch. 8.

reflected in their credit ratings. As illustrated in Figure 18 (below), the increase in modified pro-rata pay-down and decline of straight sequential pay-down are the main changes in this respect from 2004 to 2005.

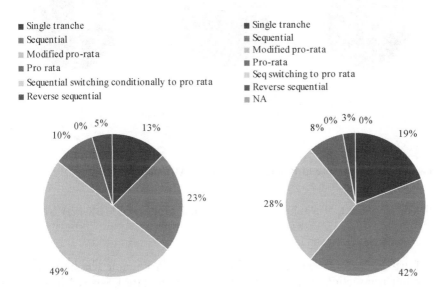

Source: Moody's Investors Service, Barclays Capital.

Figure 18: Paydown structures in European CMBS issued in 2004 and 2005.

The market has made progress in better understanding the AB and Class X note structures, now seen in most European conduit CMBS transactions. The increased importance of B notes is illustrated in Figure 19 (below). X note structures can present certain complications for bondholders of other classes, including those related to the use of liquidity.

The increase in the number of joint contributor deals, with two arrangers contributing loans to a single CMBS transaction, and the inclusion of portions of syndicated loans in various European CMBS transactions, can trigger possible servicing issues.

Linked to the growth in the introduction of Subordinate Debt into European CMBS deals, issuance from the first European Commercial Real Estate Collateralised Debt Obligation (CRE CDO) is expected in 2006, as a means for B-piece buyers to finance themselves. The introduction of a newly-managed CDO structure, allowing discretionary trading in part of the portfolio, could be expected to suit the more chunky European CMBS market well. At the same time, as the European CMBS market broadens,

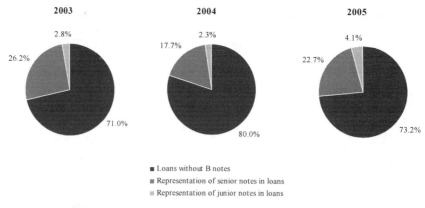

Source: Barclays Capital.

Figure 19: Relative size of B notes in European CMBS market.

the development of a market for CDOs of European CMBS may also be seen.[4]

Furthermore, the emergence of super senior AAA note classes in some conduit transactions is noted, mostly to accommodate US-based investors in the broadening investor base. Finally, the first UK synthetic CMBS transaction with EPIC (Ayton) was seen, but more non-German synthetic transactions are not expected to be seen in 2006 as most conduits originate loans with securitisation in mind and may not need to deal with reluctant borrowers required to consent to assignment of the mortgages.

Overall, with the lack of consistency among deal structures is of concern and, as a result, the implicit standardisation as a result of the increase in repeat issuance from European CMBS conduit programs is to be encouraged.

Disclosure and secondary market liquidity

Another important issue for current CMBS investors is the lack of public disclosure and the possible non-compliance with local laws and regulations as impacted by the Market Abuse Directive ("MAD").[5] In addition, for many of the transactions, the quality of disclosure does not meet investor needs, despite some of the recent efforts to define industry-wide reporting standards. These issues are linked in many respects to investors' needs for

---

[4] See Ch. 11 for a detailed discussion of CRE CDO.
[5] Dealt with in more detail in Ch. 13.

better secondary market liquidity, which will be discussed in more detail in Ch. 15.

CMBS spreads and investor preferences

This section discusses recent spread developments in a historical context. In addition, investor preferences as implied by spreads as well as based on the relative value analysis, as discussed above, are identified.

After some initial tightening in the first quarter of 2005, European CMBS spreads widened during the remainder of 2005, as illustrated in Figure 20, below. The average AAA spread was 21 bp for the entire year. Deals priced after mid-year were 24 bp on average, versus 18 bp in the first half of the year. Spreads were at their tightest levels in early March, with three very different CMBS transactions pricing at 14 bp at the AAA level. The BBB average spread was 93 bp for the full year, with deals after mid-year pricing at 106 bp on average, compared with 81 bp during the first half of the year. BBB spreads were at their tightest levels in mid- to late April, with three CMBS transactions pricing at 70 bp at the BBB level. In the second half of the year, a wide range of spreads, partly as a result of more challenging property type collateral was witnessed.

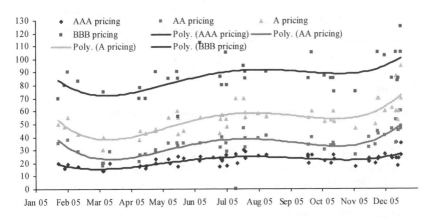

Source: Barclays Capital.

Figure 20: European CMBS primary issue spreads (bp) in 2005.

Spread drivers in 2005 included concerns over general levels of credit, especially with the GM and Ford downgrades. Additionally, after tightness in the first half of 2005, some deals priced considerably wider due to either structural or collateral concerns. Widening in the final quarter of 2005 was partly driven by the sheer volume of supply, which accounted for 34 per cent of the full year's issuance.

In the next section, year-end 2005 CMBS spreads are compared with spreads available on other ABS sectors in both Europe and the US. Barclays Capital's relative value framework also considers a number of relevant risk factors.

Despite the recent widening during 2005, it is notable that AAA spreads have tightened by approximately 45 per cent since July 2003. In addition, BBB spreads have come in from 200 to 220 bp to approximately 95 to 100 bp as of year-end 2005. Therefore, the difference between AAA and BBB spreads narrowed to approximately 70 bp at year-end 2005 from 160 bp in July 2003. This long-term tightening has made CMBS an attractive source of debt funding for an increasing range of property owners.

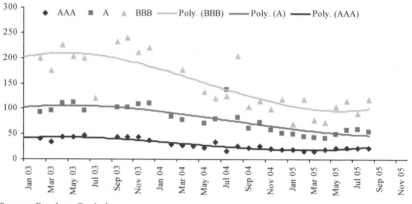

Source: Barclays Capital.

Figure 21: European CMBS primary issue spreads (bp) 2003–2005.

Prior to 2003, spreads displayed no clear trends as issuance was fairly limited between 1995 and 2002. Only approximately one-quarter of European CMBS issuance outstanding today was, in fact, issued prior to 2003. Therefore, spread movements prior to 2003 are likely to be less relevant for the current CMBS market.

As a final point, it is noted that the spreads on EUR-denominated deals and deals with better-than-average granularity seem to have priced tighter relative to the overall CMBS market. CMBS deals with particularly unusual property types, such as nursing homes, hotels and specialist care facilities, seem to carry wider spreads in the market. This seems to support the premise that the market is efficient. Also, arrangers responding by bringing more EUR-denominated and granular deals to the market than could be expected.

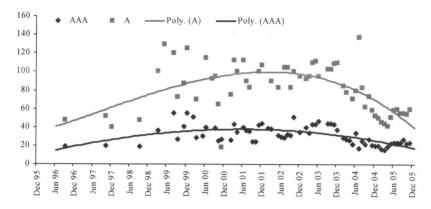

Source: Barclays Capital.

Figure 22: European CMBS primary issue spreads (bp) 1995–2005.

Figure 23, below, illustrates that, in general, during 2005 spreads for EUR-denominated CMBS were tighter than GBP-denominated CMBS, mostly due to the relative lack of EUR-denominated supply.

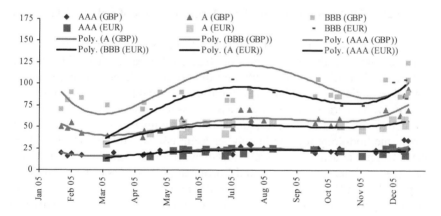

Source: Barclays Capital.

Figure 23: 2005 CMBS primary spreads—Euro versus GBP-denominated.

This final section returns to consider the relative value of CMBS across eight different US and European sectors using a top-down approach. Figure 24, below, summarises the results of Barclays Capital's analysis, plotting investment grade representative spreads against the average of six ranked risk indicators for each sector. On the basis of this analysis, in the medium-risk space, European CMBS appears to offer good value, despite the historical spread tightening over the last three years. For more risk-averse investors, European RMBS offers good value and for investors with higher risk appetites, US home equity loans (HEL) and UK pubs represent relatively good value. The consumer ABS sectors appear rich in this analysis, but this may well reflect factors not taken into consideration, such as strong historical credit performance and good secondary market liquidity.

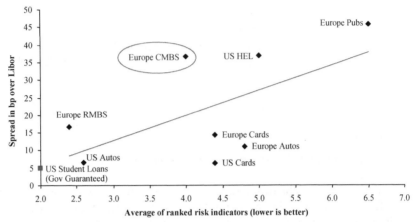

Source: Barclays Capital.

Figure 24: CSWA spreads (AAA-BBB rated) against average of ranked risk indicators.

Finding relative value in the global ABS market is as much an art as a science, owing to the complexities of structured products (i.e. wide ranging structural features and vastly different underlying collateral characteristics), varied secondary market liquidity and different legal jurisdictions. Assessing relative value across such a diverse asset class as global ABS is an enormous challenge and, in any case, it is unlikely that all investors would agree on a single methodology for conducting such an assessment. Nevertheless, Barclays Capital endeavour to create a framework (albeit simplified) to uncover relative value across major US and European ABS sectors using a top-down approach. While such a "one size fits all" approach is not entirely accurate or appropriate in all instances, at a minimum their relative value analytical framework provides a jumping off point from which investors can start their own search for that elusive goal—relative value.

CONCLUSIONS

This chapter has explored what European CMBS investors want to achieve and some of the issues that they have to deal with in the current European CMBS market. Based on the results of a recent investor survey, Barclays Capital were able to determine that there were, at the time of writing, no dedicated European CMBS investors and that most investors considered a wider range of ABS and other investment sectors. They also noted that the banks were no longer the largest investor category, with fund managers taking top honours.

In Barclays Capital's view, the broadening investor base increasingly considers CMBS in a relative value context, based on both spreads and risk factors. CMBS comes out well from their relative value analyses and is the investors' single most preferred ABS sector. Investors also indicate a strong need for growth in issuance, both to grow their ABS portfolio as well as to counteract redemptions. This strong investor demand is further focused on certain segments of the CMBS sector as a result of a large number of self imposed restrictions, related to ratings, currency-denomination and maturity. In particular, most investors in European CMBS are less restricted in AAA or investment grade, floating rate and Euro-denominated CMBS bonds.

Furthermore, investors in European CMBS are unable to use one single analytical approach for all deals, due to the lack of a standard or dominant transaction type. As result, European CMBS investors are recommended to evaluate each deal on six different levels in a qualitative manner. In addition, site visits, market research and legal document review are all part of most investors' due diligence. Other issues investors need to understand are the level of prepayments, structural complexities and public disclosure in European CMBS. Prepayments can be expected to stabilise and investors might be less concerned going forward if spreads remain range-bound. Structural complexities might be increasing, but due to more repeat issuance from CMBS conduit programs, some standardisation is also beginning to creep into the sector.

Spread tightening over the last three years implies that CMBS has been a popular sector for investors, attracting further borrowers as well. EUR-denominated spreads were tighter in 2005 compared to GBP-denominated spreads, confirming the investors preference for these type of CMBS transactions. Despite the historical spread tightening, CMBS remains relatively good value for many investors compared to most other ABS sectors and will continue to play an important role in investors' global ABS portfolios.

CHAPTER THIRTEEN

THE MARKET ABUSE RULES AND THEIR LEGAL IMPACT ON THE EUROPEAN CMBS MARKETS

James A. Spencer, Associate
Andrew V. Petersen, Senior Associate
Dechert LLP

INTRODUCTION

On the April 12, 2003, the European landscape of market abuse rules dramatically altered when the Market Abuse Directive,[1] (the "Directive") was published with a broad remit to enhance investor confidence in European financial markets and ensure the integrity of those markets and transparency of market practices by allowing equal access to price sensitive information. By extending pre-existing continuing, but rather limited, obligations and imposing additional requirements throughout Europe, the Directive aims to ultimately contribute to increased transparency and efficiency and liquidity in the secondary market by creating, for the first time, a Europe-wide uniform set of prohibitions against the use of inside information and market manipulation with a requirement that Member States each establish a designated competent authority and administrative framework to regulate against market abuse. To that end, the Directive requires issuers of financial instruments across all European regulated markets to publicly disclose inside information to the public promptly, in as synchronised a fashion as possible, thereby avoiding certain investors having advantage over others by gaining earlier or greater access to price sensitive information.

The Directive raises key issues for European CMBS, and, in particular, the dynamic and scope of investor reporting. This presents particular issues

---

[1] Directive 2003/6/EC of the European Parliament and of the Council of January 28, 2003 on insider dealing and market manipulation (market abuse).

with, as will be seen in Ch. 15, the continuing growth of the European CMBS market and the need for CMBS markets across Europe to begin to operate more professionally and with greater transparency, especially in developing a credible secondary market. Whilst, the business of investor reporting and the obligations facing the parties to a CMBS transaction will be dealt with in detail in the next chapter, this chapter will examine in detail, the key legal provisions of the Directive and the impact these have on the European CMBS markets, particularly the prohibitions against the use of inside information and market manipulation, as well as the various disclosure requirements placed on issuers of financial instruments and related European CMBS market parties.

IMPLEMENTATION OF THE DIRECTIVE

A product of the European Union's Financial Services Action Plan, it was intended that the Directive be implemented by Member States no later than October 12, 2004. However, at the time of writing, many Member States had still not implemented the Directive, whilst some introduced their own rules to implement the Directive during the course of 2005. The United Kingdom implemented the Directive on July 1, 2005 pursuant to the Market Abuse Regulations[2] (the "Regulations"). The Regulations, together with the FSA's Code of Market Conduct, introduced important changes concerning issuers of public rated instruments, their advisers and senior management, as well as anyone authorised under the Financial Services and Markets Act 2000 ("FSMA"), market participants, and those who recommend investments.

The Directive is one of the first pieces of European legislation to follow the two tier "Lamfalussy Process", whereby two levels of legislation are adopted. This is relevant, as a key component of the Lamfalussy Process, as adopted by the European Council of March 2001, is also to contribute to increased transparency, efficiency and liquidity in the secondary market, with the primary "Level 1" framework legislation introduced to set out points of principle and general objectives, followed by detailed "Level 2" implementing legislation, often drawn up by expert committees (such as the Committee of European Securities Regulators ("CESR")), that interprets and fleshes out the details, as well as determining the implementation of the Directive.

At the time of writing, the following Level 2 implementing measures had been introduced, each of which was drawn up based on consultations with, and the opinions of, the CESR:

---

[2] Financial Services and Markets Act 2000 (Market Abuse) Regulations 2005 (SI 2005/381).

(1) Commission Directive 2003/124/EEC regarding the definition and public disclosure of inside information and the definition of market manipulation;

(2) Commission Directive 2003/125/EEC regarding the fair presentation of investment recommendations and the disclosure of conflicts of interest;

(3) the Market Practices Directive[3] regarding accepted market practices, the definition of inside information in relation to derivatives on commodities, the drawing up of lists of insiders, the notification of manager's transactions and the notification of suspicious transactions; and

(4) the Market Abuse Exemptions Regulations[4] regarding exemptions for buy-back programmes and stabilisation of financial instruments.

The Directive also draws on certain terms as defined in the Investment Services Directive[5] which itself is due to be superseded by the Markets in Financial Instruments Directive[6] ("MiFID") which, at the time of writing, had been given an extended effective date of November 1, 2007.

Territorial effect

Of further significance for European CMBS, is that many deals may now be covered not just by the rules regulating their own market but also by those regulating the markets in other Member States. This is because each Member State is required under Art. 10 of the Directive to apply the provisions of the Directive to not only those actions that are carried out on a regulated market that is situated or operating within its territory, but also to actions concerning financial instruments that are admitted to trading, or for which a request for admission has been made, on a regulated market in another Member State.

The requirement for Member States to apply their own market abuse laws with extra-territorial effect will mean that, notwithstanding the steps to create a level legal and regulatory playing field, European CMBS market participants, issuers and other persons caught by the Directive, could find

---

[3] Directive 2003/72/EC of the Commission of April 29, 2004 implementing Directive 2003/6/EC as regards accepted market practices, the definition of inside information in relation to derivatives on commodities, the drawing up of lists of insiders, the notification of managers' transactions and the notification of suspicious transactions.
[4] Commission Regulation (EC) 2273/2003.
[5] Directive 93/22/EEC of May 10, 1993 on investment services in the securities field.
[6] Directive 2004/39/EC of the European Parliament and of the Council of April 21, 2004 on markets in financial instruments.

themselves in a position where they need to comply with the laws and regulations of not just one Member State, but two, possibly three Member States. To take an example, an Irish servicer of a Netherlands domiciled CMBS issuer could find themselves having to comply with inside information and disclosure requirements as applied in both Ireland and the Netherlands.

Pan-European co-operation

To counter this obvious concern, Art. 11 of the Directive requires each Member State to designate a single administrative authority that is competent to ensure that the market abuse provisions are applied. Such authorities must ensure that CMBS market participants are made aware of the changes to domestic law as a result of implementation of the Directive and each Member State should consult with market participants before making changes to the national legislation. Each competent authority will have the necessary supervisory and investigatory powers needed to exercise its functions, and will, in conformity with its national laws, be given extensive rights, including rights to access documentation in any form whatsoever, carry out on-site inspections, require existing telephone and data traffic records, require the cessation of any practice contrary to the provisions implementing the Directive, suspend trading of the financial instruments concerned, and request the freezing of assets or the temporary prohibition of the professional activity.

Provision of information

In addition to the above, each Member State's competent authority are obliged to assist each other in taking action against infringements, and making use of their powers. The Directive specifically identifies that each competent authority shall exchange information and co-operate in investigating activities. This should prove invaluable in the case of complex cross border pan-European CMBS transactions.

Moreover, a competent authority must, on request, immediately supply any information to assist another competent authority in carrying out functions. If such a competent authority cannot supply information immediately, then it must notify the requesting competent authority of the reasons. These obligations on competent authorities are, however, subject to certain limitations contained in the Directive, allowing competent authorities to refuse to act on a request for information if:

(1) it might adversely affect the sovereignty, security or public policy of a Member State,

(2) judicial proceedings have already been initiated in respect of the same actions and against the same persons, or

(3) a final judgment has already been delivered in relation to such persons for the same such actions.

In these circumstances the competent authority will still be required to provide the requesting competent authority with as much detailed information as possible regarding such proceedings or judgement.

Notification of violation in other Member States and requests for investigation

Each competent authority is obliged to notify another competent authority, in as specific a manner as possible, of any acts carried out in the territory of that other competent authority that it is convinced are contrary to the provisions of the Directive. In return, the notified competent authority must act on such information and update the notifying competent authority of the outcome. Furthermore, the Directive provides that a competent authority can request that an investigation is carried out by a competent authority in the latter's territory, and may further request that members of its own personnel be allowed to accompany the personnel of the other competent authority during the course of such an investigation. However, overall control of such investigations will be in the hands of the Member State on whose territory it is conducted and authorities may refuse to act on a request for an investigation to be conducted, and refuse to allow personnel from another competent authority to accompany its own personnel on investigations, based on the same limitations as for requests for the provision of information set out in (1) to (3), above.

THE MARKET ABUSE REGIME IN PRACTICE

The Directive requires Member States to implement rules and sanctions against the use of inside information and market manipulation (which encompasses price distortion and dissemination of false and misleading information) in relation to "financial instruments" that are admitted to trading on a "regulated market" or in respect of which a request for admission has been made.

The definition of financial instruments in the Directive is broad reaching and covers:

- transferable securities (as defined in the Investment Services Directive and discussed further below)[7];

- units in collective investment undertakings;

- money market instruments;

- financial-futures contracts, including equivalent cash settled instruments;

- forward interest rate agreements;

- interest rate, currency and equity swaps;

- options to acquire or dispose of any of the above (including cash settled instruments);

- derivatives on commodities; and

- any other instrument admitted to trading on a regulated market in a Member State or for which a request for admission has been made.

Common approach

The creation of a common legal framework for market abuse has resulted in dramatic changes to certain Member States' domestic regimes, whilst in other cases, merely adding a further level of confusion and complexity to current prohibitions. For instance, in the United Kingdom, the Directive mainly replicates (and was largely based on) the prohibitions that were already in place, with the result that, notwithstanding the Regulations, the existing market abuse regime currently contained in Pt VIII of FSMA shall remain in force until at least June 30, 2008. In essence, the detailed prohibitions contained in the Directive have been bolted on top of Pt VIII of FSMA, together with the provisions of Pt V of the Criminal Justice Act 1993, adding an additional layer of complexity. Furthermore, certain market abuse legislation contained in the FSA's Principle for Business and its Statement of Principle for Approved Persons, applying to authorised and approved persons respectively, further extends the universe of legislation and rules that govern market abuse, which must also be read alongside certain exchange rules, and the Take Over Code. This position is in total contrast to the position in Ireland, where the Directive represents a radical change to its environment where previously there was no offence of market manipulation, and the rules governing inside information have been largely repealed and replaced as result of implementing the Directive. This has an impact for the CMBS market as Ireland's structured credit market has

---

[7] As mentioned above, the Investment Services Directive is to be superseded by MiFID with an anticipated effective date of November 1, 2007.

undergone tremendous growth in recent years, both as a jurisdiction of domicile and more recently as a jurisdiction of origination, which coincided with the beginning of major market developments in European CMBS. Arrangers and originators have been quick to capitalise on the benefits of Ireland as a domicile for these deals on a cross-border basis, with Ireland's broad double-taxation treaty network facilitating payments with minimal withholding tax concerns.

The introduction of a "single passport" allows investment companies authorised in their home state to perform investment services across the EU. The Directive builds on the rules and regulations established under the Insider Dealing Directive,[8] which were confined to preventing the misuse of privileged information, and the Investment Services Directive[9] which established the legislative framework for investment services in the EU. More importantly, the Directive seeks to eradicate and harmonise the differing degrees of rules and sanctions relating to market abuse applied by Member States (notably the lack of a common position between Member States for rules against market manipulation) to create a common legal framework throughout the European Community financial markets covering insider trading and market manipulation.

KEY PROVISIONS AND IMPLICATIONS FOR CMBS

Although the prohibitions against the use of inside information and market manipulation are key provisions of the Directive (and will be dealt with below), it is the disclosure requirements that are the cause of much discussion in the European CMBS markets and especially how these impact upon the current trends for investor reporting and the access to investor information. In recognition of this, in 2005, the Commercial Mortgage Securitisation Association Europe ("CMSA Europe") and the European Securitisation Forum (ESF) (CMSA-Europe and the ESF are together the "Associations") created a joint Market Abuse Directive Task Force (the "Task Force") to explore potential issues for, amongst others, the European CMBS markets arising from the implementation of the Directive on insider dealing and market abuse.

Investor reporting

There is an obvious concern that investor reporting, and disclosure generally, to the market is commercially sensitive for transaction participants

---

[8] Directive 89/592/EEC.
[9] Directive 93/22/EEC.

and that an excessive disclosure regime could cause concerns for the European CMBS markets, and in particular could give rise to difficulties for borrowers or property management companies if they are required to disclose sensitive information. Servicers and other transaction parties are also bound by duties of confidentiality and the potential for direct conflict with the requirements of the Directive are clear. As a result, the Associations recommend that the standards for post-issuance reporting include, and identify as such, all information regarding the portfolio of securitised assets which would be considered likely to have a significant effect on the pricing of the securities relating to those assets in accordance with the Directive's definition, having regard to the "reasonable investor" test (discussed below).

In order to assist market participants with these determinations, the Associations recommend the use of existing industry standardised reports where available, such as the CMSA-Europe's European Investor Reporting Package ("E-IRP").[10]

Disclosure requirements

The Directive requires Member States to introduce a variety of disclosure and reporting obligations on issuers and other persons relating to financial instruments by placing strict obligations on issuers to publicly disclosure inside information. In doing so, the Directive fails to take account of the distinct nature of CMBS transactions and how the parties to the transaction, such as the SPV issuer and other parties such as the servicer, are responsible for reporting, or deal with the impact faced with the Directive's disclosure requirements will have on the duties placed on those parties under the transaction documents.

Member States must ensure that issuers of financial instruments disclose to the public as soon as possible inside information which directly concerns it. Where inside information is disclosed by a person to a third party in the normal course of their employment, profession or duties, that person must make complete and effective public disclosure, simultaneously in the case of intentional disclosure and promptly in the case of non-intentional disclosure.[11]

Inside information that is made public must be done so in a manner which enables fast access and complete correct and timely assessment of the information by the public. Furthermore, issuers must take reasonable care

---

[10] UK only, version 1.0 for CMBS, see Appendix 3.
[11] Except where such person owes a duty of confidentiality regardless of whether such duty is based on a law, on regulations, on articles of association or on a contract.

to ensure that the disclosure of inside information is made to the public in a synchronised manner so that all relevant classes of investors across all Member States obtain such information as closely in time as possible. When making those disclosures, issuers are specifically prohibited from combining, in a misleading manner, the provision of inside information with the marketing of its activities.

The implementing legislation incorporates, by reference, certain provisions of Directive 2001/34[12] which means that issuers must make inside information available to the public by publishing such inside information in one or more newspapers distributed throughout, or widely distributed in, the Member State(s) concerned[13] or by other equivalent means approved by the competent authorities. For example, according to local regulations implementing the Directive, issuers with securities listed in the Irish (ISE) or in the Luxembourg (LSE) Stock Exchanges, as the case may be, are allowed to disclose inside information through company announcements posted on the Stock Exchanges websites. Both the ISE and the LSE confirmed to ESF and CMSA Europe staff that they are technically capable of publishing ABS and CMBS post-issuance regular reports on their company information services (RNS). In addition, the Directive specifically requires Member States to place an obligation on issuers to post on their internet websites, for an appropriate period of time, all inside information that they are required to publicly disclose.

The need to publicly disclose inside information is a constant requirement and so any significant change to disclosed inside information must also be disclosed promptly after such a change has occurred and through the same means as the original inside information was disclosed. Given that disclosure obligations fall on issuers, a concern arises as to the adequacy of an SPV issuers' capacity in CMBS transactions to assess the information themselves and effect disclosure where applicable. Further concerns arise as to the ability or expertise of parties to transactions such as servicers, trustees or corporate service providers to assess what information regarding the portfolio of securitised assets could be price sensitive and, thus, should be disclosed according to the Directive. These concerns become more acute when one considers that SPV issuers in CMBS transactions are not generally in charge of post-issuance reporting nor have the means or the expertise to assess what is considered "inside information". Issuers will be deemed to

---

[12] Art. 102(1) and 103 of Directive 2001/34/EC of the European Parliament and of the Council of May 28, 2001 on the admission of securities to official stock exchange listing and on information to be published on those securities.

[13] Or made available to the public in writing at such places as indicated by announcements in one or more newspapers distributed throughout, or widely distributed in, the applicable Member State(s).

have disclosed the inside information as soon as possible if they have promptly informed the public and the existence of a set of circumstances or the occurrence of any event even if it is not yet formulised.

To ensure compliance with the Directive, it is clear that market transparency must be increased through regular, standardised post-issuance reporting and through the dissemination of post-issuance reports. Procedures should be put in place to ensure that potentially inside information can be clearly identified. Post-issuance reports should be made generally available to the marketplace and not limited to current security holders (including those with password-protected access, subject to limitations from applicable securities offering laws as the case may be). As they should contain all information identified as potentially price-sensitive in the offering documents so that servicers or those parties delegated with the decision-making process know what to do with such information, once appropriately disclosed to the public, they should not be capable of constituting market abuse. In those jurisdictions where the relevant competent authority requires a specific form of disclosure of inside information, issuers should ensure that such form of disclosure is technically adequate for the dissemination of post-issuance reports and inform potential investors of the same in the applicable offering documents. At a minimum, issuers should ensure that disclosure of inside information (as and when it is determined to be so) is made in accordance with the applicable rules of any home state competent authority.

INSIDE INFORMATION

The provisions of the Directive on inside information, raises complications for CMBS transactions. This is because in contrast with equity or ordinary fixed income transactions, inside information in the context of CMBS transactions may relate not to a corporate or financial institution issuer but to a securitised pool of assets serviced by an originator or other specialised third party.

Immediate disclosure

The Directive requires immediate disclosure of "inside information" as mentioned above. Throughout the market a general consensus has developed that best practise would dictate monthly reporting. Whilst some national central banks (such as the Italian and Dutch) already require SPV issuers to provide monthly investor reports, there is a level of thought that this may be difficult to comply with in a majority of European transactions due to their quarterly interest periods structure. This has the result that there remains certain intra-period risk in certain jurisdictions, that is, the risk that "inside information" arises that must be disclosed before the next reporting date. Furthermore, there is also an additional risk, though remote, that circumstances not covered by the reporting documents arise which may constitute "inside information". To address these specific concerns, in the event that the SPV issuer does not delegate the responsibility of disclosing "inside information", the transaction documents should identify a set of events occurring with respect to the securitised assets which are likely to constitute inside information. The servicer should be instructed to notify such events to the SPV issuer upon becoming aware of them and the SPV issuer or its delegate should effect disclosure in the manner determined by the applicable regulation. In the event that the SPV issuer delegates the responsibility of disclosing "inside information", servicers and other service providers within the transaction, such as the cash managers, may be the most suitable parties to carry out this function provided that they have or are provided with the resources or the expertise to assess the price sensitivity of events affecting the pool of assets.

Delayed disclosure

Notwithstanding the requirement of immediate disclosure, the Directive allows issuers to delay the disclosure of inside information so as not to prejudice its legitimate interests, provided however, that such a delay would not be likely to mislead the public and provided further that the issuer can ensure that such information remains confidential. In this regard, Member States have the ability to require issuers to inform the competent authority of any decision to delay the disclosure of inside information. Implementing Directive 2003/124 stipulates that for an issuer of information to be considered to be keeping such information confidential, it must control access to such information and, in particular:

- establish effective arrangements to deny access to such information (to persons other than those who require access by virtue of their functions within the issuer),

- take measures to ensure that any person with access to such information acknowledges the legal and regulatory duties entailed and is aware of the sanctions attached to the misuse or improper circulation of such information, and

- have in place measures which allow immediate public disclosure in case the issuer was unable to ensure the confidentiality of the relevant inside information.

Directive 2003/124 identifies two examples of when an issuer may have a legitimate interest in delaying disclosure of inside information, namely:

(1) negotiations in course where the outcome of such negotiations would likely to be affected by public disclosure. Specific reference is made to

the financial viability of the issuer being in "grave and imminent danger" where disclosure could undermine specific negotiations aimed at ensuring the long term financial recovery of the issuer, and

(2) decisions taken or contracts made by the management of the issuer which need the approval of another body of the issuer in order to become effective provided that disclosing before obtaining such approval would jeopardise the correct assessment of the information by the public.

What is inside information?

Article 1 of the Directive defines inside information as "information of a precise nature which has not been made public, relating, directly or indirectly, to one or more issuers of financial instruments or to one or more financial instruments and which, if it were made public, would be likely to have a significant effect on the prices of those financial instruments or on the price of related derivative financial instruments." In the case of those persons responsible for the execution of orders concerning financial instruments, inside information covers inside information (as defined above) which is conveyed by a client to such a person and relates to that client's pending orders.

When is information precise?

The definition of "inside information" is fleshed out in implementing Directive 2003/124 which sets out the meaning of the phrases "information of a precise nature" and "likely to have a significant effect on the prices". From these, it can be seen that information will be of a precise nature if it indicates a set of circumstances which exist, or may reasonably be expected to come into existence, or an event which has occurred, or may reasonably be expected to do so, and if it is specific enough to enable a conclusion to be drawn as to the possible effect of that set of circumstances or event on the price of financial instruments or relevant to a derivative financial instruments. However, this leaves unclear how "possible effect" is to be interpreted, and in the absence of any guidance, the safest possible route may be to err on the side of caution and assume that information may have a possible effect on the price without having a probable effect or even likely effect. For parties normally involved in CMBS transactions, such as servicers and trustees, who are not legally obliged to disclose to the public "inside information" and may not have the expertise or the time to assess whether the occurrence of an event with respect to the asset pool will have a "significant effect" on the pricing of the securities or not, this presents problems.

Moreover, given the fairly broad and vague definition of inside information provided by the Directive and the relevant implementing directive, transaction parties may not, for a number of reasons, be able to determine if information is in fact inside information. First, as stated above, such parties may not have the expertise or resources to be able to make informed decisions on the potential impact of information relating to the underlying assets of the portfolio will have on the price of any related financial instruments, and secondly they may not be capable of determining, in the context of having a "significant effect" on price, if such information would be used by a reasonable investor "as part of the basis of his investment decisions".

The reasonable investor test

Given the objective nature of the "reasonable investor" test, there is a legitimate concern within the CMBS industry about the amount of information in CMBS transactions which could be "inside information" and, although needing to be disclosed, the disclosure of which may well be viewed negatively by borrowers/originators. This is especially so, when information will be considered likely to have a significant effect on price when a "reasonable investor" would be likely to use it as "part of the basis of his investment decisions". While seemingly less vague that the interpretation of the phrase "information of a precise nature", the implementing Directive does not deal with how much information need form part of the investment decision. Therefore, it would seem that no matter how small a part of the decision making process such information holds, a person using such information could be considered to be in possession of inside information.

The E-IRP (discussed above) should contribute to improve prospective investors' understanding of the risks of the assets, of the proposed structure, as well as encourage secondary trading of CMBS. Therefore, market participants might find these reports as helpful tools to determine what information a "reasonable" investor "would be likely to use as part of the basis of his investment decisions".

A further complication arises when one considers the stratified structure of CMBS transactions at the securities level. As we saw in Ch. 8, subordinated debt tranches are in a first loss position and typically absorb losses without interrupting payments to more senior tranches, that may result in an event in the securitised pools of assets having a "significant effect" on the pricing of one tranche of the transaction but not on the others.

Therefore, for information relating directly or indirectly to a financial instrument that has not been made public to be considered inside information, it must be of a sufficiently precise nature by having a possible effect on price. The question of whether there has been a significant effect on price is answered by considering if a reasonable investor would likely use such information as part of the basis of his investment decision. As one can see from reading this definition, there is scope for interpreting what could be considered to be inside information. When one further considers that an issuer in a CMBS transaction will typically (with certain exceptions) be a special purpose vehicle (SPV) set up as a bankruptcy-remote entity, the sole purpose of which is to pass cash-flows from the underlying assets to the securities holders, the question of whether the issuer is in the best position to address the issues raised by the definition, and indeed will be capable of monitoring inside information for itself, is of concern.

In an attempt to address this concern, it is possible that the service providers of the transaction (i.e. servicers and cash managers),[14] by nature of the fact that they are the ones most likely to come across inside information as a result of them carrying out their functions, contractually assume the responsibility for assessing and disclosing "inside information" and keep the issuer indemnified for any legal liability or, failing this, the SPV issuer directly assumes this responsibility. In such a case, the SPV issuer would need to be given adequate control over a transaction post-issuance reporting.

Furthermore, the Directive requires Member States to prohibit not just natural, but also legal persons[15] who posses inside information by virtue of:

(1) their membership of the administrative, management or supervisory bodies of the issuer,

(2) their holding in the capital of the issuer,

(3) their access to the information by way of their employment, profession or duties, or

(4) their criminal activities,

from using such inside information to acquire or dispose of, or trying to acquire or dispose of, for his own account or for a third party, either directly or indirectly, financial instruments to which that information relates.[16]

The absence of any EU-wide requirement to make public a list of these financial instruments in respect of which a request for admission has been

---

[14] See Ch.14 for further discussion.
[15] A change from the Insider Dealing Directive, the Directive applies to both natural and legal persons. When concerned with the actions of legal persons the Directive applies to the natural persons who take part in the decision to carry out the transaction for the account of such legal person.
[16] Art. 2 of the Directive.

made, makes it difficult for competent authorities to determine if an instrument is caught by the Directive.

Inside information prohibitions not only relate to financial instruments that are admitted to trading on a regulated market, or for which a request for admission to trading on such a market has been made, but also to those financial instruments that are not admitted to trading on a regulated market but whose value depends on a financial instrument that is either admitted or for which an admission to trading has been made. Accordingly, the prohibition on the use of inside information will apply to those unlisted derivatives that reference publicly traded securities.

In addition, as well as prohibiting persons from using inside information as set out above, the Directive also prohibits disclosure of such inside information to any other person outside disclosure made in the normal course of the exercise of their employment, profession or duties or from recommending or inducing another person on the basis of inside information to acquire or dispose of financial instruments to which that information relates. Further, the dissemination channels provided for by certain Member States in their implementation of the Directive do not always provide the flexibility for the type of disclosure that CMBS transactions may require and do not necessarily reflect current market practice for the dissemination of information in transactions of this type.

In relation to derivatives on commodities, inside information means information of a precise nature which has not been made public, relating directly or indirectly to one or more such derivatives and which users of markets on which such derivatives are traded would expect to receive in accordance with accepted market practices on those markets.

In summary, the ultimate position seems rather unclear with almost conflicting standards to be achieved. Information need only have a possible effect on price to be considered of a precise nature but, in the final analysis, must have a significant effect on price. However, when considering if information has a significant effect on price it need only form part (rather than a "substantial" or "material" part) of the decision making process. The position is further complicated for issuers of financial instruments due to the fact that those Member States which have implemented the Directive have not interpreted the definition in the same way.

Insider lists

Issuers are also required to create and pass on to the relevant competent authority a list of those persons working for them under an employment contract or otherwise (which will include not only its employees but also its advisors and external contractors) who have access to inside information.[17] Moreover, each such list must be updated when appropriate and must be kept for at least five years after being drawn up or updated. However, because competent authorities in each Member State are free to independently apply the rules and the Directive makes no provision for mutual recognition of such lists, issuers may find themselves having to create (potentially numerous) lists of insiders which comply with the rules of each Member State in which its financial instruments are traded, creating not only a new but also potentially onerous administrative burden.

Investment research, recommendations and strategy

Persons who produce or disseminate research concerning financial instruments or issuers of financial instruments and persons who produce or disseminate other information recommending or suggesting investment strategy[18] (which includes any opinions as to the present or future value or price of that financial instrument or issuer) must take reasonable care to ensure that such information is fairly presented, and disclose their interests or indicate conflicts of interest concerning the financial instruments to which that information relates.

Implementing Directive 2003/125 fleshes out in greater detail the requirements placed on those producing investment research, recommendations and strategy, and looks specifically at the way such information should be published and the obligation on those persons to disclose all interests and conflicts of interests.[19] Any further discussion in this regard goes beyond the scope of this chapter, save that it should be mentioned that Directive 2003/125 expressly states that rating agency opinions issued on the creditworthiness of transactions do not constitute a recommendation for the purposes of the Directive. Nonetheless, the rating agencies should consider adopting internal policies and procedures designed to ensure that credit ratings published by them are fairly presented and that they appropriately

---

[17] The exact details of this obligation are contained in Art. 5 of the Market Practices Directive and require those lists to include the identity of insiders, the reason why they are on the list, and date on which such list was created or updated.

[18] Art. 1(3) of Directive 2003/125/EC defines research or other information recommending or suggesting "investment strategy" to mean (a) information produced by an independent analyst, investment firm, credit institution and any other person whose main business is to produce recommendations or a natural person working for them under a contract of employment or otherwise that directly or indirectly expresses a particular investment recommendation in respect of a financial instrument or an issuer, or (b) information produced by any other person not covered in (a) which directly recommends a particular investment decision in respect of a financial instrument.

[19] Art. 3 to 6, Directive 2003/125/EC.

disclose any significant interests of conflicts of interest concerning the financial instruments or issuers to which their rating relates.

Reporting suspicious transactions

Member States will require persons who professionally arrange transactions in financial instruments, who reasonably suspect that a transaction might constitute insider dealing or market manipulation, to notify the relevant competent authority without delay by postal mail, electronic mail, telecopy or telephone. Those who notify must provide to the competent authority, amongst other things, information regarding the transaction, reasons for suspecting market abuse and any information which may have significance in reviewing the suspicious transactions. Member States must also ensure that those people who notify a competent authority of suspicious transactions do not inform any other person, especially persons on behalf of whom the transaction was carried out. Failure to comply will not place the notifying person in liability of any kind provided that person acts in good faith.[20]

Complying with the laws of multiple Member States

Of specific relevance for the European CMBS market, is the definition of transferable securities in the Investment Services Directive (which defines transferable securities as shares in companies and other securities equivalent to shares in companies, bonds and other forms of securitised debt), in each case which are negotiated on the capital market, and any other securities normally dealt in giving the right to acquire any such transferable securities by subscription or exchange or giving rise to a cash settlement excluding instruments of payment. Once implemented, MiFID will broaden the definition of transferable securities mainly through the inclusion of depositary receipts in respect of shares, bonds and other forms of securitised debt. Accordingly, all classes of notes in CMBS transactions trading on a regulated market (or for which an admission to trading has been made) will be caught by the Directive. The prohibitions contained in Arts 2–4 of the Directive[21] will also apply to any financial instrument not admitted to trading on a regulated market, but whose value depends on a financial instrument which is so admitted or in respect of which an application for trading has been made.

The Directive incorporates the definition of "regulated market" from the Investment Services Directive. A financial market will be a regulated market

---

[20] Art. 11, Market Practices Directive.
[21] The prohibitions against the use of inside information, disclosing such information to any other person and engaging in market manipulation.

of a Member State for the purposes of the Directive if it is included in a list drawn up by the Member State of those regulated markets whose registered office, or if unregistered whose head office, is situated in that Member State and functions regularly and complies with the various admission, compliance and reporting requirements of that Member State. Under MiFID, a regulated market is defined more specifically as a multilateral system operated and/or managed by a market operator, which brings together, or facilitates the bringing together of, multiple third party buying and selling interests in financial instruments in a way that results in a contract in respect of such financial instruments and which is authorised and functions in accordance with the detailed provisions of Title III of MiFID.

Although the Directive applies to financial instruments that are subject to a request for admission to trading on a regulated market, in the absence of a requirement across Member States to maintain a public list of those instruments, it may be difficult to determine if a financial instrument is caught by the Directive.

There are, however, certain types of transactions that are expressly excluded from the provisions of the Directive.[22] Transactions carried out in the pursuit of monetary, exchange-rate or public debt-management policies by a Member State, the European System of Central Banks, by a national central bank or by any other officially designated body, or any person acting on their behalf, are not caught. Furthermore, Member States are also invited to extend the exemption to their federated states or similar local authorities in respect of the management of their public debt. In addition, transactions which amount to trading in own shares in "buy-back" programmes or to the stabilisation of a financial instrument are also excluded from the prohibitions contained in the Directive, provided however that the trading of these are carried out in accordance with the detailed prohibitions contained in the Market Abuse Exemptions Regulations.

MARKET MANIPULATION

The Directive requires Member States to prohibit any person (natural or legal) from engaging in market manipulation. The Directive provides an extensive definition of market manipulation consisting of three main elements.

---

[22] Art. 7 of the Directive.

First element

The first element covers transactions or orders to trade which:

(1) give, or are likely to give, false or misleading signals as to the supply of, demand for or price of financial instruments, or

(2) secure, by a person, or persons acting in collaboration, the price of one or several financial instruments at an abnormal or artificial level.

These types of transactions or orders to trade will not be prohibited if such person or persons, acting in collaboration, can establish that their reasons are legitimate and that such transactions or orders to trade conform to accepted market practices on the regulated market concerned.

The concept of accepted market practice is defined in the Directive as practices that are reasonably expected in one or more financial markets and which are accepted by the competent authority. The procedure for acceptance by a competent authority is detailed in Directive 2004/72 and requires Member States to consult appropriate bodies in the market place such as representatives of issuers of financial instruments, consumers, other authorities and market operators as well as competent authorities in other Member States to determine if a market practice should be accepted or not. Competent authorities are required to publicly disclose[23] their decisions regarding the acceptability of market practices concerned, and such information must be accompanied with details of factors which the relevant competent authority took into account when making their decision including any differing positions taken by other competent authorities in respect of the same market practice.

For the purposes of this element of market manipulation, Art. 4 of Directive 2003/124 sets out certain non-exhaustive factors, which although, in themselves, will not constitute market manipulation, competent authorities should take them into account when examining when transactions or orders to trade constitute market manipulation.

(1) To what extent transactions or orders to trade represent a significant proportion of the daily volume of transactions in the relevant financial instrument on the relevant regulated market.

(2) To what the extent orders to trade or transactions undertaken by a person with a significant buying or selling position in a financial

---

[23] Which includes a requirement to notify the CESR of the decision as soon as possible which the CESR must then make such information immediately available on their website.

instrument lead to a significant change in the price of the financial instrument or related derivative or underlying asset admitted to trading on a regulated market.

(3) If the transaction or order to trade leads to a change in the beneficial ownership of a financial instrument admitted to trading on a regulated market.

(4) If the transaction or order to trade represents a reversal of position in a short period of time and represents a significant proportion of the daily volume of transactions in the relevant financial instrument on a regulated market concerned, and might be associated with significant changes in the price of that financial instrument.

(5) Whether the transactions or orders to trade are concentrated in a short time span in the trading session and lead to a price change which is subsequently reversed.

(6) Whether orders to trade or transactions change the representation of the best bid or offer price of financial instruments, or more generally change the representation of the order book available to market participants, and are removed before they are executed.

(7) The extent to which orders to trade or transactions are undertaken at or around a specific time when reference prices, settlement prices and valuations are calculated and lead to price changes which have an effect on such prices and valuations.

Second element

The second element covers transactions or orders to trade which employ fictitious devices or any other form of deception or contrivance. As with the first element, Directive 2003/124 identifies certain non-exhaustive, and non-conclusive, signals which competent authorities should take into consideration when examining an order to trade or transaction, namely:

(1) whether the order to trade or transaction by a person is followed by the dissemination of false or misleading information by the same person or persons linked to them (although it is unclear what relationship is required to exist between persons for them to be linked), and

(2) whether the transaction is undertaken, or the order to trade is given, by persons before or after that same person or persons linked to them produces or disseminates research or investment recommendations which are erroneous or biased or demonstrably influenced by material interests.

Third element

The third element covers the dissemination of information through the media (which includes the internet) or any other means which gives, or is likely to give, false or misleading signals as to financial instruments. This includes the dissemination of rumours and false or misleading news where the person making that dissemination knew, or ought to have known, that the information was false or misleading. With no guidance on the phrase "ought to have known" it is unclear whether this implies an objective test of reasonableness. With some Member States simply copying out the wording from the Directive, the position remains unclear as between Member States.[24] The Directive makes specific reference to journalists who, acting in their professional capacity, disseminate such information. In such a scenario, Member States will be required to take into account the rules governing the profession, except where those persons derive, directly or indirectly, an advantage or profits from the dissemination of the information.

The Directive draws on the three elements of the definition of market manipulation discussed above and identifies the following three specific examples of market manipulation:

(1)   the conduct by a person, or persons in collaboration, to secure a dominant position over the supply or demand for a financial instrument which affects (directly or indirectly) the purchase or sale prices or creates other unfair trading conditions;

(2)   buying or selling financial instruments at the close of the market resulting in the misleading of investors acting on the basis of closing prices; and

(3)   taking advantage of the media by expressing an opinion about a financial instrument having previously taken a position on that financial instrument and profiting subsequently from the impact of such an opinion on the price of the financial instrument without having disclosed the conflict of interest to the public in a proper and effective manner.

The second of these examples seems misguided for there could be well justified reasons for trading out of a financial instrument near to the close of market, in this regard it is submitted that the Directive should have looked at the reasons for trading at close rather than the act itself of trading at close.

---

[24] The UK test is "could reasonably be expected to know".

CONCLUSION

As stated above, the overreaching purpose of the Directive is to further ensure a genuine integrated single market for financial services and efficient financial markets and to encourage public confidence in the trading of securities and derivatives through greater market transparency. By seeking to create a uniform regime against market abuse that will ensure the integrity of European Community financial markets, the introduction of the Directive and its implementation into the EU Member States have introduced significant changes in the way the European capital markets function and will in turn have a direct impact on the European CMBS markets, with those issuers listed on a regulated market being caught by the Directive and its various prohibitions and disclosure requirements. This has the result that, as discussed earlier, CMBS issuers and other transaction parties could now find themselves subject to the law of multiple Member States due to the fact that Member States must apply the Directive prohibitions not only to those actions that are carried out on its territory, but also to actions carried out on a regulated market in another Member State.

The Directive also impacts CMBS documentation. CMBS offering documents and the contractual documents for European CMBS should (to the extent they do not do so already) provide for appropriate procedures with regard to management and monitoring of the pool of securitised assets which ensure the automatic and prompt disclosure of price sensitive information in accordance with the recommended practices. In particular, clear and specific responsibilities should be allocated between and among transaction parties, such as servicers, trustees and other service providers, with regard to collecting information and assembling and distributing post-issuance reports and interim disclosures without need for a further assessment from these parties as to the nature of the information or the obligation to disclose it.

The Directive has had a significant effect on post-issuance reporting to investors in the European CMBS markets. However, notwithstanding the concerns raised above in relation to determining what information is considered inside information, the market, even before the Directive was, as a whole, calling for more transparency in the availability of information of CMBS transactions. There has been a push by investors, particularly in the secondary market, for investor reports to be made available to secondary investors, and the implementation of the Directive by Member States is proving a catalyst for change. The concern for a growing market is that the only way the market can continue to grow is for information that is made available to primary investors being more freely available to secondary investors. Without such transparency, it seems hard to envisage secondary investors willing to continue to invest in products they have little information about. As a result, this may have a negative impact on the price the seller can achieve on the pricing of CMBS bonds in the secondary market due to secondary investors' unwillingness to pay the par value of bonds where they have been unable to carry out sufficient due diligence on the underlying real estate assets of such bonds.

The public disclosure obligations on issuers, introduced by the Directive, will necessitate a change in the way investor reporting is conducted. The traditional practice in European CMBS for ongoing reporting to investors has been to make investor reports available solely to investors (or participants in clearing systems holding the securities on their behalf) and other transaction parties through password protected websites. At the time of writing this chapter, the market was already seeing a shift in allowing key transactions information to be more freely available (subject to the caveat that a general free for all disclosure regime regarding sensitive information surrounding all of the loan, may not work in all circumstances) to the public as a whole with it becoming less acceptable for material investor information to be password protected. The Directive will change the way reporting is conducted so that it will no longer be acceptable, or even legal, for material investor information to be password protected. A system of best practice will dictate that open access to information will become the order of the day, and it will be important that the market as a whole determines the best way for such information to be disclosed. Failure to do so would inevitably lead to the relevant competent authorities in Member States regulating the process themselves, which is not in anyone's interest.

CHAPTER FOURTEEN

INVESTOR REPORTING

**Jaymon Jones, Client and Investor Reporting Manager
Hatfield Philips International Ltd**

INTRODUCTION

Hatfield Philips International Ltd ("HPI"), as a third party primary and special servicer, has asset managed various types of commercial real estate and loan transactions within the UK and European markets since 1997. These transactions cover an array of real estate finance structures varying from senior, mezzanine and junior lending to pure equity positions. As one of the few true third party servicers in the European market, HPI asset manages such transactions on behalf of a number of clients.

A further component of asset management of loan portfolios is the management of CMBS securitisation programmes. Since 2004, the UK and European CMBS market has seen a tremendous level of growth and sophistication in terms of issuance, collateral, borrower type, structure and jurisdiction, to name a few. As the CMBS market has grown, so too has the need for standardisation of CMBS reporting by the various servicers in the market. In direct response to this growth HPI has developed methods of reporting to facilitate transparency and to tackle reporting issues.

CREATING A SUCCESSFUL INVESTOR REPORTING PACKAGE

An Investor Reporting Package ("IRP") is a standard information package that should aim to meet the needs of all CMBS structures and transaction types for investors. There are four key areas that need to be considered in order to create a successful IRP:

- the source of data to be used;

- data standardisation;

- the levels of information required; and

- the issues in the current European market which will affect the IRP.

Sources of data

In order to create a successful IRP package for European CMBS a starting point for a servicer is the ability to receive accurate and clear source data. The provider of source data is ultimately the borrower and the data requirements are, in the first instance, detailed in the loan documentation. The two key limitations of source data relate to timing and standardisation. In terms of timing, the unfortunate reality of borrower reporting requirements is that they are typically a final point of discussion when agreeing loan documentation and, more often than not, originating banks concede on reporting requirements that appear too onerous on certain borrowers in order to maintain a level of so-called relationship lending.

Loan documentation

Loan documentation varies immensely as each originator has its own standards and, typically, each respective law firm acting for the originator has its own standard and style of documentation. A key feature of the growing CMBS market will be the eventual standardisation of loan level documentation, which will enable efficient data management of loan details and obviously quicker execution of loan agreements.

Borrowers

As there are variations in loan documentation standards, there are similarly variations in the type of borrowers that CMBS originators are lending to. The variations range from high net-worth individuals seeking property investment through to property investment companies that invest through a fund style structure. The level of data available from the different types of borrowers also varies from very limited information provided by individual borrowers to very detailed information provided by sophisticated property investment companies. Although data from high-net individual property investors is typically limited, when compared to the data available from companies, this is usually due to the limited information available to the advisors of individual-type investors. Individual-type borrowers typically have external accountants who extract this detailed level of information and, more often than not, the loan document reporting requirements and CMBS reporting requirements are not dictated to these external parties.

A further restriction on the information available is that most borrowers are not familiar with the data requirements necessary for CMBS transactions and, unless a borrower is executing a large stand-alone CMBS-type transaction, the originating banks rarely inform borrowers of the full CMBS reporting requirements.

As the source data is ultimately provided by the borrower, it should be the given responsibility of CMBS originators to explain the reporting requirements to their borrowers. Although the servicer will need to collate and interpret the data provided, the servicer has no initial direct contact with the borrowers to fully assume this role. Furthermore, CMBS originators need to explain the loan documentation, detail the levels of information and formats required to be produced to the servicer. This will then allow the servicer to process the data in the most efficient and effective manner.

Loan coverage ratios

Offering circulars for CMBS transactions in particular, can prove to be a misleading and confusing source of loan level information as key financial ratios outlined can often be calculated in a fashion unfamiliar to a number of relative parties such as the servicer, the borrower and the bond investor, and investors should exercise caution in the interpretation of figures.

An IRP should accurately describe loan coverage ratios which can be given in various formats, but typically include interest cover, debt service cover and loan-to-value ratios. The variations are further complicated by the timescale of the coverage ratio that needs to be tested (i.e. this could be forward looking or backward looking). Loan-to-value ratios can also be complicated in terms of the reference value they refer to, that is, they could refer to original values at loan origination and not be the most recent valuation performed.

As a third party servicer, HPI always requests, from the originator, details of how ratios have been calculated to understand the ratios displayed in offering circulars against IRP standards. In essence, the offering circular reported ratios should mimic the reporting standards of the servicer, as the servicer will attempt to standardise, and the servicer will be more often than not be obligated to report according to the servicing standard.

Servicers should also work with borrowers to accurately calculate and agree borrower level figures. In particular, where borrowers are required to produce borrower certificates, the servicer should work with the borrower to calculate the ratios correctly.

Data standardisation

International organisations such as the CMSA, the European Securitisation Forum and Fitch Ratings have recently achieved great leaps towards setting new standards, which will strive towards creating market transparency and comparable transaction reporting and encouraging the growth and the secondary markets.[1] Even though different levels of standardisation are being applied to the market by different organisations, it has become apparent that, irrespective of which particular standard is adhered to, in this growth phase of the European CMBS market, there are certain levels of information which are necessary for market players to be able to track comparative deal performance.

As a start to the process of reporting standardisation, there are four main areas that borrowers on every transaction should be responsible for reporting on. These areas should be detailed as a standard on loan documentation and are not, therefore, areas where concessions are possible:

- market information,
- property management reports,
- leasing reports and strategy, and
- financial reporting.

Details of the information required in each of these areas are contained in the Annex to this chapter.

A servicer should also maintain guidelines which identify potential concerns regarding the loan, which can be applied systematically to determine whether a loan should be added to a watch list. Key criteria would be financial conditions, borrower issues, property condition issues, lease roll over, tenant issues and vacancy, maturity and other servicer discretions.

Levels of information

There are three key levels of information required in an IRP:

- loan level information;
- property level information; and
- tenant level information.

---

[1] For further details, see Ch. 15.

Information at loan level from the borrower is dynamic, however, the IRP should contain the majority of information contained in the offering circulars. Such information includes cut off balances, original note rates, maturity dates and general prepayment information as well as at issue financial data. In addition, loan level information should be updated with the remittance and reporting cycle in order to track loan changes due to scheduled and unscheduled payments as well as any modifications a loan might have.

Property level information provided in an IRP should contain static details of all properties related to a loan. In addition, property level details should be broken down into individual financial performance which will highlight the weaker properties within a portfolio.

Tenant level information should be provided at a loan level on exposure to top income producing tenants, number of leases, annual gross rental income, and overall portfolio income exposure over time.

An IRP should not focus on the current market trends but it should be written in such a way that the investor can understand what is happening in the market from a variety of sources and compare how the properties are performing in their relevant markets. Commentary is a very important aspect to this. Whilst it is very useful to follow charts and ratio trends, it is also very important to get a feeling of what is happening at the property, loan and tenancy levels. In many cases it's very useful to give a brief summary of the initial loan at closing and follow up with the progress of the loan, giving information on why a ratio has changed.

Servicer specific issues in the current European market

A number of European and UK specific issues have arisen in terms of reporting such as the lack of standards in analysing borrower financials statements, increased complexity of loans and recent disclosure requirements.

Methodology for analysing property income statements

The responsibility for collecting financial and property operating information from the borrower for each transaction is usually placed on the servicer, but it may vary with each transaction. A detailed approach to understanding borrower financial information and applying a standard which can be viewed across various loan structures, property types and regional jurisdictions has not been achieved within the market. The operating data from borrowers is used by many different parties for analysis purposes and, therefore, it is necessary to provide this information in a more standardised format. It is important that a methodology for standardising the analysis and reporting of this data be consistent across different servicers.

Reports produced on the loans should provide underwriting information and ongoing information for subsequent years, as well as the most recent financial information available. This allows for meaningful analysis based on historical data. Collecting and analysing this information is an extremely important task because the results provide investors and others with the ability to measure the performance of the underlying collateral. This, in turn, provides insight as to the performance of the loan.

Loan complexity

Loans are continually becoming more complex and, with those changes, the IRP must also be able to capture the key details which show the factors that make the loan compliant and its performance.

With the increase in AB Structures,[2] providing accurate coverage ratios has become even more difficult. The servicer is obligated to manage a loan at a whole loan level and servicing systems are also designed to report calculations on this basis. However, investors in securitised deals have usually invested in the A piece and like to view the coverage ratios on their share rather than on the whole loan. This presents a dilemma for investor reporting as to which coverage ratios to include as, if the A piece ratios only are shown within the IRP, investors would not be aware of the true performance of the loan.

Income cannot be apportioned based on the AB split as the loan covenants are based on the whole loan. Amortisation can also skew ratios when dealing with AB structures and, in some cases, the amortisation can be split pro rata. However, if amortisation is only applied to the B piece then the A piece's DSCR will not accurately show the true whole loan position.

Figures which are displayed at the property level and loan level and which are provided at the close of the origination do not clearly identify the true picture, as these can be based on gross rental income and therefore ignore tenant level expenses which can occur. Furthermore, they amount to snapshots at quarter dates and do not reveal historical trends. This is mostly due to very short duration on most commercial loans. In addition, as stated, contribution figures in offering circulars only show the A piece of a loan and, more often than not, this selected information distorts the perception of the loan.

---

[2] For full details, see Ch. 8.

Regulation and disclosure requirements

Currently there are no regulations in place that describe the level of information that can be disclosed, there is however a requirement for the disclosure of inside information, the Market Abuse Directive[3] ("MAD"). In light of MAD, which has been designed to increase transparency, efficiency and liquidity in the secondary market, and it's obligations therein, the team at HPI began by asking what information they, as a third party servicer, receive, which an issuer (legally responsible for disclosing inside information) could consider to constitute "inside information" as defined within the Directive. It was concluded that there are a number of situations where the information received by a third party servicer ought to be passed to the issuer in order that they may review its effect on the price of the notes. Those situations include:

- **Prepayments:** Any loan prepayments should be notified to the Issuer including sales and re-financing. However, this would exclude sell downs in multi-family residencies as the fact that there are a high number of prepayments will have been factored in the transaction.

- **Watch list:** Notification would be made of any loan which was entered onto the servicer's watch list. It is recommended that the notification also provide a risk rating for each watched loan and a brief description of why the loan is being monitored. The loans would be sorted in order of level of risk according to the list below:

Risk Rating	Reason
1	Risk of loss
2	Payment Default, Past Maturity or Event of Default
3	Covenant Breach
4	Programme Variance or Cost Overrun
5	Nearing Maturity
6	Inadequate or Late Reporting

- **Tenant/lease information:** This would include the purpose of any consents given by the asset managers, such as surrenders by tenants and sublettings, and the outcome of any rent reviews. It is proposed that this be limited to any lease or tenant activity which would affect a certain percentile of the gross income of a loan. It is suggested that this

---

[3] For full details, see Ch. 13.

percentage should be determined by CMBS industry participants and then be used as an industry standard.

- **Environmental:** Any environmental issues which could potentially affect the value of the property or the loan, such as, asbestos, black mould or subsidence, that was discovered as a result of an environmental survey, would be included on the notification.

- **Insurance status:** Any material insurance claims made by the borrower, such as fire, flood or legal action, that may have an impact on the property or the borrower's ability to make payments should be reported to the issuer. In addition the issuer would be notified if insurance was not in place.

- **Collateral's surrounding area:** Anything which is discovered that may materially affect the value of the property or loan should be reported. This information would be based on facts gleaned from observations made during the annual property inspection.

- **Valuation changes:** Any increases or decreases in the value of the properties that are discovered as a result of a professional valuation will be notified to the issuer.

HPI are of the opinion that, if this information is received, it could be provided to the relevant known parties to the CMBS transaction, for example, issuers, cash managers and trustees, on a monthly basis except on those months where quarterly reporting is produced, in order to prevent any duplication.

It is also felt that it is not generally within a third party servicer's range of expertise to determine whether a piece of information it receives whilst carrying out it's contractual obligations would have a significant effect on the price of the securitisation's notes and could therefore constitute "inside information". It is therefore proposed that all information of this nature be passed to the respective issuer, who would then assess its potential affect on price and disseminate the information by the required means in order to make it accessible to the public.

The sources of the majority of this information are the borrowers or property managers as a result of a loan agreement's requirements or as one of the obligations under a servicing agreement. As the loans are structured to protect asset value, it is unlikely that there would be any further information which would be received that could be described as "inside" as defined by the Directive and adhering to the reasonable investor test, although, there may be some information which is received annually upon property inspection which would be included in the annual report that the issuer could determine to be "inside".

Third party servicers would not be able to provide the issuer with any market information which may affect price as this would be beyond the scope of their contractual obligations and expertise.

CONCLUSION

The requirements of investor reporting for investors of loan and CMBS transactions have increased in-line with the growth of the CMBS market throughout Europe. It is very important for all market participants to continue to apply standardisation and to work together to set achievable rules and regulations. To achieve the goal of effective market transparency it is crucial that originators and their legal teams, along with the servicers, rating agencies and trustees, work together to implement workable standards that enable comparative deal analysis, transparency and consistency in reporting standards. This in turn will lead to the continuing growth and success of European CMBS.

ANNEX I

1. **Executive Summary/Project Overview**

2. **Market Report**

    a) Overview comments:

      i. current market conditions including local availability, prevailing rental patterns and outlook, and
      ii. relevant independent market studies incorporating area supply, demand, rental values, take-up and investment yields.

    b) Major events, competition, photos.
    c) Articles from local press.

3. **Property Management Report**

    a) Overview comments.
    b) Tenancy Schedule.
    c) New Leases signed in period.
    d) Leases maturing in next 12 months and action being taken (including forecasted increase and details of ongoing negotiations).
    e) Managing Agents reports (e.g. to include arrears and collections).
    f) Proposed sale strategy(ies) and actions taken.
    g) Maintenance and capital improvements.
    h) Tenant relations.
    i) Litigation.
    j) Valuation Changes (revised valuations).

4. **Leasing Report and Strategy**

    a) Marketing—setting initial budget and ongoing status.
    b) Target tenants.
    c) Leasing enquiries.
    d) Status of enquiries.
    e) Strategy.

5. **Finance Report**

    a) Overview Comments.
    b) Balance Sheet.
    c) Summary of Cash Receipts and Disbursements (by Property).
    d) Operating Statement (Profit & Loss Statements) (by Property).
    e) Actual v budget (for Period and Year to Date) (by Property).
    f) Loan Covenants and compliance certificates.

CHAPTER FIFTEEN

THE SECONDARY MARKET IN EUROPEAN CMBS

Rob Ford, Managing Director, Head of European ABS Trading
Hans, J. Vrensen, CFA, Drs Econ, MRE, Director of
European ABS Research
Barclays Capital

INTRODUCTION

Given the current status of the European CMBS market as a fast growing and developing, yet still immature market, it is not surprising that secondary trading in European CMBS bonds has been limited to date. Most investors view CMBS as a small (but growing) sub-sector of the overall ABS market, which has resulted in a current lack of dedicated CMBS investors and traders, and therefore this chapter will broaden its discussion to include the wider ABS universe. This chapter explores the current secondary market size and considers some structural changes currently under way that could remove some of the impediments to growth in this market.

LIMITED SIZE OF SECONDARY MARKET

Market size and limitations to growth

When discussing trading volumes in European ABS, the first point to note is the lack of any official figures. Barclays Capital believe the sector would benefit greatly if one of the clearing houses or stock exchanges that transact ABS bonds were to produce overall trading statistics on an aggregate and periodic basis. Alternatively, this could be done by the relevant industry organisations (such as ESF or CMSA) or commercial data services (like ABS Net or Markit) with the co-operation of ABS trading desks and investors.

Given the lack of industry statistics, Barclays Capital have come up with their own estimates, which for 2005 secondary market trading in European ABS is approximately €100bn.[1] This compares to the estimate of €60bn for 2003 and €80bn for 2004, which implies a compound annual growth rate (CAGR) of approximately 19 per cent over the last three years.

The estimate for trading in the first quarter of 2006 was €35bn, which represented 35 per cent of the total volume traded in 2005. In fact, the Barclays Capital secondary ABS trading volume for the same quarter was up by more than 50 per cent compared to the first quarter of 2005. However, this might be due to specific trade opportunities executed by the Barclays Capital trading desk, and therefore may not be an accurate reflection of growth in the overall market volumes (see Figure 1, below).

Compared to primary issuance (which had a CAGR of 17 per cent over the same period), it was noted that trading, as a percentage of primary issuance, had been fairly constant at around 34 per cent up to 2005, but more than doubled in the first quarter of 2006 to 70 per cent. This chapter will consider this rather large increase fully later.

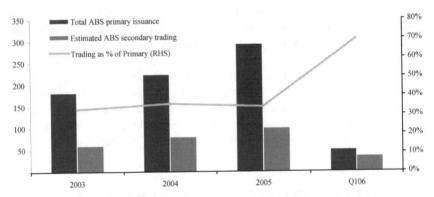

Figure 1: Primary issuance and estimated secondary ABS trading (EUR).

Source: Barclays Capital.

The historical breakdown of quarterly indexed volume in Figure 2(below) shows the distribution of Barclays Capital secondary ABS trading by sector. The following points are noted:

---

[1] These estimates are based on Barclays Capital's secondary ABS trading desk actual trading volume in 2003–2005, combined with limited data from inter-dealer brokers on third party dealer trading assuming a certain percentage of inter-dealer and investor trading.

(1) there are fairly large differences between one quarter and the next;

(2) when considering the sector breakdown, RMBS is by far the most traded asset class, representing 49 per cent of total historical trading since 2003;

(3) the "other" category, which has historically been the second most traded sector, contains many large one-off deals, such as government sponsored securitisations (such as social security contributions and delinquent tax receivables), and large SME CLO's;

(4) whole business holds a significant proportion (14 per cent) of trading volume, which is interesting considering the relatively small percentage this sector represents in the overall issuance over the same period (9 per cent); and

(5) the rest of the trading activity is relatively equally split between consumer and CMBS, each accounting for 10 per cent of total trading.[2]

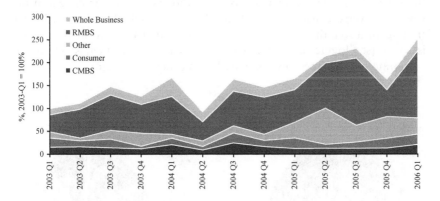

Figure 2: Secondary trading by sector (%, Q1 03 = 100).

Source: Barclays Capital.[2]

Figure 3 (below) shows clearly that secondary trading volumes by sector are broadly consistent with the relative share of different sectors in the primary issuance market.

The results for the ABS sector are not particularly surprising. However, when looking at the breakdown by coupon type, it should be noted that fixed-rate traded bonds represent a much larger proportion of traded

---

[2] Please note that all further figures in this chapter pertain to secondary trading by the Barclays Capital secondary ABS trading desk.

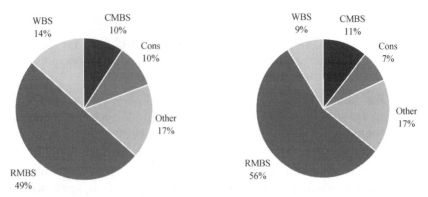

Figure 3: Trading volume (left) and primary issuance (right) since 2003 by sector.

Source: Barclays Capital.

volume (25 per cent) than their share in total issuance would imply (11 per cent). The difference is largely accounted for by whole business securitisations, which predominantly issue fixed-rate bonds. About 25 per cent of the CMBS universe consists of fixed rate bonds as well. Both have a higher trading turnover than the other sectors compared to their share of total issuance (see Figure 4, below). This is probably due to their similarity to corporate bonds, especially compared with other ABS sectors.

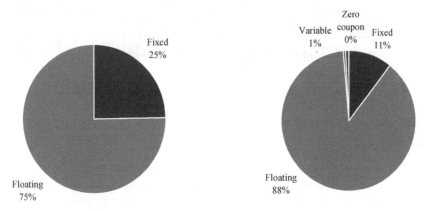

Figure 4: Breakdown of European ABS trading (left) and primary issuance (right) since 2003 by coupon type.

Source: Barclays Capital.

TRADING PATTERNS

This section explores trading patterns as a result of different trading parties as well as comparing primary issuance to trading volume per sector.

Given that investment bank trading desks and investors are the two main categories of ABS traders, we can easily categorise European ABS trading into two different categories of trades;

- trades between trading desks; and

- trades between trading desks and investors.

Trading between investors is not common in the European bond markets. However, trading between trading desks appears to be quite strong and this is probably because most medium and smaller desks trade more with other trading desks than with investor clients. The largest volume of trading between trading desks and investors is likely to be somewhat reserved for the larger trading desks, with large primary distribution volumes and capabilities. Of the 20 contributors to the ABS index (which will be discussed later in this chapter), Barclays Capital think that approximately six or seven are large desks, and the remaining desk are in the mid-size to smaller category. Estimating numbers of actively trading investors is also dealt with later in this chapter.

Figure 5 looks at trading compared to primary issuance. The figure shows the evolution of issuance in parallel with traded amounts, both expressed as a percentage of the base period, which is the first quarter of 2003. Although both series have trended upwards over the past three years, as the market has continued to mature, there seems to be a negative correlation between

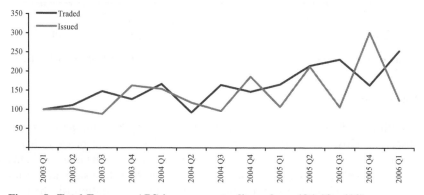

Figure 5: Total European ABS issuance vs. trading volume (Q1 03 = 100).

Source: Barclays Capital.

the rates at which they have grown. This can be explained by the fact that when primary issuance is high, most investors are busy analysing these new deals and trying to obtain the best possible allocations in the primary market rather than bidding for paper in the secondary market. Conversely, investors might be likely to use any lull or slowdown in primary issuance to more actively seek allocations in the secondary market. A contrarian strategy of buying in secondary when no other investors are focused on it and selling in secondary when other investors have time available, might be sensible.

When the break-down by sector is looked at, it is noted that RMBS exhibits the same negative correlation between the rates of growth in issuance and trading as does the overall ABS market. This is to be expected given that RMBS currently represents more that 50 per cent of total traded volumes and is therefore likely to show the highest similarity with the overall market. In contrast, CMBS shows quite a different story, with issuance increasing dramatically over the past three years while traded volumes are relatively flat. The CMBS graph is somewhat distorted given that the first quarter of 2003 was an especially low issuance quarter (see Figure 6, below). A later comparison will show that CMBS is not that much of an outlier.

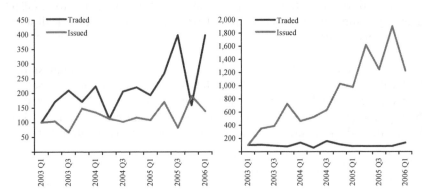

Figure 6: Issuance vs trading volume for RMBS (left chart) and CMBS (right chart), Q1 03 = 100.

Source: Barclays Capital.

Within CMBS trading, some further interesting trading patterns are observed. Most secondary CMBS trading is likely to take place with the trading desk of the bank that was the original arranger of the issuance. This might be partly due to investors seeing arrangers as their first stop, but could also be the result of the lack of publicly available information on the performance of the transactions, which is likely to render other trading desks' bids unattractive. Additionally, there are a number of other frequently

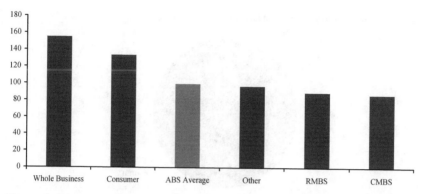

Figure 7: Barclays Capital secondary ABS trading as a percentage of issuance by sector indexed to the ABS average (%, ABS average = 100).

Source: Barclays Capital.

discussed impediments to growth in secondary trading including the fact that most investors claim to be buy-and-hold investors. The investor perspective on secondary trading is discussed in more detail below.

Furthermore, a lot of trading occurs in the few days after the primary offer has been allocated. This is probably due to the fact that many primary offerings are significantly oversubscribed, with investors getting less than their full requested allocation. In some cases, investors may even have a deliberate strategy of getting a small allocation to sell it off at a small profit in secondary right after issuance. In other cases, investors may not be in a position to actively monitor a small position if their other holdings are more significant in size. Clearly this allows those investors to match-up with other investors that want to top-up their actual allocations to be closer to their targeted allocations.

THE INVESTOR PERSPECTIVE

The main reason usually cited in explaining the limited volume of secondary trading, is that most European ABS investors are buy-and-hold investors. Barclays Capital conducted a survey among ABS investors recently, in which 84 per cent of respondents confirmed that they were indeed buy-and-hold investors. This is also confirmed by the fact that as a percentage of their overall ABS portfolio, 88 per cent of ABS assets were acquired in the primary market. This implies that the large survey respondents are a bit more likely to be buy-and-hold investors than the smaller ones (see Figure 8, below).

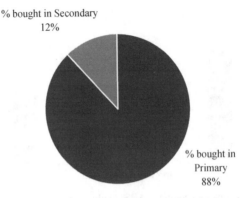

% bought in Secondary
12%

% bought in
Primary
88%

Figure 8: Investor survey respondents—ABS assets bought in primary and secondary markets.

Source: Barclays Capital.

According to the results the survey, 12 per cent of ABS assets are bought in secondary, accounting for €20bn for the survey respondents. Since the survey respondents account for 28 per cent of the overall universe, the total European ABS assets acquired via secondary trading can be estimated at approximately €75bn. However, these assets may have been acquired over a number of years. If it is assumed that the average period is 18 months, this would imply that secondary trading by investors totals around €50bn per year.

This is significantly lower than the €100bn estimate for 2005 provided by the Barclays Capital secondary trading desk. This could be partly due to the fact that the survey respondents are less interested in secondary trading compared to the overall market. However, it is more likely that the inter-dealer trading, which is not incorporated in the investor survey results, accounts for this difference. This would imply that around 50 per cent of secondary trading in European ABS takes place between banks' trading desks, which, given the current status of the market is highly plausible. it was noted that smaller trading desks were more likely to have a high per-centage of their trades with other trading desks, compared to larger trading desks which could be expected to trade more with investors.

When the investor survey results are considered further, it is important to note that only two out of 50 respondents had no ABS assets that they had acquired through secondary trading. The average of assets bought in the secondary market among the respondents was 16 per cent. The weighted average was 12 per cent, as noted in Figure 8, above. This implies that the larger investors were less likely to acquire assets in secondary trading. If an active ABS investor is defined as an investor that has acquired 20 per cent or more of its ABS assets through secondary trading, then 17 actively trading investors were noted as being included in the respondent sample (or 34 per cent of the total). Since the respondent sample makes up 28 per cent of the overall European ABS universe, the number of European ABS investors can be estimated at 180 to 200 investors. Finally, if it is assumed that the sample behaves in a similar fashion to all other investors, it can be estimated that there are 60 to 70 European investors who actively trade ABS in the secondary market.

When asked how important secondary market liquidity was, the responses were somewhat different from what might have been expected from buy-and-hold investors. On a scale of one to 10, 10 being the most important, a majority of respondents scored secondary market liquidity at seven or higher. This is interesting in light of the 84 per cent of survey respondents that claimed to be buy-and-hold investors. The exact breakdown is provided in Figure 9, below. Of course, many respondents mentioned that despite the fact that they might not use the liquidity provided by the secondary market, it would be nice to know that it is there. Furthermore, with the expansion of the European ABS investor base, structured investors and fund managers are expected to become even more prevalent. These investors might be expected to trade more actively than earlier investors. If this bears out, a decrease in the number of buy-and-hold investors in European ABS in future would be expected.

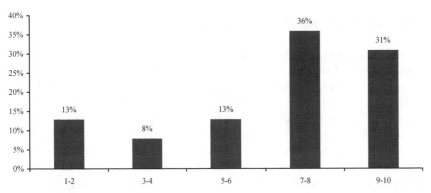

Figure 9: Survey respondents ranking of secondary liquidity (on scale from 1 = not important and 10 = most important).

Source: Barclays Capital.

If investors are keen to see better secondary market liquidity in European CMBS, then the question of how investors define secondary liquidity arises. This definition could include a sufficient number of competitive bids from trading desks, but this leaves significant room for subjective interpretation, such as, what exactly sufficient and competitive mean. To address these issues, the bid-ask spread is considered and determination is made as to a level that is sufficiently acceptable to investors. This spread might differ between ABS asset types. It should be noted that some investors may only need market pricing for their mark-to-market valuations rather than actual execution. This may mean that some investors only look for execution liquidity in a crisis situation, when it might be more difficult to obtain.

However, rather than discussing the exact definition, it might be more interesting to review some of the limitations to growth in secondary trading. These include a lack of public disclosure of investor reports, a lack of transaction structure and collateral standardisation, limited information on secondary pricing and the status of current third-party cash flow modelling. Since there has been significant progress on all of these fronts, the next section of this chapter discusses how recent developments impact these impediments.

STRUCTURAL CHANGES AND IMPROVEMENTS

A number of recent developments were under way at the time of writing that should improve the market infrastructure and are likely to accommodate further growth in secondary ABS trading.

Improvements in public data availability

Discussions amongst various market participants have been taking place over the last 12 months regarding the lack of public disclosure in certain segments of the European ABS market, especially in the CMBS sector. One of the key arguments that has increasingly been made, is that public disclosure of investor reports might be legally required by the European Commission's Market Abuse Directive (MAD). Article 6(1) of the Directive states that "Member States shall ensure that issuers of financial instruments inform the public as soon as possible of inside information which directly concerns the said issuer". The issuer is defined as one which is listed with a regulated market in an EU Member State. It has been suggested that perhaps the publication of periodic investor reports on password-protected websites would not comply with the MAD.[3] A representative of the Irish Stock Exchange confirmed that under Irish legislation, information needs to be disseminated via the proper regulatory news service. The commercial argument for making the information publicly available has not been widely made, but clearly more secondary trading by investors should bring addi-

---

[3] For further information on this, see Ch. 13.

tional investors into the ABS sector and create pricing stability in the long term.

Furthermore, the ESF has joined up with the Commercial Mortgage Securitisation Association (CMSA) to form a joint task force on MAD. During the various panels, the general consensus was that it would be far preferable for the industry (via that joint task force) to address these disclosure issues by announcing best practices, rather than having the rules enforced by a regulator or waiting for an investor to file a legal case against an issuer for insufficient disclosure. The new best practices, which include the recommendation to remove the password-protection for investor reports, have, at the time of writing, been posted and made available for comments from industry participants. Some have observed that issuers have in fact two options regarding the disclosure requirements, namely, comply or de-list from a regulated market. The last option might have a severe impact on the pricing of any bonds issued by a non-regulated issuer.

The European CMBS index

One development that is expected to improve secondary market liquidity and boost traded volumes is the expected launch of a European CMBS index in the latter half of 2006. The introduction of an index allows CMBS investors to benchmark their own performance against an independent benchmark. This index will complement the broader based iBoxx ABS50 index, launched at the beginning of 2006. The index might focus on providing a synthetic rolling index for UK and European multi-borrower CMBS conduit deals.

Similar to the ABS50 index, there will probably be "on the run" and "off the run" indices, with new series created on a regular basis and a dealer poll, formed initially of 16 to 20 dealers who will provide daily prices on each index. This is a major advantage compared to other bank-sponsored CMBS indices launched in the past, which rely on single trading desk pricing.

This new index should help improve liquidity as issuers will have a hedging tool that will enable them to lock in spreads while still building up their loan books before securitisation. In addition, structured investors, such as CDOs and SIVs, are logical counterparties that might use the index product to build up exposure quickly in their ramp-up phases.

Pricing service from Markit

Another breakthrough that is expected to improve both the quality and quantity of pricing information available to ABS investors was the launch late in 2005, by the independent service provider Markit, of a pricing service dedicated to ABS. For several years, Markit has provided asset valuation information for a variety of asset classes (such as corporate bonds, CDS, Convertibles and Loans). This recent expansion into the ABS market is expected to improve the transparency of the European ABS market going forward and possibly incentivise the use of ABS securities as collateral in the repo market, by providing a reliable source of prices for margin and haircut calculations.

Previously, most pricing information could only be obtained from individual institutions' trading desks, who, due to the complexity of the instruments and the difficulties in systemising the process, would often only provide a full list of revaluations on a monthly basis. The new pricing platform compiles prices received from more than 20 major market makers, removes the upper and lower outliers and performs an average of the remaining providers. The fact that the service aggregates prices from different sources ensures a higher degree of independence and transparency which has been lacking from the market. Whilst prices on fixed-rate bonds have been widely available for some time in the ABS and CMBS markets, the Markit service will greatly improve the availability of pricing in floating rate ABS bonds.

The service currently provides bid/offer prices, spreads and average life information on more than 3,300 European ABS bonds, of which approximately one third have three or more price contributors and represent approximately 45 per cent of the total outstanding European ABS volume.

Advancement of third-party cash flow models

Improvements in the availability of third-party cash flow modelling have been mostly related to the increased coverage of deals by third-party firms, such as Bloomberg, ABSNet, ABSXchange, Trepp and Intex. Third-party cash flow models allow investors to assess the relative value of various ABS transactions and share their models with buyers and/or sellers to allow for a more efficient and productive price negotiation. The removal of selective-deal password-protection from the websites for some of these models— expected shortly—will further improve the research coverage of the sector.

However, a few issues still remain. First, there is a lack of analytical capability of the existing models in certain sectors, such as CMBS. These do not allow investors to stress any assumptions on the property or tenant level. This is not an issue for highly diversified CMBS transactions with many loans, but this type of deal is very rare in the current European CMBS market. In fact, still more than half of the outstanding issuance is single borrower-type deals. Limiting the analysis to the loan level does not really allow investors to consider the true credit concerns with these deals. Secondly, it seems that there might be an increase in the number of third parties that will offer cash flow models. Even though this will be useful in the long term, since it will put pressure on all providers to improve the quality of the models, it might create confusion in the short term (such as determining which model is best to use).

Standardisation in European CMBS

Certain developments in deal structures might also be beneficial for secondary trading, with standardisation continuing in the RMBS and consumer ABS markets, with more issuance from master trust structures. In addition, a certain amount of standardisation is beginning to creep into the European CMBS market, by way of the increased issuance from CMBS conduit programmes. Despite the large number of such programmes, the repeat issuance from them should make things easier for investors. Repeat issuance from one programme, assuming the same collateral jurisdiction, should have a similar (if not identical) paydown and security structure. This saves investors time and allows them to focus on the new collateral pool rather than re-visit the deal structure each time.

OUTLOOK FOR SECONDARY CMBS TRADING

The structural changes and improvements discussed above seem likely to stimulate further growth in secondary CMBS turnover in the coming years, partly on the back of further growth in primary issuance. The innovations such as the introduction of the CMSA's E-IRP[4] and the discussed improvements in secondary trading could attract further investors to the European CMBS market, even if they might include different types of investors than have participated in the past. Finally, secondary trading is expected to become more relevant in the market at any point where there is saturation in primary issuance in the future.

---

[4] See Appendix 3.

INTRODUCTION TO CONTINENTAL EUROPEAN CMBS MARKETS

Recent statistics on European CMBS markets give a fairly robust picture of activity, and it is incredible to think that in recent years, European CMBS markets have grown at a faster rate than the US CMBS market, with overall European CMBS growth from 1999–2005 sitting at 888 per cent. It is even more incredible, when one considers that the European CMBS markets have achieved this growth within the backdrop of a number of jurisdictional challenges (originators, structuring and rating agencies must take into account the tax, security, enforcement, and insolvency regimes) of differing legal systems and economic realities across the continent and a wide range of deal structures.

Whilst, the vast majority of European CMBS activity (over 70 per cent in 2005) is based on UK assets and is Sterling-denominated, no book on European CMBS should be considered complete (as pointed out by Ronan Fox in the foreword to this book) without any examination of the other continental European markets and the jurisdictional challenges faced therein. This section will attempt to undertake such an examination. Of course, not every European jurisdiction can feature, however, the most active markets of Germany (second to the UK, with about 10 per cent of total European CMBS deals in 2005, with some market participants expecting the volume of German asset deals to overtake UK asset deals in 2006 with German multi-family housing leading the charge), France (where a law has recently been passed which could aid forced sales and foreclosure regimes), Italy and Spain are featured, along with a look at the Portuguese market which has recently enacted legislation in an effort to establish a more efficient framework for CMBS transactions.

The wider European markets stretching east of Germany have not featured yet, but who knows what possibilities lie across this continent. If these markets were to feature anywhere near the growth of the more established European CMBS markets, then the prediction of reaching the $100 billion annual issuance in a shorter time frame than the US will be not a prediction but a reality. We live in exciting times and, if continental Europe further adapts the legal landscape to facilitate mortgage-backed securitisation, if the kinks are worked out of securitisation programs to take into account the legal realities in the various continental European jurisdictions, and if further securitisation programs are put in place, then CMBS will continue to grow organically and remain a competitive alternative to other forms of finance in the European commercial real estate finance arena. The next five chapters will detail how the various continental European CMBS markets are adapting to differing legal and economic realities.

CHAPTER SIXTEEN

AN INSIGHT INTO GERMAN MULTI-FAMILY

Dr Olaf Fasshauer, National Partner
Dechert LLP
Andrew Currie, Senior Director
Gioia Dominedo, Associate Director
Grif Winkler, Associate Director
Stefan Baatz, Associate Director
Fitch Ratings

The German multi-family housing ("MFH") market is enjoying a period of heightened interest from international equity investors. As more transactions are being financed in the capital markets, CMBS bond investors are also starting to focus on the market. The activity in 2004, 2005 and the first two quarters of 2006 has exceeded expectations, with Germany leading the way in CMBS in continental Europe.

HISTORIC BACKGROUND OF GERMAN CMBS

Following the Second World War, the German residential market suffered from a severe housing shortage of property due to the large proportion of stock that had either been destroyed or severely damaged during the war. To address this problem, the German government encouraged third parties to provide housing and it assisted through both one-off contributions and ongoing support in the form of subsidies and low-interest loans. The Social Housing Act of 1940 (*Wohnungsgemeinnützigkeitsgesetz*), supplemented by additional legislation in the post-war period, formed the basis of the provision and organisation of social housing until 1998, when it was abolished. Residential properties were constructed by housing associations, many of which remain today, and large corporates that offered housing to their employees as part of a compensation package. In addition, government entities constructed housing stock of their own, that was offered to state employees at affordable rents.

These government policies have resulted in over 70 per cent of the current housing stock in Germany being built after the Second World War. Eighty per cent of this was built before 1979 and a further 14 per cent was built within four years after the German reunification in 1990.

Following the reunification of Germany and the subsequent migration from the east, a temporary shortage in housing supply triggered a renewed surge in construction activity. These new developments were also supported by subsidies and government loans. By the mid-1990s, however, it became apparent that the reaction had been excessive and that several local markets were suffering from over-supply, which led to increasing vacancy rates. This combined with a general economic downturn to create a stagnation of the property market. Only recently have rental levels increased slightly in major cities.

Currently, the policy focus is on decreasing state support and intervention. The new Housing Law of 2002 (*Wohnraumförderungsgesetz*) has shifted the emphasis to existing housing stock rather than new developments, including urban development projects and co-operation between housing associations and welfare associations to support lower-income citizens, single parents and larger families. In addition, responsibility has been shifted to federal states and cities to ensure that local needs are adequately addressed. Privatisation of the current housing stock is also being encouraged. Although rent restrictions gradually phase out and thus rental levels can be freely negotiated at the start of a lease; rental increases of existing leases are still regulated both at federal and municipal levels.

The situation in Eastern Germany is of particular concern. Due to the low average quality of the residential stock, extensive renovation has been required in recent years. In addition, high emigration has exacerbated vacancy rates. The combined factors of vacancy and low-quality units have prompted the launch of a €2.7 billion "Conversion of Cities in the East" programme to focus not only on renovation but also demolition of properties, to be completed by 2009. A few towns in the West have also commenced similar programmes, but on a smaller scale. Despite these policies, excess supply—especially in the East—continues to depress rental levels.

The historical emphasis by the government on the provision of housing at affordable rents led to one of the lowest residential owner-occupation rates of all major developed countries. In addition, home ownership was not possible in multi-family properties in East Germany prior to reunification. On average, today 57 per cent of Germans rent the flat they live in. However, the owner-occupation rate varies largely between the different German Länder (meaning Federal States), East and West Germany and rural areas compared to large cities. In general, the owner-occupation rate in West Germany is higher than in East Germany and more people in rural areas own the house they live in than those who live in Germany's large cities. The largest city, Berlin, has the lowest owner-occupation rate at all. Only 13 per cent of all people who live in Berlin own the flat they live in. Home ownership also varies substantially according to household size, age and income: in essence, larger, older and more affluent families have the highest probability of owning their homes.

Despite their stated goal of increasing home ownership, past governments have not affected the ownership structure of the country in a major way. The availability of relatively inexpensive rental housing continues to dissuade the acquisition of residential units. Further disincentives include significant property transaction costs (including a 3.5 per cent real estate transfer tax, costs for estate agents and notary fees), local policies that complicate the privatisation process and the absence of mortgage interest tax relief that is present in some other European countries. Consequently, home ownership remains low.

CURRENT MARKET OVERVIEW

More than two dozen large residential portfolios have been traded in recent years, and more are expected to be put under offer in the near future. A stagnant economy over more than a decade, a high unemployment rate and enormous costs for German reunification led to high debts in the public sector, affecting every level from the federal state to the Länder and the local communities. Supported by a political climate of decreasing state support and intervention, local communities started to sell off their community-owned MFH. Only recently the city of Dresden sold more than 10,000 city owned flats to an investor, paying off all of its public debt with this single transaction. Other cities are said to be interested in the same kind of transaction. It is also very likely that the Länder and the federal state will come to the conclusion that this is an appropriate way of funding for the public sector. Moreover, many corporates that previously offered accommodation as part of their employee compensation package are now finding that, in light of high unemployment, this is no longer a necessary incentive to attract employees, and are therefore selling off their housing portfolios to generate liquidity and focus on their core business. In short, an increasing supply of investment property is becoming available as the market opens up.

The sale of these portfolios—particularly the large ones—has attracted a lot of international interest, seeking the potential upside of these portfolios. Besides business plans based on the estimation that portfolios, which have been run by not-for-profit entities, can be restructured both on the operating company and property level to obtain higher returns, there are other arguments for such a potential upside: Germany has one of the lowest owner-occupation rates of all major developed countries, but as the public pension insurance suffers from an ageing society, more and more Germans are beginning to see a flat or a house owned by themselves as an integral part of the personal pension plan. In light of the lowest interest rate in post-war Europe the pension effect of a property has been a marketing tool of German lending banks in recent times. As the German economy is picking up again and interest rates are still low, it is expected that even more people will invest in a private property. It is also expected that due to demographic changes household sizes in terms of dwelling space per person will grow and overcompensate a shrinking society.

Most large portfolios of MFH are acquired with the intent to sell a portion, if not all, of the units to make a profit. Four main methods may be used to sell units in a portfolio:

(1) privatisations;

(2) block sales;

(3) share sales; and

(4) real estate funds and real estate investment trusts.

Privatisations

This option relates to the "condominiumisation" of assets into individual sale units. The most immediate source of interest in residential units lies in the tenants themselves, who may be interested in acquiring their properties rather than continuing to pay rent. This option typically offers the highest returns, but it is more time-consuming (particularly if there are restrictions on disposals of the units) and management-intensive. Given the low owner-occupation rates and the different view of a property as part of an individual pension plan, this is an option. Investors often encourage tenants to buy, and offer ready-to-sign lending packages of partner banks. However, the success of this model depends very much on the location and the quality of the property.

In addition, it is less likely to succeed in portfolios where tenants have lower average income levels, where there is greater tenant turnover and where the average unit size is smaller. This last issue is more likely to cause difficulties in the East, where the average unit size is smaller (according to the Federal Statistical Office of Germany, the average is of 76.7 sq m, compared with 92.2 sq m in the West). Finally, privatisations are to a certain extent contingent on current interest rates, which will affect the financing available to prospective buyers. The "condominiumisation" of MFH will require the permission of the local authorities.

Block sales

These permit the owner to dispose of a number of units simultaneously; however, they are usually achieved at a lower price than attainable through privatisations. This is typically an exit option for units in geographical proximity, which may be marketed to local and smaller international investors.

Under German law, the sale of a leased unit will typically not affect its lease and it may be completed without the tenant's consent.

Share sales

This option is essentially a block sale on a larger scale, which may be feasible especially when portfolios are held in various separate subsidiaries of the borrower, thus allowing for the possibility of selling entire subsidiaries to a single buyer without having to incur any real estate transfer tax. This share method is likely to target international investors.

Real estate funds and real estate investment trusts ("REITs")

A final possibility is a block sale to an existing fund or the creation of a new fund to hold the assets. This fund may in turn finance its acquisition through debt and/or through a public offering to either retail or institutional unit investors that will benefit from the upside potential of the portfolio. REITs—which benefit from tax efficiencies—provide an alternative potential exit strategy, but do not yet exist under German law. However, it is expected that REITs will be introduced in Germany in the near future to compete with other European real estate markets.

LEGAL FRAMEWORK

There are several issues to be taken into consideration in a CMBS deal involving German MFH and these are discussed below.

German trade tax

A CMBS deal is usually structured as a true sale transaction. The illiquid balance sheet assets (receivables) which generate a regular payment flow are changed into liquidity. This is achieved by the originator (typically a lending bank) selling the assets to a Special Purpose Vehicle (SPV) which issues tradeable securities to raise funds and finances the purchase price to be paid by the SPV to the originator. The true sale securitisation offers the originator therefore both, risk transfer—and therefore equity relief—and funding within a single transaction.

In general, trade tax (*Gewerbesteuer*) falls due on every business carried on in Germany, whether by a resident or a non-resident. It is a local tax in Germany and the rates vary between 12 per cent and 15 per cent, depending on the local community.

Until 2003, an SPV had to pay trade tax on 50 per cent of the interest paid to the purchasers of the securities issued by the SPV. This tax fell due, no matter if the SPV generated any profit or not. This trade tax burden often made securitisations unattractive from an economic point of view.

Even before 2003, banks located in Germany were privileged and exempted from the obligation to pay trade tax of 50 per cent on the interest paid. This, so called, bank privilege was extended by the German legislator in 2003 to include SPVs in ABS or CMBS transactions, provided they are structured properly. The purpose of this tax relief was, to promote securitisations in Germany.

Funding register (*Refinanzierungsregister*)

On September 28, 2005, an amendment to the German Banking Act (*Kreditwesengesetz—KWG*), included the regulations on a newly introduced funding register in the KWG. As far as CMBS true sale transactions are concerned, the purpose of the funding register is to give:

(1) the originator the possibility to hold in trust any collateral (such as land charges (*Grundschulden*)) for the SPV, and

(2) the SPV the right to request a separation of the collateral from the assets of the originator in case of insolvency of the originator in accordance with German insolvency law.

It is therefore no longer necessary to transfer the collateral to the SPV, or another entity controlled by the SPV, to make this collateral insolvency remote. The originator may hold any collateral in trust for the SPV and this collateral can be separated from the assets of the originator in case the originator goes bankrupt, provided that such collateral has been properly registered in the funding register. The funding register can be run by any bank located in Germany and is, in each case, monitored by an independent administrator, paid by the bank but supervised by German banking supervisory authority (*Bundesanstalt für Finanzdienstleistungsaufsicht—BaFin*).

As the originator, if it uses the funding register, can hold all collateral in trust and is no longer required to transfer such collateral, this will also save transfer costs related to the collateral, such as notary fees for the transfer of a land charge.

Banking secrecy

Banking secrecy is an integral part of the contractual relationship between a bank and its customers. In a widely recognised decision, the higher regional court of Frankfurt am Main (*Oberlandesgericht Frankfurt am Main*) ruled, in 2004, that the assignment of the claims of a bank against its customers to a third party could be illegal in cases where this could be considered a breach of banking secrecy rules (for example, because sensitive data are transferred to the purchaser of the claim), thus making an assignment of claims invalid in cases where there is no consent by the bank's customer. This court decision caused a lot of excitement and has been heavily discussed in the securitisation industry. However, in 2004 and 2005 there have been further court decisions of the regional court of Frankfurt am Main (*Landgericht Frankfurt am Main*) and other courts, making clear that banking secrecy rules do not prohibit the transfer of a bank's claim to a third party, such as a securitisation vehicle. The vast majority of legal authors are of the same opinion. It is therefore now clear, that banking secrecy rules do not prohibit the transfer of claims. However, it is strongly recommended that banking secrecy rules are respected in any CMBS deal, as a breach of these rules could lead to a claim for damages by the customer against the bank. In order to avoid any interference with banking secrecy rules, banks now include the right to transfer claims to a third party expressly in their general terms and conditions.

Data protection

The German Act on Data Protection (*Bundesdatenschutzgesetz—BDSG*) prohibits the transfer of an individual's sensitive personal data, unless this is expressly permitted by law or the relevant individual gave their consent. This can be an issue in CMBS deals involving German MFH, as a due diligence done prior to a securitisation may also reveal sensitive data pertaining to individuals, such as, names, account details and events of defaults of private tenant.

In a CMBS deal involving German MFH it is not realistic to get the express consent of each individual tenant. Therefore, the following strategies are viable:

(1) No protected data is disclosed during the due diligence process—in most cases this seems the most appropriate way to address data protection issues. In this case a transfer of tenant's data will only take place according to (3), below, after closing of the deal.

(2) The parties use a neutral data trustee that ensures compliance with the data protection rules—this can be the correct strategy in cases where additional, protected data is required, which may only rarely be the case in deals involving German MFH.

(3) The parties make use of a specific exemption of BDSG—According to BDSG a disclosure of protected data is allowed, if this is in the legitimate interest of the person or entity disclosing that data. This may be hard to argue in a due diligence process, but would apply when the deal is closed.

In any case, any issues regarding German data protection laws should be addressed properly, as a breach of German data protection rules may be regarded as a criminal offence. However, it does not make the transaction null and void.

OUTLOOK

The perspectives of the investor in German Multi-Family CMBS seem to be better than ever: A low owner occupation rate combined with an economy that's picking up again, interest rates that are still low and the people's different view on a private home as the best "pension plan" you can get, are very likely to boost the market and lead to higher real estate prices rather sooner than later. Not to forget that the German Legislator will encourage institutional and private investors even more to invest in German real estate by introducing a German Real Estate Investment Trust (G-REIT) in the near future. The introduction of the G-REIT has been agreed in the coalition agreement of the new German government and such introduction is expected for early 2007. Thus, the German MFH CMBS market may even outrun the mature UK market.

CHAPTER SEVENTEEN

THE CMBS MARKET IN FRANCE

Joseph Smallhoover, Partner
Dechert LLP, Paris

THE FRENCH SECURITISATION MARKET

The French securitisation market saw its birth with the adoption of Law no.88–1201 on December 23, 1988 (the "FFC Law") which created the FCC or *fonds commun de créances* (now codified in the French Monetary and Financial Code ("MFC"), Arts L.214–5 and L.214–43 to L.214–49). The FCC Law was implemented by regulations promulgated by Decree no. 89–158 of March 9, 1989 (the "1989 FCC Decree"), notably by Decree No. 2004–1255 of November 24, 2004 (the "2004 FCC Decree").

Fonds Commun de Créances (FCC)

The FCC Law created a new legal institution, the *fonds commun de créances* (collective debt fund or unit trust) or FCC, similar to the previously existing *fonds commun de placement* (collective investment fund) or FCP used as a vehicle for collective investment schemes, and incorporating methods used for the assignment of professional receivables under the so-called Dailly Law of 1981. The FCC is a jointly held or co-owned fund that is neither a legal entity nor an undisclosed partnership,[1] but something *sui generis* akin to and sometimes translated as unit trusts.[2]

Article L.214–43 initially provided that the "exclusive" purpose of an FCC was the acquisition of receivables and the issuing of units which represent those receivables. Following its modification by the Financial

---

[1] French Civil Code Arts 1871–1873.
[2] The translation "unit trust" is somewhat misleadingly used in the unofficial translation of the MFC published by the French Official Journal (www.legifrance.gouv.fr), as French law does not recognise the common law institution of the "trust".

Security Law (Law No. 2003–706 of August 1, 2003), the "exclusive" purpose was widened to allow FCCs to issue debt instruments[3] and enter into forward financial instruments. This latter, much welcomed, modification permits the structuring of synthetic structures by the FCC and eliminates thereby one of the drivers for structures using offshore SPVs.

The FCC is created jointly by its management company and its custodian. Whilst the management company, which acts as the legal representative of the FCC and ensures the proper financial management of the FCC, must be a French entity licensed in France by the *Autorité des Marchés Financiers* (or AMF);[4] the custodian, which holds the cash and receivables of the FCC and supervises the activities of the management company to ensure it complies with the General Regulations (*Réglement Général*) of the AMF, may be a credit institution licensed in France or elsewhere in the European Union or the European Economic Area or other credit institution licensed by the French Ministry for the Economy.

An FCC may acquire virtually any type of receivable under the MFC, although the FCC's internal rules (*réglement*) must provide for the types of receivables that it may acquire (such as trade receivables, financial leases (*crédit-bail*), rental streams and mortgage-backed debt), in order to give investors in the FCC the required security. The receivables themselves may either be governed by French law or the law of another jurisdiction and may be pre-existing at the time of their transfer, or may not yet have come into existence.[5] The now clarified ability of the FCC to acquire future receivables represents a major step forward in French securitisation law. The case law of the French Court of Cassation was, at the beginning of the decade, unclear as to whether it was possible to assign future receivables as the Commercial Chamber of the Court ruled in April 2000 that such future receivables did not pass to the FCC in the case where the assignor was ordered into judicial liquidation (*liquidation judiciaire*).[6] The First Civil Chamber of the Court, however, adopted a contrary position in a decision rendered a year later[7] with a change ensuring a remoteness from bankruptcy with respect to these receivables that was in doubt as a result of the Court of Cassation decisions. Moreover, since the doubts raised by the Court of Cassation, decisions were broadly seen as a brake on the development of the French market, the removal of those doubts is now viewed as the possible engine to drive future expansion of the CMBS market in France.

---

[3] MFC Art. 213–3.
[4] MFC, Art. L.214–47.
[5] Decree No. 2004–1255 of November 24, 2004, Arts 2 and 3.
[6] April 26, 2000 Ch. Com. *Bull. 2000* IV No.84.
[7] *Bull. civ.* I, No.76, March 20, 2001.

Mechanism of securitisation

The FCC acquires ownership of the receivables by virtue of the signature by the assignor of a private deed of transfer[8] which states that it is a deed of transfer subject to Arts L.214–43 to L.214–48 of the MFC and setting forth the identity of the assignee and designating the receivables being assigned in sufficient detail to identify them (either in written or electronic format). The transfer of the receivables identified on the transfer deed, takes place with respect not only to the assignee and the assignor on the date appearing on the transfer deed upon its handing over to the assignee, but also as regards the debtor and other third parties without any additional formalities.[9] This is a departure from the ordinary Civil Code rules which provide that an assignment is only effective as against the debtor and third parties upon notification of assignment by a bailiff or if the assignment is accepted by the debtor in a notarised deed of transfer.[10]

Unlike the instruments giving rise to the receivables themselves, which may be held by the assignor or the entity that collects the receivables,[11] the transfer deeds may only be held by the custodian.[12] The transfer of the receivables automatically gives rise to the transfer of any security related thereto, including specifically mortgages.[13]

Servicing of receivables

The servicing of the receivables will normally continue to be carried out by the assignor, although servicing can be entrusted to a licensed credit institution or the Caisse des Dépôts et Consignations ("CDC") provided the debtors are informed thereof in writing.[14] A recent trend has seen the sub-delegation of some of the servicing of receivables to entities that are not licensed credit institutions, no doubt in response to market practice in the UK where the designation of servicers and special servicers[15] has become common.[16]

---

[8] MFC, Art. L.214–43, eighth paragraph.

[9] ibid.

[10] Civil Code, Art. 1690. A similar procedure was first adopted in 1981 at the time of the adoption of the Dailly Law on the assignment of professional receivables. (Law no. 81–1 of January 2, 1981, Art. 1; MFC Arts L.313–23 et seq.).

[11] MFC, Art. L.214–48, II; 2004 Decree, Art. 20.

[12] 2004 Decree, Art. 20.

[13] MFC, Art. L. 214–43.

[14] MFC, Art. L.214–46.

[15] Dealt with in detail in Ch. 10.

[16] It is unclear whether the possibility to allow the assignor to service the receivables created by the recent changes, or the use of third parties such as junior lenders or investors as sub-servicers, also requires the assignor or sub-servicer to register as a debt collector under Decree 96–650 of July 19, 1996. See, Smallhoover and Vital-Durand, "La nouvelle réglementation du recouvrement amiable des créances : Etes-vous concerné?"—*La Semaine Juridique*, Ed. E. (no.36, 1997). There are good arguments that the Decree 96–650 does not apply in these instances—particular in the case of the assignor—but there is no reported case law on point. It would seem that current practice is to consider that Decree no. 96–650 does not apply in these instances.

In addition, the Financial Security Law amended the MFC to permit the creation by the management company and the institution that services the assigned receivables (not the assignor) of a special dedicated account against which the creditors of the servicing entity may not pursue payment of their claims even in the event of it being put into judicial reorganisation or judicial liquidation.[17] Articles 2 and 3 of the 2004 FCC Decree[18] provides that the dedicated account may be set up with any credit institution whose registered office is in a Member State of the Organisation for Economic Co-operation and Development or with the CDC or any similar foreign institution approved by the French Ministry for the Economy. The special character of the dedicated account takes effect immediately upon signature of the contract creating the account by the management company, the custodian, the servicing entity and the credit institution with which the account is opened. The creation of this dedicated account was part of the effort to increase the attractiveness of FCC structure by increasing the bankruptcy remoteness at the various points along the line of the deal structure. It is too early to tell whether this change will have a significant impact on the growth of the French CMBS market, but it is just one piece in a more complex series of changes that should improve the market's attractiveness.

THE USE OF FCC'S AS A VEHICLE FOR CMBS

The comparative weakness of the French CMBS market,[19] particularly when compared to the CMBS markets in the UK or Germany may, in fact, lie in a combination of factors having to do with both the deal structures used elsewhere (and the push toward a fairly high level of security) and the heavy tax cost associated with making transactions using the French FCC structure, which implicate existing mortgages (as opposed to deals for new financings which envisage the use of the FCC structure from the outset), bankruptcy remote.

From a purely legal point of view, the simple securitisation of financial real estate leases (*crédits-baux immobilisés*) is relatively straight forward and the tax hurdles comparatively surmountable.

---

[17] MFC, Art. L.214–46, third paragraph.
[18] Now codified at MFC Arts R.214–97 and R.214–110.
[19] Barclays Capital statistics put French levels of activity at only 4 per cent of the total European market.

Taxation

In order to be enforceable against third parties, the assignment of such rents must be filed with the local mortgage registry if it exceeds rents for more than three years.[20] The cost of such a filing is a total of 0.715 per cent of the amount of the rents assigned.[21] Moreover, the revenues generated by the assignment of the cash flow stream is taxable immediately, despite the fact that the underlying real estate would continue to be amortised over time. This disparate treatment was modified in 1999[22] to allow the financial lessor to take a provision to cover the potential loss from the sale of the real estate at the end of the financial lease, thereby attenuating the effect of the taxation of the sale of the rental stream. However, where an SPV is used to hold the real estate in order to assure further bankruptcy remoteness, it will be necessary to transfer the real estate to the SPV which, in the normal course, will give rise to real estate transfer taxes of the order of 5.09 per cent (composed of parts payable to the national, departmental and local governments), as well as the costs of the mortgage and any capital gain resulting from the transfer. The taxes that arise as a result of such a transfer can be lowered in certain circumstances, depending for instance on the nature of the real estate in question and whether it is being transferred for cash to the SPV or in exchange for shares that will be held for a minimum number of years (currently three years).

Bankruptcy risk

The recent changes in the MFC permit a bankruptcy remoteness which was not certain previously. However, even the recent changes to the French bankruptcy rules do not isolate the potential bankruptcy risk. With respect to the securitisation of rents due under financial leases, Art. L. 622–13 of the Commercial Code provides that any contract, the performance of which is on-going, may be cancelled by the bankruptcy administrator in the event the lessee is placed in judicial reorganisation. Thus, while the risk that the future receivables would not be deemed as having been validly assigned was dealt with by Arts 2 and 3 of the 2004 FCC Decree[23] in the recent reform, the risk that the financial lease itself could be terminated remains. The packaging of a series of financial leases with multiple borrowers will diminish the risk statistically but it does not eliminate it entirely.

---

[20] Decree No.55–22 of January 4, 1955, Art. 28(b).

[21] This total includes both real estate taxes (*taux de la publicité foncière*) at 0.60 per cent and the fees payable to the mortgage registrar at 0.10 per cent for publication and another 0.05 per cent for the cost of inscription in the mortgage register as at the time of writing (General Tax Code, Art. 647, Arts 296 and 293 of Annex II of the General Tax Code).

[22] General Tax Code, Art. 39 *quinquies* I.

[23] Now codified at MFC Arts R.214–93 and R.214–94.

Commercial mortgages

As for the securitisation of commercial mortgages rather than financial leases, whilst the mortgagee will hold security over the real estate, there is the risk that other super-privileged creditors could have priority over it in the event of the bankruptcy of the borrower such as employees, tax authorities and social security authorities.[24] Moreover, Art. L. 611–12 of the Commercial Code provides for an essential moratorium on enforcement actions (*suspensions des poursuites*) until the commercial court has rendered a decision on the fate of the borrower (e.g. reorganisation or liquidation). This moratorium can have a negative impact on the value of the security; even in the best of circumstances it can take many months to force a judicial sale of mortgaged property after a default and when one adds to that the time it takes the commercial court to render a decision, the time-frames can become unacceptably long. Until the promulgation of Ordinance No.2006–346 of March 23, 2006 concerning Security, French law did not recognise self-help and the enforcement of most secured obligations, including mortgages, required a judicial sale.[25] The Ordinance modified the French Civil Code[26] to highlight that the mortgage may provide that the mortgagee becomes the owner of the mortgaged property in the event of a default, so long as the property in question is not the mortgagor's principal residence. This change in the Civil Code will very likely see a fairly broad application in commercial mortgages, thereby reducing some of the uncertainty and delays that forced judicial sales have caused.

The *antichrèse* (Real estate pledge)

The French Civil Code does have an additional legal institution, the *antichrèse* (real estate pledge),[27] which would permit the beneficiary to avoid the problems that arise in the context of either the assignment of the cash streams under mortgages or financial leases. Under the *antichrèse*, the beneficiary is entitled to the "fruits" of the real estate subject to it and those "fruits" are bankruptcy remote. The *antichrèse* is not a type of security that is well understood in the common law world, and it has been suggested that this unfamiliarity is an impediment to obtaining a rating from the rating agencies commensurate with the value of the security.[28] The recent changes

---

[24] See, e.g. Art. L. 622–17 of the Commercial Code.

[25] Such judicial sales can take a minimum of twelve months to organise and in the main require more of the order of 18–24 months.

[26] Cf. Art. 30 of Ordinance No.2006–346 promulgating a new Art.2459 of the French Civil Code.

[27] Civil Code Arts 2387–2392; cf. Art. 16 of Ordinance No.2006–346.

[28] See de Kergommeaux and Van Gallebaert, "La Titrisation d'actifs immobiliés", *Bulletin Joly Bourse*, May–June 2002, pp.181–189. The CMBS Ratings process form Standard & Poor's perspective is dealt with in Ch. 4.

in the Civil Code[29] may make the *antichrèse* a more interesting form of security for use in securitisation deals, as for instance under newly promulgated Art. 2390, the beneficiary of the *antichrèse* may lease out the pledged real estate to third parties or to the debtor.

STRUCTURING THE DEAL FOR BANKRUPTCY REMOTENESS

The discussion of the use of the FCC in the previous section presupposes that the deal is structured in order to leave the existing underlying mortgages essentially untouched. This of course means that the residual risk of default of the borrower, which is always present to some extent, is coupled with the risk of bankruptcy of the mortgagee.

Special purpose vehicles

This risk would normally be dealt with at common law by making use of both a trust mechanism and the use of a special purpose bankruptcy remote SPV. As stated, whilst French law does not recognise the trust, the creation of the SPV is entirely possible, although at a potentially significant cost. The outright sale of the real estate to a bankruptcy remote SPV would give rise to real estate transfer taxes as well as to possible capital gains tax. If the transfer is done by way of contribution of the real estate to the SPV in exchange for shares in the SPV, then the transfer taxes would be at a fixed nominal amount (currently €500) rather than at the normal rates and no capital gains would be due so long as the shares in the SPV are held for three years.[30] While it has the beauty of reducing the tax implications on the event of transfer, the latter solution may not work if one of the goals of the operation is tax driven deconsolidation. Nor does the creation of the SPV in the latter type of structure entirely eliminate the bankruptcy risk, since the SPV would remain in the group and it becomes necessary to pay extra care to ensure that its independence is not compromised in a way that would permit the corporate veil to be pierced, thereby obviating the advantages of the creation of the SPV in the first place.

The concern about the negative tax consequences of using an SPV only applies to real estate that is already owned. New acquisitions of a significant size can easily be structured from the outset using an SPV and an FCC structure without the heavy cost associated with transfer of the real estate to the SPV. That said, the advantages and disadvantages of using a special

---

[29] See fn.26, above.
[30] General Tax Code, Art. 810 III.

purpose vehicle discussed above would apply regardless of whether the ultimate securitisation structure was an FCC or a deal based in the London CMBS market.

BANKING LAW CONSIDERATIONS

The French Monetary and Financial Code provides for a monopoly on credit transactions within France[31] and, as a result, any lending within France must be done by a licensed credit institution (either French or EU with a EU passportable banking license). The deal structures currently being used in the UK involving loans to a bankruptcy remote SPV by a non-French entity that is not an EU licensed credit institution could give rise to concerns about violations of the banking monopoly.[32] On the other hand, there are no prohibitions on French borrowers seeking out CMBS loans outside of France. In order to avoid a violation of the banking monopoly, which is punishable by fines of €375,000 and possible imprisonment of three years,[33] one would want to ensure that the deal structure's connections with France are as limited as possible to the real estate itself. Some commentators have expressed concern that the market is turning a blind eye to the risks that these types of structures might create as a result of imagined violations of the banking monopoly. The obvious answer to these risks under current rules is, of course, to make use of the French FCC deal structure rather than trying to adapt offshore deal structures.[34]

STANDARDISATION AND THE FUTURE OF THE CMBS MARKET IN FRANCE

The rapid growth of the CMBS market in the UK as well as elsewhere in Europe, notably in Germany and Italy, seems to be driving the market towards a European-wide standardisation. The French market is trying, to a certain extent, to resist this trend and there are discussions about a possible further reform of the French market in order to make it more competitive. In particular, reforms are being discussed that would open the securitisation market up to insurance products as well as reforms to loosen up credit for the residential mortgage market. It remains to be seen if these reforms ever come to fruition, and if they do what impact they might have on the CMBS market.

---

[31] See, Art. L. 511–1.
[32] See, de Kergommeaux and Van Gallebaert, as mentioned at fn. 28, above, at p.187.
[33] See Art. L. 571–3 MFC.
[34] See, de Kergommeaux and Van Gallebaert, as mentioned at fn. 28, above, at p.187.

Perhaps the most sizeable obstacle to MBS in France, whether commercial or residential, are the registration taxes that fall due upon transfer of the real estate to an SPV and registration of the mortgage. In order to create a more dynamic market, both for securitisation of existing mortgages as well as the securitisation of future ones, it will be necessary to revise the General Tax Code to further lower transfer taxes when the transfer is done in connection with a securitisation. Given the current budgetary pressure facing France, this will only be possible if the government becomes convinced that any upturn in the real estate and construction sectors which such a change would engender far offset the loss in registration tax revenues. Any change of this order will most likely have to wait until after the 2007 French presidential elections and parliamentary elections. On the other hand, the changes effected by the Financial and Security Law in 2003 and the 2004 Decree should give the French market a considerable push. Coupled with the innovations apparent in European CMBS, these changes are certainly a step in the right direction.

Chapter Eighteen

THE CMBS MARKET IN SPAIN

Javier Ybañez and Gonzalo Garcia-Fuertes
Garrigues
Eduardo Barrachina, Associate
Dechert LLP

INTRODUCTION

The Spanish mortgage market

Traditionally, the Spanish mortgage market has been a motor of the Spanish financial economy. This is mainly due to the nation's atavistic obsession with property ownership. This should continue in the future and be enhanced by the large number of EU citizens who are considering Spain as the place for the purchase of their second residence. For these reasons, Spain has created one of the most vibrant and dynamic property markets of the European Union.

The Spanish mortgage market is fraught with different sorts of mortgage lenders offering various financial products. Mortgage lending is reserved to financial institutions, as defined in Art. 2 of the Act 2/1981 of March 25 on the Regulation of the Mortgage Market ("Act 2/1981"). Spanish law, in particular Act 2/1981, recognises up to six different classes of financial institutions which are permitted to carry out mortgage lending activities, namely:

(1) banks, which are corporate in nature;

(2) savings banks (*cajas de ahorro*), which must adopt a legal form similar to a foundation with a social corporate purpose;

(3) credit co-operatives (*cooperativas de crédito*), which provide credit facilities for their members;

(4) the Official Credit Institute (*Instituto de Crédito Oficial*), which is a public body and part of the Finance Ministry. It offers low interest loans should a crisis arise or to specific debtors such as small and medium enterprises' or new technology companies;

(5) financial credit institutions (*establecimientos financieros de crédito*), which can carry out banking activities (lending consumer credit, mortgages, factoring and so forth) but are not permitted, however, to issue electronic money or accept deposits from the public; and

(6) specific Mortgage Lending Companies (*Sociedades de Crédito Hipotecario*).

As a result of the number of institutions, the mortgage market within banking is fairly competitive and traditionally, Spanish saving banks have been the most popular mortgage lenders, nearly followed by banks, in the last years.

The Spanish mortgage market has become extremely active as a result of the significant drop in interest rates in the last decade. Indeed, whereas in 1991 interest rates for consumer mortgages were around 18 per cent, by 1995 they had already dropped to 11 per cent and are now around 3.6 per cent (which represents a slight increase since 2005).[1] This is a radical development and small wonder that competition in the mortgage market is ferocious while lending activity is very active. However, further rates increases could cause a slow down in Spanish lending activity for 2006 and 2007.

Within the European securitisation market, Spain plays a significant role as not only does it have a specific legal framework for securitisations, including synthetics,[2] but it is also an active market with a significant number of transactions. In fact, according to the European Securitisation Forum and Fitch Ratings, issuance volumes totalled €69.3 billion in 2005, which represents a 35.7 per cent increase compared to 2004. Spain is therefore the second largest cash flow securitisation market, behind the UK, with an estimated market share of 23 per cent.

The Spanish MBS Market

In terms of the mortgage based asset market, the Spanish market is irregular with the bulk of this market being in RMBS deals. It is the second largest

---

[1] Bank of Spain.
[2] Synthetic securitisations have been regulated since 2003 (Art.97 of Act 62/2003), but no transactions with a Spanish vehicle have been carried out to date. This is essentially due to the absence of clear rules by the Bank of Spain on capital relief provided by this type of transactions although other reasons regarding the Spanish regulations have also resulted in the absence of transactions.

market in Europe after the UK by number of transactions and the third by value after the UK and the Netherlands.[3] However, CMBS have not experienced the same degree of development as RMBS and have proved somewhat erratic. In fact, although the Spanish CMBS issuance amounts, at the time of writing, to 8 per cent of the total European CMBS issuance, 2004 saw no activity.[4] In 2005, however, some new and important CMBS transactions took place in the Spanish market such as CM BANCAJA 1, FTA.[5]

Considering the low level of CMBS activity in Europe, the level of activity in the Spanish CMBS market can still be regarded as a moderately high volume when compared with countries other than the UK (47 per cent) and Italy (32 per cent). A key reason for the slow development of the Spanish market is that Spanish banks have hitherto been confident about the quality of their loans and have seen little point in engaging in CMBS.

Spain was one of the first countries within the European Union to design a mortgage backed securities (MBS) regime. Act 2/1981 and Royal Decree 685/1982, of March 17 on the development of some aspects of Act 2/1981 (Royal Decree 685/1982) established the ability of Spanish financial institutions to issue mortgage bonds (*bonos hipotecarios*), covered bonds (*cédulas hipotecarias*)[6]—similar to the German *pfandbriefe*—and some special titles defined as mortgage participations (*participaciones hipotecarias*) which have been the titles through which the majority of mortgage loans have been securitised in Spain, as detailed below. Accordingly, Spain has a fairly sound legal framework for mortgages, land registration, consumer credit, consumer protection, and so forth.

Whilst the number of transactions is likely to increase, Spanish banks have not yet been as active in the CMBS market as would have been expected in a country like Spain. However, recent data suggests that CMBS may soon begin to develop rapidly. Although there have not been any legal developments in the MBS side, it is worth noting that, at the end of last year, the Spanish Government regulated, as a development of the legislation of

---

[3] FitchRatings.com.

[4] NIBC Credit Management.

[5] Incorporate corporate collateral-mortgage loans granted to companies and was one of the first CMBS rating approach that was carried by the Spanish rating agencies.

[6] In recent years, a huge development in the issuance of structured *cédulas hipotecarias* has emerged, through Spanish special purpose vehicles, *Fondo de Titulización de Activos*—FTA—that incorporates some liquidity enhancements. The basics of those structures are to incorporate, as assets of an FTA, single covered bonds issued by different Spanish financial institutions, and then the FTA issue new securitisation notes. See *Programa Cédulas TDA, AYT Cédulas Cajas, IM Cédulas* projects. As this goes beyond the topic of this book, it has not been treated in detail.

securitisation of other assets different than mortgage (Asset Backed Securitisation or ABS), a list of future credits that could be included in a securitisation. This included the credit rights of the property owners against tenants and non-disbursed loans,[7] which could have an impact on the number of CMBS transactions in the not too distant future.

Whilst the Spanish regime for MBS is advanced for European standards, it still has a significant number of restrictions, limitations and peculiarities. Most of those made sense 25 years ago, when the Spanish market was in its infancy and Spanish law was over cautious. However, at the time of writing, the Spanish Government had begun planning a restatement of Spanish securitisation law so that a single Act would regulate all transactions. This consolidation should ease certain legal features which are currently considered troublesome. It is expected that the new securitisation Act should be passed by the end of 2006 or beginning of 2007.

THE ASSIGNMENT OF MORTGAGE LOANS

The main legal regime

In the last few years, Spain has developed an advanced system to allow most financing operations. Spain first introduced its MBS legislation back in 1992 through the passing of Act 19/1992, creating as a special purpose vehicle, the Spanish mortgage backed securitisation fund (*fondos de titulización hipotecaria* (FTH)). Act 19/1992 provides the legal framework for MBS without making any distinction between CMBS and RMBS, but with a restrictive regime that does not allow many variations or innovations in MBS structures (for example, the Act does not allow open Funds with renewable assets). It should be noted that the first MBS issuance did not occur until one year after Act 19/1992 was passed.

In 1994 a new Act was published (Act 3/1994) which extended securitisation to other financial assets, although a specific regulation from the Government was required in order to securitise non-mortgage assets. This Act was developed by Royal Decree 926/1998, of May 14, regulating Asset Securitisation Funds (*fondos de titulización de activos*) (FTA), and Management Companies (Royal Decree 926/1998) (hereinafter an FTA together with an FTH shall be referred to as the "Fund"). This Royal Decree provided that both present credits (those showing in the balance sheet of the originator) and future credits could be securitised, subject, in the case of

---

[7] Orden EHA/3536/2005, November 10, 2005.

future credits, to a specific regulation from the Government, developed partially in 2005.[8]

Due to the enormous development of the Spanish mortgage market, one might not be surprised that MBS were the first securitisations allowed in Spain, in 1992 till the passing of the ABS legislation in 1994, developed four years later.

The transfer of mortgage loans through the issuance of *participaciones hipotecarias*

One of the key characteristics of the MBS legal regime in Spain is that mortgage loans, due to taxes and the costs of filing into the different property registries, may not be securitised directly. This is in contrast to other jurisdictions where the legal framework allows a direct true sale, without the problems which could arise in Spain.

As previously mentioned, Act 2/1981 created a new instrument called *participaciones hipotecarias* (PH), which are bonds or notes issued by Spanish financial institutions that represent a portion of a single mortgage loan. This PH, created to allow banks and the rest of the Spanish financial institutions to transfer mortgage loans to the market in a simple way, is also the title used to transfer loans to securitisation vehicles.

Spanish contract law allows assignment of mortgage credits and Art. 1878 of the Spanish Civil code expressly allows for total or partial assignment of these credits provided they meet the requirements of the Decree of February 8, 1946, as amended (Spanish Mortgage Act (*Ley Hipotecaria*)). However, problems arise with Art.149 of the Mortgage Act which requires assignments of mortgage loans to be made by public deed, notice to the debtor and registration in the correspondent Land Register, irrespective of the tax consequences (up to 1 per cent of stamp duty tax). Needless to say, such incommodious and time-consuming procedures could jeopardise the smooth running of any securitisation. In addition, it will considerably increase the costs of the transaction.

In order to avoid the burden of Art.149, Act 2/1981 created the PH so that, instead of assigning the loans, the originator assigns notes that represent parts of the loan (and could represent 100 per cent of the loan, which is the standard in the securitisations). This surmounts the requirements of Spanish mortgage and contract law. As a consequence, there are no ordinary or direct sales of mortgage credits in Spain, but a prior issuance of

---

[8] See fn. 6.

notes each representing a specific mortgage loan. This method considerably eases the assignment of mortgage credits, and allows the making of a true sale of the loans, effective against third parties (and protected by the bankruptcy laws, as detailed below), without the use of deeds and registration. This method is only feasible when the purchaser of the PH is an institutional or professional investor (such as the Spanish securitisation funds), because it would be necessary to file the deed of issuance of the PH on the Land Register.

It is worthwhile considering the consequences of an assignment of mortgage loans through the issuance of PH without notice to the debtor: the assignment is still legal and valid among the parties but the debtor is entitled to pay back the original creditor and fully ignore the assignee. Also, until the debtor is notified, it has the right to set-off its rights against the original creditor.

The PH representing the pool of mortgage loans that would be transferred to the Spanish special purpose vehicle, as detailed below, should be represented by a single or a multiple nominative title, representing one or a pool of loans. It could be also represented by book entries, but that is not necessary for the purposes of a securitisation (not purported to be traded but to be treated as assets of the special purpose vehicle).

The loans represented by the PH must meet the requirements laid down in Art.2 of Act 2/1981, principally:

(1) the mortgage loans need to be transferred from certain classes of corporations. As such, only financial institutions may actually assign the loans by way of issuance of PHs;

(2) the mortgage loans must be of a particular type. The purpose of the loans must be the mortgage backed financing of buildings, rehabilitation, and acquisition of dwellings as well works of urban plan building, social equipment and the building of agrarian, tourist, industrial and commercial buildings;

(3) the assets mortgaged must be surveyed by the entities offering the mortgage loan based on those assets;

(4) the loans must be backed by first rank mortgages and their LTV cannot exceed 80 per cent where the purpose of the loan is for construction, rehabilitation or purchase of residential, or 70 per cent for other purposes; and

(5) damages insurance is compulsory.

If any of the mortgage loans do not fulfil any of the requirements of Art.2 of Act 2/1981, they could still be securitised by the issuance of PH, although such PH would have a different name: "*certificados de transmission de hipoteca*" (CTH) (mortgage transfer certificates).[9]

In addition to this nominative difference, another consequence of failing to meet the requirements of Art.2 of Act 2/1981 is that PH can be transferred to the two special purpose vehicles regulated by Spanish Law, that is to an FTH regulated under Act 19/1992 and to an FTA, regulated under Royal Decree 926/1998. However CTH can only be transferred to FTAs and not to FTHs.

Due to the limitations of the FTH vehicles created by the Act 19/1992, and other vehicles which will be analysed below, the standard, market-oriented securitisation transactions, including mortgage securitisations, RMBS and CMBS, are mainly structured with FTAs, developed by the 1998 Royal Decree 926/1998. In fact, most of the RMBS and all of the CMBS transactions developed in Spain since 1998 have been executed under Royal Decree 926/1998 through an FTA due to the more market oriented rules and flexibility of this 1998 rule in order to structuring each transaction, but we should not forget that RMBS and CMBS could also be developed under Act 19/1992.

SPECIAL PURPOSE VEHICLES AND THEIR MANAGEMENT COMPANIES

Whereas in the US or the UK the issuer may take the form of a company or trust, in Spain, the Securitisation Fund is the main[10] option that Spanish law offers to issuers.

This is not a civil law feature since, for example, Portuguese law recognises two different vehicles: funds and credit securitisation companies. The election in Spain for the fund structure was inspired by the French *fonds commun de créances* which were created in 1988. On the date of the issuance of Act 19/1992, it was understandable that Spain did not simply adopt the English trust structure as it does not expressly enforce this type of fiduciary instrument.

---

[9] This name was given by the Spanish Finance Act 2002/44, although, before that act, numerous issuances of PH without the fulfilment of the requirements of Art.2 of Act 2/1981 took place.

[10] In accordance with 3rd Additional Provision of Act 1/1999, in force, there is a specific and privileged assignment that will be applicable to some assignments of credits, and could be used by issuers fulfilling various requirements. One of those requirements is that the assignee must be a credit entity. Due to the requirements established by the Act, this possibility has not been used for standard RMBS or CMBS transactions.

Although Spain recognises legal institutions similar to a trust, these do not generally apply to companies. It is not clear why Spanish law does not allow for other structures although it seems that the Spanish legislator wished to provide securitisation with a clear and familiar vehicle with low costs and a simple structure: Spain had its first Collective Investment Schemes Funds Act in 1984 so by the time MBS were allowed in Spain the legal and banking market was already familiar with the fund structure. In addition, its simplicity and low cost favoured its election as the only vehicle permitted by Spanish law. In any case it is fair to admit that the industry has responded positively to this situation.

An FTH or an FTA adopts a double structure: they lack any legal capacity but they are represented by a management company (*Sociedad Gestora*). The management companies have an exclusive purpose and require governmental approval for their incorporation and are under the supervision of the Spanish Securities Market Commission—CNMV. Management companies can manage multiple funds and are responsible for the representation and defence of the interests of the bondholders issued by the Fund.

Securitisation Funds are different from the collective investment schemes (CIS) created and regulated by the Spanish legislation on Collective Investments Schemes (Collective Investment Schemes Act 35/2003). Indeed, the purpose of a Fund and a CIS are not only different but opposite and this distinction has not been without controversy amongst Spanish scholars and market players. Whereas Funds have only one purpose which is the securitisation of a pool of assets and the issuance of bonds, CIS are structured to channel capital and to invest it in the capital markets. In fact, while funds obtain finance from capital markets, CIS add or inject more liquidity. In addition to this, the structures for these two vehicles are also different. As explained above, funds have a double structure as they are formed by the fund and the management company. However, for CIS, Spanish law requires a third party, the custodian or depository, which is not a requirement for funds. It is also worth noting that the assets of CIS consist of any sort of negotiable notes or proprietary rights on real estate which are represented by units whereas funds assets, in the case of RMBS or CMBS, consist mainly of PH and/or CTH.

However, the clearest difference between CIS and Funds relates to ownership. The participants of CIS are the owners of the negotiable notes or proprietary rights on real estate, in proportion to their participation whereas the participants in a fund have no legal ownership of either the fund or its assets, with bondholders only having a credit right against the fund.

When using an FTH, only closed funds are authorised, whose assets consist exclusively of PH, but when using an FTA, closed or open funds are allowed, with PH and/or CTH. A fund is "closed" when, after its creation, neither the assets nor liabilities of the Fund are modified, except in cases of early repayment of assets or rectification of defects which affect such assets. On the other hand, "open" funds are those in which it is possible to make modifications to assets and/or liabilities. Liabilities are modified by providing for the successive issue of new securities in the fund, or the grant of new loans to finance the Fund while assets can be modified by renewal of assets or by an increase thereof with the correlative increase in liabilities.

The assets of the funds will consist of the PH (in case of an FTH) or PH and/or CTH and other assets (in case of an FTA). Its liabilities will consist of

(1) the notes issued by the Fund, subject to a minimum of 50 per cent, and

(2) loans granted by credit institutions. For specific characteristics of the notes, see *Issuance of Bonds*, below.

When the amount of the assets pending amortisation does not exceed 10 per cent[11] of the initial amount, an early liquidation ("claw back" clause) of the fund is possible provided that has been agreed in the foundation deed.

The fund must be set up by way of public deed (incorporation or foundation deed) which must contain the following:

(1) the pools of notes and substitution rules in case of early amortisation;

(2) a precise definition of the characteristics of the notes which are to be issued and the different tranches, if applicable; and

(3) the remaining rules which regulate the fund and the transactions or operations the fund intends to carry out, such as swaps, insurance or revolving contracts.

In principle, Spanish law does not allow amendments to the FTH incorporation deed although some amendments may be allowed in exceptional cases. This rule does not apply to an FTA.

The deed must be reviewed and registered previously to its execution at the National Securities Market Commission (*Comisión Nacional del Mercado de Valores—CNMV*), except in case of "private" funds, in which the

---

[11] In FTH. It could be a different figure in FTA.

340

notes to be issued by the Fund are not going to be listed nor offered to retail investors.

The fund will come to an end once all the notes have been amortised. It should be noted that, unlike other jurisdictions, the Spanish regulator does not accept (except in some limited and regulated circumstances), the early termination of the Fund.

ADDITIONAL REQUIREMENTS OF THE ASSIGNMENT OF THE MORTGAGE LOANS TO THE FUND

As mentioned above, the market issuance of PH has been moving lately from the use of FTHs to the use of FTAs, the latter being the funds used in ABS. Accordingly, and following the passing of Royal Decree 926/1998, it is possible to securitise MBS by using an FTA. As a consequence, in addition to the requirements for the transfer of loans by the issuance of PH and/or CTH as detailed above, it should be taken into consideration that the Spanish regulations on assignment to the Fund impose a series of "subjective" and "objective" requirements. The "subjective" requirements relate to the assignors of rights to the fund and the "objective" requirements to those which the assets to be assigned must fulfil.

In relation to the "subjective" requirements of the assignor, Art. 2.2 of Royal Decree 926/1998 provides that assignors must:

(1) have audited accounts for the last three financial years with a favourable opinion on the last accounts; the CNMV may waive this requirement when the assignor is recently formed,

(2) have filed their annual accounts with Companies House ("*Registro Mercantil*") and with the CNMV, and

(3) report in the notes to their annual accounts on credit assignment operations, including operations to secure the successful outcome of the assignment process.

It must be taken into account, however, that the requirements of (1) and (2) may be dispensed with when the debtor of the credit rights assigned is "the State, an Autonomous Region or an international body of which Spain is a member".

In relation to the "objective" requirements for assignment to the Fund:

(1) the assignments must be full and unconditional, for the whole of the period remaining until maturity;

(2) the assignor should not grant any security to the assignee or secure the successful outcome of the transaction (and this is a important issue reviewed by the regulator); and

(3) the assignor should retain administration and management of the credit right assigned, in the absence of agreement to the contrary.[12]

ISSUANCE OF BONDS

When structuring a Spanish CMBS, it should be taken into consideration that Spanish regulations establish some particular criteria for the bonds to be issued by the fund. One example is that, in the event of admission to listing, notes must have a credit rating from at least one rating agency duly recognised in Spain,[13] and the rating must appear on the prospectus. The obligation to rate notes is not without controversy since this obligation is not common in other EU Member States, and it is felt that ratings should be left to the markets which are best placed to know whether notes should be rated or not. It should also be taken in consideration that bonds are required to be quoted on a Spanish official secondary market,[14] except in case of an "institutional" offering.[15]

Also, in case of issuance of notes that are going to be listed, a prospectus concerning the incorporation of the fund should be filed, prior to listing, even in the case where there is no public offer (i.e. the offer is limited to qualified investors). This requirement has to be taken into consideration when establishing a schedule for a transaction in Spain, as it is different from other EU jurisdictions (where the prospectus for these transactions are filed after the issuance and offer, but before the admission to listing of the notes). It is for the management companies to request listing of the notes in an official exchange market in Spain.

---

[12] Art. 2.3.(b).2 of Royal Decree 926/1988.

[13] Currently only Fitch Ratings, Moody's and Standard and Poor's.

[14] Spain has the following official markets which admits securitisation notes to be listed: Stock Exchanges of Madrid, Barcelona, Valencia and Bilbao and the AIAF Fixed Rate Market. AIAF is the standard market to list securitisation notes in Spain.

[15] Due to the implementation in Spain of Directive 2003/71/CE of the Parliament and of the Council of the European Union, Spanish Securities Act 24/1988 has included the definition of "qualified investor", that includes more investors than the traditional definition of "institutional". Notwithstanding this, the securitisations laws have not been amended in consequence, and so, some mismatches among these related regulations could occur. For example, could an offering of securitisation notes directed to qualified investors, which are different from institutional investors, be excepted from quoting? No answers by the CNMV at the moment.

Other issues relating to the registration at the CNMV are dealt with by the Spanish Securities Market Act 24/1988 (*Ley del Mercado de Valores*) and Royal Decree 1310/2005 of November 4, concerning trading of securities in official secondary markets, which develops Act 24/1988 and fully incorporates into the Spanish regulations, Directive 2003/71/EC of the Parliament and the Council of the European Union.

The prospectus must be drafted in accordance with the models of Registration Document Schedule, Note Schedule with the correspondent Asset backed securities building block, as established by Commission Regulation 809/2004/EC of April 29, 2004, but with some Spanish peculiarities. For example, a lot of the information in the Registration Document is related to the Management Company instead of the Fund (which has no legal capacity).

Spanish law does not prescribe any further criteria for bonds or notes to be issued by the Fund. Consequently, Spanish law is flexible as to amortisation periods, fixed or floating rates, early amortisation and payment preferences.

CREDIT ENHANCEMENTS

In Spain, credit enhancements are regulated by law although not from a strict stance. Whereas other jurisdictions remain silent as to credit enhancements and thus leave the issue to the market itself, Spanish law has adopted a more active view. It is for the fund management companies to carry out the necessary credit enhancements, according to the fund incorporation deed. As a consequence, in order to improve or ensure regular payments, management companies of the Fund may engage in swaps, insurance contracts, revolving contracts or any other financial transactions purported to guarantee those payments. Spanish law has thus adopted a flexible approach and the use of "any other financial transaction" clearly suggests that the list is not exhaustive. In addition, Spanish law expressly allows management companies to collateralise so that they can surmount the potential mismatches between the principal and interest flows. Notwithstanding this, the Spanish regulator has interpreted this possibility in a very restrictive way, and so, the management companies are not permitted to actively manage securitised asset portfolios, even its unique purpose to act in representation, and uphold the interests, of the creditors of the Fund, as the Fund has no legal capacity.

INSOLVENCY ISSUES

In order to deal with certain insolvency and bankruptcy remoteness issues, Spain recently updated its insolvency law by passing Act 22/2003 of July 9, the Insolvency Act ("*Ley Concursal*"), which has been in force since September 2004. The text of this Act is based on the UNCITRAL models and resolves one of the traditional main problems of the Spanish bankruptcy system; the automatic resolution of every transaction. No matter its nature, it is made after a date determined by the court, at its discretion, on each insolvency proceeding.

As detailed above, the funds are a separate capital, closed-end, and do not have their own legal personality and cannot, therefore, be deemed to be subject to the bankruptcy rules under the Spanish legal system, in accordance with the provisions of Act 22/2003. Therefore, the funds early extinction or liquidation can be only ruled by the provisions of the deed and not by the general bankruptcy rules. In such a case, the rules of priority of payment set forth the in the deed should be applied. With this regulation, it is clear that the funds are a complete bankruptcy remoteness vehicle for rating agencies purposes.

Notwithstanding this, the bankruptcy regime applicable to the assignment of the PH and CTH to the Fund should be clarified. If insolvency proceedings are brought against the assignor of the PH or CTH, the issue and assignment of them may be subject to return only if an action for such return is pursued in which fraud is demonstrated to have existed in the issue and assignment[16] in accordance with the provisions of para. 4 of the Fifth Additional Provision of Act 3/1994 of April 14, 1994. Furthermore, in the event of insolvency proceedings against the assignor under the Insolvency Act, the fund, acting through its management company, will have the right of withdrawal (*derecho de separación*) in relation to the PH and/or CTH, on the terms provided in Arts 80 and 81 of the said Insolvency Act. In addition, the Fund, acting through its management company, will have the right to obtain from the assignor the amounts resulting from the PH and CTH, given that those sums will be considered property of the Fund, through the

---

[16] Even though this is not accepted without contradiction (there is no case law in Spain yet) there is a majority opinion that states that in addition to fraud, for the action of return to get fulfilled, it should also be proved that the issue and assignment is to be considered as a prejudicial acts for the assets of the insolvent and carried out within the two years prior to the date on which the insolvency was declared. For the purposes of the exercise of any reincorporation actions, the prejudice to the estate or the fraudulent character shall have to be proved by the party exercising any such action which may in no event be exercised successfully against ordinary course of business actions carried out in ordinary conditions. This interpretation should not be followed in the future, but there is no doubt as to the existence of the fraud exception.

management company, and will therefore be transferred to the management company on behalf of the Issuer.

Nevertheless, due to the fungible nature of the money, the said right of withdrawal may not be exercised with respect to the funds handled by the assignor for the account and pursuant to the orders of the Fund in its function as collections manager of the mortgage loans and with respect to the money on deposit in the Fund's accounts held in such assignor. This commingling risk should be considered when structuring a securitisation in Spain, and so it is common to establish some mechanisms to mitigate this risk. But it should be noted that the Spanish regulations have finally established an acceptable bankruptcy framework for securitisation purposes.

Finally, in the event that insolvency proceedings are brought against the management company of the Fund, the management company must be substituted in accordance with the provisions of each transaction and, in any case, in accordance with Arts 18 and 19 of Royal Decree 926/1998. Without prejudice to the above, in the event that the management company is subject to insolvency proceedings, the Fund shall have also, in accordance with the said Arts 80 and 81 of Act 22/2003, a right of withdrawal (*derecho de separación*) of the assets belonging to the Fund held by the management company.

TAXATION

PH, funds and management companies

The tax regime applicable to securitisation funds consists of the general provisions contained in Legislative Royal Decree 4/2004 of March 5, 2004 approving the consolidated text of Spanish Corporate Income Tax (*Impuesto sobre Sociedades*) and its implementing provisions, with the specific peculiarities arising from the provisions of Acts 19/1992, Act 3/1994, and Royal Decree 926/1998, which, in summary, define the following fundamental principles:

(1) Securitisation funds are independent entities liable for Corporate Income Tax, subject to the general rules for determining the tax base, to the general rate of 35 per cent, and to the common rules for deductions, set-off of losses and other substantive elements of the tax.

(2) Investment income of securitisation funds is subject to the general rules on withholdings on account of Corporate Income Tax and in particular to Art. 57-k of the Regulations approved by Royal Decree

1777/2004 of July 30, 2004 which provides that withholding does not apply to "income from *participaciones hipotecarias*, mortgage loans and other credit rights that constitute revenue items for the securitisation funds". Consequently, in addition to the income from the PH and CTH, which are the direct object of the securitisation, the withholding exemption also extends, according to the expressly stated policy of the tax authorities, to the income of the mortgage loans, to the extent that they form part of the ordinary business activity of the said funds.

(3) Article 5.10 of Act 19/1992 provides that the formation of mortgage securitisation funds is exempt from classification as "corporate operations", thereby predetermining its submission to the same.

(4) Article 16 of Royal Decree 3/1993 authorises the national government to "extend the regime provided for securitisation of mortgage participating units (*participaciones hipotecarias*) ... to the securitisation of other Mortgage Loans and credit rights". This authority was ratified and expanded by the Fifth Additional Provision of Act 3/1994.

(5) Similarly, Royal Decree 926/1998 provides that asset securitisation funds, insofar as that Decree is silent, will be subject to the rules contained in Law 19/1992 for mortgage securitisation funds, to the extent they are applicable having regard to their specific nature.

(6) The assignment to the Funds of the PH and CTH is a transaction that is subject to, but qualifies for an exemption from, Value Added Tax in accordance with the provisions of Art. 20. One.18-e of Law 37/1992 of December 28, 1992.

(7) The establishment and assignment of guarantees is subject to the general tax regime with no exceptions.

(8) In relation to Value Added Tax, the Fund will be subject to the general rules, with the sole particularity that the services provided for the Issuer by the managing company will be exempt from Value Added Tax.

(9) The bond issue itself will be exempt from Value Added Tax[17] and from Capital Transfer Tax and Stamp Duty (*Impuesto sobre Transmisiones Patrimoniales y Actos Jurídicos Documentados*).[18]

---

[17] Art.20. One.18 of the VAT Law.
[18] Art.45-I.B no.15 of the Consolidated Text of the Capital Transfer Tax and Stamp Duty Law, confirmed by the November 3, 1997 judgment of the Spanish Supreme Court.

The issued notes

Pursuant to Law 23/2005 (amending the Second Additional Disposition of Law 13/1985), securitisation bonds issued by Funds and traded on regulated markets (such as the Spanish Fixed Income Market) will enjoy the tax benefits applicable to preferred participations (i.e. they will be subject to the same regime as that governing public debt instruments), so non-residents without a permanent establishment in Spain (other than investors acting through tax havens[19]) will be exempted from Spanish withholding tax on income derived from such securitisation bonds. Individuals will also be exempted from wealth tax in relation to these bonds (companies are not subject to wealth tax).

In order to benefit for that withholding exemption and to permit the Fund to comply with its withholding and reporting obligations pursuant to Act 19/2003 (that modifies the Second Transitory Provision of Act 13/1985, Royal Decree 1778/2004 as regards non-resident holders (that modifies Royal Decree 2281/1998)), Royal Legislative Decree 4/2004 of March 5 and Order December 22, 1999, some notification of residence procedures apply to the securitisation bonds. With regard to such procedures, it should be borne in mind that the clearing systems (IBERCLEAR, EUROCLEAR and CLEARSTREAM) are, at the time of writing, in discussions to harmonise the procedure for the provision of information as required by such laws and regulations. In every transaction, holders of securitisation bonds should seek their own advice to ensure that they comply with all procedures to ensure correct tax treatment of their securitisation bonds.

CONCLUSION

Perhaps, after reading all the peculiarities of the Spanish securitisation framework, a non-familiar issuer or investor of Spanish securitisation bonds could ask how the huge development of the Spanish RMBS and CMBS transactions in recent years was possible. Although, in practice, it is not as complex as it looks and, in general terms, it is a framework that covers the rating agencies' standards. Spanish players have understood the limitations but also the possibilities of these regulations and, due to an enormous mortgage market and its continuous restlessness and their desire to improve, have executed a lot of innovative and new complex structures. If the support of the Spanish regulator and the CNMV is added to this formula, a growth in the Spanish market in the following years could be expected.

---

[19] Royal Decree 1080/1991, declared expressly in force, establish the exhaustive list of the considered tax heavens for Spanish tax administrations, including up to 48 different countries.

As we saw above, the Spanish CMBS market has not reached the levels of activity of the ABS and RMBS ones. We may conclude that no major changes will occur in the CMBS market in the near future. The levels of CMBS activity in the Spanish market are more the consequence of the market structure rather than the result of inadequate legislation. As we have seen above, the reasons may be found in banks being confident about their mortgage portfolios coupled with legislation favouring ABS transactions. Doubtless, the Spanish securitisation market will continue growing as new legislation is passed, but there are no strong signals of change on the horizon for CMBS transactions.

CHAPTER NINETEEN

THE CMBS MARKET IN ITALY

Alberto Giampieri and Andrea Giannelli
Gianni, Origoni, Grippo & Partners

INTRODUCTION

The Italian CMBS market has become extremely attractive in the last few years. The extraordinary increase of real estate financing and the need to find alternative and more convenient financing resources has certainly represented the main reason for such success. In addition, the solution of regulatory issues mainly related to the so-called "balloon risk"[1] and a certain degree of certainty on the placement of sub-investment grade notes (which must be placed to institutional investors through one to one transactions) has definitively helped to develop the CMBS market and a transactional market practice in the specific field.

The success of the Italian CMBS market is also due to a combination of reasons. Primarily, the syndication of real estate financing secured by mortgages may be extremely tax expensive since, according to the prevailing interpretation, which is also upheld by the tax authorities, the assignment of the loan would not fall within the scope of the so called substitutive tax made by the primary lender (equal to 0.25 per cent) and hence would trigger the mortgage tax at a rate of 2 per cent (plus 0.50 per cent on subsequent cancellation) if the assignee intends to be recorded as a beneficiary of the mortgage. Secondly, CMBS transactions constitute an efficient alternative to the traditional syndication structure which may reach investors which would not otherwise take any role in syndication loans. Finally, access to the capital market allows the borrower to enjoy a spread reduction and obtain a more efficient financing structure.

---

[1] The refinancing risk deriving from the inability by the borrower to generate sufficient cash flow from the sale of the assets to reimburse the loan.

On the other hand, however, the securitisation of a mortgage loan requires a certain level of comfort for the Rating Agencies and the market which, inevitably, entails a high degree of structural complexity, a more rigid structure (especially in cases where refinancing or acquisition of waivers is required), and compliance with certain fundamental features.

Although the market has already developed contractual models which meet the above requirements, it is crucial to clearly assess in advance whether a loan is envisaged to be securitised and, if so, to address well in advance (particularly in the loan documentation and in the security package) the structural issues which may be required in the context of a CMBS deal.

For instance, the length of foreclosure proceedings has induced, as a standard security, the provision of the pledge of quotas or shares of the borrower in order to facilitate, in the event of a payment default under the loan, the sale of the company through the enforcement of the pledge. The pledge will contain specific provisions to guarantee control by the lender, although the increase of control triggers inevitably increase the exposure risk for the pledgee to the extent that contractual power is exercised (dealt with below).

Although it is virtually impossible to create a complete bankruptcy remote status (except in the event of a real estate fund, in relation to which, see below), the CMBS structure must at least minimise such risk. Hence,

- the borrower should not have any employees,

- it should not have actual liabilities (or the same should be quantified in advance and be compatible with the capital structure),

- it should not incur any contingent liabilities,

- the status of the assets should be supported by a robust real estate and environmental due diligence which has identified the critical issues, and

- the lease agreements should have, in principle, a duration compatible with the tenor of the loan and provide, to the extent possible, for a triple net structure.

The control over the management of the assets is obviously a key element of the structure. While the selection of the asset manager is fundamental from a business perspective, the quality of the asset management agreement and the possibility for the lender to terminate the asset manager and replace the same is considered to be an important feature in CMBS transactions. Notwithstanding that, the so-called "contractual control provisions" may not allow specific performance remedies, these represent a significant element of pressure on both the borrower and the asset manager to comply with the business plan and the possible LTV targets contemplated by the loan. Clearly the efficiency of the asset manager may result in the success of the transaction, and the provision of appropriate remedies in the contractual documentation may enhance the position of the lender. This may play a key role in both trading portfolios (i.e. portfolio comprising assets to be sold) and stable portfolios (portfolios providing for long term leases which do not envisage a disposal plan to reimburse the loan).

An additional important element to be considered is insurance protection. Similarly, loan documentation, the co-operation of other jurisdictions, the rating of the insurer and the area of risks covered is essential. In addition, however, it is always advisable to verify the availability of the insurer to accept the loss payee clause and obtain from a third party broker a certificate confirming that the insurance policy is adequate for the business carried out in the assets.

The brief description outlined above gives a general overview of the main topics which affect an Italian CMBS transaction. Such topics will be analysed in detail in the following paragraphs. In short, a CMBS transaction may be viewed as an opportunity for both borrowers and lenders. However, the possibility to exploit the opportunity and obtain the support of the market requires a solid and clear structure, a detailed preparation of the loan documentation, the co-operation of the borrower in the securitisation phase, and the consistency between the business plan of the borrower and the contractual features of the CMBS transaction.

NATURE OF THE MORTGAGE LOAN

The typical structure used in Italy for mortgage loans, which constitute the underlying asset of a CMBS transaction, is based on either a regular mortgage loan (*mutuo ipotecario*) or a special mortgage loan that is regulated by Arts 38 (and following) of the Legislative Decree of September 1, 1993, No.358 (the "Banking Act") (*mutuo fondiario*). The lender and borrower are free to designate which type of financing they wish to use. The Banking Act provides for a peculiar regime in relation to the *fondiario* loan, the main features of which are addressed below. A mortgage loan agreement may qualify as a *fondiario* loan if the following requirements are met:

- the original lender is a bank;
- the loan has a tenor in excess of 18 months; and
- the principal amount advanced to the borrower (together with the

principal amount of any loan secured by previously recorded mortgages) does not exceed, at any time, 80 per cent of the value of the first ranking mortgaged properties constituting security for the mortgage loan.

Some of the peculiarities of the *mutuo fondiario* may give more protection to the lenders, while others create some advantages for the borrower. In particular:

(1) the hardening period applicable in respect of the mortgages which secure a *fondiario* loan is 10 days rather than the ordinary period of six months–one year provided by Art. 67 of the Royal Decree of March 16, 1942 No.267 (the "Italian Bankruptcy Law");

(2) any payment made by the relevant borrower is not subject to the claw-back regime set forth under Art. 67 of the Italian Bankruptcy Law; and

(3) the lender is entitled to commence or continue foreclosure proceedings on the assets after the date on which the borrower is declared bankrupt.

On the other hand, the borrower may enjoy the following benefits from the *fondiario* regime:

(1) the borrower of a *fondiario* loan is entitled to obtain the release of one or more mortgaged properties from the mortgage if one-fifth of the amount originally advanced is repaid and/or if, on the basis of appraisals and other documents, it is demonstrated that the remaining mortgaged properties constitute sufficient security for the outstanding amount due under the *fondiario* loan agreement. Properties will be released from the mortgage to the extent that the resulting LTV ratio of the *fondiario* loan is the highest LTV ratio permitted by law for a *fondiario* loan (80 per cent) or, according to some commentators, the original LTV ratio for the *fondiario* loan. From the lender's perspective, this may have an impact on any planned de-leveraging in the loan structure; and

(2) the lender is entitled to terminate a *fondiario* loan agreement and accelerate the loan, in the case of overdue payment, only if the borrower has delayed payment at least seven times, whether consecutively or not. A payment is considered delayed if it is made between 30 and 180 days after the due date of payment. This does not affect the lender's ability to accelerate the loan in the case of other agreed events of default.

The choice between a *fondiario* loan or an *ipotecario* loan should be clearly evaluated on a case-by-case basis and, in particular, should be based mainly on the planned de-leveraging of the loan. In any case, if it is decided to adopt a *fondiario* loan, it is possible to build mitigants to the statutory right detailed above, such as a requirement that the property appraisals are in form and substance satisfactory to the lender, and a waiver is sought by the borrower of its right to obtain the release of properties from the mortgage. However, the majority of commentators are of the opinion that such a waiver may not be enforceable in the Italian courts.

Whether a *fondiario* loan or an *ipotecario* loan is adopted, for regulatory purposes, in both instances, it is required that the mortgage loan underlying a CMBS transaction shall be structured as a real loan bearing the typical credit risk. This means, in particular, that:

(1) the lender has to obtain all relevant internal approvals (such as approval of the credit committee);

(2) the loan agreement has to be structured as a loan which may stay in place in the event that the relevant securitisation is not actually implemented; and

(3) the relevant facility agreement should not contain any condition precedent or condition subsequent represented by the implementation (or lack of implementation, as the case my be) of the securitisation within a certain period of time.

In other words, it is generally considered that a loan is created on purpose to generate a securitisation; therefore, the relevant lender should keep the loan on its books (therefore, taking the relevant credit risk of the borrower) for a certain period of time before transferring the loan to the securitisation company (the "Issuer").

Subject to any tax considerations, which will be addressed below, both an Italian bank and an EU Bank duly passported (or having a branch in Italy) are authorised to make mortgage loans in Italy (in the form of a *fondiario* loan).

BANKRUPTCY REMOTENESS OF THE BORROWER

As stated above, it is crucial for an analysis to be carried out by the Rating Agencies that the relevant borrower in a CMBS transaction is a bankruptcy remote company. However, under Italian law, it is not legally possible to render a company a full "bankruptcy remote" entity.

In any case, certain measures to limit (to the extent possible under applicable law) the risk that the borrower is declared insolvent may be adopted. As a general rule, such measures are aimed at limiting, as much as possible, the potential claims of creditors of the borrower and, in any case, to render the claims of such creditors subordinate to those of the relevant noteholders.

The following are criteria which may be generally implemented in CMBS transactions in order to reduce the risk of bankruptcy of the borrower:

(1) the borrower should be a newly incorporated company;

(2) the corporate purposes of the borrower should be, in essence, limited to the management of the real estate portfolio. The borrower should not be allowed to carry out any activity which does not relate to the purchase, sale, management and letting of the properties;

(3) the borrower should not have any employees and would obtain any service it needs in outsourcing;

(4) all the creditors or potential creditors of the borrower should issue a non-petition letter in favour of the borrower or be party to an Intercreditor Agreement and should subordinate their rights to the Issuer's rights;

(5) a liquidity line should be granted to the borrower in order to permit the latter to fulfil its obligations under the mortgage loan in the event of a default of the tenants in the payment of the rents;

(6) the Issuer should have a certain degree of control on the management of the borrower. In this respect:

    (a) the by-laws of the borrower may provide that the shareholders meeting of the company has the exclusive power to determine certain strategic matters to be agreed between the parties (such as the sale and lease of the properties, amendments to the lease agreements, etc.); and

    (b) the pledge over the borrower's shares should provide that, in a pre-default scenario, the Issuer may exercise the voting rights attached to the pledged shares with respect to, inter alia, any resolution concerning such strategic matters (on this point, see also, below);

(7) in the event that the real estate assets are transferred to the borrower by means of a demerger, appropriate indemnities should be provided for the benefit of the borrower for any contingent liability which it may incur in connection with such a demerger;

(8) the Issuer should have a control on the actual payments by the borrower of its costs, expenses and taxes. A possible instrument may be used to grant a pledge over the borrower's bank account in favour of the Issuer; and

(9) a complete legal and environmental due diligence is carried out on the real estate portfolio, in order to assess potential liabilities which may derive from the properties (for instance, in case of breach of environmental claim). If some contingent liabilities result from the due diligence, those should be quantified and a proper indemnity/ guarantee should be requested to the sponsor of the transaction or a cash reserve provided.

CASH FLOW UNDER A CMBS TRANSACTION—LEASE AGREEMENTS

The principal source of payment under a CMBS transaction is clearly represented by the rents to be paid by the relevant tenants under the lease agreements entered into in relation to the real estate portfolio. Therefore, it is crucial to structure the relevant lease agreements in order to reduce, as much as legally possible, the risk of interruption of the cash flow and to allocate to the relevant tenants all the costs and expenses to be incurred in relation to the real estate assets. Clearly, if such costs and expenses were allocated to the landlord, the cash flow deriving from the lease agreements would be used for this purpose and, accordingly, the cash flow to service the debt may potentially be adversely affected.

In light of the above, the relevant lease agreements should contain some specific provisions to address the above points. In particular:

(1) *Duration of the lease.* In order to grant to the borrower a sufficient comfort on the stability of the cash flow deriving from the leases, the tenant should not be contractually entitled to withdraw from the leases before the scheduled maturity date. However, under Italian law, the tenant has a statutory right to terminate the lease agreement at any time for serious reasons (*gravi motivi*) upon service of a six-month advance notice. Any contractual provision which limits this statutory right may be deemed null and void. In any case, since, as stated, the termination of the lease may clearly adversely affect the cash flow of the rents, appropriate mitigants to such risk should be implemented considering the actual structure of the transaction.

(2) *Maintenance works.* The tenant should be contractually obliged to bear all the costs associated with the completion of any ordinary and

extraordinary maintenance works to be carried out on the leased property in order to maintain it in good condition. However, under Italian law, the extraordinary maintenance costs in relation to leased properties have to be borne by the landlord and, in accordance with certain case law, the undertaking of the tenant to bear such costs may not be enforceable. In this case, since the landlord would be required to bear such costs, there may be a risk of shortfall in the payment of the loan by the landlord. This risk may be properly mitigated, for instance, by granting to the borrower a subordinated liquidity facility.

(3) *Ancillary costs.* The tenant should be obliged to pay all the ancillary costs associated with the use of the relevant properties, including the applicable indirect taxes. However, it should be considered that under Italian law it is prohibited for the tenant to simply undertake to pay taxes imposed on the landlord (for example, property tax). Appropriate measures have to be adopted in order to permit in any case the payment of all due taxes and to avoid the insolvency of the landlord.

(4) *Return of the properties.* The tenant has to undertake to return the properties in good condition, upon termination of the lease agreements, in order to facilitate the re-letting or the sale of the property by the landlord.

(5) *Tenant set-off.* To ensure a certain stability of the cash-flow deriving from the rent, the right for a tenant to set off its claims vis-à-vis the landlord's claims should be clearly excluded.

(6) *Rent guarantee.* Payment obligations deriving from the leases should be secured by a first demand guarantee issued by a bank of a certain rating. This guarantee, which usually covers three months of rent, may be used as a back-up in the event of a temporary shortfall in the payment obligations by the tenant.

(7) *Insurance.* The tenant should be obliged to enter into and maintain an all-risks insurance policy with a primary and reputable insurance company, meeting certain rating requirements, covering, inter alia:

(a) all the damages on the real estate units, whether deriving or not from the use of the same by the lessee and the sub-lessees and by any other third party;

(b) tort liability *vis-à-vis* third parties including, but not limited to, the lessor, the employees and consultants of the lessee, the sub-lessees and any other third party; and

(c) loss of rent.

All-risks policies sometimes exclude or limit certain risks such as terrorist attacks. It may be advisable that the risks insured and the commercial terms of the insurance policies be reviewed and certified by an insurance broker as conditions generally applied in the market for analogous buildings. The landlord would be indicated as the beneficiary of such an insurance policy. However, the ultimate beneficiary is generally the Issuer. To achieve this, there may be a loss payee clause whereby the proceeds are paid directly to the Issuer.

DESCRIPTION OF THE SECURITY PACKAGE AND OF THE MAIN ENFORCEMENT PROCEDURES

Generally, the security package for a mortgage loan to be securitised includes the following:

(1) a first ranking mortgage over the properties. The mortgage is deemed to be perfected only if it has been executed in the form of a notarised deed and it has been registered with the competent Real Estate Registries;

(2) a pledge over the quotas of the borrower (assuming, as is generally the case, that the borrower is incorporated as a *società a responsabilità limitata*). The pledge must be executed through a notarial deed and is deemed perfected once it is registered with the competent Register of Enterprises and on the shareholders book of the company;

(3) an assignment by way of security of the pecuniary receivables of the borrower arising under the lease agreements. In order to render such assignment effective vis-à-vis third parties, it shall be:

  (a) accepted by the relevant tenants by means of a deed bearing a certified date or, alternatively, notified to them through a court bailiff; and

  (b) registered with the competent Real Estate Registries;

(4) an assignment by way of security of the pecuniary receivables of the borrower arising from any agreement entered into for the purchase of the relevant real estate assets. In order to render such assignment effective vis-à-vis third parties, it shall be accepted by the relevant debtors by means of a deed bearing a certified date or, alternatively, notified to them through a court bailiff;

(5) an assignment by way of security of the pecuniary receivables of the borrower arising from hedging agreements. Such an assignment shall be accepted by the relevant hedging banks;

357

(6) a pledge over bank accounts held by the Borrower; and

(7) a loss payee clause in relation to insurance policies regarding the properties. Although the loss payee clause is not technically a security interest, it, as stated, entitles the Issuer to receive the payment of the insurance proceeds arising from time-to-time under the insurance policies and retain such proceeds to the extent necessary to satisfy its monetary claims against the borrower.

In case of default of the borrower, the Issuer will be entitled to enforce the relevant securities. In line with the Italian law principle, which prevents the automatic transfer of ownership of a security upon the mortgage borrower's default, foreclosure proceedings on attached assets are, in general, court supervised proceedings. Foreclosure proceedings on mortgaged properties (including the sale thereof) may be time-consuming, while foreclosure proceedings on the pledged quotas may be shorter.

Although rules governing enforcement proceedings vary with the kind of assets in respect of which such proceedings are commenced, in general the preservation of the attached assets during the enforcement proceedings is ensured by the attachment, served upon the borrower by the Issuer through a bailiff, whereby the bailiff orders the mortgage borrower to pay the due amount within a term of at least 10 days, and to refrain from disposing of the attached assets (to be filed by the bailiff with the court and in case of real estate properties to be registered with the Real Estate Register). After the attachment, any action taken or agreement entered into by the mortgage borrower in connection with the attached assets is ineffective vis-à-vis the Issuer. To prevent decline in the value of the attached asset, the bailiff may appoint a custodian, and the Issuer may have an influence on such an appointment depending on the kind of enforcement proceeding which has been commenced.

Not earlier than 10 days following the attachment, the Issuer files the petition for sale of the attached assets and the court sets a hearing where the conditions of such sale are established. The sale of the assets may be performed by auction (public sale to the highest bidder) or without auction (direct negotiation with any offering party). If the sale by auction is unsuccessful, the Issuer is entitled to ask the court for the assignment of the assets for an amount quantified by the court.

In relation to pledged assets, the sale may only occur after a written notice to pay is served upon the borrower and the third party pledgor, if any. If the borrower does not pay and does not challenge the sale notice within five days from the receipt of the same, the pledged assets may be sold through an auction sale or through authorised intermediaries or other entities authorised to carry out such activities (alternatively the Issuer may request the award of the pledged assets up to the amount of the secured claim through a filing with the relevant court).

The proceeds are allocated by the court, first to creditors (as the Issuer) whose credits are secured by means of a mortgage, pledge, or other privilege on the sold assets, if any, and then to unsecured creditors (in case of insolvency proceedings, the proceeds will be applied firstly toward payment of costs relating to the procedure).

THE IMPACT OF THE INSOLVENCY OF THE BORROWER: MAIN ASPECTS

As stated above, specific measures are to be adopted in order to render the borrower (to the extent possible under Italian law) a bankruptcy remote entity. Below are the key points which impact on the transaction in the case of an insolvency of the borrower:

(1) under Art. 67 of the Italian Bankruptcy Law, any security granted by the borrower during the six-month period (or, in the event the relevant security is not created contextually to the execution of the relevant mortgage loan, during the one-year period) prior to the bankruptcy declaration may be set aside, provided that certain requirements are met. As mentioned above, this general principle is derogated with respect to mortgages created to secure a *fondiario* loan, in relation to which an hardening period of 10 days would apply;

(2) the assignment by way of security of the receivables may be not effective against the insolvency receiver of the borrower with respect to claims which have still to come into existence as of the date on which the borrower is declared bankrupt (so called "*crediti futuri*"). Accordingly, the receiver may be entitled to collect the payments from the relevant tenants;

(3) under Art. 65 of the Italian Bankruptcy Law, any payments made during the two-year period prior to the bankruptcy declaration are deemed to be ineffective vis-à-vis the creditors in the event that the maturity date of such payments was provided to fall on the date of the bankruptcy declaration or thereafter. Pursuant to certain recent case law, such provisions might be also applied to any prepayments made by the borrower under a loan agreement (including a mortgage loan agreement); and

(4) as a general matter, if an insolvency proceeding is commenced, no foreclosure proceeding may be initiated and all proceedings already initiated by creditors are stayed. This means, for instance, that, upon the insolvency of the borrower, any enforcement of the security granted by the borrower has to be carried in the context of the bankruptcy proceeding. This rule does not apply (as mentioned, above) with respect to the enforcement of the mortgaged properties, which may be carried out by means of autonomous foreclosure proceedings, to the extent the relevant loan agreement is a *fondiario* loan.

In light of the above, it is clear that the noteholders would have a significant prejudice in case of insolvency of the borrower, notwithstanding all the possible mitigants which may be adopted. On this basis it remains crucial to implement all the appropriate measures, as mentioned, above, to create the bankruptcy remoteness of the borrower (to the extent legally possible).

ASSET CONTROL PROVISIONS

Also, in light of the length of the foreclosure proceedings in Italy and, in any case, in order to prevent to the extent possible the default of the borrower, rating agencies generally require to adopt specific measures (so called "Asset Control Provisions") in order to grant to the Issuer, upon the occurrence of certain "potential events of default" (for instance, in case certain LTV targets are not met), a certain degree of control on the real estate portfolio.

The Asset Control Provisions which are generally implemented are the following:

(1) Inclusion in the by-laws of the Borrower of provisions which require that certain key strategic decisions, which would ordinarily be taken by the board of directors, are taken by a meeting of the quotaholders of the borrower. Such matters should include the:

  (a) raising of finance by the borrower;
  (b) granting of security or guarantees by the borrower;
  (c) employment of personnel by the borrower;
  (d) acquisition of participation interests in other companies by the borrower; and
  (e) appointment and/or replacement of the asset manager.

(2) The pledge agreement over the quotas of the borrower should provide that:

  (a) the pledgor will give notice to the Issuer of any quotaholders' meeting, together with a description of the matters to be voted on at such quotaholders' meeting, an indication of how the pledgor, as quotaholder, proposes to vote in relation to such matters and a confirmation that such a vote will be exercised in a manner which will not cause a default under the mortgage loan;

(b) if the Issuer is of the view that the vote by the pledgor will commit the borrower to a course of action which will result in the occurrence of an event of default under the mortgage loan, the relevant matter will be voted upon at a separate quota-holders' meeting, where the right to vote will be exercised by the Issuer (acting on behalf of the secured creditors) and not by the pledgor; and

(c) for voting rights at all quotaholders' meetings to be transferred to the Issuer (acting on behalf of the secured creditors) fol-lowing the occurrence of an event of default under the mortgage loan.

(3) Inclusion in the relevant asset management agreement and in the mortgage loan agreement of certain provisions which oblige the borrower to replace the asset manager with a new one satisfactory to the Issuer in case the asset manager does not fulfil its obligations and/ or in case certain LTV targets are not met.

The Asset Control Provisions, in essence, grant to the Issuer

(1) the possibility to monitor the activity of the borrower on certain strategic matters and hence, through the instrument of the voting right, to prevent the possibility that the borrower will carry out a transaction which may significantly prejudice its rights; and

(2) in case the portfolio is not duly managed, the right to "control" the new asset manager which will be appointed to manage the real estate assets, without starting a proper foreclosure proceeding.

OVERVIEW OF A CMBS IN WHICH THE BORROWER IS A REAL ESTATE FUND

In the Italian market it is becoming common, mainly for tax reasons, to establish a real estate fund as a borrower under a mortgage loan (and, consequently under the subsequent potential CMBS). In brief terms, under Italian law, investment real estate funds are legally characterised as inde-pendent pools of assets represented by units held by participants and managed on a collective basis by a duly authorised asset management company (*società di gestione del risparmio*, "SGR").

The SGR may carry out any activity and/or enter into any agreement deemed useful or necessary in order to achieve the fund's purposes in the interest of the fund's participants, in compliance with the management rules of the fund (i.e. the by-laws of the fund) and any applicable laws and regulations. Notwithstanding that the assets of the fund are managed by the SGR, such assets are deemed to be segregated from:

- the assets of the SGR;

- any other pool of assets managed by such SGR; and

- the assets of each participant.

For the purpose of a CMBS, the main advantage in providing that the relevant borrower is a real estate fund rather than a corporate entity is represented by the fact that, in Italy, investment funds do not qualify as enterprises, and therefore the provisions contained in the Bankruptcy Law do not apply to them. This means that without the need to implement all the measures described above, the borrower will actually be a bankruptcy remote entity and, accordingly, all the risks deriving from the possible insolvency of the borrower (normally present in a CMBS in which the borrower is a corporate entity and summarised above) are not relevant in this circumstance.

On the other hand, it shall also be considered that the corporate governance of a real estate fund is different from that of a corporate entity. The management of the assets belonging to a fund must be carried out by its SGR. Certain bodies representing the interests of the participants in the fund have the power to control and verify the performance of the SGR in the management of the fund. One such body is the so-called Participants Meeting (*Assemblea dei Partecipanti*), comprising the unitholders of the fund, which is entitled to resolve on the replacement of the SGR. Any agreement attempting to derogate from these provisions may be deemed invalid or ineffective towards the unitholders.

In light of such corporate governance and considering that the units of a real estate fund are not used to secure the indebtedness of the fund itself since they belong to a different entity (i.e. the sponsor) and are generally used to secure a subordinated debt of the sponsor, the Asset Control Provisions described above and, in particular, the right for the Issuer to "control" the appointment of the asset manager, may not be fully replicated when the borrower is a fund.

Possible alternative measures which may be implemented in order to grant the Issuer a certain comfort on the quality of the entity which manages the assets may be provided. For instance, the fund management rules may provide that any management company which shall be appointed by the participants' meeting shall be a management company of primary standing and have experience in the real estate mutual funds sector.

As a further protection for the Issuer, it may be advisable to include in the mortgage loan as an event of withdrawal, permitting acceleration of the loan, the circumstance that any SGR that is appointed does not meet certain specified requirements, such as being a primary standing manager with significant experience in the management of real estate portfolios.

Clearly, such alternative measures do not grant the Issuer the same degree of protection which may be granted to it in the case where the borrower is a corporate entity. This should be carefully considered in the context of discussions with the rating agencies.

The tax regime applicable to real estate funds has been recently reformed so to provide that such entities are exempt from any income tax. Accordingly, any rent received by a real estate fund on its properties, as well as any capital gains realised by it on the disposal of the same properties, would not be subject to income tax in the hands of the fund. Proceeds earned by real estate funds are subject to tax only at the time of distribution, in the hands of the relevant unitholders.

The above represents a great incentive to the establishment of a real estate fund, which can carry out its ordinary real estate activity without triggering any tax burden, as opposed to Italian real estate companies, which are subject to both corporate income tax (IRES, at a rate of 33 per cent) and regional tax on productive activities (IRAP, generally applying at a rate of 4.25 per cent) on their income (including rents paid by the tenants and capital gains realised on the properties).

While the ongoing management of the fund is extremely efficient under an income tax perspective, no special rules are provided with respect to the contribution of properties to the same. In particular, such contribution represents a taxable event for the contributor for income tax purposes, so that it would be subject to tax on any capital gains realised thereto.

THE ITALIAN SECURITISATION LAW— TRANSFER REQUIREMENTS AND REGULATORY ASPECTS

In Italy, under a CMBS transaction the assignment of the claims deriving from a mortgage loan (and related security documents) is effected pursuant to the provisions of the law of April 30, 1999, No.130 (the "Italian Securitisation Law"). Pursuant to the Italian Securitisation Law, the relevant assignment is carried out in accordance with the procedure set forth under Art. 58, paras 2, 3 and 4, of the Italian Banking Law, which requires that the assignment shall be registered in the competent Companies Registry and a notice of the assignment published in the Official Gazette of the Republic of Italy (*Gazzetta Ufficiale della Republica Italiana*).

Upon completion of such requirements and certain other formalities required for specific security interests (such as, with respect to the pledge over quotas, a specific registration in the shareholders book of the borrower), the assignment of the claims deriving from the mortgage loan and of the relevant securities is deemed effective vis-à-vis any third party (i.e. a true sale is completed).

Article 3 of the Italian Securitisation Law provides that the claims transferred to the Issuer will be segregated from all its other assets and will only be available to the creditors of the Issuer participating in the relevant CMBS. That portfolio of claims will, therefore, be ring fenced for the benefit of, among others, the noteholders.

Under Art. 129 of the Italian Banking Act, the Issuer has to obtain a specific clearance by the Bank of Italy before it may issue the relevant notes. Such clearance is deemed as granted if the Bank of Italy does not object within 20 days from the filing of the relevant clearance request. That request shall be filed together with a term sheet describing the overall transaction (including a description of the underlying mortgage loan). The Bank of Italy may request additional information on the notes to be issued and, in general, on the overall transaction. If so, the above mentioned 20-day period shall be interrupted and will re-commence from the date on which the Bank of Italy receives the requested information.

TAX ASPECTS

Indirect tax regime of mortgage loans

As a general rule, mortgage loans granted to an Italian company and/or a real estate fund falls within the scope of VAT as a zero-rated transaction. Under certain circumstances such loans may attract the payment of a 0.25 per cent substitutive tax on the amount thereof (the "Substitutive Tax"). More precisely, the Substitutive Tax applies to loans where:

(1) the lender is an Italian resident bank, a bank resident in another country of the European Union or a permanent establishment in Italy of a foreign bank;

(2) the loan has a tenor in excess of 18 months;[2] and

(3) the relevant loan agreement is executed in Italy.

The Substitutive Tax must be paid by the lender. As a market practice, however, the related burden is switched onto the borrower.

The Substitutive Tax applies in lieu of all the indirect taxes which would be otherwise applicable to the loan, its execution, amendment and/or termination, as well as to any securities and guarantees issued in connection thereto, irrespective of whether those indirect taxes would be effectively due. In particular, the Substitutive Tax entails a substantial saving in the case of mortgage loans, since it replaces mortgage tax, which applies at a rate of 2 per cent on the registration of the mortgage with the competent Real Estate Registries and at a rate of 0.50 per cent on the subsequent cancellation thereof. In addition, the Substitutive Tax also absorbs registration tax, which applies on securities granted by a person, other than the borrower itself (for example, a pledge on the borrower's stock), at a rate of 0.50 per cent on the secured amount thereof.

The advantage provided by the application of the Substitutive Tax does not cover the syndication of a loan. In this regard, the Italian tax authorities have clarified (in several rulings) that the assignment of a loan by a lender would not fall within the scope of the Substitutive Tax paid by it and, consequently, any tax due on the security transferred to the assignee would not be absorbed. In particular, should the assignee intend to be recorded as a beneficiary of the mortgage in the competent Land Registry, registration tax at a rate of 2 per cent would be payable. Such a significant tax burden renders the syndication of real estate financings secured by a mortgage extremely expensive and hence difficult to be carried out, also considering that based on market practice the above tax burden is not borne by the borrower.

A specific exception to the above rule is set forth in case of the securitisation of loans, whereby they are assigned to an Issuer incorporated pursuant to the Italian Securitisation Law. In order to render securitisations more attractive, Art. 6 of the Italian Securitisation Law provides that, should the assigned loans be subject to Substitutive Tax, the benefits of the

---

[2] For the Substitutive Tax purposes, the term of a loan must be determined based on the relevant contractual provisions, irrespective of the effective term thereof. In the view of the Italian tax authorities the Substitutive Tax would not apply in case the relevant loan agreement does not contain a firm commitment of the lender to maintain the loan for more than 18 months (save in case of early termination due to breaches). Thus, the requirements at issue cannot be deemed as met in case the loan agreement allows the lender to terminate it whenever it desires (i.e. *ad nutum*).

latter would continue to apply and thus the transfer of the relevant securities (including the mortgage) would fall within its umbrella.

Tax regime of CMBS

The favour of the Italian legislature towards securitisations also clearly emerges from the tax regime which has been provided by the Italian Securitisation Law with respect to CMBS issued by an Issuer incorporated under that Securitisation Law, that benefit from the same tax regime applicable to bonds issued by Italian banks or Italian companies listed in an Italian regulated market.

In particular, provided that the CMBS have a term of at least 18 months, interest paid thereon (including any difference between the redemption amount and the issue price) is subject to the regime described below:

(1) interest paid to Italian resident individuals would trigger a 12.5 per cent substitutive tax. This is a final tax and it cannot be deducted from the income tax due by the noteholder;

(2) interest paid to Italian resident companies would not be subject to any withholding tax or substitutive tax and would form part of the overall taxable income of the recipient for IRES (and, in certain cases, for IRAP) purposes; and

(3) a full exemption from Italian taxation is provided with respect to interest paid to non-Italian noteholders (not having a permanent establishment in Italy), which are resident in countries providing for a satisfactory exchange of information with the Republic of Italy. Such white-list countries are typically those having entered into a tax treaty with the Republic of Italy, including exchange of information provisions. All the EU countries do in principle qualify for the exemption. The requirements to benefit from the exemption are minimal, since only the deposit of the CMBS with certain qualified intermediaries and the filing of a self-statement with the same intermediary is required.

CONCLUSION

The considerations outlined above clearly indicates that the Italian CMBS market may be considered, at least from a legal perspective, a developed market.

The legal structures which may be implemented, the solution of reg-ulatory issues which were deemed a significant burden, as well as the favourable tax treatment may be deemed the main elements for the consideration of Italy as a CMBS-friendly country.

Clearly, similarly to other jurisdictions, the financial structures envisaged for CMBS transactions need to be tested on the basis of the domestic provisions and sometimes may require adjustment or amendment. As stated above, the implementation of a CMBS deal requires a careful review of the underlying transaction and, consequently, it is always advisable to address and properly structure, in advance, the underlying loans in order to subsequently be able to securitise the assets.

The market expectation is that CMBS deals will increase in the near future and that CMBS structures will be considered as the natural exit for lenders operating in the mortgage loans market.

CHAPTER TWENTY

THE PORTUGUESE CMBS MARKET

MORTGAGE-COVERED BONDS: A BRAVE NEW TOOL

Pedro Cassiano Santos and Hugo Moredo Santos
Vieira de Almeida & Associados

THE SECURITISATION FRAMEWORK

Securitisation is a tool which has enjoyed a specific legal framework in Portugal since 1999, when Decree-Law 453/99 (the "Securitisation Law") set forth a specific regime applicable to the assignment of receivables for securitisation purposes and ruled on the incorporation and activity of the securitisation vehicles. This specific regulation was enacted in a context where securitisation in Portugal was in its infancy and transactions were carried out under the Portuguese Civil Code structure, which did not comprise a specific securitisation framework, transactions being therefore carried out under the general concept of assignment of credits (Art. 577 of Portuguese Civil Code). Taking into account this absence of a specific structure, securitisations involving mortgage-backed receivables were impracticable due to assignment and registration costs which, together with assignment formalities (which are identical to those applicable to the transfer of the underlying asset—transfer of title over real estate requires the execution of a public deed), were obstacles impossible to overcome.

In this scenario, the Securitisation Law may be seen as having established a legal framework aiming at the simplification and hence at the expansion of the Portuguese securitisation market:

(1) it has provided a standard and specific securitisation regime by regulating the creation and activity of the securitisation vehicles, the

type of receivables that may be securitised, and the entities that may assign credits for securitisation purposes;

(2) it has simplified the process by providing specific rules applicable to the assignment of receivables; and

(3) it has expanded the class of actual eligible assets so as to include mortgage loans by providing for a simplified mechanism for assignment of this type of credit.

Some key aspects of this legal framework may be summarised as follows:

(1) identification of all potential originators, including the Portuguese state and other public law entities, credit institutions, financial companies, insurance companies, pension funds, pension funds' management companies and other corporate entities having their last three-year accounts duly certified by a registered auditor;

(2) definition of the eligibility criteria that the receivables must meet so as to be capable of assignment for securitisation purposes: free assignability (hence, not limited by legal or contractual constraints), pecuniary nature, no-subordination to conditions and no submission to litigation nor to security or judicial seizure or apprehension;

(3) creation of two different structures in terms of securitisation vehicles:

   (a) credit securitisation funds (*Fundos de Titularização de Créditos*—"FTC"), operating on a tripartite structure basis which comprises the fund (autonomous pool of assets), the management company and the custodian, and

   (b) credit securitisation companies (*Sociedades de Titularização de Créditos*—"STC"), operating on a simple structure scheme, formed by the securitisation company only;

(4) establishment of special rules facilitating assignments of receivables in the context of securitisation, which includes:

   (a) the notification to the relevant debtors not to be required whenever the originator is a credit institution, financial company, insurance company, pension fund or pension fund's management company, and

   (b) the possibility for the receivables assignment agreement to be executed by private document, public deed being thus dispensed with (even in those cases where the assigned receivables are backed by mortgages);

(5) establishment of special rules aimed at the characterisation of the assignment as a true and effective sale (the sale of the assets/assignment of receivables must be treated as a complete and final transfer

from the seller—originator—to the purchaser—securitisation vehicle—so that upon such transfer the relevant receivables may no longer and for no legal purpose be seen as assets of the seller);

(6) establishment of special rules aimed at protecting investor's rights in the context of the insolvency of the originator and/or of the servicer:

    (a) unlike the general rules in this respect, the assignment of receivables for securitisation purposes even when conducted in the vicinity of insolvency is not deemed to be made in bad faith in the context of the originator's insolvency and therefore the proof of bad faith in the performance of certain acts which may be said to cause depletion of a given debtor's assets (which, in certain circumstances, is deemed to occur as per the general terms of insolvency law) lies upon the creditor whenever such acts occur for securitisation purposes;

    (b) unless it is bad faith driven, no assignment of credits for securitisation purposes may be challenged for the benefit of the originator's insolvency estate;

    (c) any payments made to the assignor in respect of receivables assigned prior to a declaration of insolvency shall not form part of its insolvency estate even when their maturity date is subsequent to any such declaration; and

    (d) any amounts held by the servicer as a result of its collection of payments in respect of credits assigned for securitisation purposes shall not form part of the servicer's insolvency estate.

Besides their specific framework, the two aforementioned different structures provide for two different investment instruments: while FTCs issue securitisation units, STCs issue securitisation notes. The creation of these two different types of securitisation vehicles may be seen as having been determined by a flexibility concern. Accordingly, it may have been felt that sticking to FTCs alone could be too limiting, particularly when the historical securitisation background is SPV-based, a structure with which Anglo-Saxon investors seem to be more familiar with. The creation of the two alternatives seems therefore to represent an adequate means of attracting a wider and more diversified range of investors.

FTCs correspond to autonomous pools of assets jointly held by individual or corporate entities (with no specific requirements applying in respect of their nature). Under no circumstances may the FTCs be liable for the debts of said entities (unitholders), of their management company (fund manager) or of the entities from which they have purchased the receivables forming part of such pools of assets (originator). With regard to their structure, FTCs may be of a variable or fixed nature, as can be defined by the applicable fund regulation (which works as the FTC's constitutional document). In those cases where the fund regulation allows for: (i) new credits to be purchased (either aimed at replacing previous receivables on their maturity date, should said receivables have a maturity date shorter than the fund's, or in addition to the ones purchased at the time of incorporation of the FTC), and/or (ii) new issues of securitisation units to be made, the FTCs will have a variable nature. When neither (i) or (ii), above, are allowed by the fund regulation, the FTC is said to be of a fixed nature.

As per the terms of the respective fund regulation, the securitisation units may grant their holders any or all of the following rights:

(1) payment of periodic income;

(2) reimbursement of the units' nominal value; and

(3) sharing of the fund's assets left upon liquidation thereof, pro rata with the relevant participation.

When the fund regulation so allows, there may be different categories of securitisation units (i.e. sets of units which grant their holders identical rights but, when compared with other sets of units, entail a different ranking insofar as the exercise of the above rights is concerned) and, provided the equal treatment of the holders of same category securitisation units is ensured, there may be early redemption of the units, either in whole or in part.

On the contrary, STCs are financial companies who are required to:

(1) qualify as *sociedade anónima* (public limited liability company) whose share capital is represented by nominative or registered bearer shares;

(2) include in its name the expression "STC" for ease of identification; and

(3) be exclusively engaged in the carrying out of securitisation transactions by means of purchasing, managing and transferring receivables, and of issuing notes as a source of financing such acquisitions.

Their main feature is that their reimbursement is guaranteed by receivables exclusively allocated to them, i.e. they are of limited recourse to the specific assets backing them. This segregation principle is made effective by the legal provisions which impose the need for the alluded receivables (i.e. those allocated to a given secured note) to be identified as such (in a codified form, the corresponding key being deposited with CMVM—the Portuguese Securities Commission) and to be treated as an autonomous pool of assets that is not available to satisfy any other debts the securitisation company may have. The holders of secured notes are further entitled to an additional creditor's privilege and their rights rank senior to those of the other creditors in respect of receivables allocated to the relevant issue of notes.

Transactions under the securitisation framework

The first securitisation transaction was carried out in Portugal in 1997 and the first AAA securitisation in 1999. However, the first transaction carried out under the Securitisation Law—which was performed by a mortgage-backed deal—only occurred in late 2001. The regime under the Securitisation Law, although investor-friendly, did not give efficient solutions for tax sensitive matters, an issue that was only overcome with the enactment of Decree-law No.219/2001, dated August 5, 2001, which established the tax regime applying to securitisation transactions.

This specific tax regime included several exemptions, notably in what concerns income inherent to securitisation units (issued by the FTCs) and securitisation notes (issued by the STCs), value added tax relating to servicing of the receivables and management thereof and stamp tax affecting assignments, interest and commissions.

From December 2001 to the present day, the Portuguese market has experienced the incorporation of more than 30 FTCs and four STCs, and the execution of nearly 20 transactions involving receivables backed by mortgages, which clearly evidences the relevant role of this type of security as a related security of a receivable assigned for securitisation purposes.

The mortgage-backed deals originated in Portugal have always related to RMBS, with the CMBS market still waiting to make its debut. Both RMBS and CMBS are subject, as concerns legal and taxation limitations, to the exact same rules as explained above. Actually, the Securitisation Law does not have any provisions specifically applicable to RMBS or to CMBS and, consequently, all key features presented in relation to potential originators, eligibility criteria, selectable securitisation vehicles, rules applicable to the assignment of receivables and investor's protection measures apply, on general terms, to both RMBS and CMBS equally.

Once there is no legal constraint applicable to CMBS when compared to RMBS, the most evident reason to explain the boom of RMBS transactions and the absence of CMBS transactions is that RMBS is a much more homogenised market (notably due to underwriting standards), thus facilitating massive assignment and avoiding complicated due diligence processes. However, things may change in the near future, for the slow-starting CMBS Portuguese market may have found a new path to develop its potentialities: mortgage-covered bonds.

MORTGAGE-COVERED BONDS

A little over four years after the first securitisation transaction carried out under the Securitisation Law and a little over six years after the enactment of that Law, and bearing in mind the fast—although smooth—growth of the Portuguese securitisation market, the Portuguese Government has decided to review Decree-law No.125/90, dated April 16, which set out the regime governing an instrument which may constitute an alternative to securitisation (although bearing different features): mortgage-covered bonds.

This review was long awaited by members of the financial community. Although the Portuguese legal environment contained regulation on mortgage-covered bonds since the beginning of the 1990's, Decree-law No.125/90 has never conquered the sympathy of market participants as a piece of legislation providing a useful and efficient tool aimed at creating conditions for debt representative instruments backed by portfolios of mortgage credits to be issued. Therefore, it does not come as a surprise that the preamble of Decree-law No.59/2006, dated March 20, identifies the purposes of avoiding bureaucratisation and creating flexibility as the most relevant targets to be achieved by granting to certain market players the ability to issue mortgage-covered bonds, hence following the European trend on this subject and profiting from the experience gathered with similar instruments in jurisdictions having this tool more efficiently developed.

Therefore, Decree-law No.59/2006 has determined several changes to the legal framework set forth by its predecessor, in particular the:

- enlargement of the type of receivables capable of being used as underlying credits of the mortgage-covered bonds, as a consequence of the adoption of more flexible eligibility criteria, thus allowing for receivables other than those mortgaged-backed to work as underlying assets;

- enlargement of the type of entities enjoying issuing capability, which resulted in the insertion of a new species of credit institution, mortgage loan credit institutions, entities which are known to the legal framework of other EU Member States; and

- acknowledgment of the useful function that risk coverage instruments may perform in the context of a transaction involving debt issuance and the consequent recognition of derivative instruments as appropriate schemes for the purposes of currency fluctuation, interest variation and liquidity shortfalls risk coverage.

Issuing capability

Decree-law No.59/2006 has not accepted the idea of all entities being entitled to issue mortgage-covered bonds. Taking into account the special nature of the typical asset which underlies debt representative instruments,[1] the law has initially limited the issuing capability to those entities which are allowed to grant mortgage loans in the context of their business activities. It is understandable that credit institutions unable to grant mortgage loans should not be entitled to issue debt representative instruments backed, primarily, by mortgage loans. This may be said to constitute a statutory limitation. However, in practice is not that relevant, as all (or, at least, the vast majority of) credit institutions are statutorily allowed to grant mortgage loans.

Even if a credit institution is allowed to grant mortgage loans in the context of its business activity, a second criterion should be also met: an appropriate level of own funds, which the law has set at €7,500,000. This may be said to constitute a prudential limitation, which is aimed at ensuring that credit institutions evidencing a low level of own funds may not obtain liquidity through the issuance of these instruments.

As previously discussed, Decree-law No.59/2006 has also introduced a new type of credit institution: mortgage loan credit institutions. These entities are credit institutions having the power to grant, acquire and sell receivables secured by mortgages over real estate for the purpose of issuing mortgage-covered bonds.[2] In order to properly conduct their activities, mortgage loan credit institutions may also perform all administrative acts relating to the assets which are collected as repayment of the receivables, as well as perform other acts proving necessary for the accomplishment of their primary role.

In conclusion, it is possible to identify as entities enjoying mortgage-covered bonds issuing capability, credit institutions legally authorised to grant mortgage loans which enjoy own funds amounting to no less than €7,500,000, including the new mortgage loan credit institutions.[3]

---

[1] Mortgage-backed receivables, resulting from a mortgage loan entered into by and between a credit institution and a given borrower.

[2] Furthermore, mortgage loan credit institutions may also grant, acquire and sell receivables due or guaranteed by central administrations or regional and local authorities of EU Member States for the purpose of issuing mortgage-covered bonds.

[3] The preamble of Decree-law No.59/2006 already anticipates that other entities—notably, financial companies—may in the future be entitled to issue mortgage-backed bonds, a possibility which is closely dependent on the evolution and experience gathered by the use of that instrument.

Main features inherent to mortgage-covered bonds

This new legal framework profited from several investor protection mechanisms introduced by the Securitisation Law, the generality of which were unknown to the former Decree-law No.125/90. Therefore, mortgage-covered bonds grant certain entitlements to their holders, which are aimed at allowing them to be detached from all risks not inherent to the securities they hold (the mortgage-covered bonds) and the receivables underlying them (the mortgage loans). In this context, the special creditor privilege (which, for flexibility and costs saving purposes, is not subject to registration) over the underlying mortgage receivables and other assets integrating the covered pool, assumes a predominant position.[4] This credit privilege allows the holders of mortgage-covered bonds to enjoy a preferential position in relation to other creditors for the purposes of principal repayment, and interest payment corresponding to their mortgage-covered bonds.[5]

Additionally, as the mortgage receivables and other assets allocated to the mortgage-covered bonds, including the proceeds relating to interest and repayments, constitute an autonomous pool of assets, they are incapable of being used for the payment of other debts incurred by the issuer, to the extent the amounts due to the holders of the mortgage-covered bonds are not fully discharged. This segregation structure, which is already familiar to investors in securitisation units (on a fund by fund basis) and on securitisation notes (on a issuance by issuance basis) issued by FTCs and STCs respectively, demands mortgage receivables and other assets forming part of the autonomous pool of assets allocated to the mortgage-covered bonds, to be registered in segregated accounts of the issuer, and identified in a codified manner in the issuance documents.[6] The key to the code, following the solution that already applies to securitisation notes,[7] must be deposited with the Bank of Portugal, as supervising entity of the issuer. Decree-law No.59/2006 has not provided for specific rules governing the access by holders of mortgage-covered bonds to the code, entrusting the matter to the Bank of

---

[4] In its main features, notably the preference status granted thereby and the absence of registration, this entitlement is very similar to the one awarded to the holders of securitisation bonds and entities rendering services connected with the issuance thereof under Portuguese Securitisation Law.

[5] This credit privilege is extendable to the counterparts of eligible derivative transactions, insofar as the receivables resulting from such transactions are concerned. See "Risk Coverage Instruments", below.

[6] The Portuguese securitisation funds dispense with the need for such a segregated registration, as each fund works as an autonomous pool of assets, and is thus capable of being used for only one transaction, even if the same involves multiple issuances and multiple series of securitisation units.

[7] The key to the code of the securitisation bonds' accounts shall be deposited with the CMVM (Portuguese Securities Commission), as supervising entity of the STCs.

Portugal, who must establish, by means of regulation, the conditions under which such access may, in the event of default, take place.

Another relevant feature of mortgage-covered bonds is the ring fencing mechanism set forth by the legislator, so as to safeguard those instruments and respective holders, from events having a negative patrimonial impact on the issuer, notably its insolvency. Hence, in the event of dissolution and winding-up (including on grounds of insolvency) of the issuer, the mortgage receivables and remainder assets allocated to the mortgage-covered bonds will be segregated from the insolvency estate and thus will not form part thereof. This segregation allows for the mortgage receivables and assets to be autonomously managed until full repayment of the amounts due to the holders of the mortgage-covered bonds, notwithstanding the bondholders meeting being entitled to approve the immediate acceleration of those securities. Also in this respect, the Bank of Portugal is required to provide the procedures that must be adopted during such autonomous management and the terms of the liquidation of the estate (mortgage receivables and other assets) allocated to the mortgage-covered bonds following the acceleration of the securities.

What type of assets can back mortgage-covered bonds?

Decree-law No.59/2006 provides for two different categories of underlying assets:

- unconditioned pecuniary non-matured mortgage-backed receivables, and
- other assets.

Unconditioned pecuniary non-matured mortgage-backed receivables

These include three different sorts of receivables:

(1) pecuniary receivables that are not matured, nor subject to conditions, nor encumbered, nor judicially seized or apprehended and which are secured by first ranking mortgages over residential or commercial real estate located in a EU Member State;

(2) receivables secured by junior mortgages where all receivables secured by senior mortgages over the same real estate are held by the issuer and allocated to the same bond issuance; and

(3) receivables enjoying the benefit of a personal guarantee granted by a credit institution or by an appropriate insurance policy, with a mortgage counter guarantee evidencing the characteristics identified above.

It should be noted that, when establishing the eligibility criteria for assets which may back mortgage-covered bonds, Decree-law No.59/2006 has followed in the footsteps of the Securitisation Law with regard to the definition of the receivables capable of assignment for securitisation purposes. In fact, only in respect of maturity and transferability the features of eligible unconditioned pecuniary non-matured receivables differ from those of receivables eligible for securitisation purposes.

Regarding maturity, it should be stressed that the original version of the Securitisation Law also prevented the use of matured and unpaid receivables for securitisation purposes, a restriction which has been eliminated so as to "leave to market players the role of evaluating the quality of the transactions they wish to enter in light of the rating attributed by the relevant rating agency".[8] Securitisation regulation has not always been as it currently is; the legislator has originally chosen a prudent approach on the eligibility criteria and has later removed some of the limitations initially imposed in order to meet the market development and to achieve a full undertaking by investors, as decision makers, of the investment risk inherent to the purchased securities. It remains to be seen if the same happens in respect of this requisite for mortgage-covered bonds.

The absence of transferability (a key, indeed critical, feature of receivables hoping to qualify as suitable for assignment for securitisation purposes) among the mortgage-covered bonds eligibility criteria means that there must be no transfer of the mortgage loan and relevant mortgage to any third party, as happens in standard securitisation (as opposed to synthetic securitisation). As happens in securitisation transactions, the proceeds inherent to mortgage loans are allocated to the mortgage-covered bonds. However, the benefit of the holders of mortgage-covered bonds to receive all principal and interest collections resulting from those loans is not the consequence of a transfer of title but rather of an allocation of proceeds and security scheme, thus implying no variation at the creditor position level.

Other assets

In the "other assets" category, the law has included deposits with the Bank of Portugal, in cash or in securities eligible for credit transactions of the Eurosystem; current or term account deposits with credit institutions (which are not in a domination or group relationship with the issuer) having a rating equal to or higher than "A-" or equivalent; and other assets complying simultaneously with the requisites of low risk and high liquidity.

---

[8] Preamble of Decree-law No.303/2003, dated December 5, which enacted the second amendment to the Portuguese Securitisation Law.

In addition to their specific features, the main difference between the two types of underlying assets stems from the fact that the total value of the "other assets" may not exceed 20 per cent of the global value of the mortgage receivables and other assets allocated as security over the mortgage-covered bonds.

Risk coverage instruments

The need to ensure, at all times, that the relevant periodic payments are duly performed as and when they fall due is one of the major concerns inherent to the issuance of bonds and other debt representative securities. Therefore, it is critical to permit the use by the issuer of certain tools whenever, for any reason whatsoever, proceeds originated by the mortgage-backed receivables and other assets allocated to the issued mortgage-covered bonds prove to be insufficient to meet the scheduled payment obligations.

In order to face temporary liquidity shortfalls, irrevocable credit lines may be contracted and, if needed, activated, the corresponding funds being exclusively used for purposes of repayment and interest payments of the relevant mortgage-covered bonds. Following the same rating level requirement which has been presented above in relation to current or term account deposits with credit institutions (which may be comprised within the "other assets" category), those credit facilities may only be contracted with credit institutions rated at least "A-".

On the other hand, and with the exclusive purpose of ensuring risk coverage, namely interest rate, currency exchange and liquidity shortfalls, the issuer is entitled to conduct transactions involving derivative financial instruments. Those instruments would form part of the autonomous pool of assets allocated to the performance of the corresponding mortgage-covered bonds, and should be considered for calculation of the relevant limits and registered in the applicable segregated accounts of the issuer.[9]

As happens with the credit facilities, there is a restriction on where derivative financial instruments may be entered into. Decree-law No.59/2006 identifies regulated markets functioning in Member States or recognised markets of a full member of the Organisation for Economic Co-operation and Development (OECD) as eligible transaction markets for this type of transaction. The entering into of transactions involving derivative financial

---

[9] This registration shall additionally include, in respect of each derivative financial instrument, the following conditions: the mortgage-covered bonds to which such instrument is allocated, asset or assets underlying such mortgage-covered bonds, transaction amount, identification of the counterpart and initial date and maturity date.

instruments outside those restrictions is only acceptable if the respective counter part is a credit institution rated at least "A-".

Derivative financial instruments grant to the counterpart of the issuer the credit privilege referred to earlier in this chapter, insofar as the receivables resulting from such transactions are concerned.

It should be noted that the Bank of Portugal may define, by means of regulation approved for such purpose, the terms in which the derivative financial instruments are to be considered for the purposes of determining the prudential limits explained in the next part of this chapter, or set forth the application of further conditions on the use of derivative financial instruments.

Prudential rules

As illustrated by provisions such as those relating to segregation and ring fencing, the whole purpose of mortgage-covered bonds, is allocation, asset-backing and a direct connection between a particular asset and the securities whose performance it secures. Therefore, the existence of certain ratios is crucial for the prudent relationship between the backing assets and the performing securities. Therefore, Decree-law No.59/2006 provided that the nominal global value of the outstanding mortgage-covered bonds may not exceed 95 per cent of the nominal global value of the mortgage receivables and other assets allocated thereto. Similar rules apply to interest payments, and thus the nominal global amount of interest to be paid to the holders of mortgage-covered bonds may not exceed, from time-to-time, the amount of interest pertaining to the mortgage receivables and other assets allocated to the mortgage-covered bonds. The calculation of these limits, as well as other limits or conditions, and relevant calculation methods, namely in what relates to risk coverage and management, may still be complemented by regulations enacted by the Bank of Portugal.

While these two references relate to the mortgage-covered bonds themselves, another reference, working as an eligibility criterion, also results from the law: the relationship between the amount of a mortgage receivable and the value of the mortgage securing it, i.e. the loan-to-value ratio. Contrary to the position under the Securitisation Law, Decree-law No.59/2006 has defined a minimally acceptable ratio to the agreement that parties may achieve in the transaction documents determining that the amount of any mortgage receivable allocated to mortgage-covered bonds may not exceed the value of the respective mortgage (i.e. that amount secured thereby); neither 80 per cent of the value of the secured asset, in the case of residential real estate, nor 60 per cent of that value in the case of commercial real estate.

Should any of the above limits be exceeded the issuer shall ensure that the excess is not prejudicial to the performance of the issued mortgage-covered bonds and that the balance which the law has defined as a minimum—and which is evidenced by the referred ratios—is promptly re-established. For such a purpose, the issuer may:

(1) enlarge the set of assets allocated to the mortgage-covered bonds, improving the deficient backing level (rebalance at the underlying asset level) by the allocation of new mortgage receivables, with or without substitution of the mortgage receivables allocated to the mortgage-covered bonds, or other authorised assets; and/or

(2) decrease the number of outstanding mortgage-covered bonds and improve the backing level (rebalance at the mortgage-covered bonds level), through the acquisition of mortgage-covered bonds in the secondary market.

Tax implications

Provided certain requisites are met, income generated by mortgage-covered bonds may be exempt from corporate or personal income tax (including capital income and capital gains). This exemption is provided for in Decree-law No.193/2005, dated November 7, which sets forth a special taxation regime applicable to securities qualifying as debt representative instruments issued by public or private entities and traded in a centralised system recognised by Portuguese Securities Code.

Additionally, and in order for those securities to be released from tax contingencies, a second requisite must be met: the effective beneficiaries thereof may not have their residence, head office, effective management or permanent establishment in Portuguese territory to which the alluded income may be allocated, a structure which is very close to the one provided for in Decree-law No.219/2001, which establishes the tax regime applying to securitisation transactions carried out under the Securitisation Law.

CONCLUSION AND EXPECTATIONS

Legislation on mortgage-covered bonds has been awaited for several years by Portuguese market players, particularly credit institutions having strong shares in residential mortgage markets. The Portuguese legislator has closely followed the already tested and efficient framework of the Securitisation Law notably in matters such as the entitlements of holders of mortgage-covered bonds, including:

- the special creditor privilege over the underlying mortgage receivables,

- the account's segregation mechanism,

- the ring fencing structure,

- the definition of eligible underlying assets, where the criteria applicable to receivables qualifying for securitisation purposes have been *mutatis mutandis* adopted, and

- admissibility of risk coverage instruments.

Decree-law No.59/2006 has thus chosen to follow solutions that have been successfully used by the legal framework under which dozens of securitisation transactions, including those of mortgage-backed receivables, were carried out in Portugal.

It is to be hoped that the inefficiencies that doomed the now revoked Decree-law No.125/90 have been identified. In its place, a brave new tool has now been made available granting market players, from originators to arrangers, an alternative tool to manage mortgage loan portfolios which may be more useful in all those cases where balance sheet release is not critical asset class diversification for investors is also an achievement of their new legislation.

As discussed, most of the legal solutions have already crossed the market hurdle with regard to securitisation structures. The adoption of those same solutions for the issuance of mortgage-covered bonds demonstrates that the Portuguese legislator has followed the path of flexibility and market and investors protection, for the benefit of transactions originating out of Portugal. The legislator has done its job and it remains to be seen how market participants will respond.

CHAPTER TWENTY ONE

AN INNOVATION IN FINANCING—ISLAMIC CMBS

Michael J.T. McMillen, Partner
Abradat Kamalpour, Partner
Dechert LLP

INTRODUCTION AND OVERVIEW

Islamic finance, in its modern incarnation, is in its infancy, having emerged in the 1970s and only taken form in the mid to late 1990s. The growth of Islamic finance has been explosive over the last decade. Real estate has been a (if not the) primary focus of the industry since the 1990s. Islamic real estate investments began in the residential housing sector, but quickly moved to commercial properties, and commercial property investments now dominate this sector throughout the world. Initial investments were, and continue to be, effected primarily through investment fund structures. However, the emergence of the *sukuk* (Islamic bonds and Islamic securitisations) in 2003 and its continuing accelerated growth portend significant changes in Islamic finance, particularly Islamic real estate finance. Although *sukuk* offerings to date have mostly been Islamic bonds backed by sovereign credits (rather than the credit of isolated pools of *Shari'ah*-compliant obligations), attention is now turning to true private sector securitisations, and commercial real estate securitisations are the first area of focus.

While figures are difficult to substantiate, it is reputably estimated that funds immediately available for investments that are compliant with the principles and precepts of Islamic *shari'ah*[1] (the "*Shari'ah*") are approximately \$250–500 billion and real estate is a preferred investment for *Shari'ah*-compliant investors. Thus, the potential Islamic CMBS market has to be judged enormous by any standard.

---

[1] Islamic religious law as applied to commercial and financial activities.

Current discussions regarding *Shari'ah*-compliant CMBS products focus on:

(1) the sale of securitisation instruments backed by US and European properties into the markets dominated by Muslim investors (which, for convenience, this chapter will refer to as the *"OIC Markets"* although, to date, these are primarily Middle Eastern markets); and

(2) securitisation of properties within the OIC Markets.

Noticeably, there are no true Islamic CMBS products at present. Given the high level of creativity in, and the rapid expansion of, the Islamic finance field, this absence of product, of itself, is surprising. The securitisation industry is populated by highly creative entrepreneurs that embrace innovations and are constantly searching for new product opportunities: why have none of them identified the obvious opportunities afforded by the burgeoning Islamic finance markets?

However, things are usually not what they seem, nor are they as simple as they seem, and money clearly does not grow on trees. *Shari'ah*-compliant securitisation is a different animal than conventional securitisation as practiced in North America and Europe. First, there is the necessity of learning a bit about the *Shari'ah* and the constraints that it imposes. This is not the easiest task given that there are few written sources of information on the *Shari'ah* (fewer still that are accurate). Obtaining accurate knowledge of the *Shari'ah* is largely an oral process at this time in history, and the sources are limited to only a handful of individuals. Secondly, one finds that what one learns is a bit confusing, and sometimes downright discouraging, if one is steeped in conventional Western learning and conventional Western securitisation practices.

For example, firstly, the payment and receipt of interest are prohibited by the *Shari'ah*, making it particularly difficult to make use of most of the world's existing mortgages, credit card receivables, and other debt instruments for *Shari'ah*-compliant securitisations. Then there is the *Shari'ah* prohibition on the sale of debt or any other instrument that does not represent an ownership interest in a tangible asset. That principle would seem to limit the entire industry to 1983 pass-through certificates—and maybe some aircraft, vessel and equipment leases. Then one realises that the securitised lease must itself be *Shari'ah*-compliant and triple-net leases (i.e. most of the foregoing leases) are not *Shari'ah*-compliant. Then there is the fact that the Accounting and Auditing Organisation for Islamic Financial Institutions ("AAOIFI") has provided a rather precise definition of acceptable *sukuk* and the 14 permissible categories of *sukuk*, and most of them relate to leasing arrangements or joint venture arrangements that are divergent from conventional securitisation concepts. This raises the question of whether the ability to develop an Islamic CMBS industry in harmony with the existing Western securitisation industry is limited? Furthermore, will the AAOIFI standard induce a broadening of conventional securitisation concepts or will Islamic securitisation be partly harmonious with Western securitisation and partly outside existing conventional concepts? These are questions that this chapter will attempt to answer.

Notwithstanding this initial alarm, most of those practicing in the field of Islamic finance believe that Islamic CMBS present a rare and realisable opportunity unlike any that has previously been witnessed. They look at the future with creative enchantment and envision unrealised opportunities realised. This chapter attempts to provide an indication of why they have this belief, and in so doing it needs to provide an introduction to Islamic finance as it affects CMBS.

The chapter begins with an introduction to Islamic finance and the *Shari'ah* and those who determine what the *Shari'ah* actually is in a given business or with respect to a given structure or product, the *Shari'ah* scholars and the *Shari'ah* supervisory boards (the "*Shari'ah* Boards" or the "Boards"). To provide necessary context and an indication of a few of the constraints that affect the structure and issuance of Islamic CMBS products, it summarises a handful of substantive *Shari'ah* precepts and the essential structural nature of *sukuk*. Thereafter, it works through examples of some of the primary *sukuk* structures that will play into the Islamic CMBS markets and provides an analysis of some of the primary limitations and constraints on the development and growth of those markets.

WHAT IS ISLAMIC FINANCE?

Islamic finance, as an economic discipline, is the conduct of commercial and financial activities in accordance with the *Shari'ah*. The *Shari'ah*, for present purposes, is Islamic religious law as applied to commercial and financial activities. As in all areas, it is a combination of theology, religion and law. The *Shari'ah* is a guide to how a Muslim leads life (it means, literally, "the Way" or "the Right Path"). Thus, it is the perfect, immutable, divine law as revealed in the *Qur'an* and the *sunna*.

Fiqh, meaning literally, "understanding", is the sum of human comprehension of that divine law; the practical rules of *Shari'ah* as determined by the *Shari'ah* scholars. The primary methodology used in this determinative and interpretive effort is *ijtihad* (literally, "effort"), or legal reasoning, using the "roots of the law" (*usul al-fiqh*). The roots (*usul*) upon which Islamic jurisprudence are based are the:

(1) *Qur'an*, being the holy book of Islam and the revealed word of Allah (notably, less than 3 per cent of the *Qur'an* is legal in nature);

(2) *sunna* of the Prophet Mohammed, which are the binding authority of his dicta and decisions;

(3) *ijma*, or "consensus" of the community of scholars; and

(4) *qiyas*, or analogical deductions and reasoning.

The *Shari'ah* is comprised of principles and precepts. In its explication and application, it is largely oral (there are a limited number of written compilations, such as the 1839 compilation for the Ottoman Empire, the *Majelle* or *Majalat al-Ahkam al-Adliyah*). Further, there are a number of schools of Islamic jurisprudence (the four main *Sunni* schools are Hanafi, Hanbali, Maliki and Shafi). Historically, the different schools are frequently in conflict with respect to the application of the *Shari'ah* to different factual or structural situations. Even within a school there are variant interpretations with respect to any given matter. There is also considerable divergence between Southeast Asia (particularly Malaysia, Indonesia and Brunei) on the one hand, and the Middle East and Western Asia (particularly Pakistan), on the other hand.

As explicated by *Shari'ah* scholars over the last 1400 years, and as applied to Islamic finance, the *Shari'ah* is a fulsome body of law. It covers virtually every aspect of commerce and finance that is addressed by a mature body of secular law. Thus, for example, it addresses contracts, concepts of consideration, legal capacity, mutuality, sales, leasing, construction activities, partnerships and joint ventures of various types, guarantees, estates, equity and trust, litigation, and many other activities and legal structures. As such, it influences all aspects of the formation of an investment fund as well as every aspect of the operation and conduct of business by an investment fund.

SHARI'AH SUPERVISORY BOARDS: COMPOSITION

How does an investor that wants to make *Shari'ah*-compliant investments ensure that his or her investment is in fact compliant? Most individuals do not have the expertise to make that determination for themselves. Over the last few decades, the mechanism that has evolved to provide comfort with respect to *Shari'ah* compliance is the *Shari'ah* Board.

Most Islamic banks and financial institutions, and many of the higher net worth families and individuals, have retained one or more *Shari'ah* scholars that comprise a *Shari'ah* Board. Each Board oversees the complete range of investment practices, and the principles, methodology and activities of operation of all aspects of the business, of the entity or individual that has retained that particular Board. Each *Shari'ah* Board is comprised of a different group of individual scholars; no two Boards are identically comprised. Each Board renders determinations with respect to structures and undertakings that are confidential and proprietary to the entity that retains that Board, with the result that explication of the *Shari'ah*, as applied in competitive financial markets, has occurred in isolated pockets rather than a manner that is co-ordinated across markets or even schools of Islamic jurisprudence.

The education of individual *Shari'ah* scholars is not centrally regulated or co-ordinated. There are no established curricula for the education of a *Shari'ah* scholar; it is largely a matter of self-selection and personal choice on the part of both the incipient scholar and that scholar's teachers, including as to the school of Islamic jurisprudence and the substantive areas of study within the chosen school, and of peer recognition. Overwhelmingly, the education of any given scholar has been a process of "sitting and studying at the knee" of another scholar. Until quite recently, many of the more learned scholars had little practical experience; their learning had been primarily academic. The lack of practical experience was, in part, the result of the domination of an interest-based economic system for a period of over five centuries and the concomitant interregnum in the development of Islamic finance.

The practical effect of the foregoing and other factors, particularly the diversity of interpretation of the *Shari'ah* across and within schools of Islamic jurisprudence, has been that the determinations of any one *Shari'ah* Board were fairly restricted and of narrow application—often being applicable to only a single entity. One investor or company would accept a new product as being compliant while others would determine that same product to be non-compliant. Obviously, few entrepreneurs were willing to invest heavily in product development in such an environment.

As discussed below under the heading "Modern Islamic Finance", commencing in the 1970s, but particularly in the 1990s, and to the present, there were a number of developments that profoundly affected the field of Islamic finance. In summary, there was a sanctioned movement toward interpretive uniformity and harmony, with the concomitant decrease in entrepreneurial and transactional risks. An entrepreneur is now able to develop a new product with much greater certainty that it will be accepted by most investors. This, of itself, spurred the development of *Shari'ah*-compliant investment funds, many of which now retain their own *Shari'ah* Boards. This substantially increases the likelihood of agreed compliance and wider market acceptance. As many of the members of an investment fund's

Shari'ah Board are also members of investor Boards, the risk of market (investor) rejection of a given fund or product are minimised. The last point is worth considering a bit further as it has resulted in significant benefits to the industry, but is also the focus of conflict of interest concerns.

Shari'ah Boards may be comprised of one scholar or a group of scholars. Frequently, a Board is comprised of one or more of the leading "internationalist" scholars, some regional scholars, and some local scholars. This brings international, regional and local expertise, experience and political sensitivity to bear on compliance issues. Frequently, the internationalist scholars (who most often populate the Boards of the investment funds) have expertise and experience in sophisticated financial transactions in a wide range of jurisdictions throughout the world, including variant secular tax, securities law and other legal and regulatory regimes and the interplay between those regimes and the *Shari'ah* as applied and considered by specific investors.

Separate, and only informally co-ordinated, *Shari'ah* Boards for individual entities are the norm in the Middle East, North America and Europe. However, numerous other developments exert pressure away from that model and toward uniformity, which is important for the development of a buoyant secondary market in *sukuk*. For example, certain jurisdictions have adopted approaches that are more centralising or unifying, thus decreasing developmental and transactional risks. Malaysia is an example of a jurisdiction in which there is a central *Shari'ah* Board operating under the aegis of the government regulatory structure (via the central bank). AAOIFI and the Islamic Financial Services Board ("IFSB") are also strong forces in promoting greater uniformity across the jurisprudential schools and across the divide between Southeast Asian jurisdictions, on the one hand, and Middle Eastern and Western Asian jurisdictions, on the other. As a greater number and variety of multi-national conventional banks and investment banks enter, and expand their range within, the Islamic finance field, there will be increased pressure toward uniformity, if only to facilitate the implementation of internal policies and procedures of these institutions.

SHARI'AH SUPERVISORY BOARDS: ROLES AND *FATAWA*

The role of a *Shari'ah* Board varies from fund-to-fund and entity-to-entity based upon the nature, extent and degree of *Shari'ah* compliance and monitoring desired by the target investors. The fund or other entity and the individual members of the Board will enter into a consulting agreement specifying the duties and standards to be applied in the performance of the

Shari'ah consultation. Each individual *Shari'ah* scholar brings his unique perception to the relevant *Shari'ah* issues and interpretive matters although many scholars consult among themselves, both informally and through organisations such as the Organisation of the Islamic Conference ("OIC") Fiqh Academy. Thus, the relationship between each *Shari'ah* Board and its related fund or entity is unique, despite trends toward uniformity and convergence. In each case, however, the Board will perform a number of different roles, including, typically, the following:

(1) participation in product development activities;

(2) review and approval of the fund or entity structure and its objectives, criteria and guidelines and issuance of a *fatwa* in respect thereof;

(3) review and approval of disclosure and offering documents and issuance of a *fatwa* in respect thereof;

(4) review, approval and oversight of investment and business operational structures and methodology, and issuance of a *fatwa* in respect thereof;

(5) on-going review, oversight and approval of transactional or operational variances or applications to unique or changing circumstances on an ongoing basis; and

(6) annual audit of the operations of the fund or entity and issuance of an annual certification of *Shari'ah* compliance.

Decisions of the Board are usually unanimous and *fatawa* are almost always executed by all Board members. Frequently, multi-member *Shari'ah* Boards will appoint one of their members as the administrative member to be available for, and address matters needing resolution prior to, the next regularly scheduled meeting (which are periodic, often quarterly). That administrative member will exercise discretion as to whether to convene discussion with other members on operational or interpretive matters that arise from time-to-time.

A *fatwa* (singular; *fatawa* is the plural) is a written certification of a *Shari'ah* scholar or Board. It has no binding legal effect under secular law, unless the *Shari'ah*, as incorporated in the secular law of the land, were to give it binding effect (that is not presently true in any known jurisdiction). Historically, a *fatwa* was a short, conclusory statement, providing only a summary of the reasoning behind the determination or a few salient *Shari'ah* precepts or precedents. More recently, and betraying the involvement of some western lawyers, *fatawa* have been structured more like Anglo-American judicial opinions, with discussion of the underlying *Shari'ah* precepts and a view toward its precedential value. It is common to see a copy of a more general *fatwa* reproduced in the offering circular of a *sukuk* issue.

MODERN ISLAMIC FINANCE

After centuries of dormancy, modern Islamic finance re-emerged in the 1970s. Since then, but particularly since the late 1990s, the number and type of *Shari'ah*-compliant investments has expanded exponentially, as has the dollar volume of compliant investments. The expansion continues to the present and is expected to accelerate over the foreseeable future.

Middle Eastern investors have led the growth of Islamic finance internationally and within the Middle East. In Pakistan, Malaysia and Indonesia, with limited exceptions, investment and growth is more internal. International Islamic finance focused first on the United States (from the late 1990s to the present) and, later, on Europe (commencing in 2003 to the present). International Islamic finance has been, and is, dominated by *Shari'ah* scholars from the Sunni branch of Islam in the Middle East and West Asia (particularly Pakistan), although some Malaysian scholars have become prominent among the "internationalists".

Before the 1990s (and certainly before the 1970s) there were relatively few Islamic banks and financial institutions, there were relatively few *Shari'ah* scholars with knowledge and practical experience in financial and commercial transactions, the focus was primarily on the deposit side of Islamic banking, discourse took place primarily in the Arabic language, and the dominant *Shari'ah*-compliant financing structures were based strictly upon the nominate contracts and financing structures that were developed in the earliest years of Islam.

Commencing in the 1970s, and increasingly from the 1990s to the present, there were a number of profound changes in the field of Islamic finance, virtually all of which are ongoing. Among them are the following:

(1) renewed focus on Islamic banking and finance, including investment activities both within and without the Middle East, often as a result of increased oil wealth;

(2) a movement of focus away from the deposit side of Islamic banking to the investment side and the larger realm of Islamic finance;

(3) a significant number of Islamic and conventional multinational banks, investment banks and financial institutions, as well as Western asset managers, lawyers, accountants and other professionals, entered the field of Islamic finance;

(4)   *Shari'ah* scholars gained significant practical experience in an expanding range of financial and commercial transactions of increasing complexity;

(5)   a significant increase in discourse on Islamic finance in the English language;

(6)   a group of *Shari'ah* scholars made a decision and undertook concerted efforts to move toward consensus (*ijma*), which had the effect of reducing (although not eliminating) differences between schools of Islamic jurisprudence;

(7)   the shortage of *Shari'ah* scholars ensured that some of the key individuals in the movement toward consensus sat on multiple Boards, thus moving the entire industry toward greater harmony, uniformity and consensus;

(8)   a transformative move away from the historical rigidity in the use of static nominate contract and early *Shari'ah*-compliant structures towards the use of nominate contracts and accepted structures as building blocks that may be constituted and constructed creatively in new combinations;

(9)   significant internationalisation and globalisation necessitating that *Shari'ah* compliance be achieved in harmony with a various secular legal systems;

(10) AAOIFI was created and generated uniform standards for accounting for Islamic financial institutions and transactions;

(11) the IFSB was created and is undertaking the development of uniform standards for capital adequacy, prudential banking standards, corporate governance, capital markets activities and securities laws; and

(12) establishment of a broad range of other co-ordinative entities, with particular focus, to date, on Islamic banking.

Prior to the late 1990s, most *Shari'ah*-compliant investments were single transactions, such as a single property acquisition. Commencing in the late 1990s, tax efficient fund structures became the dominant form. Western interest-based banks and, later investment banks, began moving into the Islamic finance field around 2004 (a few were involved earlier, but those were exceptions). These entities have considerable experience with investment fund structures and securitisation structures, and they have begun to focus on opportunities in these fields.

Shari'ah-compliant real estate funds emerged in the mid-1990s, and the number of such funds multiplied markedly after the dot.com slide. Initially, they invested in United States residential real estate projects, beginning with multi-family housing and moving on to single-family developments, gated communities, golf course communities and other projects. Five primary factors drove the emphasis on residential funds:

(1) the *Shari'ah* rules prohibiting tenants of *Shari'ah*-compliant investments from engaging in Prohibited Business Activities (as defined, below) are not applicable to individual residential tenants;

(2) the development of workable *Shari'ah*-compliant *istisna'a—ijara* (construction—lease) financing structures in the United States;

(3) the flexibility of the United States legal system in accommodating financing and investment structures that were both *Shari'ah*-compliant and used conventional interest-based financing in a manner that met the underwriting standards and criteria of conventional banks;

(4) the short-term nature of construction financing was desirable to Middle Eastern investors; and

(5) the boom in the United States real estate markets during this period.

Commencing in late 2002 and early 2003, real estate funds in the United States began investing in single-tenant, credit-tenant leased, commercial office and warehouse properties with remaining lease terms longer than the expected hold periods. These investments were *ijara*-based (lease-based) acquisition financing investments rather than construction investments, and thus of longer tenor. These funds were designed to move into the strong United States commercial real estate markets during a growth period and in a manner that minimised the *Shari'ah* issues with respect to Prohibited Business Activities by tenants (only a single tenant and its lease need be reviewed and re-leasing issues were avoided).

Shari'ah-compliant commercial real estate funds began to focus on Europe in late 2003 and 2004. At the same time, in both the United States and Europe, investment began in multi-tenant properties and a wide range of other properties (such as hotels, outpatient treatment centres and hospitals). The movement to Europe was based upon the economics of European real estate investments and the increasing competition with conventional investors in the United States. The movement toward multi-tenant properties was driven by:

• increased familiarity of fund managers and fund investors with the *Shari'ah* compliance issues,

• the shrinking pool of single tenant properties, and

- increased sophistication of *Shari'ah* scholars in addressing complex multi-tenant issues.

The last point is especially important because it has had spill-over effects into the realm of re-leasing issues. Resolution of those issues is opening the real estate funds markets to *Shari'ah*-compliant investments in multi-tenant properties where leases expire and are renewed or replaced by new leases.

Many large office buildings and complexes have tenants that engage in Prohibited Business Activities, such retail branch banks, restaurants that serve alcohol, or grocery stores that sell pork, wine and beer. In the purest case, the entire building or complex would be an impermissible investment. However, the *Shari'ah* scholars have taken a pragmatic view. Rules are now being developed that would allow investment in these properties for certain impermissible uses, such as those just mentioned. For example, if the branch bank serves a retail market, there are insufficient other banking opportunities in the defined area, and the branch bank occupies a small percentage of the property (say, 1 per cent or less), some *Shari'ah* Boards will permit the property acquisition and allow renewal of the lease to that branch bank. The development of these rules as to *de minimis* impermissible tenancies is greatly expanding the universe of properties available for investment and is likely to enhance the development of these funds.

SOME *SHARI'AH* PRECEPTS

As noted above, the *Shari'ah*, as explicated over the last 1400 years, addresses most, if not all, matters addressed by a modern secular legal system. It also addresses a number of business matters that go beyond law and into the realm of ethics. An example is the prohibition of involvement in certain types of businesses and business activities, in the same manner as other ethical investment funds. This section provides a rudimentary summary of some of the major *Shari'ah* principles pertaining to Islamic real estate finance, including securitisations.

At its core, the *Shari'ah* embodies the essence of "ethical investing": it prohibits investment in, or the conduct of, businesses whose core activities:

(1) include the manufacture or distribution of alcoholic beverages or pork products for human consumption or, in the case of certain *Shari'ah* Boards, firearms;

(2) have a significant involvement in gaming (gambling, including casinos), brokerage, interest-based banking or impermissible insurance;

(3) include certain types of entertainment elements (particularly porno-graphy); or

(4) have impermissible amounts of interest-based indebtedness or interest income.

The activities referred to in clauses (a) to (c) are referred to as "Prohibited Business Activities". Some *Shari'ah* Boards also include the growing, manufacture and distribution of tobacco within Prohibited Business Activities. Some Boards interpret the entertainment exclusion more broadly and include cinema and music generally because of the possibly porno-graphic elements of these industries. Hotels are often included because of the presence of alcohol in bars and mini-bars. Entities that have Prohibited Business Activities may not be tenants in properties owned and leased by a *Shari'ah*-compliant investor. These prohibitions fundamentally influence the nature and operations of funds and businesses.

A fundamental *Shari'ah* precept is the prohibition of *riba*, best known by its prohibition on the payment or receipt of interest. This prohibition extends to direct or indirect benefit concepts. This precept affects every aspect of the manner in which a *Shari'ah*-compliant transaction is structured and implemented. In the securitisation field, it (and other precepts) preclude pooling of conventional mortgages, credit card receivables, and all interest-bearing debt instruments.

In the area of joint ventures (including partnerships), numerous precepts address allocation of work, profit and loss allocations and distributions and virtually all other operational matters. For example, as a general statement, all distributions of profits and losses must be pro rata. Preferred stock is impermissible. In certain types of partnerships (*mudaraba*), one person contributes services and another person contributes capital. If the arrangement suffers a loss, only the capital provider may be monetarily penalised. In other types of partnerships (*sharikat* and *musharaka*), work and capital contribution may be allocated over all partners with correlative loss sharing. Obviously, these rules affect business and fund structures and many operational activities and, directly, *sukuk*.

Shari'ah precepts pertaining to leasing are of particular import because leasing is the primary tool used in the implementation of *Shari'ah*-compliant transactions. Examples include the requirement that a property lessor must maintain the integrity of the leased property. The lessor may not pass structural maintenance obligations, or correlative obligations such as the maintenance of casualty insurance, to a lessee. In short, the pervasive triple net lease is prohibited. The end-user tenant may not have Prohibited

Business Activities and the lease to the end-user tenant must itself be *Shari'ah*-compliant. These precepts have a critical impact on Islamic CMBS.

As one would expect in light of the development of the *Shari'ah* in Middle Eastern societies that were so heavily focused on trading activities, the *Shari'ah* precepts applicable to sales are especially well refined. Leasing, in fact, is treated as a type of sale—sale of the usufruct of property. With only limited exceptions, one can sell only tangible assets. Debt cannot be sold, nor can other financial instruments that do not represent an ownership interest in tangible assets. Further, one cannot sell property that one does not own and possess. These principles operate as the primary restrictions on the development of *Shari'ah*-compliant short sales, options trading and derivatives transactions. They also have a major influence on the structure of Islamic bonds and CMBS. In addition, there are very particular rules addressing delivery, receipt, ownership, allocation of risk, down-payments and virtually all other aspects of sales transactions. These rules affect both the ability to create secondary markets, the tradability of equity and CMBS instruments.

Shari'ah precepts that preclude gambling and uncertainty also preclude most types of insurance and investments in insurance companies, although the unavailability of *takaful* (*Shari'ah*-compliant insurance) has led to some practical accommodations to the prohibition on the use of insurance. In the views of some *Shari'ah* scholars, the *Shari'ah* also precludes the provision of guarantees for compensation; a guarantee must be a non financial charitable transaction.

UNDERLYING REAL ESTATE, SALE AND JOINT VENTURE STRUCTURES

To understand Islamic securitisation instruments and envisage the future of Islamic CMBS, it is necessary to have some knowledge of the component structures that may be securitised. Some of these structures relate to the assets, usufruct or services that are securitised. These are primarily the lease (*ijara*) and sale (particularly *murabaha* and *salam*) structures. Two structures, the *mudaraba* and *musharaka*, are joint venture structures. Each structure (other than the *salam*) is briefly summarised in this section, and each of these structures is the basis or a component of Islamic bond and CMBS structures.

Ijara (lease) structures

The predominant acquisition and operating financing structure in Islamic real estate finance is the *ijara* (lease). Figure 1, below, graphically depicts a basic leasing structure. This example assumes 75 per cent conventional interest-based financing and 25 per cent contribution by the *Shari'ah*-compliant investors (the "Investors"); these percentages will vary with each transaction.

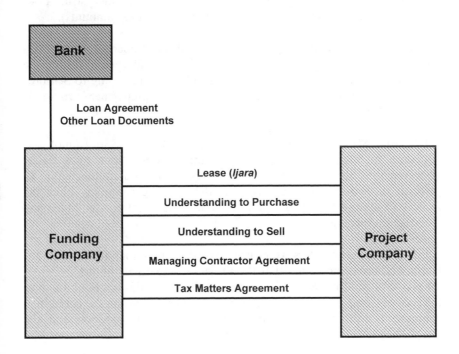

Figure 1: *Ijara* structure.

The Investors make their investment into the "Project Company". For tax reasons, this investment is usually made through a "fund" and at least one entity is intermediate between that fund and the Project Company. A special purpose vehicle, the "Funding Company", is established to acquire and hold title to the property in which the *Shari'ah*-compliant investment is to be made (the "Property"). The Project Company contributes its investment (25 per cent of the acquisition price) to the Funding Company. A conventional interest-bearing commercial mortgage loan is made by the "Bank" (the "Bank Loan") to the Funding Company (equal to 75 per cent of the acquisition price). The Funding Company then acquires the property from the seller.

Thereafter, the Funding Company enters into an *ijara* (lease) with the Project Company, as lessee. The rent payable under the *ijara* is identical to the debt service on the Bank Loan and provides the funds to pay that debt service. Future rents cannot be accelerated under a *Shari'ah*-compliant lease.

Given that the outstanding principal is paid through the *ijara*, an acceleration mechanism is necessary outside the *ijara* itself. The Understanding to Purchase performs that function (it also mirrors all mandatory prepayment provisions of the Bank Loan). The Bank, through the Funding Company, "puts" the property to the Project Company at a strike price equal to the outstanding principal (and other outstanding amounts).

The Project Company may also want to sell the Property (or a portion thereof, such as a single condominium or single family home) during the period that the Bank Loan is outstanding. The Understanding to Sell provides the mechanism (and also mirrors the voluntary prepayment provisions of the Bank Loan).

Under the *Shari'ah* precepts noted above, and others, a lessor cannot pass structural maintenance and casualty insurance obligations to a lessee. However, in a building block analysis, a lessor can hire another entity to perform those functions. In this case, the Funding Company hires the Project Company to perform those activities pursuant to the Managing Contractor Agreement.

Finally, the Tax Matters Agreement provides a road map for the relevant taxing authority, indicating that the Project Company is the tax owner of the property and for income tax (and other) purposes, this is a Bank Loan to the Project Company. The Tax Matters Agreement delineates the correlative components as between the conventional loan documentation and the *Shari'ah*-compliant leasing documentation.

The foregoing structure is used in essentially all *Shari'ah*-compliant commercial real estate transactions in North America and Europe (with some relatively minor country variations, as appropriate, under relevant tax and real estate laws) and, as noted below, it is easily modified to effect a *Shari'ah*-compliant CMBS.

Murabaha (sale at a mark-up) structures

A widely-used sales structure, and one that is used in some *sukuk* and in many working capital financings, is the *murabaha*. Most simply defined, the *murabaha* is a sale at a mark-up. Figure 2, below, sets for the graphic depiction of a simple *murabaha* transaction.

In the simple *murabaha*, "OpCo", a client of "MBank", desires to purchase a commodity, piece of equipment, or other asset. OpCo negotiates the terms of the purchase, including payment terms and precise specifications, with the Commodity Seller. OpCo then asks MBank to finance the purchase of that asset. OpCo and MBank enter into a *Murabaha* Agreement pursuant

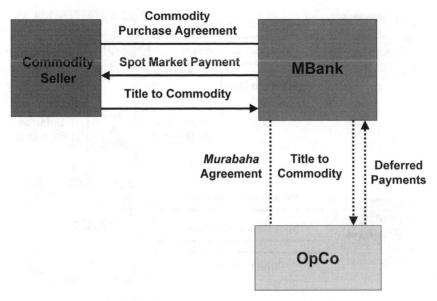

Figure 2: Basic *murabaha* structure.

to which MBank agrees to supply to OpCo a commodity or asset meeting the precise specifications that were negotiated with the Commodity Seller. The *Murabaha* Agreement will require OpCo to make payment to MBank for that commodity on a deferred purchase basis. MBank, in turn, will enter into a Commodity Purchase Agreement with the Commodity Seller and will purchase the commodity from the Commodity Seller for immediate payment in full.

Upon accepting delivery of the commodity, MBank will fulfil its obligations under the *Murabaha* Agreement by re-selling the commodity to OpCo. While there are numerous other applicable precepts, two are of particular note:

(1) MBank must have ownership risk with respect to the asset; and

(2) OpCo can, under most schools of Islamic jurisprudence at the present time, act as the agent for MBank in consummating the arrangements between MBank and the Commodity Seller.

A metals *murabaha* is graphically depicted in Figure 3, below. This structure is used, in variant forms, in *sukuk* and working capital structures.

The transaction is substantially identical to the *murabaha* transaction illustrated in Figure 2, above. The additional element is that OpCo, upon taking title to the commodity (here a permissible metal), immediately sells

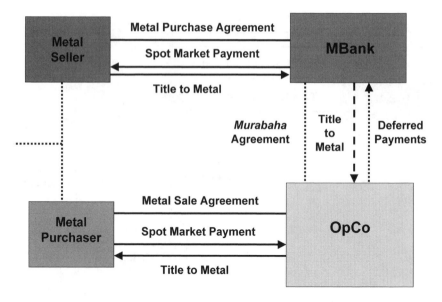

Figure 3: Working capital *murabaha*.

that metal to the Metal Purchaser for a cash payment at the same spot market price as obtained in MBank's purchase of that metal from the Metal Seller (fees ignored). The Metal Purchaser and Metal Seller are frequently affiliates. The net result is that OpCo ends up with cash equal to the spot market price of the metal and a deferred *murabaha* payment obligation to MBank in respect of that amount plus a profit factor.

Mudaraba (service provider—capital provider) structures

A *mudaraba* is a type of joint venture. It is most frequently formulated as a limited partnership or limited liability company. The base structure involves one partner providing services and management (the *mudarib*). Usually, the *mudarib* does not provide cash or other in-kind capital. Some *Shari'ah* Boards prohibit *mudarib* capital; all prohibit it without the consent of the other partner. The other partner(s) (the *rabb ul-maal*) provides capital, in cash or in kind, and generally may not interfere in the management or service component. A simple *mudaraba* arrangement with multiple capital providers is depicted in Figure 4, below.

As a general matter, and with a few modifications, a conventional limited partnership agreement or limited liability company operating agreement works well to structure a *mudaraba*. For example, while a capital provider may not interfere in the management function, most *Shari'ah* Boards permit "minority rights" protections such as are afforded to limited partners, and

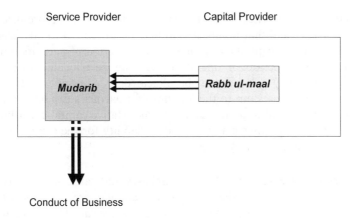

Figure 4: *Mudaraba* **structure**.

other rights are permissible in *mudarib* default, breach and infringement scenarios.

Profit in a *mudaraba* is that amount that exceeds the capital after deduction of all allowable *mudaraba* expenses. Conversely, loss is the diminishment in the *mudaraba* capital. The critical *Shari'ah* precept pertaining to losses is that all losses are borne by the capital provider (the service provider has lost its services and is not assessed pecuniary losses). Profit allocations must be specified, and must be pro rata (although formulas specifying different allocations upon satisfaction of hurdles have been accepted). Importantly, there can be no predetermined or conclusive profit allocation to any of the parties and arrangements allocating all profit to a single party are impermissible. More difficult issues arise with respect to scenarios in which a clawback of distributions may be necessitated, as with losses subsequent to distributions.

Musharaka (capital provider) structures

Al-sharika is a partnership for profit, *sharikat ul-amwaal* is a property partnership, and *al-musharaka* is a finance method derived from a partnership contract in which a bank participates with one or more clients. In more recent parlance, the term *musharaka* refers to a wide range of partnership or joint venture arrangements without further delineation. In a *musharaka*, each of the partners contributes capital, and there is significantly greater flexibility in allocating management responsibilities between and among partners; joint rights of management are frequent and usual.

Limited partnership agreements and limited liability company operating agreements are also useful models for structuring *musharaka* arrangements. Profit and loss definitions are largely the same as with *mudaraba*, with some fundamental differences. Profits may be allocated in accordance with a points system, and that points system may be structured to take cognisance of the amount of capital contributed and the period of participation. Profit from a specific period or operation may not be allocated to a specified partner, nor may a lump sum be allocated to a specific partner. In the majority view, losses, up to the amount of a partner's capital contribution, must be distributed in accordance with the relative capital contributions of the partners. A partner may not assume liability for the capital of another partner, including by way of guarantee.

Shari'ah precepts applicable to purchases and sales of interests (*hissas*) from one partner to another (as well as *murabaha* precepts) form the basis for securitisation transactions involving *musharaka*. These are discussed below.

SUKUK (ISLAMIC BONDS AND SECURITISATIONS)

One of the most active and fastest-growing areas of Islamic finance is *sukuk* issuance. As an indication, Dow Jones and Citigroup recently launched the "Dow Jones Citigroup Sukuk Index". *Sakk* (singular; *sukuk* is the plural) means, in ancient Arabic, "to strike" or "to hit", as in to strike or imprint one's mark on a document or tablet, and, as a derived term, means "minting coins".

Sukuk are of two general types: Islamic bonds and Islamic securitisations. Islamic bonds are based upon the credit of an entity that is participating in the transaction (issuer, guarantor or other credit support provider). Securitisations involve asset transfers from an originator into a trust or similar special purpose vehicle ("SPV") with *sukuk* issuance by that SPV and payments on the *sukuk* derived from the payments received in respect of those transferred assets. Most *sukuk* offerings to date have been of the bond type, and the ultimate credit in most of those bond offerings has been a sovereign entity. There have been very few, if any, true securitisations, largely because of the inability to obtain ratings from major international ratings firms for the securitisation *sukuk* issuances (ratings have been obtained for the sovereign bond issuances based upon the rating of the sovereign credit).

Under the AAOIFI *sukuk* standard, *sukuk* are defined as certificates of equal value put to use as common shares and rights in tangible assets, usufructs and services or as equity in a project or investment activity. The AAOIFI standard carefully distinguishes *sukuk* from equity, notes and bonds. It emphasises that *sukuk* are not debts of the issuer; they are fractional or proportional interests in underlying assets, usufructs, services, projects or investment activities. *Sukuk* may not be issued on a pool of receivables. Further, the underlying business or activity, and the underlying transactional structures (such as the underlying leases) must be *Shari'ah*-compliant (the business or activity cannot engage in Prohibited Business Activities, for example).

AAOIFI has specified 14 categories of permissible *sukuk*. In broad summary, they are securitisations:

(1) of an existing or to be acquired tangible asset (*ijara*);

(2) of an existing or to be acquired leasehold estate (*ijara*);

(3) of presales of services (*ijara*);

(4) of presales of the production of goods or commodities at a future date (*salam* (forward sale));

(5) to fund construction (*istisna'a* (construction contract));

(6) to fund the acquisition of goods for future sale (*murabaha*);

(7) to fund capital participation in a business or investment activity (*mudaraba* or *musharaka*); and

(8) to fund various asset acquisition and agency management (*wakala* (agency)), agricultural land cultivation, land management and orchard management activities.

The parenthetical in each of the foregoing indicates the relevant *Shari'ah* structure.

It is clear that the markets will move to securitisation *sukuk* as soon as possible. At present, however, it is difficult to obtain ratings from major international ratings agencies on transactions that are dependent, at any level, upon laws in most of the OIC jurisdictions. The main impediments relate to the inability to obtain satisfactory legal opinions with respect to true sales of assets, and bankruptcy law matters, particularly non-consolidation of assets of the issuer SPV into the originator of the assets, fraudulent transfers and other transfer avoidance doctrines, bankruptcy remoteness covenants, and a range of general legal enforceability matters, among others. Briefly, with respect to enforceability in OIC jurisdictions, judicial decisions are frequently not published, the concept of binding precedent is often not embodied in the juridical system, and there is substantial variance of the degree to which *Shari'ah* is itself incorporated in secular law (with the potential for modification of contractual agreements negotiated under accepted secular legal premises). Each of these factors adversely influences certainty and predictability and the quality of legal opinions that are necessary to support the *sukuk* financings.

The movement toward securitisation *sukuk* in these jurisdictions is likely to be gradual given the necessity of considerable legal reform as a prerequisite to the issuance of satisfactory legal opinions. However, there are organised efforts to define the necessary legal reforms. For example, the IFSB is undertaking a broad survey of trust laws, securities laws, capital markets laws and bankruptcy laws in an effort to identify and suggest necessary legal reforms so as to facilitate the development and growth of capital markets, including *sukuk* issuances and secondary trading. Efforts of this type will ultimately facilitate the issuance of securitisation *sukuk* in OIC jurisdictions.

Another factor that impinges upon the structuring and issuance of *sukuk* and *Shari'ah*-compliant CMBS transactions is the lack of *Shari'ah*-compliant hedging mechanisms;[2] there are no broadly approved *Shari'ah*-compliant equivalents to conventional currency or interest rates swaps such as those approved by the International Swaps and Derivatives Association ("ISDA"). Frequently, the viability of an issuance is significantly affected by the efficacy of these hedging mechanisms. The *Shari'ah*-compliant hedging techniques that do exist have not yet achieved broad market acceptance; some institutions are willing to enter into the alternative structures and some are not. There are various initiatives (including an ISDA initiative) to develop viable and broadly accepted *Shari'ah*-compliant hedging mechanisms. However, given *Shari'ah* requirements that tradeable instruments represent an ownership interest in tangible assets, and the prohibitions on the sale and purchase of debt and other purely financing instruments, this is one of the more challenging areas of Islamic finance.

It seems probable that the initial CMBS *sukuk* issuances will emanate from United States and European jurisdictions. These are likely to be securitisations of assets in those jurisdictions, rather than assets located in OIC jurisdictions. The reasons for this are:

(1) increased involvement in Islamic finance by international banks and investment banks;

(2) those banks and investment banks have substantial *Shari'ah*-compliant assets (such as leased equipment and real estate) that are desirable investments for *Shari'ah*-compliant investors;

---

[2] See Ch.7 for more details.

(3) those banks and investment banks have significant CMBS experience; and

(4) importantly, those banks and investment banks can obtain the necessary ratings because the transactions can be structured entirely within jurisdictions where necessary legal opinions are readily obtainable.

Unrated CMBS *sukuk* may involve assets in OIC jurisdictions, but the issuing SPV for even those *sukuk* are likely to be located outside OIC jurisdictions to minimise bankruptcy and true sale issues to the greatest possible extent. However, the market for unrated *sukuk* is likely to be dwarfed by the market for rated *sukuk* in the medium to long term.

Prohibitions on *riba* (interest), and on the sale of instruments that do not represent fractional undivided ownership interest in tangible assets, present a seemingly insurmountable problem for CMBS. Many commercial mortgages may never be made *Shari'ah*-compliant in and of themselves, but it seems likely that bifurcated structures will be developed to securitise these assets (just as conventional interest-based financing is now used in most international *Shari'ah*-compliant real estate and private equity financings).

The *Ijara al-Sukuk*

The *ijara* structure that is so widely used in Islamic finance (see Figure 1, above) is readily adaptable to CMBS in a number of different ways. First, consideration is given to two simple securitisations which could be readily accomplished at the present time due to the fact that virtually all *Shari'ah*-compliant commercial real estate transactions to date have been effected using the *ijara* structure shown in Figure 1. The simplest securitisation of the *ijara* structure is summarised in Figure 5, below. In this structure, a *sukuk* issuance replaces the conventional Bank loan; the Funding Company issues a *sukuk* to the *Sukuk* Holder rather than utilising conventional bank financing.

A slight variation on that structure is the pooled *sukuk* illustrated in Figure 6, below. In the pooled securitisation, each Funding Company issues a *sukuk* to the Master Issuer, and the Master Issuer then sells a Master *Sukuk* to the *Sukuk* Holders.

In each of these structures, the rental stream from the various *ijara* can be structured to produce a precise cash flow on the *sukuk*, fixed or variable, based upon an amortisation schedule or a bullet repayment. Other adaptations of the *ijara* structure have recently been used to create *sukuk* that have economic qualities similar to standard bonds, and these structures are

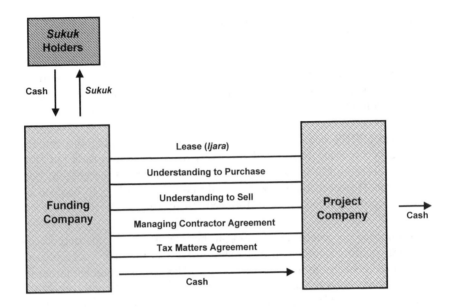

Figure 5: *Ijara sukuk*.

currently common in the market. Some of these structures have addressed circumstances in which the party seeking the financing does not wish to own an asset but needs financing for other purposes.

An example of successfully adopting the *ijara* structure for a global issuance was the Malaysian government's issue of Sukuk Trust Certificates in August 2002. This issue was listed on the Luxembourg Stock Exchange and rated by both Standard & Poor's and Moody's. Although a sovereign credit issuance, this *sukuk* is one of the seminal transactions laying the groundwork for the issuance of securitisation *sukuk*. Figure 7, below, presents a generalised illustration of this transaction.

The structure used was simple and clean in order to appeal to the broadest possible base of Islamic investors. The *sukuk* issuer ("Issuer SPV"), Malaysian Global Sukuk Inc. ("MGS"), was incorporated in Labuan and owned by a Malaysian state entity. MGS used the issuance proceeds to purchase parcels of land from another Malaysian state entity. MGS then leased those parcels to the Federation of Malaysia. At the expiry of the lease term, the Malaysian government agreed to purchase the parcels from MGS at the face value of the initial issue amount of the *sukuk*.

Pursuant to a declaration of trust, the land parcels are held by MGS in favour of the *Sukuk* Holders. All returns made on the parcels are and will be conveyed to the *Sukuk* Holders (including lease payments and the final

404

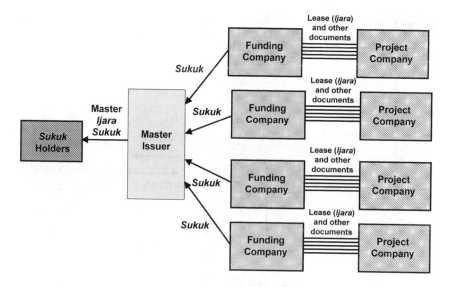

Figure 6: *Ijara sukuk.*

repurchase proceeds). The resulting cash flow is similar to a bond flow. The lease payments are like coupons and the repurchase proceeds paid at the end of the term are akin to principal. The lease payments are determined based on a spread over LIBOR (a permissible benchmark for lease pricing).

Trading in debt above or below par would obviously breach *riba* precepts (being interest) and be impermissible. On the other hand, the ability to trade freely in capital market instruments is critical for the creation of liquidity. The resolution of the apparent *riba* issue lies in the fact that an *ijara sukuk* represents an interest in the underlying tangible assets and not debts. Therefore, those *sukuk* can be traded above or below par.

There are some limitations to the use of the *ijara sukuk*. For example, many originators do not own appropriate underlying assets that are subject to *Shari'ah*-compliant leases or can be made available for such leases during the *sukuk* term, and, in many jurisdictions, there are significant adverse tax consequences associated with the introduction of the assets into a *sukuk* structure.

Ijara sukuk transactions, to date, have not been true pooled securitisations. They have used a limited number of discrete assets and are rated, not on the basis of pooled asset performance, but on the basis of the ultimate credit, the lessee and the ultimate purchaser of the asset at maturity or default. Thus, most transactions, to date, are akin to bond financings.

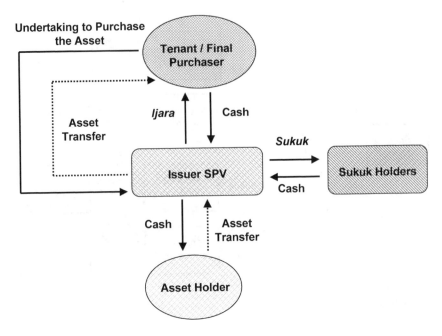

Figure 7: *Ijara sukuk*.

The *Sukuk al-Mudaraba*

The *mudaraba* structure may also be incorporated into a *sukuk* offering in a number of different variants of the *sukuk al-mudaraba*. A generalised generic form of a *sukuk al-mudaraba* is set forth in Figure 11, below.

The *sukuk al-mudaraba* is quite similar to the standard *mudaraba* structure presented in Figure 4, above. The *Rabb ul-maal* Issuer sells the *Sukuk* to the *Sukuk* Holders and the proceeds of that issuance provide the capital for the *mudaraba*. The *Mudarib* will conduct the business of the *mudaraba* as the provider of services. As noted above, this is similar to a limited partnership or limited liability company.

This *mudaraba* may constitute the only entity necessary for the conduct of the relevant business. Or, as is more likely in a complex project or under-taking, this *mudaraba* may enter into joint venture and/or other contractual arrangements with other parties. For example, in a complex project financing this *mudaraba* may enter into a further joint venture with a project sponsor in connection with the financing, construction and operation of the project.

Some of the primary structural considerations will focus, at each level of the transaction, on principles pertaining to allocation and distribution of

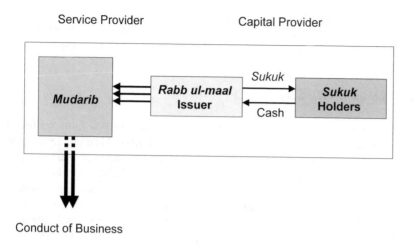

Figure 8: *Sukuk al-mudaraba.*

profits and losses, and the permissibility of capital contributions by the *Mudarib*. A separate set of issues arise in any financing in which capital is needed periodically (these issues also affect other structures, such as the *musharaka*). Consider, for example, the construction of a large-scale project where the construction cycle extends over a period of years and there is no project income during that period. All involved parties will desire that there be a certainty of capital availability throughout the construction period. Periodic *sukuk* issuances do not provide that certainty. An initial *sukuk* issuance for the full amount of the construction costs will provide that certainty, but is economically inefficient. The issuance proceeds in excess of immediate needs will be invested in short-term investments (such as *murabaha*) that have low rates of return. Further, the *Sukuk* Holders will probably expect periodic returns from the inception of the transaction. The project itself will be generating no income (it is in the construction phase) and the reinvestment income will be low. Payments on the *Sukuk* during the construction and ramp-up phase are essentially self-funded by the *Sukuk* Holders.

There have been very few *sukuk al-mudaraba* issuances. Conventional financiers view a partnership arrangement of this type with scepticism and reticence; their initial reaction has been "banks do not enter into partnerships with their clients, particularly where the client controls the partnership and the client cannot contribute equity capital". As a result, there is no history of involvement of conventional banks in this type of structure (such as there is with the *ijara*). The successful use of the *sukuk al-musharaka* is changing this perception, which is likely to have overflow effects on the use of the *sukuk al-mudaraba*. It seems probable that the "limited partnership—limited liability company" nature of the *mudaraba*, which is well accepted in conventional financing, together with creative structuring efforts, are a sound basis for an expansion in the use of this type of *sukuk*.

The *Sukuk al-Musharaka*

In the *sukuk al-musharaka* the SPV "Issuer" enters into a joint venture or partnership arrangement, pursuant to a "*Musharaka* Management Agreement", with the party seeking financing (the "*Musharaka* Partner"). As noted above, each party may contribute capital to the *musharaka*. Each of the partners receives "units" or "*hissas*" in the *musharaka* in accordance with their respective capital contributions. The Issuer's capital contribution is in cash and equals the proceeds of the *sukuk* issuance. The contribution of the Musharaka Partner is usually an in-kind contribution of a tangible asset. A generic *musharaka* structure is depicted in Figure 9, below.

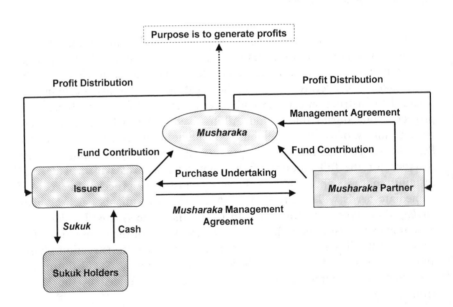

Figure 9: *Sukuk al-musharaka.*

The Issuer and the *Musharaka* Partner enter into a Purchase Undertaking (sometimes structured as a *murabaha* agreement) pursuant to which the Issuer can require the *Musharaka* Partner to purchase designated units or *hissas* on specified dates during the term of the *sukuk*. The Issuer will receive profit distributions from the *musharaka* and the proceeds from sales of the units or *hissas*, which are then distributed to the *sukuk* holders in accordance with agreed formulae.

One of the authors structured and implemented one of the first such *musharaka sukuk* issuances, in 1997, for Saudi Arabian electric generation and transmission assets. Three banks contributed both fixed and variable rate financing for the construction of the electric assets by purchasing *hissas* in an undisclosed *sharikat mahassa* (the *musharaka*) as construction mile-stones were completed. One bank acted as the administrative and finance manager of the *sharika*, and the electric utility acted as the technical manager (the *Musharaka* Partner in the previous example). At defined times, in accordance with a financing amortisation schedule, *hissas* were sold by the banks to the utility pursuant to a *murabaha* agreement in order to effect repayment of the financing.

The *musharaka* structure has not been unanimously accepted by *Shari'ah* scholars. One area of discussion among the scholars relates to the pricing of the *hissas* being sold to the Musharaka Partner. Some scholars take the position that the price of the *hissas* must be established at the time of the sale to the Musharaka Partner and cannot be established at the inception of the Purchase Agreement for a serial purchase arrangement. The reasoning is that a sale price that is in excess of the market price would represent a disproportionate share of the *musharaka* profit. Another line of discussion focuses on the compulsory nature of the *hissa* purchase and sale. A selling partner would be obligated to sell if the buying partner (the *Musharaka* Partner) elects to purchase, but the buying partner cannot be compelled to purchase. Some *Shari'ah* scholars have required that a series of Purchase Agreements be executed, one at the time of each *hissa* sale and purchase. A further point of discussion relates to the provisions of the Musharaka Management Agreement that restrict profit entitlements and limit loss allocations to the bank partners (or the *Sukuk* Holders). Careful structuring in respect of the matters addressed above, and the acceptance of existing *musharaka sukuk* structures by some of the most prominent *Shari'ah* scholars, will ensure that the *musharaka sukuk* will remain a securitisation vehicle in Islamic finance.

Sukuk al-murabaha

There have been a number of *sukuk* issuances based upon *murabaha* transactions. These are of three types:

(1) OpCo purchases an asset using the proceeds of a *sukuk* issuance and retains ownership of that asset;

(2) the *Sukuk* Holders are participating in a *murabaha* transaction itself (akin to a bond); and

(3) a number of deferred *murabaha* payment obligations constitute the pool upon which the *sukuk* is issued (akin to a true securitisation).

Figure 2, above, illustrates the first type of *sukuk*. This *sukuk* is generally *Shari'ah*-compliant and the assets can be made available as collateral for the *sukuk*. Figure 10, below, illustrates a bond-type *sukuk*. The transaction is essentially identical to the structure depicted in Figure 4, above.

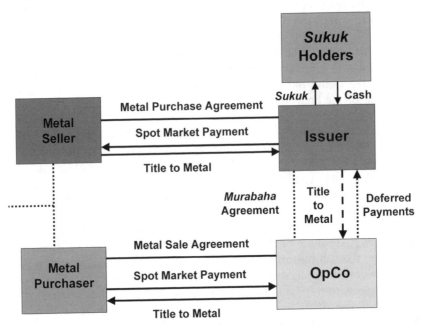

Figure 10: *Sukuk al-murabaha.*

The *sukuk al-murabaha* is issued to the *Sukuk* Holders by the Issuer. The *sukuk* represents a "participation interest" in the underlying *murabaha* transaction. The issuance proceeds are used to purchase a metal on the spot market, the metal is then sold to OpCo on a deferred payment basis, and OpCo sells the metal to the Metal Purchaser on the spot market. This net result is that OpCo holds cash equal to the spot market price of the metal which it can use in its operations and OpCo has a deferred payment obligation on the *Murabaha* Agreement that is used to service the *sukuk*. Periodic issuances are possible.

Figure 11, below, illustrates a *murabaha sukuk* in which the deferred *murabaha* payment obligations under a pool of *murabaha* transactions are pooled, and the Issuer sells a *sukuk* off that pool.

It is clear from a review of the latter two *murabaha sukuk* structures that the party needing financing (OpCo) obtains cash only by selling the tangible asset (the metal or other asset). Thus, on an on-going basis, this *sukuk* does not represent an ownership interest in a tangible asset—it has been sold—

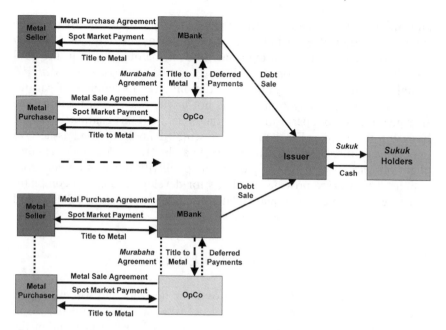

Figure 11: *Sukuk al-murabaha.*

and only the deferred debt obligation remains after sale of the asset. *Ijara sukuk* are tradeable above and below par because they are structured to represent fractional undivided ownership interests in tangible assets. The issue is significantly more difficult for a securitisation or pooled *murabaha sukuk*.

Some scholars have taken the position that *murabaha* debt is not tradeable unless it continues to be backed by assets. Other scholars have taken the position that a *murabaha sukuk* that is not backed by assets is tradeable at par, but not at a premium or discount to par. Other scholars, mostly in Southeast Asia, have taken the position that the deferred debt obligation arose in and through a *Shari'ah*-compliant transaction and may thereafter be the basis for a tradeable *sukuk*, including at a premium or discount. The purchase of the *murabaha* debt (the "Debt Sale" element in Figure 11, above) can therefore be problematic from a *Shari'ah* point of view. This issue is particularly acute if the debt needs to be sold at a discount (as is the case in many conventional securitisations) in order to achieve credit enhancement of the underlying pool of *murabaha* debt that will ultimately back the *sukuk* for ratings purposes.

A seminal *sukuk* issuance, the 2003 Solidarity Trust Services Limited trust certificates issuance of the Islamic Development Bank ("IDB"), addressed these issues. The pool of assets underlying the *sukuk* were *ijara*, *murabaha* and *istisna'a* (construction contract) payment obligations. In order for the *sukuk* to be tradeable, including at a premium or discount, the *Shari'ah* Board required that not less than one-third of the obligations in the pool must be *ijara* obligations on tangible assets owned and leased in a *Shari'ah*-compliant manner. Although this structure involved the pooling of various *Shari'ah*-compliant obligations, it was not a true rated securitisation. The IDB guaranteed pool performance to the Issuer, and this guarantee was the basis for the rating. The issue thus resembled an IDB bond issue. An important feature of the structure was the ability to replace *Shari'ah*-compliant obligations constituting part of the pool with other compliant obligations. This feature provides the basis for developing *Shari'ah*-compliant structures akin to conventional collateralised debt obligations (CDOs) and collateralised loan obligations (CLOs).

THE FUTURE

Shari'ah-compliant CMBS is coming over the horizon, and will eventually emerge as an enormous market. Emergence will occur on a limited basis in the near term. Full realisation of market potentials will depend upon the rapidity of at least some legal reform in OIC jurisdictions (including matters pertaining to bankruptcy, trust concepts and laws, securities laws and capital markets laws), and the development of a wider range of *Shari'ah*-compliant products (such as hedging structures).

While these may seem daunting challenges, the Islamic finance industry is cognisant of the needs and has undertaken efforts to identify and implement the necessary changes in a concerted effort to enhance the Islamic capital markets. Securitisation is at the heart of these undertakings and is likely to reap the earliest benefits of these efforts. Participants in the conventional capital markets, particularly the securitisation markets, have a great deal of knowledge and experience to contribute, whatever the state of their knowledge of the *Shari'ah*-compliant markets. Effective integration of the conventional and Islamic markets depends upon the contributions of the conventional market participants. The process is one of exceptional creativity and the rewards will be fulsome: financially, socially, culturally and ethically.

CHAPTER TWENTY-TWO

RISK ASSESSMENT GROWS UP

US-STYLE TITLE INSURANCE IN THE EUROPEAN SECURITISATION MARKET

Jean-Bernard Wurm, Managing Director
LandAmerica (Europe)

BACKGROUND

This chapter reviews the reasons why title insurance has become a universal instrument for RMBS and CMBS transactions in the US, and examines the increasingly important role that it is playing in Europe. Once only available in the US, title insurance is now a well-established financial instrument for mitigating risks in property acquisition, financing and securitisation in Canada, Latin America, the Caribbean and Australia.

In Europe, especially Central and Eastern Europe (CEE), the demand for title insurance has increased along with the growth and sophistication of cross-border real estate transactions. According to a survey by Jones Lang LaSalle, the worldwide flow of these investments in 2004 reached almost $100 billion. European cross-border transactions grew to $54.1 billion, a 70 per cent increase over a four-year period.

WHAT IS TITLE INSURANCE?

Title Insurance indemnifies against loss suffered by buyers and lenders if title is not good, or there are issues with mortgage GAP recording or rank. For a one-time premium, it provides coverage against financial loss arising from title defects and other irregularities relating to real estate, such as compliance with zoning, codes and permits. Title insurance also frees investors and their lenders from having to understand complex legal opinions in various languages, formats, contexts and degrees of reliability.

Financial protection against both known and unknown title defects

The original purpose of title insurance was to insure against "unknown" defects, with "known" defects shown as exceptions in the policy. That coverage has evolved, and now title companies often provide insurance for "known" or existing defects or title problems.

Protection beyond a legal opinion

Lawyers provide an *opinion*. Title insurance provides an indemnity against loss. A legal opinion, especially in a large securitisation transaction, is fundamentally a disclosure document, in which counsel carefully defines the state of title and related issues, identifying—but not eliminating—risks. Title insurance goes beyond a legal opinion to underwrite risks due to faulty records, ambiguities, negligence, fraud, or even simple mistakes.

A BRIEF HISTORY OF TITLE INSURANCE IN THE UNITED STATES

Title insurance was created in the last part of the nineteenth century. Until then, buyers could acquire insurance for errors and omissions only from their lawyers.

Unifying a complex series of local property laws

At that time—as in Europe today—each state in the US operated with different laws for conveyance and property rights. States still have a multitude of counties, with different sets of regulations for zoning, permit or deed recording. Certain states operated under a system of deed recording similar to France, others under registration of rights similar to the UK. Title insurance competed with land registration systems, such as Torrens, which 22 states adopted between 1900 and 1922. After the First World War, the title insurance industry began to create a national market and became the preferred mechanism.

It is important to keep in mind that until 1974, US banks could not have offices or branches outside their own state and, some, outside their county.[1] Banks that wished to operate nationwide could not rely on their own net-

---

[1] In Chicago, banks were limited to one branch.

work to perform due diligence or have local expertise. They required two elements:

(1) assurance that there were no potential legal problems for the assets that backed their financing, and

(2) a common standard throughout the maze of laws and regulations that still exists in the US. Insurers were successful in convincing lenders that title insurance was critical for financing residential mortgages. As a national market grew, title insurance policies helped standardise loan documentation and create a secondary mortgage market.

The intervention of the Federal government in the housing market during the Depression, and the ensuing evolution of loans into long-term amortising mortgages, broadened the need for title insurance. The trend accelerated with the housing boom that followed World War II and the creation of Federal mortgage refinancing agencies such as the Federal National Mortgage Association (FNMA) and the Government National Mortgage Association (GNMA). By 1969, the industry passed the $1 billion mark in total premiums and in 2005, it represented over $17 billion in annual revenues.

A key role in the development of the US securitisation market

When the securitisation market started in the US in the mid-1980s, title insurance was already universally accepted—every asset behind every mortgage, and every mortgage, whether residential or commercial, already benefited from title insurance.

THE EUROPEAN MARKET FOR TITLE INSURANCE

Until recently, title insurance was unknown in Europe except for the UK, where a more limited type of insurance, Legal indemnity, has existed for over a hundred years. Several American title insurance companies, and one European, recently entered the European market and provide coverage similar to ALTA (American Land Title Association) policies in the US. These not only cover *known* defects or restrictive use of a property but also issues that are *unknown* at the time of closing.

UK legal indemnity addresses only specific title flaws

Unlike title insurance, which covers defects *unknown* at the time of closing, legal indemnity addresses *specific* title flaws or restrictive covenants. Land

Registry (the Queen's Registry) only appeared in the UK in the second half of the twentieth century, much later than in the rest of Europe. Consequently the Land Registry is of no use for properties that have not changed hands since it was established. The abundant tracks of land not yet entered in the Registry have created a growing demand for policies that will cover defective title or restrictive covenants.

Defective titles and restrictive covenants limit the sale of a property

Defective titles can include a gap in the chain of recorded ownership, missing documents or invalid signatures. *Restrictive covenants* can affect the use of a property but may no longer be enforceable, such as deeds dating back to the 1850s that limit the sale of dwellings on a property to "upstanding Christian families."

These covenants may be so old that it is impossible to determine who has a right to have them enforced, such as church deeds that forbid serving alcohol on the land. With title insurance or legal indemnity, a developer can go ahead with a residential or commercial project and obtain financing, without going through the court system, in order to have those problems resolved before starting construction.

Traditionally, the various European land titling systems, through registration or deed recording, appear to have generated fewer errors and claims than in the US. There is, however, no hard data available in most countries to know the exact extent of title litigation taking place every year. This lack of demand to cover domestic direct acquisitions, whether commercial or residential, presents different opportunities for title insurance in Europe:

(1) Notaries or lawyers are responsible only for errors and omissions. Once they have disclosed a potential issue, title insurance can assume the risk, freeing the buyer from assuming the risk himself.

(2) Most European countries have created a favourable regulatory framework for real estate companies, whether unlisted or in the form of Real Estate Investment Trusts (REITs). There is an increasing number of indirect transactions—through acquisition of shares of real estate companies or units of Limited Partnerships—that are not recorded in Land Registry or by a notary. With title insurance, buyers of shares or units can obtain coverage assuring that they benefit from a clean title as of the day of the transaction.

(3) There are several countries in Central and Eastern Europe (CEE), Poland in particular, where confirmation of title and mortgage registration can take up to 18 months. Title insurance companies

416

provide *Registration Gap* coverage, which allows owners and lenders to operate with the assurance of a clean title and mortgage rank as of the day of closing.

A two-fold benefit: protection and standardisation

Acquisition or lending has traditionally been considered safer in one's own country than abroad. Consequently, there is a two-fold benefit to title insurance in cross-border transactions:

(1) The *traditional* role of insurance, since participants often feel uncomfortable with risks taken abroad that they would readily assume in their own country.

(2) A form of *standardisation*. Title insurance provides lenders and buyers with a standard text in English that applies (with only limited variations) in every single country of the European Union and in most CEE countries. For investors or lenders that are active in many European countries, it can eliminate the need to refer to lengthy legal documentation translated from a variety of languages.

Furthermore, sellers may be not be in a position (or reluctant) to provide legal representations and warranties:

- Public companies have to disclose contingent liabilities and carry explanations in the footnotes of their annual reports.

- Private companies may not want to continue having exposure on a property that they no longer own.

- Special Purpose Vehicles (SPVs) that are commonly used may not be dissolved immediately after a transaction and may have to keep a portion of the sales proceeds to back up those "Reps and Warranties."

TITLE INSURANCE: A CRITICAL ROLE IN EUROPEAN CMBS/RMBS SECURITISATION

By the time securitisation appeared in the US in the 1980s, title insurance had already become the norm for commercial and residential loans. In Europe, however, the securitisation market developed *before* the appearance of title insurance.

Title insurance makes securitisation more efficient

Title insurance enhances the efficiency and liquidity of CMBS/RMBS markets by:

(1) helping mortgage-backed securities achieve satisfactory credit ratings;

(2) providing a *private* solution to harmonising legal due diligence across different laws, regulations and languages, especially critical in multi-country transactions; and

(3) allowing fund managers to respond to investor demands for safety and common standards for legal due diligence and thus helping fulfil their fiduciary requirements.

CMBS/RMBS—A financial product growing in importance in Europe

Title insurance played a critical role in the largest ever European CMBS transaction—Terra Firma Capital's July 2006 securitisation of a €5.4 billion residential portfolio in Germany. By guaranteeing rank and registration for thousands of mortgages, title insurance greatly streamlined and accelerated the legal due diligence process for issuers, ratings agencies and investors.

Nevertheless, volumes in Europe still lag 10 years behind those in the US. Although European CMBS grew by 89 per cent last year,[2] Europe may not witness the sharp increase that the mortgage securitisation market experienced in the US after 1995.

There are specific traits of the European securitisation market that have, so far, limited its ability to follow the US pattern of growth:

(1) The European securitisation process has been driven more by issuers than investors. While the European Securitisation Forum (ESF) and Commercial Mortgage Securitisation Association (CMSA) have set up procedures/standards, and are active in lobbying the European governments and institutions to create favourable legal frameworks for the securitisation market, there are still no European standards for loan documentation or legal due diligence. Issuers have attempted to follow certain formats, but there are still significant differences in the information disclosed to the public for each issue.

---

[2] Deutsche Bank, 2005 Review and Outlook for 2006.

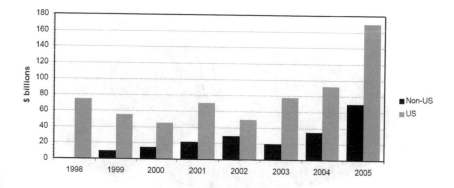

Figure 1: CMBS Volume Trends: US vs. non–US.

Source : Commercial Mortgage Alert.

(2) The focus of European issuers has been to obtain the most favourable financing rather than unload various risks off their balance
sheet.

In the US, AAA tranches represent less than 40 per cent and AA another
20 per cent of all MBS issues. By contrast, in Europe, over 90 per cent are
AAA and AA with some issues rated 95 per cent or even 100 per cent AAA.

The MBS market continues to be dominated by the UK, which still
represented 60 per cent of new issues in 2005. The percentage of pan-
European securitisation was only 4 per cent in 2005, but is expected to grow
significantly. For Pan-European issues, it is much easier to provide rating
agencies and investors with a standard title policy that covers all countries,
rather than with translations of legal documentation from different jurisdictions, languages and formats.

There will also be new market entrants from countries where the perceived legal risks are much greater and the need for title insurance more
compelling.[3] Single-borrower/single-property issues, where title conditions
are easier to grasp, represent 28 per cent of transactions to date, but this
percentage is expected to diminish.

---

[3] "Industry analysts predict that Russian mortgage lenders could have $45 bio of MBS out-
standing" (Asset-Backed Alert, March 17, 2006), and Turkish bank, Isbank, is considering $1.4
bio MBS program (Security News, March 13, 2006).

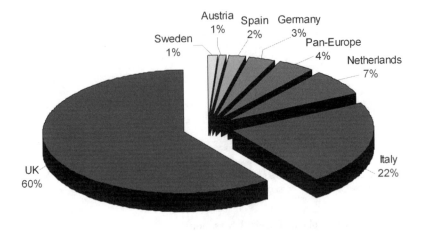

Figure 2: European CMBS Issuance by Country: January—September 2005.

Source : Commercial Mortgage Alert.

Basel II and its impact on the European securitisation market

According to a credit policy report published by Fitch Ratings in September 2005, "Basel II will establish strong capital incentives for banks to securitise commercial mortgages." All financial institutions in the European Union will have to operate under the Basel II guidelines.

(1) This will put pressure on banks to securitise a large share of their commercial mortgages (as well as credit card receivables).

(2) The capital ratios will not penalise banks that retain investment grade tranches in their books. It will, however, force them to sell a larger share of sub-investment grade positions in commercial mortgages to market participants not subject to Basel II (such as hedge funds and investment groups). It is clear that the current average 90 per cent AAA and AA rating of European issues does not reflect the true nature of the balance sheet of the issuing banks.

The same study goes on to show that while Basel II may have minimal impact on a bank's decision to securitise residential mortgage assets, it will have a major impact on the securitisation of CMBS.

Title insurance and growing importance of junior tranches

As a consequence of Basel II, the proportion of sub-investment grade tranches in CMBS issues will increase substantially and, with it, the need to attract investors and provide them with title insurance.

Buyers and traders of junior notes need to perform a thorough due diligence. While trained to assess the credit, financial or economic risks, they are rarely equipped to evaluate the legal ones, thus underlining the need for title insurance.

The institutions or groups that specialise in lower-rated paper are, for a large part, from the US. They are used to having legal risks covered by title insurance, and show little inclination to have their attorneys also review the legal opinions provided by the issuer.

In the wake of Basel II implementation, title insurance can play a key role in broadening the risk profile of European MBS issues.

SUMMARY AND CONCLUSIONS

The formation of a global real estate market in Europe over the last 20 years has created a context similar, in many ways, to the situation in the US at the end of the nineteenth Century: investors and lenders operating through different jurisdictions, with different laws or rules, as well as very different methods to record and guarantee title.

This chapter has reviewed the use of title insurance as a tool to mitigate real estate transaction risks, thus promoting investment in a securitised instruments beyond the AA and AAA products typically purchased in Europe.

Title insurance has evolved into a universal standard in the US real estate market with over $17 billion in annual premiums in 2005. While no one expects the European need for title insurance to generate similar volumes, demand for title insurance has increased in Europe due to the rising volume of cross-border investments, the increase in indirect real estate transactions, and the development of a securitisation market.

As for securitisation, real estate professionals, bankers and rating agencies are becoming increasingly aware of the role title insurance can play in simplifying and expediting issuance, covering known and *unknown* legal risks, thereby enhancing the safety and liquidity of CMBS/RMBS markets.

While there are efforts to harmonise mortgage markets within the European Union, it may take years to move forward. In addition, there is a growing demand from American and European investors, rating agencies, and auditors for additional disclosures and stronger guarantees. Title insurance provides a private solution that allows investors, as well financial institutions, to benefit from a vast unified market.

CHAPTER TWENTY-THREE

WHAT NEXT FOR EUROPEAN CMBS?

Jack Toliver, Managing Director—CMBS
Dominion Bond Rating Service, Chicago

INTRODUCTION

Throughout history, people ranging from the subsistence farmers of Polynesia to the bankers of modern-day Canary Wharf have intuitively understood the importance of cycles. Whether the growth of crops or the progression of interest rates, human beings have always known that the cycle rules.

Globally, since the beginning of the millennia, real estate values have risen at unprecedented rates and the CMBS market volume has risen to meet it. This has caused some to call for the end of the market's expansion, others to declare a shift in how real estate is valued, still others to celebrate its beginning and most to wonder where it really is in the cycle. This chapter examines the real estate cycle, various points in the cycle and identifies a list of market structural features that investors should consider. It does this by first examining the cycle and what has influenced cyclical shifts in the past. Secondly, it highlights which issues are unique to the CMBS market at any point in the cycle. Thirdly, it explains why, and where in the world, the CMBS market is most likely to continue its progress.

THE STAGES OF THE REAL ESTATE CYCLE

Before you can understand where you are headed in a cycle, it's important to know where you are. The real estate cycle has four stages: expansion, contraction, recession and recovery. Transitions from one cycle to another are often marked by an extreme in the balance between the influence of lenders, borrowers and tenants.

When the market favours lenders, interest spreads are high, loan terms become more restrictive, overall leverage is reduced and new construction requires substantial pre-leasing and significant equity. As a result rental rates increase and land prices weaken.

When the market favours borrowers, capital is plentiful and cheap, lenders bend their underwriting parameters and development accelerates. Land prices spike with development activity and this increased supply erodes rental rate pricing power.

When tenants have the upper hand, rental rates decline and concessions such as free rent and tenant improvement allowances abound. Borrower equity is eroded as cash flow declines diminish their ability to service or refinance debt.

It all sounds like an orderly process, but tax incentives for lenders and developers, regulatory expansion activity and the influence of capital markets can compound the volatility. The near future of this market cycle will certainly be roiled by the capital markets.

Adding to the confusion in the cycle, the balance between lenders, borrowers and tenants is different from region to region. Where you are in the cycle also depends on where you are in the world.

THE GROWTH OF CMBS MARKETS

The market in the United States in the 1980s is a particularly poignant example of desperate times and the desperate measures that they bring about. By 1980, virtually every Savings & Loan (S&L) in the US found itself with a cost of capital that exceeded the yields on their investment portfolios, which were primarily comprised of single family residential mortgages. Although successive years of double-digit inflation had grown the values of the underlying assets, the S&Ls, as lenders, were unable to take advantage of it. With few, if any viable alternatives, the regulatory limitations were changed, allowing S&Ls to finance commercial real estate and get into the development business through wholly owned service companies which entered into joint ventures with developers. Although this was initially a profitable business for many of the early participants, exposure limitations diluted the effects of impressive returns. To increase profits, the S&Ls took on more and more risk until the development partners effectively shifted all risk to the lending institutions. With no financing risk and substantial tax incentives for the developers as well as the lenders, the developers began a massive building campaign that begat the overbuilding of the late 1980s and the subsequent bear market.

It should be noted that this downturn had one very positive outcome: it primed the pumps of the great CMBS pipeline. As we discovered in Ch. 1, in order to bail out the failed S&Ls and restore public confidence, the US government enacted the Financial Institutions Reform, Recovery, and Enforcement Act of 1989 that created the Resolution Trust Company (RTC). One of the RTCs strategies was to buy non-performing commercial loans from the failed banks and work them out. With so many loans coming its way, the government needed a liquidity strategy and was able to take advantage of the 1986 REMIC laws making it possible to create pools of loans that would pay their interest out in a senior/subordinate bond structure to investors. The wide range of qualities of the underlying loans quickly developed a need for rating agencies that would provide professional and objective due diligence on the loan pools, and quantify the risk by assigning ratings to the various classes of certificates. In the following years, the US market developed excellent industry best practices that have more recently been stretched due to competition within the market—causing some firms to cut corners to increase profitability. Although the credit worthiness of many of the underlying loans has taken a beating in recent years, the underlying loans have maintained the structural features and enforceable documentation that was adapted in the illiquid lending environments of the early 1990s.[1]

Shortly after the birth of the CMBS market in the US the European market began to develop. The European market, however, did not evolve from a real estate market recession. The liquid lending environment required securitised lenders to compete directly with traditional commercial mortgage portfolio lenders. To gain acceptance of the CMBS product, lenders needed to offer the same or greater flexibility in loan structural features. In addition, the European governments were less apt to regulate the market and create the hurdles that constrained the US market, thereby allowing the greater flexibility that has led to the creation of highly structured loans.[2]

During this time the market was beginning in Canada as well. Like the European market, the Canadian market was uninhibited by the overreaching legal structures of the US. But the Canadian market got its start with experienced conduit players, whose US model was not immediately transferable to Canada. The market struggled until a daisy chain of bank and life company mergers led to a liquidity crunch. In an effort to consolidate business lines to meet strategic objectives, seasoned portfolios of performing as well as non-performing loans were securitised or sold creating a critical mass of transactions. Possibly as a result of the bitter sting of

---

[1] See Ch. 1 for further details on the emergence of CMBS.
[2] See Ch. 3 for further details on the emergence of European CMBS.

sudden illiquidity in their real estate market, the Canadian CMBS industry quickly adopted the more credit positive features from the US and Europe in terms of transaction structure, loan recourse and shorter amortisation schedules. The Canadian market has also been positively impacted by the high due diligence requirements that that country's institutional investors impose and a natural urge for its constituents to catch up to the others by creating a transparent and fair market.

More recently, the global CMBS market has been impacted by the use of reverse inquiries. These are transactions that allow institutional investors to buy a specific group of cash flows or rights within the loan pool that is being offered. To help the institution hedge other risks in its portfolio, it may want to purchase only the interest-only notes in a pool with excessive balloon or refinance risk. Alternatively, they may prefer to balance out their allocation by only taking on the loans on multi-family mortgages. This kind of transaction helped to craft investment products that were effective in their ability to increase investment in the CMBS market because they became available at a difficult point in the market cycles. Institutions had been hurt by the implosion of several currencies and the rapid expansion of other equity markets increased their risk management and diversification needs. These highly structured bonds offered both.

ISSUES AFFECTING THE EUROPEAN CMBS MARKET

Clearly, the rise of each of these markets varied based on the relationship between lenders and borrowers and the amount and variety of regulation in the market. Regardless of its place in the cycle, investors in the European CMBS market should consider several challenges before entering into it, detailed below.

Jurisdictional nuances

Local cultures and regulatory environments are an issue for many types of investors. However, those considering CMBS have a greater due diligence obligation in the European Union than in many other locations. The most transparent of the CMBS markets in Europe is Sweden's, where a national governing body publishes details on each deal and requires valuation professionals to pass a written test and spend five years in the industry before they may begin their work. Contrast this to Sweden's EU cousin, France, which tracks no price information and requires no qualification for valuation experts and generally recognises tenants occupancy rights to have precedence over borrower and lender rights.[3] Beyond Europe, other jurisdictional aspects distinguish markets. The US market strictly prohibits secondary debt due at the sale. Canadian loans feature recourse covenants and amortisation, and covenants in the UK are bank-oriented, requiring borrowers to provide high amounts of collateral and de-lever their interest in the event that the property's cash flow declines.

Covenants

These terms specify special agreements to protect the lender and they can have a very large impact on the investor. One common covenant, for example, governs the amount of debt that properties may take on. Generally, CMBS covenants are much stricter than those in bank loans because CMBS loans are subject to static governmental regulations while bank loan covenants ebb and flow with the real estate cycle. Enforcement of these covenants frequently requires additional security, increased debt service coverage or reversion of the sequential pay structure. Enforcing of such covenants is more effective when accompanied by cash management agreements, recourse to the borrower or other structural features in place at the loan origination.

Documentation and reporting standards

CMBS reporting has become more globally standard, but it still has some way to go. For example, the creation of the E-IRP[4] sought to standardise these regulations. While it is useful for investors in deals in the UK, its value is limited in jurisdictions as close by as France. It is also generally limited by the nature of CMBS. The E-IRP is not aggregated for specific loans so pools with little diversification may be poorly represented in the E-IRP.

Servicers[5]

These professionals are probably the most under-appreciated part of the CMBS marketplace. Servicers add to the standardisation of the industry because they subject loans to the same requirements, every time. Servicers also eliminate cronyism in the industry by ensuring that all investors are treated equally and special servicers bring significant value to the investors when they need it the most: when a borrower has defaulted. They have developed the expertise in the appropriate enforcement and modification of loans that bring them back to performing status, thereby protecting an investor's interest.

---

[3] "Commercial Real Estate and CMBS in Europe," *CMBS World*, Fall 2005.
[4] See Appendix 3.
[5] See Ch. 10 for further details.

THE FUTURE FOR EUROPEAN CMBS

Due in part to the increased due diligence requirements, the future seems bright for the European CMBS market. The expansion of the market in several different legal jurisdictions has been measured and steady. But there are two imminent challenges that the European CMBS market will face, and overcome, which will ensure the growth of the market in the future.

The main one is the development of a secondary market. Investors have thus far held to maturity or have been able to trade between the initial investors of a transaction. Broadening liquidity and the development of a secondary market will require the standardised structure, documentation and comprehensive performance data throughout the life of the transaction that investors need.

But perhaps the greater contributor to the Global CMBS market's growth will be the real estate cycle's changes. Testing the effectiveness of CMBS through the entire range of up and down markets will prove to investors that the diversification and presence of servicers and rating agencies, that are unique to CMBS, make it an effective asset class.

At the end of the day, the cycle will rule and the European CMBS market will continue to expand. It will also go through periods of reflection, where investors and issuers will find the ability to add some of the key structural features brought about by an illiquid market. While it evolves to a mature market, CMBS will continue to help investors to ride the cycle up and provide diversification for the downs.

APPENDICES

APPENDIX 1

INTERCREDITOR AGREEMENT

by and between

[_____],

as Senior Lender

and

[_____],

as Mezzanine Lender

Dated as of [_____], 200__

Premises: _____
_____
_____

APPENDIX 1

INTERCREDITOR AGREEMENT

THIS INTERCREDITOR AGREEMENT (this "Agreement"), dated as of [_____],
200[__] by and between [_____], a [_____], having an office at [_____]
("Senior Lender"), and [_____], a [_____], having an office at [_____]
("Mezzanine Lender").

RECITALS

WHEREAS, pursuant to the terms, provisions and conditions set forth in that certain Loan
Agreement, dated as of [_____], 200[__], between [_____], a [_____]
("Borrower") and Senior Lender (the "Senior Loan Agreement"), Senior Lender is the owner
and holder of a loan to Borrower in the original principal amount of $[_____] (the
"Senior Loan"), which Senior Loan is evidenced by a certain [_____] Note dated as of
[_____], 200[__], made by Borrower to Senior Lender in the amount of the Senior Loan
(the "Senior Note"), and secured by, among other things, a [_____], dated as of
[_____], 200[__], made by Borrower in favor of Senior Lender (the "Senior Mortgage"),
which Senior Mortgage encumbers the real property described on Exhibit A attached hereto
and made a part hereof, and all improvements thereon and appurtenances thereto (collectively,
the "Premises"); and

WHEREAS, pursuant to the terms, provisions and conditions set forth in that certain
Mezzanine Loan Agreement, dated as of [_____], 200[__], between [_____], a
[_____] ("Mezzanine Borrower") and Mezzanine Lender (the "Mezzanine Loan
Agreement"), Mezzanine Lender is the owner and holder of a loan to Mezzanine Borrower in
the original principal amount of $[_____] (the "Mezzanine Loan"), which Mezzanine
Loan is evidenced by a certain [_____] Note, dated as of [_____], 200[__], made
by Mezzanine Borrower in favor of Mezzanine Lender in the amount of the Mezzanine Loan
(the "Mezzanine Note"), and secured by, among other things, a [_____], dated as of
[_____], 200[__], from Mezzanine Borrower pursuant to which Mezzanine Lender is
granted a first priority security interest in all of Mezzanine Borrower's ownership interests in
Borrower (the "Pledge Agreement"); and

WHEREAS, Senior Lender and Mezzanine Lender desire to enter into this Agreement to
provide for the relative priority of the Senior Loan Documents (as such term is hereinafter
defined) and the Mezzanine Loan Documents (as such term is hereinafter defined) on the terms
and conditions hereinbelow set forth, and to evidence certain agreements with respect to the
relationship between the Mezzanine Loan and the Mezzanine Loan Documents, on the one
hand, and the Senior Loan and the Senior Loan Documents, on the other hand.

NOW, THEREFORE, in consideration of the foregoing recitals and for other good and
valuable consideration, the receipt and sufficiency of which are hereby acknowledged, Senior
Lender and Mezzanine Lender hereby agree as follows:

Section 1. Certain Definitions; Rules of Construction.

(a) As used in this Agreement, the following capitalized terms shall have the following
meanings:

"Affiliate" means, as to any particular Person, any Person directly or indirectly, through one
or more intermediaries, Controlling, Controlled by or under common Control with the Person
or Persons in question.

"Agreement" means this Agreement, as the same may be amended, modified and in effect
from time to time, pursuant to the terms hereof.

"Award" has the meaning provided in Section 9(d) hereof.

"Borrower" has the meaning provided in the Recitals hereto.

"Borrower Group" has the meaning provided in Section 10(c) hereof.

"Business Day" means a day on which commercial banks are not authorized or required by
law to close in New York, New York.

"CDO" has the meaning provided in the definition of the term "Qualified Transferee."

"CDO Asset Manager" with respect to any Securitization Vehicle which is a CDO, shall
mean the entity which is responsible for managing or administering the Mezzanine Loan as an
underlying asset of such Securitization Vehicle or, if applicable, as an asset of any Intervening

Trust Vehicle (including, without limitation, the right to exercise any consent and control rights available to the holder of the Mezzanine Loan).

"Certificates" means any securities (including all classes thereof) representing beneficial ownership interests in the Senior Loan (or in any one or more participation interests therein) or in a pool of mortgage loans including the Senior Loan (or in any one or more participation interests therein) issued in connection with a Securitization of the Senior Loan (or in any one or more participation interests therein).

"Conduit" has the meaning set forth in Section 15(b) hereof.

"Conduit Credit Enhancer" has the meaning set forth in Section 15(b) hereof.

"Conduit Inventory Loan" has the meaning set forth in Section 15(b) hereof.

"Continuing Senior Loan Event of Default" means an Event of Default under the Senior Loan, which has not been cured, for which (i) Senior Lender has provided notice of such Event of Default to Mezzanine Lender in accordance with Section 11(a) of this Agreement and (ii) the cure period provided to Mezzanine Lender in Section 11(a) of this Agreement has expired.

"Control" means the ownership, directly or indirectly, in the aggregate of more than fifty percent (50%) of the beneficial ownership interests of an entity and the possession, directly or indirectly, of the power to direct or cause the direction of the management or policies of an entity, whether through the ability to exercise voting power, by contract or otherwise. "Controlled by," "Controlling" and "under common Control with" shall have the respective correlative meaning thereto.

"Directing Mezzanine Lender" has the meaning provided in Section 4(c) hereof.

"Eligibility Requirements" means, with respect to any Person, that such Person (i) has total assets (in name or under management) in excess of $600,000,000 and (except with respect to a pension advisory firm or similar fiduciary) capital/statutory surplus or shareholder's equity of $250,000,000 and (ii) is regularly engaged in the business of making or owning (or, in the case of a pension advisory firm or other fiduciary) managing commercial real estate loans, participations or notes (including, without limitation, mezzanine loans, participations or notes with respect to commercial real estate) or operating commercial mortgage properties.

"Enforcement Action" means any (i) judicial or non-judicial foreclosure proceeding, the exercise of any power of sale, the taking of a deed or assignment in lieu of foreclosure, the obtaining of a receiver or the taking of any other enforcement action against the Premises or any portion thereof or Borrower, including, without limitation, the taking of possession or control of the Premises or any portion thereof, (ii) acceleration of, or demand or action taken in order to collect, all or any indebtedness secured by the Premises (other than giving of notices of default and statements of overdue amounts) or (iii) exercise of any right or remedy available to Senior Lender under the Senior Loan Documents, at law, in equity or otherwise with respect to Borrower and/or the Premises.

"Equity Collateral" means the direct and indirect equity interests in Borrower pledged pursuant to the Pledge Agreement.

"Equity Collateral Enforcement Action" means any action or proceeding or other exercise of Mezzanine Lender's rights and remedies commenced by Mezzanine Lender, in law or in equity, or otherwise, in order to realize upon the Equity Collateral, in whole or in part, or any transaction, whether in the nature of a transfer in lieu of foreclosure or otherwise, in order to acquire the Equity Collateral, in whole or in part.

"Event of Default" as used herein means (i) with respect to the Senior Loan and the Senior Loan Documents, any Event of Default thereunder which has occurred and is continuing (i.e., has not been cured by Borrower or by the Mezzanine Lender in accordance with the terms of Section 11 of this Agreement and (ii) with respect to the Mezzanine Loan and the Mezzanine Loan Documents, any Event of Default thereunder which has occurred and is continuing (i.e., has not been cured by Mezzanine Borrower).

"Intervening Trust Vehicle" with respect to any Securitization Vehicle which is a CDO, shall mean a trust vehicle or entity which holds the Mezzanine Loan as collateral securing (in whole or in part) any obligation or security held by such Securitization Vehicle as collateral for the CDO.

"Loan Pledgee" has the meaning provided in Section 15 hereof.

"Loan Purchase Price" has the meaning provided in Section 13(a) hereof.

"Mezzanine Borrower" has the meaning provided in the Recitals hereto.

"Mezzanine Lender" has the meaning provided in the first paragraph of this Agreement.

"Mezzanine Loan" has the meaning provided in the Recitals hereto.

"Mezzanine Loan Agreement" has the meaning provided in the Recitals hereto.

"Mezzanine Loan Cash Management Agreement" means any cash management agreement executed in connection with, or the cash management provisions of, the Mezzanine Loan Documents.

"Mezzanine Loan Documents" means the Mezzanine Loan Agreement, the Mezzanine Note, the Pledge Agreement, the Mezzanine Loan Cash Management Agreement, and all the documents and instruments set forth on Exhibit C hereto, as any of the foregoing may be modified, amended, extended, restated, supplemented, restated or replaced from time to time, subject to the limitations and agreements contained in this Agreement.

"Mezzanine Loan Modification" has the meaning provided in Section 7(b) hereof.

"Mezzanine Note" has the meaning provided in the Recitals hereto.

"Monetary Cure Period" has the meaning provided in Section 11(a) hereof.

"Permitted Fund Manager" means any Person that on the date of determination is (i) one of the entities listed on Exhibit D or any other nationally-recognized manager of investment funds investing in debt or equity interests relating to commercial real estate, (ii) investing through a fund with committed capital of at least $250,000,000 and (iii) not then subject to a bankruptcy proceeding.

"Person" means any individual, sole proprietorship, corporation, general partnership, limited partnership, limited liability company or partnership, joint venture, association, joint stock company, bank, trust, estate unincorporated organization, any federal, state, county or municipal government (or any agency or political subdivision thereof) endowment fund or any other form of entity.

"Pledge" has the meaning provided in Section 15 hereof.

"Pledge Agreement" has the meaning provided in the Recitals hereto.

"Premises" has the meaning provided in the Recitals hereto.

"Proceeding" has the meaning provided in Section 10(c) hereof.

"Property Manager" means [_____], a [_____], or any successor thereto as property manager of the Premises.

"Protective Advances" means all sums advanced for the purpose of payment of real estate taxes (including special payments in lieu of real estate taxes), maintenance costs, insurance premiums or other items (including capital items and operating expenses incurred in the ordinary course) reasonably necessary to protect the Premises or the Separate Collateral, respectively, from forfeiture, casualty, loss or waste, including, with respect to the Mezzanine Loan, amounts advanced by Mezzanine Lender pursuant to Section 11 hereof.

"Purchase Option Event" has the meaning provided in Section 13(a) hereof.

"Purchase Option Notice" has the meaning provided in Section 13(a) hereof.

"Qualified Manager" has the meaning provided in the Senior Loan Agreement.

"Qualified Transferee" means (i) Mezzanine Lender or any Person Controlled by, Controlling or under common Control with Mezzanine Lender, or (ii) one or more of the following:

(A) a real estate investment trust, bank, saving and loan association, investment bank, insurance company, trust company, commercial credit corporation, pension plan, pension fund or pension advisory firm, mutual fund, government entity or plan, provided that any such Person referred to in this clause (A) satisfies the Eligibility Requirements;

(B) an investment company, money management firm or "qualified institutional buyer" within the meaning of Rule 144A under the Securities Act of 1933, as amended, or an institutional "accredited investor" within the meaning of Regulation D under the Securities Act of 1933, as amended, provided that any such Person referred to in this clause (B) satisfies the Eligibility Requirements;

(C) an institution substantially similar to any of the foregoing entities described in clauses (ii)(A) or (ii)(B) that satisfies the Eligibility Requirements;

(D) any entity Controlled by, Controlling or under common Control with any of the entities described in clause (i) or clauses (ii)(A), (ii)(B) or (ii)(C) above or clause (ii)(F) below;

(E) a Qualified Trustee (or in the case of a CDO, a single purpose bankruptcy-remote entity which contemporaneously pledges its interest in the Mezzanine Loan to a Qualified Trustee) in connection with (1) a securitization of, (2) the creation of collateralized debt obligations ("CDO") secured by, or (3) a financing through an "owner trust" of, the Mezzanine Loan (any of the foregoing, a "Securitization Vehicle"), provided that (a) one or more classes of securities issued by such Securitization Vehicle is initially rated at least investment grade by each of the Rating Agencies which assigned a rating to one or more classes of securities issued in connection with such a Securitization (it being understood that with respect to any Rating Agency that assigned such a rating to the securities issued by such Securitization Vehicle, a Rating Agency Confirmation will not be required in connection with a transfer of the Mezzanine Loan to such Securitization Vehicle); or (b) in the case of a Securitization Vehicle that is not a CDO, the special servicer of such Securitization Vehicle has a Required Special Servicer Rating (such entity, an "Approved Servicer") and such Approved Servicer is required to service and administer such Mezzanine Loan in accordance with servicing arrangements for the assets held by the Securitization Vehicle which require that such Approved Servicer act in accordance with a servicing standard notwithstanding any contrary direction or instruction from any other Person; or (c) in the case of a Securitization Vehicle that is a CDO, the CDO Asset Manager and, if applicable, each Intervening Trust Vehicle that is not administered and managed by a CDO Asset Manager which is a Qualified Transferee, are each a Qualified Transferee under clauses (ii)(A), (B), (C), (D), or (F) of this definition;

    (F)   an investment fund, limited liability company, limited partnership or general partnership where a Permitted Fund Manager or an entity that is otherwise a Qualified Transferee under clauses (ii)(A), (B), (C) or (D) of this definition investing through a fund with committed capital of at least $250,000,000 acts as the general partner, managing member or fund manager and at least 50% of the equity interests in such investment vehicle are owned, directly or indirectly, by one or more entities that are otherwise Qualified Transferees under clauses (ii)(A), (B), (C) or (D) of this definition; or

    (G)   any Qualified Transferee that is acting in an agency capacity for a syndicate of lenders, provided more than 50% of the committed loan amounts or outstanding loan balance are owned by lenders in the syndicate that are Qualified Transferees.

"Qualified Trustee" means (i) a corporation, national bank, national banking association or a trust company, organized and doing business under the laws of any state or the United States of America, authorized under such laws to exercise corporate trust powers and to accept the trust conferred, having a combined capital and surplus of at least $100,000,000 and subject to supervision or examination by federal or state authority, (ii) an institution insured by the Federal Deposit Insurance Corporation or (iii) an institution whose long-term senior unsecured debt is rated either of the then in effect top two rating categories of each of the Rating Agencies.

"Rating Agencies" shall mean, prior to a Securitization, each of S&P, Moody's Investors Service, Inc., and Fitch, Inc., or any other nationally-recognized statistical rating agency which has been designated by Senior Lender and, after a Securitization, shall mean any of the foregoing that have rated any of the Certificates.

"Rating Agency Confirmation" means each of the Rating Agencies shall have confirmed in writing that the occurrence of the event with respect to which such Rating Agency Confirmation is sought shall not result in a downgrade, qualification or withdrawal of the applicable rating or ratings ascribed by such Rating Agency to any of the Certificates then outstanding. In the event that no Certificates are outstanding or the Senior Loan is not part of a Securitization, any action that would otherwise require a Rating Agency Confirmation shall require the consent of the Senior Lender, which consent shall not be unreasonably withheld or delayed.

"Redirection Notice" has the meaning provided in Section 15 hereof.

"Required Special Servicer Rating" means (i) a rating of "CSS1" in the case of Fitch, (ii) on S&P's Select Servicer List as a U.S. Commercial Mortgage Special Servicer in the case of S&P and (iii) in the case of Moody's, such special servicer is acting as special servicer in a commercial mortgage loan securitization that was rated by Moody's within the twelve (12) month period prior to the date of determination, and Moody's has not downgraded or withdrawn the then-current rating on any class of commercial mortgage securities or placed any class of commercial mortgage securities on watch citing the continuation of such special servicer as special servicer of such commercial mortgage securities.

"S&P" means Standard & Poor's Ratings Services, a division of The McGraw-Hill Companies, Inc.

"Securitization" means the sale or securitization of the Senior Loan (or any portion thereof) in one or more transactions through the issuance of securities, which securities may be assigned ratings by the Rating Agencies.

"Senior Lender" has the meaning provided in the first paragraph of this Agreement.

"Senior Loan" has the meaning provided in the Recitals hereto.

"Senior Loan Agreement" has the meaning provided in the Recitals hereto.

"Senior Loan Cash Management Agreement" means any cash management agreement or agreements executed in connection with, or cash management provisions of, the Senior Loan Documents.

"Senior Loan Default Notice" has the meaning provided in Section 11(a) hereof.

"Senior Loan Documents" means the Senior Loan Agreement, Senior Note, the Senior Mortgage, the Senior Cash Management Agreement, and all the instruments and documents set forth on Exhibit B hereto, as any of the foregoing may be modified, amended, extended, supplemented, restated or replaced from time to time, subject to the limitations and agreements contained in this Agreement.

"Senior Loan Liabilities" shall mean, collectively, all of the indebtedness, liabilities and obligations of Borrower evidenced by the Senior Loan Documents and all amounts due or to become due pursuant to the Senior Loan Documents, including interest thereon and any other amounts payable in respect thereof or in connection therewith, including, without limitation, any late charges, default interest, prepayment fees or premiums, exit fees, advances and post-petition interest.

"Senior Loan Modification" has the meaning provided in Section 7(a) hereof.

"Senior Mortgage" has the meaning provided in the Recitals hereto.

"Senior Note" has the meaning provided in the Recitals hereto.

"Separate Collateral" means (i) the Equity Collateral, (ii) the accounts (and monies therein from time to time) established pursuant to the Mezzanine Cash Management Agreement, (iii) any letter of credit established as collateral or security for the Mezzanine Loan, and (iv) any other collateral (including, without limitation, guarantees, UCC insurance policies, letters of credit, and rate cap agreements) now or hereafter given as security for the Mezzanine Loan pursuant to the Mezzanine Loan Documents, in each case not directly constituting security for the Senior Loan.

"Separate Collateral Enforcement Action" means any action or proceeding or other exercise of Mezzanine Lender's rights and remedies commenced by Mezzanine Lender, under the Mezzanine Loan Documents, at law or in equity, or otherwise, in order to realize upon the Separate Collateral, in whole or in part, or any transaction, whether in the nature of a transfer in lieu of foreclosure or otherwise, in order to acquire the Separate Collateral, in whole or in part.

"Third Party Agreement" has the meaning provided in Section 5(a) hereof.

"Third Party Obligor" has the meaning provided in Section 5(a) hereof.

"Transfer" means any assignment, pledge, conveyance, sale, transfer, mortgage, encumbrance, grant of a security interest, issuance of a participation interest, or other disposition, either directly or indirectly, by operation of law or otherwise.

(b) For all purposes of this Agreement, except as otherwise expressly provided or unless the context otherwise requires:

(i) all capitalized terms defined in the Recitals to this Agreement shall have the meanings ascribed thereto whenever used in this Agreement and the terms defined in this Agreement have the meanings assigned to them in this Agreement, and the use of any gender herein shall be deemed to include the other genders;

(ii) terms not otherwise defined herein shall have the meaning assigned to them in the Senior Loan Agreement;

(iii) all references in this Agreement to designated Sections, Subsections, Paragraphs, Articles, Exhibits, Schedules and other subdivisions or addenda without reference to a document are to the designated sections, subsections, paragraphs and articles and all other subdivisions of and exhibits, schedules and all other addenda to this Agreement, unless otherwise specified;

(iv) a reference to a subsection without further reference to a Section is a reference to such Subsection as contained in the same Section in which the reference appears, and this rule shall apply to Paragraphs and other subdivisions;

(v) the terms "includes" or "including" shall mean without limitation by reason of enumeration;

(vi) the words "herein", "hereof", "hereunder" and other words of similar import refer to this Agreement as a whole and not to any particular provision;

(vii) the words "to Mezzanine Lender's knowledge" or "to the knowledge of Mezzanine Lender" (or words of similar meaning) shall mean to the actual knowledge of officers of Mezzanine Lender with direct oversight responsibility for the Mezzanine Loan without independent investigation or inquiry and without any imputation whatsoever; and

(viii) the words "to Senior Lender's knowledge" or "to the knowledge of Senior Lender" (or words of similar meaning) shall mean to the actual knowledge of officers of Senior Lender with direct oversight responsibility for the Senior Loan without independent investigation or inquiry and without any imputation whatsoever.

Section 2. Approval of Loans and Loan Documents.

(a) Mezzanine Lender hereby acknowledges that (i) it has received and reviewed and, subject to the terms and conditions of this Agreement, hereby consents to and approves of the making of the Senior Loan and, subject to the terms and provisions of this Agreement, all of the terms and provisions of the Senior Loan Documents, (ii) the execution, delivery and performance of the Senior Loan Documents will not constitute a default or an event which, with the giving of notice or the lapse of time, or both, would constitute a default under the Mezzanine Loan Documents, (iii) Senior Lender is under no obligation or duty to, nor has Senior Lender represented that it will, see to the application of the proceeds of the Senior Loan by Borrower or any other Person to whom Senior Lender disburses such proceeds, and (iv) any application or use of the proceeds of the Senior Loan for purposes other than those provided in the Senior Loan Documents shall not affect, impair or defeat the terms and provisions of this Agreement or the Senior Loan Documents.

(b) Senior Lender hereby acknowledges that (i) it has received and reviewed, and, subject to the terms and conditions of this Agreement, hereby consents to and approves of the making of the Mezzanine Loan and, subject to the terms and provisions of this Agreement, all of the terms and provisions of the Mezzanine Loan Documents, (ii) the execution, delivery and performance of the Mezzanine Loan Documents will not constitute a default or an event which, with the giving of notice or the lapse of time, or both, would constitute a default under the Senior Loan Documents, (iii) Mezzanine Lender is under no obligation or duty to, nor has Mezzanine Lender represented that it will, see to the application of the proceeds of the Mezzanine Loan by Mezzanine Borrower or any other Person to whom Mezzanine Lender disburses such proceeds and (iv) any application or use of the proceeds of the Mezzanine Loan for purposes other than those provided in the Mezzanine Loan Documents shall not affect, impair or defeat the terms and provisions of this Agreement or the Mezzanine Loan Documents. Senior Lender hereby acknowledges and agrees that any conditions precedent to Senior Lender's consent to mezzanine financing as set forth in the Senior Loan Documents or any other agreements with the Borrower, as they apply to the Mezzanine Loan Documents or the making of the Mezzanine Loan, have been either satisfied or waived.

(c) Notwithstanding anything in this Agreement to the contrary, Senior Lender agrees that no default or Event of Default under the Mezzanine Loan Documents shall, in and of itself, constitute or give rise to a default or Event of Default under the Senior Loan Documents, entitle Senior Lender to accelerate payments under the Senior Loan Documents or entitle Senior Lender to modify any provisions of the Senior Loan Documents; provided, however, the circumstances giving rise to a default or Event of Default under the Mezzanine Loan Documents may give rise to a default or Event of Default under the Senior Loan Documents.

Section 3. Representations and Warranties.

(a) Mezzanine Lender hereby represents and warrants as follows:

(i) Exhibit C attached hereto and made a part hereof is a true, correct and complete listing of all of the Mezzanine Loan Documents as of the date hereof. To Mezzanine Lender's knowledge, there currently exists no default or event which, with the giving of notice or the lapse of time, or both, would constitute a default under any of the Mezzanine Loan Documents.

(ii) Mezzanine Lender is the legal and beneficial owner of the entire Mezzanine Loan free and clear of any lien, security interest, option or other charge or encumbrance, other than any lien or security interest granted to any Loan Pledgee (as hereinafter defined) as contemplated by the provisions of Section 15 hereof.

(iii) There are no conditions precedent to the effectiveness of this Agreement against Mezzanine Lender that have not been satisfied or waived.

(iv) Mezzanine Lender has, independently and without reliance upon Senior Lender and based on such documents and information as it has deemed appropriate, made its own credit analysis and decision to enter into this Agreement.

(v)   Mezzanine Lender is duly organized and is validly existing under the laws of the jurisdiction under which it was organized with full power to execute, deliver, and perform this Agreement and consummate the transactions contemplated hereby.

(vi)   All actions necessary to authorize the execution, delivery, and performance of this Agreement on behalf of Mezzanine Lender have been duly taken, and all such actions continue in full force and effect as of the date hereof.

(vii)   Mezzanine Lender has duly executed and delivered this Agreement and this Agreement constitutes the legal, valid, and binding agreement of Mezzanine Lender enforceable against Mezzanine Lender in accordance with its terms subject to (x) applicable bankruptcy, reorganization, insolvency and moratorium laws, and (y) general principles of equity which may apply regardless of whether a proceeding is brought in law or in equity.

(viii)   To Mezzanine Lender's knowledge, no consent of any other Person and no consent, license, approval, or authorization of, or exemption by, or registration or declaration or filing with, any governmental authority, bureau or agency is required in connection with the execution, delivery or performance by Mezzanine Lender of this Agreement or consummation by Mezzanine Lender of the transactions contemplated by this Agreement, other than those obtained.

(ix)   None of the execution, delivery and performance of this Agreement nor the consummation of the transactions contemplated by this Agreement will (v) violate or conflict with any provision of the organizational or governing documents of Mezzanine Lender, (w) to Mezzanine Lender's knowledge, violate, conflict with, or result in the breach or termination of, or otherwise give any other Person the right to terminate, or constitute (or with the giving of notice or lapse of time, or both, would constitute) a default under the terms of any contract, mortgage, lease, bond, indenture, agreement, or other instrument to which Mezzanine Lender is a party or to which any of its properties are subject, (x) to Mezzanine Lender's knowledge, result in the creation of any lien, charge, encumbrance, mortgage, lease, claim, security interest, or other right or interest upon the properties or assets of Mezzanine Lender pursuant to the terms of any such contract, mortgage, lease, bond, indenture, agreement, franchise, or other instrument (provided, however, that Mezzanine Lender and any participant in the Mezzanine Loan shall have the right to grant a lien, charge, encumbrance, claim or security interest in the Mezzanine Loan or any portion thereof to a Loan Pledgee as contemplated by the provisions of Section 15 hereof), (y) violate any judgment, order, injunction, decree, or award of any court, arbitrator, administrative agency or governmental or regulatory body of which Mezzanine Lender has knowledge against, or binding upon, Mezzanine Lender or upon any of the securities, properties, assets, or business of Mezzanine Lender or (z) to Mezzanine Lender's knowledge, constitute a violation by Mezzanine Lender of any statute, law or regulation that is applicable to Mezzanine Lender.

(x)   The Mezzanine Loan is not cross-defaulted with any loan other than the Senior Loan. The Premises do not directly secure any loan from Mezzanine Lender to Mezzanine Borrower or any other Affiliate of Borrower.

(b)   Senior Lender hereby represents and warrants as follows:

(i)   Exhibit B attached hereto and made a part hereof is a true, correct and complete listing of the Senior Loan Documents as of the date hereof. To Senior Lender's knowledge, there currently exists no default or event which, with the giving of notice or the lapse of time, or both, would constitute a default under any of the Senior Loan Documents.

(ii)   Senior Lender is the legal and beneficial owner of the Senior Loan free and clear of any lien, security interest, option or other charge or encumbrance.

(iii)   There are no conditions precedent to the effectiveness of this Agreement that have not been satisfied or waived.

(iv)   Senior Lender has, independently and without reliance upon Mezzanine Lender and based on such documents and information as it has deemed appropriate, made its own credit analysis and decision to enter into this Agreement.

(v)   Senior Lender is duly organized and is validly existing under the laws of the jurisdiction under which it was organized with full power to execute, deliver, and perform this Agreement and consummate the transactions contemplated hereby.

(vi)   All actions necessary to authorize the execution, delivery, and performance of this Agreement on behalf of Senior Lender have been duly taken, and all such actions continue in full force and effect as of the date hereof.

(vii)   Senior Lender has duly executed and delivered this Agreement and this Agreement constitutes the legal, valid, and binding agreement of Senior Lender enforceable against Senior Lender in accordance with its terms subject to (x) applicable bankruptcy, reorganization, insolvency and moratorium laws and (y) general principles of equity which may apply regardless of whether a proceeding is brought in law or in equity.

(viii)   To Senior Lender's knowledge, no consent of any other Person and no consent, license, approval, or authorization of, or exemption by, or registration or declaration or filing with, any governmental authority, bureau or agency is required in connection with the execution, delivery or performance by Senior Lender of this Agreement or consummation by Senior Lender of the transactions contemplated by this Agreement.

(ix)   None of the execution, delivery and performance of this Agreement nor the consummation of the transactions contemplated by this Agreement will (v) violate or conflict with any provision of the organizational or governing documents of Senior Lender, (w) to Senior Lender's knowledge, violate, conflict with, or result in the breach or termination of, or otherwise give any other Person the right to terminate, or constitute (or with the giving of notice or lapse of time, or both, would constitute) a default under the terms of any contract, mortgage, lease, bond, indenture, agreement, or other instrument to which Senior Lender is a party or to which any of its properties are subject, (x) to Senior Lender's knowledge, result in the creation of any lien, charge, encumbrance, mortgage, lease, claim, security interest, or other right or interest upon the properties or assets of Senior Lender pursuant to the terms of any such contract, mortgage, lease, bond, indenture, agreement, franchise or other instrument, (y) violate any judgment, order, injunction, decree or award of any court, arbitrator, administrative agency or governmental or regulatory body of which Senior Lender has knowledge against, or binding upon, Senior Lender or upon any of the securities, properties, assets, or business of Senior Lender or (z) to Senior Lender's knowledge, constitute a violation by Senior Lender of any statute, law or regulation that is applicable to Senior Lender.

(x)   The Senior Loan is not cross-defaulted with any other loan. The Premises do not secure any other loan from Senior Lender to Borrower, Mezzanine Borrower or any other Affiliate of Borrower.

(xi)   The Senior Loan is not secured by any direct or indirect equity interest in the Borrower.

Section 4.   Transfer of Mezzanine Loan or Senior Loan.

(a)   Mezzanine Lender shall not Transfer more than 49% of its beneficial interest in the Mezzanine Loan unless either (i) a Rating Agency Confirmation has been given with respect to such Transfer, in which case the related transferee shall thereafter be deemed to be a "Qualified Transferee" for all purposes of this Agreement, or (ii) such Transfer is to a Qualified Transferee. Any such transferee (other than a participant or Loan Pledgee, both of which shall take subject to this Agreement) must assume in writing the obligations of Mezzanine Lender hereunder and agree to be bound by the terms and provisions hereof. Such proposed transferee (other than a participant or Loan Pledgee, both of which shall take subject to this Agreement) shall also remake each of the representations and warranties contained herein for the benefit of the Senior Lender.

(b)   At least five (5) days prior to a transfer of more than 49% of its beneficial interest in the Mezzanine Loan to a Qualified Transferee, the Mezzanine Lender shall provide to Senior Lender and, if any Certificates are outstanding, to the Rating Agencies, a certification that such transfer will be made in accordance with this Section 4, such certification to include the name and contact information of the Qualified Transferee, as the case may be. The provisions of this Section 4(b) are not intended to apply to a Pledge granted under Section 15 of this Agreement.

(c)   If more than one Person shall hold a direct interest in the Mezzanine Loan (or if Mezzanine Lender has sold one (1) or more participation interests in the Mezzanine Loan), the holder(s) of more than 50% of the principal amount of the Mezzanine Loan (or, in the case of a sale of one (1) or more participation interest(s), the owner(s) of the beneficial interest of the agreement(s)) shall designate by written notice to Senior Lender one of such Persons (the

"Directing Mezzanine Lender") to act on behalf of all such Persons holding an interest in the Mezzanine Loan (or the beneficial owners of the principal amount of the Mezzanine Loan set forth in the applicable participation agreement(s)). The Directing Mezzanine Lender shall have the sole right to receive any notices which are required to be given or which may be given to Mezzanine Lender pursuant to this Agreement and to exercise the rights and power given to Mezzanine Lender hereunder, including any approval rights of Mezzanine Lender; provided, that until the Directing Mezzanine Lender has been so designated, the last Person known to the Senior Lender to hold more than a 50% direct interest in the Mezzanine Loan (or if none of the Persons holding a direct interest own more than 50%, then the last Person known to the Senior Lender to hold a plurality of such interests) shall be deemed to be the Directing Mezzanine Lender. Once the Directing Mezzanine Lender has been designated hereunder, Senior Lender shall be entitled to rely on such designation until it has received written notice from the holder(s) of more than 50% (or if none of the Persons holding a direct interest own more than 50%, then the Person holding a plurality of such interests) of the principal amount of the Mezzanine Loan of the designation of a different Person to act as the Directing Mezzanine Lender. As of the date hereof, the Directing Mezzanine Lender is Mezzanine Lender.

(d) Mezzanine Lender acknowledges that any Rating Agency Confirmation may be granted or denied by the Rating Agencies in their sole and absolute discretion and that such Rating Agencies may charge customary fees in connection with any such action.

(e) Senior Lender may, from time to time, in its sole discretion Transfer all or any of the Senior Loan or any interest therein, provided that the terms and provisions of this Agreement shall be binding on Senior Lender's successors and assigns, and notwithstanding any such Transfer or subsequent Transfer, the Senior Loan and the Senior Loan Documents shall be and remain a senior obligation in the respects set forth in this Agreement to the Mezzanine Loan and the Mezzanine Loan Documents in accordance with the terms and provisions of this Agreement. In no event shall any such Transfer by Senior Lender be to the Borrower, or knowingly to any Affiliate of Borrower (provided that nothing contained herein shall restrict Borrower or any Affiliate of Borrower from acquiring any Certificates).

Section 5. Foreclosure of Separate Collateral.

(a) Mezzanine Lender shall not complete a foreclosure or other realization upon the Equity Collateral (including, without limitation, obtaining title to the Equity Collateral or selling or otherwise transferring the Equity Collateral) without a Rating Agency Confirmation unless (i) the transfer of title to the Equity Collateral is to a Qualified Transferee, (ii) the Premises will be managed by a Qualified Manager promptly after the transfer of title to the Equity Collateral and (iii) if not in place prior to the transfer of title to the Equity Collateral, hard cash management and adequate reserves for taxes, insurance, debt service, ground rents, capital repair and improvement expenses, tenant improvement expenses and leasing commissions and operating expenses will be implemented under the Senior Loan promptly after the transfer of title to the Equity Collateral; provided, that the implementation of such hard cash management and reserves would not cause a "significant modification" of the Senior Loan, as such term is defined in Treasury Regulations Section 1.860G–2(b). Additionally, if a non-consolidation opinion was delivered in connection with the closing of the Senior Loan, the transferee of the Equity Collateral shall deliver a new non-consolidation opinion relating to the transferee acceptable to the Rating Agencies within ten (10) Business Days of the transfer of title to the Equity Collateral. The Mezzanine Lender shall provide notice of the transfer and an officer's certificate from an officer of Mezzanine Lender certifying that all conditions set forth in this Section 5(a) have been satisfied to Senior Lender and the Rating Agencies upon consummation of any transfer of the Equity Collateral pursuant to this Section 5(a). Senior Lender may request reasonable evidence that the foregoing requirements have been satisfied. In the event that such Transfer results in the removal of any guarantor, indemnitor, pledgor, or other obligor under the Senior Loan Documents (each, a "Third Party Obligor"), such transferee or an Affiliate thereof reasonably satisfactory to the Senior Lender shall: (A) execute and deliver to Senior Lender a guaranty, indemnity, pledge agreement or other agreement which provides for the obligations of such obligor (each, a "Third Party Agreement"), in each case, in a form substantially similar to the Third Party Agreement that it is replacing, pursuant to which the Third Party Obligor shall undertake the obligations set forth therein, and (B) if there are Certificates then outstanding, deliver (or cause to be delivered) to Senior Lender and each Rating Agency, an opinion of counsel that the substitution of the original Third Party Obligor and the original

Third Party Agreement with a substitute Third Party Obligor and a substitute Third Party Agreement, would not cause a "significant modification" of the Senior Loan, as such term is defined in Treasury Regulations Section 1.860G–2(b).

(b)   Nothing contained herein shall limit or restrict the right of Mezzanine Lender to exercise its rights and remedies, in law or in equity, or otherwise, in order to realize on any Separate Collateral that is not Equity Collateral (including, without limitation, exercising any remedy pursuant to any guaranty or additional insurance given in connection with the Mezzanine Loan), provided that Mezzanine Lender shall not exercise any rights or remedies with respect to any guarantor if the Senior Lender is simultaneously exercising its rights or remedies against the same guarantor.

(c)   In the event Mezzanine Lender or any purchaser at a UCC sale obtains title to any Separate Collateral, Senior Lender hereby acknowledges and agrees that any transfer or assumption fee in the Senior Loan Agreement shall be waived as a condition to such transfer and any such transfer shall not constitute a breach or default under the Senior Loan Documents, provided the conditions in Section 5(a) are met. Senior Lender also acknowledges and agrees that it will not impose any fees or unreasonable delays in connection with such Transfer. No transfer or assumption fee under the Senior Loan shall be payable in connection with any transfer resulting from the exercise of Mezzanine Lender's remedies under the Mezzanine Loan Documents or, in lieu thereof, an assignment of any Separate Collateral.

(d)   Nothing contained in this Section 5 is intended (i) to limit a Loan Pledgee's right under its financing documents with Mezzanine Lender to foreclose against Mezzanine Lender, provided that Loan Pledgee complies with the applicable provisions of Section 15, or (ii) if any such Loan Pledgee has foreclosed under its financing documents as aforesaid, to limit such Loan Pledgee's right to foreclose against Mezzanine Borrower's interest in the Separate Collateral, provided that Loan Pledgee complies with the applicable provisions of Section 5.

Section 6.   Notice of Rating Confirmation. Mezzanine Lender promptly shall notify Senior Lender of any intended action relating to the Mezzanine Loan which would require Rating Agency Confirmation pursuant to this Agreement and shall cooperate with Senior Lender in obtaining such confirmation. Senior Lender promptly shall notify Mezzanine Lender of any intended action relating to the Senior Loan which would require Rating Agency Confirmation pursuant to this Agreement and shall cooperate with Mezzanine Lender in obtaining such confirmation. Mezzanine Lender shall pay all fees and expenses of the Rating Agencies in connection with any request for any Rating Agency Confirmation pursuant to this Agreement.

Section 7.   Modifications, Amendments, Etc.

(a)   Senior Lender shall have the right without the consent of Mezzanine Lender in each instance to enter into any amendment, deferral, extension, modification, increase, renewal, replacement, consolidation, supplement or waiver (collectively, a "Senior Loan Modification") of the Senior Loan or the Senior Loan Documents provided that no such Senior Loan Modification shall (i) increase the interest rate or principal amount of the Senior Loan (except for increases in principal to cover Protective Advances and for enforcement and workout costs), increase the amount of any principal payments required under the Senior Loan, or modify any related principal amortization schedule in a manner which would increase the amount of principal payments, (ii) increase in any other material respect any monetary obligations of Borrower under the Senior Loan Documents or impose any additional financial covenants on Borrower, (iii) extend or shorten the scheduled maturity date of the Senior Loan (except that Senior Lender may permit Borrower to exercise any extension options in accordance with the terms and provisions of the Senior Loan Documents), (iv) convert or exchange the Senior Loan into or for any other indebtedness or subordinate any of the Senior Loan to any indebtedness of Borrower, (v) amend or modify the provisions regarding Transfers of interests (direct or indirect) in the Borrower or the Premises, (vi) amend, modify, waive, terminate or otherwise change any term or provision of any Senior Loan Cash Management Agreement, or any Senior Loan Document with respect to the manner, priority, payment, timing, use, withdrawal, or method of the application of payments under the Senior Loan Documents or the Mezzanine Loan Documents (including, without limitation, the amount of any escrows or reserves or terms and conditions of any "cash trap", "cash sweep" or similar provisions), (vii) cross default the Senior Loan with any other indebtedness, (viii) consent to a higher strike price with respect to any new or extended interest rate cap agreement entered into in connection with the extended term of the Senior Loan, (ix) obtain any direct or indirect equity interest in Borrower or Mezzanine Borrower or provide for any contingent interest, additional interest or so-called "kicker" measured on the basis of the cash flow or appreciation of the Premises, (or other similar equity participation), (x) extend the period during which voluntary prepayments are prohibited or during which prepayments require the payment of a prepayment fee or premium or yield maintenance charge, impose any prepayment fee or premium or yield maintenance charge in connection with a prepayment of the Senior Loan when none is now required or increase the amount of any prepayment fee, premium or yield maintenance charge, or waive any prohibition on prepayment of the Senior Loan without contemporaneous prepayment of the Mezzanine Loan; (xi) amend, modify or waive the material insurance requirements set forth in the Senior Loan Agreement, (xii) amend or modify the definition of "Event of Default" under the Senior Loan Documents or add any additional Events of Default; or (xiii) shorten any notice or cure period provided in the Senior Loan Document; provided, however, in no event shall Senior Lender be obligated to obtain Mezzanine Lender's consent to a Senior Loan Modification in the case of a work-out or other surrender, compromise, release, renewal, or indulgence relating to the Senior Loan during the existence of a Continuing Senior Loan Event of Default, except that under no conditions shall clause (i) ((with respect to increases in principal amounts only, except for increases in principal to cover Protective Advances, workout costs and enforcement costs), or clause (x) be modified without the written consent of Mezzanine Lender. In addition and notwithstanding the foregoing provisions of this Section 7, any amounts funded by the Senior Lender under the Senior Loan Documents as a result of (A) the making of any Protective Advances or other advances by the Senior Lender, or (B) interest accruals or accretions and any compounding thereof (including default interest), shall not be deemed to contravene this Section 7(a).

(b)   Mezzanine Lender shall have the right without the consent of Senior Lender in each instance to enter into any amendment, deferral, extension, modification, increase, renewal, replacement, consolidation, supplement or waiver (collectively, a "Mezzanine Loan Modification") of the Mezzanine Loan or the Mezzanine Loan Documents provided that no such Mezzanine Loan Modification shall (i) increase the interest rate or principal amount of the Mezzanine Loan (except for increases in principal to cover Protective Advances and for enforcement and workout costs), increase the amount of any principal payments required under the Mezzanine Loan, or modify any related principal amortization schedule in a manner which would increase the amount of principal payments (ii) increase in any other material respect any monetary obligations of Mezzanine Borrower under the Mezzanine Loan Documents, (iii) extend or shorten (other than by acceleration) the scheduled maturity date of the Mezzanine Loan (except that Mezzanine Lender may permit Mezzanine Borrower to exercise any extension options in accordance with the terms and provisions of the Mezzanine Loan Documents), (iv) convert or exchange the Mezzanine Loan into or for any other indebtedness or subordinate any of the Mezzanine Loan to any indebtedness of Mezzanine Borrower, (v) provide for any additional contingent interest, additional interest or so-called "kicker" measured on the basis of the cash flow or appreciation of the Premises or (vi) cross default the Mezzanine Loan with any other indebtedness (other than the Senior Loan). Notwithstanding the foregoing provisions of this Section 7(b), any amounts funded by the Mezzanine Lender under the Mezzanine Loan Documents as a result of the making of any Protective Advances or other advances, or interest accruals or accretions and any compounding thereof (including default interest), shall not be deemed to contravene this Agreement. Notwithstanding anything to the contrary contained herein, if an Event of Default exists under the Mezzanine Loan Documents, Mezzanine Lender shall be permitted to modify or amend the Mezzanine Loan Documents in connection with a work-out or other surrender, compromise, release, renewal or modification of the Mezzanine Loan except that under no conditions shall clause (i) (with respect to increases in principal amounts only, except for increases in principal to cover Protective Advances, workout costs and enforcement costs), clause (ii), clause (iii) (with respect to shortening the maturity only), clause (iv) or clause (v) be violated without the written consent of the Senior Lender.

(c)   Senior Lender shall deliver to Mezzanine Lender copies of any and all modifications, amendments, extensions, consolidations, spreaders, restatements, alterations, changes or revisions to any one or more of the Senior Loan Documents (including, without limitation, any side letters, waivers or consents entered into, executed or delivered by Senior Lender) within a reasonable time after any of such applicable instruments have been executed by Senior Lender.

(d)   Mezzanine Lender shall deliver to Senior Lender copies of any and all modifications, amendments, extensions, consolidations, spreaders, restatements, alterations, changes or revisions to any one or more of the Mezzanine Loan Documents (including, without limitation, any side letters, waivers or consents entered into, executed or delivered by Mezzanine Lender) within a reasonable time after any of such applicable instruments have been executed by Mezzanine Lender.

(e) Senior Lender agrees that, notwithstanding anything to the contrary set forth in the Senior Loan Documents, any amendment to or modification of the Mezzanine Loan Documents that is not prohibited by this Section 7 shall not be a default under the Senior Loan, and Senior Lender shall not declare the existence of a default under the Senior Loan solely as a result of any amendment or modification to the Mezzanine Loan Documents that is not prohibited by this Agreement.

(f) Mezzanine Lender agrees that, notwithstanding anything to the contrary set forth in the Mezzanine Loan Documents, any amendment to or modification of the Senior Loan Documents that is not prohibited by this Section 7 shall not be a default under the Mezzanine Loan, and Mezzanine Lender shall not declare the existence of a default under the Mezzanine Loan solely as a result of any amendment or modification to the Senior Loan Documents that is not prohibited by this Agreement.

Section 8. Subordination of Mezzanine Loan and Mezzanine Loan Documents.

(a) Except with respect to the Separate Collateral and subject to the provisions of Section 8(c), Mezzanine Lender hereby subordinates and makes junior the Mezzanine Loan, the Mezzanine Loan Documents and the liens and security interests created thereby, and all rights, remedies, terms and covenants contained therein to (i) the Senior Loan, (ii) the liens and security interests created by the Senior Loan Documents (and (iii) all of the terms, covenants, conditions, rights and remedies contained in the Senior Loan Documents, and no amendments or modifications to the Senior Loan Documents (implemented in accordance with this Agreement) or waivers of any provisions thereof (implemented in accordance with this Agreement) shall affect the subordination thereof as set forth in this Section 8(a). Mezzanine Lender hereby acknowledges and agrees that the Mezzanine Loan is not secured by a lien on the Premises or any of the other collateral securing the Senior Loan or any other assets of the Borrower.

(b) Except with respect to the Separate Collateral and subject to the provisions of Section 8(c), every document and instrument included within the Mezzanine Loan Documents shall be subject and subordinate to each and every document and instrument included within the Senior Loan Documents and all extensions, modifications, consolidations, supplements, amendments, replacements and restatements of and/or to the Senior Loan Documents (implemented in accordance with this Agreement).

(c) This Agreement shall not be construed as subordinating and shall not subordinate or impair Mezzanine Lender's first lien priority right, estate and interest in and to the Separate Collateral and Senior Lender hereby acknowledges and agrees that Senior Lender does not have and shall not hereafter acquire, any lien on, or any other interest whatsoever in, the Separate Collateral, or any part thereof, and that the exercise of remedies and realization upon the Separate Collateral (and the application of proceeds therefrom) by Mezzanine Lender, a Loan Pledgee or other transferee in accordance with the terms and provisions of this Agreement are expressly permitted and shall not constitute a default or an Event of Default under the Senior Loan Documents or under this Agreement.

Section 9. Payment Subordination.

(a) Subject to Section 9(b) hereof, except (i) as otherwise expressly provided in this Agreement or any Senior Loan Document, and (ii) in connection with the exercise by Mezzanine Lender of its rights and remedies with respect to the Separate Collateral in accordance with the terms of this Agreement, all of Mezzanine Lender's rights to payment of the Mezzanine Loan and the obligations evidenced by the Mezzanine Loan Documents are hereby subordinated to all of Senior Lender's rights to payment by Borrower of the Senior Loan and the obligations secured by the Senior Loan Documents, and Mezzanine Lender agrees that it shall not, from and after receipt by Mezzanine Lender of written notice of the occurrence of an Event of Default under the Senior Loan Documents and during the continuance thereof, accept or receive payments (including, without limitation, whether in cash or other property and whether received directly, indirectly or by set-off, counterclaim or otherwise) from Borrower prior to the date that all obligations of Borrower to Senior Lender under the Senior Loan Documents are paid. Except as otherwise expressly provided in this Agreement or in connection with realizing on the Separate Collateral in accordance with the terms of this Agreement, if a Proceeding shall have occurred or a Continuing Senior Loan Event of Default shall have occurred and be continuing, Senior Lender shall be entitled to receive payment and performance in full of all amounts due or to become due to Senior Lender before Mezzanine Lender is entitled to receive any payment on account of the Mezzanine Loan. Notwithstanding anything to the contrary in this Agreement, Mezzanine Lender shall be entitled to retain (A) funds deposited in the Mezzanine Lender's account for the Mezzanine Loan (other than funds deposited therein in error), (B) any proceeds generated as a result of an Equity Collateral Enforcement Action, and (C) payments or proceeds generated from the exercise of Mezzanine Lender's remedies with respect to any Separate Collateral, in each case to the extent permitted by this Agreement. All payments or distributions upon or with respect to the Mezzanine Loan which are received by Mezzanine Lender contrary to the provisions of this Agreement shall be received and held in trust by the Mezzanine Lender for the benefit of Senior Lender and shall be paid over to Senior Lender in the same form as so received (with any necessary endorsement) to be applied (in the case of cash) to, or held as collateral (in the case of non-cash property or securities) for, the payment or performance of the Senior Loan in accordance with the terms of the Senior Loan Documents. Nothing contained herein shall prohibit the Mezzanine Lender from making Protective Advances (and adding the amount thereof to the principal balance of the Mezzanine Loan) notwithstanding the existence of a default under the Senior Loan at such time.

(b) Notwithstanding anything to the contrary contained in this Agreement, including, without limitation, Section 9(a), but subject to Section 7(b), provided that no Continuing Senior Loan Event of Default shall then exist under the Senior Loan Documents, Mezzanine Lender may accept and retain payments (i) of any amounts (both current and delinquent) due and payable from time to time which Mezzanine Borrower is obligated to pay Mezzanine Lender (together with all prepayments and applicable fees, premiums and related charges not prohibited from being made) in accordance with the terms and conditions of the Mezzanine Loan Documents and (ii) made to Mezzanine Lender in accordance with the Senior Loan Cash Management Documents, and, in each case, Mezzanine Lender shall have no obligation to pay over to Senior Lender any such amounts. Notwithstanding the foregoing, nothing contained in this Agreement shall prohibit Mezzanine Lender from accepting payments from Mezzanine Borrower or any of its Affiliates (other than Borrower) to the extent that such payments are sourced from Mezzanine Borrower's or such Affiliate's own funds and are not directly or indirectly derived from the Premises or any other collateral for the Senior Loan or any proceeds thereof (it being understood and agreed that Mezzanine Lender shall in any event be entitled to retain funds sourced or derived from the Premises to the extent the same have previously been distributed to Borrower or Mezzanine Borrower provided such distribution did not violate any provision of the Senior Loan Documents); provided, however, that in the event Senior Lender and Mezzanine Lender each have claims or rights of collection with respect to any such Affiliate (including, without limitation, in pursuant to any guaranty), Mezzanine Lender's rights shall be subordinate to those of Senior Lender. If funds are deposited into the Mezzanine Lender's account for the Mezzanine Loan, or otherwise paid to Mezzanine Lender, Senior Lender agrees that, absent clear evidence of error, such amounts shall be deemed to have been properly paid to Mezzanine Lender and may be accepted and retained by Mezzanine Lender.

(c) Mezzanine Lender may (in its sole and absolute discretion without Senior Lender's consent) take any Equity Collateral Enforcement Action and/or Separate Collateral Enforcement Action which is permitted under Section 5 hereof; provided, however, that (i) Mezzanine Lender shall, prior to commencing any Equity Collateral Enforcement Action, give the Senior Lender written notice of the default which would permit Mezzanine Lender to commence any such Equity Collateral Enforcement Action, and (ii) Mezzanine Lender shall provide Senior Lender with copies of any and all material notices, pleadings, agreements, motions and briefs served upon, delivered to or with any party to any Equity Collateral Enforcement Action and otherwise keep Senior Lender reasonably apprised as to the status of any Equity Collateral Enforcement Action.

(d) In the event of a casualty to the buildings or improvements constructed on any portion of the Premises or a condemnation or taking under a power of eminent domain of all or any portion of the Premises, Senior Lender shall have a first and prior interest in and to any payments, awards, proceeds, distributions, or consideration arising from any such event (the "Award"). If the amount of the Award is in excess of all amounts owed to Senior Lender under the Senior Loan Documents, however, and either the Senior Loan has been paid in full or

Borrower is entitled to a remittance of same under the Senior Loan Documents other than to restore the Premises, such excess Award or portion to be so remitted to Borrower shall, to the extent not prohibited by the Senior Loan Documents, be paid to or at the direction of Mezzanine Lender, unless other Persons have claimed the right to such awards or proceeds, in which case Senior Lender shall only be required to provide notice to Mezzanine Lender of such excess Award and of any other claims thereto. In the event of any competing claims for any such excess Award, Senior Lender shall continue to hold such excess Award until Senior Lender receives an agreement signed by all Persons making a claim to the excess Award or a final order of a court of competent jurisdiction directing Senior Lender as to how and to which Person(s) the excess Award is to be distributed. Notwithstanding the foregoing, in the event of a casualty or condemnation, Senior Lender shall release the Award from any such event to the Borrower if and to the extent required by the terms and conditions of the Senior Loan Documents in order to repair and restore the Premises in accordance with the terms and provisions of the Senior Loan Documents. Any portion of the Award made available to the Borrower for the repair or restoration of the Premises shall not be subject to attachment by Mezzanine Lender.

Section 10. Rights of Subrogation; Bankruptcy.

(a) Each of Mezzanine Lender and Senior Lender hereby waives any requirement for marshaling of assets thereby in connection with any foreclosure of any security interest or any other realization upon collateral in respect of the Senior Loan Documents or the Mezzanine Loan Documents, as applicable, or any exercise of any rights of set-off or otherwise. Each of Mezzanine Lender and Senior Lender assumes all responsibility for keeping itself informed as to the condition (financial or otherwise) of Borrower, Mezzanine Borrower, the condition of the Premises and all other collateral and other circumstances and, except for notices expressly required by this Agreement, neither Senior Lender nor Mezzanine Lender shall have any duty whatsoever to obtain, advise or deliver information or documents to the other relative to such condition, business, assets and/or operations. Mezzanine Lender agrees that Senior Lender owes no fiduciary duty to Mezzanine Lender in connection with the administration of the Senior Loan and the Senior Loan Documents and Mezzanine Lender agrees not to assert any such claim. Senior Lender agrees that Mezzanine Lender owes no fiduciary duty to Senior Lender in connection with the administration of the Mezzanine Loan and the Mezzanine Loan Documents and Senior Lender agrees not to assert any such claim.

(b) No payment or distribution to Senior Lender pursuant to the provisions of this Agreement and no Protective Advance by Mezzanine Lender shall entitle Mezzanine Lender to exercise any right of subrogation in respect thereof prior to the payment in full of the Senior Loan Liabilities, and Mezzanine Lender agrees that, except with respect to the enforcement of its remedies under the Mezzanine Loan Documents permitted hereunder, prior to the satisfaction of all Senior Loan Liabilities it shall not acquire, by subrogation or otherwise, any lien, estate, right or other interest in any portion of the Premises or any other collateral now securing the Senior Loan or the proceeds therefrom that is or may be prior to, or of equal priority to, any of the Senior Loan Documents or the liens, rights, estates and interests created thereby.

(c) Subject to Section 30 of this Agreement, the provisions of this Agreement shall be applicable both before and after the commencement, whether voluntary or involuntary, of any case, proceeding or other action against Borrower under any existing or future law of any jurisdiction relating to bankruptcy, insolvency, reorganization or relief of debtors (a "Proceeding"). For as long as the Senior Loan shall remain outstanding, Mezzanine Lender shall not, and shall not solicit any person or entity to, and shall not direct or cause Mezzanine Borrower to direct or cause either the Borrower or any entity which Controls Borrower (the "Borrower Group") to: (i) commence any Proceeding; (ii) institute proceedings to have Borrower adjudicated a bankrupt or insolvent; (iii) consent to, or acquiesce in, the institution of bankruptcy or insolvency proceedings against Borrower (iv) file a petition or consent to the filing of a petition seeking reorganization, arrangement, adjustment, winding-up, dissolution, composition, liquidation or other relief by or on behalf of Borrower; (v) seek or consent to the appointment of a receiver, liquidator, assignee, trustee, sequestrator, custodian or any similar official for Borrower, the Premises (or any portion thereof) or any other collateral securing the Senior Loan (or any portion thereof); (vi) make an assignment for the benefit of any creditor of Borrower; (vii) seek to consolidate the Premises or any other assets of the Borrower with the assets of the Mezzanine Borrower or any member of the Borrower Group in any proceeding relating to bankruptcy, insolvency, reorganization or relief of debtors; or (viii) take any action in furtherance of any of the foregoing.

(d) If Mezzanine Lender is deemed to be a creditor of Borrower in any Proceeding (i) Mezzanine Lender hereby agrees that it shall not make any election, give any consent, commence any action or file any motion, claim, obligation, notice or application or take any other action in any Proceeding by or against the Borrower without the prior consent of Senior Lender, except to the extent necessary to preserve or realize upon Mezzanine Lender's interest in any or all of the Equity Collateral or Separate Collateral; provided, however, that any such filing shall not be as a creditor of the Borrower, (ii) Senior Lender may vote in any such Proceeding any and all claims of Mezzanine Lender, and Mezzanine Lender hereby appoints the Senior Lender as its agent, and grants to the Senior Lender an irrevocable power of attorney coupled with an interest, and its proxy, for the purpose of exercising any and all rights and taking any and all actions available to the Mezzanine Lender in connection with any case by or against the Borrower in any Proceeding, including without limitation, the right to file and/or prosecute any claims, to vote to accept or reject a plan, to make any election under Section 1111(b) of the Bankruptcy Code; provided, however, that with respect to any proposed plan of reorganization in respect of which creditors are voting, Senior Lender may vote on behalf of Mezzanine Lender only if the proposed plan would result in Senior Lender being "impaired" (as such term is defined in the United States Bankruptcy Code) and (iii) Mezzanine Lender shall not challenge the validity or amount of any claim submitted in such Proceeding by Senior Lender in good faith or any valuations of the Premises or other Senior Loan collateral submitted by Senior Lender in good faith, in such Proceeding or take any other action in such Proceeding, which is adverse to Senior Lender's enforcement of its claim or receipt of adequate protection (as that term is defined in the Bankruptcy Code). Senior Lender shall not have the rights provided herein if Senior Lender is an Affiliate of Borrower (other than by virtue of being the holder of any Certificates).

(e) To the extent any payment under the Mezzanine Loan Documents (whether by or on behalf of Mezzanine Borrower, as proceeds of security or enforcement of any right of setoff or otherwise) is declared to be fraudulent or preferential, set aside or required to be paid to a trustee, receiver or other similar party under any bankruptcy, insolvency, receivership or similar law, the Mezzanine Loan or part thereof originally intended to be satisfied shall for all purposes of this Agreement be deemed to be reinstated and outstanding as if such payment had not occurred.

Section 11. Rights of Cure.

(a) Prior to Senior Lender commencing any Enforcement Action under the Senior Loan Documents, Senior Lender shall provide written notice of the default which would permit the Senior Lender to commence such Enforcement Action to Mezzanine Lender and any Loan Pledgee entitled to notice thereof pursuant to Section 15 of this Agreement, whether or not Senior Lender is obligated to give notice thereof to Borrower (each, a "Senior Loan Default Notice") and shall permit Mezzanine Lender and any such Loan Pledgee an opportunity to cure such default in accordance with the provisions of this Section 11(a). If the default is a monetary default, Mezzanine Lender and Loan Pledgee shall have until five (5) days (with respect to Borrower's failure to make scheduled payments of principal and/or interest) and five (5) Business Days (with respect to any other monetary default) after the later of (A) receipt or deemed receipt from Senior Lender of the Senior Loan Default Notice in accordance with Section 18 of this Agreement and (B) the expiration of Borrower's cure provision, if any (a "Monetary Cure Period") to cure such monetary default; provided, however, in the event it elects to cure any such monetary default, Mezzanine Lender shall reimburse the Senior Lender for any interest on Protective Advances and/or advances for monthly payments of principal and/or interest on the Senior Loan made at the rate charged by Senior Lender for such interest on such advances pursuant to the applicable pooling and servicing agreement, if any. Mezzanine Lender shall not be required, in order to effect a cure hereunder other than the reimbursement of interest on advances for monthly payment of principal and/or interest on any Protective Advances, as aforesaid, to pay any default interest, late charges or any similar amounts under the Senior Loan Documents, and no default interest, late charges or any similar amounts shall accrue against Mezzanine Lender during the Monetary Cure Period. Mezzanine Lender shall not have the right to cure as hereinabove set forth with respect to monthly scheduled debt service payments on the Senior Loan for a period of more than six (6) consecutive months

446

unless Mezzanine Lender has commenced and is continuing to diligently pursue its rights against the Separate Collateral. If the default is of a non-monetary nature, Mezzanine Lender shall have until ten (10) Business Days after the later of (i) receipt or deemed receipt from Senior Lender of the Senior Loan Default Notice in accordance with <u>Section 18</u> of this Agreement and (ii) the same period of time as the Borrower under the Senior Loan Documents to cure such non-monetary default as if the first notice to Borrower of same was the date of giving of the Senior Loan Default Notice (if such date is after the date on which Borrower is so notified); provided, however, if such non-monetary default is susceptible of cure but cannot reasonably be cured within such period and if curative action was commenced within the applicable cure period and is being diligently pursued by Mezzanine Lender (or with respect to a non-monetary default that is not susceptible to cure without the foreclosure of its Equity Collateral or not susceptible to cure at all, if Mezzanine Lender shall be diligently pursuing the foreclosure of the Equity Collateral), Mezzanine Lender shall be given an additional period of time as is reasonably necessary for Mezzanine Lender in the exercise of due diligence to cure such non-monetary default (or to foreclose on the Equity Collateral, if the non-monetary default is not susceptible to cure without the foreclosure of the Equity Collateral or not susceptible to cure at all) for so long as (A) timely payments of Borrower's regularly scheduled monthly principal and/or interest payments under the Senior Loan and any other amounts due under the Senior Loan Documents are made, (B) such additional period of time does not exceed thirty (30) days, unless such non-monetary default is of a nature that can not be cured within such thirty (30) days, without ownership of the Equity Collateral or otherwise, in which case, Mezzanine Lender shall have such additional time as is reasonably necessary to cure such non-monetary default, (C) such default is not caused by a bankruptcy, insolvency or assignment for the benefit of creditors of Borrower and (D) during such non-monetary cure period (or such period during which Mezzanine Lender is pursuing foreclosure of the Equity Collateral in the case of defaults not susceptible of cure), there is no further material impairment to the value, use or operation of the Premises. Any additional cure period granted to the Mezzanine Lender hereunder shall automatically terminate upon the bankruptcy of the Borrower.

(b) To the extent that any Qualified Transferee acquires the Equity Collateral in accordance with the provisions and conditions of this Agreement, such Qualified Transferee shall acquire the same subject to the Senior Loan and the terms, conditions and provisions of the Senior Loan Documents for the balance of the term thereof, which shall not be accelerated by Senior Lender solely due to such acquisition and shall remain in full force and effect; provided, however, that (i) such Qualified Transferee shall have caused Borrower to reaffirm in writing, subject to such exculpatory provisions as shall be set forth in the Senior Loan Documents, all of the terms, conditions and provisions of the Senior Loan Documents on Borrower's part to be performed, other than those that cannot be performed by a transferee and do not materially impair the value, use or operation of the Premises, and (ii) all monetary defaults under the Senior Loan which remain uncured as of the date of such acquisition have been cured or waived by Senior Lender. Upon such acquisition, all non-monetary defaults under the Senior Loan that are not susceptible to being cured by such Qualified Transferee shall be deemed waived provided the same do not materially impair the value, use or operation of the Premises. Notwithstanding anything to the contrary in this Agreement, the Senior Loan Documents or the Mezzanine Loan Documents, no acquisition or other fee, charge, payment or similar amount shall be due in connection with such Qualified Transferee's acquisition of any direct or indirect interest in Borrower or the Premises as the result of an Equity Collateral Enforcement Action, a Separate Collateral Enforcement Action or other negotiated settlement in lieu of any of the foregoing.

(c) So long as no Continuing Senior Loan Event of Default shall exist under the Senior Loan Documents, all funds held and applied pursuant to the Senior Loan Documents, shall continue to be applied pursuant thereto and shall not be applied by Senior Lender to prepay outstanding principal balance of the Senior Loan.

Section 12. <u>No Actions; Restrictive Provisions.</u>

Senior Lender consents to Mezzanine Lender's right, pursuant to the Mezzanine Loan Documents, under certain circumstances, to cause the termination of the Property Manager. In the event both Mezzanine Lender and Senior Lender shall have such rights at any time, and Senior Lender shall fail to exercise such rights, Mezzanine Lender may exercise such rights, provided such exercise may be superseded by any subsequent exercise of such rights by Senior Lender pursuant to the Senior Loan Documents. Upon the occurrence of any event which would entitle Mezzanine Lender to cause the termination of the Property Manager pursuant to the Mezzanine Loan Documents, Mezzanine Lender shall have the right to select, or cause the selection, of a replacement property manager (including any asset manager) or leasing agent for the Premises, which replacement manager, asset manager and/or leasing agent shall either (a) be subject to Senior Lender's reasonable approval and, if any Certificates are then outstanding, be subject to a Rating Agency Confirmation or (b) be a Qualified Manager. Notwithstanding anything in this Section 12 to the contrary, if an Event of Default under the Senior Loan then exists or any other event shall have occurred pursuant to which Senior Lender has the right to select any replacement manager, asset manager and/or leasing agent pursuant to the Senior Loan Documents, Senior Lender shall have the sole right to select any replacement manager, asset manager and/or leasing agent, whether or not a new manager or agent was retained by Mezzanine Lender.

Section 13. Right to Purchase Senior Loan.

(a) If (i) the Senior Loan has been and continues to be accelerated, (ii) any Enforcement Action has been commenced and is continuing under the Senior Loan Documents, (iii) a monetary or a material non-monetary Event of Default under the Senior Loan Documents has occurred, (iv) the Senior Loan is a "specially serviced mortgage loan" under the applicable pooling and servicing agreement, or (v) Borrower has become a debtor in any Proceeding (each of the foregoing, a "Purchase Option Event"), upon ten (10) Business Days prior written notice to Senior Lender (the "Purchase Option Notice"), Mezzanine Lender (or its trustee or designee) shall have the right to purchase, in whole but not in part, the Senior Loan for a price equal to the sum of (x) the outstanding principal balance of the Senior Loan at the time of such purchase, together with all accrued and unpaid interest and other amounts due thereon (including, without limitation, any late charges, default interest, exit fees, advances and post petition interest) and (y) any Protective Advances made by or other costs and expenses incurred by Senior Lender in connection with the enforcement of the Senior Loan Documents that have not been reimbursed, together with interest charged thereon pursuant to the applicable pooling and serving agreement, if any (the "Loan Purchase Price"). If Mezzanine Lender notifies Senior Lender in a timely manner that it desires to purchase the Senior Loan by giving the Purchase Option Notice, the closing of such acquisition shall occur on the date ("Closing Date") designated by Mezzanine Lender which Closing Date shall occur not later than the earlier of (i) ten (10) Business Days after the date the Purchase Option Notice is received by Senior Lender or (ii) the Business Day preceding the date of any scheduled foreclosure sale under the Senior Loan Documents. Concurrently with payment to the Senior Lender of the Loan Purchase Price, Senior Lender shall deliver or cause to be delivered to the purchaser all Senior Loan Documents held by or on behalf of Senior Lender and will execute in favor of the purchaser assignment documentation, in form and substance reasonably acceptable to the purchaser, at the sole cost and expense of the purchaser to assign the Senior Loan and Senior Lender's rights under the Senior Loan Documents (without recourse, representations or warranties, except for representations as to (a) the power and authority of Senior Lender to transfer the Senior Loan, (b) the documentation that constitutes the Senior Loan Documents, (c) the outstanding balance of the Senior Loan, all other components constituting the Loan Purchase Price and the reserves held under the Senior Loan, and (d) Senior Lender's being the holder of and not having assigned, transferred, participated or encumbered its rights in the Senior Loan). The right of Mezzanine Lender to purchase the Senior Loan shall automatically terminate (i) upon a transfer of the Premises by foreclosure sale, sale by power of sale or, subject to the next proviso, delivery of a deed in lieu of foreclosure or (ii) if a Purchase Option Event ceases to exist. In addition to any and all other rights of Mezzanine Lender herein, if Borrower offers to deliver or actually delivers to Senior Lender a deed in lieu of foreclosure to the Premises (each, a "Deed in Lieu"), Senior Lender shall provide Mezzanine Lender not less than seven (7) Business Days written notice prior to accepting a Deed in Lieu to the Premises, and if Mezzanine Lender shall deliver a Purchase Notice to Senior Lender prior to the expiration of such seven (7) Business Day period Senior Lender shall not accept the Deed in Lieu to the Premises, provided that Mezzanine Lender pays the Loan Purchase Price to Senior Lender and acquires the Senior Loan as and when otherwise required under this Section 13. Senior Lender shall give Mezzanine Lender written notice of each Purchase Option Event (and of any transfer of title to the Premises to Senior Lender (or its designee)) promptly after Senior Lender obtains knowledge of same.

(b) Mezzanine Lender covenants not to enter any agreement with the Borrower or any

Affiliate thereof to purchase the Senior Loan pursuant to subsection (a) above or in connection with any refinancing of the Senior Loan in any manner designed to avoid or circumvent the provisions of the Senior Loan Documents which require the payment of a prepayment fee or yield maintenance charge in connection with a prepayment of the Senior Loan by the Borrower.

Section 14. Additional Understandings. For as long as the Mezzanine Loan remains outstanding:

(a) Notices of Transfer; Consent. Senior Lender promptly shall notify Mezzanine Lender if Borrower seeks or requests a release of all or any portion of the lien of the Senior Loan or seeks, or requests Senior Lender's consent, to take any action in connection with or in furtherance of a sale or transfer of all or any portion of the Premises, the granting of a further mortgage, deed of trust or similar encumbrance against all or any portion of the Premises, a prepayment or refinancing of the Senior Loan, any Transfer (as defined in the Mezzanine Loan Agreement) and any offer to purchase all or any portion of the Senior Loan by Borrower, any of its Affiliates or a Property Related Party. In the event of a request by the Borrower for Senior Lender's consent to either (i) the sale or transfer of all or any portion of the Premises, (ii) the granting of a further mortgage, deed of trust or similar encumbrance against all or any portion of the Premises, or (iii) any Transfer, Senior Lender shall, if Senior Lender has the right to consent, obtain the prior written consent of Mezzanine Lender prior to Senior Lender's granting of its consent or agreement thereto. Nothing contained in this paragraph is intended to limit or affect the rights granted to Mezzanine Lender under the Mezzanine Loan Documents.

(b) Annual Budget. The Mezzanine Lender shall have the right to approve the annual operating budget of Borrower in accordance with the terms of the Mezzanine Loan Documents. In the event the Mezzanine Lender objects to any such proposed budget, the Mezzanine Lender shall advise the Senior Lender of such objections, along with its suggestions for changes, within ten (10) days after its receipt of such budget in accordance with the Mezzanine Loan Documents. Senior Lender agrees to consult with the Mezzanine Lender with respect to such objections and suggestions but such consultation shall not be binding on Senior Lender. The Mezzanine Lender shall consent to any changes in the budget reasonably requested by the Senior Lender.

(c) Reserves and Escrows. If Senior Lender waives any reserves or escrow accounts under the Senior Loan Documents and such reserves or escrow accounts are also required under the Mezzanine Loan Documents, then Senior Lender acknowledges that Mezzanine Lender may require that Mezzanine Borrower (i) deposit such amounts that would have been deposited into any reserves or escrow accounts under the Senior Loan to be transferred to and deposited with Mezzanine Lender and (ii) enter into a cash management agreement with Mezzanine Lender substantially similar to the arrangement entered into by Borrower with Senior Lender at the closing of the Senior Loan.

Section 15. Financing of Mezzanine Loan.

(a) Notwithstanding any other provision hereof, Senior Lender consents to Mezzanine Lender's pledge (a "Pledge") of the Mezzanine Loan, the Mezzanine Loan Documents, and of the Separate Collateral (or any portion thereof) to any entity which has extended a credit facility to Mezzanine Lender that is a Qualified Transferee or a financial institution whose long-term unsecured debt is rated at least "A" (or the equivalent) or better by each Rating Agency (a "Loan Pledgee"), on the terms and conditions set forth in this Section 15(a); it being further agreed that a financing provided by a Loan Pledgee to Mezzanine Lender, or to an entity which owns, directly or indirectly, substantially all of the interests in Mezzanine Lender, and that is secured by Mezzanine Lender's interest in the Mezzanine Loan and is structured as a repurchase arrangement shall qualify as a Pledge, provided all applicable terms and conditions of this subsection (a) are complied with; and provided further that a Loan Pledgee which is not a Qualified Transferee may not take title to the Equity Collateral without a Rating Agency Confirmation. Upon written notice by Mezzanine Lender or any participant in the Mezzanine Loan to Senior Lender that the Pledge has been effected, Senior Lender agrees to acknowledge receipt of such notice and thereafter agrees: (a) to give Loan Pledgee written notice of any default by Mezzanine Lender under this Agreement of which default Senior Lender has actual knowledge; (b) to allow Loan Pledgee a period of ten (10) Business Days (in respect of a monetary default) and a period of thirty (30) days (in respect of a non-monetary default), in each case from receipt of such notice, to cure a default by Mezzanine Lender in respect of its obligations to Senior Lender hereunder, but Loan Pledgee shall not be obligated to cure any such default; (c) that no amendment, modification, waiver or termination of this Agreement shall be effective against Loan Pledgee without the written consent of Loan Pledgee, which consent shall not be unreasonably withheld; (d) that Senior Lender shall give to Loan Pledgee copies of any Senior Loan Default Notice simultaneously with the giving of same to the Mezzanine Lender and accept any cure thereof by Loan Pledgee made in accordance with the provisions of Section 11 of this Agreement as if such cure were made by the Mezzanine Lender; (e) that Senior Lender shall deliver to Loan Pledgee such estoppel certificate(s) as Loan Pledgee shall reasonably request, provided that any such estoppel certificate(s) shall be in the form contemplated by Section 19 and no such request shall be made more than once during any twelve month period and (f) that, upon written notice (a "Redirection Notice") to Senior Lender by Loan Pledgee that Mezzanine Lender is in default, beyond applicable cure periods, under Mezzanine Lender's obligations to Loan Pledgee pursuant to the applicable credit agreement between Mezzanine Lender and Loan Pledgee (which notice need not be joined in or confirmed by Mezzanine Lender), and until such Redirection Notice is withdrawn or rescinded by Loan Pledgee, Senior Lender shall remit to Loan Pledgee and not to Mezzanine Lender, any payments that Senior Lender would otherwise be obligated to pay to Mezzanine Lender from time to time pursuant to this Agreement, any Mezzanine Loan Document, any Senior Loan Document or any other agreement between Senior Lender and Mezzanine Lender that relates to the Senior Loan or the Mezzanine Loan. Mezzanine Lender hereby unconditionally and absolutely releases Senior Lender from any liability to Mezzanine Lender on account of Senior Lender's compliance with any Redirection Notice believed by Senior Lender to have been delivered by Loan Pledgee. Loan Pledgee shall be permitted to fully exercise its rights and remedies against Mezzanine Lender, and realize on any and all collateral granted by Mezzanine Lender to Loan Pledgee (and accept an assignment in lieu of foreclosure as to such collateral), in accordance with applicable law. In such event, the Senior Lender shall recognize Loan Pledgee (and any purchaser or transferee which is also a Qualified Transferee at any foreclosure or similar sale held by Loan Pledgee or any transfer in lieu of such foreclosure), and its successors and assigns, as the successor to Mezzanine Lender's rights, remedies and obligations under this Agreement and the Mezzanine Loan Documents and any such Loan Pledgee or Qualified Transferee shall assume in the writing the obligations of the Mezzanine Lender hereunder accruing from and after such Transfer and agrees to be bound by the terms and provisions hereof (it being agreed that, notwithstanding anything to the contrary contained herein, such Loan Pledgee shall not be required to so assume Mezzanine Lender's obligations hereunder prior to such realization on such collateral). The rights of Loan Pledgee under this Section 15 shall remain effective unless and until Loan Pledgee shall have notified the Senior Lender in writing that its interest in the Mezzanine Loan has terminated.

(b) Notwithstanding any provisions herein to the contrary, if a conduit ("Conduit") which is not a Qualified Transferee provides financing to Mezzanine Lender then such Conduit will be a permitted "Loan Pledgee" despite the fact it is not a Qualified Transferee if the following conditions are satisfied:

(i) The loan (the "Conduit Inventory Loan") made by the Conduit to Mezzanine Lender to finance the acquisition and/or holding of its interest in Mezzanine Loan will require a third party (the "Conduit Credit Enhancer") to provide credit enhancement;

(ii) The Conduit Credit Enhancer will be a Qualified Transferee;

(iii) The Mezzanine Lender will pledge its interest in the Mezzanine Loan to the Conduit as collateral for the Conduit Inventory Loan;

(iv) The Conduit Credit Enhancer and the Conduit will agree that, if Mezzanine Lender defaults under the Conduit Inventory Loan, or if the Conduit is unable to refinance its outstanding commercial paper even if there is no default by the Mezzanine Lender, the Conduit Credit Enhancer will purchase the Conduit Inventory Loan from the Conduit, and the Conduit will assign the pledge of the Mezzanine Lender's interest in the Mezzanine Loan to the Conduit Credit Enhancer; and

(v) Unless the Conduit is in fact then a Qualified Transferee, the Conduit will not, without obtaining a Rating Agency Confirmation, have any greater right to acquire the interests in the Mezzanine Loan, by foreclosure or otherwise, than would any other purchaser that is not a Qualified Transferee at a foreclosure sale conducted by a Loan Pledgee.

Section 16. <u>Intentionally Omitted</u>.

Section 17. <u>Obligations Hereunder Not Affected</u>.

(a) All rights, interests, agreements and obligations of Senior Lender and Mezzanine Lender under this Agreement shall remain in full force and effect irrespective of:

  (i) any lack of validity or enforceability of the Senior Loan Documents or the Mezzanine Loan Documents or any other agreement or instrument relating thereto;

  (ii) any taking, exchange, release or non-perfection of any other collateral, or any taking, release or amendment or waiver of or consent to or departure from any guaranty, for all or any portion of the Senior Loan or the Mezzanine Loan;

  (iii) any manner of application of collateral, or proceeds thereof, to all or any portion of the Senior Loan or the Mezzanine Loan, or any manner of sale or other disposition of any collateral for all or any portion of the Senior Loan or the Mezzanine Loan or any other assets of Borrower or Mezzanine Borrower or any other Affiliate of Borrower;

  (iv) any change, restructuring or termination of the corporate structure or existence of Borrower or Mezzanine Borrower or any other Affiliates of Borrower; or

  (v) any other circumstance which might otherwise constitute a defense available to, or a discharge of, Borrower, Mezzanine Borrower or a subordinated creditor or a Senior Lender subject to the terms hereof.

(b) This Agreement shall continue to be effective or be reinstated, as the case may be, if at any time any payment of all or any portion of the Senior Loan is rescinded or must otherwise be returned by Senior Lender or Mezzanine Lender upon the insolvency, bankruptcy or reorganization of Borrower or otherwise, all as though such payment had not been made.

Section 18. <u>Notices</u>. All notices, demands, requests, consents, approvals or other communications required, permitted, or desired to be given hereunder shall be in writing sent by facsimile (with answer back acknowledged) or by registered or certified mail, postage prepaid, return receipt requested, or delivered by hand or reputable overnight courier addressed to the party to be so notified at its address hereinafter set forth, or to such other address as such party may hereafter specify in accordance with the provisions of this <u>Section 18</u>. Any such notice, demand, request, consent, approval or other communication shall be deemed to have been received: (a) three (3) Business Days after the date mailed, (b) on the date of sending by facsimile if sent during business hours on a Business Day (otherwise on the next Business Day), (c) on the date of delivery by hand if delivered during business hours on a Business Day (otherwise on the next Business Day) and (d) on the next Business Day if sent by an overnight commercial courier, in each case addressed to the parties as follows:

To Mezzanine Lender:

_____
_____
_____

Attention:
Facsimile No.:

With a copy to:

_____
_____
_____

Attention:
Facsimile No.:

APPENDIX 1

To Senior Lender:

_____
_____
_____
_____

Attention:
Facsimile No.:

With a copy to:

_____
_____
_____

Attention:
Facsimile No.:

Section 19. Estoppel.

(a) Mezzanine Lender shall, within ten (10) Business Days following a request from Senior Lender, provide Senior Lender with a written statement setting forth the then current outstanding principal balance of the Mezzanine Loan, the aggregate accrued and unpaid interest under the Mezzanine Loan, and stating whether to Mezzanine Lender's knowledge any default or Event of Default exists under the Mezzanine Loan.

(b) Senior Lender shall, within ten (10) Business Days following a request from Mezzanine Lender, provide Mezzanine Lender with a written statement setting forth the then current outstanding principal balance of the Senior Loan, the aggregate accrued and unpaid interest under the Senior Loan, and stating whether to Senior Lender's knowledge any default or Event of Default exists under the Senior Loan.

Section 20. Further Assurances. So long as all or any portion of the Senior Loan and the Mezzanine Loan remains unpaid and the Senior Mortgage encumbers the Premises, Mezzanine Lender and Senior Lender will each execute, acknowledge and deliver in recordable form and upon demand of the other, any other instruments or agreements reasonably required in order to carry out the provisions of this Agreement or to effectuate the intent and purposes hereof.

Section 21. No Third Party Beneficiaries; No Modification. The parties hereto do not intend the benefits of this Agreement to inure to Borrower, Mezzanine Borrower or any other Person (other than the successors and permitted assigns of the parties hereto and any Loan Pledgees pursuant to Section 15). This Agreement may not be changed or terminated orally, but only by an agreement in writing signed by the party against whom enforcement of any change is sought. If any Certificates are outstanding, this Agreement shall not be amended unless a Rating Agency Confirmation has been obtained with respect to such amendment.

Section 22. Successors and Assigns. This Agreement shall bind all successors and permitted assigns of Mezzanine Lender and Senior Lender and shall inure to the benefit of all successors and permitted assigns of Senior Lender and Mezzanine Lender.

Section 23. Counterpart Originals. This Agreement may be executed in counterpart originals, each of which shall constitute an original, and all of which together shall constitute one and the same agreement.

Section 24. Legal Construction. In all respects, including, without limitation, matters of construction and performance of this Agreement and the obligations arising hereunder, this Agreement shall be governed by, and construed in accordance with, the internal laws of the State of New York applicable to agreements intended to be wholly performed within the State of New York.

Section 25. <u>No Waiver; Remedies</u>. No failure on the part of the Senior Lender or Mezzanine Lender to exercise, and no delay in exercising, any right hereunder shall operate as a waiver thereof, nor shall any single or partial exercise of any right hereunder preclude any other or further exercise thereof or the exercise of any other right. The remedies herein provided are cumulative and not exclusive of any remedies provided by law.

Section 26. <u>No Joint Venture</u>. Nothing provided herein is intended to create a joint venture, partnership, tenancy-in-common or joint tenancy relationship between or among any of the parties hereto.

Section 27. <u>Captions</u>. The captions in this Agreement are inserted only as a matter of convenience and for reference, and are not and shall not be deemed to be a part hereof.

Section 28. <u>Conflicts</u>. In the event of any conflict, ambiguity or inconsistency between the terms and conditions of this Agreement and the terms and conditions of any of the Senior Loan Documents or the Mezzanine Loan Documents, the terms and conditions of this Agreement shall control.

Section 29. <u>No Release</u>. Nothing herein contained shall operate to release Borrower from (a) its obligation to keep and perform all of the terms, conditions, obligations, covenants and agreements contained in the Senior Loan Documents or (b) any liability of Borrower under the Senior Loan Documents or to release Mezzanine Borrower from (x) its obligation to keep and perform all of the terms, conditions, obligations, covenants and agreements contained in the Mezzanine Loan Documents or (y) any liability of Mezzanine Borrower under the Mezzanine Loan Documents.

Section 30. <u>Continuing Agreement</u>. This Agreement is a continuing agreement and shall remain in full force and effect until the earliest of (a) payment in full of the Senior Loan, (b) transfer of the Premises by foreclosure of the Senior Mortgage or the exercise of the power of sale contained therein or by deed-in-lieu of foreclosure or similar agreement (except as provided in <u>Section 13(a)</u> above), (c) transfer of title to the Mezzanine Lender of the Equity Collateral, or (d) payment in full of the Mezzanine Loan; <u>provided, however</u>, that any rights or remedies of either party hereto arising out of any breach of any provision hereof occurring prior to such date of termination shall survive such termination.

Section 31. <u>Severability</u>. In the event that any provision of this Agreement or the application hereof to any party hereto shall, to any extent, be invalid or unenforceable under any applicable statute, regulation, or rule of law, then such provision shall be deemed inoperative to the extent that it may conflict therewith and shall be deemed modified to conform to such statute, regulation or rule of law, and the remainder of this Agreement and the application of any such invalid or unenforceable provisions to parties, jurisdictions or circumstances other than to whom or to which it is held invalid or unenforceable, shall not be affected thereby nor shall same affect the validity or enforceability of any other provision of this Agreement.

Section 32. <u>Expenses</u>.

(a) To the extent not paid by Borrower or out of or from any collateral securing the Senior Loan which is realized by Senior Lender, Mezzanine Lender agrees upon demand to pay to Senior Lender the amount of any and all reasonable expenses, including, without limitation, the reasonable fees and expenses of its counsel and of any experts or agents, which Senior Lender may incur in connection with the (i) exercise or enforcement of any of the rights of Senior Lender against Mezzanine Lender hereunder to the extent that Senior Lender is the prevailing party in any dispute with respect thereto or (ii) failure by Mezzanine Lender to perform or observe any of the provisions hereof.

(b) To the extent not paid by Mezzanine Borrower out of or from any collateral securing the Mezzanine Loan which is realized by Mezzanine Lender, Senior Lender agrees upon demand to pay to Mezzanine Lender the amount of any and all reasonable expenses, including, without limitation, the reasonable fees and expenses of its counsel and of any experts or agents, which Mezzanine Lender may incur in connection with the (i) exercise or enforcement of any of the rights of Mezzanine Lender against Senior Lender hereunder to the extent that Mezzanine

Lender is the prevailing party in any dispute with respect thereto or (ii) failure by Senior Lender to perform or observe any of the provisions hereof.

Section 33. Injunction. Senior Lender and Mezzanine Lender each acknowledge (and waive any defense based on a claim) that monetary damages are not an adequate remedy to redress a breach by the other hereunder and that a breach by either Senior Lender or Mezzanine Lender hereunder would cause irreparable harm to the other. Accordingly, Senior Lender and Mezzanine Lender agree that upon a breach of this Agreement by the other, the remedies of injunction, declaratory judgment and specific performance shall be available to such non-breaching party.

Section 34. Mutual Disclaimer.

(a) Each of Senior Lender and Mezzanine Lender are sophisticated lenders and/or investors in real estate and their respective decision to enter into the Senior Loan and the Mezzanine Loan is based upon their own independent expert evaluation of the terms, covenants, conditions and provisions of, respectively, the Senior Loan Documents and the Mezzanine Loan Documents and such other matters, materials and market conditions and criteria which each of Senior Lender and Mezzanine Lender deem relevant. Each of Senior Lender and Mezzanine Lender has not relied in entering into this Agreement, and respectively, the Senior Loan, the Senior Loan Documents, the Mezzanine Loan or the Mezzanine Loan Documents, upon any oral or written information, representation, warranty or covenant from the other, or any of the other's representatives, employees, Affiliates or agents other than the representations and warranties of the other contained herein. Each of Senior Lender and Mezzanine Lender further acknowledges that no employee, agent or representative of the other has been authorized to make, and that each of Senior Lender and Mezzanine Lender have not relied upon, any statements, representations, warranties or covenants other than those specifically contained in this Agreement. Without limiting the foregoing, each of Senior Lender and Mezzanine Lender acknowledges that the other has made no representations or warranties as to the Senior Loan or the Mezzanine Loan or the Premises (including, without limitation, the cash flow of the Premises, the value, marketability, condition or future performance thereof, the existence, status, adequacy or sufficiency of the leases, the tenancies or occupancies of the Premises, or the sufficiency of the cash flow of the Premises, to pay all amounts which may become due from time to time pursuant to the Senior Loan or the Mezzanine Loan).

(b) Each of Senior Lender and Mezzanine Lender acknowledges that the Senior Loan and the Mezzanine Loan Documents are distinct, separate transactions and loans, separate and apart from each other.

Section 35. Venue. Any legal suit, action or proceeding against Senior Lender or Mezzanine Lender arising out of or relating to this Agreement shall be instituted in any federal or state court in New York, and Senior Lender and Mezzanine Lender waives any objection which it may now or hereafter have to the laying of venue of any such suit, action or proceeding, and Senior Lender and Senior Mezzanine Lender hereby irrevocably submits to the jurisdiction of any such court in any suit, action or proceeding.

Section 36. NO TRIAL BY JURY. Each of the parties hereto, to the fullest extent that they may lawfully do so, hereby waives trial by jury in any action or proceeding brought by any party hereto with respect to this Agreement or the matters covered hereby.

IN WITNESS WHEREOF, Senior Lender and Mezzanine Lender have executed this Agreement as of the date and year first set forth above.

SENIOR LENDER:

[_____],

a [_____]

By:_____

Name:

Title:

MEZZANINE LENDER:

[_____],

a [_____]

By:_____

Name:

Title:

EXHIBIT A

(Legal Description)

EXHIBIT B

Senior Loan Documents

EXHIBIT C

Mezzanine Loan Documents

EXHIBIT D

Permitted Fund Managers

Westbrook Partners
DLJ Real Estate Capital Partners
iStar Financial Inc.
Capital Trust
Lend-Lease Real Estate Investments
Archon Capital, L.P.
Whitehall Street Real Estate Fund, L.P.
The Blackstone Group International Ltd.
Apollo Real Estate Advisors
Colony Capital, Inc.
Praedium Group
J.E. Robert Companies
Fortress Investment Group, LLC
Lonestar Opportunity Fund
Clarion Partners
Walton Street Capital, LLC
Starwood Financial Trust
BlackRock, Inc.

DATED_____

_____

AS ISSUER

_____

AS FACILITY AGENT, CASH MANAGER, BORROWER SECURITY TRUSTEE AND

_____

AS SERVICER

_____

AS SPECIAL SERVICER

_____

AS NOTE TRUSTEE

_____

AS SUBORDINATED LENDERS[1]

_____

SERVICING AGREEMENT

_____

160 Queen Victoria Street, London EC4V 4QQ
Tel: 020 7184 7000 Fax: 020 7184 7001

_____

[1] This form agreement contemplates a multi-loan pool, with some loans having related subordinate tranches.

Appendix 2

TABLE OF CONTENTS

European Servicing Agreement

THIS SERVICING AGREEMENT (the "**Agreement**") is dated as of_____20___ (the "**Closing Date**"),

BETWEEN:

_____, a _____ having its registered office at _____ (the "**Issuer**");

_____, acting through its office at _____ as facility agent under the Facility Agreement (the "**Facility Agent**", and which expression will, without limitation, include any successor facility agent);

_____, acting through its office at _____ as cash manager (the "**Cash Manager**", and which expression will, without limitation, include any successor cash manager);

_____, acting through its office at _____ as security trustee (the "**Borrower Security Trustee**", and which expression will, without limitation, include any such successor security trustee);

_____, acting through its office at _____ as note trustee (the "**Note Trustee**", which expressions will respectively include, without limitation, any successor note trustee);

_____, acting through its office at _____ as subordinated lender (the "**Subordinated Lender**", which expressions will respectively include, without limitation, any subordinated lender that accedes to the relevant Intercreditor Deed and this Agreement);

_____, acting through its office at _____ as servicer (the "**Servicer**", and which expression will, without limitation, include any successor servicer); and

_____, acting through its office at _____ as special servicer (the "**Special Servicer**", which expression shall, without limitation, include any successor special servicer).

WHEREAS

(A) Pursuant to a Loan Sale Agreement dated on or about the date hereof (the "**Closing Date**"), _____ (the "**Originator**") has agreed to sell and the Issuer has agreed to purchase the Originator's right, title, interest and benefit in and to the Mortgage Loans on the Closing Date as well as the Originator's corresponding interest in the Related Security.

(B) Upon the acquisition by the Issuer of the Mortgage Loans and its Related Security the Issuer will charge or assign by way of security to the Note Trustee, amongst other things, its interest in the Mortgage Loans and its interest in the Related Security as security for, among other things, its obligations in relation to the issue of the Notes.

(C) The Subordinated Lenders shall purchase the Subordinated Loans and upon the relevant purchase, shall enter into the applicable Intercreditor Deed. Pursuant to the Intercreditor Deeds, the rights of each Subordinated Lender in respect of its Subordinated Loan shall be subordinated to the interests of the Issuer under the related Senior Loan.[2]

(D) The Servicer is willing to act on behalf of the Issuer, the Subordinated Lender, the Facility Agent, the Borrower Security Trustee, and the Note Trustee as servicer of the Mortgage Loans, Whole Mortgage Loans and the Related Security in the ordinary course of business, and the Special Servicer is willing to act on behalf of the parties as aforesaid as special servicer of the Mortgage Loans, Whole Mortgage Loans and the

---

[2] If the securitization transaction involves one or more Subordinated Lenders whose rights are detailed in one or more Intercreditor Deeds, then language such as this will often be a part of the servicing agreement.

Related Security following the occurrence of a Servicing Transfer Event, in consideration of their receipt of the Servicing Fee and the Special Servicing Fee (each defined herein), respectively, and the other amounts set forth herein, on the terms set forth in this Agreement.

1. **DEFINITIONS AND INTERPRETATION**

Unless otherwise defined in this Servicing Agreement or the context requires otherwise, words and expressions used in this Servicing Agreement have the meanings and constructions ascribed to them in the Additional Definitions Schedule set out in Schedule 1 attached hereto.

2. **APPOINTMENT OF THE SERVICER AND THE SPECIAL SERVICER**

2.1. Each of the Servicer and the Special Servicer is hereby appointed by the Issuer and the Note Trustee to act as its agent and to exercise all of the rights, powers and discretions as Lender and the Note Trustee in relation to the Mortgage Loans and Whole Mortgage Loans and to perform the other services specified in this Agreement on the terms and subject to the conditions set forth in this Agreement.

2.2. Each of the Servicer and Special Servicer is hereby appointed by the Issuer to exercise all of the Issuer's rights, powers and discretions under the related Intercreditor Deeds on the terms or subject to the conditions set forth in this Agreement. For the avoidance of doubt, to the extent that an Intercreditor Deed expressly grants a right or power to a Subordinated Lender, such Subordinated Lender shall continue to exercise that right or power on its own behalf and shall not, by this Agreement, delegate the same to the Servicer or the Special Servicer.[3]

2.3. Each of the Servicer and the Special Servicer is hereby appointed by the Facility Agent to exercise all of the rights, powers and discretions given to the Facility Agent (expressly or impliedly) by, under or pursuant to the Facility Agreement and to perform the other services specified in this Agreement on the terms and subject to the conditions set forth in this Agreement.

2.4. Each of the Servicer and the Special Servicer is hereby appointed by the Borrower Security Trustee to exercise all of the rights, powers and discretions given to the Borrower Security Trustee by, under or pursuant to the Finance Documents and to perform the other Services specified in this Agreement on the terms and subject to the conditions set forth in this Agreement. Notwithstanding the foregoing, the Borrower Security Trustee shall remain as the legal owner of the Related Security and shall continue to exercise any rights, powers and discretions which may only be exercised by the legal owner of the Related Security provided that the Borrower Security Trustee shall only exercise such rights, powers and discretions in accordance with the instructions of the Servicer or the Special Servicer (which shall be given in accordance with the requirements of this Agreement).

2.5. Each appointment made by the Issuer, the Borrower Security Trustee and the Facility Agent of the Servicer and of the Special Servicer in relation to the Mortgage Loans shall take effect immediately upon the transfer to the Issuer of the Mortgage Loans on the Closing Date. The appointment made by a Subordinated Lender shall take effect on the transfer of such Subordinated Loan to the Subordinated Lender and entry by the Subordinated Lender into the related Intercreditor Deed.

2.6. Each of the Servicer and the Special Servicer accepts the appointments made by the Issuer, the Subordinated Lenders, the Facility Agent and the Borrower Security Trustee made pursuant to this Clause 2, to perform the duties and obligations as set out herein (together, the "**Services**") such appointments to take effect immediately upon the execution of this Agreement.

---

[3] If the securitization transaction involves one or more Subordinated Lenders, then language such as this, providing for the ability of the Servicer or Special Servicer to exercise the Issuer's rights under the relevant Intercreditor Deeds, will often be a part of the servicing agreement.

3. **SERVICING STANDARD**

3.1.   Each of the Servicer and the Special Servicer shall exercise all rights, powers and discretions relating to the Mortgage Loans, Whole Mortgage Loans and the Related Security which have been delegated to it by the Issuer, the Subordinated Lenders, the Facility Agent and/or the Borrower Security Trustee and all other services to be provided by it under this Agreement in accordance with and subject to the Servicing Standard.

3.2.   The "**Servicing Standard**" shall mean diligent servicing and administration or special servicing, as applicable, of the Mortgage Loans and Whole Mortgage Loans pursuant to the Servicing Agreement in the best interests of and for the benefit of the holders of the Notes and related Subordinated Lenders as a collective whole, taking into account the subordinated nature of the Subordinated Loans, in accordance with applicable law, the terms of the Finance Documents, any relevant Intercreditor Deed, and the terms of this Agreement, and to the extent consistent with the foregoing, in accordance with the customary and usual standards of practice prudent commercial mortgage lenders servicing their own mortgage loans, with a view to the timely collection of all sums due in respect of the Mortgage Loans or Whole Mortgage Loans, or if a Mortgage Loan or Whole Mortgage Loan comes into default, the maximization of value on the present value basis of the Mortgage Loan or Whole Mortgage Loan as determined by the Servicer or the Special Servicer, as applicable, in its reasonable judgment.

3.3.   Without prejudice to any of its other obligations under this Agreement (including, without limitation, Clause 3.2), the Servicer or, if at the relevant time any Mortgage or Whole Mortgage Loan is a Specially Serviced Mortgage Loan, the Special Servicer, shall perform all duties which the relevant Intercreditor Deed provides are to be performed by the Servicer or, as the case may be, the Special Servicer.

3.4.   In applying the Servicing Standard, neither the Servicer nor the Special Servicer shall have regard to:

3.4.1.   any fees or other compensation to which the Servicer or the Special Servicer are entitled;

3.4.2.   any relationship the Servicer or the Special Servicer or any of their respective affiliates may have with any party to the transaction entered into in connection with the Notes or with any Borrower or any affiliate of any Borrower;

3.4.3.   the ownership of any Note or any interest in a Subordinated Loan by the Servicer or Special Servicer or any affiliate thereof; and/or

3.4.4.   the ownership of any interest in the Notes or a Subordinated Loan by the Servicer or the Special Servicer. Each of the Servicer or Special Servicer may become the owner or otherwise hold an interest in respect of the Notes or a Subordinated Loan with the same rights as each would have if it were not the Servicer or Special Servicer, as the case may be.

4. **PERFORMANCE OF THE SERVICES**

The Servicer will service and administer the Mortgage Loans and Whole Mortgage Loans and will render the Services provided for herein (including without limitation those provided for in Clauses 5, 6, 7, and 21 hereof), in accordance with the Servicing Standard. The Special Servicer will specially service any Mortgage Loan or Whole Mortgage Loan while it is a Specially Serviced Mortgage Loan and will render the Services as are provided for herein, in accordance with the Servicing Standard.

4.1.   Subject to the provisions of this Agreement, the Servicer or, as applicable, the Special Servicer (while any Mortgage Loan or Whole Mortgage Loan is a Specially Serviced Mortgage Loan) will:

4.1.1.   have full power and authority, acting alone, to exercise the rights and powers of the Issuer, the Facility Agent and the Borrower Security Trustee under the Finance Documents in performing their respective duties in relation to the Mortgage Loans, Whole Mortgage Loans and the Related Security under this

Agreement and to do or cause to be done any and all things in connection with such duties or obligations which it may deem necessary or desirable; and

4.1.2. conduct all communications and dealings with the Borrower in relation to all matters concerning the Mortgage Loans, Whole Mortgage Loans and the Related Security, including, without limitation, the giving of any notices, consents or approvals on behalf of the Issuer, the Subordinated Lenders, the Facility Agent or the Borrower Security Trustee under or in relation to the Finance Documents.

4.2. In all dealings referred to in Clause 4.1, the Servicer or the Special Servicer, as applicable, will make it clear that it is acting as servicer or special servicer, as applicable, of the Mortgage Loans, the Whole Mortgage Loans the Related Security and related matters for and on behalf of the Issuer, the Facility Agent and/or the Borrower Security Trustee, as appropriate.

4.3. Nothing in this Agreement or in any power of attorney granted in furtherance of this Agreement will be construed:

4.3.1. so as to give the Servicer or the Special Servicer any powers, rights, authorities or discretions relating to the operating and financial policies of the Issuer, and the Servicer and the Special Servicer hereby acknowledge that all such powers, rights, authorities and discretions are, and will at all times remain, vested in the Issuer and its directors; or

4.3.2. except as contemplated pursuant to the Issuer Deed of Charge, to permit the Servicer or the Special Servicer to dispose of the Mortgage Loans, Whole Mortgage Loans or any of the Related Security on behalf of the Issuer or the Note Trustee.

4.4. In order to enable the Servicer and the Special Servicer to perform the Services on behalf of the Issuer, the Subordinated Lenders, the Facility Agent and the Borrower Security Trustee:

4.4.1. the Issuer will deliver to each of the Servicer and the Special Servicer on or before the Closing Date a power of attorney;

4.4.2. each Subordinated Lender will deliver to each of the Servicer and the Special Servicer on or before the Closing Date a power of attorney;

4.4.3. the Borrower Security Trustee will deliver to each of the Servicer and the Special Servicer on or before the Closing Date, a power of attorney;

4.4.4. the Note Trustee will deliver to each of the Servicer and the Special Servicer on or before the Closing date, a power of attorney; and

4.4.5. the Facility Agent will deliver to each of the Servicer and the Special Servicer on or before the Closing Date, a power of attorney.

5. PAYMENTS, OTHER COLLECTIONS AND INTEREST RATES

5.1. On each loan payment date under each of the Facility Agreements, the Servicer will calculate, and will in accordance with the Facility Agreements, procure the withdrawal from the applicable Borrower accounts of all amounts due from the Borrower to the Lender under the Facility Agreements. All amounts withdrawn from such accounts under this Clause 5.1 will be deposited into the Collection Account, *provided, however*, that if the loan is a Whole Mortgage Loan, then all amounts so withdrawn in relation to that Whole Mortgage Loan will be deposited into the related accounts for that Whole Mortgage Loan in accordance with the relevant Intercreditor Deed whereupon amounts paid to the Issuer under such Intercreditor Deed will be transferred to the Collection Account.

5.2. If the Servicer or the Special Servicer receives any money whatsoever arising from the Mortgage Loans or Whole Mortgage Loans, subject to Section 5.1 such money shall be paid or otherwise transferred to the Issuer, the relevant Subordinated Lenders, the Borrower Security Trustee or the Note Trustee for onward payment into the Collection

Account pursuant to this Agreement or any Transaction Document. Until such time as the money is paid as aforesaid, the Servicer or Special Servicer, as appropriate, will hold such money on trust for the Issuer, the Borrower Security Trustee or the Note Trustee, as the case may be, and will keep such money separate from all other money belonging to the Servicer or Special Servicer.

6.   **SWAP AGREEMENT**

6.1. Upon receiving notification from a Borrower that it intends to prepay all or any part of a Mortgage Loan or Whole Mortgage Loan the Servicer will seek confirmation from the relevant swap provider as to:

6.1.1. the amount of swap termination payments (if any) that would be payable to or by the Issuer or related Subordinated Lender if the relevant swap transaction was to be terminated (in whole or in part) on that day in order to take account of such prepayment; and

6.1.2. the amount of any Break Adjustment to be applied to the Mortgage Loan or Whole Mortgage Loan, assuming that the Mortgage Loan or Whole Mortgage Loan, as applicable, was to be repaid (in full or in the amount specified by the related Borrower) on that day.

The Servicer shall advise the Borrower of the amount of the Break Adjustment notified to the Servicer pursuant to this Clause 6.1 and shall, upon receiving confirmation that the prepayment will proceed as notified by the related Borrower, make the necessary adjustments to the redemption statement provided to the related Borrower.

6.2. Upon being notified by the Issuer that a swap agreement has terminated (whether because of a Rating Agency downgrade of the swap provider or otherwise) the Servicer shall provide to the Issuer such assistance as the Issuer may reasonably require in order to comply with its obligations under the Transaction Documents relating to the pro-curement of a replacement swap agreement. The Issuer shall reimburse, subject to the Priority of Payments, the Servicer for all out-of-pocket costs and expenses incurred by it in performing its duties under this Clause 6.2.

6.3. Upon any reduction in the principal amount outstanding of any Mortgage Loan or Whole Mortgage Loan and at any other time upon reasonable request by the swap provider, the Servicer shall notify the swap provider and the Issuer and any related Subordinated Lender of the principal amount outstanding under that Mortgage Loan or Whole Mortgage Loan.

7.   **INSURANCE AND HEADLEASES**

7.1. The Servicer will establish, administer and maintain procedures to monitor compliance by the Borrower with the requirements of the Facility Agreement relating to insurance. The Special Servicer will provide to the Servicer all information then in its possession or control relating to the Specially Serviced Mortgage Loan that may reasonably be required and requested by the Servicer in order to enable the Servicer to monitor compliance by the Borrower under the Specially Serviced Mortgage Loan with its obligations relating to insurance. The Servicer will use reasonable efforts to procure that all insurance policies are maintained in the form, in the amounts and with insurers as required under the relevant Facility Agreement.

7.2. The Servicer will not knowingly take any action or omit to take any action which would result in the avoidance, termination or non-renewal of any insurance policy or which would reduce the amount payable on any claim thereunder.

7.3. Each of the Servicer and Special Servicer shall at all times during the term of this Agreement keep in force a policy or policies of insurance covering loss occasioned by the errors, acts and omissions of its officers, employees and agents in connection with its servicing obligations hereunder, which policy or policies shall be in such form and amount as may be required by the Rating Agencies, from time to time. Each Servicer shall be deemed to have complied with the foregoing provisions if an affiliate thereof has such insurance and, by the terms of such policy or policies, the coverage afforded thereunder extends to the Servicer or the Special Servicer, as the case may be.

7.4. Notwithstanding the foregoing, for so long as the long-term debt obligations of the Servicer or the Special Servicer, as the case may be, are rated at least "A" by S&P, "A1" by Moody's and "A" by Fitch (or any lower rating as will not result in an Adverse Rating Event, as evidenced in writing by each Rating Agency then rating the Notes), such entity may self-insure with respect to the risks described in Clause 7.3.

7.5. Headlease; Prevention of Forfeiture

7.5.1 To the extent that it receives the relevant information, the Servicer shall:

a. maintain accurate records with respect to each related Property reflecting the status of any rents payable in respect of any Headlease; and

b. make enquiries to confirm, from time to time, the payment of such items.

7.5.2 The Servicer shall use efforts consistent with the Servicing Standard to monitor the compliance of, and, to the extent reasonably practicable, to cause the Borrowers (subject to any requirements of the related Facility Agreements) to make payments in respect of rents payable pursuant to any Headlease at the time they first become due and, in any event, prior to the institution of enforcement or forfeiture or similar proceedings with respect to the related Mortgaged Property for non-payment of such items. Subject to sub-Clause 7.5.3 below, the Servicer or Special Servicer, as applicable, shall in respect of such unpaid rent, make a Property Protection Drawing or, at the Servicer's or Special Servicer's absolute discretion, a Property Protection Advance pursuant to Clause 8 below.

7.5.3 Notwithstanding the provisions of sub-Clause 7.5.2 above, neither the Servicer nor the Special Servicer shall pay or be required to instruct the payment of any amount or take any action pursuant to this Clause 7.5 if, in its reasonable opinion, acting in accordance with the Servicing Standard, the expense of making such payment and/or taking such action would not be to the benefit of the Noteholders and any related Subordinated Lender as a collective whole (taking into account the subordinate nature of the Subordinated Loan).

7.5.4 Except as otherwise set forth herein, if the landlord exercises its right of forfeiture (or any equivalent proceedings) under any relevant Headlease, the Servicer or the Special Servicer will, on behalf of the Issuer apply for relief against such forfeiture if the Issuer holds a legal mortgage over the property. For the avoidance of doubt, if the Servicer or Special Servicer obtains such relief, the new lease will be granted in favour of the Issuer (or its designee) who will be directly responsible for such lease.

8. PROPERTY PROTECTION ADVANCES

8.1. In the event a Borrower fails to pay certain amounts to third parties, such as insurers and persons providing services in connection with the operation of the Mortgaged Properties (and there are insufficient funds available in the Borrower's accounts to pay it), and

8.1.1. the relevant Facility Agreement entitles the lender to pay or discharge the obligation to the third party,

8.1.2. the relevant Facility Agreement requires the Borrower to reimburse the lender for any payments so made,

8.1.3. the Servicer or Special Servicer is satisfied that such amounts will, in addition to all other amounts due, be recoverable from the relevant Borrower, and

8.1.4. the Servicer or, as the case may be, the Special Servicer, is otherwise satisfied that it would be in accordance with the Servicing Standard to do so,

then the Servicer or Special Servicer may make arrangements to ensure that the relevant payment is made (any such payment being a "**Property Protection Advance**").

8.2. If the Servicer or the Special Servicer (as the case may be) decides in its sole discretion to do so, it may (but shall have no obligation to) make a Property Protection Advance from its own funds. If the Servicer or the Special Servicer makes a Property Protection Advance from its own funds, it will be repaid, in priority to the Notes and subject to the Priority of Payments together with interest thereon at the Reimbursement Rate on the Distribution Date immediately following the date on which such Property Protection Advance was made. Alternatively, the Servicer or the Special Servicer (as the case may be) may instruct the Issuer or Cash Manager, as applicable, to make a Property Protection Drawing under the Liquidity Facility.

8.3. The Servicer or, if at the relevant time any Mortgage Loan is a Specially Serviced Mortgage Loan, the Special Servicer, shall from time to time use all reasonable endeavors consistent with the Servicing Standard to ensure that an amount equal to all Property Protection Advances is, in addition to all other sums then due under the Finance Documents, recovered from the Borrower. The Servicer or the Special Servicer (as the case may be) shall ensure that any amount from time to time recovered from the Borrower as contemplated in this Clause 8.3 shall forthwith be deposited into the Collection Account.

9. MODIFICATIONS, WAIVERS, AMENDMENTS AND CONSENTS

9.1. The Servicer or, if any Mortgage Loan or Whole Mortgage Loan is a Specially Serviced Mortgage Loan, the Special Servicer will be responsible for responding to requests by a Borrower for consent to modifications, waivers or amendments relating to the relevant Facility Agreement and the other Finance Documents, or grant any consent requested by a Borrower under the Finance Documents.

[To the extent required by the related Intercreditor Deed, neither the Servicer nor the Special Servicer will be permitted at any time during its appointment hereunder to consent to any change to the margin, maturity date or principal balance of a Whole Mortgage Loan without the consent of the relevant Subordinated Lender (the "**Subordinated Lender Veto Rights**") and, notwithstanding any other provision of this Agreement, neither the Servicer nor the Special Servicer will be liable for the consequences of failing to take any action in respect of which such consent is sought above pending receipt of the Subordinated Lender's consent, *provided always* that in no circumstances shall the Servicer or the Special Servicer follow any direction of any Subordinated Lender if such action would contradict the Servicing Standard and none of the above rights of the Subordinated Lender shall prevent the Special Servicer from completing any enforcement action, or otherwise realizing upon the security for the related Whole Mortgage Loan in connection with any action otherwise taken in accordance with the Servicing Agreement other than to the extent limited by the provisions set forth under Clause 12 (*Operating Advisor*) below. [4]]

9.2. In issuing any consent or agreeing to any modification or waiver of the Finance Documents, the Servicer or Special Servicer must comply with the requirements of Clause 12.

9.3. Except as otherwise set forth herein, the Servicer and the Special Servicer may not consent to any request by the Borrower for consent under, or to waive, modify or amend the terms of, any Facility Agreement or the other Finance Documents unless the following conditions are satisfied:

9.3.1. the consent, modification, waiver or amendment would be in accordance with the Servicing Standard; and

---

[4] When subordinated lenders are involved in a securitization transaction, they often possess additional consent rights to significant loan modifications and this bracketed language providing for Subordinated Lender Veto Rights may be added to the servicing agreement. These rights may also be contained in the Intercreditor Deed, and may terminate upon a significant decrease in the value of the Related Security.

9.3.2.   the granting of such consent, modification, waiver or amendment would not result in an Adverse Rating Event.

9.4.   The Servicer or the Special Servicer (for as long as any Mortgage Loan or Whole Mortgage Loan is a Specially Serviced Mortgage Loan) may, without any Rating Agency Confirmation:

(A)   consent to the Mortgaged Property being subject to an easement or right-of-way for utilities, access, parking, public improvements or another purpose, provided the Servicer or Special Servicer (as the case may be) shall have determined in accordance with the Servicing Standard that such easement or right-of-way shall not materially interfere with the then-current use of the Mortgaged Property, or the security intended to be provided by the Finance Documents, the Borrower's ability to repay a Mortgage Loan or Whole Mortgage Loan, or materially or adversely affect the value of the Mortgaged Property;

(B)   grant waivers of minor covenant defaults (other than financial covenants) including late financial statements;

(C)   grant releases of non-material parcels of a Mortgaged Property (provided that if the Finance Documents expressly require such releases upon the satisfaction of certain conditions, such release shall be made as required by the Finance Documents); and

(D)   consent to any request for a consent, modification, waiver or amendment that the Servicer or the Special Servicer, as applicable, determines would not result in a material modification to the terms of any Mortgage Loan or Whole Mortgage Loan,

provided that any such consent, modification, waiver or amendment:

9.4.2.   would be consistent with the Servicing Standard; and

9.4.3.   would not violate the terms, provisions or limitations of this Agreement or any other Transaction Document.

9.5.   The Servicer or, if any Mortgage Loan or Whole Mortgage Loan is a Specially Serviced Mortgage Loan, the Special Servicer may agree to any request by the Borrower to provide a consent if the provisions of the relevant Finance Document require such consent to be granted subject to certain conditions being satisfied provided that the Servicer or the Special Servicer, as applicable, is acting in accordance with the Servicing Standard.

9.6.   The Servicer or, if any Mortgage Loan or Whole Mortgage Loan is a Specially Serviced Mortgage Loan, the Special Servicer may modify or amend the terms of the Mortgage Loan or Whole Mortgage Loan in order to:

9.6.1.   cure any ambiguity or mistake therein; or

9.6.2.   correct or supplement any provisions therein which may be inconsistent with any other provisions therein,

provided that, in each case, to do so would be in accordance with the Servicing Standard.

9.7.   Where necessary following any consent, waiver or modification, the Servicer will liaise with the swap provider with a view to arranging for the Issuer to amend its existing hedging arrangements to cause the Issuer to be hedged in a manner consistent with the hedging arrangements effected on the Closing Date.

9.8.   Each of the Servicer and the Special Servicer will execute on behalf of the Issuer, any related Subordinated Lender, the Facility Agent and/or the Borrower Security Trustee any documents necessary in order to effect any consent, modification, waiver or amendment pursuant to this Clause 9. The Issuer, any related Subordinated Lender, the Facility Agent and/or the Borrower Security Trustee will give further or other authority as may be reasonably requested by the Servicer or the Special Servicer for the purpose of giving a consent or modifying or waiving any provision of the Finance Documents pursuant to this Clause 9.

9.9.   If the relevant Borrower has failed to repay a Mortgage Loan or Whole Mortgage Loan, as applicable, on the relevant loan maturity date, then except as otherwise set forth in this Agreement, the Special Servicer may grant an extension of the relevant loan maturity date where the following conditions are satisfied:

9.9.1.   the Special Servicer will have commenced discussions with the Borrower for the sale of the Mortgaged Property or the refinancing of the Mortgage Loan or Whole Mortgage Loan, as applicable, and the Special Servicer has determined, acting in accordance with the Servicing Standard, that the Borrower has a credible plan to refinance or liquidate the Mortgaged Property;

9.9.2.   the Borrower is not in material breach of any of the covenants under the Finance Documents (except for the breach with respect to the repayment of the Mortgage Loan or Whole Mortgage Loan, as applicable, at the expiry of its term); and

9.9.3.   Special Servicer determines, acting in accordance with the Servicing Standard, that the likely recovery on the Mortgage Loan or Whole Mortgage Loan, as applicable, on a net present value basis, will be higher by allowing an extension of the Mortgage Loan or Whole Mortgage Loan, as applicable, rather than enforcing the Mortgage Loan or Whole Mortgage Loan, as applicable, and the Related Security,

provided that the Special Servicer shall not be authorised to extend the Mortgage Loan or Whole Mortgage Loan maturity date to a date which falls later than the date falling two calendar years before the maturity date of the Notes unless the granting of such consent, modification, waiver or amendment will not result in an Adverse Rating Event.

9.10.   The Servicer or, if any Mortgage Loan or Whole Mortgage Loan is a Specially Serviced Mortgage Loan, the Special Servicer shall, as a condition to granting any request by the Borrower for consent, modification, amendment or waiver in accordance with this Clause 9, require that the Borrower pay any related out-of-pocket costs and expenses (including, but not limited to, all reasonable legal fees incurred by the Servicer or the Special Servicer, as applicable, in connection therewith) provided that to do so would be in accordance with the Servicing Standard. If such costs and expenses are recovered from the Borrower prior to the Distribution Date immediately following the date on which they are incurred, the Issuer may pay, subject in the case of the Issuer to the Priority of Payments, the same to the Servicer or, as the case may be, the Special Servicer in order to discharge the Issuer's obligations to the Servicer or Special Servicer in relation to such costs and expenses under this Clause 9.

9.11.   Provided that the Servicer, or, as the case may be, the Special Servicer determines that it would not be inconsistent with the Servicing Standard to do so, it may require that the Borrower pay a reasonable and customary fee which may be charged in addition to any out of pocket costs and expenses in consideration for the performance of Services by or on behalf of the Issuer, the Facility Agent or the Borrower Security Trustee in connection with any waivers or amendments made to any Finance Documents or any consents issued thereunder (a "**Restructuring Fee**") to the Servicer, or, if at any relevant time the Mortgage Loan or Whole Mortgage Loan is a Specially Serviced Mortgage Loan to the Special Servicer, prior to agreeing to any waiver or modification of the Finance Documents or issuing any consent thereunder. If a Restructuring Fee is charged to and recovered from the Borrower, such Restructuring Fee shall, on receipt, be paid to the Servicer or, if at the relevant time the Mortgage Loan or Whole Mortgage Loan is a Specially Serviced Mortgage Loan, the Special Servicer. For the avoidance of doubt, in no circumstances shall the Issuer have any obligation to pay any Restructuring Fee if it has not first been recovered from the Borrower, nor shall the Servicer or the Special Servicer be entitled to charge a Restructuring Fee if to do so would be inconsistent with the Servicing Standard.

9.12.   The Servicer or, if the Mortgage Loan or Whole Mortgage Loan is a Specially Serviced Mortgage Loan, the Special Servicer will notify the Issuer (for onward transmission to the Noteholders), the Borrower Security Trustee, the Rating Agencies, the Facility Agent, the Special Servicer (if applicable), any related Subordinated Lender and the

471

Note Trustee in writing of any consent, modification, extension, waiver or amendment of any term of any Mortgage Loan or Whole Mortgage Loan to which it has agreed. Such notice will include the date of the consent, modification, waiver or amendment and any fees, costs and expenses charged to the Borrower. The Servicer will retain for deposit or, in the case of a Specially Serviced Mortgage Loan, the Special Servicer will promptly provide to the Servicer for deposit in the related Servicing File, an executed counterpart of the agreement relating to such consent, modification, waiver or amendment promptly following execution and delivery thereof. Upon reasonable prior written notice to the Servicer, copies of each agreement by which any consent, modification, waiver or amendment of any term of any Finance Documents has been effected will be available for review during normal business hours at the offices of the Servicer.

10.   SPECIAL SERVICING TRANSFER EVENTS

10.1.   Upon determining that a Special Servicing Transfer Event has occurred, the Servicer will, as soon as is reasonably practicable, give written notice thereof to the Issuer (for onward transmission to the Noteholders), the Borrower Security Trustee, the Operating Advisor, the Note Trustee, any related Subordinated Lender and the Special Servicer whereupon the Facility will become a "**Specially Serviced Mortgage Loan**", provided, however in the case of a Whole Mortgage Loan, if the Special Servicer Transfer Event arises as a result of the non-payment of principal or interest by a Borrower and the related Subordinate Lender has made a cure payment which makes good the shortfall that would otherwise be caused by such non-payment or if the applicable cure period has not expired, the relevant Whole Mortgage Loan shall not become a Specially Serviced Mortgage Loan.

10.2.   The Special Servicer may conclusively rely on any determination by the Servicer that a Special Servicing Transfer Event has occurred.

10.3.   Upon a Mortgage Loan or Whole Mortgage Loan becoming a Specially Serviced Mortgage Loan, the Servicer will deliver a copy of the related Mortgage File to the Special Servicer and will use reasonable efforts to provide the Special Servicer with all information, documents (or copies thereof) and records (including records stored electronically on computer tapes, magnetic discs and the like) relating to the Mortgage Loan or Whole Mortgage Loan either in the Servicer's or any of its directors', officers', employees', affiliates' or agents' possession or control or otherwise available to the Servicer without undue burden or expense, and reasonably requested by the Special Servicer, to enable it to assume its functions.

10.4.   The Servicer will use reasonable efforts to comply with the requirements of Clause 10.3 within three business days of the appointment of the Special Servicer and within three business days of any later request of the Special Servicer; provided however, that if the information, documents and records requested by the Special Servicer are not contained in the Mortgage Files, the Servicer will have such period of time as reasonably necessary to make such delivery.

10.5.   Upon compliance with the requirements of Clause 10.3, the obligations of the Servicer to perform those duties in relation to that Mortgage Loan or Whole Mortgage Loan which according to the terms of this Agreement shall, after the occurrence of a Servicing Transfer Event, be undertaken by the Special Servicer, will terminate (in each case until such time (if any) that the Mortgage Loan or Whole Mortgage Loan becomes a Corrected Mortgage Loan), and the obligations of the Special Servicer to specially service the Mortgage Loan or Whole Mortgage Loan as set out in this Agreement will commence.

10.6.   The Special Servicer will not be liable or in default hereunder for any reasonable act or failure to act arising out of the Servicer's failure to deliver information, documents or records with respect to a Specially Serviced Mortgage Loan in accordance with the requirements of this Agreement.

10.7.   Upon determining that a Specially Serviced Mortgage Loan has become a Corrected Mortgage Loan, the Special Servicer will promptly give written notice thereof to the Issuer (for onward transmission to the Noteholders), the Operating Advisor (if appointed), the Borrower Security Trustee, the Note Trustee, any related Subordinated Lender and the Servicer, and will within five business days of such determination return the related Servicing File, together with any and all new information, documents and records which have become part of the Servicing File, to the Servicer (or such other person as may be directed by the Servicer). Upon compliance with the preceding sentence, the Special Servicer's obligation to specially service the Mortgage Loan or Whole Mortgage Loan and its right to receive the Special Servicing Fee will terminate (in each case until such time (if any) that the Mortgage Loan or Whole Mortgage Loan once more becomes a Specially Serviced Mortgage Loan) and the obligations of the Servicer which had been transferred to the Special Servicer with respect to the Mortgage Loan or Whole Mortgage will resume. The Servicer will not be liable or in default hereunder for any reasonable act or failure to act arising out of the Special Servicer's failure to deliver information, documents or records with respect to a Corrected Mortgage Loan in accordance with the requirements of this Clause 10.7.

10.8. Notwithstanding any of the foregoing provisions of this Clause 10, after a Mortgage Loan or Whole Mortgage Loan becomes a Specially Serviced Mortgage Loan, the Servicer will continue to service the Mortgage Loan or Whole Mortgage Loan in all respects as provided for in this Agreement other than in respect of those duties which are contemplated to be performed by the Special Servicer, and shall, among other things and without limitation, continue to collect information, prepare reports and perform administrative functions (but will not be responsible for any special servicing functions and will not be entitled to receive the Special Servicing Fee with respect thereto).

10.9. The Special Servicer shall, not later than thirty (30) days after the occurrence of a Servicing Transfer Event in relation to any Mortgage Loan or Whole Mortgage Loan, use reasonable efforts to obtain a valuation by an independent valuer (being a member of the Royal Institution of Chartered Surveyors) of the Mortgaged Property. The costs of obtaining such a valuation will be paid by the Special Servicer, subject to being reimbursed by the Issuer in accordance with and subject to the Priority of Payments. However the Special Servicer will not be obliged to obtain such a valuation if a valuation has been obtained during the immediately preceding 12 months and the Special Servicer is of the opinion (without any liability on its part) that neither the Mortgaged Property nor the relevant property markets have experienced any material change since the date of such previous valuation.

10.10. Following receipt of the valuation report, the Special Servicer will determine whether or not an Appraisal Reduction applies to the Mortgage Loan or Whole Mortgage Loan secured by the Mortgaged Property so valued and shall notify the other parties hereto, any related Subordinated Lender and the Liquidity Facility Provider thereof forthwith.

11. ENFORCEMENT OF THE MORTGAGE LOAN

11.1. If the Servicer determines, in its discretion (which shall be applied in accordance with the Servicing Standard) that a Mortgage Loan event of default has occurred, the Servicer will forthwith give notice pursuant to the Facility Agreement to the Borrower and any other party as required under the relevant Finance Documents, with a copy to the Issuer, the Note Trustee, the Borrower Security Trustee, any related Subordinated Lender, the Special Servicer, and Operating Advisor, if applicable.

11.2. Each of the Servicer or, once a Servicing Transfer Event has occurred, the Special Servicer is hereby authorized by the Issuer, the Borrower Security Trustee and the Facility Agent to determine, in accordance with the Servicing Standard, the best strategy for exercising the rights, powers and discretions of the Issuer, the Facility Agent and the Borrower Security Trustee following the occurrence of a Mortgage Loan event of default.

11.3. To the extent that the Issuer is required under any applicable Intercreditor Deed, the Servicer or Special Servicer, as applicable, shall give notice of a Mortgage Loan event of default to any relevant Subordinated Lender and shall provide reasonable assistance to that relevant Subordinated Lender if such Subordinated Lender chooses to tender any cure.

11.4. With respect to any Whole Mortgage Loan, the Servicer or the Special Servicer, as applicable, shall promptly provide notice to the relevant Subordinated Lender and the Rating Agencies of the occurrence of a Purchase Event with respect to the related Senior Loan. The Servicer or the Special Servicer, as applicable, is authorised to take all action, and is required to take all action requested by the related Subordinated Lender (acting reasonably) in order to permit the related Subordinated Lender to exercise its right under the related Intercreditor Deed to acquire the related Senior Loan. If, pursuant to its rights under the related Intercreditor Deed, the respective Subordinated Lender notifies the Servicer or the Special Servicer, as applicable, that it intends to acquire the Senior Loan pursuant to the terms of the Intercreditor Deed, the Servicer or the Special Servicer, as applicable, shall calculate the purchase price of the relevant Senior Loan, based upon the calculation prescribed in the related Intercreditor Deed. The Servicer or the Special Servicer, as applicable, will notify the related Subordinated Lender of such purchase price, which the Subordinated Lender will be required to pay on the next loan payment date. All reasonable costs and expenses (including legal fees) incurred by the Servicer or the Special Servicer, as applicable, in connection with this Clause 11.3 shall be paid by the relevant Subordinated Lender to the Servicer or Special Servicer, as applicable, on completion of the relevant purchase. If the purchase price is not paid by the Subordinated Lender on or before such loan payment date, the Servicer or the Special Servicer, as applicable, will be required to recalculate the amount for the next following loan payment date. Upon payment by the Subordinated Lender of such purchase price, the Servicer, the Special Servicer, the Issuer, Borrower Security Trustee and the Note Trustee, as applicable, will take all action necessary to assign the related Senior Loan and the Related Security as directed by the related Subordinated Lender. The relevant Subordinated Loan will be deemed not to be a Specially Serviced Mortgage Loan (and accordingly no Special Servicing Fee shall accrue thereon) at any time during which the related Subordinated Lender is exercising its right under the related Intercreditor Deed to acquire the related Senior Loan.

11.5. Pending receipt of a satisfactory environmental report, the Servicer or the Special Servicer, as applicable, will use their best efforts to ensure that no action will be taken in relation to the Mortgaged Property if, as a result of such action, the Issuer, any related Subordinated Lender, the Borrower Security Trustee or the Facility Agent could be considered to be an owner or operator of such Mortgaged Property within the meaning of any applicable law.

11.6. As soon as the Special Servicer makes a Final Recovery Determination with respect to the Mortgage Loan or Whole Mortgage Loan it will promptly notify the Servicer, the Issuer and the Cash Manager (and, to the extent that such Final Recovery Determination is in respect of a Whole Mortgage Loan, the relevant Subordinated Lender) of the amount of such Final Recovery Determination. The Special Servicer will maintain accurate record of the Final Recovery Determination (if any) and the basis of determination thereof.

11.7. Each of the Servicer and the Special Servicer (for so long as the Mortgage Loan or Whole Mortgage Loan is a Specially Serviced Mortgage Loan) will procure that in relation to the Mortgage Loan, Whole Mortgage Loan and the Related Security if, after enforcement of such Related Security, an amount in excess of all sums due from the Borrower under the Facility Agreement is recovered or received, the balance (after discharge of all such sums) is paid to the person entitled thereto.

12. OPERATING ADVISOR

12.1. In relation to any Mortgage Loan or Whole Mortgage Loan, the Controlling Party will be entitled to appoint an Operating Advisor to represent their interests and shall notify the Servicer and the Special Servicer of the appointment thereof. The Operating Advisor shall have a duty of care only to the Controlling Party (as applicable).

12.2. Except as otherwise set forth herein, the Servicer or Special Servicer will not: for at least 5 business days, after notifying an Operating Advisor (if any has been appointed) of its intention to do so, agree to waive or amend any Finance Document relevant to any

Mortgage Loan or Whole Mortgage Loan in relation to which such Operating Advisor has been appointed if the effect of such waiver or amendment would be to:

1. make an amendment to the relevant Facility Agreement which would result in the extension or shortening of the final maturity date;

2. modify the interest rate on all or any part thereof;

3. modify the amount or timing of any payment of interest or principal;

4. forgive any interest or principal;

5. make any further advance;

6. agree to the release of any Mortgaged Property from the security created by the relevant Related Security and/or to the substitution of any Mortgaged Property that secures the relevant Mortgage Loan or Whole Mortgage Loan, with any other Mortgaged Property (other than in circumstances which are contemplated by the relevant Facility Agreement);

7. release the relevant Borrower from its obligations;

8. agree to the further encumbrance of any assets which secure the relevant Mortgage Loan or Whole Mortgage Loan;

9. waive or reduce any prepayment fee, late payment charge or default interest;

10. confirm to the relevant Borrower the amount of breakage costs or prepayment fees payable on a redemption (in whole or in part);

11. cross-default the relevant Mortgage Loan or Whole Mortgage Loan to any other indebtedness of the relevant Borrower;

12. approve any material capital expenditure;

13. agree to the modification in any material respect of any Headlease by which any Borrower holds an interest in a Mortgaged Property;

14. agree to change any reporting requirements under the relevant Facility Agreement;

15. consent to the creation of any mezzanine debt of any direct or indirect owner of the relevant Borrower that would be paid from distributions of net cash flows from any Mortgaged Property;

16. accept any insurance company or underwriter pursuant to the relevant Facility Agreement;

17. consent to the grant of any new occupational lease or the modification or termination of any existing occupational lease unless in accordance with the relevant Loan Documents or, as the circumstances require, as determined by the Servicer or the Special Servicer acting in accordance with the Servicing Standard, consent cannot be unreasonably withheld or delayed;

18. commence formal enforcement proceedings in respect of any Related Security for the repayment of the relevant Mortgage Loan or Whole Mortgage Loan, including the appointment of a receiver or administrator or similar or analogous proceedings;

19. take any action to remedy an environmental problem at any relevant Mortgaged Property;

20. waive any Mortgage Loan event of default;

21. approve a restructuring plan in insolvency of the relevant Borrower;

22. defer interest on all or any part of the relevant Mortgage Loan or Whole Mortgage Loan for more than ten (10) business days;

23. modify any provision of the relevant Facility Agreement relating to the rights of a relevant lender to assign its interest therein; or

475

24. modify any provision of the relevant Loan Documents relating to any of the following:

   (1) reserve requirements;

   (2) rent collection;

   (3) cash management;

   (4) financial covenants;

   (5) hedging requirements;

   (6) insurance requirements;

   (7) the basis on which all or any part of the security for the relevant Mortgage Loan or Whole Mortgage Loan may be released or substituted;

   (8) the basis on which all or any of the Borrowers may be released from their obligations under the relevant Loan Documents; and

   (9) the basis on which further encumbrances of any relevant Mortgaged Property may be created.

12.3. If the Issuer (or the Servicer on behalf of the Issuer) has notified the Special Servicer of the appointment of an Operating Adviser, the Special Servicer must notify the Operating Advisor and the Borrower Security Trustee in writing in advance of any action it intends to take with regard to the matters set out in 12.2 above and must take due account of the advice and representations of the Operating Advisor, although if the Special Servicer determines that immediate action is necessary to protect the interest of the Noteholders, the Special Servicer may take whatever action it reasonably considers necessary without waiting for the Operating Advisor's response, provided that the Special Servicer acts in accordance with the Servicing Standard. If the Special Servicer does take such action and the Operating Advisor objects in writing to the actions taken within five (5) business days after being notified of the action and being provided with all reasonably requested information, the Special Servicer must take due account of the advice and representations made by the Operating Advisor regarding any further steps that it considers should be taken. The Operating Advisor will be considered not to have objected to any action taken by the Special Servicer without the prior consultation with the Operating Advisor if the Operating Advisor does not object within five (5) business days of receiving such notice.

12.4. The Special Servicer will not be obliged to consult further with the Operating Advisor in respect of any actions to be taken by the Special Servicer with respect to any Specially Serviced Mortgage Loan if:

   12.4.1. the Special Servicer has, as provided in subclause 12.3, notified the Operating Advisor in writing of various actions that the Special Servicer proposes to take with respect to the Specially Serviced Mortgage Loan; and

   12.4.2. for thirty (30) days following the notice, the Operating Advisor has objected to all of those proposed actions and has failed to suggest any alternative actions that the Special Servicer considers to be consistent with the Servicing Standard.

12.5. Upon reasonable request, the Special Servicer will provide the Operating Advisor with any information in the Special Servicer's possession with respect to any matter regarding any Specially Serviced Mortgage Loan, including its reasons for determining to take a proposed action and such information will also be promptly provided upon written request, in a written format, to the Issuer, the Borrower Security Trustee and the Note Trustee. However, the Special Servicer may require the Operating Advisor to execute a confidentiality agreement, in a form acceptable to the Special Servicer and the Operating Advisor, with respect to any such information that is, by its terms, confidential.

12.6. If the Issuer (or the Servicer on behalf of the Issuer) has notified the Special Servicer of the appointment of an Operating Advisor, the Special Servicer will notify the Operating Advisor of any release or substitution of any Related Security for the Specially Serviced

Mortgage Loan even if such release or substitution is in accordance with the provisions of the Finance Documents.

12.7. Notwithstanding anything herein to the contrary, no advice, direction or objection from or by the Operating Advisor may (and the Servicer or Special Servicer will ignore and act without regard to any such advice, direction or objection) require or cause the Servicer or Special Servicer to violate any applicable law or any other provision of this Agreement, the Facility Agreement, the Finance Documents, any applicable Intercreditor Deed or to service the Mortgage Loan or Whole Mortgage Loan, if applicable, other than in accordance with the Servicing Standard.

12.8. The Operating Advisor will have no liability to the Issuer, the Borrower Security Trustee, the Facility Agent, or the Note Trustee for any action taken, or for refraining from the taking of any action, in good faith pursuant to this Agreement, or for errors in judgement.

12.9. Furthermore, without prejudice to the Servicer and the Special Servicer's obligations to act in accordance with the Servicing Standard and/or its obligation to take action in circumstances where this clause requires it do so, neither the Servicer nor the Special Servicer will be liable for the consequences of any delay caused by the compliance with their obligations under this clause relating to consultation with the Operating Advisor.

13. APPOINTMENT OF SUB-CONTRACTORS OR DELEGATES

13.1. The Servicer and the Special Servicer may enter into sub-servicing agreements to provide for the performance by third parties of any or all of its respective obligations hereunder, provided that, in each case:

13.1.1. the Servicer or the Special Servicer, as the case may be, will use reasonable skill and care in the selection of any sub-servicer;

13.1.2. if the arrangements involve the custody or control of any files, deeds, policies or other material documents relating to Mortgage Loans, Whole Mortgage Loans or the Related Security for the purpose of performing any sub-contracted or delegated Services, the sub-Servicer or the sub-Special Servicer, as the case may be, has executed an acknowledgement to the effect that all such files, deeds, policies and other material documents are and will be held to the order of the Issuer or the Borrower Security Trustee, as the case may be, prior to the serving by the Note Trustee of a Note Acceleration Notice and thereafter to the order of the Note Trustee;

13.1.3. prior to the commencement of the proposed arrangement, any such sub-servicer has executed a written waiver of any Encumbrance (present or future) which has arisen or which may arise in connection with such delegated Services (to the extent that such Encumbrance relates to any of the Related Security or the Issuer Security);

13.1.4. the Servicer and the Special Servicer will procure that no sub-servicer will be entitled to sub-contract or delegate the performance of all or any of the Services sub-contracted or delegated to it by the Servicer or, as the case may be, the Special Servicer without the prior written consent of the Servicer or, as the case may be, the Special Servicer;

13.1.5. the entry into of such sub-servicing agreements will be in conformity with all applicable laws and regulations, including, without limitation, any applicable data protection legislation or license, consent or registration required to carry out the Services;

13.1.6. in the event of any breach in the performance of the obligations of the Servicer or the Special Servicer (as applicable) by a sub-servicer then, if such breach is not remedied or if such sub-servicer is not terminated, by the Servicer or the Special Servicer (as applicable), within 30 days of the earlier of the Servicer or the Special Servicer becoming aware of the breach (or such shorter period which if exceeded would result in a Note event of default) and receipt by the Servicer or the Special Servicer (as applicable) of written notice from the Issuer, the Borrower Security Trustee or the Note Trustee requiring the same to be remedied, such breach will be treated as a breach of this Agreement by the Servicer or the Special Servicer (as applicable);

13.1.7. where the sub-servicing arrangements referred to in the foregoing provisions of this Clause 13 involve or may involve the receipt by the sub-servicer of any money arising from any Mortgage Loan or Whole Mortgage Loan, which money is to be paid or otherwise transferred to the Issuer, the Borrower Security Trustee or the Note Trustee or any related Subordinated Lender or into the Collection Account pursuant to this Agreement or any other Transaction Document, the Servicer or the Special Servicer will arrange for the sub-servicer, as the case may be, to acknowledge that such sub-servicer will hold such money on trust for the Issuer, the Borrower Security Trustee or the Note Trustee or any related Subordinated Lender, as the case may be, and that such money is subject to a security interest in favor of the Note Trustee and Secured Parties and will keep such money separate from all other money belonging to such sub-servicer and will promptly following receipt thereof pay the same into the Collection Account;

13.1.8. any sub-servicing arrangements do not lead to an Adverse Rating Event;

13.1.9. the appointment of such sub-servicer will not cause the Issuer to become subject to any tax which it would not otherwise have become subject to, either directly or indirectly, or would not cause the imposition of any withholding tax; and

13.1.10. subject to Clause 13.2, the fees, costs, charges and expenses of any such appointment will be borne by the Servicer or the Special Servicer (as applicable).

13.2. If the Servicer or the Special Servicer appoints a lawyer, banker, valuer, surveyor, broker, auctioneer, financial adviser, securities dealer, investment bank, computer consultant or other expert or professional adviser to perform some of the obligations of the Servicer or the Special Servicer (as applicable) under this Agreement pursuant to Clause 13.3, then Clause 13.1.10 will not apply to the engagement of such person and the costs, charges and expenses payable to or incurred by such person will be reimbursed to the Servicer or the Special Servicer (as applicable) pursuant to Clause 17.

13.3. Each of the Servicer and the Special Servicer may, in relation to its authorities, rights, powers, duties and discretions conferred or imposed by or referred to in this Agreement or by operation of law, act on the opinion or advice of, or a certificate or any information obtained from any lawyer, banker, valuer, surveyor, broker, auctioneer, accountant, financial adviser, securities dealer, investment bank, computer consultant or other expert or professional adviser (whether obtained by the Servicer, the Special Servicer, its sub-servicer, the Issuer, the Note Trustee or the Borrower) provided in relation to any of such persons, it will use reasonable care in the selection of the foregoing and will not, provided that it will not have acted fraudulently or negligently in the selection of the foregoing, be responsible for any loss occasioned by so acting; any such opinion, advice, certificate or information may be sent or obtained by letter or facsimile and each of the Servicer and the Special Servicer will not be liable for acting on any opinion, advice, certificate or information purporting to be so conveyed although the same will contain some error or will not be authentic, provided that such error or lack of authenticity will not be manifest.

13.4. Notwithstanding any sub-contract or delegation of the performance of any of their obligations under this Agreement pursuant to this Clause 13 (but without prejudice to Clause 13.3 or Clause 13.1.10, neither the Servicer nor the Special Servicer will thereby be released or discharged from any liability hereunder and each will remain responsible for the performance of its duties and obligations under this Agreement and the performance or non-performance or the manner of performance of any sub-servicer of any of the Services will not affect the Servicer's or the Special Servicer's duties or obligations under this Agreement.

13.5. Upon request from the Issuer and/or the Note Trustee and with effect from the date of occurrence of any event referred to in Clause 13.6 below, the Servicer and the Special Servicer agree to assign to the Issuer and the Note Trustee any rights which the Servicer or the Special Servicer may have against any sub-servicer arising from the performance of the Services by such sub-servicer.

13.6. The events referred to in Clause 13.5 above are that:

13.6.1. the Note Trustee has delivered a notice terminating the appointment of the Servicer or the Special Servicer pursuant to Clause 24.1;

13.6.2. the Servicer and/or the Special Servicer has delivered a notice of voluntary termination pursuant to Clause 24.2; or

13.6.3. by reason of failure by any sub-servicer to properly perform its obligations the Servicer or the Special Servicer is in breach of its obligations under this Agreement and such breach could reasonably be expected, in the sole opinion of the Note Trustee, to have a material adverse effect in respect of the Mortgage Loans, the Whole Mortgage Loans and the Related Security and the Servicer or the Special Servicer is not pursuing such rights as it may have against such sub-servicer to the reasonable satisfaction of the Note Trustee or has failed to pursue such rights within 30 days of receipt of notice from the Note Trustee requiring it to do so.

13.7. The Servicer and the Special Servicer, for the benefit of the Issuer, any related Sub-ordinated Lender, the Facility Agent, the Borrower Security Trustee and the Note Trustee, will, at their own cost and expense, monitor the performance and enforce the obligations of their respective sub-servicers under the related sub-servicing agreements. Such enforcement, including the legal prosecution of claims, termination of sub-servicing agreements in accordance with their respective terms and the pursuit of other appropriate remedies, will be in such form and carried out to such an extent and at such time as the Servicer or the Special Servicer, in their good faith business judgement, would require were it the beneficial owner of the Mortgage Loan or Whole Mortgage Loan if applicable.

14. NO LIABILITY

14.1. Neither the Servicer nor the Special Servicer will have any liability for any obligation of the Borrower under any Facility Agreement or with respect to the Related Security, and nothing in this Agreement will constitute a guarantee, or similar obligation, by the Servicer or the Special Servicer of the Mortgage Loans or Whole Mortgage Loan if applicable or the Related Security or any other obligation of any Borrower.

14.2. Without prejudice to the obligations of the Servicer and the Special Servicer to the Issuer, the Facility Agent, the Borrower Security Trustee and the Note Trustee under this Agreement and other Transaction Documents to which the Servicer and the Special Servicer, respectively, are a party, neither the Servicer nor the Special Servicer will have any liability to any third party for the obligations of the Issuer, the Facility Agent, the Borrower Security Trustee, the Note Trustee or of any other party to the Transaction Documents under any of the Transaction Documents or any related Subordinated Lender and nothing herein will constitute a guarantee, or similar obligation, by the Servicer or the Special Servicer of the Issuer, the Facility Agent, the Borrower Security Trustee, the Note Trustee or any other party in respect thereof.

14.3. Except as is expressly set out in this Agreement, neither the Servicer nor the Special Servicer will at any time lend or provide any sum to the Issuer.

14.4. The Servicer and the Special Servicer will have no liability whatsoever to the Issuer, the Facility Agent, the Borrower Security Trustee, the Note Trustee, the Noteholders or any other person for any failure by the Issuer to make any payment due by it under the Notes or any of the Transaction Documents unless such failure by the Issuer results from a direct failure by the Servicer or the Special Servicer, as the case may be, to perform its obligations under this Agreement in accordance with the terms hereof.

14.5.   Neither the Servicer nor the Special Servicer shall be liable to any person for the breach by the other of their respective obligations under this Agreement.

14.6.   Subject to Clause 22.2, the Issuer (in the manner set forth herein) shall indemnify and hold harmless the Servicer or, as the case may be, the Special Servicer against any liabilities, actions, proceedings, claims, demands and properly incurred costs or expenses which the Servicer or the Special Servicer may have incurred in consequence of this Agreement or as a result of the performance of the functions and services provided for hereunder, and except as a result of a breach by the Servicer or Special Servicer of a representation given hereunder, or the negligence, willful default, dishonesty or fraud of the Servicer or the Special Servicer, as applicable. This indemnity shall expressly inure to the benefit of any current or future director, officer, employee or agent of the Servicer or the Special Servicer and to the benefit of any successor of the Servicer or the Special Servicer (as applicable) hereunder and shall survive the termination of this Agreement. Notwithstanding any other provision contained herein, the Servicer or Special Servicer may refrain from taking any action or incurring any costs or expenses unless indemnified to their satisfaction by the Issuer.

14.7.   The Issuer agrees to pay to the Servicer or the Special Servicer (as applicable) an amount equal to any stamp, documentary, transfer, excise, registration, filing and other similar duties, levies, fees, taxes, assessments, imposts, deductions, charges and withholdings to which the Servicer or the Special Servicer may be subject as a result of the performance by the Servicer or the Special Servicer (as applicable) of its obligations under this Agreement other than any tax assessed on the Servicer or the Special Servicer (as applicable) in respect of its overall net income (and taxes imposed in lieu thereof) or in respect of which an amount is payable under Clause 17.

15.   REDEMPTION OF THE MORTGAGE LOAN

15.1.   Subject to the terms of the relevant Issuer Deed of Charge, upon payment in full of all sums and the satisfaction in full of all obligations under any Facility Agreement, the Servicer or the Special Servicer (for as long as any Mortgage Loan or Whole Mortgage Loan is a Specially Serviced Mortgage Loan) will (subject to the continued existence of all necessary powers of attorney) execute on behalf of the Issuer or any applicable Subordinated Lender and the Borrower Security Trustee, and will procure that any directors or employees of the Servicer or the Special Servicer who are at that time attorneys-in-fact (directly or indirectly) of the Issuer or the Borrower Security Trustee or any applicable Subordinated Lender execute on behalf of the Issuer and the Borrower Security Trustee or any applicable Subordinated Lender, a reconveyance, receipt or discharge of any mortgage or other security for the repayment of a Mortgage Loan or Whole Mortgage Loan, as applicable, which receipt, discharge or other such document will be registered or recorded if required by applicable law and be delivered to or to the order of the person entitled thereto.

15.2.   The Issuer, the Borrower Security Trustee, the Note Trustee and any applicable Subordinated Lender will, subject as aforesaid and promptly upon payment in full as aforesaid, release, and shall authorize the Servicer (or any delegate or sub-contractor thereof) or the Special Servicer (or any delegate or sub-contractor thereof) to release, the relevant Mortgage Files to the person or persons entitled thereto.

15.3.   The Servicer will provide to the Borrower Security Trustee and the Note Trustee, upon the request of the Borrower Security Trustee or the Note Trustee (as the case may be), a redemption statement or other statement in respect of the balance of the relevant Mortgage Loan or Whole Mortgage Loan.

16.   NOTIFICATIONS AND REGISTRATIONS

16.1.   Promptly, upon becoming aware of the same, the Servicer or the Special Servicer (in the case of the Specially Serviced Mortgage Loan) will notify the Issuer, the Facility Agent, the Borrower Security Trustee and the Note Trustee in writing of any matter or thing which becomes known to the Servicer or the Special Servicer, respectively, which is a breach of any of the representations, warranties and undertakings of the Originator contained in the Loan Sale Agreement and the Servicer (or, for as long as the Mortgage Loan or Whole Mortgage Loan is a Specially Serviced Mortgage Loan, the Special Servicer) will promptly serve a notice of such breach on the Originator as contemplated by the Loan Sale Agreement.

16.2. The Servicer (or, for as long as the Mortgage Loan or Whole Mortgage Loan is a Specially Serviced Mortgage Loan, the Special Servicer) may consult with the Originator regarding the steps to be taken by the Originator in attempting to cure any breach which is the subject of a notice referred to in Clause 16.1, but in doing so will not waive the obligation of the Originator to repurchase a Mortgage Loan or Whole Mortgage Loan if the breach in question has not been remedied within the cure periods specified in the Loan Sale Agreement. If such breach has not been cured within the applicable cure period, the Servicer (or, for as long as a Mortgage Loan is a Specially Serviced Mortgage Loan, the Special Servicer) will act on behalf of the Issuer and the Borrower Security Trustee in relation to the repurchase by the Originator of a Mortgage Loan, Whole Mortgage Loan and its Related Security in accordance with the Loan Sale Agreement.

16.3. The Servicer (or, for as long as the Mortgage Loan or Whole Mortgage Loan is a Specially Serviced Mortgage Loan, the Special Servicer) will take all reasonable action, at the expense of the Originator, to effect any buy-back of the Mortgage Loan or Whole Mortgage Loan effected pursuant to the terms of the Loan Sale Agreement.

16.4. Upon becoming aware of the same, the Servicer and Special Servicer (in the case of a Specially Serviced Mortgage Loan) will promptly notify the Issuer, the Facility Agent, the Borrower Security Trustee and the Note Trustee (and, to the extent that any breach is in respect of a Subordinated Loan, the relevant Subordinated Lender) of any material breach by the Borrower of the terms of the Facility Agreement or any other Finance Documents.

17. FEES AND PAYMENTS TO THE SERVICER AND THE SPECIAL SERVICER

17.1. On each Distribution Date the Issuer will pay to the Servicer a fee (the "Servicing Fee") equal to [0.10]% per annum (plus VAT, if any) of the outstanding principal balance of the Mortgage Loans and Whole Mortgage Loans as at the first day of the Mortgage Loan interest period to which such Distribution Date relates.

17.2. Following any termination of the Servicer's appointment as Servicer, the Servicing Fee will be paid to any substitute servicer appointed; provided that the Servicing Fee that may be payable to any substitute servicer may not exceed the rate then commonly charged by providers of loan servicing services in relation to commercial properties.

17.3. The Servicing Fee will:

17.3.1. be calculated on the basis of the actual number of days to elapse from and including the most recently preceding Distribution Date; and

17.3.2. be payable by the Issuer on each Distribution Date in accordance with the provisions of the Cash Management Agreement along with all other compensation payable by the Issuer to the Servicer under this Agreement.

17.4. On each Distribution Date, for so long as a Mortgage Loan or Whole Mortgage Loan is a Specially Serviced Mortgage Loan, the Issuer will, in addition to the Servicing Fee payable to the Servicer, pay to the Special Servicer a fee (the "**Special Servicing Fee**") equal to [0.25]% per annum (plus VAT, if any) of the aggregate outstanding principal balance of the Mortgage Loan or Whole Mortgage Loan as at the first day of the Mortgage Loan interest period to which such Distribution Date relates.

17.5. The fees in Clause 17.4 and this Clause 17.5 shall be paid in addition to the Servicing Fee. The Special Servicing Fee will accrue on a daily basis based on the number of days in an Mortgage Loan interest period in which the Mortgage Loan or Whole Mortgage Loan is a Specially Serviced Mortgage Loan and will be payable on each Distribution Date:

17.5.1. starting on the Distribution Date following the date on which the Mortgage Loan or Whole Mortgage Loan becomes a Specially Serviced Mortgage Loan; and

17.5.2. ending on the Distribution Date following the date on which the Mortgage Loan or Whole Mortgage Loan becomes a Corrected Mortgage Loan.

The Special Servicing Fee will cease to accrue on the date on which the Specially Serviced Mortgage Loan becomes a Corrected Mortgage Loan.

17.6. The Servicing Fee and the Special Servicing Fee will cease to accrue in relation to the Mortgage Loan or Whole Mortgage Loan if any of the following events (each, a "**Liquidation Event**") occurs:

17.6.1. the Mortgage Loan or Whole Mortgage Loan is repaid in full; or

17.6.2. a Final Recovery Determination is made with respect to the Mortgage Loan or Whole Mortgage Loan.

17.7. On each Distribution Date the Issuer will:

17.7.1. pay to the Servicer or, as the case may be, the Special Servicer, all out-of-pocket costs and expenses incurred by the Servicer or the Special Servicer (including any Property Protection Advances) made or incurred on behalf of the Lender under the Finance Documents; and

17.7.2. pay to the Special Servicer:

(a) a liquidation fee (the "**Liquidation Fee**") equal to [1.00]% (plus VAT, if any) of the proceeds of sale, net of costs and expenses of sale, if any, arising from the sale of a Mortgage Loan or a Whole Mortgage Loan (including to a Subordinated Lender) or of any part of the Mortgaged Property following the enforcement of the Mortgage (or deed in lieu thereof) (such proceeds, "**Liquidation Proceeds**"); or

(b) a Workout Fee (the "**Workout Fee**") in an amount equal to [1.00]% (plus VAT, if any) of each payment of principal and interest collected under the Finance Documents, for so long as the relevant Mortgage Loan or Whole Mortgage Loan, having been a Specially Serviced Mortgage Loan, remains a Corrected Mortgage Loan.

17.8. If the Issuer is required by the terms of this Agreement to make any payment to the Servicer or the Special Servicer in respect of any out-of-pocket costs and expenses incurred by the Servicer or the Special Servicer in connection with its duties hereunder, the Issuer will make such payment together with interest at the Reimbursement Rate from:

17.8.1. the date on which such expense is incurred by the Servicer or the Special Servicer; until

17.8.2. the date on which such out-of-pocket expense is paid by the Issuer to the Servicer or the Special Servicer, as appropriate.

17.9. The Issuer will be obliged to reimburse the Servicer and the Special Servicer in respect of any VAT incurred by the Servicer or the Special Servicer on any out-of-pocket costs and expenses incurred by them in the course of the performance of their respective duties hereunder as contemplated by Clause 17.7.1 but only to the extent that such VAT is not recovered by the Servicer or the Special Servicer, as the case may be, from the Borrower, as applicable. Payments of costs and out-of-pocket expenses due to the Servicer and/or the Special Servicer in relation to the Mortgage Loans or Whole Mortgage Loans shall be due and payable by the Issuer.

17.10. Each payment by the Issuer to the Servicer and the Special Servicer under this Agreement will be made subject to and in accordance with the provisions of the Cash Management Agreement and the Priority of Payments.

18. **DEALINGS WITH MANAGING AGENTS**

Neither the Servicer nor the Special Servicer will require the Borrower under any Facility Agreement to terminate the appointment of a managing agent unless a replacement satisfactory to the Servicer or, if relevant, the Special Servicer, has been or will, immediately on such termination, be appointed. Furthermore, if a managing agent gives notice of its intention to terminate its appointment or suspend the provision of its services, the Servicer or, if relevant, the Special Servicer will use all reasonable endeavors consistent with the Servicing Standard to prevent it from doing so until a suitable replacement managing agent has been appointed on terms acceptable to the Servicer or, if applicable, the Special Servicer.

19. **CUSTODY OF MORTGAGE FILES AND SERVICING FILES**

19.1. The Facility Agent will ensure that as soon as practicable, and in any event no later than twenty (20) days after the Closing Date, copies of the Mortgage Files are in the possession of the Servicer (which will include for these purposes deeds and documents held by solicitors who have given an undertaking to hold such documents on behalf of the Borrower Security Trustee who will instruct such solicitors to take such action as is required by the Servicer in order for it to comply with its obligations under this Clause 19).

19.2. The Servicer will keep or cause to be kept the Mortgage Files in a secure place and will maintain in an adequate form such records as are necessary to enforce the Mortgage Loans or Whole Mortgage Loans and the Related Security; provided that this will not impose any obligation on the Servicer to visit or inspect the offices of any solicitors by whom any of the foregoing are held on behalf of the Issuer, the Borrower Security Trustee or the Note Trustee.

19.3. The Servicer will keep or cause to be kept the Mortgage Files, and Servicing Files in such a way that they can be clearly distinguished from the loan files, deeds and other documentation relating to other loans or mortgages serviced by the Servicer.

19.4. The Servicer will deliver, or request the delivery by the relevant holder of the Mortgage Files and Servicing Files, the Mortgage Files and/or Servicing Files and any other deeds, documents or correspondence relating to the Mortgage Loans or Whole Mortgage Loans and the Related Security, or any of them, to or to the order of the Borrower Security Trustee upon its written request made at any time and from time to time and will provide or cause to be provided access at all reasonable times during normal business hours, to the Mortgage Files and Servicing Files and any other deeds, documents or correspondence relating to the Mortgage Loans or Whole Mortgage Loans and the Related Security to the Borrower Security Trustee or the Note Trustee and their respective agents.

19.5. The Servicer acknowledges that the Mortgage Files and Servicing Files in its possession, custody or control will, after the Closing Date, be held to the order of the Borrower Security Trustee and that it has no beneficial interest therein whatsoever and irrevocably waives any rights, lien or encumbrance which it might have therein or to which it might at any time be entitled.

19.6. The Servicer will upon request, inform the Special Servicer and the Borrower Security Trustee of the location of the Mortgage Files and Servicing Files.

20. **THE MORTGAGE LOAN AND MORTGAGED PROPERTY REVIEW AND REPORTING REQUIREMENTS**

20.1. No later than 5:00pm on each Distribution Date in respect of the immediately preceding Mortgage Loan interest period, the Servicer will deliver to the Cash Manager and the Special Servicer, in respect of the immediately preceding Mortgage Loan interest period, a report setting forth, among other things, quarterly payments on the Mortgage Loans and Whole Mortgage Loans as well as the tracking of both scheduled and unscheduled payments on the Mortgage Loans and Whole Mortgage Loans.

20.2. The Servicer will also provide, during each Mortgage Loan interest period, a report (a "**Servicer Quarterly Report**") (based, where necessary, on information provided to the Servicer by the Special Servicer), with the following information regarding the Mortgage Loans, Whole Mortgage Loans and the Mortgaged Properties in relation to the preceding Mortgage Loan interest period:

20.2.1. a report setting forth the information provided by the Borrower pursuant to the information covenants contained in the Facility Agreement;

20.2.2. a report setting forth, among other things, general information in relation to the Mortgage Loans or Whole Mortgage Loans including cut-off balance, original mortgage rate, maturity date and general payment information, as well as financial data; and

20.2.3. a report setting forth, among other things, information regarding the Mortgaged Properties.

20.3. The Servicer will also deliver to the Issuer, the Special Servicer, the Cash Manager and the Borrower Security Trustee the following reports:

20.3.1. on the Mortgage Loan payment date immediately following a modification of the Mortgage Loans or Whole Mortgage Loans, a report setting forth, among other things, the original and revised terms of the Mortgage Loans or Whole Mortgage Loans, as of the related Mortgage Loan interest period and as of the Mortgage Loans or Whole Mortgage Loans closing date; and

20.3.2. on the Mortgage Loan payment date following a liquidation of the Mortgage Loans, Whole Mortgage Loans or Mortgaged Properties following enforcement of the security (or deed in lieu thereof), a report setting forth, among other things, the amount of Liquidation Proceeds and liquidation expenses in connection with such liquidation.

20.4. The Servicer will prepare the reports referred to in this Clause 20 in an electronic format which is reasonably acceptable to the Cash Manager. The Issuer, the Cash Manager and the Note Trustee may, absent manifest error, conclusively rely on the reports so provided by the Special Servicer to the extent that the underlying information is solely within the control of the Special Servicer (including, for the avoidance of doubt, any sub-servicer).

20.5. The Servicer's ability to provide the reports referred to in this Clause 20 may, in the case of any Specially Serviced Mortgage Loan depend on the timely receipt of the necessary information from the Special Servicer.

20.6. The Servicer will undertake an annual review of the Mortgage Loans or Whole Mortgage Loans and may conduct more frequent reviews if it has cause for concern as to the ability of the Borrower to meet its obligations under the Facility Agreements and a review (annual or otherwise) may, but need not necessarily, include an inspection of the Mortgaged Properties. The Special Servicer will assist the Servicer by providing such information as it may have which may be needed by the Servicer for the carrying out of any such review.

21. **MAINTENANCE OF ISSUER'S RECORDS AND STATUTORY OBLIGATIONS**

21.1. The Servicer will prepare or cause to be prepared and submit or cause to be submitted on behalf of the Issuer all necessary applications and requests for any approval, authorization, consent or license requested by the Issuer in connection with the business of the Issuer insofar as it relates to the duties to be performed by the Servicer or the Special Servicer under this Agreement, and the Servicer and the Special Servicer hereby agree to perform the Services in such a way as not to prejudice the continuation of any such approval, authorisation, consent or license.

21.2. In performing the Services, the Servicer will not take any action which in its good faith and reasonable judgement would cause the Issuer to breach any applicable legal or regulatory requirements of which the Servicer has actual knowledge or the terms of any Transaction Document to which the Servicer is a party.

21.3. The Servicer will promptly upon reasonable request provide to the Issuer and the Facility Agent any information concerning the Mortgage Loans, Whole Mortgage Loans and the Related Security which is available to the Servicer and which is required to enable the Issuer to prepare a profit and loss account, balance sheet and directors' report and any other reports or information required under or pursuant to applicable laws or regulations in respect of each statutory accounting reference period of the Issuer and to enable the Issuer to prepare and file all other reports, annual returns, statutory forms and other returns which the Issuer is required under or pursuant to applicable laws or regulations to prepare and file.

21.4. Each of the Servicer and (in the case of any Specially Serviced Mortgage Loan) the Special Servicer will keep records, books of account and documents (which can be in electronic form if it so decides) for the Issuer in relation to the Mortgage Loans and Whole Mortgage Loans.

21.5. Each of the Servicer and (in the case of any Specially Serviced Mortgage Loan) the Special Servicer will assist the auditors of the Issuer and provide information to such auditors upon reasonable request and will permit the auditors of the Issuer and any other person nominated by the Issuer or the Note Trustee at any time upon reasonable notice to have access to all books of record and account relating to the administration of the Mortgage Loans, Whole Mortgage Loans and the Related Security, the Servicing Files and related matters in accordance with this Agreement.

21.6. The Servicer will provide to the Issuer any information concerning the books of account maintained by any Servicer pursuant to this Agreement and each of the Servicer and (in the case of the Specially Serviced Mortgage Loan) the Special Servicer will provide to the Issuer any information concerning any other matter relating to the Issuer for which the Servicer or the Special Servicer is responsible under this Agreement, which the Issuer informs the Servicer or the Special Servicer from time to time is required under or pursuant to applicable law or which the Issuer may reasonably request to enable the Issuer to comply with its filing other obligations under any applicable laws or regulations.

21.7. Following receipt of a written request, the Servicer and, for as long as any Mortgage Loan or Whole Mortgage Loan is a Specially Serviced Mortgage Loan, the Special Servicer will prepare and deliver to the Issuer and the Note Trustee such further information reports whether in writing or otherwise as the Issuer and the Note Trustee may reasonably require.

22. REPRESENTATIONS AND COVENANTS

22.1. As at the date hereof, each of the Servicer and the Special Servicer hereby represents and warrants to the Issuer, the Subordinated Lenders, the Borrower Security Trustee, the Facility Agent and the Note Trustee that, without prejudice to any of its specific obligations hereunder that:

22.1.1. it is duly incorporated with full power and authority for it to own its assets, carry on its business as it is now being conducted, and to execute, sign, deliver and perform the transactions contemplated in the Transaction Documents to which it is a party and the Transaction Documents to which it is a party constitute its legal, valid and binding obligations, enforceable against it in accordance with their terms;

22.1.2. as far as it is aware, neither the signing and delivery of this Agreement nor any other Transaction Document to which it is a party contravenes or constitutes a default under, or causes to be exceeded any limitation on it or the powers of its directors imposed by or contained in (i) any law or regulation by which it or any of its assets is bound or affected, (ii) its constitutive documents, or (iii) any agreement to which it is a party or by which it or any of its assets is bound;

22.1.3. it has duly obtained or made each authorization, approval, consent, license, exemption, registration or declaration required on its part for or in connection with the execution, validity, enforceability and performance of each of the

Transaction Documents to which it is a party and any matters contemplated thereby have been unconditionally obtained and are in full force and effect, and there has been no default in the observance of any conditions or restrictions imposed in, or in connection with, the same;

22.1.4. it is not a party to any litigation, arbitration or administrative proceedings which could be expected to have a material adverse effect on its ability to perform the Services and, to its knowledge, no such litigation, arbitration or administrative proceedings are pending or threatened against it; and

22.1.5. no Servicer Insolvency Event has occurred in respect of it, and it is not insolvent.

22.2. As at the date hereof, each of the Servicer and the Special Servicer hereby covenants with each of the Issuer, the Subordinated Lenders, the Borrower Security Trustee, the Facility Agent and the Note Trustee that, without prejudice to any of its specific obligations hereunder that:

22.2.1. it will not knowingly fail to comply with any legal or regulatory requirements relating directly to the performance of the Services or its obligations under this Agreement;

22.2.2. it will make any payments required to be made by it pursuant to this Agreement on the date when such payments are due in [euros] (or as otherwise specified under the Transaction Documents in immediately available funds for value on such day without set-off (including, without limitation, for any fees owed to it) or counterclaim but subject to any deductions required by applicable law;

22.2.3. subject to and in accordance with the terms of this Agreement, it will take all reasonable steps to recover any sums due to the Issuer, the Facility Agent, the Borrower Security Trustee, the Note Trustee and any related Subordinated Lender from the Borrower, or any other third party;

22.2.4. it will notify the Issuer, the Facility Agent, the Borrower Security Trustee and the Note Trustee as soon as it becomes aware of any breach by it of any of its obligations under this Agreement;

22.2.5. it will obtain and maintain the necessary consents, licenses and regulatory or other approvals enabling it to continue administering the Mortgage Loans or Whole Mortgage Loans and the Related Security; and

22.3. The covenants of the Servicer and the Special Servicer in Clause 22.2 will remain in force until the appointment of the Servicer or, as the case may be, the Special Servicer is terminated or until this Agreement is terminated but without prejudice to any right or remedy of the Issuer, the Subordinated Lenders, the Facility Agent, the Borrower Security Trustee, the Issuer Security the Note Trustee arising from breach of any such covenant prior to the date of termination of the relevant appointment or of this Agreement.

22.4. The Issuer will not amend, vary or terminate the Cash Management Agreement without the prior written consent of the Servicer or the Special Servicer (which consent will not be unreasonably withheld or delayed).

22.5. The Issuer will not assign or transfer any of its rights or obligations under any Transaction Document without the prior written consent of the Note Trustee and the Servicer (which latter consent will not be unreasonably withheld or delayed) except by way of the Issuer Deed of Charge.

22.6. Each of the Servicer and the Special Servicer covenants with the other parties hereto that it will not pay or cause to be paid any monies received from the Borrower, or from the Originator into an account in its own name.

22.7. If for any reason a withholding is imposed on any payments made under any Mortgage Loan or Whole Mortgage Loan or in respect of the Related Security, then the Servicer the Special Servicer will, with the co-operation, where necessary, of the Issuer and the

Note Trustee, take all reasonable steps to avoid the necessity to make any such deduction or withholding and the costs incurred in doing so will be borne by the Issuer.

22.8. Nothing in this Agreement will prevent the Servicer or the Special Servicer from rendering services similar to those provided for in this Agreement to other persons or from carrying on business similar to or in competition with the business of the Issuer, the Originator, the Borrower or any other party to the Transaction Documents.

23 SERVICER EVENTS OF DEFAULT

23.1. If any of the following events (each, a "**Servicer Event of Default**") occurs:

23.1.1. the Servicer fails to procure the transfer of sums required to be transferred on any Mortgage Loan payment date from the relevant Borrower account to the Collection Account in the time or otherwise in the manner required pursuant to Clause 5.1 hereof, other than in circumstances which are beyond the control of the Servicer;

23.1.2. the Servicer or the Special Servicer, as the case may be, defaults in making payment due and payable by it under this Agreement and such default continues for a period of five business days after the earlier of:

(a) the Servicer or the Special Servicer, respectively, becoming aware of such default; and

(b) receipt by the Servicer or the Special Servicer, respectively, of written notice by the Note Trustee requiring the same to be remedied;

23.1.3. default (other than a failure to pay) is made by the Servicer or the Special Servicer in the performance or observance of any of its other covenants and obligations under this Agreement, or breach of any of the representations and warranties of the Servicer or the Special Servicer contained herein, which in the opinion of the Note Trustee is materially prejudicial to the interests of the holders of the most senior class outstanding of the Notes and such default continues unremedied for a period of thirty (30) days after receipt by the Servicer or the Special Servicer of written notice from the Note Trustee requiring the same to be remedied, or such longer time (but no longer than 90 days) as the Note Trustee may agree is necessary to cure the relevant breach, provided that the Servicer or the Special Servicer is proceeding with all due diligence required to cure such breach;

23.1.4. except in connection with a Permitted Reorganization, an order is made or an effective resolution passed for winding up the Servicer or the Special Servicer;

23.1.5. except in connection with a Permitted Reorganization, the Servicer or the Special Servicer ceases to own the whole of its business or ceases to own the whole or substantially the whole of its commercial mortgage servicing business;

23.1.6. except in connection with a Permitted Reorganization, the Servicer or the Special Servicer stops payment of its debts or the Servicer or the Special Servicer is deemed unable to pay its debts within the meaning of the insolvency laws applicable to such entity or becomes unable to pay its debts as they fall due or otherwise becomes insolvent (any such event, a "**Servicer Insolvency Event**");

23.1.7. except in connection with a Permitted Reorganization, proceedings are initiated (including the presentation of a petition or filing of documents with the court for administration (other than proceedings for dissolution or winding-up which are contested in good faith and discharged within ninety (90) days)) against the Servicer or the Special Servicer under any applicable laws concerning liquidation, administration, bankruptcy, insolvency, examinership, composition or reorganization (save where such proceedings are frivolous or vexatious or are being contested in good faith by the Servicer or the Special Servicer) or an encumbrancer will take possession of all or a substantial part of the undertaking or assets of the Servicer or the Special Servicer in respect of a secured debt exceeding [€150,000] or more and it will not be discharged or stayed within ninety (90) days or a distress or execution or other process will be levied or enforced upon or sued out against all or a substantial part of the undertaking or assets of the Servicer or the Special Servicer in respect of a judgement debt of [€150,000] or more and such distress, execution or other process will not be discharged or stayed within 90 days;

23.1.8. except in connection with a Permitted Reorganization, an effective resolution is passed for a moratorium of or in respect of the Servicer or the Special Servicer;

23.1.9. if it becomes unlawful for the Servicer or the Special Servicer to perform any material part of the Services except in circumstances where no other person could perform such material part of the Services lawfully; or

23.1.10. if any Rating Agency gives notice that the continued appointment of the Servicer or Special Servicer is likely to result in or does result in an Adverse Rating Event,

then the Issuer may, with the written consent of the Note Trustee, (or, after the service of a Note acceleration notice, the Note Trustee may) by notice in writing to the party to which the Servicer Event of Default in question applies, terminate the appointment under this Agreement of the Servicer or the Special Servicer (as the case may be), with effect from a date (not earlier than the date of such notice) specified in such notice provided that the termination of the appointment of the Servicer or the Special Servicer and the appointment of a successor Servicer or Special Servicer satisfies the requirements of Clause 24.4.

23.2. The Servicer or the Special Servicer will deliver to the Issuer and the Note Trustee as soon as practicable (but in any event within thirty (30) days of becoming aware thereof) a notice in writing of any Servicer Event of Default that has occurred in respect of it.

24   TERMINATION OF APPOINTMENT

24.1. On or after the occurrence of a Note event of default the Note Trustee shall, if so directed in writing by seventy-five per cent. (75%) of the Noteholders, terminate the appointment under this Agreement of the Servicer or the Special Servicer (as the case may be), by notice in writing to the Servicer or the Special Servicer with effect from a date (not earlier than the date of such notice) (as the case may be) specified in such notice provided that the termination of the appointment of the Servicer or the Special Servicer and the appointment of a successor Servicer or Special Servicer satisfies the requirements of Clause 24.4. The Note Trustee shall have no responsibility to appoint a replacement servicer or special servicer subsequent to such termination.

24.2. Subject to the requirements of Clause 24.4, the Servicer or the Special Servicer may terminate its appointment under this Agreement upon the expiry of not less than three months' written notice of termination given to each of the Issuer, the Facility Agent, the Borrower Security Trustee, the Servicer (in the case of notice by the Special Servicer), the Special Servicer (in the case of notice by the Servicer) and the Note Trustee.

24.3. Subject to the requirements of Clause 24.4, the appointment of the person then acting as Special Servicer in relation to the Mortgage Loan or Whole Mortgage Loan may also be terminated upon the Operating Advisor notifying the Issuer that it requires a replacement Special Servicer to be appointed.

24.4. No termination of the appointment of the Servicer or the Special Servicer under Clauses 23.1, 24.1 or 24.3 will take effect unless:

24.4.1. a successor Servicer or, as the case may be, a successor Special Servicer is appointed by or on behalf of the Issuer, such appointment to be effective no later than the date of termination of the outgoing Servicer or Special Servicer and the successor Servicer or successor Special Servicer, as applicable, agrees in writing to be bound by the terms of this Agreement and the other Transaction Documents (and if no substitute Servicer or Special Servicer, as applicable, is appointed within 60 days of the termination of appointment of the Servicer or

Special Servicer, as applicable, the Special Servicer may petition a court of competent jurisdiction to appoint such successor);

24.4.2. the Servicer or, as the case may be, the Special Servicer will have notified each of the Rating Agencies in writing of the identity of the successor Servicer or successor Special Servicer and the Rating Agencies have confirmed to the Note Trustee or Issuer that the appointment of the successor Servicer or Special Servicer will not result in an Adverse Rating Event, unless each class of Noteholders has approved, in accordance with the Note Conditions, the successor Servicer or successor Special Servicer, as applicable; and

24.4.3. the successor Servicer or, as the case may be, Special Servicer enters into an agreement substantially on the terms of this Agreement but subject to the Issuer Deed of Charge and such successor Servicer or Special Servicer has experience in servicing mortgages of commercial property on similar terms to that required under this Agreement and is approved by the Issuer and the Note Trustee.

24.5. Upon termination of the appointment of the Servicer or Special Servicer, as the case may be, the terminated Servicer or Special Servicer will:

24.5.1. (subject to any applicable legal or regulatory requirements) promptly deliver a copy of the related Servicing Files, or in the case of the Special Servicer, so much thereof which is in its possession (in electronic form or such other form as the file is maintained) to the successor Servicer or Special Servicer, as the case may be, and will provide the successor Servicer or Special Servicer, as the case may be, with all books and records (including records stored electronically on computer tapes, magnetic discs and the like) relating to the Mortgage Loans and Whole Mortgage Loans, either in the Servicer's or Special Servicer's or any of its directors', officers', employees', affiliates' or agents' possession or control or otherwise to the Servicer or Special Servicer, and reasonably requested by the successor Servicer or Special Servicer, to enable it to assume its functions hereunder with respect thereto;

24.5.2. co-operate with the successor Servicer or Special Servicer, as the case may be, in ensuring that all computer records and files can be transferred in a compatible form to the computer system of the successor Servicer or Special Servicer, as the case may be; and

24.5.3. take such further lawful action as the successor Servicer or successor Special Servicer may reasonably request, (without incurring any additional costs or expenses), to enable the Services of the terminated Servicer or Special Servicer as the case may be, to be performed by a successor Servicer or successor Special Servicer, as the case may be.

24.6. The Issuer will, promptly following the execution of a servicing agreement (which servicing agreement must be substantially similar to this Agreement) with a successor Servicer or Special Servicer at its own cost execute a security interest over its interest in such agreement in favor of the Note Trustee on the terms of the Issuer Deed of Charge, to the satisfaction of the Note Trustee.

24.7. On and after termination of the appointment of the Servicer or Special Servicer, as the case may be, or the termination of this Agreement pursuant to this Clause 24, all authority and power of the Servicer or the Special Servicer, as the case may be, under this Agreement will be terminated and be of no further force and effect, and the Servicer or Special Servicer will not thereafter hold itself out in any way as the agent of the Issuer, the Facility Agent, the Borrower Security Trustee or the Note Trustee.

24.8. On termination of the appointment of the Servicer or the Special Servicer under this Clause 24, the Servicer or Special Servicer, as the case may be, will be entitled to receive, subject as applicable to the terms of this Agreement, the Cash Management Agreement and the Issuer Deed of Charge, all fees and other monies accrued up to the date of termination (but, except as set forth in this Clause 24 will not be entitled to any other or further compensation in respect of the Servicing Fee or the Special Servicing Fee), as the case may be, payable on the dates on which they would otherwise have fallen due hereunder. Without prejudice to the provisions of the Cash Management Agreement and the Issuer Deed of Charge, the Servicer or Special Servicer will have no right whatsoever of set-off nor any right whatsoever to any lien or encumbrance over any of the Issuer's assets in respect of such amounts held by it on behalf of the Issuer. Notwithstanding the foregoing, if any Workout Fee is payable to the replaced Special Servicer, such replaced Special Servicer will continue to be entitled to receive the Workout Fee until such time (if ever) as the Mortgage Loan or Whole Mortgage Loan again becomes a Specially Serviced Mortgage Loan, at which time, such replaced Special Servicer's entitlement to be paid a Workout Fee shall cease permanently.

24.9. This Agreement will terminate at such time as neither the Issuer nor the Note Trustee has any further interest in the Mortgage Loan, Whole Mortgage Loan or the Related Security.

25. PURCHASE OF ISSUER ASSETS BY THE SERVICER

25.1. If, at any time, the principal amount outstanding of all the Notes is less than ten per cent. (10%) of the principal amount outstanding as at the Closing Date then, the Servicer will have the option (but not the obligation) to purchase the Mortgage Loans on any Distribution Date thereafter, provided that not earlier than sixty (60) and not later than forty (40) days prior to such Distribution Date the Servicer has served on the Issuer and the Note Trustee a written notice notifying them of its intention to so purchase the Mortgage Loans.

25.2. If the Servicer serves on the Issuer and the Note Trustee the written notice referred to in Clause 25.1 above, the Issuer will sell and the Servicer will purchase (at the Servicer's expense) all the right, title, interest and benefit of the Issuer in, to and under the Mortgage Loans.

25.3. Completion of any purchase by the Servicer under this Clause 25 will take place on the Distribution Date following the service of the notice referred to in Clause 25.1 above, when the Servicer will pay to or to the order of the Note Trustee the amount necessary to discharge the Issuer's liabilities in respect of the Notes as the purchase price for the Mortgage Loans.

25.4. Against payment of the amount referred to in Clause 25.3 in respect of a purchase of the Mortgage Loan, the Issuer, the Borrower Security Trustee and the Note Trustee will, at the Servicer's expense, execute and complete such documentation as is necessary to transfer to the Servicer (subject to the Servicer carrying out any necessary registrations) all the right, title and interest of the Issuer in, to and under the Mortgage Loans and the Related Security (as applicable) and any documentation relating to the Mortgage Loans and the Related Security, which will continue to be held by the Issuer, the Note Trustee or the Borrower Security Trustee, as the case may be and further, in the case of the Note Trustee or the Borrower Security Trustee, as the case may be, to perfect a release or discharge of the security created pursuant to the Issuer Deed of Charge. For the avoidance of doubt, the Servicer will pay on a full indemnity basis all costs and expenses of the Issuer and the Note Trustee (including, without limitation, legal fees and expenses) in connection with such purchase and transfer of the Mortgage Loans and the release of the Related Security.

26 MISCELLANEOUS PROVISIONS

26.1. The parties hereto agree that they will co-operate fully to do all such further acts and things and execute any further documents as may be necessary or desirable to give full effect to the arrangements contemplated by this Agreement, but, in the case of the Note Trustee and the Note Trustee, only if indemnified and/or secured to its respective satisfaction.

26.2. Without prejudice to the generality of the forgoing and to the provisions of Clause 4, each of the Issuer, the Facility Agent and the Borrower Security Trustee will, upon request by the Servicer or the Special Servicer, promptly give to the Servicer or the Special Servicer, as the case may be, such further powers of attorney or other written authorizations or mandates and instruments as are considered necessary by the Servicer or the Special Servicer to enable the Servicer or the Special Servicer to the Services.

26.3. Unless stated otherwise in this Agreement, any notice or communication to be given pursuant to this Agreement by any of the parties hereto will be given in accordance with the notice provisions in the Incorporated Terms Memorandum.[5]

26.4. This Agreement may be enforced and relied upon solely by the parties hereto.

26.5. This Agreement may be executed (manually or by facsimile) in one or more counterparts, and each such counterpart (when executed) will be an original. Such counterparts will together constitute one and the same instrument.

26.6. This Agreement may be amended from time to time by the mutual agreement of the parties hereto, without the consent of any other party.

26.7. If any one or more of the covenants, agreements, provisions or terms of this Agreement will be for any reason whatsoever held invalid, then such covenants, agreements, provisions or terms will be deemed severable from the remaining covenants, agreements, provisions or terms of this Agreement and will in no way affect the validity or enforceability of the other provisions of this Agreement or of the Notes or the rights of the Noteholders.

26.8. The Servicer will promptly provide notice to each Rating Agency with respect to each of the following of which it has actual knowledge:

26.8.1. any material change or amendment to this Agreement;

26.8.2. the occurrence of any Servicer Event of Default;

26.8.3. the resignation or termination of the Servicer or the Special Servicer;

26.8.4. the appointment of any replacement Servicer or Special Servicer in relation to the Mortgage Loans or Whole Mortgage Loans (including, for the avoidance of doubt the identity of any replacement Servicer or Special Servicer),

and shall provide a copy of each such notice to the Special Servicer and the Issuer.

26.9. The Servicer or, if any Mortgage Loan or Whole Mortgage Loan is a Specially Serviced Mortgage Loan, the Special Servicer, will promptly notify the Rating Agencies of any repurchase by the Originator of the Mortgage Loan or Whole Mortgage Loan pursuant to the Loan Sale Agreement.

26.10. The Servicer, or if any Mortgage Loan or Whole Mortgage Loan is a Specially Serviced Mortgage Loan, the Special Servicer will promptly upon request provide such information regarding:

26.10.1. the Mortgage Loan, the Whole Mortgage Loan and the Related Security for which it is responsible;

26.10.2. compliance by the Servicer or the Special Servicer with its obligations hereunder,

as a Rating Agency may from time to time request or the Note Trustee may from time to time request and which the Servicer or the Special Servicer can provide in accordance with applicable law.

26.11. If this Agreement requires Rating Agency Confirmation to be obtained in relation to a particular matter, the Servicer (or, in the case of matters pertaining to a Specially Serviced Mortgage Loan, the Special Servicer) will, as soon as is practicable following a request therefor, provide each Rating Agency with all information as is reasonably necessary and available to it to enable such Rating Agency to determine whether, and on what basis, confirmation should be given.

---

[5] The Incorporated Terms Memorandum is one of the Transaction Documents that provides the definitions for defined terms used throughout the Transaction Documents.

26.12. In the event that there is any change in the identity of the Note Trustee or the Borrower Security Trustee in accordance with the Note Trust Deed, the Issuer Deed of Charge, or the Finance Documents, the retiring Note Trustee or retiring Borrower Security Trustee (as the case may be) and the Servicer, the Special Servicer, the Facility Agent, the Note Trustee (without duplication), the Borrower Security Trustee (without duplication) and the Issuer, will execute such documents and take such actions as the new note trustee or the new security trustee may reasonably require for the purpose of vesting in such new note trustee or new security trustee the rights and obligations (if any) of such Note Trustee or Borrower Security Trustee, as applicable, under this Agreement, the Note Trust Deed, the Issuer Deed of Charge, and the Finance Documents and for releasing the retiring note trustee or retiring security trustee from further obligations hereunder and thereunder. While any Notes remain outstanding, the Issuer will give written notice to each Rating Agency of such change.

26.13. Nothing herein contained will impose any obligation or liability on the Note Trustee to assume or perform any of the obligations of the Issuer, Borrower, the Originator, the Facility Agent, the Borrower Security Trustee, the Servicer, the Cash Manager or the Special Servicer hereunder or render it liable for any breach thereof.

26.14. This Agreement embodies the complete agreement among the parties and may not be varied or terminated except by a written agreement conforming to the provisions of Clause 26.6. All prior negotiations or representations of the parties are merged into this Agreement and will have no force or effect unless expressly stated herein.

26.15. The Issuer may not assign or transfer any of its rights or obligations under this Agreement without the prior written consent of the Note Trustee.

26.16. Neither the Servicer nor the Special Servicer may assign or transfer any of its respective rights or obligations under this Agreement without the prior written consent of the Note Trustee.

IN WITNESS WHEREOF the parties hereto have executed this Agreement on the date first mentioned above.

SCHEDULE 1

ADDITIONAL DEFINITIONS

"**Adverse Rating Event**" means, with respect to any Rating Agency, an event that would cause a downgrade, qualification or withdrawal of the then current ratings by such Rating Agency of any class of Notes.

"**Appraisal Reduction**" will be deemed to have occurred when the positive difference between (i) the balance of the relevant Mortgage Loan or Whole Mortgage Loan, as applicable, then outstanding and (ii) the principal amount of the relevant Mortgage Loan or Whole Mortgage Loan, as applicable, then outstanding, together with any unpaid interest, all currently due and unpaid taxes and assessments, insurance premiums, ground rents (if applicable), in respect of the Mortgaged Properties (net of any amount placed into an escrow account in respect of such items), and outstanding drawings on the Liquidity Facility including any interest thereon, (without duplication) Property Protection Advances including any interest thereon, exceeds 90% of the appraised value of the relevant Mortgaged Properties as determined by the relevant Valuation;

"**Borrower**" means the obligor under a Mortgage Loan or Whole Mortgage Loan, as applicable;

"**Break Adjustment**" means an amount to be determined by the Lender upon any prepayment or repayment of principal under a Mortgage Loan, by reference to the amount upon parties dealing at arm's length would reasonably reach a mutual agreement to terminate an interest rate swap transaction with a notional amount equal to the amount of such prepayment or repayment;

"**Cash Management Agreement**" means the agreement so named between _____ dated as of the Closing Date;

"**Cash Manager**" has the meaning provided in the Cash Management Agreement;

"**Collection Account**" means an account of the Issuer opened at the [Operating Bank], or such other account or accounts as may, with the prior written consent of the Note Trustee, be designated by the Issuer as such account;

"**Controlling Party**" shall have the meaning ascribed to it in the Transaction Documents, except in relation to a Whole Mortgage Loan, the Controlling Party will be the relevant Subordinated Lender, provided a Control Valuation Event has not occurred in relation to that Whole Mortgage Loan;

"**Control Valuation Event**" will exist on any date if the difference between (a) the then outstanding principal balance of Mortgage Loan or Whole Mortgage Loan, minus (b) the applicable Reduction Amount, is less than [25]% of the Whole Mortgage Loan;

"**Corrected Mortgage Loan**" means a Mortgage Loan:

(a)   after it became a Specially Serviced Mortgage Loan; and

(b)   after the Special Servicing Transfer Event which resulted in the Mortgage Loan or Whole Mortgage Loan so becoming a Specially Serviced Mortgage Loan, is remedied; and

(c)   for so long as no Special Servicing Transfer Event is continuing;

"**Distribution Date**" means _____ [dates of payments on Notes];

"**Encumbrance**" means in relation to any Mortgage Loan or Whole Mortgage Loan, any encumbrance having priority over, or being on par with, the first ranking security of the mortgage;

493

"**Extraordinary Resolution**" means a resolution passed at a meeting duly convened and held in accordance with the provisions for meetings of Noteholders by a majority of not less than three quarters of the votes cast;

"**Facility Agreement**" means, with respect to any Mortgage Loan or Whole Mortgage Loan, the loan facility agreement between the Originator and the Borrower;

"**Final Recovery Determination**" means a determination at any time by the Special Servicer, acting reasonably, with respect to a Mortgage Loan or Whole Mortgage Loan that there has been a recovery of all liquidation proceeds and other payments or recoveries that, in the Special Servicer's judgment (such judgment to be exercised in accordance with the Servicing Standard), will ultimately be recoverable;

"**Finance Document**" means, with respect to a Mortgage Loan or Whole Mortgage Loan, the "Finance Documents" as defined in the relevant Facility Agreement;

"**Headlease**" means each lease under which a Borrower or other obligor holds an interest in a property;

"**Intercreditor Deed**" means an intercreditor deed between the Issuer and a Subordinated Lender on or prior to the Closing Date, as amended from time to time;

"**Issuer Deed of Charge**" means the deed so named dated on or about the Closing Date between, *inter alios*, the Issuer and the Note Trustee;

"**Issuer Security**" means the security created in favor of the Note Trustee and the Secured Parties pursuant to the Issuer Deed of Charge;

"**Lender**" means, as applicable, the Issuer and Subordinated Lenders subject, in each case, to the terms of the relevant Intercreditor Deed;

"**Liquidation Event**" means, in relation to any Mortgage Loan or Whole Mortgage Loan, the following events:

(a) the Mortgage Loan or Whole Mortgage Loan is repaid in full;

(b) a Final Recovery Determination is made with respect to the Mortgage Loan or Whole Mortgage Loan; or

(c) the Mortgage Loan is repurchased by the Originator in accordance with and pursuant to the terms of the Loan Sale Agreement;

"**Liquidity Facility**" means the revolving liquidity facility made available to the Issuer by the liquidity facility provider in accordance with the terms of the Liquidity Facility Agreement;

"**Liquidity Facility Agreement**" means the agreement so named dated on or about the Closing Date between the Issuer, the Liquidity Facility Provider and the Note Trustee;

"**Mortgage File**" means the documents listed below pertaining to any Mortgage Loan or Whole Mortgage Loan as the case may be and any additional documents required to be added to such Mortgage File pursuant to the express provisions of the Servicing Agreement, or any other Transaction Documents:

(a) the Facility Agreement and all the documents relating to the Related Security and all amendments and supplements thereto;

(b) the original or a copy of the mortgages and/or other security agreements for each Mortgaged Property, in each case with evidence of recording indicated thereon;

(c) copies of the original environmental reports of each Mortgaged Property made in connection with the origination of the Mortgage Loan;

(d) copies of the management agreements and duty of care agreements or similar agreements for each Mortgaged Property;

(e) the Loan Sale Agreement and any transfer certificate or documents relating to the Mortgage Loan;

(f)   originals or copies of all amendment, assumption, modification, written assurance and substitution agreements, with evidence of recording thereon if appropriate, in those instances where the terms or provisions of the Facility Agreement, a management agreement, a duty of care agreement, any mortgage or any related security document or other document listed herein have been modified;

(g)   the original or a copy of any guarantee (if any) of the obligations of the Borrower under the Mortgage Loan; and

(h)   any other documents and any other material written agreements or documents related to the Mortgage Loan, including lease agreements and insurance policies;

(i)   any applicable Intercreditor Deed;

"**Mortgage Loan**" means those loans, including, in the event of a Whole Mortgage Loan, the Senior Loans, sold to the Issuer pursuant to the Loan Sale Agreement;

"**Mortgaged Property**" means the freehold, heritable or leasehold property or properties secured, mortgaged or charged as security for the repayment of any Mortgage Loan;

"**Note Acceleration Notice**" means a notice delivered by the Note Trustee to the Issuer which declares the Notes to be immediately due and payable and the Issuer Security to be immediately enforceable;

"**Noteholders**" means at any particular time, the then holders of the Notes;

"**Notes**" means the notes in the denominations of _____ in registered form, each comprising the _____ Notes due _____, constituted in relation to the Trust Deed;

"**Operating Advisor**" means the party appointed by the Controlling Party to represent their interests in the servicing of any Specially Serviced Mortgage Loan;

"**Permitted Reorganisation**" means a reorganisation or restructuring:

(a)   in respect of which the terms has been notified to the Note Trustee; and

(b)   in respect of which the identity of the relevant surviving entity has been notified to the Note Trustee; and

(c)   in respect of which the surviving party meets the requirements with respect to successors contained in the relevant Transaction Document; and

(d)   in relation to which the relevant surviving entity demonstrates to the satisfaction of the Note Trustee that, following the completion of the reorganization or restructuring, it will:

      (i)   not be insolvent; and

      (ii)   have assumed all of the liabilities and obligations of the Servicer or the Special Servicer, as applicable;

"**Priority of Payments**" means the Pre-Enforcement Priority of Payments and the Post-Enforcement Priority of Payments as defined in the Cash Management Agreement and/or the Issuer Deed of Charge;

"**Property Protection Drawing**" means a liquidity drawing made by or on behalf of the Issuer under the Liquidity Facility on any business day in order to fund a Property Protection Shortfall, or a payment made by or on behalf of the Issuer, on any business day in order to fund a Property Protection Shortfall;

"**Property Protection Shortfall**" means a shortfall arising if, on any day, the Issuer is required to pay certain amounts to third parties, such as insurers, and persons providing services in connection with a Mortgaged Property that have not been paid by a Borrower due to insufficient funds to pay such amounts and making such payment would preserve or enhance the value of the relevant Mortgage Property as determined by the Servicer or Special Servicer, as applicable, in accordance with the terms of the Servicing Agreement;

"**Purchase Event**" means any event that gives rise to a Subordinated Lender right to acquire the related Senior Loan in accordance with the relevant Intercreditor Deed;

"**Rating Agencies**" means [the applicable Rating Agencies on the deed], and "**Rating Agency**" means any of them;

"**Rating Agency Confirmation**" means, in respect of any action to be taken, written confirmation from each Rating Agency then ascribing a rating to the Notes that the then outstanding Rating will not be withdrawn or downgraded as a result of such action;

"**Reduction Amount**" means the positive difference between (i) the balance of the relevant Mortgage Loan or Whole Mortgage Loan, as applicable, then outstanding and (ii) the principal amount of the relevant Mortgage Loan or Whole Mortgage Loan, as applicable, then outstanding, together with any unpaid interest, all currently due and unpaid taxes and assessments, insurance premiums, ground rents (if applicable), in respect of the Mortgaged Properties (net of any amount placed into an escrow account in respect of such items), and any swap breakage costs, outstanding drawings on the Liquidity Facility including any interest thereon, (without duplication) Property Protection Advances including any interest thereon, less 90% of the appraised value of the relevant Mortgaged Properties as determined by the relevant Valuation. For the avoidance of doubt, the Reduction Amount is first applied to reduce the Subordinated Loan before any application to reduce the Senior Loan;

"**Reimbursement Rate**" means a per annum rate which is equal to the base lending rate of _____ (or such other) bank which may be agreed upon by the Servicer (or Special Servicer, as the case may be) and the Note Trustee;

"**Related Security**" means all property of whatever nature and wherever located which constitutes security for any Mortgage Loan;

"**Secured Parties**" means, as applicable in the relevant context, each of the Noteholders, the Note Trustee, any receiver appointed pursuant to the terms of the Issuer Deed of Charge, the Borrower Security Trustee, the Corporate Services Provider, the Servicer, the Special Servicer, the Cash Manager, the Liquidity Facility Provider, the Swap Provider, the Agents, the Agent Bank, the Operating Bank and the Originator;

"**Senior Loan**" means the senior portion of each Whole Mortgage Loan advanced pursuant to the relevant Facility Agreement;

"**Servicing File**" means, with respect to a Mortgage Loan or Whole Mortgage Loan to the extent such documentation exists, copies of the following items:

(a)   all of the items delivered to the Servicer pursuant to the Servicing Agreement;

(b)   property inspection reports;

(c)   financial statements for the related Borrower and each Mortgaged Property;

(d)   valuation reports;

(e)   environmental reports;

(f)   building surveys;

(g)   if applicable, asset summaries and financial information on the related Borrower; and

(h)   any escrow analysis performed with respect to the Mortgage Loan or Whole Mortgage Loan;

"**Special Servicing Transfer Event**" means the occurrence of any of the following events:

(i)   a payment default on any Mortgage Loan or Whole Mortgage Loan on its final maturity date;

(ii)   any payment on any Mortgage Loan or Whole Mortgage Loan scheduled to be made by the Borrower (other than on the Mortgage Loan maturity date) is more than 45 days overdue;

(iii)   any Borrower becoming the subject of insolvency proceedings;

(iv)   the Servicer or the Special Servicer, as the case may be, receiving a notice of the enforcement of any other security on a Mortgaged Property; and

(v)   any other material default occurring which is not cured within the applicable cure period or which in the opinion of the Servicer is not likely to be cured within 30 days, that would, in the opinion of the Servicer, be likely to have a material adverse effect upon the Issuer or the Mortgage Loan or Whole Mortgage Loan.;

"Subordinated Lender" means the holder of the Subordinated Loan;

"Subordinated Loan" means the subordinated portion of each Whole Mortgage Loan advanced pursuant to the relevant Facility Agreement;

"Transaction Documents" means [list securitization transaction documents];

"Trust Deed" means the deed so named dated on or about the Closing Date between the Issuer and the Note Trustee;

"Valuation" means valuation in relation to each Loan and its Related Security, by internationally recognized real property valuers (each, a **"Valuer"**) of the relevant Mortgaged Properties;

"Whole Mortgage Loan" means, with respect to a loan for which there is a Subordinated Loan, the Senior Loan and the Subordinated Loan.

CMSA-EUROPEAN INVESTOR REPORTING PACKAGE™, UK

(CMSA E-IRP™)

Version 1.0

CMSA-European Investor Reporting Package, UK, Version 1.0

I. Overview of the CMSA-European Investor Reporting Package UK

Version 1.0

Overview of the CMSA-European Investor Reporting Package, UK (E-IRP)

GENERAL COMMENTS

This package constitutes Version 1.0 of the Commercial Mortgage Securities Association European Investor Reporting Package, UK (CMSA E-IRP). It should be utilised whenever the reporting requirements in a Servicing Agreement call for reporting on UK deals according to the CMSA standard reporting package/IRP. In some Servicing Agreements, the reporting requirements identify the CMSA standard reporting package/IRP "as it may be modified from time to time". While it is hoped the CMBS marketplace will adopt the CMSA E-IRP as the exclusive reporting standard, to the extent that a particular Serving Agreement or Cash Management Agreement requires different reporting formats or different methodologies, then the user should adhere to the terms of that Agreement.

Users of the CMSA E-IRP should be advised that the data contained within the CMSA data files and reports do not take into account every different Securitisation structure. It is the responsibility of the user to understand the structure of particular transactions and utilise the data files and reports provided accordingly. Also, at the current time, this package has been designed for UK transactions only.

In order to maximise the usefulness and effectiveness of the CMSA E-IRP for the investor community, the European Investor Reporting Committee of CMSA-Europe has established a process for the consideration of modifications or additions to the CMSA E-IRP. The CMSA European Investor Reporting Committee consists of a representative group of investors, servicers, cash managers, trustees, managers, arrangers and rating agencies. (A listing of committee participants is included in Section III). If your company is not represented and you are interested in participating in the ongoing work of this committee, contact Carol Wilkie, Director, CMSA-Europe at carol@cmbs.org. Together, they have designed this standard information package, which will hopefully meet the needs of all types of CMBS investors. Users are invited to make comments to the CMSA European Investor Reporting Committee on a yearly basis during an open period for questions, comments, suggested changes and enhancements. The Committee will take all comments and suggestions under advisement and issue modifications to the CMSA E-IRP as necessary.

For questions or comments contact Carol Wilkie.

SUMMARY OF INFORMATION AVAILABLE

CMSA-Europe is devoted to meeting the needs of all types of investors who are monitoring CMBS transactions. The CMSA E-IRP has been designed accordingly. The medium of distribution is dependent on the strategy of the Cash Manager or the Servicer. Information can be found on the Internet and can be obtained by fax, e-mail or regular mail. There are various formats of information. One or all of the following can be used to better understand a transaction:-

1) The Offering Circular
2) The CMSA European Investor Reporting Package, UK Only
3) The Statement to Noteholders
4) Other electronic information found on the Internet or Bloomberg

CMSA DATA FILE OVERVIEW

The information in the CMSA E-IRP is contained in electronic data files. An overview of the data files is provided below. All data files are designed to provide standard formats that facilitate a smooth transfer of information from the Servicer to the Cash Manager and from the Cash Manager to the Investor (or user of this data). These standard data files are essential to support continued growth and liquidity within the secondary market. Standardisation provides investors and rating agencies with more consistent and reliable information, which is necessary so that an evaluation as to the probability of the timely receipt of interest and principal payments can be made.

The following lists the files or data available to end-users:-
1)   CMSA E-IRP Loan Setup File
2)   CMSA E-IRP Loan Periodic Update File
3)   CMSA E-IRP Property File
4)   CMSA E-IRP Bond Level File – due to be released September 2006

Note:
In the data file and the report descriptions which follow, whenever there is a reference to the Master Servicer, this reference is intended to mean the Servicer that reports to the Cash Manager.

CMSA E-IRP Loan Setup File
This data file is provided by the Master Servicer using information that is prepared by the Arranger at the time of issuance. This file generally contains static information. The Arranger should provide the CMSA E-IRP Loan Setup File to the Master Servicer. The file should be made available to investors by the Cash Manager on its website and should be updated by the Master Servicer when necessary (e.g., if information changes or loans are added to a transaction). The Loan Setup File will contain the majority of the loan-level information found in the offering circular. Such information includes cut-off balance, original loan interest rate, loan maturity date and general prepayment information, as well as "at securitisation closing" financial data.

CMSA E-IRP Loan Periodic Update File
This data file is prepared by the Master Servicer and delivered to the Cash Manager in conjunction with the remittances according to the remittance and reporting cycle in the transaction. This file is necessary in order to track loan changes due to scheduled and unscheduled payments as well as any modifications a loan might have. *When a loan pays off (or is repurchased or substituted), it will stay on the file with a zero balance for one reporting period then will drop off.*

CMSA E-IRP Property File
This data file is always produced for each loan in a transaction regardless of whether the loan is secured by one property or multiple properties. The underwriter should provide the 'securitisation date' data in the Property File to the Master Servicer and the Cash Manager. The Master Servicer should also furnish an updated file to the Cash Manager each successive quarter or as required by the Servicing Agreement or Cash Management Agreement. The file data can change over time for many fields. Major file changes may occur if a loan allows for substitution of different properties as collateral for a particular loan. *When a loan pays off (or is repurchased or substituted) all the properties for the Loan will stay on the file for one quarter then drop off. If the loan was subject to a partial release, the released property will stay on the file for one quarter and then drop off.*

CMSA E-IRP Bond Level File
This data is prepared by the Cash Manager and consists of updated remittance period information on the notes. This file reports such items as updated note balances, the amount of interest and principal received on the notes, and other information typically contained in a statement to noteholders. It also contains note ratings whenever provided by the Rating Agencies to the Cash Manager.

II. CMSA Data Files

Please refer to the individual excel files located on the CMSA website.

European Commercial Mortgage Securities Association
CMSA "Loan Setup" File
(Data Record Layout)
Cross Refrenced as "ES"

E - CMSA Grouping	Field Name	UK / European Field Number	US Field Number	Field Type	Format Example	Description / Comments	European Definitions
Loan Identifiers (ES1 - ES7)	Transaction Identifier	ES1	S1	Alpha Numeric	XXX97001	Unique issue identification string	The name assigned to the securitisation or issue, this can be as identified in the Offering Circular or assigned by the Servicer.
	Group Identifier	ES2	S2	Alpha Numeric	XXX97001A	Unique identification number assigned to each loan group within an issue	The alpha-numeric code assigned to each loan group within an issue. A Group ID may not be applicable for every transaction.
	Servicer Loan Identifier	ES3	S3	Alpha Numeric	0000000012345	Unique number assigned by Servicer to each Loan	The Servicer's unique identification number assigned to each loan in the pool.
	Offering Circular Loan Identifier	ES4	S4	Alpha Numeric	123	Unique number assigned to each Loan in Offering Circular	The identification number(s), if any, assigned to each loan in the offering circular.
	Blank Field	ES5				Blank Field	
	Blank Field	ES6				Blank Field	
	Blank Field	ES7				Blank Field	
Original Loan Terms (ES8 - ES19)	Currency	ES8		Alpha Numeric		In what currency is the loan denominated?	
	Original Loan Amount	ES9	S5	Numeric	1000000.00	The mortgage loan balance at inception of the loan	The amount of the loan/commitment at origination. IF the committed amount was not fully drawn, enter the total amount drawdown.
	Original Term of Loan	ES10	S6	Numeric	240	Original number of months until maturity of loan	The number of months from the loan origination date until the maturity date of the loan.
	Start Date of Amortisation	ES11		Alpha Numeric	YYYYMMDD	Start Date	The date that amortisation will commence on the loan (this may be a date prior to the Securitisation date).
	Index Code	ES12	S22	Alpha Numeric	A	See Index Code Legend	Refer to the Index Code Legend to select the code describing the interest rate type for the loan
	Original Loan Interest Rate	ES13	S8	Numeric	0.095	Loan all-in interest rate at inception of loan	
	First Loan Payment Due Date	ES14	S10	Alpha Numeric	YYYYMMDD	First payment date on the mortgage loan not first payment date after securitisation	The date that the first interest payment was due on the loan following origination (not first date after securitisation).
	Blank Field	ES15				Blank Field	
	Blank Field	ES16				Blank Field	
	Blank Field	ES17				Blank Field	
	Blank Field	ES18				Blank Field	
	Blank Field	ES19				Blank Field	
Collateral Details (ES20 -ES37)	Number of Properties At Issue Date	ES20	S54	Numeric	13	The number of properties underlying the mortgage loan	The number of properties that serve as security for the loan at the Issue Date.
	Property Name	ES21	S55	Alpha Numeric	Text	If multiple properties, print "Various"	The name of the property that serves as security for the loan. If multiple properties, print "Various."
	Property Address	ES22	S56	Alpha Numeric	Text	If multiple properties, print "Various"	The address of the property that serves as security for the loan. If multiple properties, print "Various."
	Property City	ES23	S57	Alpha Numeric	Text	If multiple properties have the same city then print the city, otherwise print "Various". Missing information print " Incomplete".	The city name where the property or properties are located. If multiple properties have the same city then print the city, otherwise print "Various". Missing information print "Incomplete".
	Postal Code	ES24	S59	Alpha Numeric	Text	If multiple properties have the same postal code then print the postal code, otherwise print "Various". Missing information print " Incomplete".	The postal code (or equivalent) for the property or properties that serve as security for the loan. If multiple properties have the same code, print "Various." For missing information print "Incomplete"

505

European Commercial Mortgage Securities Association
CMSA "Loan Setup" File
(Data Record Layout)
Cross Refenced as "ES"

E - CMSA Grouping	Field Name	UK / European Field Number	US Field Number	Field Type	Format Example	Description / Comments	European Definitions
	Region (NUTS)	ES25	S60	Alpha Numeric	Text	If multiple properties have the same region then print the region, otherwise print "Various". Missing information print " Incomplete".	The region in which the property or properties thath serve as security are located. - Use the standard regions as defined by Eurostat. Their website is: www.europa.eu.int/comm/eurostat/ramon/nuts/splash_regions.html NUTs stands for "Nomenclature of Territorial Units for Statistics". If multiple properties, print "Various". Missing information print "Incomplete".
	Property Country	ES26		Alpha Numeric	Text	If multiple properties have the same country then print the country, otherwise print "Various". Missing information print " Incomplete".	If multiple properties have the same country then print the country, otherwise print "Various". Missing information print "Incomplete".
	Property Type Code	ES27	S61	Alpha Numeric	MF	See Property Type Code Legend. If multiple properties have the same property type code then print the property code, otherwise print "XX" to represent various. Missing information print "ZZ".	Refer to the Property Type Code Legend and use the code that is most suitable for the property or properties.
	Net Square Feet At Issue Date	ES28	S62	Numeric	25000	For multiple properties, if all the same property type. sum the values. Otherwise, leave empty.	The total net rentable area of the properties in square feet that serve as security for the loan at the Issue Date. For multiple properties, if not all information available, leave blank. Complete either square feet or square metres field (or both if easier)
	Net Square Metre At Issue Date	ES29		Numeric	2322	For multiple properties, if all the same property type. sum the values. Otherwise, leave empty.	The total net rentable area of the properties in square metres that serve as security for the loan at the Issue Date. For multiple properties, if not all information available, leave blank. Complete either square feet or square metres field (or both if easier)
Collateral Details (ES20 -ES37)	Number of Units/Beds/Rooms At Issue Date	ES30	S63	Numeric	75	For multiple properties, if all the same property type. sum the values. Otherwise, leave empty.	For property type Multifamily enter number of units, for Hospitality/Hotel/Healthcare - beds, for Caravan Parks - units, Lodging=rooms, Self Storage=units. For Multiple properties, if all the same Property Type, sum the values. If missing any, leave empty.
	Year Built	ES31	S64	Alpha Numeric	1960	If the multiple properties have the same Year Built then print Year Built, otherwise leave empty. If multiple years then put in "Various"	The year the property was built. For multiple properties, if all the same print the year, else leave empty.
	Form of Title	ES32	S74	Alpha Numeric	Y	Freehold, Leasehold or Mixed	Would the property(ies) be described as leasehold (or equivalent) rather than freehold. If multiple properties and various types, or single property, enter M. F = Freehold, L =Leasehold, M=Mixed.
	Blank Field	ES33				Blank Field	
	Blank Field	ES34				Blank Field	
	Blank Field	ES35				Blank Field	
	Blank Field	ES36				Blank Field	
	Blank Field	ES37				Blank Field	
	ICR Covenant	ES38		Alpha Numeric	Text	If there is an ICR financial covenant, the threshold for a breach of such covenant.	If there is an ICR financial covenant stipulated in the loan agreement, enter the threshold for a breach of such covenant.
Loan Covenant Details (ES38 - ES44)	DSCR Covenant	ES39		Alpha Numeric	Text	If there is a DSCR financial covenant, the threshold for a breach of such covenant.	If there is a DSCR financial covenant stipulated in the loan agreement, enter the threshold for a breach of such covenant.
	LTV Covenant	ES40		Alpha Numeric	Text	If there is an LTV financial covenant, the threshold for a breach of such covenant.	If there is an LTV covenant stipulated in the loan agreement, enter the threshold for a breach of such covenant.
	Other Financial Covenant	ES41		Alpha Numeric	Text	Y=Yes N=No. Are there any other types of financial covenants for the Loan?	Y=Yes N=No. Are there any other types of financial covenants for the Loan?

European Commercial Mortgage Securities Association
CMSA "Loan Setup" File
(Data Record Layout)
Cross Refrenced as "ES"

E - CMSA Grouping	Field Name	UK / European Field Number	US Field Number	Field Type	Format Example	Description / Comments	European Definitions
Loan Statistics at Issue Date (ES45 -ES72)	Revenue At Issue Date	ES45	S70	Numeric	10000	If multiple properties, then sum the value, if missing any then use the DSCR Indicator Legend. Should match the Offering Circular if available	The total underwritten revenue from all sources for a property as described in the Offering Circular. If multiple properties, sum the values in the Property File. If missing data or if all received/consolidated, use the DSCR Indicator Legend rule.
	Operating Expenses At Issue Date	ES46	S71	Numeric	10000	If multiple properties, then sum the value, if missing any then use the DSCR Indicator Legend. Should match the Offering Circular if available.	Total underwritten operating expenses for the properties a described in the offering Circular. These may include real estate taxes, insurance, management, utilities, maintenance and repairs and direct property costs to the landlord; capital expenditures and leasing commissions are excluded, total the operating expenses of the underlying properties. If multiple properties exist and data is not available for all properties or if received/consolidated, refer to the DSCR Indicator Legend rule.
	NOI At Issue Date	ES47	S65	Numeric	10000	NOI relates to Net Operating Income on the Properties at the Issue Date, as set forth in the Offering Circular.	Revenue less Operating Expenses at Issue Date (Field ES45 minus ES46). If multiple properties, sum the values. If missing data or if all received/consolidated, refer to the DSCR Indicator Legend rule.
	Capital Expenditures at Issue Date	ES48		Numeric	10000	If multiple properties, then sum the value, if missing any then use the DSCR Indicator Legend. Should match the Offering Circular if available	Capex at Issue Date (as opposed to repairs and maintenance) if identified in the Offering Circular. If missing date or if all received/consolidated refer to the DSCR Indicator Legend rule
	NCF At Issue Date	ES49	S83	Numeric	10000	Net Cash Flow on the Properties at the Issue Date, as set forth in the Offering Circular	NOI less Capex at Issue Date (Field ES47 less ES48). If missing data or if all received/consolidated refer to the DSCR Indicator Legend rule.
	ICR (NOI) At Issue Date	ES50		Numeric	2.11	If multiple properties, use the DSCR Indicator Legend. ICR At Issue Date using NOI. Should match the Offering Circular if available.	The ICR as described in the Offering Circular (if available). otherwise calculate using the NOI as Issue Date and the interest based on the Loan Rate at Issue Date (Field ES62) and Actual Principal Balance at Issue Date (Field ES60). If multiple properties and not all information available refer to the DSCR Indicator Legend rule.
	ICR (NCF) at Issue Date	ES51		Numeric	2.11	If multiple properties use the DSCR Indicate Legend. ICR At Issue Date using NCF to calculate. Should match the Offering Circular if available.	The ICR based on NCF at Issue date as described in the Offering Circular (if available), otherwise calculated using the NCF at Issue Date and the interest based on the Loan Rate at Issue Date (Field ES62) and Actual Principal Balance at Issue Date (Field ES60). If multiple properties and not all available refer to the DSCR Indicator Legend rule.
	DSCR (NOI) At Issue Date	ES52	S66	Numeric	2.11	If multiple properties, use the DSCR Indicator Legend. DSCR At Issue Date using NOI. Should match the Offering Circular if available.	The DSCR as described in the Offering Circular (if available), otherwise calculate using the NOI as Issue Date and the debt service amount by annualising the Periodic P & I Payment at Issue Date (Field ES61). If multiple properties and not all information available refer to the DSCR Indicator Legend rule.
	DSCR (NCF) At Issue Date	ES53		Numeric	2.11	DSCR based upon NCF at the Issue Date as set forth in the Offering Circular	The DSCR as described in the Offering Circular (if available), otherwise calculate using the NCF as Issue Date and the debt service amount by annualising the Periodic P & I Payment at Issue Date (Field ES61). If multiple properties and not all information available refer to the DSCR Indicator Legend rule
Loan Statistics at Issue Date (ES45 -ES72)	DSCR Indicator At Issue Date	ES54	S85	Alpha Numeric	Text	Flag used to explain how the DSCR was calculated when there are multiple properties. See DSCR Indicator Legend	Code describing how the DSCR is calculated/applied when a loan has multiple properties. See DSCR Indicator Legend for codes.
	Original Loan to Value (LTV) Ratio at Issue Date	ES55		Numeric	0.75	Should match the Offering Circular if available.	The Loan to Value ratio as described in the Offering Circular (if available), otherwise calculate using Actual Principal Balance at Issue Date (Field ES60) and Portfolio Value at Issue Date (Field ES56)

507

European Commercial Mortgage Securities Association
CMSA "Loan Setup" File
(Data Record Layout)
Cross Refrenced as "ES"

E - CMSA Grouping	Field Name	UK / European Field Number	US Field Number	Field Type	Format Example	Description / Comments	European Definitions
	Portfolio Value At Issue Date	ES56	S67	Numeric	1000000.00	If multiple properties, sum the values. If missing any then leave empty.	The valuation of the properties securing the loan at Issue Date as described in the Offering Circular. If multiple properties sum the value in the Property File, otherwise leave blank.
	Valuation Date At Issue Date	ES57	S68	Alpha Numeric	YYYYMMDD	If multiple properties and all the same then print the date. If missing any then leave empty.	The date the valuation was prepared for the values disclosed in the Offering Circular. For multiple properties, leave blank.
	Economic Occupancy At Issue Date	ES58	S69	Numeric	0.95	If multiple properties, use weighted average by using the calculation [Current Allocated %(Prop) * Occupancy(Oper)] for each Property. If missing one then leave empty.	The percentage of rentable space with signed leased in place at Issue Date if disclosed in Offering Circular (tenants may not be in occupation but are paying rent). If multiple properties use weighted average by using the calculation (Current Allocated % (Prop)*Occupancy)) for each property. If missing some date leave blank.
	Committed Principal Balance At Issue Date	ES59		Numeric	1000000.00	The committed balance, including current undrawn amounts, of the mortgage loan at issue date	The committed balance, including any undrawn amounts, of the loan at Issue Date.
	Actual Principal Balance At Issue Date	ES60	S44	Numeric	1000000.00	The actual drawn principal balance of the mortgage loan at issue date	Actual Principal Balance of the loan at the Issue Date as identified in the Offering Circular
	Periodic P&I Payment At Issue Date	ES61	S53	Numeric	100000.00	The periodic scheduled principal & interest payment at issuance monthly/quarterly	The scheduled principal & interest payment that is due on the next Loan Payment Date as at the Issue Date.
	Loan Rate At Issue Date	ES62	S45	Numeric	0.04563	Gross interest rate applicable to the calculation of scheduled interest at issue date	The total interest rate (eg Libor + Margin) that is being used to calculate interest due on the loan at the Issue Date.
	Ranking of Charge at Issue Date	ES63	S78	Numeric	1	1=First, 2=Second	Is the security granted to the Issue a first ranking security, ie does it have priority over all other lenders/parties (enter 1); or is it second ranking, ie subordinated in some way (enter 2).
	Financials reported at issuance as of Date	ES64	S72	Alpha Numeric	YYYYMMDD	The as of date for the property financials provided issuance. If missing leave blank.	The end date of the financials used to support the Revenue and Expenses amounts disclosed in the Offering Circular if available, otherwise the Issue Date. If multiple properties and the dates are the same, enter the date, or if different or missing any leave blank.
	Remaining Term At Issue Date	ES65	S41	Numeric	240	Remaining number of months until maturity of loan at issue date	The number of months remaining to maturity of loan at the Issue Date.
	Remaining Amort Term At Issue Date	ES66	S42	Numeric	240	Remaining number of months loan amortised at issue date	The number of months loan amortised at the Issue Date. If amortisation has not commenced at the Issue Date this will be less than the Remaining Term at Issue Date.
Loan Statistics at Issue Date (ES45 -ES72)	Loan Maturity Date at Issue Date	ES67	S43	Alpha Numeric	YYYYMMDD	The scheduled maturity date of the mortgage loan at issue	The maturity date of the loan as defined in the loan agreement. This would not take into account any extended maturity date that may be allowed under the loan agreement, but the initial maturity date
	Blank Field	ES68				Blank Field	
	Blank Field	ES69				Blank Field	

European Commercial Mortgage Securities Association
CMSA "Loan Setup" File
(Data Record Layout)
Cross Refrenced as "ES"

E - CMSA Grouping	Field Name	UK / European Field Number	US Field Number	Field Type	Format Example	Description / Comments	European Definitions
	Blank Field	ES70				Blank Field	
	Blank Field	ES71				Blank Field	
	Blank Field	ES72				Blank Field	
	Amounts Held in Escrow at Issue Date	ES73		Numeric	10000	Total amounts held in escrow accounts at the time of securitisation	Total balance of the reserve accounts at the loan level at the Issue Date.
	Collection Of Escrows (Y/N)	ES74	S76	Alpha Numeric	N	Y=Yes, N=No - Referring to ground rents	Enter Y - (yes) if any payments are held in reserve accounts to cover ground lease payments, insurance or taxes only (not maintenance, improvements, capex etc) as required under the loan agreement, otherwise N - (No).
Loan Escrow & Reserve Details	Collection Of Other Reserves (Y/N)	ES75	S77	Alpha Numeric	N	Y=Yes, N=No - Referring to reserves other than ground rents	Are any amounts other than round rents taxes or insurance held in reserve accounts as required under the terms of the loan agreement for tenant improvements, leasing commissions and similar items in respect of the related property or for purpose of providing additional collateral for such loan. Y= Yes or N =No
(ES73 - ES81)	Escrow Held Upon Trigger Event	ES76		Alpha Numeric	N	Y=Yes N=No	Does the loan agreement require reserve amounts to be made upon the occurrence of any trigger events. Y= Yes or N =No
	Trigger for Escrow to be Held	ES77		Alpha Numeric	ICRT	Trigger Event Legend	If yes, refer the Trigger Event Legend and describe type of trigger event.
	Blank Field	ES78				Blank Field	
	Blank Field	ES79				Blank Field	
	Blank Field	ES80				Blank Field	
	Blank Field	ES81				Blank Field	
Loan Grouping & Substitutions Details	Cross-Collateralised Loan Grouping	ES82	S75	Alpha Numeric	Text	Indicator of loans that are cross collateralised (Example: loans 1 and 44 are cross collateralised as are loans 4 and 47). First pair will be assigned value of 1; second pair assigned value of 2	Indicator of loans that are cross collateralised within the pool (Example: loans 1 and 44 are cross collateralised as are loans 4 and 47). First pair will be assigned value of 1; second pair assigned value of 2
(ES82 - ES91)	Substituted Loan (Y/N)	ES83		Alpha Numeric	Y	Y=Yes N=No. Was loan substituted for another loan on a date after the Issue Date?	Is this loan a substitute for another loan on a date after the Issue Date? Y=Yes N=No
	Date of Substitution	ES84	S11	Alpha Numeric	YYYYMMDD	If loan was substituted after the Issue Date, the date of such substitution	If loan was substituted after the Issue Date, the date of such substitution
	Grace Days Allowed	ES85	S89	Numeric	5	Number of days from due date borrower is permitted to remit payment	The number of days after a payment is due in which the lender will not charge a late penalty or report the payment as late.
	Additional Financing Indicator	ES86		Numeric	0	See Additional Financing Indicator Code Legend	Code indicating whether additional financing/mezzanine debt is present. See Additional Financing Indicator Legend
	Blank Field	ES87				Blank Field	
	Blank Field	ES88				Blank Field	
	Blank Field	ES89				Blank Field	
	Blank Field	ES90				Blank Field	
Loan Grouping & Substitutions Details	Blank Field	ES91				Blank Field	
(ES82 - ES91)	Interest Rate Type	ES92	S14	Numeric	1	1=Fixed, 2=Floating, 3=Step, 4=Mixed/Fixed Floating, 9=Other	Use a code to describe the type of interest rate applied to the loan. 1=Fixed, 2=Floating, 3=Step, 4=Mixed/Fixed Floating, 9=Other

European Commercial Mortgage Securities Association
CMSA "Loan Setup" File
(Data Record Layout)
Cross Refrenced as "ES"

E - CMSA Grouping	Field Name	UK / European Field Number	US Field Number	Field Type	Format Example	Description / Comments	European Definitions
Loan Interest Rate Details (ES92 - ES98)	Interest Accrual Method Code	ES93	S15	Numeric	1	1=30/360, 2=Actual/365, 3=Actual/360, 4=Actual/Actual, 5=Actual/366, 6=Simple	Code indicating the 'number of days' convention used to calculate interest. 1=30/360, 2=actual/365, 3=actual/360, 4=actual/actual, 5=actual/366, 6=simple.
	Interest in Arrears (Y/N)	ES94	S16	Alpha Numeric	Y	Y=Yes N=No	Is the interest that accrues on the loan paid in arrears Y(es) or N(o)
	Blank Field	ES95				Blank Field	
	Blank Field	ES96				Blank Field	
	Blank Field	ES97				Blank Field	
	Blank Field	ES98				Blank Field	
Loan Amortisation Details (ES99 - ES107)	Amortisation Type Code	ES99		Numeric	1	See Amortisation Type Code Legend	Refer to the Amortisation Code legend to describe the type of amortisation that applies to the loan
	Original Length of IO Period	ES100		Numeric	24	Number of months that loan is interest only	Number of months that loan is interest only (from the date of origination not from the Issue Date)
	Amortisation Trigger	ES101		Alpha Numeric	Y	Y=Yes N=No. Identify if a trigger event caused the loan to amortise in addition to scheduled amortisation	Y=Yes N=No. Identify if a trigger event caused the loan to amortise in addition to scheduled amortisation.
	Amortisation Trigger Types	ES102		Alpha Numeric	LTVT	Trigger Events Legends	If yes, refer the Trigger Event Legend and describe type of trigger event.
	Amortisation Trigger Levels	ES103		Numeric	2	If multiple triggers, leave empty. Otherwise, indicate number for trigger	What level of amortisation will be required if a trigger event occurs. Describe as a % of the loan balance at origination if possible. If multiple triggers or not easily described leave blank
	Accrual of Interest Allowed	ES104		Alpha Numeric	Y	Y=Yes N=No - Do the loan documents allow for interest to be accrued and capitalised	Do the loan documents allow for interest to be accrued and capitalised - Y=Yes N=No
	Blank Field	ES105				Blank Field	
	Blank Field	ES106				Blank Field	
	Blank Field	ES107				Blank Field	
Loan Prepayment Details (ES108 - ES114)	Prepayment Lock-out End Date	ES108	S18	Alpha Numeric	YYYYMMDD	Date after which loan can be prepaid	The date after which the lender allows prepayment of the loan. If there are no restrictions leave blank
	Yield Maintenance End Date	ES109	S19	Alpha Numeric	YYYYMMDD	Date after which loan can be prepaid without yield maintenance	The date after which the lender allows prepayment of the loan without requirement for a prepayment fee or yield maintenance to be paid
	Prepayment Premium End Date	ES110	S20	Alpha Numeric	YYYYMMDD	Date after which loan can be prepaid without penalty	The date after which the lender allows prepayment of the loan without requirement for a prepayment fee to be paid
	Prepayment Terms Description	ES111	S21	Alpha Numeric	Text	Should reflect the information in Offering Circular. For Instance, if the prepayment terms are the payment of a 1% fee in year one of the loan, 0.5% in year two and 0.25% in year three of the loan this may be shown in the OC as: 1%(12), 0.5%(24), 0.25%(36)	Should reflect the information in Offering Circular. For Instance, if the prepayment terms are the payment of a 1% fee in year one of the loan. 0.5% in year two and 0.25% in year three of the loan this may be shown in the OC as 1%(12), .5%(24) 0.25%(36)

European Commercial Mortgage Securities Association
CMSA "Loan Setup" File
(Data Record Layout)
Cross Refrenced as "ES"

E - CMSA Grouping	Field Name	UK / European Field Number	US Field Number	Field Type	Format Example	Description / Comments	European Definitions
	Blank Field	ES112				Blank Field	
	Blank Field	ES113				Blank Field	
	Blank Field	ES114				Blank Field	
Loan Hedging Details (ES115 - ES134)	Margin	ES115		Numeric	0.013	Rate added to index used in the determination of the gross interest rate	The rate added to the index rate used to calculate the interest paid on the loan
	Lifetime Rate Cap	ES116	S26	Numeric	0.0603	Maximum rate that the borrower must pay on a Floating loan per the loan agreement	Maximum rate that the borrower must pay on a floating rate loan as required under the terms of the loan agreement
	Lifetime Rate Floor	ES117	S27	Numeric	0.0403	Minimum rate that the borrower must pay on a Floating loan per the loan agreement	Minimum rate that the borrower must pay on a floating rate loan as required under the terms of the loan agreement
	Type of Loan Level Swap	ES118		Alpha Numeric	C	C = Currency Swap; I = Interest Rate Swap; CI = Currency and Interest Rate Swap	Describe the type of loan level swap that applies - C = Currency Swap, I = Interest Rate Swap, CI = Currency and Interest Rate Swap
	Loan Swap Provider	ES119		Alpha Numeric	Text	Name of Swap Counterparty	The name of the swap provider for the loan if the Borrower has the direct contract with the swap counterparty. Leave blank if the loan has been hedged with the lender having the contract with the swap counterparty
	Type of Interest Rate Loan Level Swap	ES120		Alpha Numeric	L	L=Fixed to LIBOR, E=Fixed to Euribor, O=Other (Identify)	Describe the type of interest rate swap that applies to the loan - L=Fixed to LIBOR, E=Fixed to Euribor, O=Other (Identify)
	Type of Currency Loan Level Swap	ES121		Alpha Numeric	OS	OE=Other currency to Euros, OS=Other currency to Sterling, O=Other (Identify)	Describe the type of currency rate swap that applies - OE=Other currency to Euros, OS=Other currency to Sterling, O=Other (Identify)
	Payment Obligations by Loan Swap provider	ES122		Numeric	0.013	The spread over Index (if any) payable by Loan Swap Provider on an Interest Rate Swap	The spread over Index (if any) payable by Loan Swap Provider on an Interest Rate Swap
	Swap Rate payable by borrower	ES123		Numeric	0.013	The strike price that is payable by the Borrower under the Interest Rate Swap	The strike price that is payable by the Borrower under the Interest Rate Swap
	Exchange Rate for Loan Level Swap	ES124		Numeric	0.013	Exchange Rate for Loan Level Swap	The exchange rate that has been set for a currency loan level swap
Loan Hedging Details (ES115 - ES134)	Start date of Loan Level Swap	ES125		Alpha Numeric	YYYYMMDD	Start Date	
	End Date of Loan Level Swap	ES126		Alpha Numeric	YYYYMMDD	End Date	
	Required Ratings of Loan Swap Provider	ES127		Alpha Numeric	Text	Identify the minimum rating requirements of Loan Swap Provider	Identify the minimum rating requirements of Loan Swap Provider either as required under the loan or servicing agreement
	Actual Ratings of Loan Swap Provider	ES128		Alpha Numeric	Text	Identify the ratings of the Swap Counterparty as of the date of issuance of the Notes at Issue Date	Identify the ratings of the Swap Counterparty as at the Issue Date
	Borrower's Obligation to Pay Breakage on Loan Level Swap	ES129		Alpha Numeric	TI	Extent to which Borrower is obligated to pay breakage costs to Loan Swap Provider (see Swap Breakage Legend)	Refer to Swap Breakage Legend for code to describe what level of indemnification is given by the borrower to pay breakage costs on the swap
	Reset Date for Loan Level Swap	ES130		Alpha Numeric	YYYYMMDD	The reset date for any Interest Rate Swap	What date will the rate on the swap be reset (give the next date that is due)
	Blank Field	ES131				Blank Field	
	Blank Field	ES132				Blank Field	
	Blank Field	ES133				Blank Field	
	Blank Field	ES134				Blank Field	
	First Rate Adjustment Date	ES135	S23	Alpha Numeric	YYYYMMDD	First date on which the interest rate on the Loan could change (not the first date after securitisation on which it could change)	For adjustable rate loans, enter the first date that the interest rate was due to change. For fixed rate loans, enter the first interest payment date (not the first date after securitisation on which it could change).

European Commercial Mortgage Securities Association
CMSA "Loan Setup" File
(Data Record Layout)
Cross Refenced as "ES"

E - CMSA Grouping	Field Name	UK / European Field Number	US Field Number	Field Type	Format Example	Description / Comments	European Definitions
Rate Adjustment Details (ES135 - ES147)	First Payment Adjustment Date	ES136	S24	Alpha Numeric	YYYYMMDD	First date on which the payment on the Loan could change (not the first date that the payment could change after securitisation)	For adjustable rate loans, the next date that the amount of scheduled principal and/or interest is due to change. For fixed rate loans, enter the next payment date (not the first date after securitisation on which it could change).
	Payment Frequency	ES137	S32	Numeric	3	Frequency of payments on Loan according to original loan documents. 1=Monthly, 3=Quarterly, 6=Semi-Annually, 12=Annually	Frequency of payments on Loan according to original loan documents. 1=Monthly, 3=Quarterly, 6=Semi-Annually, 12=Annually, 365=Daily
	Rate Reset Frequency	ES138	S33	Numeric	3	Frequency with which the interest rate is reset according to original loan documents. 1=Monthly, 3=Quarterly, 6=Semi-Annually, 12=Annually, 365=Daily	Frequency with which the interest rate is reset according to original loan documents. 1=Monthly, 3=Quarterly, 6=Semi-Annually, 12=Annually, 365=Daily
	Pay Reset Frequency	ES139	S34	Numeric	3	Frequency with which the P&I payment is reset according to original loan documents. 1=Monthly, 3=Quarterly, 6=Semi-Annually, 12=Annually, 365=Daily	Frequency with which the P&I payment is reset according to original loan documents. 1=Monthly, 3=Quarterly, 6=Semi-Annually, 12=Annually, 365=Daily
	Index Look Back In Days	ES140	S37	Numeric	3	Use Index in Effect X Days Prior to Adjustment Date	The number of days prior to the interest payment date that the interest rate is set (eg Euribor set 2 days prior to interest payment date)
	Index Determination Date	ES141		Alpha Numeric	YYYYMMDD	Specific dates (if any) at which Index will be determined	If the Loan Agreement states specific dates for the index to be set, enter brief description in field. Eg. 15 Jan/Apr/July/Oct.
	Blank Field	ES142				Blank Field	
	Blank Field	ES143				Blank Field	
	Blank Field	ES144				Blank Field	
	Blank Field	ES145				Blank Field	
	Blank Field	ES146				Blank Field	
	Blank Field	ES147				Blank Field	
Rate Adjustment Details (ES135 - ES147)	Loan Structure Code	ES148	S90	Alpha Numeric	WL	See Loan Structure Code Legend	Refer to the Loan Structure Code to describe what structure applies to this loan eg whole loan, A/B splits, syndicated. Use multiple codes is applicable.
	Syndicated Loan	ES149		Alpha Numeric	N	Y=Yes, N=No	Is the loan part of a syndicated loan? Y= Yes or N =No.
	Date of Syndication	ES150		Alpha Numeric	YYYYMMDD		
	Type of Syndication	ES151		Alpha Numeric	FP	See Participation Legend	See Participation Legend.
	Participation of Issuer in Syndicated Loan	ES152		Alpha Numeric	FP	See Participation Legend	Refer to Participation Legend to describe the method used by the Issuer to acquire ownership in the syndicated loan.
	Total Loan Balance	ES153		Numeric	1000000.00	Total balance of loan that has been syndicated	Enter the total balance of the syndicated loan at Issue Date.
	Total Issuer Loan Balance	ES154		Numeric	1000000.00	Balance of loan in the securitisation	Enter the balance of the syndicated loan that is owned by the Issuer at the Issuer Date
	% of Issuer Facility being Securitised	ES155		Numeric	0.30	% of total loan in securitisation at Issue Date	What % of the syndicated loan is owned by the Issuer at the Issue Date.
	Name of Controlling Syndicate Member	ES156		Alpha Numeric	Text	Name of controlling participant	Name of the party that controls or is the majority for decision making of the syndication

European Commercial Mortgage Securities Association
CMSA "Loan Setup" File
(Data Record Layout)
Cross Refrenced as "ES"

E - CMSA Grouping	Field Name	UK / European Field Number	US Field Number	Field Type	Format Example	Description / Comments	European Definitions
Loan Syndication & Participation Details (ES148 - ES168)	Relationship of Controlling Syndicate Member	ES157		Alpha Numeric	Text	Investor or Third Party Provider	Describe the relationship of the controlling syndicate member to the Issuer eg investor or other syndicate lender.
	Other Material Syndicate Members (>33% interest)	ES158		Alpha Numeric	Text	Name of material participants defined as banks owning 33% or more of the loan	Name of material syndicate members defined as banks owning 33% or more of the loan
	Rights of Controlling Party for Material Decisions	ES159		Alpha Numeric	Text	See Controlling Party Rights (Material Decisions) Legend. Does owner of any participation other than the issuer have the right to make major decisions and if so, Who is it? Y=Yes N=No add Name	See Controlling Party Rights (Material Decisions) Legend. Does owner of any participation other than the issuer have the right to make major decisions and if so, Who is it? Y=Yes N=No - add Name.
	Rights of Issuer's Loan	ES160		Alpha Numeric	Text	See Controlling Party Rights (Material Decisions) Legend. Does issuer have right to make material decisions?	Refer to Controlling Party Rights (Material Decisions) Legend to describe the rights the Issuer may have on material decisions.
	Method of Notification for Material Decisions	ES161		Alpha Numeric	Text	Mail, Verbal, Electronic	What method must the facility agent use to advise about matters relating to material decisions eg mail, verbal, electronic.
	Major Decision Notification Period	ES162		Numeric	10	Number of Days required notice	How many days notice is required to respond on matters relating to material decisions.
	Participant Deadlock Resolutions Methods	ES163		Alpha Numeric	Text	Shot Gun Buy-Sell, Independent Arbitrator, Other Method	What methods can be used to resolve deadlocks on material decisions eg Shot Gun Buy-Sell, Independent Arbitrator, Other Method.
	Method of Notification	ES164		Alpha Numeric	Text	Mail, Verbal, Electronic	What method must the facility agent use to advise about matters relating to deadlocks eg mail, verbal, electronic.
	Deadlock Notification Period	ES165		Numeric	10	Number of Days required notice	How many days notice is allowed to respond when there is a deadlock.
	Blank Field	ES166				Blank Field	
	Blank Field	ES167				Blank Field	
	Blank Field	ES168				Blank Field	
Loan Syndication & Participation Details (ES148 - ES168)	Last Setup Change Date	ES169	S82	Alpha Numeric	YYYYMMDD	Payment date that the information was last changed by loan	The Loan Payment Date that any information in the Loan Set Up File was last changed, following any amendments/modifications to the loan agreement
	Remedy for Breach of Financial Covenant	ES170		Numeric	1	Indicate types of remedies for a breach of a financial covenant by populating with "Remedies Upon Breach of Financial Covenants' Legend	Refer to the "Remedies Upon Breach of Financial Covenants" Legend to select the code describing the remedy for the financial covenant breach.
	Loan Contributor to Securitisation	ES171	S86	Alpha Numeric	Text	Name of entity ultimately responsible for the reps and warranties of the loan	Name of the originator that sold the loan to the Issuer.
Misc. Loan Details (ES169 - ES179)	Credit Tenant Lease	ES172	S87	Alpha Numeric	Y	Y=Yes, N=No. Single tenant with lease term at least as long as the loan term	Enter Y - (yes) if there is a single tenant whose lease is at least as long as the term of the loan, otherwise N - (no). If there are multiple properties and at least one of the properties has a CTL enter Y/P to show the CTLs apply to part of the security.
	Financial Information Submission Penalties	ES173	S88	Alpha Numeric	N	Indicator for penalties for borrower's failure to submit required financial information (Op. Stmt. Schedule, etc.) as per loan documents. M=Monetary, N=No penalties allowed in documents, O=Other penalties	Indicator for penalties for borrower's failure to submit required financial information (Op. Stmt, Schedule, etc.) as per loan documents. M=Monetary, N=No penalties allowed in documents, O=Other penalties.
	Recourse (Y/N)	ES174	S73	Alpha Numeric	Y	Y=Yes N=No Is the loan recourse to any party?	Is there recourse to another party (eg guarantor) if the event the borrower defaults on an obligation under the loan agreement? Y=Yes N=No.
	Rounding Code	ES175	S35	Numeric	1	Rounding method for sum of index plus margin (See Rounding Code Legend)	Refer to Rounding Code Legend to describe the method for rounding the interest rate.
	Rounding Increment	ES176	S36	Numeric	1	Used in conjunction with rounding code	The incremental percentage by which an index rate should be rounded in determining the interest rate as set out in the loan agreement.
	Servicing Fee Rate	ES177	S46	Numeric	1000.00	Amount of fee deducted from interest transferred to Issuer	The % rate per annum paid to the servicer.
	Blank Field	ES177				Blank Field	
	Blank Field	ES178				Blank Field	
	Blank Field	ES179				Blank Field	

version 1.0

Field Type Codes	
D	Date: DD/MM/YYYY
I	Integer
R	Real Number
T	Text
Z	Postcode
Property Type Code Legend	
CP	Caravan Park
CPK	Car Park
HC	Health Care
HO	Hospitality/Hotel
IN	Industrial
LA	Land
LE	Leisure
MF	Multifamily
MU	Mixed Use
OF	Office
OT	Other
RT	Retail
SS	Self Storage
WH	Warehouse
NOI/NCF Indicator Code Legend	
CMSA	Calculated using CMSA standard
PSA	Calculated using a definition given in the PSA
U/W	Calculated using the underwriting method
Property Status Codes	
1	In Foreclosure
2	Real Estate Owned
3	Defeased
4	Partial Release
5	Released
6	Same as at Issue Date

European Commercial Mortgage Securities Association
CMSA "Loan Periodic Update" File
(Data Record Layout)
Cross Refenced as "EL"

E - CMSA Grouping	Field Name	UK / European Field Number	US Field Number	Field Type	Format Example	Description / Comments	European Definitions
	Transaction Identifier	EL1	L1	Alpha Numeric	XXX97001	Unique Issue Identification String	The name assigned to the securitisation or issue, this can be as identified in the Offering Circular or assigned by the Servicer.
	Group Identifier	EL2	L2	Alpha Numeric	XXX97001A	Unique identification number assigned to each loan group within an issue	The alpha-numeric code assigned to each loan group within an issue. A Group ID may not be applicable for every transaction.
	Servicer Loan Identifier	EL3	L3	Alpha Numeric	0000000012345	Unique number assigned to each loan by the Servicer	The Servicer's unique identification number assigned to each loan in the pool.
	Offering Circular Loan Identifier	EL4	L4	Alpha Numeric	123	Unique number assigned to each loan in the Offering Circular	The identification number(s), if any, assigned to each loan in the offering circular.
	Number of Properties	EL5	L86	Alpha Numeric	13.00	The Number of Properties Underlying the Mortgage Loan	The number of properties that serve as security for the loan.
	Loan Payment Date	EL6	L6	Alpha Numeric	YYYYMMDD	Date payments made to the Issuer	The date principal and interest is paid to the Issuer, this would normally be the interest payment date of the loan.
Loan Identifiers & Payment Date Details	Paid through Date	EL7	L8	Alpha Numeric	YYYYMMDD	Last loan interest payment date for which full payment has been received	The date at which all payments have been paid in full with no shortfalls. On a performing loan this will be the Loan Payment Date immediately prior to the date in Field EL6.
	Next Rate Adjustment Date	EL8	L21	Alpha Numeric	YYYYMMDD	Date Loan Interest Rate Is Next Scheduled to Change	For adjustable rate loans, the next date that the interest rate is due to change. For fixed rate loans, enter the next interest payment date.
(EL1 - EL15)	Next Payment Adjustment Date	EL9	L22	Alpha Numeric	YYYYMMDD	Date Scheduled P&I Amount Is Next Scheduled To Change	For adjustable rate loans, the next date that the amount of scheduled principal and/or interest is due to change. For fixed rate loans, enter the next payment date.
	Current Loan Maturity Date	EL10	L11	Alpha Numeric	YYYYMMDD	Date Loan Is Scheduled To Make Its Final Payment	The maturity date of the loan as defined in the loan agreement. This would not take into account any extended maturity dates that may be allowed under the loan agreement, but the initial maturity date.
	Blank Field	EL11				**Blank Field**	
	Blank Field	EL12				**Blank Field**	
	Blank Field	EL13				**Blank Field**	
	Blank Field	EL14				**Blank Field**	
	Blank Field	EL15				**Blank Field**	
	Current Index Rate	EL16	L9	Numeric	0.09	The index rate used to determine the Current Loan Interest Rate.	The interest rate (before margin) used to calculate the interest paid on the Loan Payment Date in Field EL6.
Rate Details	Current Margin Rate	EL17		Numeric	0.09	Margin used to determine the Current Loan Interest Rate	The margin being used to calculate the interest paid on the Loan Payment Date in Field EL6.
	Current Loan Interest Rate	EL18	L10	Numeric	0.09	Gross Rate per annum used to calculate the current period scheduled interest	The total interest rate being used to calculate the interest paid on the Loan Payment Date in Field EL6 (sum of Field EL16 and EL18).
(EL16 - EL23)	Blank Field	EL19				**Blank Field**	
	Blank Field	EL20				**Blank Field**	
	Blank Field	EL21				**Blank Field**	
	Blank Field	EL22				**Blank Field**	
	Blank Field	EL23				**Blank Field**	

European Commercial Mortgage Securities Association
CMSA "Loan Periodic Update" File
(Data Record Layout)
Cross Refenced as "EL"

E - CMSA Grouping	Field Name	UK / European Field Number	US Field Number	Field Type	Format Example	Description / Comments	European Definitions
Principal Details (EL24 - EL34)	Current Beginning Opening Balance	EL24	L6	Numeric	100000.00	Outstanding balance at beginning of current period	The outstanding balance of the loan at the beginning of the interest period used the calculate the interest due on the Loan Payment Date in Field EL6
	Scheduled Principal Amount	EL25	L24	Numeric	1000.00	Scheduled Principal Payment Due on the Loan for the current period	The principal payment due to be paid to the Issuer on the Loan Payment Date in Field EL6 eg amortisation but not prepayments
	Current Ending Scheduled Balance	EL26	L7	Numeric	100000.00	Outstanding Sched Prin Bal of Loan at End of current period following amortisation but prior to any prepayments	The principal balance of the loan that would be outstanding following the scheduled principal payment but prior to any prepayments (Field EL24 minus EL25)
	Unscheduled Principal Collections	EL27	L27	Numeric	1000.00	Unscheduled payments of principal received during the current period	Other principal payments received during the interest period that will be used to pay down the loan. This may relate to sales proceeds, voluntary prepayments or liquidation amounts.
	Other Principal Adjustments	EL28	L28	Numeric	1000.00	Unscheduled principal adjustments for interest period, not associated with movement of cash.	Any other amounts that would cause the balance of the loan to be decreased or increased in the current period which are not considered Unscheduled Principal Collections and are not Scheduled Principal. Examples include write offs and adjustments necessary to synchronize the Servicer's records with the value of the bonds.
Principal Details (EL24 - EL34)	Actual Balance	EL29	L36	Numeric	100000.00	Outstanding Actual Principal Balance At The End Of The Current Period	The actual balance of the loan outstanding for the next interest period following all principal payments
	Blank Field	EL30				Blank Field	
	Blank Field	EL31				Blank Field	
	Blank Field	EL32				Blank Field	
	Blank Field	EL33				Blank Field	
	Blank Field	EL34				Blank Field	
Interest Details (EL35 - EL45)	Scheduled Interest Amount	EL35	L23	Numeric	1000.00	Gross interest for period assuming no repayment in current period	The total interest that is due on the Loan Payment Date, assuming no prepayments are made during the interest period.
	Prepayment Interest Excess (Shortfall)	EL36	L31	Numeric	1000.00	Shortfall or excess of actual interest payment for the current period that is not related to a loan default.	Results from a prepayment received on a date other than a scheduled payment due date: Shortfall – The difference by which the amount of interest paid is less than the scheduled interest that was due on the Loan Payment Date. (this would only apply if there is a shortfall after the borrower has paid any break costs). Excess – Interest collected in excess of the accrued interest due for the loan interest accrual period. A negative number displays shortfall and excess is displayed as a positive number.
	Other Interest Adjustment	EL37	L102	Numeric	1000.00	Companion field for EL30 to show Unscheduled Interest Adjustments for the related Collection Period	Companion field for Other Principal Adjustments (Field EL28) to show unscheduled interest adjustments for the related collection period
Interest Details (EL35 - EL45)	Reimbursed Interest on Advances	EL38	L107	Numeric	1000.00	Indicates any reimbursed interest on property protection advances in the calculation of the reconciliation of funds	Cumulative amount of interest paid to the Servicer for any property protection advances.
	Negative Amortisation / Deferred Interest / Capitalised Interest	EL39	L26	Numeric	1000.00	Negative Amortisation/Deferred Interest/Capitalised Interest	Negative amortisation occurs when interest accrued during a payment period is greater than the scheduled payment and the excess amount is added to the outstanding loan balance. Deferred interest is the amount by which the interest a borrower is required to pay on a mortgage loan is less than the amount of interest accrued on the outstanding loan balance. Capitalised interest is where interest is added to the loan balance at the end of the interest period in accordance with loan agreement.

European Commercial Mortgage Securities Association
CMSA "Loan Periodic Update" File
(Data Record Layout)
Cross Refrenced as "EL"

E - CMSA Grouping	Field Name	UK / European Field Number	US Field Number	Field Type	Format Example	Description / Comments	European Definitions
	Actual Interest Paid	EL40		Numeric	1000.00	Actual Interest Paid	Total amount of interest paid by the borrower during the interest period or on the Loan Payment Date.
	Blank Field	EL41				Blank Field	
	Blank Field	EL42				Blank Field	
	Blank Field	EL43				Blank Field	
	Blank Field	EL44				Blank Field	
	Blank Field	EL45				Blank Field	
Principal & Interest Details (EL46 - EL58)	Total Scheduled Principal & Interest due	EL46	L25	Numeric	1000.00	Scheduled Principal & Interest Payment Due on the Loan For The Current Period for the Issuer	The total scheduled principal and interest due on the Loan Payment Date (sum of Fields EL25 and EL35) - can be used for DSCR calculations.
	Total Shortfalls in Principal & Interest Outstanding	EL47		Numeric	1000.00	Cumulative outstanding P&I Amounts due on Loan At The End Of The Current Period	The cumulative amount of any unpaid principal and interest on the Loan Payment Date
	Total Other Amounts Outstanding	EL48		Numeric	1000.00	Cumulative outstanding Amounts on Loan (e.g., Insurance Premia, Ground Rents) At The End Of The Current Period That Have Been Expended by Issuer/Servicer	The cumulative amount of any property protection advances or other sums that have been advanced by the Servicer or Issuer and not yet reimbursed by the borrower.
	Cumulative Amount Outstanding	EL49		Numeric	1000.00	The sum of Field EL47 and EL48	The sum of Field EL47 and EL48.
	Amortisation Trigger Reached	EL50		Alpha Numeric	Y	Y=Yes N=No If the Loan has an amortisation trigger, has the trigger been met	Y=Yes N=No If the Loan has an amortisation trigger, has the trigger been met.
	Current Amortisation Type	EL51		Alpha Numeric	1	See Amortisation Type Code Legend	Refer to Amortisation Type Legend for description to use
	Annuity Full Amortisation Period	EL52		Alpha Numeric	YYYYMMDD	If Annuity amortisation, period over which loan would fully amortise if scheduled annuity payment continued to paid until zero balance was achieved	If the amortisation type is Annuity, what is the date the loan would reduce to zero if the annuity payments continue to be paid.
Principal & Interest Details (EL46 - EL58)	Linear Amortisation per Annum	EL53		Numeric	1000.00	If Linear amortisation, percentage of amortisation per annum, calculated as percentage of day 1 loan balance	If the amortisation type is Linear, what is the percentage of amortisation being paid per annum based on the original loan balance (not the balance when the securitisation closed).
	Blank Field	EL54				Blank Field	
	Blank Field	EL55				Blank Field	
	Blank Field	EL56				Blank Field	
	Blank Field	EL57				Blank Field	
	Blank Field	EL58				Blank Field	

European Commercial Mortgage Securities Association
CMSA "Loan Periodic Update" File
(Data Record Layout)
Cross Refrenced as "EL"

E - CMSA Grouping	Field Name	UK / European Field Number	US Field Number	Field Type	Format Example	Description / Comments	European Definitions
Most Recent YTD Financial Details (EL59 - EL85)	Most Recent Financial As of Start Date	EL59	L72	Alpha Numeric	YYYYMMDD	If multiple properties and all the same then print the date, if missing any then leave empty	The first day of the financials used for the most recent financial operating statement (e.g. year to date or trailing 12 months) - will be the day after the date for preceding fiscal year end statement Field EL86. If multiple properties and all the same date, print date. If missing any, leave empty.
	Most Recent Financial As of End Date	EL60	L73	Alpha Numeric	YYYYMMDD	If multiple properties and all the same then print the date, if missing any then leave empty	The end date of the financials used for the most recent financial operating statement (e.g. year to date or trailing 12 months). If multiple properties and all the same date, print date. If missing any, leave empty.
	Most Recent Financial Indicator	EL61	L82	Alpha Numeric	TA	(TA = Trailing 12 months Actual TN = Trailing 12 months Normalised. YA = Year to Date Actual. YN = Year to Date Normalised.) Check Start & End Date Applies to fields EL66 to EL84.	This field is used to describe the period for which the most recent financial data is reflected. TA=Trailing 12 months actual. TN=Trailing 12 months normalized. YA=Year to Date actual. YN=Year to Date normalized. Check Start & End Date applies to fields EL66 to EL84. If there are multiple properties that are all the same, print the value. If missing any values or they are not the same, use combination of statements covering the same period with the same value.
	NOI / NCF Indicator	EL62	L90	Alpha Numeric	Text	Indicates how NOI or Net Cash Flow was calculated should be the same for each financial period. See NOI/NCF Indicator Legend. P84 - If multiple Properties and all the same then print value, if missing any or if the values are not the same, then leave empty	Refer to the NOI/NCF Indicator Legend to describe which method is being used to calculate the NOI/NCF used in these reports.
	Financial Covenant Breach	EL63		Alpha Numeric	DSCR	If there has been a financial covenant breach, indicate which type of breach by populating with "Financial Covenant Legend"	Refer to Financial Covenant Legend for descriptions of the types of financial covenants. Complete if there has been a breach, otherwise leave blank.
	Breach in delivery of Reports	EL64		Alpha Numeric	Y	Y = Yes, N = No Is Borrower in breach of its obligation to deliver reports to lender?	Y = Yes, N = No Is Borrower in breach of its obligation to deliver reports to lender?
	Most Recent Revenue	EL65	L66	Numeric	1000.00	If multiple properties then sum the value, if missing any then populate using the "DSCR Indicator Legend" rule	Total revenues for the period covered by the most recent financial operating statement (i.e year to date or trailing 12 months) for all the properties. If multiple properties then sum the revenue (should match figures for sum of properties in Property File for this loan) , if missing any or if all received/consolidated, then populate using the DSCR Indicator Legend rule. May be normalised if required by the applicable servicing agreement.
	Most Recent Operating Expenses	EL66	L67	Numeric	1000.00	If multiple properties then sum the value, if missing any then populate using the "DSCR Indicator Legend" rule	Total operating expenses for the period covered by the most recent financial operating statement (i.e. year to date or trailing 12 months) for all properties. These may include real estate taxes, insurance, management, utilities, maintenance and repairs and direct property costs to the landlord, capital expenditures and leasing commissions are excluded. If multiple properties exist, total the operating expenses of the underlying properties. If multiple properties exist and data is not available for all properties or if received/consolidated, refer to the DSCR Indicator Legend rule. May be normalised if required by the applicable servicing agreement.

European Commercial Mortgage Securities Association
CMSA "Loan Periodic Update" File
(Data Record Layout)
Cross Refrenced as "EL"

E - CMSA Grouping	Field Name	UK / European Field Number	US Field Number	Field Type	Format Example	Description / Comments	European Definitions
Most Recent YTD Financial Details (EL59 - EL85)	Most Recent NOI	EL67	L68	Numeric	1000.00	If multiple properties then sum the value. If missing any then populate using the "DSCR Indicator Legend" rule	Total revenues less total operating expenses for the period covered by the most recent financial operating statement (Field EL65 minus EL66) If multiple properties exist and not all information available or consolidated refer to the DSCR Indicator Legend.
	Most Recent Capital Expenditure	EL68		Numeric	1000.00	If multiple properties then sum the value. If missing any then populate using the "DSCR Indicator Legend" rule	Total capex (as opposed to repairs and maintenance) for the period covered by the most recent financial operating statement (ie year to date or trailing 12 months) for all the properties. If multiple properties exist and data is not available for all properties or if all received/consolidated refer to the DSCR Indicator Legend rule.
	Most Recent NCF	EL69	L96	Numeric	1000.00	Most Recent Net Cash Flow related to Financial As of Ending Date EL73. If multiple properties then sum the value. If missing any then populate using the "DSCR Indicator Legend" rule	Total NOI less total capex for the period covered by the most recent financial operating statement (Field EL67 minus EL68) If multiple properties and not all information is available. refer to the DSCR Indicator Legend.
	Most Recent Interest Paid	EL70		Numeric	1000.00	Sum of interest paid in Financial YTD	Total interest due for the period covered by the most recent financial operating statement (ie year to date or trailing 12 months)
	Most Recent ICR (NOI)	EL71		Numeric	2.55	If multiple properties populate using the "DSCR Indicator Legend" rule. Most Recent Interest Coverage Ratio using NOI	Calculate the ICR based on NOI for the period covered by the most recent financial operating statement (ie year to date or trailing 12 months). If multiple properties and not all information available or consolidated, refer to DSCR Indicator Legend.
	Most Recent Debt Service Amount	EL72	L69	Numeric	1000.00	If multiple properties then sum the value. If missing any then populate using the "DSCR Indicator Legend" rule	Total scheduled payments of principal and interest due during the period covered by the most recent financial operating statement (ie year to date or trailing 12 months). Should equal the sum of the values for properties securing this loan shown in the Property File Field EP67.
	Most Recent DSCR (NOI)	EL73	L70	Numeric	2.55	If multiple properties populate using the "DSCR Indicator Legend" rule. Most Recent Debt Service Coverage Ratio using NOI	Calculate the DSCR based on NOI for the period covered by the most recent financial operating statement (ie year to date or trailing 12 months). If multiple properties and not all information available. refer to DSCR Indicator Legend)
	Most Recent DSCR (NCF)	EL74	L97	Numeric	2.55	Most Recent Debt Service Coverage Ratio using Net Cash Flow related to Financial As of Ending Date EL73. If multiple properties populate using the "DSCR Indicator Legend" rule	Calculate the DSCR based on NCF for the period covered by the most recent financial operating statement (ie year to date or trailing 12 months). If multiple properties and not all information available, refer to DSCR Indicator Legend)
	Most Recent DSCR Indicator	EL75	L89	Alpha Numeric	Text	Flag used to explain how the DSCR was calculated when there are multiple properties. See DSCR Indicator Legend	Code describing how DSCR is calculated/applied when a loan has multiple properties. See DSCR Indicator Legend.

European Commercial Mortgage Securities Association
CMSA "Loan Periodic Update" File
(Data Record Layout)
Cross Reffenced as "EL"

E - CMSA Grouping	Field Name	UK / European Field Number	US Field Number	Field Type	Format Example	Description / Comments	European Definitions
	Most Recent Economic Occupancy	EL76		Numeric	0.85	If multiple properties, use weighted average by using the calculation [Current Allocated % (Prop) * Occupancy] for each Property. If missing any then leave empty	The most recent available percentage of rentable space with signed leases in place (tenants may not be in occupation but are paying rent). Should be derived from a rent roll or other document indicating occupancy consistent with most recent financial year information. If missing any or the information is not available, leave empty.
	Most Recent Physical Occupancy	EL77	L71	Numeric	0.85	If multiple properties, use weighted average by using the calculation [Current Allocated % (Prop) * Occupancy (Physical)] for each Property. If missing any then leave empty	The most recent available percentage of rentable space actually occupied (ie where tenants are actually in occupation and not vacated). Should be derived from a rent roll or other document indicating occupancy consistent with most recent financial year information. If missing any or the information is not available, leave empty.
	Most Recent Valuation Date	EL78	L74	Alpha Numeric	YYYYMMDD	If multiple properties and all the same then print the date. If missing any then leave empty	The date the most recent valuation/appraisal was prepared. If multiple properties and all the same date, print date. If missing any, leave empty
Most Recent YTD Financial Details (EL59 - EL85)	Most Recent Valuation, BPO or Internal Value	EL79	L75	Numeric	100000.00	If multiple properties then sum the value. If missing any then leave empty	The most recent valuation of all properties securing the loan. If multiple properties, sum the value. If missing any, leave empty.
	LTV at Loan Payment Date	EL80		Numeric	0.85	The Loan to Value ratio of the properties securing the loan.	The Loan to Value ratio of the properties securing the loan. Field EL29 (Actual Balance)/Field EL79 (Most recent valuation). Leave blank if not all valuation figures available.
	Blank Field	EL81				Blank Field	
	Blank Field	EL82				Blank Field	
	Blank Field	EL83				Blank Field	
	Blank Field	EL84				Blank Field	
	Blank Field	EL85				Blank Field	
	Preceding Financial Year As of Date	EL86	L58	Alpha Numeric	YYYYMMDD	If multiple properties and all the same then print the date. If missing any then leave empty	The end date of the financials used for the preceding year financial operating statement (e.g. year to date or trailing 12 months). If multiple properties and all the same date, print date. If missing any, leave empty.
	Preceding Financial Year Revenue	EL87	L52	Numeric	1000.00	If multiple properties then sum the value, if missing any then populate using the "DSCR Indicator Legend" rule	Total normalised revenues for the period covered by the preceding year financial operating statement (i.e year to date or trailing 12 months) for all the properties. If multiple properties then sum the revenue (should match figures for sum of properties in Property File for this loan). If missing any or if all received/consolidated, then populate using the DSCR Indicator Legend rule.

520

European Commercial Mortgage Securities Association
CMSA "Loan Periodic Update" File
(Data Record Layout)
Cross Refrenced as "EL"

E - CMSA Grouping	Field Name	UK / European Field Number	US Field Number	Field Type	Format Example	Description / Comments	European Definitions
Preceding Fiscal Year Financial Details (EL86 - EL101)	Preceding Financial Operating Expenses	EL88	L53	Numeric	1000.00	If multiple properties then sum the value, if missing any then populate using the "DSCR Indicator Legend" rule	Total normalised operating expenses for the period covered by the preceding Financial year financial operating statement (i.e. year to date or trailing 12 months) for all properties. Typically included are real estate taxes, insurance, management, utilities and maintenance repairs, but capital expenditures and leasing commissions are excluded. If multiple properties exist, total the operating expenses of the underlying properties. If multiple properties exist and data is not available for all properties or if received/consolidated, refer to the DSCR Indicator Legend rule
	Preceding Financial Year NOI	EL89	L54	Numeric	1000.00	If multiple properties then sum the value, if missing any then populate using the "DSCR Indicator Legend" rule	Total revenues less total operating expenses for the period covered by the preceding year financial operating statement (Field EL87 minusField EL88). If multiple properties exist and not all information available or consolidated refer to the DSCR Indicator Legend
	Preceding Financial Year NCF	EL90	L92	Numeric	1000.00	Preceding Fiscal Year Net Cash Flow related to Financial As of Date EL86. If multiple properties then sum the value, if missing any then populate using the "DSCR Indicator Legend" rule	Total NOI less total capex for the period covered by the preceding year financial operating statement. If multiple properties exist and not all information is available, refer to the DSCR Indicator Legend.
	Preceding Financial Year ICR (NOI)	EL91		Numeric	2.55	If multiple properties populate using the "DSCR Indicator Legend" rule. Preceding Fiscal Yr Interest Cvrge Ratio using NOI	Calculate the ICR based on NOI for the period covered by the preceding year financial operating statement (ie year to date or trailing 12 months). If multiple properties exist and not all information available or consolidated, refer to DSCR Indicator Legend.
	Preceding Financial Year Debt Svc Amount	EL92	L55	Numeric	1000.00	If multiple properties then sum the value, if missing any then populate using the "DSCR Indicator Legend" rule	Total scheduled payments of principal and interest due during the period covered by the preceding year financial operating statement (ie year to date or trailing 12 months). If multiple properties and not all information available refer to DSCR Indicator Legend
	Preceding Financial Year DSCR (NOI)	EL93	L56	Numeric	2.55	If mmultiple properties populate using the "DSCR Indicator Legend" rule. Preceding Fiscal Yr Debt Svc Cvrge Ratio using NOI	Calculate the DSCR based on NOI for the period covered by the preceding year financial operating statement (ie year to date or trailing 12 months). If multiple properties and not all information available, refer to DSCR Indicator Legend).
	Preceding Financial Year DSCR (NCF)	EL94	L93	Numeric	2.55	Preceding Fiscal Year Debt Service Coverage Ratio using NCF related to Financial As of Date L58. If multiple properties populate using the "DSCR Indicator Legend" rule	Calculate the DSCR based on NCF for the period covered by the preceding year financial operating statement (ie year to date or trailing 12 months). Field EL89(Preceding Financial Year NOI) Field EL92 (Preceding Financial Year Debt Svc Amount). If multiple properties and not all information available, refer to DSCR Indicator Legend).
	Preceding Year DSCR Indicator	EL95	L87	Alpha Numeric	Text	Flag used to explain how the DSCR was calculated when there are multiple properties. See DSCR Indicator Legend	Code describing how DSCR is calculated/applied when a loan has multiple properties. See DSCR Indicator Legend.

521

European Commercial Mortgage Securities Association
CMSA "Loan Periodic Update" File
(Data Record Layout)
Cross Refrenced as "EL"

E - CMSA Grouping	Field Name	UK / European Field Number	US Field Number	Field Type	Format Example	Description / Comments	European Definitions
Preceding Fiscal Year Financial Details (EL86 - EL101)	Preceding Financial Year Economic Occupancy	EL96	L57	Numeric	0.85	If multiple properties, use weighted average by using the calculation (Current Allocated % (Prop) * Occupancy (Oper) for each Property. If missing any then leave empty	The percentage of rentable space actually occupied (ie where tenants may not be in occupation but are paying rent) at the preceding financial year as of date. Should be derived from a rent roll or other document indicating occupancy consistent with preceding year financial information. If multiple properties, populate with weighted average, using the calculation (Current Allocated % (Prop) * Occupancy (Oper)) for each Property. If missing any or the information is not available, leave empty.
	Blank Field	EL97				Blank Field	
	Blank Field	EL98				Blank Field	
	Blank Field	EL99				Blank Field	
	Blank Field	EL100				Blank Field	
	Blank Field	EL101				Blank Field	
	Second Preceding Financial Year Financial As of Date	EL102	L65	Alpha Numeric	YYYYMMDD	If multiple properties and all the same then print the date, if missing any then leave empty	The date 12 months prior to the preceding financial year as of date Field EL86. If multiple properties and all the same date, print date. If missing any, leave empty.
	Second Preceding Financial Year Revenue	EL103	L59	Numeric	1000.00	If multiple properties then sum the value, if missing any then populate using the "DSCR Indicator Legend" rule	Total normalised revenues for the period covered by the second preceding year financial operating statement (i.e year to date or trailing 12 months) for all the properties. If multiple properties then sum the revenue (should match figures for sum of properties in Property File for this loan). If missing any or of all received/consolidated, then populate using the DSCR Indicator Legend rule
	Second Preceding Financial Year Operating Expenses	EL104	L60	Numeric	1000.00	If multiple properties then sum the value, if missing any then populate using the "DSCR Indicator Legend" rule	Total normalised operating expenses for the period covered by the second preceding Financial year financial operating statement (i.e. year to date or trailing 12 months) for all properties. Typically included are real estate taxes, insurance, management, utilities and maintenance repairs, but capital expenditures and leasing commissions are excluded. If multiple properties exist, total the operating expenses of the underlying properties. If multiple properties exist and data is not available for all properties or if received/consolidated, refer to the DSCR Indicator Legend rule.
Second Preceding Fiscal Year Financial Details (EL102 - EL117)	Second Preceding Financial Year NOI	EL105	L61	Numeric	1000.00	If multiple properties then sum the value, if missing any then populate using the "DSCR Indicator Legend" rule	Total revenues less total operating expenses for the period covered by the second preceding year financial operating statement (Field EL103 minus EL104). If multiple properties exist and not all information available or consolidated then refer to the DSCR Indicator Legend.
	Second Preceding Financial Year NCF	EL106	L94	Numeric	1000.00	Second Preceding Fiscal Year Net Cash Flow related to Financial As of Date L65. If multiple properties then sum the value, if missing any then populate using the "DSCR Indicator Legend" rule	Total NOI less total capex for the period covered by the second preceding year financial operating statement. If multiple properties and not all information is available, refer to the DSCR Indicator Legend
	Second Preceding Financial Year ICR (NOI)	EL107		Numeric	2.55	If multiple properties populate using the "DSCR Indicator Legend" rule. Second Preceding Fiscal Year Interest Coverage Ratio using NOI	Calculate the ICR based on NOI for the period covered by the second preceding year financial operating statement (ie year to date or trailing 12 months). If multiple properties and not all information available or consolidated, refer to DSCR Indicator Legend.

European Commercial Mortgage Securities Association
CMSA "Loan Periodic Update" File
(Data Record Layout)
Cross Refrenced as "EL"

E - CMSA Grouping	Field Name	UK / European Field Number	US Field Number	Field Type	Format Example	Description / Comments	European Definitions
	Second Preceding Financial Year Debt Service Amount	EL108	L62	Numeric	1000.00	If multiple properties then sum the value, if missing any then populate using the "DSCR Indicator Legend" rule	Total scheduled payments of principal and interest due during the period covered by the second preceding year financial operating statement (ie year to date or trailing 12 months). If multiple properties and not all information available refer to DSCR Indicator Legend.
	Second Preceding Financial Year DSCR (NOI)	EL109	L63	Numeric	2.55	If multiple properties populate using the "DSCR Indicator Legend" rule. Second Preceding Fiscal Year Debt Service Coverage Ratio using NOI	Calculate the DSCR based on NOI for the period covered by the second preceding year financial operating statement (ie year to date or trailing 12 months). If multiple properties and not all information available, refer to DSCR Indicator Legend).
Second Preceding Fiscal Year Financial Details (EL102 - EL117)	Second Preceding Financial Year DSCR (NCF)	EL110	L95	Numeric	2.55	Second Preceding Fiscal Year Debt Service Coverage Ratio using Net Cash Flow related to Financial As of Date L65. If multiple properties populate using the "DSCR Indicator Legend" rule	Calculate the DSCR based on NCF for the period covered by the second preceding year financial operating statement (ie year to date or trailing 12 months). Field EL105(Second Preceding Financial Year NOI)/ Field EL108 (Second Preceding Financial Year Debt Service Amount. If multiple properties and not all information available, refer to DSCR Indicator Legend).
	Second Preceding Year DSCR Indicator	EL111	L88	Alpha Numeric	Text	Flag used to explain how the DSCR was calculated when there are multiple properties. See DSCR Indicator Legend	Code describing how DSCR is calculated/applied when a loan has multiple properties. See DSCR Indicator Legend.
	Second Preceding Financial Year Economic Occupancy	EL112	L64	Numeric	0.85	If multiple properties, use weighted average by using the calculation [Current Allocated % (Prop) * Occupancy (Oper)] for each Property, if missing any then leave empty	The percentage of rentable space actually occupied (ie where tenants may not be in occupation but are paying rent) at the second preceding financial year as of date. Should be derived from a rent roll or other document indicating occupancy consistent with second preceding year financial information. If multiple properties, populate with weighted average, using the calculation [Current Allocated % (Prop) * Occupancy (Oper)] for each Property. If missing any or the information is not available, leave empty.
	Blank Field	EL113				Blank Field	
	Blank Field	EL114				Blank Field	
	Blank Field	EL115				Blank Field	
	Blank Field	EL116				Blank Field	
	Blank Field	EL117				Blank Field	
Reserve & Escrow Details (EL118 - EL125)	Total Reserve Balance	EL118	L104	Numeric	1000.00	Total Reserves at the loan level undisbursed at the end of the current period. Includes Maintenance, Repairs & Environmental, etc. Excludes Insurance escrows. Should be populated if value in Setup File field 116 or 117 is "Y".	Total balance of the reserve accounts at the loan level at the Loan Payment Date. Includes Maintenance, Repairs & Environmental, etc. (excludes Tax & Insurance escrows). Includes LC's for reserves (excludes LC for Tax & Insurance reserves). Should be completed if Field ES75 Collection of Other Reserves in Loan Set up is "Y".
	Escrow Trigger Event Occurred	EL119		Alpha Numeric	Y	Y=Yes N=No	Enter Yes if an event has occurred that has caused reserve amounts to be established. (not if payments are built up as a normal condition of the loan agreement).
	Amounts Added to Escrows in Current Period	EL120		Numeric	1000.00	Amount that has been added to any escrows or reserves during Current Period	Total amounts added to escrow or reserve accounts during the current period.
	Blank Field	EL121				Blank Field	
	Blank Field	EL122				Blank Field	
	Blank Field	EL123				Blank Field	
	Blank Field	EL124				Blank Field	

European Commercial Mortgage Securities Association
CMSA "Loan Periodic Update" File
(Data Record Layout)
Cross Refrenced as "EL"

E - CMSA Grouping	Field Name	UK / European Field Number	US Field Number	Field Type	Format Example	Description / Comments	European Definitions
Liquidation & Prepayment Details (EL126 - EL133)	Liquidation / Prepayment Code	EL127	L32	Numeric	1	See Liquidation/Prepayment Codes Legend	Code assigned to any unscheduled principal payments or liquidation proceeds received during the collection period. Specific codes apply. See Liquidation/Prepayment Code Legend.
	Prepayment Fee	EL128	L30	Numeric	1000.00	Prepayment fee paid in addition to any break funding payment for the current period	Amount collected from the borrower as the fee due for making prepayments as required under the terms of the loan agreement. This is not intended to include any amounts paid as a "break cost" to make up interest payments up to the Loan Payment Date.
	Blank Field	EL129				Blank Field	
	Blank Field	EL130				Blank Field	
	Blank Field	EL131				Blank Field	
	Blank Field	EL132				Blank Field	
	Blank Field	EL133				Blank Field	
Loan Hedging Details (EL134 - EL147)	Borrower Level / Name of Loan Swap Provider	EL134		Alpha Numeric	Text	Borrower Level/Name of Swap Provider	The name of the Swap provider for the loan if the Borrower has the direct contract with the swap counterparty. Leave blank, if the loan has been hedged with the lender having the contract with the swap counterparty
	Actual Ratings of Loan Swap Provider	EL135		Alpha Numeric	Text	Identify the ratings of the Swap Counterparty as of the (Loan Payment Date) date current Payment Date of the Notes	List the current rating (i.e. Fitch, Moodys S & P) of the borrower swap counterparty.
	Full or Partial Termination Event of Loan Level Swap for Current Period	EL136		Alpha Numeric	RD	If swap has been terminated during current period, identify reason (see Loan Level Swap Termination Legend)	Refer to Loan Level Swap Termination Legend for code to reflect the reason for termination.
	Net Periodic Payment due to Loan Swap Provider	EL137		Numeric	1000.00	Amount of payment due to the Swap Counterparty (other than swap breakage costs)	Amount of payment made by the borrower to the swap counterparty on the Loan Payment Date as required by the Swap contract. This does not include any breakage or termination payments.
	Net Periodic Payment due from Loan Swap Provider	EL138		Numeric	1000.00	Amount of payment due from the Swap Counterparty (other than swap breakage costs)	Amount of payment made by the swap counterparty to the borrower on the Loan Payment Date as required by the Swap contract. This does not include any breakage or termination payments.
	Breakage Costs Due to Loan Swap Provider	EL139		Numeric	1000.00	Amount of any breakage costs due to Loan Swap Provider	Amount of any payment due from the borrower to the swap counterparty for partial or full termination of the Swap.
	Shortfall in Payment of Breakage Costs on Loan Level Swap	EL140		Numeric	1000.00	Amount of any shortfall in collections from Borrower necessary to pay any Loan Level Breakage Costs	Amount of any shortfall, if any, of breakage costs resulting from full or partial termination of the swap, paid by the borrower.
	Breakage Costs Due from Loan Level Swap Counterparty	EL141		Numeric	1000.00	Amount of breakage costs, if any, due from Loan Swap Provider	Amount of any breakcosts (ie gains) paid by the swap counterparty to the borrower on full or partial termination.
	Next Reset Date for the Loan Level Swap	EL142		Alpha Numeric	YYYYMMDD	Date of next reset date on the Loan Level Swap	The next date when the rates are re-set on the loan level swap.
	Blank Field	EL143				Blank Field	
	Blank Field	EL144				Blank Field	
	Blank Field	EL145				Blank Field	
	Blank Field	EL146				Blank Field	
	Blank Field	EL147				Blank Field	

European Commercial Mortgage Securities Association
CMSA "Loan Periodic Update" File
(Data Record Layout)
Cross Refrenced as "EL"

E - CMSA Grouping	Field Name	UK / European Field Number	US Field Number	Field Type	Format Example	Description / Comments	European Definitions
Loan Status Details (EL148 - EL163)	Status of Loan	EL148	L40	Alpha Numeric	1	See Status of Loan Legend	Refer to the Status of Mortgage Loan Legend to determine the code used to explain the loan status (ie current, non payment etc.). If a loan has multiple Status Codes triggered, Servicer discretion to determine which codes reported.
	Enforcement Start Date	EL149	L42	Alpha Numeric	YYYYMMDD	If multiple properties have the same date then print the same date otherwise leave empty	The date on which foreclosure proceedings or alternative enforcement procedures were initiated against or agreed by the borrower.
	Special Servicing	EL150		Alpha Numeric	Y	"Y" for Yes or "N" for NO	Is the loan currently being specially serviced? Y= Yes or N =No
	Workout Strategy Code	EL151	L76	Numeric	1	See Workout Strategy Codes Legend	The code assigned that best describes the steps being taken to resolve the loan. Specific codes apply. See Workout Strategy Code Legend.
	Date Asset Expected to Be Resolved or Foreclosed	EL152	L79	Alpha Numeric	YYYYMMDD	If multiple properties then print the latest date from the affiliated properties. If in Enforcement - Expected Date of Completion of Enforcement and if REO - Expected Sale Date	Estimated date the Special Servicer expects resolution. If multiple properties, print latest date from the affiliated properties. If in foreclosure = Expected Date of Foreclosure and if Property Possession = Expected Sale Date.
	In Insolvency	EL153		Alpha Numeric	Y	Insolvency Status of Loan (If In Insolvency "Y", Else "N")	Insolvency Status of Loan (If In Insolvency "Y", Else "N").
	Insolvency Date	EL154		Alpha Numeric	YYYYMMDD	Date Of Insolvency	Date Of Insolvency
	Property Possession Date	EL155	L43	Alpha Numeric	YYYYMMDD	If multiple properties have the same date then print the same date otherwise leave empty	The date on which title to (or an alternative form of effective control and ability to dispose of) the collateral property were obtained.
	Net Proceeds Received on Liquidation	EL156	L45	Numeric	10000.00	Net Proceeds Rec'd On Liquidation Used To Determine Loss to the Issuer per the Transaction Documents	The amount of the net proceeds of sale received, this will determine whether there is a loss or shortfall on the loan.
	Liquidation Expense	EL157	L46	Numeric	10000.00	Expenses Associated With The Liq'n To Be Netted from the Other Assets of Issuer to Determine Loss per the Trust Documents	Amount of any liquidation expenses that will be paid out of the net sales proceeds to determine whether there will be any loss.
	Realised Loss to Securitisation	EL158	L47	Numeric	10000.00	Outstanding Balance of Loan (plus Liquidation Expenses) Less Net Liquidation Proceeds Received	The amount of any loss to the issuer after deducting liquidation expenses from the net sales proceeds.
	Blank Field	EL159				Blank Field	
	Blank Field	EL160				Blank Field	
	Blank Field	EL161				Blank Field	
	Blank Field	EL162				Blank Field	
Loan Status Details (EL148 - EL163)	Blank Field	EL163				Blank Field	
	Last Setup Change Date	EL164	L83	Alpha Numeric	YYYYMMDD	Payment Date that information changed last in the setup file by loan	The Loan Payment Date that any information in the Loan Set Up File was last changed, following any amendments/modifications to the loan agreement.
	Last Loan Sale Date	EL165	L84	Alpha Numeric	YYYYMMDD	Date the loan was sold to Issuer	The date the loan was sold to the Issuer, if the loan was part of the original securitisation, then this will be the Issue Date.
	Last Property Issue Date	EL166	L85	Alpha Numeric	YYYYMMDD	Date the latest property or properties print the latest date from the affiliated properties	Date the latest property or properties were contributed to this securitisation. If any properties have been substituted, enter the date of the last substitution. If the properties was part of the original transaction, this will be the Issue Date.

European Commercial Mortgage Securities Association
CMSA "Loan Periodic Update" File
(Data Record Layout)
Cross Refrenced as "EL"

E - CMSA Grouping	Field Name	UK / European Field Number	US Field Number	Field Type	Format Example	Description / Comments	European Definitions
Loan Modification Details (EL164 - EL178)	Date of Assumption	EL167	L91	Alpha Numeric	YYYYMMDD	Date the loan last assumed by a new borrower - empty if never assumed	Date the assignment/innovation or assumption was executed by the new borrower (leave blank if original borrower).
	ARA Date	EL168	L100	Alpha Numeric	YYYYMMDD	The effective date of the last Appraisal Reduction Amount, not the date of the appraisal used to derive the ARA amount	Date the ARA was calculated and approved (initial or updated calculation as of date). The calculation may be performed monthly, annually, etc. and is triggered by an Appraisal Reduction Event. The ARA is then reported as of the loan or note payment date that follows the ARA calculation date.
	Date of Last Modification	EL169	L48	Alpha Numeric	YYYYMMDD	Date Loan Was Modified	Last effective date the loan was modified, leave blank if no changes.
	Modification Code	EL170	L49	Numeric	1	See Modification Codes Legend	Refer to Modification Code Legend for code to describe type of modification
	Modified Payment Rate	EL171	L51	Numeric	0.09	Payment Rate Loan Modified To	If the loan has been restructured (probably during a workout process), and the amortisation schedule has been amended, then the new amount, expressed as a % of the loan balance, should be entered, otherwise leave blank.
	Modified Loan Interest Rate	EL172	L50	Numeric	0.09	Loan Interest Rate Loan Modified To	If the loan has been restructured (probably during a workout process), and the interest rate/margin has been amended, then the new rate should be entered, otherwise leave blank.
	Credit Tenant Lease	EL173	L101	Alpha Numeric	Y	Single tenant with lease term at least as long as the loan term.	Enter Yes if there is a single tenant whose lease is at least as long as the term of the loan, otherwise leave blank. If there are multiple properties and at least one of the properties has a CTL, enter Yes/partial to show CTLs apply to part of the security
	Blank Field	EL174				Blank Field	
	Blank Field	EL175				Blank Field	
	Blank Field	EL176				Blank Field	
	Blank Field	EL177				Blank Field	
	Blank Field	EL178				Blank Field	
Loan Syndication & Participation Details (EL179 - EL188)	% of Issuer Facility being Securitised	EL179		Numeric	0.09	% of total loan in securitisation at Issue Date	If the loan has been split or in the case of a syndicated loan, the Issuer owns a part of the loan, give the % of the loan that is sold to the Issuer at the Issue Date.
	Change in Controlling Party	EL180		Alpha Numeric	Y	Y=yes, N=no: If the Loan is syndicated, has there been a change in the Controlling Party since the prior reporting period?	Y=yes, N=no: Has there been a change in the Controlling Party since the prior reporting period?
	Name of Old Controlling Party	EL181		Alpha Numeric	Text	Name of Institution	Name of Institution
	Name of New Controlling Party	EL182		Alpha Numeric	Text	Name of Institution	Name of Institution
	Date of change of Controlling Party	EL183		Alpha Numeric	YYYYMMDD	Date that Controlling Party under Syndicated Loan has changed	Date that Controlling Party under Syndicated Loan has changed
	Blank Field	EL184				Blank Field	
	Blank Field	EL185				Blank Field	
	Blank Field	EL186				Blank Field	
	Blank Field	EL187				Blank Field	
	Blank Field	EL188				Blank Field	
Loan Syndication & Participation Details (EL179 - EL188)	Date Added to Watchlist	EL189	L105	Alpha Numeric	YYYYMMDD	Date corresponds to the first Determination Date that the loan was added to the watchlist	The first or Loan Payment Date/Determination Date that a loan was placed on the Watchlist. If loan came off the Watchlist in a prior period and is now coming back on, use the new entry date.

European Commercial Mortgage Securities Association
CMSA "Loan Periodic Update" File
(Data Record Layout)
Cross Refrenced as "EL"

E - CMSA Grouping	Field Name	UK / European Field Number	US Field Number	Field Type	Format Example	Description / Comments	European Definitions
Special Servicing Details (EL189 - EL202)	Most Recent Special Servicer Transfer Date	EL190	L77	Alpha Numeric	YYYYMMDD	Date Transferred To The Special Servicer	The date a loan was transferred to the special Servicer following a servicing transfer event. Note: If the loan has had multiple transfers, this should be the last date transferred to special servicing.
	Most Recent Master Servicer Return Date	EL191	L78	Alpha Numeric	YYYYMMDD	Date Returned To The Master Servicer or Primary Servicer	The date a loan becomes a "corrected mortgage loan", which is the date the loan was returned to the master/primary Servicer from the special Servicer. Note: If the loan has had multiple transfers, this should be the last date returned to the master/primary Servicer from special servicing.
	Special Servicing Fee Amount plus Adjustments	EL192	L106	Numeric	1000.00	A Summation of the Special Servicer Base fee, other fees and misc adjustments. Total fees charged by special Servicer in current period.	The total of all amounts paid to the special Servicer during the current period. this will include the basic fee plus any other amounts paid whether expenses or fees.
	Servicer Fee Amount	EL193	L12	Numeric	1000.00	Fee Paid To The Servicer	The amount of the fee paid to the Servicer for the current period as calculated in accordance with the Servicing Agreement.
	Costs other that the servicing fee that are deducted from the current net loan interest rate	EL194		Numeric	1000.00	Costs other that the servicing fee that are deducted from the gross loan interest payment to derive the current net loan interest rate	Any other amounts that may be deducted from the interest paid by the borrower at the loan level that would reduce the amounts payable to the Issuer
	Workout Fee Amount	EL195	L108	Numeric	1000.00	Workout Fee Amount	The amount of any workout fee being paid to the special Servicer for the current period on a loan that has become a corrected loan.
	Liquidation Fee Amount	EL196	L109	Numeric	1000.00	Liquidation Fee Amount	The amount of any liquidation fee paid to the special Servicer for the current period on a specially serviced loan following the liquidation of a property securing the loan.
	Non Recoverability Determined	EL197	L110	Alpha Numeric	Y	Y or N to describe if Servicer has determined property protection advances non-recoverable	Indicator (Yes/No) as to whether the Servicer/Special has determined that there will be a shortfall in recovering any advances it has made and the outstanding loan balance and any other amounts owing on the loan from proceeds upon sale or liquidation of the property or Loan.
	Blank Field	EL198				Blank Field	
	Blank Field	EL199				Blank Field	
	Blank Field	EL200				Blank Field	
	Blank Field	EL201				Blank Field	
	Blank Field	EL202				Blank Field	

527

European Commercial Mortgage Securities Association
CMSA "Property" File
(Data Record Layout)
Cross Refrenced as "EP"

E - CMSA Grouping	Field Name	UK / European Field Number	US Field Number	Field Type	Format Example	Description / Comments	European Definitions
	Transaction Identifier	EP1	P1	Alpha Numeric	XXX97001	Unique issue identification string	The name assigned to the securitisation or issue, this can be as identified in the Offering Circular or assigned by the Servicer.
	Servicer Loan Identifier	EP2	P2	Alpha Numeric	0000000012345	Unique number assigned by servicer to each Loan	The Servicer's unique identification number assigned to each loan in the pool.
	Offering Circular Loan Identifier	EP3	P3	Alpha Numeric	123	Unique number assigned to each Loan in OC	The identification number(s), if any, assigned to each loan in the offering circular.
	Property Identifier	EP4	P4	Alpha Numeric	123	Unique servicer property number assigned to each property	The Servicer's unique identification number assigned to each property serving as security for a loan in the pool.
Loan Identifiers & Payment Date Details (EP1 - EP11)	Distribution Date	EP5	P5	Alpha Numeric	YYYYMMDD	Bond payment date corresponding to data in file	Bond payment date for which the data in the files corresponds
	Cross-Collateralised Loan Grouping	EP6	P6	Text		Indicator of loans that are cross collateralised (Example: loans 1 and 44 are cross collateralised as are loans 4 and 47). First pair will be assigned value of 1; second pair assigned value of 2	Indicator of loans that are cross collateralised within the pool (Example: loans 1 and 44 are cross collateralised as are loans 4 and 47). First pair will be assigned value of 2
	Blank Field	EP7				Blank Field	
	Blank Field	EP8				Blank Field	
	Blank Field	EP9				Blank Field	
	Blank Field	EP10				Blank Field	
	Blank Field	EP11				Blank Field	
	Property Name	EP12	P7	Alpha Numeric	Text	Name of property	The name of the property that serves as security for the loan. If multiple properties, print "Various."
	Property Address	EP13	P8	Alpha Numeric	Text	Address	The address of the property that serves as security for the loan. If multiple properties, print "Various."
	Property City	EP14	P9	Alpha Numeric	Text	City	The city name where the property or properties are located. If multiple properties have the same city then print the city, otherwise print "Various". Missing information print "Incomplete"
	Region (NUTS)	EP15	P12	Alpha Numeric	Text	Region	The region in which the property or properties thath serve as security are located. - Use the standard regions as defined by Eurostat. Their website is: www.europa.eu.int/comm/eurostat/ramon/nuts/splash_regions.html. NUTs stands for "Nomenclature of Territorial Units for Statistics". If multiple properties, print "Various." Missing information print "Incomplete"
Collateral Details (EP12 -EP38)	Property Postal Code	EP16	P11	Alpha Numeric	Text	Post Code	The postal code (or equivalent) for the property or properties that serve as security for the loan. If multiple properties have the same code, print "Various." For missing information print "Incomplete"
	Property Country	EP17		Alpha Numeric	Text	Country	If multiple properties have the same country then print the country, otherwise print "Various." Missing information print "Incomplete"
	Property Type Code	EP18	P13	Alpha Numeric	OF	See Property Type Code Legend	Refer to the Property Type Code Legend and use the code that is most suitable for the property or properties.
	Year Built	EP19	P14	Alpha Numeric	1990	Year property was built	The year the property was built. For multiple properties, if all the same print the year, else leave empty.
	Year Last Renovated	EP20	P15	Numeric	1990	Current last year renovated	Year that last major renovation/new construction was completed on the property.
	Net Square Metres At Issue Date	EP21		Numeric	1000.00	Rentable area in property	The total net rentable area of the properties in square metres that serve as security for the loan at the Issue Date. For multiple properties, (if not all information available, leave blank. Complete either square feet or square metres field (or both if easier).

European Commercial Mortgage Securities Association
CMSA "Property" File
(Data Record Layout)
Cross Refrenced as "EP"

E - CMSA Grouping	Field Name	UK / European Field Number	US Field Number	Field Type	Format Example	Description / Comments	European Definitions
	Net Square Feet At Issue Date	EP22	P16	Numeric	1000.00	Rentable area in property	The total net rentable area of the properties in square feet that serve as security for the loan at the Issue Date. For multiple properties, if not all information available, leave blank. Complete either square feet or square metres field (or both if easier)
	Number of Units/Beds/Rooms At Issue Date	EP23	P17	Numeric	1000	Number of units in property (i.e., rooms, beds, pads, etc)	For property type Multifamily enter number of units, for Hospitality/Hotel/Healthcare - beds, for Caravan Parks - units, Lodging=rooms, Self Storage=units. For Multiple properties, if all the same Property Type, sum the values. If missing any, leave empty.
	Property Status	EP24	P18	Numeric	2	See Property Status Codes	Refer to the Property Status Code Legend and use the code that is most suitable for the property or properties eg whether sold, part sold, in foreclosure.
	Property Condition Legend	EP25	P89	Alpha Numeric	E	E = Excellent, G = Good, F = Fair, P = Poor	Refer to Property Condition Code Legend to describe the condition of the property based on the latest inspection results. Codes pursuant to CMSA/MBA standard property inspection report results.
	Date of Last Property Inspection	EP26	P52	Alpha Numeric	YYYYMMDD	Date of last physical site inspection	Date of last physical site inspection. If not inspected since the last valuation enter that date.
	Form of Title	EP27	P22	Alpha Numeric	Text	Freehold, Leasehold or Mixed	A lease of land only, on which the borrower usually owns a building or is required to build as specified in the lease. Such leases are usually long-term net leases; the borrower's rights and obligations continue until the lease expires or is terminated through default. Y=Yes, N=No, S=Subordinate. If multiple properties and any one is 'Y' or S, print Y.
Collateral Details (EP12 -EP38)	Leasehold Expiry	EP28		Alpha Numeric	YYYYMMDD	Enter the date the ground lease/head lease expires	Enter the date the ground lease/head lease expires.
	Ground Rent Payable	EP29		Numeric	1000.00	If leasehold, the current annual Leasehold rent payable	If the property is Leasehold enter the amount of the annual leasehold payment. If calculated in another way enter brief description.
	Date of Most Recent Valuation	EP30	P24	Alpha Numeric	YYYYMMDD	The date of the latest available appraised value for the property	The date the valuation was prepared for the values disclosed in the Offering Circular. For multiple properties, if several dates, leave blank.
	Most Recent Valuation, BPO, or Internal Value	EP31	P25	Alpha Numeric	Text	Name of valuer if it was carried out by a valuer. If it wasn't, who did? (e.g. Servicer/Lender)	The most recent valuation of all properties securing the loan. If multiple properties, sum the value. If missing any, leave empty.
	Most Recent Valuation Source	EP32	P90	Alpha Numeric	Text	Source of most recent property valuation	Source of most recent property valuation eg 3rd party external valuer or special servicer estimate.
	Total Reserve Balance allocated to Property	EP33	P23	Numeric	1000.00	Total property reserve balance at Loan Payment Date?	Total balance of the reserve accounts for the property at the Loan Payment Date. Includes Maintenance, Repairs & Environmental, etc. (excludes Tax & Insurance reserves). Includes LCs for reserves (excludes LC for Tax & Insurance reserves). Should be completed if Field ES75 Collection of Other Reserves in Loan Set up is "Y".
	Blank Field	EP34				Blank Field	
	Blank Field	EP35				Blank Field	
	Blank Field	EP36				Blank Field	
	Blank Field	EP37				Blank Field	
	Blank Field	EP38				Blank Field	
Issue Date Details	Property Issue Date	EP39	P67	Alpha Numeric	YYYYMMDD	Date property was contributed. If defeased, populated with effective date of defeasance	Date the property was contributed to this securitisation. If this property has been substituted, enter the date of the substitution. If the property was part of the original transaction, this will be the Issue Date.
	Allocated Percentage of Loan at Issue Date	EP40	P19	Numeric	0.1100	Issuer to allocate loan % attributable to property for multi-property loans	Allocated loan % attributable to property at Issue Date where there is more than one property securing the loan. This may be set out in the Loan Agreement, otherwise assign by valuation or NOI.

529

European Commercial Mortgage Securities Association
CMSA "Property" File
(Data Record Layout)
Cross Refenced as "EP"

E - CMSA Grouping	Field Name	UK / European Field Number	US Field Number	Field Type	Format Example	Description / Comments	European Definitions
(EP39 - EP54)	Date of Financials at Issue Date	EP41	P44	Alpha Numeric	YYYYMMDD	Date of financials at issue date	The end date of the financials for the information used in the Offering Circular (e.g. year to date or trailing 12 months). If multiple properties and at the same date, print date. If missing any, leave empty.
	Property Revenue at Issue Date	EP42	P45	Numeric	1000.00	Property revenue at issue date as disclosed in offering circular (actual)	The total underwritten revenue from all sources for a property as described in the Offering Circular. If multiple properties, sum the values in the Property File. If missing data or if all received/consolidated, use the DSCR Indicator Legend rule.
	Operating Expenses At Issue Date	EP43	P46	Numeric	1000.00	Property expenses at issue date	Total underwritten operating expenses for the properties a described in the offering Circular. These may include real estate taxes, insurance, management, utilities, maintenance and repairs and direct property costs to the landlord, capital expenditures and leasing commissions are excluded. If multiple properties exist, total the operating expenses of the underlying properties. If multiple properties exist and data is not available for all properties or if received/consolidated, refer to the DSCR Indicator Legend rule.
	NOI at Issue Date	EP44	P47	Numeric	1000.00	Securitisation NOI	Revenue less Operating Expenses at Issue Date (Field EP42 minus EP43) If multiple properties, sum the values. If missing date or if all received/consolidated, refer to the DSCR Indicator Legend rule
	Capital Expenditure at Issue Date	EP45		Numeric	1000.00	Capital Expenses at Issue Date	Capex at Issue Date (as opposed to repairs and maintenance) if identified in the Offering Circular. If missing date or if all received/consolidated refer to the DSCR Indicator Legend rule.
	NCF at Issue Date	EP46	P76	Numeric	1000.00	Securitisation NCF	NOI less Capex at Issue Date (Field EP44 less EP45). If missing data or if all received/consolidated refer to the DSCR Indicator Legend rule.
Issue Date Details	DSCR (NOI) at Issue Date	EP47	P48	Numeric	1.50	Securitisation DSCR based upon NOI	The DSCR at Issue Date. Calculate by using the NOI at Issue Date and applying the Allocated % of Loan at Issue Date (EP40) to the Periodic P & I Payment at Issue Date (Field ES61. If multiple properties and not all information available refer to the DSCR Indicator Legend rule.
(EP39 - EP54)	Valuation at Issue Date	EP48	P49	Numeric	1000.00	Securitisation appraised value	The date the valuation was prepared for the values disclosed in the Offering Circular. For multiple properties, if several dates, leave blank.
	Date of Valuation at Issue Date	EP49	P50	Alpha Numeric	YYYYMMDD	Date of securitisation appraised value	The valuation of the properties securing the loan at Issue Date as described in the Offering Circular. If multiple properties sum the value in the Property File, otherwise leave blank.
	Blank Field	EP50				Blank Field	
	Blank Field	EP51				Blank Field	
	Blank Field	EP52				Blank Field	
	Blank Field	EP53				Blank Field	
	Blank Field	EP54				Blank Field	
	Current Allocated Percentage	EP55	P20	Numeric	0.11	Allocated percentage of loan as of latest distribution date	Allocated loan % attributable to property at Loan Payment Date where there is more than one property securing the loa, the sum of all % should total 100%. This may be set out in the Loan Agreement, otherwise assign by valuation or NOI.
	Current Allocated Ending Loan Amount	EP56	P21	Numeric	1,000.00	Current allocated ending loan amount	Apply the Current Allocated % to the Actual Balance outstanding on the Loan (EL29).
Most Recent YTD Financial Details	Most Recent Financial As of Start Date	EP57	P73	Alpha Numeric	YYYYMMDD	Most recent Financial Reporting year to date start date	The first day of the financials used for the most recent financial operating statement (e.g. year to date or trailing 12 months) - will be the day after the date for preceding fiscal year end statement Field EP74. If multiple properties and all the same date, print date. If missing any, leave empty.

European Commercial Mortgage Securities Association
CMSA "Property" File
(Data Record Layout)
Cross Refrenced as "EP"

E - CMSA Grouping	Field Name	UK / European Field Number	US Field Number	Field Type	Format Example	Description / Comments	European Definitions
(EP55 - EP73)	Most Recent Financial As of End Date	EP58	P74	Alpha Numeric	YYYYMMDD	Most recent Financial Reporting year to date end date	The end date of the financials used for the most recent financial operating statement (e.g. year to date or trailing 12 months). If multiple properties and all the same date, print date. If missing any, leave empty.
	Last Month of Year used for Reporting Financials	EP59	P43	Alpha Numeric	Text	Last month of year used for reporting financials	Enter the month that the financials for each year (most recent, preceding and second preceding) will end.
	NOI / NCF Indicator	EP60	P84	Alpha Numeric	CMSA	Indicates how NOI or NCF were calculated; should be the same for each financial period. See NOI/NCF Indicator Code Legend	Refer to the NOI/NCF Indicator Legend to describe which method is being used to calculate the NOI/NCF used in these reports
	Most Recent Financial Indicator	EP61	P75	Alpha Numeric	YA	TA = Trailing 12 months actual. TN = Trailing 12 months normalised. YA = Year to date actual. YN = Year to date normalised (Applies to fields 70-77)	This field is used to describe the period for which the most recent financial data is reflected. TA=Trailing 12 months actual. TN=Trailing 12 months normalized. YA=Year to Date actual. YN=Year to Date normalized. Check Start & End Date applies to fields EL66 to EL84. If there are multiple properties that are all the same, print the value. If missing any values or they are not the same, use combination of statements covering the same period with the same value.
	Most Recent Revenue	EP62	P68	Numeric	1000.00	Most recent Financial Reporting year to date revenue	Total revenues for the period covered by the most recent financial operating statement (i.e year to date or trailing 12 months) for all the properties. If multiple properties then sum the revenue (should match figures for sum of properties in Property File for this loan). If missing any or if all received/consolidated, then populate using the DSCR Indicator Legend rule May be normalised if required by the applicable servicing agreement.
	Most Recent Operating Expenses	EP63	P69	Numeric	1000.00	Most recent Financial Reporting year to date operating expenses	Total operating expenses for the period covered by the most recent financial operating statement (i.e. year to date or trailing 12 months) for all properties. These may include real estate taxes, insurance, management, utilities, maintenance and repairs and direct property costs to the landlord; capital expenditures and leasing commissions are excluded. If multiple properties exist, total the operating expenses of the underlying properties. If multiple properties exist and data is not available for all properties or if received/consolidated, refer to the DSCR Indicator Legend rule. May be normalised if required by the applicable servicing agreement.
Most Recent YTD Financial Details (EP55 - EP73)	Most Recent NOI	EP64	P70	Numeric	1000.00	Most recent Financial Reporting year to date NOI	Total revenues less total operating expenses for the period covered by the most recent financial operating statement (Field EP62 minus EP63) If multiple properties exist and not all information available or consolidated refer to the DSCR Indicator Legend.
	Most Recent Capital Expenditure	EP65		Numeric	1000.00	Most recent Financial Reporting year to date capital expenses	Total capex (as opposed to repairs and maintenance) for the period covered by the most recent financial operating statement (ie year to date or trailing 12 months) for all the properties. If multiple properties exist and data is not available for all properties or if all received/consolidated refer to the DSCR Indicator Legend rule.
	Most Recent NCF	EP66	P82	Numeric	1000.00	Most recent NCF	Total NOI less total capex for the period covered by the most recent financial operating statement (Field EP64 minus EP65) If multiple properties and not all information is available, refer to the DSCR Indicator Legend.
	Most Recent Debt Service Amount	EP67	P71	Numeric	1000.00	Most Recent Debt Service Amount	Total scheduled payments of principal and interest due during the period covered by the most recent financial operating statement (ie year to date or trailing 12 months). Calculate by applying the Current Allocated % to the Most Recent DSCR amount in EL72.

European Commercial Mortgage Securities Association
CMSA "Property" File
(Data Record Layout)
Cross Refenced as "EP"

E - CMSA Grouping	Field Name	UK / European Field Number	US Field Number	Field Type	Format Example	Description / Comments	European Definitions
	Most Recent DSCR (NOI)	EP68	P72	Numeric	1.50	Most recent Financial Reporting year to date DSCR based upon NOI	Calculate the DSCR based on NOI for the period covered by the most recent financial operating statement (ie year to date or trailing 12 months). If multiple properties and not all information available, refer to DSCR Indicator Legend).
	Blank Field	EP69				Blank Field	
	Blank Field	EP70				Blank Field	
	Blank Field	EP71				Blank Field	
	Blank Field	EP72				Blank Field	
	Blank Field	EP73				Blank Field	
	Preceding Financial Reporting Year as of Date	EP74	P53	Alpha Numeric	YYYYMMDD	Refers to end date of financial period	The end date of the financials used for the preceding year financial operating statement (e.g. year to date or trailing 12 months). If multiple properties and all the same date, print date. If missing any, leave empty.
	Preceding Financial Reporting Year Revenue	EP75	P54	Numeric	1000.00	Preceding Financial Reporting year revenue	Total normalised revenues for the period covered by the preceding year financial operating statement (i.e year to date or trailing 12 months) for all the properties. If multiple properties then sum the revenue (should match figures for sum of properties in Property File for this loan). If missing any or if all received/consolidated, then populate using the DSCR Indicator Legend rule.
	Preceding Financial Reporting Year Operating Expenses	EP76	P55	Numeric	1000.00	Preceding Financial Reporting year operating expenses	Total normalised operating expenses for the period covered by the preceding fiscal year financial operating statement (i.e. year to date or trailing 12 months) for all properties. Typically included are real estate taxes insurance, management, utilities and maintenance repairs, but capital expenditures and leasing commissions are excluded. If multiple properties exist, total the operating expenses of the underlying properties. If multiple properties exist and data is not available for all properties or if received/consolidated, refer to the DSCR Indicator Legend rule.
Preceding Fiscal Year Financial Details (EP74 - EP86)	Preceding Financial Reporting Year NOI	EP77	P56	Numeric	1000.00	Preceding Financial Reporting year NOI	Total revenues less total operating expenses for the period covered by the preceding year financial operating statement (Field EL87 minusField EL88). If multiple properties exist and not all information available or consolidated refer to the DSCR Indicator Legend.
	Preceding Financial Reporting Year Capital Expenditure	EP78		Numeric	1000.00	Preceding Financial Reporting year Capital Expenses	Total capex (as opposed to repairs and maintenance) for the period covered by the preceding year financial operating statement (ie year to date or trailing 12 months) for all the properties. If multiple properties exist and data is not available for all properties or if all received/consolidated refer to the DSCR Indicator Legend.
	Preceding Financial Reporting Year NCF	EP79	P78	Numeric	1000.00	Preceding Financial Reporting year NCF	Total NOI less total capex for the period covered by the preceding year financial operating statement. If multiple properties and not all information is available, refer to the DSCR Indicator Legend
	Preceding Financial Reporting Year Debt Service Amount	EP80	P57	Numeric	1000.00	Preceding Financial Reporting Year Debt Service	Total scheduled payments of principal and interest due during the period covered by the preceding year financial operating statement (ie year to date or trailing 12 months). If multiple properties and not all information available refer to DSCR Indicator Legend.
	Preceding Financial Reporting Year DSCR (NOI)	EP81	P58	Numeric	1.50	Preceding Financial Reporting Year DSCR (NOI)	Calculate the DSCR based on NOI for the period covered by the preceding year financial operating statement (ie year to date or trailing 12 months). If multiple properties and not all information available, refer to DSCR Indicator Legend)
	Blank Field	EP82				Blank Field	

European Commercial Mortgage Securities Association
CMSA "Property" File
(Data Record Layout)
Cross Refrenced as "EP"

E - CMSA Grouping	Field Name	UK / European Field Number	US Field Number	Field Type	Format Example	Description / Comments	European Definitions
	Blank Field	EP83				Blank Field	
	Blank Field	EP84				Blank Field	
	Blank Field	EP85				Blank Field	
	Blank Field	EP86				Blank Field	
Second Preceding Fiscal Year Financial Details **(EP87 -EP99)**	Second Preceding Financial Reporting Year Financial As of Date	EP87	P60	Alpha Numeric	YYYYMMDD	Second preceding Financial Reporting year financial as of date	The date 12 months prior to the preceding financial year as of date Field EP74. If multiple properties and all the same date, print date. If missing any, leave empty.
	Second Preceding Financial Reporting Year Revenue	EP88	P61	Numeric	1000.00	Second preceding Financial Reporting year revenue	Total normalised revenues for the period covered by the second preceding year financial operating statement (i.e year to date or trailing 12 months) for all the properties. If multiple properties then sum the revenue (should match figures for sum of properties in Property File for this loan) . If missing any or if all received/consolidated, then populate using the DSCR Indicator Legend rule.
	Second Preceding Financial Reporting Year Operating Expenses	EP89	P62	Numeric	1000.00	Second preceding Financial Reporting year operating expenses	Total normalised operating expenses for the period covered by the second preceding Financial year operating statement (i.e. year to date or trailing 12 months) for all properties. Typically included are real estate taxes, insurance, management, utilities and maintenance repairs, but capital expenditures and leasing commissions are excluded. If multiple properties exist, total the operating expenses of the underlying properties. If multiple properties exist and data is not available for all properties or if received/consolidated, refer to the DSCR Indicator Legend rule.
	Second Preceding Financial Reporting Year NOI	EP90	P63	Numeric	1000.00	Second preceding Financial Reporting year NOI	Total revenues less total operating expenses for the period covered by the second preceding year financial operating statement (Field EP88 minus EP89). If multiple properties exist and not all information available or consolidated refer to the DSCR Indicator Legend.
	Second Preceding Financial Reporting Year Capital Expenditure	EP91		Numeric	1000.00	Second Preceding Financial Reporting Year Capital Expenses	Total capex (as opposed to repairs and maintenance) for the period covered by the second preceding year financial operating statement (ie year to date or trailing 12 months) for all the properties. If multiple properties exist and data is not available for all properties or if all received/consolidated refer to the DSCR Indicator Legend rule.
	Second Preceding Financial Reporting Year NCF	EP92	P80	Numeric	1000.00	Second preceding Financial Reporting year NCF	Total NOI less total capex for the period covered by the second preceding year financial operating statement. If multiple properties and not all information is available. refer to the DSCR Indicator Legend.
	Second Preceding Financial Reporting Year Debt Service Amount	EP93	P64	Numeric	1000.00	Second Preceding Financial Reporting Year Debt Service Amount	Total scheduled payments of principal and interest due during the period covered by the second preceding year financial operating statement (ie year to date or trailing 12 months). If multiple properties and not all information available refer to DSCR Indicator Legend.
Second Preceding Fiscal Year Financial Details **(EP87 -EP99)**	Second Preceding Financial Reporting Year DSCR (NOI)	EP94	P65	Numeric	1.50	Second Preceding Financial Reporting Year DSCR (NOI)	Calculate the DSCR based on NOI for the period covered by the second preceding year financial operating statement (ie year to date or trailing 12 months). If multiple properties and not all information available, refer to DSCR Indicator Legend).
	Blank Field	EP95				Blank Field	
	Blank Field	EP96				Blank Field	
	Blank Field	EP97				Blank Field	
	Blank Field	EP98				Blank Field	
	Blank Field	EP99				Blank Field	

European Commercial Mortgage Securities Association
CMSA "Property" File

(Data Record Layout)
Cross Refrenced as "EP"

E - CMSA Grouping	Field Name	UK / European Field Number	US Field Number	Field Type	Format Example	Description / Comments	European Definitions
Occupancy Details (EP100 - EP110)	Occupancy As of Date	EP100	P30	Alpha Numeric	YYYYMMDD		Date of most recently received rent roll (for hospitality (hotels), and health care properties use average occupancy for the period for which the financial statements are reported).
	Physical Occupancy at Issue Date	EP101	P51	Numeric	0.11	Most recent economic occupancy as of date	The most recent available percentage of rentable space actually occupied (ie where tenants are actually in occupation and not vacated). Should be derived from a rent roll or other document indicating occupancy consistent with most recent financial year information. If multiple properties, populate with weighted average, using the calculation [Current Allocated % (Prop) Occupancy (Open)] for each Property. If missing any or the information is not available, leave empty.
	Most Recent Physical Occupancy	EP102	P29	Numeric	0.11	Percentage of lettable area occupied	The most recent available percentage of rentable space actually occupied (ie where tenants are actually in occupation and not vacated). Should be derived from a rent roll or other document indicating occupancy consistent with most recent financial year information.
	Most Recent Economic Occupancy	EP103	P59	Numeric	0.11	Percentage of lettable area occupied	The most recent available percentage of rentable space with signed leases in place (tenants may not be in occupation but are paying rent). Should be derived from a rent roll or other document indicating occupancy consistent with most recent financial year information.
	Preceding Financial Reporting Year Economic Occupancy	EP104	P66	Numeric	0.11	Percentage of rentable area that is subject to contractual leases	The percentage of rentable space actually occupied (ie where tenants may not be in occupation but are paying rent) at the preceding financial year as of date. Should be derived from a rent roll or other document indicating occupancy consistent with preceding year financial information.
Occupancy Details (EP100 - EP110)	Second Preceding Financial Reporting Year Economic Occupancy	EP105		Numeric	0.11	Preceding Financial Reporting Year Economic Occupancy	The percentage of rentable space actually occupied (ie where tenants may not be in occupation but are paying rent) at the second preceding financial year as of date. Should be derived from a rent roll or other document indicating occupancy consistent with second preceding year financial information.
	Blank Field	EP106				Second Preceding Financial Reporting Year Economic Occupancy	
	Blank Field	EP107				Blank Field	
	Blank Field	EP108				Blank Field	
	Blank Field	EP109				Blank Field	
	Blank Field	EP110				Blank Field	
	% Income expiring 1-12 months	EP111	P32	Numeric	0.11	Percentage of income expiring in 1 to 12 months	Percentage of income expiring in 1 to 12 months from Occupancy as of Date (Field EP100).
	% Income expiring 13-24 months	EP112	P33	Numeric	0.11	Percentage of income expiring in 13 to 24 months	Percentage of income expiring in 13 to 24 months.
	% Income expiring 25-36 months	EP113	P34	Numeric	0.11	Percentage of income expiring in 25 to 36 months	Percentage of income expiring in 25 to 36 months.
	% Income expiring 37-48 months	EP114	P35	Numeric	0.11	Percentage of income expiring in 37 to 48 months	Percentage of income expiring in 37 to 48 months.
	% Income expiring 49+ months	EP115	P36	Numeric	0.11	Percentage of income expiring in 49 or more months	Percentage of income expiring in 49 or more months.
	Largest Tenant by income (Net)	EP116	P37	Alpha Numeric	Text	Name of largest current tenant by net rent	Name of largest current tenant by net rent.
	Date of Lease Expiration of Largest Tenant	EP117	P86	Alpha Numeric	YYYYMMDD	Expiration date of lease of largest current tenant (by net rent)	Expiration date of lease of largest current tenant (by net rent).
	Rent Payable by Largest Tenant	EP118		Numeric	1000.00	Annual Rent payable by largest current tenant	Annual Rent payable by largest current tenant.
Top Three Tenant Details	2nd Largest Tenant by Income (Net)	EP119	P39	Alpha Numeric	Text	Name of second largest current tenant (by net rent)	Name of second largest current tenant (by net rent).

534

European Commercial Mortgage Securities Association
CMSA "Property" File

(Data Record Layout)
Cross Refrenced as "EP"

E - CMSA Grouping	Field Name	UK / European Field Number	US Field Number	Field Type	Format Example	Description / Comments	European Definitions
(EP111 - EP129)	Date of Lease Expiration of 2nd Largest Tenant	EP120	P87	Alpha Numeric	YYYYMMDD	Expiration date of lease of second largest current tenant (net annual rent)	Expiration date of lease of second largest current tenant (net annual rent).
	Rent Payable by 2nd Largest Tenant	EP121		Numeric	1000.00	Rent Payable by second largest current tenant	Rent Payable by second largest current tenant.
	3rd Largest Tenant by Income (Net)	EP122		Alpha Numeric	Text	Name of third largest current tenant (by net rent)	Name of third largest current tenant (by net rent)
	Date of Lease Expiration of 3rd Largest Tenant	EP123	P88	Alpha Numeric	YYYYMMDD	Expiration date of lease of third largest current tenant (net annual rent)	Expiration date of lease of third largest current tenant (net annual rent).
	Rent Payable by 3rd Largest Tenant	EP124		Numeric	1000.00	Rent Payable by third largest current tenant	Rent Payable by third largest current tenant.
	Blank Field	EP125				Blank Field	
	Blank Field	EP126				Blank Field	
	Blank Field	EP127				Blank Field	
	Blank Field	EP128				Blank Field	
	Blank Field	EP129				Blank Field	
Foreclosure Details (EP130 -EP137)	Date Asset Expected to Be Resolved or Foreclosed	EP130	P26	Alpha Numeric	YYYYMMDD	Date asset expected to be resolved	Estimated date the Special Servicer expects resolution. If multiple properties, print latest date from the affiliated properties. If in foreclosure = Expected Date of Foreclosure and if Property Possession = Expected Sale Date.
	Possession Proceedings Start Date	EP131	P27	Alpha Numeric	YYYYMMDD	Date proceedings were started	The date on which foreclosure proceedings or alternative enforcement procedures were initiated against or agreed by the borrower.
	Date of Receivership	EP132	P28	Alpha Numeric	YYYYMMDD	Date loan became real estate owned	The date on which title to (or an alternative form of effective control and ability to dispose of) the collateral property were obtained.
	Blank Field	EP133				Blank Field	
	Blank Field	EP134				Blank Field	
	Blank Field	EP135				Blank Field	
	Blank Field	EP136				Blank Field	
	Blank Field	EP137				Blank Field	

European Commercial Mortgage Securities Association
Investor Reporting Package
Data Dictionary

UK / European Related Field Numbers	UK / European Field Number	Field Name	European Definitions
	ES20	Number of Properties At Issue Date	The number of properties that serve as security for the loan at the Issue Date
ES30, EP23	ES30	Number of Units/Beds/Rooms At Issue Date	For property type Multifamily enter number of units, for Hospitality/Hotel/Healthcare - beds, for Caravan Parks - units, Lodging=rooms, Self Storage=units. For Multiple properties, if all the same Property Type, sum the values. If missing any, leave empty.
	EP111	% Income expiring 1-12 months	Percentage of income expiring in 1 to 12 months from Occupancy as of Date (Field EP100)
	EP112	% Income expiring 13-24 months	Percentage of income expiring in 13 to 24 months
	EP113	% Income expiring 25-36 months	Percentage of income expiring in 25 to 36 months
	EP114	% Income expiring 37-48 months	Percentage of income expiring in 37 to 48 months
	EP115	% Income expiring 49+ months	Percentage of income expiring in 49 or more months
ES155, EL179	ES155	% of Issuer Facility being Securitised	What % of the syndicated loan is owned by the Issuer at the Issue Date
	EP119	2nd Largest Tenant by Income (Net)	Name of second largest current tenant (by net rent)
	EP122	3rd Largest Tenant by Income (Net)	Name of third largest current tenant (by net rent)
	ES104	Accrual of Interest Allowed	Do the loan documents allow for interest to be accrued and capitalised - Y=Yes N=No
	EL29	Actual Balance	The actual balance of the loan outstanding for the next interest period following all principal payments
	EL40	Actual Interest Paid	Total amount of interest paid by the borrower during the interest period or on the Loan Payment Date
ES128, EL135	ES60	Actual Principal Balance At Issue Date	Actual Principal Balance of the loan at the Issue Date as identified in the Offering Circular.
	ES128	Actual Ratings of Loan Swap Provider	Identify the ratings of the Swap Counterparty as at the Issue Date
	ES86	Additional Financing Indicator	Code indicating whether additional financing/mezzanine debt is present. See Additional Financing Indicator Legend
	EP40	Allocated Percentage of Loan at Issue Date	Allocated loan % attributable to property at Issue Date where there is more than one property securing the loan. This may be set out in the Loan Agreement, otherwise assign by valuation or NOI.
	ES101	Amortisation Trigger	Y=Yes N=No. Identify if a trigger event caused the loan to amortise in addition to scheduled amortisation.
	EL103	Amortisation Trigger Levels	What level of amortisation will be required if a trigger event occurs. Describe as a % of the loan balance at origination if possible. If multiple triggers or not easily described leave blank.
	EL50	Amortisation Trigger Reached	Y=Yes N=No. If the Loan has an amortisation trigger, has the trigger been met
	EL102	Amortisation Trigger Types	If yes, refer the Trigger Event Legend and describe type of trigger event.
	ES99	Amortisation Type Code	Refer to the Amortisation Code legend to describe the type of amortisation that applies to the loan
	EL120	Amounts Added to Escrows in Current Period	Total amounts added to escrow or reserve accounts during the current period
	ES73	Amounts Held in Escrow at Issue Date	Total balance of the reserve accounts at the loan level at the Issue Date
	EL52	Annuity Full Amortisation Period	If the amortisation type is Annuity, what is the date the loan would reduce to zero if the annuity payments continue to be paid
	EL168	ARA Date	Date the ARA was calculated and approved (initial or updated calculation as of date). The calculation may be performed monthly, annually, etc. and is triggered by an Appraisal Reduction Event. The ARA is then reported as of the loan or note payment date that follows the ARA calculation date.
		Blank Fields	To be utilised as and when future versions of the CMSA European IRP are released.
	EL134	Borrower Level / Name of Loan Swap Provider	The name of the Swap provider for the loan if the Borrower has the direct contract with the swap counterparty. Leave blank, if the loan has been hedged with the lender having the contract with the swap counterparty
	ES129	Borrower's Obligation to Pay Breakage on Loan Level Swap	Refer to Swap Breakage Legend for code to describe what level of indemnification is given by the borrower to pay breakage costs on the swap.
	EL64	Breach in delivery of Reports	Y = Yes, N = No. Is Borrower in breach of its obligation to deliver reports to lender?
	EL141	Breakage Costs Due from Loan Level Swap Counterparty	Amount of any breakcosts (ie gains) paid by the swap counterparty to the borrower on full or partial termination
	EL139	Breakage Costs Due to Loan Swap Provider	Amount of any payment due from the borrower to the swap counterparty for partial of full termination of the Swap
EP45, ES48	EP45	Capital Expenditure at Issue Date	Capex at Issue Date (as opposed to repairs and maintenance) if identified in the Offering Circular. If missing date or if all received/consolidated refer to the DSCR Indicator Legend rule
	EL180	Change in Controlling Party	Y=yes, N=no. Has there been a change in the Controlling Party since the prior reporting period?
	ES74	Collection Of Escrows (Y/N)	Enter Y - (yes) if any payments are held in reserve accounts to cover ground lease payments, insurance or taxes only (not maintenance, improvements, capex etc) as required under the loan agreement, otherwise N - (no)
	ES75	Collection Of Other Reserves (Y/N)	Are any amounts other than round rents taxes or insurance held in reserve accounts as required under the terms of the loan agreement for tenant improvements, leasing commissions and similar items in respect of the related property or for purpose of providing additional collateral for such loan. Y or N
	ES59	Committed Principal Balance At Issue Date	The committed balance, including any undrawn amounts, of the loan at Issue Date

536

European Commercial Mortgage Securities Association
Investor Reporting Package
Data Dictionary

UK / European Related Field Numbers	UK / European Field Number	Field Name	European Definitions
	EL194	Costs other that the servicing fee that are deducted from the gross loan interest payment to derive the current net loan interest rate	Any other amounts that may be deducted from the interest paid by the borrower at the loan level that would reduce the amounts payable to the Issuer
ES172, EL173	ES172	Credit Tenant Lease	Enter Y - (yes) if there is a single tenant whose lease is at least as long as the term of the loan, otherwise N - (no). If there are multiple properties and at least one of the properties has a CTL enter Y/P to show the CTLs apply to part of the security
ES82, EP6	ES82	Cross-Collateralised Loan Grouping	Indicator of loans that are cross collateralised within the pool (Example: loans 1 and 44 are cross collateralised as are loans 4 and 47). First pair will be assigned value of 1: second pair assigned value of 2
	EL49	Cumulative Amount Outstanding	The sum of Field EL47 and EL48
	ES8	Currency	
	EP56	Current Allocated Ending Loan Amount	Apply the Current Allocated % to the Actual Balance outstanding on the Loan (EL29).
	EP55	Current Allocated Percentage	Allocated loan % attributable to property at Loan Payment Date where there is more than one property securing the loa, the sum of all % should total 100%. This may be set out in the Loan Agreement, otherwise assign by valuation or NOI.
	EL51	Current Amortisation Type	Refer to Amortisation Type Legend for description to use
	EL24	Current Beginning Opening Balance	The outstanding balance of the loan at the beginning of the interest period used the calculate the interest due on the Loan Payment Date in Field EL6
	EL26	Current Ending Scheduled Balance	The principal balance of the loan that would be outstanding following the scheduled principal payment but prior to any prepayments (Field EL24 minus EL25)
	EL16	Current Index Rate	The interest rate (before margin) used to calculate the interest paid on the Loan Payment Date in Field EL6
	EL18	Current Loan Interest Rate	The total interest rate being used to calculate the interest paid on the Loan Payment Date in Field EL6 (sum of Field EL16 and EL18)
	EL10	Current Loan Maturity Date	The maturity date of the loan as defined in the loan agreement. This would not take into account any extended maturity dates that may be allowed under the loan agreement, but the initial maturity date
	EL17	Current Margin Rate	The margin being used to calculate the interest paid on the Loan Payment Date in Field EL6
	EL189	Date Added to Watchlist	The first or Loan Payment Date?Determination Date that a loan was placed on the Watchlist. If loan came off the Watchlist in a prior period and is now coming back on, use the new entry date.
EL152, EP130	EL152	Date Asset Expected to Be Resolved or Foreclosed	Estimated date the Special Servicer expects resolution. If multiple properties, print latest date from the affiliated properties. If in foreclosure = Expected Date of Foreclosure and if Property Possession = Expected Sale Date.
	EL167	Date of Assumption	Date the assignment/novation or assumption was executed by the new borrower (leave blank if original borrower).
	EL183	Date of change of Controlling Party	Date that Controlling Party under Syndicated Loan has changed
	EP41	Date of Financials at Issue Date	The end date of the financials for the information used in the Offering Circular (e.g. year to date or trailing 12 months). If multiple properties and all the same date, print date. If missing any, leave empty.
	EL169	Date of Last Modification	Last effective date the loan was modified, leave blank if no changes
	EP26	Date of Last Property Inspection	Date of last physical site inspection, if not inspected since the last valuation enter that date.
	EP120	Date of Lease Expiration of 2nd Largest Tenant	Expiration date of lease of second largest current tenant (net annual rent)
	EP123	Date of Lease Expiration of 3rd Largest Tenant	Expiration date of lease of third largest current tenant (net annual rent)
	EP117	Date of Lease Expiration of Largest Tenant	Expiration date of lease of largest current tenant (by net rent)
	EP30	Date of Most Recent Valuation	The date the valuation was prepared for the values disclosed in the Offering Circular. For multiple properties, if several dates, leave blank
	EP132	Date of Receivership	The date on which title to (or an alternative form of effective control and ability to dispose of) the collateral property were obtained.
	ES84	Date of Substitution	If loan was substituted after the Issue Date, the date of such substitution
	ES150	Date of Syndication	
	EP49	Date of Valuation at Issue Date	The valuation of the properties securing the loan at Issue Date as described in the Offering Circular. If multiple properties sum the value in the Propety File, otherwise leave blank
	ES165	Deadlock Notification Period	How many days notice is allowed to respond when there is a deadlock
	EP6	Distribution Date	Bond payment date for which the data in the files corresponds
	ES53	DSCR (NCF) At Issue Date	The DSCR as described in the Offering Circular (if available), otherwise calculate using the NCF as Issue Date and the debt service amount by annualising the Periodic P & I Payment at Issue Date (Field ES61). If multiple properties and not all information available refer to the DSCR Indicator Legend rule
ES52, EP47	ES52	DSCR (NOI) At Issue Date	The DSCR as described in the Offering Circular (if available), otherwise calculate using the NOI as Issue Date and the debt service amount by annualising the Periodic P & I Payment at Issue Date (Field ES61). If multiple properties and not all information available refer to the DSCR Indicator Legend rule
	ES39	DSCR Covenant	If there is an DSCR financial covenant stipulated in the loan agreement, enter the threshold for a breach of such covenant.

European Commercial Mortgage Securities Association
Investor Reporting Package

Data Dictionary

UK / European Related Field Numbers	UK / European Field Number	Field Name	European Definitions
	ES54	DSCR Indicator At Issue Date	Code describing how the DSCR is calculated/applied when a loan has multiple properties. See DSCR Indicator Legend for codes.
	ES58	Economic Occupancy At Issue Date	The percentage of rentable space with signed leased in place at Issue Date if disclosed in Offering Circular (tenants may not be in occupation but are paying rent). If multiple properties use weighted average by using the calculation (Current Allocated % ('Prop')*Occupancy)) for each property. If missing some date leave blank.
	ES126	End Date of Loan Level Swap	
	EL149	Enforcement Start Date	The date on which foreclosure proceedings or alternative enforcement procedures were initiated against or agreed by the borrower.
	ES76	Escrow Held Upon Trigger Event	Does the Loan agreement require reserve amounts to be made upon the occurrence of any trigger events. Y or N
	EL119	Escrow Trigger Event Occurred	Enter Yes if an event has occurred that has caused reserve amounts to be established (not if payments are built up as a normal condition of the loan agreement)
	ES124	Exchange Rate for Loan Level Swap	The exchange rate that has been set for a currency loan level swap
	EL63	Financial Covenant Breach	Refer to Financial Covenant Legend for descriptions of the types of financial covenants. Complete if there has been a breach, otherwise leave blank
	ES173	Financial Information Submission Penalties	Indicator for penalties for borrower's failure to submit required financial information (Op. Stmt, Schedule, etc.) as per loan documents. M=Monetary, N=No penalties allowed in documents, O=Other penalties
	ES64	Financials reported at issuance as of Date	The end date of the financials used to support the Revenue and Expenses amounts disclosed in the Offering Circular if available, otherwise the Issue Date. If multiple properties and the dates are the same, enter the date, or if different or missing any leave blank.
	ES14	First Loan Payment Due Date	The date that the first interest payment was due on the loan following origination (not first date after securitisation).
	ES136	First Payment Adjustment Date	For adjustable rate loans, the next date that the amount of scheduled principal and/or interest is due to change. For fixed rate loans, enter the next payment date (not the first date after securitisation on which it could change).
	ES135	First Rate Adjustment Date	For adjustable rate loans, enter the first date that the interest rate was due to change. For fixed rate loans, enter the first interest payment date (not the first date after securitisation on which it could change).
ES32, EP27	ES32	Form of Title	Would the property(ies) be described as leasehold (or equivalent) rather than freehold. If multiple properties and various types, or single property, enter M. F = Freehold, L =Leasehold, M=Mixed
	EL136	Full or Partial Termination Event of Loan Level Swap for Current Period	Refer to Loan Level Swap Termination Legend for code to reflect the reason for termination.
	ES85	Grace Days Allowed	The number of days after a payment is due in which the lender will not charge a late penalty or report the payment as late.
	EP29	Ground Rent Payable	If the property is Leasehold enter the amount of the annual leasehold rent payable. If calculated in another way enter brief description.
ES2, EL2	ES2	Group Identifier	The alpha-numeric code assigned to each loan group within an issue. A Group ID may not be applicable for every transaction.
	ES51	ICR (NCF) at Issue Date	The ICR based on NCF at Issue date as described in the Offering Circular (if available), otherwise calculated using the NCF at Issue Date and the interest based on the Loan Rate at Issue Date (Field ES62) and Actual Principal Balance at Issue Date (Field ES60). If multiple properties and not all available refer to the DSCR Indicator Legend rule.
	ES50	ICR (NOI) At Issue Date	The ICR as described in the Offering Circular (if available), otherwise calculate using the NOI as Issue Date and the interest based on the Loan Rate at Issue Date (Field ES62) and Actual Principal Balance at Issue Date (Field ES60). If multiple properties and not all information available refer to the DSCR Indicator Legend rule
	ES38	ICR Covenant	If there is an ICR financial covenant stipulated in the loan agreement, enter the threshold for a breach of such covenant.
	EL153	In Insolvency	Insolvency Status of Loan (If In Insolvency "Y", Else "N")
	ES12	Index Code	Refer to the Index Code Legend to select the code describing the interest rate type for the loan
	ES141	Index Determination Date	If the Loan Agreement states specific dates for the index to be set, enter brief description in field. Eg. 15 Jan/Apr/July/Oct.
	ES140	Index Look Back In Days	The number of days prior to the interest payment date that the interest rate is set (eg Euribor set 2 days prior to interest payment date)
	EL154	Insolvency Date	Date Of Insolvency
	ES93	Interest Accrual Method Code	Code indicating the 'number of days' convention used to calculate interest. 1=30/360, 2=actual/365, 3=actual/360, 4=actual/actual, 5=actual/366, 6=simple.
	ES94	Interest in Arrears (Y/N)	Is the interest that accrues on the loan paid in arrears Y(es) or N(o)
	ES92	Interest Rate Type	Use a code to describe the type of interest rate applied to the loan. 1=Fixed, 2=Floating, 3=Step, 4=Mixed/Fixed Floating, 9=Other
	EP116	Largest Tenant by Income (Net)	Name of largest current tenant by net rent
	EL165	Last Loan Sale Date	The date the loan was sold to the Issuer, if the loan was part of the original securitisation, then this will be the Issue Date.
	EP59	Last Month of Year used for Reporting Financials	Enter the month that the financials for each year (most recent, preceding and second preceding) will end
	EL166	Last Property Issue Date	Date the latest property or properties were contributed to this securitisation. If any properties have been substituted, enter the date of the last substitution. If the properties was part of the original transaction, this will be the Issue Date

European Commercial Mortgage Securities Association
Investor Reporting Package

Data Dictionary

UK / European Related Field Numbers	UK / European Field Number	Field Name	European Definitions
ES169, EL164	ES169	Last Setup Change Date	The Loan Payment Date that any information in the Loan Set Up File was last changed, following any amendments/modifications to the loan agreement
	EP28	Leasehold Expiry	Enter the date the ground lease/head lease expires
	ES116	Lifetime Rate Cap	Maximum rate that the borrower must pay on a floating rate loan as required under the terms of the loan agreement
	ES117	Lifetime Rate Floor	Minimum rate that the borrower must pay on a floating rate loan as required under the terms of the loan agreement
	EL53	Linear Amortisation per Annum	If the amortisation type is Linear, what is the percentage of amortisation being paid per annum based on the original loan balance (not the balance when the securitisation closed)
	EL127	Liquidation / Prepayment Code	Code assigned to any unscheduled principal payments or liquidation proceeds received during the collection period. Specific codes apply. See Liquidation/Prepayment Code Legend.
	EL126	Liquidation / Prepayment Date	Can't find a Liquidation prepayment code? The date on which an unscheduled principal payment or liquidation proceeds are received.
	EL157	Liquidation Expense	Amount of any liquidation expenses that will be paid out of the net sales proceeds to determine whether there will be any loss
	EL196	Liquidation Fee Amount	The amount of any liquidation fee paid to the special Servicer for the current period on a specially serviced loan following the liquidation of a property securing the loan.
	ES171	Loan Contributor to Securitisation	Name of the originator that sold the loan to the Issuer
	ES67	Loan Maturity Date at Issue Date	The maturity date of the loan as defined in the loan agreement. This would not take into account any extended maturity date that may be allowed under the loan agreement, but the initial maturity date.
	EL6	Loan Payment Date	The date principal and interest is paid to the Issuer, this would normally be the interest payment date of the loan.
	ES62	Loan Rate At Issue Date	The total interest rate (eg Libor + Margin) that is being used to calculate interest due on the loan at the Issue Date
	ES148	Loan Structure Code	Refer to the Loan Structure Code to describe what structure applies to this loan eg whole loan, A/B splits, syndicated. Use multiple codes is applicable.
	ES119	Loan Swap Provider	The name of the swap provider for the loan if the Borrower has the direct contract with the swap counterparty. Leave blank if the loan has been hedged with the lender having the contract with the swap counterparty.
	EL80	LTV at Loan Payment Date	The Loan to Value ratio of the properties securing the loan. Field EL29 (Actual Balance)/Field EL79 (Most recent valuation). Leave blank if not all valuation figures available
	ES40	LTV Covenant	If there is an LTV covenant stipulated in the loan agreement, enter the threshold for a breach of such covenant.
	ES162	Major Decision Notification Period	How many days notice is required to respond on matters relating to material decisions
	ES115	Margin	The rate added to the index rate used to calculate the interest paid on the loan
	ES164	Method of Notification	What method must the facility agent use to advise about matters relating to deadlocks eg mail, verbal, electronic.
	ES161	Method of Notification for Material Decisions	What method must the facility agent use to advise about matters relating to material decisions eg mail, verbal, electronic.
	EL170	Modification Code	Refer to Modification Code Legend for code to describe type of modification
	EL172	Modified Loan Interest Rate	If the loan has been restructured (probably during a workout process), and the interest rate/margin has been amended, then the new rate should be entered, otherwise leave blank.
	EL171	Modified Payment Rate	If the loan has been restructured (probably during a workout process), and the amortisation schedule has been amended, then the new amount expressed as a % of the loan balance, should be entered, otherwise leave blank.
EL68, EP65	EL68	Most Recent Capital Expenditure	Total capex (as opposed to repairs and maintenance) for the period covered by the most recent financial operating statement (ie year to date or trailing 12 months) for all the properties. If multiple properties exist and data is not available for all properties or if all received/consolidated refer to the DSCR Indicator Legend rule.
EL72, EP67	EL72	Most Recent Debt Service Amount	Total scheduled payments of principal and interest due during the period covered by the most recent financial operating statement (ie year to date or trailing 12 months).
	EL74	Most Recent DSCR (NCF)	Calculate the DSCR based on NCF for the period covered by the most recent financial operating statement (ie year to date or trailing 12 months). If multiple properties and not all information available, refer to DSCR Indicator Legend)
EL73, EP68	EL73	Most Recent DSCR (NOI)	Calculate the DSCR based on NOI for the period covered by the most recent financial operating statement (ie year to date or trailing 12 months). If multiple properties and not all information available, refer to DSCR Indicator Legend)
	EL75	Most Recent DSCR Indicator	Code describing how DSCR is calculated/applied when a loan has multiple properties. See DSCR Indicator Legend
EL76, EP103	EL76	Most Recent Economic Occupancy	The most recent available percentage of rentable space with signed leases in place (tenants may not be in occupation but are paying rent). Should be derived from a rent roll or other document indicating occupancy consistent with most recent financial year information. If missing any or the information is not available, leave empty.
EL60, EP58	EL60	Most Recent Financial As of End Date	The end date of the financials used for the most recent financial operating statement (e.g. year to date or trailing 12 months). If multiple properties and all the same date, print date. If missing any, leave empty.

European Commercial Mortgage Securities Association
Investor Reporting Package

Data Dictionary

UK / European Related Field Numbers	UK / European Field Number	Field Name	European Definitions
EP57, EL59	EP57	Most Recent Financial As of Start Date	The first day of the financials used for the most recent financial operating statement (e.g. year to date or trailing 12 months) - will be the day after the date for preceding fiscal year end statement. If multiple properties and all the same date, print date. If missing any, leave empty.
EL61, EP61	EL61	Most Recent Financial Indicator	This field is used to describe the period for which the most recent financial data is reflected. TA=Trailing 12 months actual. TN=Trailing 12 months normalized, YA=Year to Date actual, YN=Year to Date normalized. Check Start & End Date applies to fields EL66 to EL84. If there are multiple properties that are all the same, print the value. If missing any values or they are not the same, use combination of statements covering the same period with the same value.
	EL71	Most Recent ICR (NOI)	Calculate the ICR based on NOI for the period covered by the most recent financial operating statement (ie year to date or trailing 12 months). If multiple properties and not all information available or consolidated, refer to DSCR Indicator Legend
	EL70	Most Recent Interest Paid	Total interest due for the period covered by the most recent financial operating statement (ie year to date or trailing 12 months)
	EL191	Most Recent Master Servicer Return Date	The date a loan becomes a "corrected mortgage loan", which is the date the loan was returned to the master/primary Servicer from the special Servicer. Note: If the loan has had multiple transfers, this should be the last date returned to the master/primary Servicer from special servicing.
EL69, EP66	EL69	Most Recent NCF	Total NOI less total capex for the period covered by the most recent financial operating statement. If multiple properties and not all information is available, refer to the DSCR Indicator Legend
EL67, EP64	EL67	Most Recent NOI	Total revenues less total operating expenses for the period covered by the most recent financial operating statement. If multiple properties exist and not all information available or consolidated refer to the DSCR Indicator Legend
EL66, EP63	EL66	Most Recent Operating Expenses	Total operating expenses for the period covered by the most recent financial operating statement (i.e. year to date or trailing 12 months) for all properties. These may include real estate taxes, insurance, management, utilities, maintenance and repairs and direct property costs to the landlord; capital expenditures and leasing commissions are excluded. If multiple properties exist, total the operating expenses of the underlying properties. If multiple properties exist and data is not available for all properties or if received/consolidated, refer to the DSCR Indicator Legend rule. May be normalised if required by the applicable servicing agreement.
EL77, EP102	EL77	Most Recent Physical Occupancy	The most recent available percentage of rentable space actually occupied (ie where tenants are actually in occupation and not vacated). Should be derived from a rent roll or other document indicating occupancy consistent with most recent financial year information. If missing any or the information is not available, leave empty.
EL65, EP62	EL65	Most Recent Revenue	Total revenues for the period covered by the most recent financial operating statement (i.e year to date or trailing 12 months) for all the properties. If multiple properties then sum the revenue (should match figures for sum of properties in Property File for this loan), if missing any or if all received/consolidated, then populate using the DSCR Indicator Legend rule. May be normalised if required by the applicable servicing agreement.
	EL190	Most Recent Special Servicer Transfer Date	The date a loan was transferred to the special Servicer following a servicing transfer event. Note: If the loan has had multiple transfers, this should be the last date transferred to special servicing
	EL78	Most Recent Valuation Date	The date the most recent valuation/appraisal was prepared. If multiple properties and all the same date, print date. If missing any, leave empty.
EP32	EP32	Most Recent Valuation Source	Source of most recent property valuation eg 3rd party external valuer or special servicer estimate
EL79, EP31	EL79	Most Recent Valuation, BPO or Internal Value	The most recent Valuation of all properties securing the loan. If multiple properties, sum the value. If missing any, leave empty
ES156	ES156	Name of Controlling Syndicate Member	Name of the party that controls or is the majority for decision making of the syndication
EL182	EL182	Name of New Controlling Party	Name of Institution
EL181	EL181	Name of Old Controlling Party	Name of Institution
EP46, ES49	EP46	NCF at Issue Date	NOI less Capex at Issue Date If missing data or if all received/consolidated refer to the DSCR Indicator Legend rule.
EL39	EL39	Negative Amortisation / Deferred Interest / Capitalised Interest	Negative amortisation occurs when interest accrued during a payment period is greater than the scheduled payment and the excess amount is added to the outstanding loan balance. Deferred interest is the amount by which the interest a borrower is required to pay on a mortgage loan is less than the amount of interest accrued on the outstanding principal balance. Deferred interest is not added to the outstanding loan balance. Capitalised interest is where interest is added to the loan balance at the end of the interest period in accordance with loan agreement.
	EL138	Net Periodic Payment due from Loan Swap Provider	Amount of payment made by the swap counterparty to the borrower on the Loan Payment Date as required by the Swap contract. This does not include any breakage or termination payments.
	EL137	Net Periodic Payment due to Loan Swap Provider	Amount of payment made by the borrower to the swap counterparty on the Loan Payment Date as required by the Swap contract. This does not include any breakage or termination payments.
	EL156	Net Proceeds Received on Liquidation	The amount of the net proceeds of sale received, this will determine whether there is a loss or shortfall on the loan

European Commercial Mortgage Securities Association
Investor Reporting Package
Data Dictionary

UK / European Related Field Numbers	UK / European Field Number	Field Name	European Definitions
ES28, EP22	ES28	Net Square Feet At Issue Date	The total net rentable area of the properties in square feet that serve as security for the loan at the Issue Date. For multiple properties, if not all information available, leave blank. Complete either square feet or square metres field (or both if easier)
ES29, EP21	ES29	Net Square Metre At Issue Date	The total net rentable area of the properties in square metres that serve as security for the loan at the Issue Date. For multiple properties, if not all information available, leave blank. Complete either square feet or square metres field (or both if easier)
	EL9	Next Payment Adjustment Date	For adjustable rate loans, the next date that the amount of scheduled principal and/or interest is due to change. For fixed rate loans, enter the next payment date.
	EL8	Next Rate Adjustment Date	For adjustable rate loans, the next date that the interest rate is due to change. For fixed rate loans, enter the next interest payment date.
	EL142	Next Reset Date for the Loan Level Swap	The next date when the rates are re-set on the loan level swap
EL62, EP60	EL62	NOI / NCF Indicator	Refer to the NOI/NCF Indicator Legend to describe which method is being used to calculate the NOI/NCF used in these reports
ES47, EP44	ES47	NOI At Issue Date	Revenue less Operating Expenses at Issue Date. If multiple properties, sum the values. If missing data or if all received/consolidated, refer to the DSCR Indicator Legend rule
	EL197	Non Recoverability Determined	Indicator ('Yes/No) as to whether the Servicer/Special has determined that there will be a shortfall in recovering any advances it has made and the outstanding loan balance and any other amounts owing on the loan from proceeds upon sale or liquidation of the property or Loan.
	EL5	Number of Properties	The number of properties that serve as security for the loan.
	EP100	Occupancy As of Date	Date of most recently received rent roll (for hospitality (hotels), and health care properties use average occupancy for the period for which the financial statements are reported).
ES4, EP3	ES4	Offering Circular Loan Identifier	The identification number(s), if any, assigned to each loan in the offering circular.
ES46, EP43	ES46	Operating Expenses At Issue Date	Total underwritten operating expenses for the properties a described in the offering Circular. These may include real estate taxes, insurance, management, utilities, maintenance and repairs and direct property costs to the landlord; capital expenditures and leasing commissions are excluded. If multiple properties exist, total the operating expenses of the underlying properties. If multiple properties exist and data is not available for all properties or if received/consolidated, refer to the DSCR Indicator Legend rule.
	ES100	Original Length of IO Period	Number of months that loan is interest only (from the date of origination not from the Issue Date)
	ES9	Original Loan Amount	The amount of the loan/commitment at origination. IF the committed amount was not fully drawn, enter the total amount drawndown.
	ES13	Original Loan Interest Rate	
ES55	ES55	Original Loan to Value (LTV) Ratio at Issue Date	The Loan to Value ratio as described in the Offering Circular (if available), otherwise calculate using Actual Principal Balance at Issue Date (Field ES60) and Portfolio Value at Issue Date (Field ES66)
	ES10	Original Term of Loan	The number of months from the loan origination date until the maturity date of the loan.
	ES41	Other Financial Covenant	Y=Yes N=No. Are there any other types of financial covenants for the Loan?
	EL37	Other Interest Adjustment	Companion field for Other Principal Adjustments (Field EL28) to show unscheduled interest adjustments for the related collection period.
	ES158	Other Material Syndicate Members (>33% interest)	Name of material syndicate members: defined as banks owning 33% or more of the loan
	EL28	Other Principal Adjustments	Any other amounts that would cause the balance of the loan to be decreased or increased in the current period which are not considered Unscheduled Principal Collections and are not Scheduled Principal. Examples include write offs and adjustments necessary to synchronize the Servicer's records with the value of the bonds.
	EL7	Paid through Date	The date at which all payments have been paid in full with no shortfalls. On a performing loan this will be the Loan Payment Date immediately prior to the date in Field EL6
	ES163	Participant Deadlock Resolutions Methods	What methods can be used to resolve deadlocks on material decisions eg Shot Gun Buy-Sell, Independent Arbitrator, Other Method
	ES152	Participation of Issuer in Syndicated Loan	Refer to Participation Legend to describe the method used by the Issuer to acquire ownership in the syndicated loan.
	ES139	Pay Reset Frequency	Frequency with which the P&I payment is reset according to original loan documents. 1=Monthly, 3=Quarterly, 6=Semi-Annually, 12=Annually, 365=Daily
	ES137	Payment Frequency	Frequency of payments on Loan according to original loan documents. 1=Monthly, 3=Quarterly, 6=Semi-Annually, 12=Annually
	ES122	Payment Obligations by Loan Swap provider	The spread over Index (if any) payable by Loan Swap Provider on an Interest Rate Swap
	ES61	Periodic P&I Payment At Issue Date	The scheduled principal & interest amount that is due on the next Loan Payment Date as at the Issue Date.

European Commercial Mortgage Securities Association

Investor Reporting Package

Data Dictionary

UK / European Related Field Numbers	UK / European Field Number	Field Name	European Definitions
	EP101	Physical Occupancy at Issue Date	The most recent available percentage of rentable space actually occupied (ie where tenants are actually in occupation and not vacated). Should be derived from a rent roll or other document indicating occupancy consistent with most recent financial year information. If multiple properties, populate with weighted average, using the calculation [Current Allocated % (Prop) * Occupancy (Oper)] for each Property. If missing any or the information is not available, leave empty
	ES56	Portfolio Value At Issue Date	The valuation of the properties securing the loan at Issue Date as described in the Offering Circular. If multiple properties sum the value in the Property File, otherwise leave blank
	EP131	Possession Proceedings Start Date	The date on which foreclosure proceedings or alternative enforcement procedures were initiated against or agreed by the borrower.
	ES24	Postal Code	The postal code (or equivalent) for the property or properties that serve as security for the loan. If multiple properties have the same code, print "Various." For missing information print "Incomplete"
	EP74	Preceding Financial Reporting Year as of Date	The end date of the financials used for the preceding year financial operating statement (e.g. year to date or trailing 12 months). If multiple properties and all the same date, print date. If missing any, leave empty.
	EP78	Preceding Financial Reporting Year Capital Expenditure	Total capex (as opposed to repairs and maintenance) for the period covered by the preceding year financial operating statement (ie year to date or trailing 12 months) for all the properties. If multiple properties exist and data is not available for all properties or if all received/consolidated refer to the DSCR Indicator Legend rule.
	EP80	Preceding Financial Reporting Year Debt Service Amount	Total scheduled payments of principal and interest due during the period covered by the preceding year financial operating statement (ie year to date or trailing 12 months). If multiple properties and not all information available refer to DSCR Indicator Legend.
	EP81	Preceding Financial Reporting Year DSCR (NOI)	Calculate the DSCR based on NOI for the period covered by the preceding year financial operating statement (ie year to date or trailing 12 months). If multiple properties and not all information available, refer to DSCR Indicator Legend)
	EP104	Preceding Financial Reporting Year Economic Occupancy	The percentage of rentable space actually occupied (ie where tenants may not be in occupation but are paying rent) at the preceding financial year as of date. Should be derived from a rent roll or other document indicating occupancy consistent with preceding year financial information.
	EP79	Preceding Financial Reporting Year NCF	Total NOI less total capex for the period covered by the preceding year financial operating statement. If multiple properties and not all information is available, refer to the DSCR Indicator Legend.
	EP77	Preceding Financial Reporting Year NOI	Total revenues less total operating expenses for the period covered by the preceding year financial operating statement (Field EL87 minusField EL88) If multiple properties exist and not all information available or consolidated refer to the DSCR Indicator Legend
	EP76	Preceding Financial Reporting Year Operating Expenses	Total normalised operating expenses for the period covered by the preceding fiscal year operating statement (i.e. year to date or trailing 12 months) for all properties. Typically included are real estate taxes, insurance, management, utilities and maintenance repairs, but capital expenditures and leasing commissions are excluded. If multiple properties exist, total the operating expenses of the underlying properties. If multiple properties exist and data is not available for all properties or if received/consolidated, refer to the DSCR Indicator Legend rule.
	EP75	Preceding Financial Reporting Year Revenue	Total normalised revenues for the period covered by the preceding year financial operating statement (i.e year to date or trailing 12 months) for all the properties. If multiple properties then sum the revenue (should match figures for sum of properties in Property File for this loan) .if missing any or if all received/consolidated, then populate using the DSCR Indicator Legend rule.
	EL88	Preceding Financial Operating Expenses	Total normalised operating expenses for the period covered by the preceding Financial year financial operating statement (i.e. year to date or trailing 12 months) for all properties. Typically included are real estate taxes, insurance, management, utilities and maintenance repairs, but capital expenditures and leasing commissions are excluded. If multiple properties exist, total the operating expenses of the underlying properties. If multiple properties exist and data is not available for all properties of if received/consolidated, refer to the DSCR Indicator Legend rule.
	EL92	Preceding Financial Year Debt Svc Amount	Total scheduled payments of principal and interest due during the period covered by the preceding year financial operating statement (ie year to date or trailing 12 months). If multiple properties and not all information available, refer to DSCR Indicator Legend.
	EL94	Preceding Financial Year DSCR (NCF)	Calculate the DSCR based on NCF for the period covered by the preceding year financial operating statement (ie year to date or trailing 12 months). Field EL89(Preceding Financial Year NOI)/ Field EL92 (Preceding Financial Year Debt Svc Amount). If multiple properties and not all information available, refer to DSCR Indicator Legend)
	EL93	Preceding Financial Year DSCR (NOI)	Calculate the DSCR based on NOI for the period covered by the preceding year financial operating statement (ie year to date or trailing 12 months). If multiple properties and not all information available, refer to DSCR Indicator Legend)
	EL96	Preceding Financial Year Economic Occupancy	The percentage of rentable space actually occupied (ie where tenants may not be in occupation but are paying rent) at the preceding financial year as of date. Should be derived from a rent roll or other document indicating occupancy consistent with preceding year financial information. If multiple properties, populate with weighted average, using the calculation [Current Allocated % (Prop) * Occupancy (Oper)] for each Property. If missing any or the information is not available, leave empty.
	EL86	Preceding Financial Year As of Date	The end date of the financials used for the preceding year financial operating statement (e.g. year to date or trailing 12 months). If multiple properties and all the same date, print date. If missing any, leave empty

Version 1.0

European Commercial Mortgage Securities Association
Investor Reporting Package

Data Dictionary

UK / European Related Field Numbers	UK / European Field Number	Field Name	European Definitions
	EL91	Preceding Financial Year ICR (NOI)	Calculate the ICR based on NOI for the period covered by the preceding year financial operating statement (ie year to date or trailing 12 months). If multiple properties and not all information available or consolidated, refer to DSCR Indicator Legend.
	EL90	Preceding Financial Year NCF	Total NOI less total capex for the period covered by the preceding year financial operating statement. If multiple properties and not all information is available, refer to the DSCR Indicator Legend
	EL89	Preceding Financial Year NOI	Total revenues less total operating expenses for the period covered by the preceding year financial operating statement (Field EL87 minusField EL88). If multiple properties exist and not all information available or consolidated refer to the DSCR Indicator Legend
	EL87	Preceding Financial Year Revenue	Total normalised revenues for the period covered by the preceding year financial operating statement (i.e year to date or trailing 12 months) for all the properties. If multiple properties then sum the revenue (should match figures for sum of properties in Property File for this loan) . if missing any or if all received/consolidated, then populate using the DSCR Indicator Legend rule.
	EL95	Preceding Year DSCR Indicator	Code describing how DSCR is calculated/applied when a loan has multiple properties. See DSCR Indicator Legend
	EL128	Prepayment Fee	Amount collected from the borrower as the fee due for making prepayments as required under the terms of the loan agreement. This is not intended to include any amounts paid as a "break cost" to make up interest payments up to the Loan Payment Date
	EL36	Prepayment Interest Excess (Shortfall)	Results from a prepayment received on a date other than a scheduled payment due date: Shortfall – The difference by which the amount of interest paid is less than the scheduled interest that was due on the Loan Payment Date, (this would only apply if there is a shortfall after the borrower has paid any break costs). Excess – Interest collected in excess of the accrued interest due for the loan interest accrual period. A negative number displays shortfall and excess is displayed as a positive number.
	ES108	Prepayment Lock-out End Date	The date after which the lender allows prepayment of the loan. If there are no restrictions leave blank
	ES110	Prepayment Premium End Date	The date after which the lender allows prepayment of the loan without requirement for a prepayment fee to be paid
	ES111	Prepayment Terms Description	Should reflect the information in Offering Circular. For Instance, if the prepayment terms are the payment of a 1% fee in year one of the loan, 0.5% in year two and 0.25% in year three of the loan this may be shown in the OC as: 1% (12) .5% (24) 0.25%(36)
ES22, EP13	EP13	Property Address	The address of the property that serves as security for the loan. If multiple properties, print "Various."
ES23, EP14	EP14	Property City	The city name where the property or properties are located. If multiple properties have the same city then print the city, otherwise print "Various." Missing information print "Incomplete"
	EP25	Property Condition Legend	Refer to Property Condition Code Legend to describe the condition of the property based on the latest inspection results. Codes pursuant to CMSA/MBA standard property inspection report results.
ES26, EP17	EP17	Property Country	If multiple properties have the same country then print the country, otherwise print "Various". Missing information print " Incomplete"
	EP4	Property Identifier	The Servicer's unique identification number assigned to each property serving as security for a loan in the pool
	EP39	Property Issue Date	Date the property was contributed to this securitisation. If this property has been substituted, enter the date of the substitution. If the property was part of the original transaction, this will be the Issue Date.
ES21, EP12	EP12	Property Name	The name of the property that serves as security for the loan. If multiple properties, print "Various."
	EL155	Property Possession Date	The date on which title to (or an alternative form of effective control and ability to dispose of) the collateral property were obtained.
	EP16	Property Postal Code	The postal code (or equivalent) for the property or properties that serve as security for the loan. If multiple properties have the same code, print "Various." For missing information print "Incomplete"
	EP42	Property Revenue at Issue Date	The total underwritten revenue from all sources for a property as described in the Offering Circular. If multiple properties, sum the values in the Property File. If missing data or if all received/consolidated, use the DSCR Indicator Legend rule.
	EP24	Property Status	Refer to the Property Status Code Legend and use the code that is most suitable for the property or properties eg whether sold, part sold, in foreclosure
ES27, EP18	EP18	Property Type Code	Refer to the Property Type Code Legend and use the code that is most suitable for the property or properties
	ES63	Ranking of Charge at Issue Date	Is the security granted to the Issue a first ranking security, ie does it have priority over all other lenders/parties (enter 1); or is it second ranking. ie subordinated in some way (enter 2).
	ES138	Rate Reset Frequency	Frequency with which the interest rate is reset according to original loan documents. 1=Monthly, 3=Quarterly, 6=Semi-Annually, 12=Annually, 365=Daily
	EL158	Realised Loss to Securitisation	The amount of any loss to the issuer after deducting liquidation expenses from the net sales proceeds
	ES174	Recourse (Y/N)	Is there recourse to another party (eg guarantor) if the event the borrower defaults on an obligation under the loan agreement? Y=Yes N=No
ES25, EP15	ES25	Region (NUTS)	The region in which the property or properties thath serve as security are located. - Use the standard regions as defined by Eurostat. Their website is: www.europa.eu.int/comm/eurostat/ramon/nuts/splash_regions.html. NUTS stands for "Nomenclature of Territorial Units for Statistics". If multiple properties, print "Various." Missing information print "Incomplete"
	EL38	Reimbursed Interest on Advances	Cumulative amount of interest paid to the Servicer for any property protection advances.
	ES157	Relationship of Controlling Syndicate Member	Describe the relationship of the controlling syndicate member to the Issuer eg investor or other syndicate lender

European Commercial Mortgage Securities Association
Investor Reporting Package

Data Dictionary

UK / European Related Field Numbers	UK / European Field Number	Field Name	European Definitions
	ES66	Remaining Amort Term At Issue Date	The number of months remaining to maturity of the loan of the amortisation term. If amortisation has not commenced at the Issue Date this will be less than the Remaining Term at Issue Dat
	ES65	Remaining Term At Issue Date	The number of months remaining to maturity of loan at the Issue Date
	ES170	Remedy for Breach of Financial Covenant	Refer to the "Remedies Upon Breach of Financial Covenants" Legend to select the code describing the remedy for the financial covenant breach.
	EP121	Rent Payable by 2nd Largest Tenant	Rent Payable by second largest current tenant
	EP124	Rent Payable by 3rd Largest Tenant	Rent Payable by third largest current tenant
	EP118	Rent Payable by Largest Tenant	Annual Rent payable by largest current tenant
	ES127	Required Ratings of Loan Swap Provider	Identify the minimum rating requirements of Loan Swap Provider either as required under the loan or servicing agreement
	ES130	Reset Date for Loan Level Swap	What date will the rate on the swap be reset (give the next date that is due)
	ES45	Revenue At Issue Date	The total underwritten revenue from all sources for a property as described in the Offering Circular. If multiple properties, sum the values in the Property File. If missing data or if all received/consolidated, use the DSCR Indicator Legend rule.
	ES159	Rights of Controlling Party for Material Decisions	See Controlling Party Rights (Material Decisions) Legend. Does owner of any participation other than the Issuer have the right to make major decisions and if so, Who is it? Y=Yes N=No - add Name
	ES160	Rights of Issuer's Loan	Refer to Controlling Party Rights (Material Decisions) Legend to describe the rights the Issuer may have on material decisions.
	ES175	Rounding Code	Refer to Rounding Code Legend to describe the method for rounding the interest rate.
	ES176	Rounding Increment	The incremental percentage by which an index rate should be rounded in determining the interest rate as set out in the loan agreement.
	EL35	Scheduled Interest Amount	The total interest that is due on the Loan Payment Date, assuming no prepayments are made during the interest period.
	EL25	Scheduled Principal Amount	The principal payment due to be paid to the Issuer on the Loan Payment Date in Field EL6 eg amortisation but not prepayments
	EP91	Second Preceding Financial Reporting Year Capital Expenditure	Total capex (as opposed to repairs and maintenance) for the period covered by the second preceding year financial operating statement (ie year to date or trailing 12 months) for all the properties. If multiple properties exist and data is not available for all properties or if all received/consolidated refer to the DSCR Indicator Legend rule.
	EP93	Second Preceding Financial Reporting Year Debt Service Amount	Total scheduled payments of principal and interest due during the period covered by the second preceding year financial operating statement (ie year to date or trailing 12 months). If multiple properties and not all information available refer to DSCR Indicator Legend.
	EP94	Second Preceding Financial Reporting Year DSCR (NOI)	Calculate the DSCR based on NOI for the period covered by the second preceding year financial operating statement (ie year to date or trailing 12 months). If multiple properties and not all information available, refer to DSCR Indicator Legend.
	EP105	Second Preceding Financial Reporting Year Economic Occupancy	The percentage of rentable space actually occupied (ie where tenants may not be in occupation but are paying rent) at the second preceding financial year as of date. Should be derived from a rent roll or other document indicating occupancy consistent with second preceding year financial information.
	EP87	Second Preceding Financial Reporting Year Financial As of Date	The date 12 months prior to the preceding financial year as of date Field EP74. If multiple properties and all the same date, print date. If missing any, leave empty.
	EP92	Second Preceding Financial Reporting Year NCF	Total NOI less total capex for the period covered by the second preceding year financial operating statement. If multiple properties and not all information is available, refer to the DSCR Indicator Legend
	EP90	Second Preceding Financial Reporting Year NOI	Total revenues less total operating expenses for the period covered by the second preceding year financial operating statement (Field EP88 minus EP89). If multiple properties then sum the revenue (should match figures for sum of properties in Property File for this loan) . If missing any or all received/consolidated, then populate using the DSCR Indicator Legend rule.
	EP89	Second Preceding Financial Reporting Year Operating Expenses	Total normalised operating expenses for the period covered by the second preceding Financial year operating statement (i.e. year to date or trailing 12 months) for all properties. Typically included are real estate taxes, insurance, management, utilities and maintenance repairs, but capital expenditures and leasing commissions are excluded. If multiple properties exist, total the operating expenses of the underlying properties. If multiple properties exist and data is not available for all properties or if received/consolidated, refer to the DSCR Indicator Legend rule.
	EP88	Second Preceding Financial Reporting Year Revenue	Total normalised revenues for the period covered by the second preceding year financial operating statement (i.e year to date or trailing 12 months) for all the properties. If multiple properties then sum figures for sum of properties in Property File for this loan) .if missing any or all received/consolidated, then populate using the DSCR Indicator Legend rule.
	EL108	Second Preceding Financial Year Debt Service Amount	Total scheduled payments of principal and Interest due during the period covered by the second preceding year financial operating statement (ie year to date or trailing 12 months). If multiple properties and not all information available refer to DSCR Indicator Legend.
	EL110	Second Preceding Financial Year DSCR (NCF)	Calculate the DSCR based on NCF for the period covered by the second preceding year financial operating statement (ie year to date or trailing 12 months). Field EL105(Second Preceding Financial Year NOI)/ Field EL108 (Second Preceding Financial Year Debt Service Amount. If multiple properties and not all information available, refer to DSCR Indicator Legend)

Version 1.0

European Commercial Mortgage Securities Association
Investor Reporting Package

Data Dictionary

UK / European Related Field Numbers	UK / European Field Number	Field Name	European Definitions
	EL109	Second Preceding Financial Year DSCR (NOI)	Calculate the DSCR based on NOI for the period covered by the second preceding year financial operating statement (ie year to date or trailing 12 months). If multiple properties and not all information available, refer to DSCR Indicator Legend)
	EL112	Second Preceding Financial Year Economic Occupancy	The percentage of rentable space actually occupied (ie where tenants may not be in occupation but are paying rent) at the second preceding financial year as of date. Should be derived from a rent roll or other document indicating occupancy consistent with second preceding year financial information. If multiple properties, populate with weighted average, using the calculation [Current Allocated % (Prop) * Occupancy (Oper)] for each Property. If missing any or the information is not available, leave empty.
	EL102	Second Preceding Financial Year Financial As of Date	The date 12 months prior to the preceding financial year as of date Field EL86. If multiple properties and all the same date, print date. If missing any, leave empty.
	EL107	Second Preceding Financial Year ICR (NOI)	Calculate the ICR based on NOI for the period covered by the second preceding year financial operating statement (ie year to date or trailing 12 months). If multiple properties and not all information available or consolidated, refer to DSCR Indicator Legend.
	EL106	Second Preceding Financial Year NCF	Total NOI less total capex for the period covered by the second preceding year financial operating statement. If multiple properties and not all information is available, refer to the DSCR Indicator Legend
	EL105	Second Preceding Financial Year NOI	Total revenues less total operating expenses for the period covered by the second preceding year financial operating statement (Field EL103 minus EL104). If multiple properties exist and not all information available or consolidated refer to the DSCR Indicator Legend
	EL104	Second Preceding Financial Year Operating Expenses	Total normalised operating expenses for the period covered by the second preceding Financial year financial operating statement (i.e. year to date or trailing 12 months) for all properties. Typically included are real estate taxes, insurance, management, utilities and maintenance repairs, but capital expenditures and leasing commissions are excluded. If multiple properties exist, total the operating expenses of the underlying properties. If multiple properties exist and data is not available for all properties or if received/consolidated, refer to the DSCR Indicator Legend rule.
	EL103	Second Preceding Financial Year Revenue	Total normalised revenues for the period covered by the second preceding year financial operating statement (i.e year to date or trailing 12 months) for all the properties. If multiple properties then sum the revenue (should match figures for sum of properties in Property File for this loan). If missing any or if all received/consolidated, then populate using the DSCR Indicator Legend rule.
	EL111	Second Preceding Financial Year DSCR Indicator	Code describing how DSCR is calculated/applied when a loan has multiple properties. See DSCR Indicator Legend.
	ES193	Servicer Fee Amount	The amount of the fee paid to the Servicer for the current period as calculated in accordance with the Servicing Agreement
ES3, EL3, EP2	ES3	Servicer Loan Identifier	The Servicer's unique identification number assigned to each loan in the pool.
	ES177	Servicing Fee Rate	The % rate per annum paid to the servicer
	EL140	Shortfall in Payment of Breakage Costs on Loan Level Swap	Amount of any shortfall, if any, of breakage costs resulting from the full or partial termination of the swap, paid by the borrower.
	EL150	Special Servicing	Is the loan currently being specially serviced
	EL192	Special Servicing Fee Amount plus Adjustments	The total of all amounts paid to the special Servicer during the current period, this will include the basic fee plus any other amounts paid whether expenses or fees.
	ES11	Start Date of Amortisation	The date that amortisation will commence on the loan (this may be a date prior to the Securitisation date)
	ES125	Start date of Loan Level Swap	
	EL148	Status of Loan	Refer to the Status of Mortgage Loan Legend to determine the code used to explain the loan status (ie current, non payment etc). If a loan has multiple Status Codes triggered, Servicer discretion to determine which codes reported.
	ES83	Substituted Loan (Y/N)	Is this loan a substitute for another loan on a date after the Issue Date? Y=Yes N=No
	ES123	Swap Rate payable by borrower	The strike price that is payable by the Borrower under the Interest Rate Swap
	ES149	Syndicated Loan	Is the loan part of a syndicated loan Y or N
	EL4	Offering Circular Loan Identifier	The identification number(s), if any, assigned to each loan in the offering circular.
	ES154	Total Issuer Loan Balance	Enter the balance of the syndicated loan that is owned by the Issue at the Issuer Date
	ES153	Total Loan Balance	Enter the total balance of the syndicated loan at Issue Date
	EL48	Total Other Amounts Outstanding	The cumulative amount of any property protection advances or other sums that have been advanced by the Servicer or Issuer and not yet reimbursed by the borrower
	EL118	Total Reserve Balance	Total balance of the reserve accounts at the loan level at the Loan Payment Date. Includes Maintenance, Repairs & Environmental, etc. (excludes Tax & Insurance escrows). Includes LC's for reserves (excludes LC for Tax & Insurance reserves). Should be completed if Field ES75 Collection of Other Reserves in Loan Set up is "Y"
	EP33	Total Reserve Balance allocated to Property	Total balance of the reserve accounts for the property at the Loan Payment Date. Includes Maintenance, Repairs & Environmental, etc. (excludes Tax & Insurance escrows). Includes LC's for reserves (excludes LC for Tax & Insurance reserves). Should be completed if Field ES75 Collection of Other Reserves in Loan Set up is "Y".
	EL46	Total Scheduled Principal & Interest due	The total scheduled principal and interest due on the Loan Payment Date (sum of Fields EL25 and EL35) - can be used for DSCR calculations
	EL47	Total Shortfalls in Principal & Interest Outstanding	The cumulative amount of any unpaid principal and interest on the Loan Payment Date

Version 1.0

545

European Commercial Mortgage Securities Association
Investor Reporting Package

Data Dictionary

UK / European Related Field Numbers	UK / European Field Number	Field Name	European Definitions
ES1, EL1, EP1	ES1	Transaction Identifier	The name assigned to the securitisation or issue, this can be as identified in the Offering Circular or assigned by the Servicer
	ES77	Trigger for Escrow to be Held	If yes, refer the Trigger Event Legend and describe type of trigger event.
	ES121	Type of Currency Loan Level Swap	Describe the type of currency rate swap that applies - OE=Other currency to Euros, OS=Other currency to Sterling, O=Other (Identify)
	ES120	Type of Interest Rate Loan Level Swap	Describe the type of interest rate swap that applies to the loan - L=Fixed to LIBOR, E=Fixed to Euribor, O=Other (Identify)
	ES118	Type of Loan Level Swap	Describe the type of loan level swap that applies - C = Currency Swap, I = Interest Rate Swap, CI = Currency and Interest Rate Swap.
	ES151	Type of Syndication	See Legend
	EL27	Unscheduled Principal Collections	Other principal payments received during the interest period that will be used to pay down the loan. This may relate to sales proceeds, voluntary prepayments or liquidation amounts.
	EP48	Valuation at Issue Date	The date the valuation was prepared for the values disclosed in the Offering Circular. For multiple properties, if several dates, leave blank
	ES57	Valuation Date At Issue Date	The date the valuation was prepared for the values disclosed in the Offering Circular. For multiple properties, if several dates, leave blank
	EL195	Workout Fee Amount	The amount of any workout fee being paid to the special Servicer for the current period on a loan that has become a corrected loan
	EL151	Workout Strategy Code	The code assigned that best describes the steps being taken to resolve the loan. Specific codes apply. See Workout Strategy Code Legend.
ES31, EP19	ES31	Year Built	The year the property was built. For multiple properties, if all the same print the year, else leave empty.
	EP20	Year Last Renovated	Year that last major renovation/new construction was completed on the property.
	ES109	Yield Maintenance End Date	The date after which the lender allows prepayment of the loan without requirement for a prepayment fee or yield maintenance to be paid.

Appendix 4

 CMSA-Europe™ is part of Commercial Mortgage Securities Association (CMSA®), an international trade association dedicated to promoting the ongoing strength, liquidity and viability of commercial real estate capital market finance ™ worldwide.

With more than 400 member companies worldwide, CMSA offers unparalleled leadership in the commercial real estate finance markets. Our diverse membership base spans the globe and represents the full range of the industry's market participants, from senior executives at the largest money-center banks and investment banks, rating agencies, insurance companies, and investors to service providers.

Member-driven, CMSA is dedicated to insightful, forward thinking that encourages vision, innovation and continuous professional growth for market participants. It is committed to being responsive to its members and providing them a culture of collaboration, collegiality, open and inclusive dialogue, consensus building and respect for diverse views.

CMSA-Europe
Tokenhouse
Room 213
12 Tokenhouse Yard
London EC2R 7AS
United Kingdom
Tel: +44 (0) 20 7073 2815
Fax: +44 (0) 20 7073 2770

Contact:
Carol Wilkie
Director
carol@cmbs.org

APPENDIX 5

GLOSSARY OF TERMS

A

AAOIFI
Accounting Auditing Organisation For Islamic Financial Institutions.

AB Structure
A senior-subordinate debt structure whereby the ownership of a single mortgage loan is tranched into one or more senior tranches and one or more subordinate tranches.

Accrued interest
Interest charged or due on a loan which is unpaid. This is often added to the outstanding principal balance and must be paid before any reduction in the principal balance is allowed.

Accrued rate
The rate at which interest is charged or is due on a loan.

Adjustable Rate Mortgage (ARM)
A mortgage loan whereby the interest rate changes on specific dates.

Administration rate
The annual servicing fee as a percentage of the outstanding principal balance of each loan.

Administrator
The agent responsible for managing a conduit or an SPE. Their responsibilities may include maintaining the bank accounts into which payments received from securitised assets are deposited, making payments to the investors using this cash flow and monitoring the performance of the securitised assets.

Advances
Payments by the special servicer (in respect of delinquent loans) or the master servicer (in respect of performing loans) so that note payments can continue as scheduled. These can be required for a variety of payments alongside principal and interest payments (for example taxes and insurance) but do not include fees which the trustee or an officer of the trustee deems "non-recoverable".

Adverse selection
The process by which the risk profile of an asset pool is assumed to worsen over time due to the presumption that those more creditworthy borrowers are more likely to prepay their loans resulting over time in less creditworthy borrowers predominating.

All in cost
The total cost of a securitisation to the issuer or sponsor (including the interest rate paid to investors' underwriting expenses and various other expenses such as legal and documentation fees) amortised over the expected average life of the issue. This is often quoted in basis points to indicate what would have been added to the yield had these expenses not been incurred in the creation of the security.

Allocated percentage
The proportion of the principal amount of a mortgage loan secured by multiple properties which is associated with each individual property. The proportion is usually calculated by dividing the net operating income or net cash flow produced by the one property by the cumulative net operating income or net cash flow produced by all of the properties that secure the loan. Consequently, the sum of all of the "allocated percentages" should be 100 per cent.

A Loan
The senior tranche in an AB Structure.

Al-Musharaka
An Islamic financing method derived from a partnership contract in which a bank participates with one or more clients.

Al-Sharika
An Islamic finance term meaning a partnership for profit.

Alternative A loan
A first ranking residential mortgage loan that generally conforms to traditional "prime" credit guidelines, although the LTV ratio, loan documentation, occupancy status, property type, or other factors cause the loan not to qualify under standard underwriting programmes. Less than full documentation is typically the reason for classifying a loan as "alternative A".

Amortisation
The process whereby the principal amount of a liability is reduced gradually by repayment over a period of time until it is paid off. The contrast to amortisation is a bullet repayment whereby the entire principal amount is repaid at closing. Scheduled amortisation is not prepayment, which is the repayment of principal in advance of its scheduled date for payment.

Amortisation polled
A period during which the outstanding balance of any related securities of a transaction are partially repaid. This may follow the revolving period of a transaction.

Annual payment cap
In relation to an ARM loan, the maximum percentage in any one year by which the due payments of principal and interest can be increased.

A Notes
The most senior tranche of an ABS or MBS issue. These rank senior to other tranches both in priority of repayment of principal, interest and credit terms.

Arbitrage
The simultaneous purchase and sale of an asset in order to profit from a difference in its price, usually on different exchanges or marketplaces. An example of this is where a domestic stock also trades on a foreign exchange in another country, where its price has not adjusted in line with the exchange rate. A trader purchases the stock where it is undervalued and short sells the stock where it is overvalued, thus profiting from the difference.

Arbitrage CDO
A CDO transaction which is based on issuing securities the aggregate yield of which is less than the aggregate yield of the underlying pool of assets.

Asking rent
A prospective rent offered by the landlord to a prospective tenant. The actual rent paid will often be less than this following negotiations and concessions.

Asset-Backed Securities (ABS)
Bonds or notes backed by pools of financial assets. Such financial assets will generally have predictable income flows (for example credit card or trade receivables), and are originated by banks and other credit providers.

Asset-Independent Approach
An approach to rating synthetic securities which is not based on a credit evaluation of the SPE's assets. Instead the credit rating is in accordance with the creditworthiness of the swap counterparty or its guarantor.

Glossary of Terms

Asset originator
The party that has originated an asset or group of assets by extending credit to one or more creditors.

Assignment
The transfer of an interest, right, claim or property from one party to another.

Available funds
All funds available or collected from the borrower or borrowers (for example principal and interest payments and prepayments).

Available funds cap
A ceiling applied to the amount of interest payable to noteholders, being the extent of interest accrued on a pool of loans.

Average life
The time span until it is anticipated that all scheduled and unscheduled payments of principal will have been made. This therefore gives a measure of the duration of an investment. Unscheduled payments of principal include prepayments. The average life is calculated by multiplying each repayment of principal by the time elapsed between making the investment and receiving the principal repayment, calculating the sum of the results, and dividing by the total amount invested. The average life of a CMBS is typically compared to the comparable Treasury to determine the expected yield on the CMBS.

B

Backstop facility
A facility provided by a highly rated entity which can be drawn on should the entity with the primary obligation to make the payment be unable to do so.

Balance-sheet CDO
A CDO transaction in which the sponsor securitises assets which it already owns.

Balloon loan
A loan in which monthly payments of principal and interest during the period until maturity are not sufficient to fully amortise the loan. The balloon payment is the amount of remaining principal which is due upon maturity of the loan.

Bank for International Settlements (BIS)
An international bank based in Basel, Switzerland, which monitors and collects data on international banking activity and circulates rules concerning international bank regulation.

Bankruptcy-remote
A description of an entity which is unlikely to: (a) have an incentive to voluntarily institute insolvency proceedings, and (b) have involuntary insolvency proceedings instituted against it by third party creditors.

Basel Committee on Banking Supervision
A committee established in 1974 which aims to improve the supervisory guidelines which central banks or similar authorities impose on both wholesale and retail banks. The committee makes banking policy guidelines and helps authorities implement these.

Basel II
The guidelines set out in *International Convergence of Capital Measurement and Capital Standards: A Revised Framework* published in June 2004 by the Basel Committee on Banking Supervision.

Basis point (bp)
One-hundredth of one percentage point. One basis point is the smallest measure used to quote yields on bills, notes, and bonds.

Basis risk
The risk that payments received from the underlying mortgage loans do not match the necessary payments out to bondholders. This arises from discrepancy between the indices to which the mortgage and the bonds are linked. For example, if mortgages are at fixed rates but bonds are at

551

floating rates the bonds could accrue interest at a higher rate than the underlying mortgage loans. The resulting shortfall is known as the basis risk shortfall.

Bifurcation
The process of splitting a loan into a senior and a junior tranche.

B Loan
The subordinate tranche in an AB Structure.

B Notes
A subordinated tranche in a CMBS structure or other securitisation issuance.

Bond
A certificate of short-term debt.

B Pieces
Tranches of a CMBS issuance which are rated BB or lower and are therefore below investment grade.

Bracket
Categorising loans according to a sole shared attribute. For example in a "term bracket" all loans will have the same average life.

Bullet Loan
A loan whereby principal is repaid in its entirety through a single payment at maturity.

C

Callable
A loan or security over which the borrower or noteholder has the option to require repayment ahead of schedule.

Call protection
Protection against the risk that loans will be prepaid early, or protection against prepayment risk.

Capital adequacy
The obligation on a regulated entity (such as a bank or building society) to maintain a certain minimum level of capital in proportion to the risk profile of its assets. Such regulated entities may be able to meet the capital adequacy requirement by securitising their assets and removing them from their balance sheet without recourse, thereby negating the obligation to maintain capital with respect to the securitised assets.

Capitalisation rate
A measure of a property's value based on current performance and also a measure of investor's expectations. Calculated by dividing the net operating income for the year by the value of the property.

Capped floating-rate note
A floating rate note with an upper limit or cap on the coupon rate. This prevents the investor from benefiting from interest rate movements which would take the coupon above the cap.

Cash collateral
A reserve fund that can be accessed in the event of credit losses and subsequent claims by investors and therefore a type of credit enhancement. The account in which the funds are held is the Cash Collateral Account (CCA) and is lent to the issuer by a third party under a loan agreement.

Cash flow note
A note which is not based on an interest rate but repaid periodically based on a portion of cash flow derived by the secured property.

Cash flow waterfall
The order in which the cash flow available to an issuer, after covering all expenses, is allocated to the debt service owed to holders of the various classes of issued securities.

Cash-on-cash return
A measure of the short term return on property investment calculated by dividing cash flow received from the property by the equity invested in the property.

Cash-out refinance mortgage loan
A mortgage loan taken in order to refinance an existing mortgage loan in a situation where the amount of the new loan exceeds (by more than 1 per cent) the amount required to cover repayment of the existing loan, closing costs and repayment of any outstanding subordinate mortgage loans. The borrower can put the additional cash to whatever use it pleases.

Cash trap
A provision often seen in intercreditor agreements whereby all amounts that would be distributable to a junior lender commencing immediately on a payment default or borrower insolvency are held in escrow ("trapped") pending the senior lender's decision to enforce or the junior leader's decision to cure the borrower default.

Casualty
Unexpected damage or destruction to a property.

Centre of Main Interest (COMI)
A term relevant with respect to insolvency. An entity's centre of main interests is generally (in an EU context) where the main insolvency proceedings against that entity will be taken.

Certificate
A formal certificate evidencing beneficial ownership in a trust fund. Owned by a certificate holder.

Cherry-picking
The practice of applying specific criteria to select assets from a portfolio; the opposite of a sample selected at random.

Clean-up call
An optional redemption of securities at a point when there is 15 per cent or less of the original principal balance of the underlying collateral pool outstanding and the cost of servicing the remaining pool of assets has become uneconomic. The issuing SPE will sell the remaining assets (usually at par) to the senior or the originator/sponsor of the assets and use the proceeds to effect the redemption. The benefit to investors of such a redemption is that it provides assurance that they will not be left with a tiny, illiquid fraction of their original investment.

Clearstream International
A subsidiary of Deutsche Borse AG that provides clearing, settlement and custody services for stocks and bonds traded in European domestic and cross-border markets.

CMSA
Commercial Mortgage Securities Association.

Collar
The lowest rate acceptable to a note purchaser or the lowest price acceptable to the issuer.

Collateral
Assets that have value to both a borrower and a lender and which the borrower pledges to the lender as security for the funds borrowed. Should the borrower default on its obligations under the loan agreement, the lender can apply these pledged assets to make good the default.

Collateral Support Agreements (CSA)
A document which governs the nature, type and amount of collateral required to support the payment obligations of a swap counterparty which no longer meets minimum rating requirements. See also Credit Support Annex.

Collateralised Bond Obligation (CBO)
A security backed by a pool of corporate bonds.

Collateralised Debt Obligation (CDO)
A security backed by a pool of various types of debt, which may include corporate bonds sold in the capital markets, loans made to corporations by institutional lenders, tranches of securitisations and other Asset Backed Securities. See also CRE CDOs.

553

Collateralised Loan Obligation (CLO)
A security backed by a pool of loans made to corporations by institutional lenders, usually commercial banks.

Collateralised Mortgage Obligation (CMO)
A security backed by a pool of mortgage loans or some combination of residential mortgage loans and agency securities. CMO issuances usually involves multiple classes of securities with varying maturities and coupons.

Collection account
The account into which (generally) all payments and collectables received on mortgages are deposited.

Collective Investment Scheme (CIS)
An investment vehicle which allows multiple parties to pool resources to create a well diversified portfolio.

Combined LTV Ratio
An LTV ratio calculated in situations where a property secures more than one mortgage loan.

Comfort letter
Either: (a) a letter from one party to an agreement to the other that certain actions which are not contemplated by the agreement will not taken; or (b) an independent auditor's letter providing assurance that information in the registration statement and prospectus is correct and that no material changes have occurred since its preparation (this does not positively state the information is correct, only that the accountants are not aware of anything to indicate it is not correct and is therefore sometimes called a cold comfort letter).

Commercial Mortgage Backed Securities or Commercial Mortgage Backed Securitisations (CMBS)
The CMBS abbreviation is used in two contexts. The former refers to securities that are backed by one or more pools of mortgage secured by commercial real estate, such as shopping centres, industrial parks, office buildings and hotels. All principal and interest from the mortgages flow to the noteholders in a pre-determined sequence. The latter refers to the overall transaction by which the securities are issued and sold in the capital markets.

Commercial Paper (CP)
Short-term promissory notes with a maturity of generally less than 270 days and most commonly between 30 and 50 days or less.

Commingling risk
The risk that cash belonging to an issuing SPE is mixed with cash belonging to a third party (for example, the originator or servicer) with the result that, should the third party become insolvent/bankrupt, such cash cannot be separately identified or such cash is frozen in the accounts of the third party.

Compound Annual Growth Rate (CAGR)
The year-on-year growth rate of an investment over a specified period of time.

Concentration risk
A risk that a pool which is not particularly diverse will suffer disproportionately from certain economic or market developments or changes. Having a diverse pool of loans mitigates this risk.

Concessions
An incentive offered to attract and retain tenants whereby payments under a lease are reduced, most often through a rent free period. These make the calculation of net cash flow (and correspondingly debt service coverage ratios) difficult to calculate.

Conduit
The legal entity which provides the link between the lender(s) originating loans and the ultimate investor(s). The conduit purchases loans from third parties and once sufficient volume has been accumulated, pools these loans to sell in the CMBS market. In the European CMBS market the pool is generally of less than 20 loans with a wide or narrow range of properties. On the other

hand, in the US market the pool may consist of anything between 50 to 100 loans secured on a wide range of properties.

Constant prepayment rate
The percentage of the outstanding principal which will theoretically be prepaid in one year, estimated based on a constant (rather than variable) rate of prepayment.

Control valuation event
Such an event occurs if the value of the property serving as collateral has decreased to such an extent that the subordinated lender(s) are not likely to get a meaningful economic recovery on their investment.

Controlled amortisation
A period that may follow the revolving period of a transaction, during which the outstanding balance of the related securities is partially repaid. A controlled amortisation period is usually 12 months in length.

Controlling party
A specified party with the right to approve and direct certain acts of the special servicer.

Corporate guarantee
A form of credit enhancement whereby the issuer or a third party provides a guarantee in respect of certain losses up to a specified sum. The guarantor will be subject to minimum rating requirements.

Corrected loan
A loan which, after being transferred to the special servicer for handling has been corrected and is now reperforming.

Covenant
In a legal context, a promise to do or not to do something.

CRE CDOs or Commercial Real Estate CDOs
A security backed by a portfolio of loans, securities or other interests related to commercial real estate.

Credit Default Swap (CDS)
A credit default swap is a contract whereby the protection seller agrees to pay to the protection buyer the settlement amount should certain credit events occur. This gives protection to the protection buyer, in return for which the protection buyer will pay the protection seller a premium.

Credit derivatives
Instruments used in the capital markets to re-allocate credit risk from one party to another, such as credit default swaps, total return swaps and credit-linked notes.

Credit enhancement
An instrument or mechanism which operates alongside the mortgage collateral to enhance the credit quality of the mortgage backed securities and thereby support the desired credit rating of the securities. Basically these are elements within the structure of a securitisation which are designed to ensure that investors do not suffer from decreases in the value of the underlying assets.

Credit enhancer
A party that agrees to provide credit enhancement for a pool of assets by making payments, usually up to a specified amount, should the cash flow produced by the underlying pool of assets be less than the amounts contractually required due to defaults by the underlying obligors.

Credit-linked note
A note, payment of which is dependant on a credit event occurring or credit measure existing with respect to a reference entity or pool of assets.

Credit risk
The risk that the lender will be either: (1) repaid less than the amount owed to it, (2) repaid over a longer period than orginally agreed or, in the worst case, (3) not repaid at all.

555

Credit Support Annex
A type of collateral support agreement produced by ISDA.

Credit tenant
A tenant which is rated as investment grade.

Credit tenant lease
A lease of part or all of a commercial property to a credit tenant.

Credit tenant lease loans
Mortgage loan secured by commercial properties occupied by investment-grade credit tenants. The loans are underwritten and structured based on the anticipated cash flow from the leases rather than on the value of the underlying real estate.

Cross-collateralisation
A provision by which collateral for one mortgage also serves as collateral for other mortgage(s) in the structure. This is a technique for enhancing the protection provided to a leader which adds value to the structure and therefore is a form of credit enhancement. Generally seen in connection with commercial mortgage loans.

Cure payments
See Cure rights.

Cure rights
These are rights often given to subordinated lenders giving them the right to cure the default giving rise to a special servicing transfer event within a certain time period.

Current delinquency status
The delinquency status of a loan as of the current date.

Cut off date
The date the underlying pool of assets which secures a CMBS issuance is identified, calculations are based on this before issuing the securities.

D

Dark space
Empty space in a property for which the tenant continues to pay rent. Tenants in large properties may exercise break rights in leases should any other tenant go dark.

Debenture
A document evidencing the indebtedness of one party to another and the terms and conditions governing the relationship between the creditor who lends funds to the debtor who in turn repays the principal amount lent to it with or without interest.

Debt service
The scheduled payments on a loan, including principal, interest and other fees stipulated in the credit agreement.

Debt Service Coverage Ratio (DSCR)
The net cash flow generated by an income-generating property on an annual basis divided by the annual debt service payments required under the terms of the mortgage loan or loans entered into for the purpose of financing the property. This is generally expressed as a multiple and gives a measure of a property's ability to cover debt service payments. Should this ratio drop below 1.0, there will be insufficient cash flow from the property to cover debt payments.

Debt service payments
Payments which the borrower is required to make under the relevant credit agreement.

Default Probability (PD)
A measure of the likelihood that a party will default on its obligations under an agreement.

Defeasance
The setting aside of cash or a portfolio of high-quality assets to cover the remaining interest and principal payments due with respect to a debt.

Deferred interest
The amount by which the interest accrued on the outstanding principal balance exceeds the interest a borrower is required to pay on a mortgage loan. This amount is usually added to the outstanding principal balance of the mortgage loan.

Deferred maintenance account
An account set up by a borrower to cover the cost of any repairs or future maintenance of a property.

Delinquency
Failure to comply with a debt obligation by the specified due date.

Demand notes
Short term loans or notes which include a provision that repayment can be demanded or the note called should the lender choose. Such notes often require all cash flows net of debt service to be applied to amortise a loan should the borrower fail to demonstrate progress towards refinancing. These can be "fast pay" whereby if the balloon payment of a balloon mortgage is not met, the borrower must apply excess cash flows to pay down the loan balance.

Determination date
The date for the calculation of the payments due on securities.

Discount margin
The difference between the price and the face value of a security.

Distressed mortgage loan
Another term for a non-performing loan.

Distribution date
The date of the month when payments on securities are made to investors. Necessarily this falls a few days after the determination date.

Due diligence
In practical terms this is the investigation and fact finding exercise carried out by a potential purchaser to allow him to make a more well-informed decision about whether to purchase or invest. In legal terms this is a measure of the prudence as can be expected from a reasonable and prudent person in the circumstances of the particular deal. The degree of prudence depends on the facts of the case and is judged on industry standards. In a CMBS investors rely on the expertise of the professionals involved in a transaction as it is impossible for them to inspect properties, financial records and the due diligence such professionals have carried out.

E

Earn out loans
A credit agreement under which the original principal balance can be resized for further advances should the operating performance of a property be able to service the additional debt.

Enforceability opinion
A legal opinion stating that the obligations imposed on a party by an agreement will be legal, valid and binding on that party in accordance with its terms, subject to certain standard assumptions and qualifications.

Enforcement
The process whereby the lender takes control of the collateral including the cash flow from the mortgaged property.

Environmental risk
The risk of the value of a property being decreased by the presence of hazardous materials (for example asbestos). Rating agencies may include the possibility of non-compliance with future environmental standards in their analysis even if a property complies with current environmental standards.

Equitable transfer
The transfer of the beneficial ownership, as opposed to legal ownership, of property. This is

often seen in European securitisation transactions as it is often significantly cheaper to arrange than a legal transfer.

Equity
A subordinated and predominantly unrated note holding in a securitisation which allows the holder to receive all surplus cash flows as a transaction, analogous to holding equity capital.

Equity capital
The contribution of shareholder capital in a company which entitles such shareholders to receive a return by reference to and subject to the company's profitability.

ERISA (or Employee Retirement Income Security Act of 1974)
US legislation which stipulates the standard of risk suitable and acceptable for private pension plan investments.

Euroclear
One of two principal clearing systems in the Eurobond Market, functioning much like the Depository Trust Company in the US market. Euroclear began operations in 1968, is located in Brussels and is managed by Morgan Guaranty Bank.

Euro Interbank Offered Rate (EURIBOR)
The interest rate at which interbank term deposits denominated in Euros are offered by one prime bank in the euro zone to another prime bank in the euro zone. EURIBOR is established by a panel of about 60 European banks. As with LIBOR, there are EURIBOR rates for deposits of various maturities.

Event of default
A negotiated set of events the failure of which to satisfy (such as failure to pay when due) will result in loan repayment or bond/note redemption together with enforcement of any related security.

Event risk
Certain events (for example natural disaster, industrial accident and takeover) cannot be predicted via a standard method of credit analysis. The risk that such events pose to an issuer's ability to make its debt service payments is the event risk.

Excess interest/excess spread
Interest received from repayments which exceeds interest on the notes.

Excess servicing fee
The portion of the interest charged to underlying obligors in a securitisation structure that is in excess of the interest portion of debt service payments or the regular servicing fee.

Excess spread
The return to the loan originator for securitisation.

Expected Loss (EL)
The loss which a lender anticipates it will suffer should a borrower default on its obligations.

Expected maturity
The date as of which securities are expected to be repaid in full based on a specified assumption regarding the rate of repayment of the underlying assets.

Expense ratio
The ratio of operating expenses and operating revenues.

Expense stops
Lease clauses which limit the amount of a landlords obligation for expense on a property, with expenses in excess of this amount being met by the tenant.

Exposure at default (EAD)
The exposure of a lender should borrow default on its obligations.

Extension adviser
A third party with the right or obligation to approve loan extensions or notifications recommended by the master or special servicer.

Extension/extension option
A "grace period" following the contractual termination date given to a borrower to repay a loan (through refinancing or sale). Used to prevent foreclosing on the property and the additional cost this incurs.

Extension risk
The potential inability to refinance balloon mortgages in a timely manner, with the result that the life of the security may be extended beyond the expected life.

External credit enhancement
Credit support provided by a highly rated third-party to enhance the rating of the securitisation structure.

F

Face rent
Rental payments without adjustments for any lease concessions (for example rent-free periods).

Fast pay
A descriptive term applied to a security or a transaction structure aimed at ensuring repayment of principal on an accelerated schedule.

Fannie Mae (or Federal National Mortgage Association or FNMA)
A quasi-private US corporation which purchases and pools conventional mortgages then issues securities using these as collateral. Holders of Fannie Mae certificates are guaranteed full and timely payment of principal and interest.

Fatwa/fatawah
A written confirmation of a *Shari'ah* scholar or board. This has no binding effect under secular law. Historically this was a short summary of the decision, and more recently these have been structured like Anglo-American legal opinions.

Financial covenants
Positive or negative obligations on the borrower relating purely to financial matters, for example to maintain LTV to a certain percentage.

First loss piece
The most junior class of a securitisation which suffers losses from the underlying pool of assets before any other classes suffer.

Fixed income investor
An investor seeking a fixed (and therefore certain) rate of return on their investments.

Floating-rate notes
A class of securities having a variable or floating (rather than fixed) interest rate, typically at a margin above a market index such as LIBOR.

Fonds Commun de Créance (FCC)
A type of closed-end mutual debt fund used as a funding vehicle in French securitisations.

Foreclosure
A proceeding, in or out of court, brought by a lender holding a mortgage on real property seeking to enable the lender to sell the property and apply the sale proceeds to satisfy amounts owned by the owner under the related loan.

Freddie Mac (or Federal Home Loan Mortgage Corporation or FHCMC)
A quasi-private US corporation. This entity is charged with providing liquidity to the secondary market for single family mortgages and issues securities using these mortgages as the underlying collateral. Holders of Freddie Mac certificates are assured of timely payment of interest and eventual payment of principal.

Fusion deals
A CMBS which features a combination of conduit loans, small loans and large loans.

G

GAAP
Acronym for "generally accepted accounting principals". There are various sets of generally accepted accounting principals worldwide, such as US, UK and German.

Gearing
An accounting term used to define the debt-to-equity ratio of a company. SPEs will typically be more highly geared than operating companies.

Government National Mortgage Association (Ginnie Mae or GNMA)
This is a US government related agency which guarantees securities which use mortgages initially issued by approved lenders as their underlying collateral.

Government Sponsored Enterprise (GSE)
The collective description for the US government agencies formed to provide a secondary market for residential real estate loans. Includes Fannie Mae, Freddie Mac and Ginnie Mae.

Graduated payment mortgage
A mortgage where the individual loan payments are graduated on the basis of pre-defined schedules.

Granularity
This is achieved where an underlying pool of loans is made up of smaller loans. Pools which contain a small number of higher value loans are said to be less granular, or more lumpy.

Gross full service lease
A lease which provides that the landlord pays all building expenses. Also called a full service lease or a gross rent lease.

Ground lease
A lease either of undeveloped land or the land excluding any buildings and structures thereon.

Guaranteed Investment Contract (GIC)
A deposit account provided by a financial institution that guarantees a minimum rate of return, thereby mitigating interest rate risk.

H

Haircut
The expression given to the reduction in the value attributed to an asset or the income or cash flow anticipated to be received from a property, usually by applying a percentage to this value.

Hedging
A general term used to refer to strategies adopted to offset investment risks. Examples of hedging include the use of derivative instruments to protect against fluctuations in interest rates or currency exchange rates, or investment in assets whose value is expected to rise faster than inflation to protect against inflation (interest rate hedging, currency hedging and inflation rate hedging respectively).

High Volatility Real Estate (HVRE)
Real estate which requires more specialised lending (for example development and infra-structure) which may exhibit highly volatile losses.

Hissas
An Islamic finance term referring to the sale and purchase of partnership interests from one partner to another.

Hurdle rate
A break-even debt service calculation which establishes the maximum interest rate a mortgaged property can handle at maturity if the property must be refinanced. Also called "break even debt service analysis".

Hybrid
A term used to refer to a whole-business securitisation. Such a transaction entails risks that are a hybrid of pure corporate risk and the risks associated with traditional securitisations backed by financial assets or diversified pools of corporate credits.

Hyper-amortisation
The accelerated paydown of a CMBS class achieved through the allocation of all principal and interest to that class.

I

IDB
Islamic Development Bank.

IFSB
The Islamic Financial Services Board.

Ijara
An Islamic finance term meaning a lease. A predominant structure in Islamic real estate finance. Securitisations which use this structure are termed *Ijara al Sukuk*.

Illiquid
An asset which is not easily tradable, the opposite of liquid.

Impound or escrow account
An account jointly held by the borrower and lender containing funds for capital expenses, such as improvement or insurance.

Independent director
A key component of SPEs. This is a member of the board of directors of the borrowing or issuing entity where a vote is required for certain important acts of the entity such as declaration of bankruptcy. This removes control of the entity from the hands of affiliated principals.

Intercreditor agreement
An agreement which governs the relationship between the holders of senior and junior loans. Whilst this is expressed as an "agreement", this document will usually be executed as a deed.

Interest Cover Ratio (ICR)
A ratio used to determine how easily a borrower can pay interest on an outstanding debt. Calculated by dividing the borrower's income during a certain period by its interest expenses of the same period.

Interest Only Strip (IO Strip)
Should the interest rate on the underlying loans exceed the interest paid on the issued securities backed by the same, the surplus is removed and added as a further class, the IO strip. Usually sold for a small percentage of the price of the whole security, these can be very volatile, for example if there is a large amount of pre-payment this could remove the interest stream to pay the IO strip, usually curtailing the life span of the IO strip.

Interest paid vs. interest impacted
This clause in the CMBS structure determines how and when losses are allocated, for example before or after principal is paid. This has a major impact on the yield of the most junior noteholders.

Interest Payment Date (IPD)
The date (usually quarterly) on which interest is paid.

Interest rate cap
Limits the rate to a maximum or "cap" thereby protecting the borrower from rising rates. Often purchased by the borrower.

Interest rate risk
A change in interest rates may mean that interest earned on assets in a low interest rate environment will not be sufficient to service payments required in a higher interest rate environment, thereby leading to shortfall. The risk of such shortfall (and the corresponding change in a security's value), is the interest rate risk.

Interest rate swap
A binding agreement between two counterparties to exchange periodic interest payments on a predetermined principal amount, which is referred to as the notional amount. Typically, to hedge against basis risk by exchanging counterparty will pay interest at a fixed rate in return for interest at a variable rate.

Interest shortfall
The difference between the aggregate amount of interest payments received from the borrowers and the accrued interest due to the noteholders.

Internal credit enhancement
Mechanisms inherent within the securitisation structure designed to improve the credit quality of the senior classes of securities, most commonly involving the channelling of asset cash flow in ways that protect those senior classes from experiencing shortfalls.

Internal Rate of Return (IRR)
The rate which an investor anticipates/desires to receive on an investment.

In the pool
A tranche of a loan which is included in the pool of loans which is to be securitised.

Investment grade
Investments rated BBB- or higher.

Involuntary repayment
Pre-payment on a mortgage loan due to default.

Issue credit rating
A rating agency opinion of the creditworthiness of an obligor with respect to a specific financial obligation, a specific class of financial obligations, or a specific financial program (including MTN programs and CP programs). Relevant factors in determining the issue credit rating are the creditworthiness of guarantors, insurers, the currency of the obligation as well as other forms of credit enhancement.

Issuer
A legal entity that has approved the creation and sale of securities to investors. In a securitisation structure, the issuer will usually be an SPE (in the case of CMBS) or other special purpose vehicle established in a jurisdiction that offers a favourable legal and tax regime in terms of the ability to achieve bankruptcy-remote status for the issuer and the security arrangements provided for the investors. Common jurisdictions used for establishing SPEs are The Netherlands, Ireland, Italy, Luxemburg and Jersey.

Issuer collection account
An account opened in the name of the Issuer at the Issuer's cash management bank into which the servicer deposits payments from the borrower.

Issuer Credit Rating (ICR)
A rating agency opinion of an obligor's overall financial capacity to pay its financial obligations. This is basically an opinion of creditworthiness. An ICR focuses on the obligor's general capacity and willingness to meet its financial commitments as they fall due. Unlike the issue credit rating, this does not apply to any specific financial obligations.

Istisna'a
An Islamic finance term meaning construction contract. One of the 14 categories of permissible sukuk specified by the AAOIFI.

***Istisna'a—Ijara* structure**
An Islamic finance term meaning a construction-lease financing structure.

J

Junk bonds
A term used to determine below investment grade securities.

L

Lead manager
An investment bank or securities dealer that manages a syndicate of dealer banks and agrees to place a securities issuance. It usually subscribes to a larger share of the issuance and therefore has an increased interest in ensuring the success of the marketing and placement of the securities. The lead manager is responsible for structuring the securities to be issued and liaising with other parties such as rating agencies, lawyers and credit enhancers.

The lead manager is also closely involved in the preparation of the offering circular and advises its client on the pricing of the related securities. The lead manager may have legal liability as to the compliance of the issuance with relevant securities laws and regulations.

Leakage
Cash which escapes or is lost during its movement through a securitisation structure from underlying tenants to the issuer which has not been built into the structure and is unexpected.

Lease assignment
A form of credit enhancement whereby lease payments are made directly to the servicer.

Legal final maturity
The date by which the principal balance of securities must be repaid.

Letter of Credit (LOC or LC)
Another form of credit enhancement whereby a third party agrees to guarantee the payment of another party's debts (usually up to a stated amount and for a specified period). The third party rating is generally required to be at least equal to the highest rating of the securities.

Lien
An encumbrance against a property which may be voluntary (as in the case of a mortgage) or involuntary (as in the case of a lien for unpaid property taxes), and acts as security for amounts owed to the holder of the lien.

Limited Purpose Entity (LPE)
A corporate vehicle (whether in the form of a limited company, partnership, trust, limited partnership or other form) which complies with rating agency LPE criteria. An LPE is usually the property owner. Due to inherent risks which stem from property ownership, LPEs are not fully insolvency remote but instead are structured so that insolvency risks are mitigated to the fullest possible extent. Characteristics which mitigate insolvency risk include: use of newly formed entities, contractual restrictions on activities and powers, non-petition covenants, separateness covenants and no employees.

Line-of-Credit Mortgage Loan
A mortgage loan that is linked to a revolving line of credit upon which the borrower can draw at any time during the life of the loan. The interest rate charged on the loan is usually variable and accrues on the basis of the outstanding balance only, while the undrawn principal limit grows at an annual rate.

Liquidation fee
The fee the special servicer is entitled to from the proceeds remaining from any sale of a mortgage loan or related mortgaged property.

Liquidity
The adjective applied to the ease with which assets are actively traded. Those traded more readily are said to be more liquid.

Liquidity facility
A facility, such as an LOC, used to enhance the liquidity (but not the creditworthiness) of securitised assets. This facility provides cash to make the necessary payments of principal and interest on securities in the event of a shortfall in the cash available to the Issuer to make these payments. Amounts drawn on this facility become a senior obligation of the Issuer and will rank at least *pari passu* with the related securities.

Liquidity provider
The provider of a liquidity facility.

Liquidity risk
The risk that there will only be a limited number of buyers interested in buying an asset if and when the current owner of the asset wishes to sell it. Basically the risk that an owner of an asset will not be able to dispose of that asset.

Listing agent
The agent responsible for carrying out the procedures required to have securities listed on the appropriate stock exchange.

Loan files
A record maintained by the servicer of, amongst other things, debt service payments, property protection advances, property inspection reports, financial statements, property level intelligence, modifications to any loan documents and records of special servicing transfer events.

Loan-to-Value (LTV) Ratio
The balance of a mortgage loan over either the value of the property financed by the loan or the price paid by the borrower to acquire the property and provides a measure of the equity the borrower has in the asset that secures the loan. The greater the LTV ratio, the less equity the borrower has at stake and the less protection is available to the lender by virtue of the security arrangement.

Lock box provision
A provision giving trustees the control of the underlying properties in a CMBS so that property owners only have a claim to cash flows net of expenses.

Lock-out period
The time period following origination during which the borrower cannot prepay the mortgage loan.

London Interbank Offered Rate (LIBOR)
The rate of interest that major international banks in London charge each other for borrowings. There are LIBOR rates for deposits of various maturities.

Loss curve
A graphical representation of the pattern of losses experienced over time regarding a sample of loans or receivables, based on plotting the defaults or losses that occur over the life of all loans or receivables in the sample.

Loss security
The ratio of the outstanding principal paid on the loans minus the realised loss to the outstanding principal on the mortgage loans. Gives a rate of loss on a liquidated mortgage.

Loss Given Default (LGD)
The loss suffered by a lender should a borrower default on its obligations.

Loss to lease
The difference between the rent being paid for property and the market rental rate for such a property.

M

Mark to market
To re-state the value of an asset based on its current market price.

Master servicer
The party responsible for servicing mortgage loans.

Master servicing fee
The main fee paid to the master servicer for the servicing services it provides. Generally payable monthly from interest on the loan.

Master trust
An SPE that issues multiple series of securities backed by a single pool of assets, with the cash flow generated by the assets being allocated between the series according to a predetermined formula.

Mayfair
The term used to describe the most valuable property in the underlying pool of assets. If the Mayfair amounts to a very high percentage of the value of the entire pool, the pool is said to be Mayfair heavy.

Medium-Term Note (MTN)
A corporate debt instrument that is continuously offered over a period of time by an agent of the issuer. Investors can select from varying maturity bands ranging from short term, medium term to long term.

Member States
The Member States of the European Union from time-to-time. There are currently 25 Member States. Ordered chronologically from the date of membership they are as follows: Belgium, France, Germany, Italy, Luxembourg, The Netherlands (1957); Denmark, Ireland, United Kingdom (1972); Greece (1981); Portugal, Spain (1986); Austria, Finland, Sweden (1995); Cyprus, the Czech Republic, Estonia, Hungary, Latvia, Lithuania, Malta, Poland, Slovakia and Slovenia (2004). In addition there are five "candidate countries" which are not yet Member States: Bulgaria, Croatia, Former Yugoslav Republic of Macedonia, Romania and Turkey. These are in the process of becoming Member States.

Mezzanine debt
Debt which is paid off after repayment of a senior debt.

Mezzanine pieces
Classes or tranches rated in the middle range of a multi-class security. These are more secure than the first loss piece but less secure than senior classes.

Mezzanine investor
A party who actively invests in mezzanine debt.

Modelling/cash flow modelling
When converted into securities, all payments are chronologically collated to the class created in the issuance. Cash flows are estimated in a variety of circumstances using multiple variables (or models).

Monoline insurer
An insurance company which is only allowed, pursuant to its charter, to write insurance policies relating to a single type of risk. The monoline insurer unconditionally guarantees the repayment of certain securities issued in connection with specified types of transactions (usually a securitisation) in return for the payment of a fee or premium.

The financial guarantee provided by a monoline insurer will generally allow the insured class or classes of a securitisation to be rated based on the financial guarantee rating of the insurer, with the result that the classes are rated higher than they would be were the financial guarantee not in place.

Mortgage
A security interest in real property given as security for the repayment of a loan.

Mortgage-Backed Securities (MBS)
MBS include all securities whose security for repayment consists of a mortgage loan (or a pool of mortgage loans) secured on real property. Payments of interest and principal to investors are derived from payments received on the underlying mortgage loans.

Mortgagee
The lender with respect to a mortgage loan.

Mortgagor
The borrower with respect to a mortgage loan.

Mudaraba
An Islamic finance term meaning a partnership whereby one party contributes services and another party capital. Securitisations which use this structure are termed Sukuk al-Mudaraba.

Mudarib
An Islamic finance term meaning the partner in a mudaraba structure which provides services and capital and usually no cash.

Multi-family property
A building with at least five residential units, often classed as high rise, low rise or garden apartments. The quality of such properties is distinguished as:
  (a) Class A—command the highest rental rates in the market due to design/construction/ location. Usually managed by large management companies.
  (b) Class B—command average rental rates in the market due to outdated design and finish but still which are of adequate construction quality and are well maintained. Again usually managed by large management companies. This class compiles the majority of properties collateralising up RMBS.
  (c) Class C—command below average rental rates due to poor maintenance/build in less desirable areas/occupied by tenants in less stable income streams. Generally managed by smaller, local property management companies.

Murabaha
Islamic finance term meaning sale at a mark-up. A prevalent structure in Islamic financing. Securitisations which use this structure are termed *Sukuk al-Murabaha*.

Murabaha
Islamic finance term meaning a partnership. Securitisations which use this structure are termed Sukuk al-Murubaha.

Musharaka
An Islamic finance term meaning a capital provider structure. Here each partner contributes capital and there is a much greater flexibility in allocating management responsibilities among partners, with joint rights of management being frequent and usual.

N

Negative amortisation
This occurs when the principal balance of a loan based on the amount paid periodically by the borrower is less than the amount required to cover the amount of interest due. The unpaid interest is generally added to the outstanding principal balance.

Negative amortisation limit
The maximum amount by which the balance of a negatively amortising loan can increase before the LTV ratio exceeds a pre-defined limit. When this limit is reached, the repayment schedule for the loan is revised to ensure that the full balance will be repaid by maturity.

Net effective rent
The gross rent less all operating expenses, rental concessions, tenant improvements, etc. This can be a negative figure.

Net net lease (or double net lease)
A lease which requires the tenant to pay for property taxes and insurance in addition to the rent.

Net net net lease (or triple net lease)
A lease which requires the tenant to pay for property taxes, insurance and maintenance in addition to the rent.

Net Operating Cash Flow (NOCF)
Total income less operating expenses and adjustments but before mortgage payments, tenant improvements, replacement revenues and leasing commissions. This is used as the basis for many financial calculations (for example debt service coverage ratios).

Net receivables
The principal balance of receivables minus any portion of the interest due with respect to those receivables.

Non-consolidation opinion
A key feature of an SPE or bankruptcy remote entity. This is a legal opinion which confirms that the assets of an entity would not be substantially consolidated with those of its affiliates.

Non-performing

A loan or other receivable with respect to which the obligor has failed to make at least three scheduled payments.

Note

A certificate of medium or long-term debt.

Notice rights

Rights often given to subordinated lenders allowing them notice that the loan is non-performing, or that a special servicing transfer event has occurred. Twinned with cure rights.

Notional amount

The figure used as the basis for calculating the interest due with respect to an obligation that either has no principal balance or has a principal balance that is not the balance used for calculating interest.

Novation

The transfer of all rights and obligations from one party to the other requires the consent of all parties to the original contractual arrangement and the new party assuming such rights and obligations.

O

Obligor

The party that has taken on the responsibility of certain obligations under the terms of a contractual agreement. These actions often include making payments to parties. In a securitisation structure, the term generally refers to the parties making payments on the assets being securitised; these payments are the source of cash flows from which investors are repaid.

Offering circular

A document used to promote a new securities issuance to prospective investors containing all material informtion about the security. This describes the transaction, including the features of each class of securities to be issued (such as the basis for interest payments, credit rating, expected average life and priority with respect to other classes). In a securitisation structure, the offering circular also gives details of the underlying assets, for example the type of assets and their credit quality. The offering circular is usually prepared by the lead manager of the securities issurance and its legal advisors. If prepared pursuant to, and in accordance with, the Prospectus Directive the offering circular will be called a "Prospectus".

OIC

The Organisation of the Islamic Conference.

One-tier transaction

A securitisation in which the transferor sells or pledges assets directly to the issuing SPE and/or the note trustee or custodian and so does not involve multiple transfers of the assets and one or more intermediate SPEs (thereby reducing transaction costs).

OpCo—PropCo structure

This arises where an operating borrower with significant property assets (such as pubs and care homes) is acquired and restructured into two separate companies. "OpCo" is the operating company and operates the business, "PropCo" holds all the property assets. OpCo then takes a lease from PropCo on all of the operating properties.

Open pre-payment

A clause permitting prepayment of all or a portion of a loan without incurring a fee or penalty often restricted to a specified period.

Option adjusted spreads

A representation of incremental return incorporating interest rate volatility and variations in cash flow due to changes in rates. Used in RMBS to price the prepayment risk to an investor. Less relevant to CMBS given the prevalence of prepayment penalties.

Operating advisor

A party appointed by the controlling class whom the servicer or special servicer must consult with before making certain decisions with respect to the loans.

Optional termination
A clause in a CMBS defining who can liquidate a CMBS prior to the last payment of the mortgages in the pool. Will also specify when and under what circumstances this can occur.

Original issue discount
A bond which is sold below, or at a discount to, par.

Original LTV ratio
The original amount owed with respect to a mortgage loan divided by the value of the property on which the loan is secured. In the case of commercial mortgage loans, "value" is generally taken to mean the current market value of the property.

Origination
The process of making loans.

Originator
An entity that underwrites and makes loans; the obligations arising with respect to such loans are originally owed to this entity before the transfer to the SPE issuer.

Out of the pool
A tranche of a loan which is not included in the pool of loans which are to be securitised.

Overcollateralisation
A capital structure in which the principal par value of assets exceeds the principal par value of the liabilities and therefore a form of credit enhancement (used most regularly in CDOs and others asset-backed transactions).

P

Pay rate
The periodic rate at which interest is paid on a mortgage. May differ from the accrual rate.

Paying agent
A bank of international standing and reputation that is responsible for making payments on CMBS and other securitisation transactions. In general, payment is made via a clearing system (in Europe usually through Euroclear or Clearstream International). In Europe, this role is often assumed by an entity affiliated with the trustee or the administrator; whilst, in the US, the trustee itself is generally responsible for making payments to investors.

Payment history
A record of a borrower's payments.

Percentage lease
Rent payments which include overage as a percentage of gross expenses which exceed a certain amount as well as minimum of base rent. Common in large rental stores.

Performing
Term used to describe a loan or other receivable with respect to which the borrower has made all scheduled interest and principal payments under the terms of the loan.

Pfandbriefe
A debt instrument issued by German mortgage banks and certain German financial institutions. There are two types of *Pfandbriefe*: "*Hypothekenpfandbriefe*" that banks use to finance their lending activities and "*Offentliche Pfandbriefe*" that they use to finance their lending to public sector entities.

Phase rent
Rental payments without adjustments for any lease concessions (for example rent free periods).

Plumbing
To remedy or cure any leakage from a securitisation structure.

Pool factor
The percentage of the original aggregate principal balance of a pool of assets which is still outstanding as of a particular date.

Pooling and servicing agreement (PSA)
A contract that documents a transaction in which a defined group of financial assets are aggregated and details how the future cash flows to be generated by those assets will be divided between the parties to the contract. This also details the responsibilities of the master servicer and the special servicer for managing a CMBS.

Portfolio manager
A regulated institution or entity that manages a portfolio of investments.

Preferred equity
Financing that is similar to mezzanine loan but structured to a senior equity position rather than as a loan. A preferred equity interest will typically have a stated preferred return and control rights similar to or greater than those of a mezzanine lender.

Preliminary prospectus (or Red Herring or the Red)
A prospectus which includes all or nearly all the information which will be included in the final version, identified by red printing on the front cover. This is essentially a marketing tool allowing investors to assess the utility of the security for meeting their investment objectives and allows the issuer to gauge interest in the proposed issuance.

Premium
An amount in excess of the regular price paid for an asset (or the par value of a security), usually as an inducement or incentive.

Prepayment
A payment by the borrower which is greater than and/or earlier than the scheduled repayments.

Prepayment interest shortfall
The shortfall between the interest accured on the corresponding mortgages and that accured from a prepayment, generally when interest received from the prepayment is less than the interest on notes. Such shortfall may be allocated to certain classes of notes and, if so, that class will be adversely affected.

Prepayment penalty or prepayment premium
A levy imposed on prepayments made on a mortgaged loan to discourage prepayment.

Prepayment rate
The rate at which the mortgage loans (or other receivables in discrete pools) are reported to have been prepaid, expressed as a percentage of the remaining principal balance of the pool. Prepayment rates are often sensitive to market rates of interest.

Prepayment risk
The risk that the yield on an investment will be adversely affected if some or all of the principal amount invested is repaid ahead of schedule. Commercial mortgages often reduce this risk through lockout periods, prepayment premiums and/or yield maintenance. Prepayment risk can also be taken to include extension risk, which is related to the repayment of principal more slowly than expected.

Pricing
The process of determining the coupon and the price for securities prior to their issuance. The price of any financial instrument should be equal to the present value of the cash flow that it is expected to produce. In a securitisation structure, due to the effect of prepayment on the timing of the cash flows, the pricing process generates expected cash flows using a prepayment scenario.

Priority of distributions
Provisions which dictate how, when and to whom available funds will be distributed.

Private placement
The sale of securities to investors who meet certain criteria who are deemed to be sophisticated investors (for example insurance companies, pension funds).

Professional market parties (PMP)
Dutch law restrictions which provide that certain debt obligations can only be transferred to entities which qualify as PMPs.

Profit stripping
The process whereby a company that has sold its assets in a securitisation continues to extract value from those assets by siphoning off the profits earned by the securitisation vehicle. The company therefore retains the economic benefits of ownership of the securitised assets.

Prohibited business activities
In an Islamic finance context, the conduct of business whose core activities: (a) include manufacture or distribution of alcohol beverages or pork products for human consumption (or in some cases firearms); (b) have a significant involvement in gaming, brokerage, interest based banking or impermissible insurance; (c) involve certain types of entertainment elements (especially pornography); or (d) have impermissible amounts of interest based indebtedness or interest income. Activities (a) to (c) are prohibited under the Shari' ah.

Property manager
The party responsible for the management of a property.

Property protection advance
A mechanism by which the servicer or special servicer can provide amounts required to protect the property serving as collateral for the loan, for example payment of insurance premiums. In the event that a property protection payment is not made by the borrower, the servicer or special servicer can require a property protection advance to be made either by the borrower drawing on a liquidity facility or the servicer or special servicer making the payment out of its own funds then being reimbursed by the issuer.

Prospectus
See "Offering circular".

Protection buyer
The party transferring the credit risk associated with certain assets to a protection seller in return for payment to the protection seller. Often seen in transactions such as credit default swaps. Payment is typically an up-front premium.

Protection seller
The party that accepts the credit risk associated with certain assets (often seen in transactions such as credit default swaps, as mentioned above) from a protection buyer. Should losses on the assets exceed a specified amount, the protection seller makes credit protection payments to the protection buyer.

100 per cent PSA
The benchmark mortgage prepayment scenario. Under this scenario, the monthly prepayment rate is assumed to be 0.2 per cent per annum in the first month after issuance and to increase by 20 bps per year each month for the next 28 months. Beginning in the 30th month after issuance, the monthly prepayment rate is assumed to level off at 6 per cent per annum and to remain at that level for the life of the mortgage pool to which the scenario is being applied.

200 per cent PSA
A prepayment scenario in which prepayments are assumed to be made twice as fast as under the benchmark mortgage prepayment scenario. Under the 200 per cent PSA scenario, the monthly prepayment rate is assumed to be 0.4 per cent per year in the first month after issuance and to increase by 40 bps per year each month for the next 28 months. Beginning in the 30th month after issuance, the monthly prepayment rate is assumed to level off at 12 per cent per year and to remain at that level for the life of the mortgage pool to which the scenario is being applied.

Property protection payment
A payment required to be made by the borrower in respect of the property serving as collateral such as insurance, real estate taxes or rent due under a headlease.

Purchase event of default
A right given to subordinated lenders to purchase the senior portion of a loan which has gone into default.

Q

Qualified mortgage
A mortgage which can appropriately be included in a CMBS.

R

Rabb ul-Maal
An Islamic finance term meaning partners in a mudaraba structure which provide capital in cash or in kind and generally do not interfere with the management or service component.

Rake bonds
Loan specific securities backed by a B Note, or the junior component of a single commerical mortgage loan.

Rate creep
This arises where the principal amount allocated sequentially (to the senior loan in priority to the junior) causes the weighted average rate on the senior and junior loans set out in the intercreditor agreement to creep above the weighted coverage whole loan rate that the tenant pays, with the result that there is an available funds shortfall with an increasing portion of junior loan interest becoming non-recoverable.

Rate step-ups
Agreed increases in interest rates. These can occur at certain specified times or upon the occurrence of certain events, for example if the borrower is unable to obtain a signed sales contract on the underlying property.

Rated obligations
The obligation on an issuer to pay principal and interest which has been assigned a rating by a rating agency according to the likelihood they would be able to comply with those obligations.

Rated securities
Securities to which a rating agency has given an issuer credit rating.

Rating agency
The agencies that, in the context of securitisation, examine securities and their underlying collateral and attribute a credit rating to the securities based on compliance with their criteria. Ratings range from AAA (highest) to CCC (lowest).

Real Estate Investment Trust (REIT)
A tax election option which allows a specially formed vehicle to invest in real estate and/or securities backed by real estate. Such entities receive favourable tax breaks.

Real Estate Mortgage Investment Conduit (REMIC)
A pass-through entity which can hold loans secured by real property which again receives favourable tax breaks. Such entities help facilitate the sale of interest in mortgage loans in the secondary market.

Realised loss
The amount unrecovered when a foreclosed loan is sold, equal to: (i) the unpaid balance of the loan; plus (ii) all unpaid scheduled interest; plus (iii) all fees applied to the sale of the property; minus (iv) the amount received from the sale.

Receivables
General term referring to principal and interest related cash flows generated by an asset which are payable to (or receivable by) the owner of the asset.

Red herring or the Red
The preliminary prospectus identified by the red printing on the front cover. Despite the name this is no way diversionary although it is subject to amendment. See also preliminary prospectus.

Refinancing risk
The risk that a borrower will not be able to refinance the underlying asset on maturity or early repayment thus extending the life of a security which uses such assets as collateral. See also Balloon Risk.

Reinvestment risk
The risk of an adverse affect on the yield on an investment if the interest rate at which interim cash flows can be reinvested is lower than expected.

REIT debt securities
Securities issued by a real estate investment trust which are generally unsecured and may be subordinated to other obligations of the issuer.

Release provision
Either: (a) a provision to release collateral under a mortgage for a pre-agreed amount, or (b) a provision which requires the borrower, if it prepays the loan associated with one property in the pool which is consolidated and cross collaterised, to prepay a portion of all other loans in the pool (thereby stopping the borrower "cherry picking" properties in a pool and preparing the loans relating to these properties).

Remittance report
A report sent to noteholders on each distribution date by the servicer containing information about the current distribution.

Rent set-up
A lease whereby the rent increases at set intervals for a certain pre-agreed period or for the life of the lease.

Representations and warranties
Clauses in an agreement in which various parties to the agreement confirm certain factual matters and agree that, should those statements of fact be untrue or incorrect, they will take steps to ensure that the statements are corrected or otherwise compensate the other parties to the agreement because the statements are not correct. In the context of a securitisation, the representations and warranties usually cover the condition and quality of the assets at the time of their transfer from the originator to the SPE or an intermediate transferor. They generally also specify the remedies available to the SPE or the intermediate transferor in the event that any of the representations are subsequently found to have been untrue. These may still be enforceable once the asset has been included in a securitised pool of assets.

Reserve account
A funded account available for use by an SPE for certain specified purposes and often used as a form of credit enhancement. Virtually all reserve accounts are at least partially funded at the start of the related transactions, but many are structured to be built up over time using the excess cash flow that is available after making payments to investors. \

Residential Mortgage-Backed Securities (RMBS)
These securities involve the issuance of debt secured by a homogenous pool of mortgage loans which have been secured on residential properties as opposed to being secured on commercial properties as in a CMBS.

Residual
The term applied to any cash flow remaining after the liquidation of all security classes in a CMBS.

Reverse earn-out loans
Loans in respect of which provisions concerning resizing are made at origination on the basis of criteria not yet met, or not yet achieved consistently. Criteria will be specified and, if these are not met by specified dates, then the loan will be resized downwards. The difference between the original balance of the loan and the resized balance must be paid down by the borrower.

Reversion
The ultimate sale of property after a holding period (can be a theoretical sale).

Reversionary cap rate
The capitalisation rate applied to the expected sale price of a property after a holding period. This will be higher than the going-in capitalisation rate.

Reversionary value
The expected value of a property upon reversion.

Revolving period
The period during which newly originated loans or other receivables may be added to the asset pool of a revolving transaction.

Riba
An Islamic finance term meaning interest. The payment or receipt of *riba* is prohibited under *Shari'ah* law.

Right to cure
The right for a specified interested third party to assume the responsibilities of a party who has breached a contractual obligation with a view to remedying the breach and preserving their interests.

Right of substitution
The right to replace collateral, parties or other components in a contractual obligation.

Risk Based Capital (RBC)
An amount of capital or net worth an investor must identify and allocate to absorb a potential loss on an instrument. The amount of RBC varies amongst asset classes and is usually expressed as a percentage of the amount at risk.

Risk diversity
The pooling of diverse loans to avoid and reduce concentration risk.

Risk-weighting
The practice of classifying assets on the basis of the degree of risk that they entail.

Risk-weighting bucket
A risk-weighting category which includes assets that involve a similar degree of risk.

Russell NCREIF Index
Numerous indexes complied by the Frank Russell Company and the National Council and Real Estate Investment Fiduciaries on commercial real estate performance. Often used in the US as a benchmark for real estate investment performance.

S

Sakk
An Islamic finance term which is the singular of *Sukuk*.

Salam
An Islamic finance term meaning forward sale. One of the 14 categories of permissible *Sukuk* specified by the AAOIFI.

Scheduled interest
The amount of interest due and payable during the relevant payment or interest period.

Scheduled principal
The amount of principal scheduled to be repaid during the relevant payment or interest period.

Schuldschein or Schuldscheindarlehen
Loans made in the domestic German market that are evidenced by a promissory note.

Seasoning
Descriptive term used to refer to the age of an asset being securitised. This gives an indication of how long the obligor has been making payments and satisfying its other obligations with respect to the asset prior to its securitisation. An asset becomes more "seasoned" as the period it has been performing to its terms increases. It is presumed that more seasoned assets have a lower likelihood of default.

Secondary market
The market in which existing securities are re-traded (as opposed to a primary market in which securities are issued and subscribed to by investors).

Secondary mortgage market
The market for the buying, selling and trading of individual mortgage loans and MBS.

Second-lien mortgage loan
A loan secured by a mortgage or trust deed, the security of which is junior to the security of another mortgage or trust deed.

Secured debt
Borrowing that is made, in part, on the basis of security pledged by the borrower to the lender.

Securities and Exchange Commission (SEC)
A US government agency which issues regulations and enforces provisions of federal securities laws and its own regulations, including regulations governing the disclosure of information provided in connection with offering securities for sale to the public. The SEC is also responsible for regulating the trading of these securities.

Securitisation
An issuance of securities representing an undivided interest in a segregated pool of specific assets such as commercial mortgages.

Security
Assets that the borrower pledges to the lender to ensure that the borrower will live up to its obligations under a loan agreement. In the event of default by the borrower, the lender can use the assets pledged to recover some or all of the funds owed to it by the borrower.

Self-amortising loans
A loan whereby the full amount of principal will be paid off at termination.

Senior/junior
A common structure of securitisations that provides credit enhancement to one or more classes of securities by ranking them ahead of (or senior to) other classes of securities (junior classes). In a basic two-class senior/junior relationship, the senior classes are often called the class A notes and the junior (or subordinated) classes are called the class B notes. The class A notes will receive all cash flow up to the required scheduled interest and principal payments. The class B notes provide credit enhancement to the class A notes and experience 100 per cent of losses on the security until the amount of the class B notes is exceeded, when class A will experience all future losses.

Senior pieces
Classes or tranches rated above BBB (or an investment grade) which are appropriate for regulated institutional investors.

Servicer
The organisation that is responsible for collecting loan payments from individual borrowers and for remitting the aggregate amounts received to the owner or owners of the loans.

Servicer event of default
An event allowing the issuer to terminate the appointment of the servicer or special servicer. Typical examples of servicer events of default are set out in Ch. 10 and Appendix 2.

Servicing advances
The customary, necessary and reasonable out-of-pocket expenses incurred by the master servicer or special servicer in performing their duties. These are generally paid directly and then reimbursed from future payments.

Servicing standard override
The rights of the controlling class (in particular in any concert rights they may have) can be overridden by the servicer if it determines that following the course of action proposed by the operating advisor or the controlling class would violate the servicing standard.

Servicing standard
The standard that the servicer and special servicer must adhere to when performing their respective functions. The wording of the standard will be set out in the Servicing Agreement and an example of a typical servicing standard is set out in Ch. 10 and Appendix 2.

Servicing tape
A record maintained by the servicer of the current and historical loan payment profile of a loan.

Shari'ah board or Shari'ah supervisory board
The panel of Islamic scholars who determine whether an Islamic financial structure is *Sharia'ah*-compliant.

Sharikat
An Islamic finance term meaning a partnership whereby work and capital may be allocated over all persons with correlative loss sharing.

Sharkat ul-amwaal
An Islamic finance term meaning a musharaka which is a property partnership.

Shell rent
A portion of rental rates intended to amortise the cost of extraordinary tenant improvements.

Special-Purpose Entity (SPE)
A bankruptcy-remote corporate vehicle (whether in the form of a limited company, partnership, trust, limited partnership or other form) that satisfies rating agency special-purpose criteria. The bankruptcy remoteness protects the noteholders from having the underlying assets involved in insolvency proceedings against the borrower or issuer.

Special servicer
This can be the same or a different party to the master servicer, but is responsible for managing loans which have defaulted.

Special servicing fee
The portion of the special servicer's fee which accrues with each specially serviced mortgaged loan.

Special servicing transfer event
An event triggering the transfer of the servicing responsibilities from the master servicer to the special servicer. The trigger event is generally when the borrower has defaulted or, in the master servicer's reasonable opinion, is likely to default and be unable to cure the same within a reasonable time.

Sponsor
The entity that sponsors a securitisation.

Spread
In a CMBS context the difference: (1) between yields on securities of the same quality but different maturities, or (2) between yields on securities with the same maturity but different quality.

Spread accounts
A revenue account into which is paid any collateral interest which is in excess of note interest which is not directed at any particular class. This provides credit enhancement in that it absorbs mortgage losses up to a stated cap.

Stand alone securitisation
A securitisation based on a single loan. This has a very high concentration risk.

Standard prepayment assumption
This is a measure of prepayment rates on loans based on a variable rate of prepayments each month relative to the outstanding principal balance of the loans. Contrast with the constant prepayment rate which assumes a constant rate of prepayment each month.

Static pool
A pool of assets made up solely of assets originated or purchased during a finite period of time, and which does not change during the course of a transaction.

Stress testing
The process used to evaluate whether the assets that will form the collateral for a securitisation are likely to produce sufficient cash flows in a variety of economic scenarios to be able to continue to make the principal and interest payments due on the related securities. The scenarios generally include a "worst case" and provide an indication of whether the proposed structure and level of credit enhancement is sufficient to achieve a particular credit rating for some or all of the various tranches issued in connection with the transaction. (See also WAFF.)

Stripped interest notes
Note classes entitled to interest distributions but no (or a nominal) distribution of principal.

Stripped principal notes
Note classes entitled to principal distribution but no (or a nominal) distribution of interest.

Structured finance
A type of financing in which the credit quality of the debt is assumed to be based not on the financial strength of the debtor itself, but on a direct guarantee from a creditworthy entity or on the credit quality of the debtor's assets, with or without credit enhancement.

Structured Investment Vehicle (SIV)
A type of SPE that funds the purchase of its assets, which consist primarily of highly rated securities, through the issuance of both CP and MTNs. Should an SIV default, its pool of assets may need to be liquidated; therefore, the rating on an SIV reflects the risks associated with potential credit deterioration in the portfolio and market value risks associated with selling the assets.

Structuring
The process by which combinations of mortgages and security classes are put together to achieve the highest price for a CMBS based on the current market position.

Structuring bank
The investment bank responsible for co-ordinating the execution of a securitisation with respect to the originator/client, law firms, rating agencies, and other third parties. Typically, the structuring bank performs a due diligence exercise with respect to the assets to be securitised and the capacity of the servicer including an identification of historical information and often an asset audit. The structuring bank is also responsible for developing and documenting the legal structure of the transaction and for identifying and resolving accounting and tax issues. In the case of a public issue, the structuring bank oversees the preparation of an information memorandum or offering circular to be used for the offering and listing of the related securities. The structuring bank ensures that the transaction complies with local regulatory requirements.

Subordinated class
A class of securities with rights that are subordinate to the rights of other classes of securities issued in connection with the same transaction. Subordination usually relates to the rights of holders of the securities to receive promised debt service payments, particularly where there is a shortfall in cash flow to pay promised amounts to the holders of all classes of securities, although this could be related to the voting rights of noteholders.

Subordinated debt
Debt which ranks junior to other debt. Such debt is usually paid after amounts currently due (or previously due) to holders of senior debt before paying amounts currently due (or previously due) to holders of the subordinated debt.

Subordination
A form of credit enhancement whereby the risk of credit loss is disproportionately collected amongst classes.

Sub-performing loan
A loan which is producing payments (even the full principal and interest payments required) but with an unacceptable debt coverage ratio. Some investors also apply this term to loans making all necessary payments but the LTV ratio (or other indicatory value) suggest it is unlikely to be fully paid off at maturity.

Subrogation
The succession by one party, often an insurer, to another party's legal right to collect a debt from or enforce a claim against a third partly.

Sub-servicing
This is when the servicer and/or the special servicer sub-contracts some or all of their obligations. This is generally prohibited if it would result in the downgrade in the rating of the notes. The servicer and special servicer would remain liable for any breach by the sub-servicer of their obligations under the servicing agreement.

Sukuk
An Islamic finance term which refers to both Islamic bonds and Islamic securitisations.

Supervisory Formula (SF)
A formula used to calculate the capital requirement for unrated securitised tranches based on internal factors and tranche specifics such as thickness, size, enhancement level and pool diversity.

Survivability
A term applied to contractual terms which are still enforceable once the loan has been included in a CMBS. Often the case with representations and warranties.

Swap
An agreement pursuant to which two counterparties agree to exchange one cash flow stream for another, for example fixed-to-floating interest-rate swaps, currency swaps, or swaps to change the maturities or yields of a bond portfolio.

Swap provider
The party that writes a swap contract.

Synthetic CDO or Synthetic CMBS
A CDO or CMBS transaction in which the transfer of risk is effected through the use of a credit derivative as opposed to a true sale of the assets.

Synthetic securities
Securities designed to modify the cash flows generated by underlying asset securities that are rated primarily on the creditworthiness of the asset securities and currency or interest rate swaps or other similar agreements.

T

Takeover Code
The City Code on Takeovers and Mergers as published from time to time by the UK Panel on Takeovers and Mergers.

Tenant improvements
The expense, generally met by the tenant, of physically improving the leased property or space.

Third party pool insurance
A form of credit enhancement whereby the issuer pays a bond issuer an annual premium, in return for which the issuer will absorb the loss on mortgaged loans. This therefore protects investors from any losses on the mortgage loans. The CMBS is usually never rated higher than the credit rating of the third party insurer. See also monoline insurer.

Top-down approach to investing
A strategy adopted by an investor whereby large scale trends in the general economy are examined and industries and companies to invest in selected which are likely to benefit from those trends, contrast with a bottom-up approach to investing.

Tranche
The collective description of the discreetly rated classes of CMBS securities. Each class is paid a pre-determined coupon and principal based on a payment sequence. The lower rated tranches generally have higher coupons (to compensate for increased risk) and longer life spans as they do not receive principal payments until higher rated tranches have been paid off.

Tranching account
An account opened by the security trustee pursuant to the terms of the intercreditor agreement pursuant to which it agrees to hold all amounts received on the whole mortgage loan in its entirety on trust for the holders of each tranche and to disburse such amounts pursuant to the terms of the intercreditor agreement.

Treasuries
Negotiable debt obligations of the US government issued with varying maturities. These are backed by the credit of the US government.

577

Trigger event

In a securitisation structure, the occurrence of an event which indicates that the financial condition of the issuer or some other party associated with the transaction is deteriorating. Such events will often be defined in the transaction documents, as are the changes to the transaction structure and/or priority of payments that are to be made following the occurrence of such an event.

Trophy asset

A large commercial property that enjoys a high profile as a result of some combination of prestigious location, highly visible owners, prominent tenants and often striking design.

True sale opinion

With respect to a securitisation, a legal opinion to the effect that the assets that are being securitised have been transferred from the originator to the issuing SPE that these assets will not form part of the bankruptcy estate of the originator or be subject to any applicable automatic stay or moratorium provisions.

Trustee

Often a specialist trust corporation or the trustee part of a bank, appointed to act on behalf of investors. In a securitisation, the trustee is given responsibility for making certain key decisions that may arise during the life of the transaction on behalf of the investors. This role is typically referred to as the Note Trustee.

The trustee is most likely to also hold the security created by the Issuer over the securitised assets on trust on behalf of the secured parties. This role is typically referred to as the Security trustee.

U

Underwriter

Any party that takes on risk. In the context of the capital markets, a securities dealer will act as underwriter to an issuance and commit to purchasing all or part of the securities at a specified price thereby giving the issuer certainty that the securities will be placed and at what price and eliminating the market risk. In return for assuming this risk, the underwriter will charge a fee.

Unexpected loss

The loss suffered by a lender should a borrower default on its obligations under a loan which it did not anticipate.

V

Value

Unless specified to the contrary the fair market value of a property determined in an appraisal made by the originator when the loan is first made.

Voluntary prepayments

Prepayments by the borrower so to reduce or pay off the outstanding principal, often due to the borrower refinancing at lower interest rates.

W

Wakala

An Islamic finance term meaning agency. One of the 14 categories of permissible *Sukuk* specified by the AAOIFI.

Waterfall

The term applied to the cash flow pay-out priority in a securitisation. Typically with separate waterfalls for interest proceeds and principal proceeds. Both interest and principal will generally be applied to pay down interest and principal (respectively) on each class of securities in order of the highest rated tranche first down to the lower rated tranches. Certain expenses and fees, as well as hedging payments are paid in priority to interest and principal on the securities. The sequence will be stipulated in the prospectus or offering circular at the time of issue.

Weighted-average cost of funds

The weighted-average rate of return that an issuer must offer to investors in the event of a combination of borrowed funds and equity investments. Also referred to as the weighted-average cost of capital.

Weighted-Average Coupon (WAC)
The "average" interest rate for a group of loans or securities, calculated by multiplying the coupon applicable to each loan or security in the group by the proportion of the outstanding principal balance of the entire pool made up by the loan or security to which the coupon relates.

Weighted-Average Foreclosure Frequency (WAFF)
The estimated percentage of assets in the securitisation pool that will go into default under an economic scenario designed to test whether the cash flow that is expected to be generated by the pool plus available credit enhancement will be sufficient to repay all securities rated at a certain rating category or higher. The WAFF is used in conjunction with the WALS to determine the expected level of losses at different rating categories.

Weighted-Average Loss Severity (WALS)
The average loss that is expected to be incurred in the event that any one asset in a securitisation pool goes into default, expressed as a percentage of outstanding principal balance of such asset as of the date of the default.

The expected loss is predicted by making various assumptions about the potential decline in the market value of collateral that may secure the asset. The WALS is used in conjunction with the WAFF to determine the expected level of losses at different rating categories.

Weighted-Average Maturity (WAM)
A measure of the remaining term to maturity of a group of loans, calculated by multiplying the remaining months to maturity of each loan in the group by the proportion of the outstanding principal balance of the entire pool made up by the loan or security to which the coupon relates.

Whole business securitisation
A whole-business or corporate securitisation refers to the issuance of bonds backed by a company's cash flow generating assets and/or its inventory. The security may have been legally isolated in favour of the holders of the notes and might be managed by a backup operator, thereby prolonging the security's cash flow generating capacity in favour of the noteholders should insolvency proceedings be brought against the company or the company become insolvent. With appropriate enhancements to the securitised debt structure in place, securitisation can achieve a higher rating on (and longer term of) the securitised debt than a company's secured or unsecured corporate debt.

Workout fee
The fee the special servicer is entitled to for any specialist serviced loan which becomes corrected. It provides an incentive for the special servicer to correct a non-performing loan as soon as possible. This fee is paid only whilst the loan remains a corrected mortgaged loan.

X

X-notes
The term usually given to the notes which form the IO strip in a CMBS.

Y

Yield maintenance
A prepayment provision to ensure investors attain the same yield as if the borrower had made all scheduled payments until maturity, therefore removing the prepayment risk.

Yield spread
The difference in yield between a security and a separate benchmark (for example UK treasuries of the same maturity).

Yield to average life
A calculation based on the expected term of the class rather than its final stated maturity. Used in lieu of yield to maturity.

Yield to maturity
The calculation of the return an investor will receive if a note is held to its maturity date. This

takes into account purchase price, redemption value, time to maturity, coupon and the time between interest payments.

Z

Zero coupon note
A note that does not pay interest and therefore does not have a coupon but is traded at a deep discount, rendering profit at maturity when the bond is redeemed for its full face value. Another name for a stripped interest note.

INDEX